Czyzewo synagogue, now a storage building, and the Brok River, August 2018.
Old house and the synagogue western wall with "stone tablets" brickwork, May 2012.
Photos courtesy of Hazel and John Boon and Stephen and Marian Rothstein.

Czyzewo Memorial Book

(Czyżew-Osada, Poland)

Translation of Sefer Zikaron Czyzewo

Memorial Book of Czyzewo

Original Book edited by: Shimon Kanc

Published by former residents of Czyzewo in Israel and the USA

In Tel Aviv, 1961

Published by JewishGen

An Affiliate of the Museum of Jewish Heritage—A Living Memorial to the Holocaust
New York

Czyzewo Memorial Book (Czyżew-Osada, Poland)
Translation of *Sefer Zikaron Czyzewo*
Memorial Book of Czyzewo

Copyright © 2020 by JewishGen, Inc.
All rights reserved.
First Printing: January 2021, Tevet 5781

Editor of Original Yizkor Book: Shimon Kanc
Project Coordinator: Jennifer L. Mohr
Layout: Donni Magid
Cover Design: Nina Schwartz, Impulse Graphics
Name Indexing: Jonathan Wind

This book may not be reproduced, in whole or in part, including illustrations in any form (beyond that copying permitted by Sections 107 and 108 of the U.S. Copyright Law and except by reviewers for public press), without written permission from the publisher.

Published by JewishGen, Inc.
An Affiliate of the Museum of Jewish Heritage
A Living Memorial to the Holocaust
36 Battery Place, New York, NY 10280

JewishGen, Inc. is not responsible for inaccuracies or omissions in the original work and makes no representations regarding the accuracy of this translation. Digital images of the original book's contents can be seen online at the New York Public Library website.

The mission of the JewishGen organization is to produce a translation of the original work, and we cannot verify the accuracy of statements or alter facts cited.

Printed in the United States of America by Lightning Source, Inc.

Library of Congress Control Number (LCCN): 2020952324

ISBN: 978-1-954176-01-0 (hard cover: 618 pages, alk. paper)

Cover Credits:

Front Cover top:

The Market on fair day, c.1925. Courtesy of Jennifer Mohr.

Front cover, bottom:

Cavalry officer Yitzchak Blizniak and his bride, c.1925. Courtesy of Marshall Cohen.

Back cover, top:

Lepak family at the train station, 1932 or 1933. Courtesy of Jennifer Mohr. Right to left: Yehoshua Lepak, Yosel Baruch Lepak, Yental Lepak, Ben-Tsion Markovsky, Peshe Lepak Markovsky, and (woman next to Peshe) Gitel Lepak. The Markovskys were on their way to Israel (Palestine). Family at left (husband, wife and daughter) is unknown; possibly also going to Palestine.

Back cover, top right:

Czyzewo, from 1935 Military Geographical Institute Map of Poland, p. 37, loc. 35-I. Public domain. Source: Wikipedia.org.

Back cover, right:

Mordchai (Motel) Szczupakiewicz at his power plant (Łepak and Szczupakiewicz), the first electric concession in Czyzewo, 1929. Courtesy of Enid and Eric Stubin.

Back cover, bottom:

David Isaac Winkelstein and his parents, Shmuel Meir and Henya Basha, c.1935. Courtesy of Shmuel Even-Zohar.

JewishGen and the Yizkor Books in Print Project

This book has been published by the **Yizkor Books in Print Project**, as part of the **Yizkor Book Project** of JewishGen, Inc.

JewishGen, Inc. is a non-profit organization founded in 1987 as a resource for Jewish genealogy. Its website [www.jewishgen.org] serves as an international clearinghouse and resource center to assist individuals who are researching the history of their Jewish families and the places where they lived. JewishGen provides databases, facilitates discussion groups, and coordinates projects relating to Jewish genealogy and the history of the Jewish people. In 2003, JewishGen became an affiliate of the **Museum of Jewish Heritage—A Living Memorial to the Holocaust** in New York.

The **JewishGen Yizkor Book Project** was organized to make more widely known the existence of Yizkor (Memorial) Books written by survivors and former residents of various Jewish communities throughout the world. Later, volunteers connected to the different destroyed communities began cooperating to have these books translated from the original language—usually Hebrew or Yiddish—into English, thus enabling a wider audience to have access to the valuable information contained within them. As each chapter of these books was translated, it was posted on the JewishGen website and made available to the general public.

The **Yizkor Books in Print Project** began in 2011 as an initiative to print and publish Yizkor Books that had been fully translated, so that hard copies would be available for purchase by the descendants of these communities and also by scholars, universities, synagogues, libraries, and museums.

These Yizkor books have been produced almost entirely through the volunteer effort of researchers from around the world, assisted by donations from private individuals. The books are printed and sold at near cost, so as to make them as affordable as possible. Our goal is to make this important genre of Jewish literature and history available in English in book form, so that people can have the personal histories of their ancestral towns on their bookshelves for themselves and for their children and grandchildren.

A list of all published translated Yizkor Books in the project with prices and ordering information can be found at:
http://www.jewishgen.org/Yizkor/ybip.html

Lance Ackerfeld, Yizkor Book Project Manager
Joel Alpert, Yizkor-Book-in-Print Project Coordinator
Susan Rosin, Yizkor-Book-in-Print Project Associate Coordinator

This book is presented by the
Yizkor-Books-In-Print Project
Project Coordinator: Joel Alpert

Part of the Yizkor Books Project of JewishGen. Inc.
Project Manager: Lance Ackerfeld

These books have been produced solely through efforts of volunteers from around the world. The books are printed using the Print-on-Demand technology and sold at near cost, to make them as affordable as possible.

Our goal is to make this intimate history of the destroyed Jewish shtetls of Eastern Europe available in book form in English, so that people can experience the near-personal histories of their ancestral town on their bookshelves and those of their children and grandchildren.

All donations to the Yizkor Books Project, which translated the books, are sincerely appreciated.

Please send donations to:

Yizkor Book Project
JewishGen, Inc.
36 Battery Place
New York, NY, 10280

JewishGen, Inc. is an affiliate of the
Museum of Jewish Heritage
A Living Memorial to the Holocaust

Notes to the Reader:

We apologize ahead of time for the poor quality of images in the book. Often these images had been scanned from the original Yizkor books which were of poor quality to begin with, being copies of old photographs. Each transfer results in loss of quality. We have done the best we could, given the original material and the resources and technology at hand. Even though images often appear of higher quality on computer screens, that does not transfer to high quality images in print. A reader can view the original scans on the web sites listed below.

Within the text the reader will note "{34}" standing ahead of a paragraph. This indicates that the material translated below was on page 34 of the original book. However, when a paragraph was split between two pages in the original book, the marker is placed in this book after the end of the paragraph for ease of reading.

Also please note that all references within the text of the book to page numbers, refer to the page numbers of the original Yizkor Book.

The original book can be seen online at the New York Public Library site:

https://digitalcollections.nypl.org/search/index?utf8=%E2%9C%93&keywords=czyzewo

or at the Yiddish Book Center web site:

https://www.yiddishbookcenter.org/collections/yizkor-books/yzk-nybc313736/kanc-shimon-yizker-bukh-nokh-der-horev-gevorener-yidisher-kehile-tshizsheve

In order to obtain a list of all Shoah victims from Czyzew, the reader should access the Yad Vashem web site listed below; one can also search for specific family names using family name option. These lists are continually updated by Yad Vashem, so it is worthwhile to periodically search these lists.

There is much valuable information available on this web site, including the Pages of Testimony, etc.
http://yvng.yadvashem.org

A list of this book and all books available in the Yizkor-Book-In-Print Project along with prices is available at:
http://www.jewishgen.org/Yizkor/ybip.html

Geopolitical Information:

Czyżew-Osada, Poland is located at 52°48' N 22°19' E
And 67 miles NE of Warszawa

Period	Town	District	Province	Country
Before WWI (c. 1900):	Czyżew	Ostrów	Łomża	Russian Empire
Between the wars (c. 1930):	Czyżewo	Wysokie Mazowieckie	Białystok	Poland
After WWII (c. 1950):	Czyżewo			Poland
Today (c. 2000):	Czyżew-Osada			Poland

Alternate names for the town:
Czyżew-Osada [Pol], Czyżewo [Pol], Chizeva [Yid], Chizhev-Osada [Rus], Czyżew, Chizheva, Chizhevo, Tshizsheve, Tshizheva, Tzizhav

Nearby Jewish Communities:

Andrzejewo 7 miles WNW
Zareby Koscielne 8 miles WSW
Nur 9 miles S
Jablonka 11 miles N
Wysokie Mazowieckie 12 miles NE
Ciechanowiec 12 miles SE
Wyszonki Koscielne 13 miles E
Zambrow 13 miles NNW
Szumowo 13 miles NW
Malkinia Gorna 15 miles WSW
Sterdyn 15 miles S
Kosow Lacki 15 miles SSW
Prostyn 17 miles SW
Ostrow Mazowiecka 17 miles W
Kosewo 19 miles WNW
Gac 20 miles N
Sokoly 20 miles NE
Brok 21 miles WSW
Sniadowo 21 miles NW
Rutki 21 miles NNE
Bransk 23 miles E
Stoczek 25 miles SW
Miedzna 25 miles SSW
Czerwin 26 miles WNW
Lapy 26 miles ENE
Poreba Srednia 27 miles WSW
Poreba-Koceby 27 miles WSW
Wasewo 28 miles W
Wizna 28 miles N
Sokolow Podlaski 28 miles S
Zawady 28 miles NNE
Piatnica 28 miles NNW
Lomza 28 miles NNW
Suraz 28 miles ENE
Baczki 29 miles SW
Lopianka 30 miles SW
Dlugosiodlo 30 miles W
Wegrow 30 miles SSW

Jewish Population in 1900: 1596

Map of Poland with Czyzewo (Czyzew-Osada)

Czyzewo Memorial Book

Yizkor Book

of the

Jewish Community

Czyzewo

Where the majority were Jews

Published by the Czyzewer

Landsmanschaft in Israel and America

1961   1 Tevet   Tel-Aviv

[Column 11]

Memoriel Book
TSHIJEVO

All rights reserved
Printed in Israel 1961
Printed by A. Ben-Hur, Tel-Aviv
19 Halutsim Street, Telephone 83748

Editor:

Shimon Kanc

Editorial Board:

Dov Brukarz Dov Gorzalczany

Gerszon Gora

Ahron Jablonka

The Hebrew material edited and corrected:

Yitzchak Szlaski

LET STAND TO BE BLESSED

To those who were very loyal, devoted and fervent supporters of the publication of the Czyzewo Yizkor Book and who rendered large financial help with their contributions.

Motl Szczupakiewicz
New York

Simcha Prawda Kopczyński
Mexico

Yehoshua Wolmer
Nicaragua

TABLE OF CONTENTS

Article Title	Author	Page
Preface to the Book		2
Song Of The Murdered Jewish People	Yitzchak Kacenelson	3
Introduction	Shimon Kanc	6
Let Us Remember!		8
Remember What Amalek Did To You	The Editorial Board	11
So We Started	Czyzewer landsmanschaft	12
The History of the Town		
Once, Once…		19
A Tear For A Generous Friend	I. Dawidowicz	20
An Overview of the Development and Growth of the Jewish Community in Czyzewo	Dov Gorzalczany	20
A Small Detail	Arthur Szrajer	33
The Development and Growth of Czyzewo	Dov Gorzalczany	33
Community Life		
The Jewish Kehila	Dov Gorzalczany	35
The Cooperative Bank	Dov Gorzalczany	40
Gmiles Khsodim (loans without interest)	Dov Gorzalczany	42
Linat Hazedek, Bikur Holim, Hakhnasas Orhim	Dov Brucarz	44
"Centos" – The Organization That Helped Jewish Children	Dov Abu Szmuel	45
Hasidim		54
Hasidic Shtiblach (prayer houses)	Dov Brucarz	55
My Great Father	Freidel Levinson	59
The Ger Shtibl	Gerszon Gora	68
My Aleksander Shtibl	Berl Szajes	72
The Amszynower Congreation in Shtetl	Pinchas Frydman	78
The Fire Brigade	Yitzchak Bursztajn	80
The Daf-Yomi Ended	Yitzchak Bursztajn	80
A Day in Czyzewo	Shmuel Abarbanel	81
A Maskil (enlightened man) Among Hasidim	Gad Zaklilowski	84
The Great Quarrel	Hyman (Anshel) Kowadla	87
The Great Peace	A. Wiewiurka	89
Hassidim in the Town	aron Jablonka	92
The Gaon Reb Szmuel Dawid of Holy Blessed Memory	Rabbi Levinson	96
Rabbi Szmuel Dawid Zabludower of Holy Blessed Memory	Gerszon Gora	99

The Rabbinate of Czyzewo	Gerszon Gora	104
My Grandfather	Gerszon Gora	109
One of the Five	Gerszon Gora	112
Reb Zebulun Grosbard	aron Tapuchi	115
The Admor Rabbi Boruch of Czyzewo	Rabbi Tankhum Rubinsztajn	118

Youth Movements and Political Parties

Youth Organizations and the Zionist Movement	Yitzchak Szlaski	125
The Mizrachi Organization in Czyzewo	Eliahu Gora	139
Memories from the Hachsharah Kibbutz in Czyzewo	Aryeh Porat	142
The Zionist Organziations in Czyzewo	Yitzchak Szlaski	145
The Movement for "A Working Eretz–Yisrael"	Malka Szejman	147
Freiheit	Leah Dimentman (Bursztajn)	151
My Father's Agony and Ecstasy When Organizing the Mizrakhi	Matisyahu Prawda	154
Agudas Yisrael	Gershon Gora	156
I Say Goodbye to the Shtetl	Gerszon Gora	160
The First Buds of Communism	Yitzchak Gora	162
Communists	Dov Gorzalczany	164
Bundists	Dov Gorzalczany	167

Theater

The First Flash of the Yiddish Theater in Czyzewo	Dov Brukarz	169
Days and Nights on the Magic Stage	Simcha Gromadzyn	171
The Third and Last Period of Yiddish Theater in Czyzewo	Dov Gorzalczany	175
The Library – The Center of Cultural Life	Dov Gorzalczany	178
We Build a Beis Am[1]		181

Way of Life

Jewish shtetlekh in Poland	Chaim Grade	185
Our Guardians	Aron Jablonka	187
They Come and Demand Their Due	Aron Jablonka	188
The First Strike	Dov Brukarz	190
Khederim, Schools, Teachers and Melamdim	Dov Brukarz	191
A Ray of Light from Past Years	Dov Brukarz	193
New Winds	Dov Brukarz	195
A Regular Market Day	Dov Brukarz	198
My Melamdim	Dov Brukarz	203
Types in the Shtetl	Dov Brukarz	208
Czyzewo's Tzitzis Maker	Dov Brukarz	211
Reb Binyamin the Tailor	Arya Gorzalczany	218
Yitzchak-Ahron – the Modest Man	Dov Brukarz	220

The Purim Shpiler	Dov Brukarz	221
A Visit to the Shtetl After Thirteen Years	Dov Brukarz	222
In the Days of the Polish–Bolshevik War	Dvora Brukarz (Dwasza)	225
How Cossacks Arrested Me as a German Spy	Simcha Glina, Tel Aviv	227
My Good Father	Simcha Prawda	230
My Homily	Simcha Prawda	233
The Holy Billy Goat	Simcha Prawda	235
Czyzewo Klezmorim (musicians)	Avraham Yosef Ritholc	238
Gentle Souls and Kind Hearts of My Little Town Czyzewo	Chaikeh Cikrovich (Prawda)	241
Khevra Mishnius	Simcha Gromadzyn	245
The Bridge	Elihu Gora	247
Bright and Dark Days	M. Szczupakiewicz	249
My Shtetele	Arya Gorzalczany	253
Chaim–Judel Tracz	Arja Gorzalczany	254
Yudel Wapniak	Arja Gorzalczany	255
Yitzchak, son of Bunim	Arya Gorzalczany	258
The Testament of Leyzer, the son of Yosl	Arya Gorzalczany	260
The Nightmare Persecutes Me	Malka Lubelczyk-Malinowicz	262
What My Grandfather Said -The Apothecary's Friendship	Malka Lubelczyk-Malinowicz	263
Nuska Szejman	Yitzchak Szlaski	264
My Mother – the Teacher	Yitzchak Szlaski	266
The Light From Our Home	Berl and Chantsha	269
The Pogrom in Czyzewo Described in the Yiddish Press of That Time		279
The Scroll of Blood	Gerszon Gur	293
Once Upon A Time There Was A Shtetl	Yitzchak Bursztajn	294
A Walk Through Czyzewo's Streets	Gerszon Góra	302
Water Carriers	Dov Brukarz	317
The Dear and Naïve Water Carriers	Aron Jablonka	320

People and Personalities

Meyer Richter	Yisrael Wajntraub	323
Reb Yechiel Asher Prawda	D. Gorzalczany	325
Reb Alter the Sofer Stam of blessed memory	Y. Szlaski	327
The Shofar Blower	G. Gora	332
Reb Alter Wolmer	Dov Gorzalczany	335
Reb Szmuel Zeev and Lea Kandel	Kandel sons	337
The Lithuanian	G. Gora	338
The Waker	G. Gora	340
The Cantor of the Town	G. Gora	343
In the Sukkah of Reb Itzel	G. Gora	345

The Prayer Leader	G. Gora	348
Shmuele the Walker	G. Gora	352
Flocks of Holy Ones	G. Gora	353
My Parents	Isachar Okon	357
Our Parents	Ch. Kirszenbojm	358
Reb Mendel, the Son of Israel–Shlomo	D. Gorzalczany	361
Reb Fishl Lubelczyk	Bat–Sheva and Shlomo	363

Memories

The Jewish Town that Was Destroyed	Yerucham HaLevi–Kopiec	366
Czyzewo – One Among Many	Pinchas Frydman	367
My Town on Weekdays and Festivals	Aron Jablonka	368
The Bridge	Eliahu Gora	373
The Footsteps of the Early Ones	Yerachmiel Eliasz	374
My Small town	Dalia Schneiderman	376
Father!	Rachel Wengorz (Gorzalczany)	378

Destruction and Holocaust

The Death of the Jewish Population in Czyzewo	Shimon Kanc	379
During the "Quiet" Days	Yitzchak Worona	381
Desolate Days and Nights	Yentl Kitaj	382
The Walk Through Every Hell	M. Kitaj	395
The Road of Suffering	I. Nowinsztern	405
In the Valley of Lament and Fear	Etka Cukerman	429
How I Smuggled Food into tho Zambrower Barracks	I. Wyprawnik	435
In the Circle of Death's Agony	Sz. Moncarz	436
In the Ghetto and On The Way to Auschwitz	Shmuel (Wajsbart) Ben Zahavi	441
I Escaped from Auschwitz	Sura Ben–Ari	445
In the Abyss of Terrible Death	Moshe Rajczik	447
Across Rivers of Tears and Seas of Blood	Yisroelke Fenster	454
In the First Days of Burning Hate	Avraham Kandel, Chaim Belfer & Arya Gorzalczany	455
My Experiences during the Years of the Second World War	Mirl Wolmer-Biderman	459
Through Flames and Smoke	B. Bolender	464
Czyzewo – Siberia – Canada	Moshel Blajwajs	468
Propelled by Fear of the Swastika	Freidel Levinson	475
Years of Banishment	Sheva Lubelczyk	482
Blind Fate	D. Saba	489
Majdanek	Gershuni	492

After the Deluge

A Look At My Destroyed Shtetl	Ch. Gromadzyn–Gotlib	493

On the Ruins of Czyzewo	Dov Saba	496
Czyzewo – Today On the Vestiges of a Disappeared Jewish Life	Y. Dawidowicz	504
Czyzewo Jews – Where Are They?	I. Dawidowicz	511
We Will Guard Your Holy Memory in Our Hearts	Dov Gorzalczany	513
Czyzewo Benevolent Association	Itsl Kirszenbojm	516
Activities of the Czyzewo Landsmanschaft in Israel	D. Aba Yitzchaki	517
Dedicated to the Anonymous Donor	Editorial Board	521
Memorial Candles		522
Index of Names in the Hebrew/YiddishCyzewo Yizkor Book		554
Name Index of the English Translation		587

[Column 17]

Preface to the Book

Translated from Hebrew by Jerrold Landau

In this book before us, we unite ourselves with the holy memory of the dear natives of our town, who were murdered in such a terrible and frightful manner, of which there are no human words to describe.

There was a Jewish community in Czyzewo, and it is no longer.

We, the survivors, come with awe and trepidation to erect a monument to it.

We attempted to gather and weave together chapters about the life in the town, a life of toil and creativity, the physical and the spiritual life, a vibrant life in all its dimensions and all its eras.

Generation followed generation in the chain of Jewish life of Czyzewo. A multi-faceted Jewish life grew here, and laid down roots.

Generations to come will find in this book, as in all memorial books to the victims of the Holocaust, a testimony and mirror into what it was like in the Diaspora of Europe prior to the great destruction, when all vestiges of Jewish life were erased from our town.

This book that is before us cannot purport to portray all facets of the variegated life of our small town, and it should not be approached as an ordinary book of literature, science, or history. The various ways of life presented on these pages cannot be weighed on the scales of literature, or on the scales of history and science. The importance of this memorial book, even for science, is that its authors are not men of science.

We who came from the community of Czyzewo, who remain a few of many, and who merited to join ourselves with the builders of our homeland in the Land of Israel, felt that it is upon us to fulfil this holy duty – to erect a memorial to our community. We did not rest or silence ourselves until we completed the task.

This was a holy task, of agony and grief.

We will kindle an eternal light to the holy and pure martyrs; we will erect an eternal monument to the memory of the community that was destroyed and annihilated.

May this book serve as an eternal memorial!

Yisgadal Veyiskadash… (the first words of the Jewish Kaddish memorial prayer).

[Column 21]

The Song of the Murdered Jewish People
Yitzchak Kacenelson

Translated from Yiddish by Judie Ostroff-Goldstein

Translation donated by Jane Prawda

How can I sing – so that the world will know?
How can I play with broken hands?
Where are my dead? G-d, I am searching for my dead,
In every hill of ash: - Oh, tell me, where are they?

Shout out from the sand, from under every stone,
From all the dust, shout, from all the flames, from all the smoke –
It is your blood and sap, it is the marrow from your bones,
It is your body and your life! Shout, Scream, loud!

Shout out from animal entrails in the forest, from fish in the river –
I want a shriek, an outcry, a voice from you,
They ate you. Scream from the lime kiln, scream small and big,
Scream murdered Jewish people, shout out!

Oh, alas, my people appear. Raise your hands
Out of the deep, mile long graves and sealed shut,
Layer upon layer, doused with lime and burned,
Up! Up! Ascend from the obstacle, the deepest layer!

Everybody come, from Treblinka, from Sobibor, from Ostrolenka,
From Belzec come, come from Ponar and from others, from others, from other!
With eyes torn open, raise a cry and without a voice,
Come from the swamps, from deep in the mud, from Poland -

[Columns 23-24]

Come, you who are drained, ground down, crushed. Come. Stand up,
In a circle, a large circle around me, one large ring –
Grandfathers, grandmothers, mothers with babies in their wombs –
Come, Jewish babies of powder, of a bit of soap.

I am the man who watched, who saw
How men threw my children, my wives, my young, my old
Into wagons, like stones you were flung in there, like discards,

And they beat you without pity and spoke to you as wantons.

And now? You see wagons, trucks now, you watch,
You silent witness of such burdens and of such pain and of such distress!
Silent and closed, you watched, Oh, tell me wagons, where
You are traveling to. You the people, the Jewish people, have departed to death?

The first killed were the children, forlorn, little orphans. They are called
The best of the world, the most beautiful that the dark earth possesses!
Oh, from the loneliest little orphans and children's homes should grow our comfort, from the cheerless, mute, little faces, the gloominess will not be allowed to take us!

They were the first to be taken to their deaths, the first ones on the wagon,
Men threw all of them in the wagons, like a handful of garbage, like rubbish –
And took them away, murdered them, destroyed them, there is no trace
Of them, of my best, no more remains! Akh, alas, woe is me!

[Columns 25-26]

The sun will rise once more over small villages in Lithuania and Poland never to meet a Jew again
A light in the dark, an old man, a man reciting a chapter of Psalms, a man going into the synagogue -
After all, the peasants will travel in wagons on all the roads, they will travel to the fair after all,
So many gentiles – good gracious! Yet more than before! And the market, the market is dead. The market is full and is not full!

There is no longer a Jew to beautify the fair for great distances around, they are no longer lively, there is no longer any spirit
And no longer will a Jewish long, black coat flap over the market with a sack of potatoes, flour and grain, and a Jewish hand
Will no longer raise a pot, a soft chicken, caress a calf…the peasant a drunk, whips
His horse in grief pulls the full wagon back to the village… gone! Gone, there are no longer any Jews in the country!

And Jewish children – they will not wake up from sleeping, from dreams, every one of them bright in the morning –
They will no longer go to school, no longer let their minds wander, no longer play pranks, no longer play in the sand,
Oh, you Jewish youngsters, oh, bright eyes! Little angels…where are you from? From here, in this town? And not from here!
Oh, beautiful young girl, your brightness, your neatness, everything in order, your little face is not messy.

They are gone already! Oh, on the other side of the ocean, do not ask, do not search in Kasrylewka, nor in Jehupiec…leave it alone!
Do not search for any one…not the Menachem-Mendels, the Tuwia Milkhikers, the Shlomo Nagids, the Motke ganefs, oh, do not search!
Like your prophets, Yeshaya, Jermia, Jehezkiel, Hosza and Amos, from the eternal Bible

[Columns 27-28]

They will cry out to you from Bialik, speak to you from Scholem Aleichem, from Scholem Ash, from one of their books.

It is that lost voice from the Torah no longer heard from any yeshivas, from any study house and pale yeshiva students,
Noble in learning, poring over the Talmud, deep in thought…no, no, not pale, there is such a glow!
Already extinguished…rabbis, heads of yeshivas, Jews studying, geniuses thin, dry, weak and full of Talmud,
With post Talmudic commentators, small Jews with large heads, with high foreheads, clear eyes, they are already gone, they will no longer be.

[Column 29]

Introduction

Shimon Kanc

Translated from Yiddish by Judie Ostroff Goldstein

The subjective element, those who experienced events and automatically, the individual manner of seeing events – puts a stamp on all the descriptions of the Czyzewer Jews and are factors, as they do not pretend to be all encompassing and answer all the problems that emerged in various eras.

Only the first articles about one-time Czyzewo are an attempt to find the synthesis of the economic development process of the Jewish community in Czyzewo. In all the articles, which are in the part "Between the Two World Wars", there is a tendency to analyze the facts and events. These are imparted as memories, warm and simple. It is important to mention the proficiency, in all cases, of the people who wrote articles. Examples of this are the works about the Jewish Community Council and about Tzentos (children's homes/orphanages) and the Merchant's Union. They bring out important scholarly problems that first had to be systematically and fundamentally elaborated.

The memories about the Zionist youth organizations are told with love and enthusiasm. They can be useful not only in studies of the shtetl, but also in studying the Zionist movement in Poland.

The part "Way of Life" and Folklore takes you further into the large feuds caused by the Hasidim and Mitnagdim (those opposed to Hassidism) shoykhet (ritual slaughterer) and the various institutions, types of people and images that created the flavor of the village.

The important entries are the eyewitness accounts by those who miraculously were survivors and who clearly describe everything that happened during the Holocaust in the Czyzewo ghetto.

From the ghetto material you can see that the Germans were in no small measure responsible for precipitating the annihilation of morality. People forced Jews into physical closeness, in order to intensify their spiritual distance. It is true there was a moral decline by those who worked on behalf of the Germans. But there was no stealing and looting, no scenes of Jewish cruelty, of detachment from the suffering of brothers. There were also no cases of suicide.

[Columns 31-32]

There is an interesting description by I. Dawidowicz of the town today, almost twenty years after its destruction. "The screams of the murdered hang over the houses and people. The confusion that has been visited on the Poles is seen in all the misfortune that came to the town, the hand of justice and persecution for helping murder the Jews who truly built the town."

One senses in the articles the reliability of the various people who brought out facts from oblivion.

The entire town was used as an important and valuable source of material. It serves the historian as a basis for research and scholarly synthesis and as a source to create material to illuminate our fundamental problems, but does not give any clear answers.

Despite the lack of analysis, these simple people created descriptions that give us a picture of life and death of the Jewish population in Czyzewo. The historian can learn about the way of life and the struggle led by the Czyzewo Jews to exist. Small articles, facts and figures give an idea about community activities that were of course led by parties (political) and organizations. The immense vitality, the great will to live and endure which existed even in the worst ghetto conditions will be found in these pages.

The characteristic common to all the articles, even the drier, documentary material, is the warmth with which they are written. This is the warmth of the Czyzewo Jew that he guards even in far off places.

[Columns 33-34]

Shma Yisrael

(Hear, O Israel)

Take a look and see, there is such suffering here,
my suffering, that is my burden. (Lamentations)

[Column 37]

Let Us Remember!

Translated from Hebrew by Jerrold Landau

Let us remember with grief and indignation the souls of our holy and pure brothers and sisters who fell at the hands of the impure murderers, who were bereft of the Divine image.

Let us remember the loss of the treasuries of Torah and wisdom, the nobles of the Children of Israel, the choicest of the old and new culture, the glory of humanity, from the elderly to the children, possessing of all proper traits: charity, doing of good deeds, love of the fellowman, and dedication.

Let us remember all of the splendorous abilities, the G-dly lights that lit up the masses, the dreams, hopes, and desires of the souls, the lofty aspirations, the love of Jews and the love of the Land of Israel, the faith and might, the hatred and disdain for the human beasts.

Let us remember the synagogues and Beis Midrashes, the institutions of charity and good works, the houses of study, the libraries, and the houses that were dedicated to the service of the people and the Land.

Let us also remember the cemeteries, the graves of our fathers, an all of the fruits of their faithful labor.

Let us remember them all, who were killed, annihilated and destroyed at the hands of the wild evildoers who were impure of soul. Let us remember – we will not forget!

[Column 39]

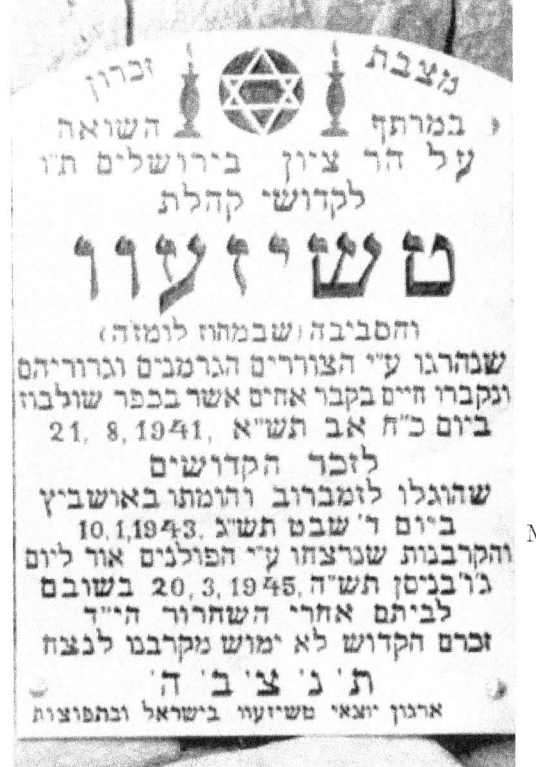

**A Memorial Tablet
In the Holocaust Cellar
On Mount Zion in Jerusalem, may it be built and established
For the martyrs of the community of
CZYZEWO**

And the surrounding area (in the Lomza region)
Who were murdered by the German enemies and their accomplices
And buried alive in a communal grave in the village of Szulborze
On the 28th of Av, 5601, August 21, 1941.
In memory of the martyrs
Who were exiled to Zambrów and murdered in Auschwitz
On the 4th of Shvat 5703, January 10, 1943
And the victims who were murdered by the Poles on
Monday evening, 6th of Nisan 5705, March 20, 1945 when they returned
To their homes after the liberation. May G-d avenge their deaths
Their holy memory will never leave us
May their souls be bound in the bonds of eternal life.
The organization of Czyzewo émigrés in Israel and the Diaspora.

[Column 41]

G-d full of mercy, the judge of widows and the father or orphans,
Do not ignore and overlook the blood of Jews that was spilled
Like water. Grant proper repose under the wings of the Divine presence
In the holy an pure heavens, in the radiance of the splendorous heavens,
To the souls of the thousands of martyrs of
Czyzewo
Men, women, boys, and girls, who were murdered, slaughtered,
Burned, drowned, strangled and buried alive. All are holy
And pure. May the Master of Mercy bind their
Souls in the bonds of eternal lie, and remember their sacrifice for us.
May the land not cover their blood![1]

[Column 43]

Top translated from Yiddish by Judie Ostroff Goldstein
Bottom paragraph translated from Hebrew by Jerrold Landau

My heart trembles and shakes, but my hands do not cease their shaking and trembling. We stand in deep sorrow over the martyrs, our dear ones, our own folk, but a consolation is here:

The consolation is the Land of Israel.

Let us allow our sorrow to leave us like flames, but let us not allow the flames to incinerate our spirit.

The bright memory of our anguish demands from us a strong and courageous heart, in order that their deaths should fight for redress in building our bright future.

The head of my father appeared unto me, a holy skull from its habitation, as if it was removed from its shoulders. It flew in the clouds of smoke, with its face pained from agony, and it eyes exuding blood.

(Ch. N. Bialik)

Translator's note:

1. This prayer is a close adaptation of the "Kel Male" prayer recited at Yizkor services, funerals, and other memorial occasions.

[Column 45]

Remember What Amalek[1] Did to You

The Editorial Board

Translated from Yiddish by Judie Ostroff Goldstein

Words alone are the matzevah-Czyzewo (gravestone) unfolding before our eyes. It is difficult to do because my heart bleeds so, for the atrocious destruction and the tragedy of the huge grave on which the "gravestone" will now be erected.

This memorial book does not need a preface or an explanation. This is the only matzevah that we can erect for the martyrs from our town who drained the cup of Hitler's poison to the bottom. As long as there are still living witnesses, it is our holy duty to gather all the material possible, everything that we remember, know and feel about our shtetl.

This material was gathered from the small number of those who clawed their way out of the mass graves. Some of them, in those terrible days, wandered through fields and forests, staying there overnight in the snow and cold and imbibed in their limbs the lot of every dark day and listened in the quiet to the rattle of our dying brothers during their last minutes.

None of us are professional writers or historians. Only the shocking agony that appeared with the horrible Holocaust opened our mute lips and made them speak. Every note, even when it was written with a gentle smile and light humor, is still an expression of concentrated grief. Therefore, every line has a place in this matzevah book in memory of our nearest and dearest.

Only a part of the Czyzewer Jews were saved from the Nazi authorities. Several only remained alive to be able to tell about the Holocaust. In Czyzewo, as in hundreds of other towns and villages, there aren't any Jews. Therefore, it was many years after the Hitler deluge before we found in ourselves the courage and gathered the strength needed to erect this memorial, this Yizkor Book from our shtetl Czyzewo.

It is clear and understandable, that in most notes and dissertations that are in this book, one hears the mourning cries; in the memoirs everyone can hear the sounds of lament and elegy, the lament of the destruction. For the participants in this book, the destruction of Czyzewo, like the general tragedy of the Jews in Europe, is a personal tie to the tragedy, with grief for our own dear ones. Perhaps you will see here and there repetition in some of the articles, mentioning some of the same affairs, events and people, but the first reinforces the second and creates the picture of a way of life, of the disappointments and accomplishments. Everything together tells the story of how much we have lost, how large and truly incomprehensible this loss is.

The heart cries for the tortured, the lost. But their illustrious memory requires us to be strong of spirit and to take heart in order that their deaths can fight to build and improve our future.

Telling the story about these people and personalities permeates our hearts with affection and longing for all of them – those who were and are no more. Reading about them, we still see the faces of our brothers and sisters, for all of them were a part of us body and soul.

Those of us who have had the honor to be saved from that immense conflagration, always see before our eyes our ancestors' commandment that remains engraved with letters of fire and blood: "remember what Amalek did to you" – the Amalek of the twentieth century.

This is actually the designated role of this book; not an ordinary memoir of the distant and not so distant past, not just a memorial light for the pure and holy souls who were murdered, put to death through various, horrible means. By recording our memoirs we felt that we needed to bring out the distinct illustriousness of the Jewish people in our shtetl. This book should give future generations an idea of the beauty that was killed.

With our heads bowed and wringing our hands, we stand at the modest monument to our murdered Jewish community in Czyzewo. We are united with the holy memory of the murdered martyrs.

Alas for those who have been killed, but will not be forgotten!

This yizkor book should stand for generations as a remembrance. For all those who read this book it should be a document that reflects the rich way of life that is no more.

Their screams that come from this book should not be stilled and should not cease to demand their due for generations to come.

[Column 49]

So We Started

Translated from Yiddish by Judie Ostroff Goldstein

Excerpt from the resolution that was passed during a meeting of the Czyzewer landsmanschaft in Israel in 1957.

For hundreds of years our ancestors built their homes in Czyzewo, to create a place of repose in the shtetl, to build a warm home for future generations.

To our great regret and pain their hopes became drowned in blood. Our parents, sisters, brothers, friends and comrades were savagely murdered. The enemy did not even spare young children or infants. Our town was suddenly transformed into a murderous slaughterhouse, from which it was impossible to get out alive.

True, the daily needs and problems of each of us have compelled us to forget the great misfortune that our people met. It is also possible that we simply are not able to comprehend the horrible Holocaust that took place in our former home.

But the day must come, in which all of us who came from Czyzewo and are now located in all the countries throughout the world, must mention our martyrs. We must mention our dear ones and loved ones. In the very recent past they lived and hoped to see a better, calmer and more beautiful life in the future. But they did not live to see it.

We must mention and therefore care that they should not be forgotten by us, all of them for whom the possibility of living was so brutally discontinued.

We must remember that not so long ago, we had received living greetings full of warmth, affection and worry and today all of this has become silent. Dead!

We must remember that there in Szulborze, murder "was the solution" through which the German assassins and their Polish assistants answered the Jewish question in Czyzewo. There lies in one

[Columns 51-52]

large "mass grave" the bones of all of those whose last wish before giving up their holy souls was: – that we, all the survivors, wherever we find ourselves, should live united and keep their memory holy!

In the ruins of the two Czyzewo desecrated, shamed and destroyed cemeteries lie the bones of our great-great grandfathers, the founders and builders of the town. We stand today with bowed heads, to erect a memorial, for the murdered martyrs, in the form of a Yizkor Book that must serve all of them as a "cemetery" in which the souls of our nearest and dearest may rest.

For all of us survivors there lies a holy duty to erect a matzevah (gravestone) for all of those we will never forget. This we will do in the Yizkor Book for our annihilated shtetl Czyzewo.

Every Czyzewer is duty bound to help create this Yizkor Book, in which he must see a matzevah for his dear ones. He must see in this Yizkor Book not just any printed, mute words, but the voice of the souls of his so brutally murdered relatives who call out:

Remember! You should not forget us!

As a result, the following appeal was sent to all countries:

[Columns 53-54]

To Our Fellow Czyzewers In All Cities, In All Countries!

Sixteen years have passed since the murderous catastrophe, like a hellish fire, that engulfed the town where we were born, Czyzewo.

A dreadful slaughter, unequaled in the history of our martyred people, was carried out by Hitler's hordes in our shtetl.

It is only sixteen years later and already there is not even a trace remaining of the place where the bloody tragedy, in our old home, was played out. Every bit of ground there is drenched with Jewish blood, with the blood of our holy ones and dear ones, fathers, mothers, brothers, sisters, relatives, friends and comrades, all of them our own dear people with whom we spent the best years of our youth.

From generations of Jews and yiddishkeit (Jewishness) there remains only enormous mass graves without gravestones, without the smallest memorial that should shout out to the world about the terrible tragedy that happened there.

On the huge mass graves wild grass is already growing. It covers and erases the traces of the horrible murders and they will be forgotten along with our entire past life in Czyzewo.

We must not tolerate this!

This would be a great injustice on our part, a desecration of the honor of our martyrs who knew in the last minutes of their lives to believe in us.

Therefore a large, holy duty lies on all of us. We must answer to that tragically mowed down Czyzewo community in which we lived together, grew up, dreamed, struggled and strove for better times, for a better life.

We must erect a matzevah, an eternal memorial! A matzevah that should tell our children and the future generations about this tragedy and to perpetuate the memory of our martyrs!

[Columns 55-56]

We know what an appropriate matzevah should be. And if we would be able to build it, it would be a large cultural or holy building in Israel. It would simultaneously symbolize the realization of the ideal of all Czyzewer Jews who were permeated with the idea of "love of Zion" and suffered, not living to see the great miracle of our time – **the establishment of the Land of Israel**. But, due to enormous monetary difficulties, with which such a project is tied, we must, with great regret, resign ourselves.

To begin with:

To perpetuate the memory of our town in a matzevah book. We must create a memorial book for Czyzewo.

Our shtetl was small and poor, but it had a rich way of life, firmly established in yiddishkeit and Jewish traditions. Jews had lived in Czyzewo for hundred of years, withstanding afflictions and tortures, pogroms and hooligan attacks, evil decrees and persecution. And yet they struck deep roots.

In Czyzewo there was everything that characterized Jewish life. Our town had an interesting variety of wholesome ordinary Jews, learned men, Hasidim and various superb figures. There are too many to tell about here and would necessitate an article in itself.

For this purpose, the Czyzewer landsmanschaft in Israel created a committee that will be in charge of collecting material, written articles, pictures, historical data that is relevant to Czyzewo, to take testimonies and documents from Czyzewer Jews.

To start with, local committees should be created wherever there are fellow Czyzewers, for the purpose of taking charge of the work.

[Columns 57-58]

All together we will establish this holy work. Every Jew who comes from Czyzewo must give a hand to this holy work either by writing or receiving from others, memoirs, facts, happenings, events, legends, everything related to Czyzewo, to life in Czyzewo, to Czyzewo's Jews. It must be written in simple language, in a language that is comfortable, without artificial fanciness, without stylistic effort, only genuineness and truth, like the hearts of the simple Czyzewer Jews. This must be the holy task of every Czyzewer regardless of where he is.

At the same time, we must make every effort to create a monetary base to publish the mentioned collective creation. The responsibility lies with every one of us, a holy duty to contribute according to one's means, in order to help. The Czyzewo memorial book should be rich and valuable in its contents, as well as esthetically pleasing in its outward appearance.

The Czyzewo landsmanschaft in Israel will direct the subscription collection among our fellow Czyzewers to create the first basic sum needed for the task. We will then rely on the local committees that will be created in every country and city to find the appropriate means to collect money for this holy task.

No Czyzewer Jew should refuse to give his fair share for this modest keepsake – the Czyzewo memorial book, that will remain as an everlasting remembrance for our children and also for everyone for generations.

> Sister and brothers, fellow Czyzewers!
> Step forward immediately to work.
> Create local committees.
> Let us know the addresses of your committees soon.

With brotherly greetings:
The committee in Israel.

> Okon, Isachar / Tel-Aviv   Jablonka, Ahron / Tel-Aviv
> Brukarz, Dov / Tel-Aviv   Surowicz, Gedalia / Ein Harod
> Bodla, Izak / Yerushalayem   Eliasz, Yechiel / Tel-Aviv
> Gorzalczany, Dov / Tel-Aviv   Cukrowicz, Avraham / Haifa
> Gorzalczany, Arija / Petach-Tkod Kandel, Jakob / Tel-Aviv
> Gora, Gerszon / Bnei Brak   Kupiec, Fiszel / Tel-Aviv
> Gora, Eliahu / Tel-Aviv   Rabinowicz, Alisza / Tel-Aviv
> Held, Josef / Yerushalayim   Szlaski, Yitzchak / Tel-Aviv
> Worona, Chaim / Haifa

To the Natives of Czyzewo in All Places

Translated from Hebrew by Jerrold Landau

Sixteen years have gone by since the terrible disaster passed over us like a fiery downpour upon our native town of Czyzewo.

The Nazi warriors perpetrated a terrible slaughter in our town, which has no comparison in the annals of the tribulations of our people.

Only sixteen years have passed since then, and already there is no remnant from that place, our old birthplace, where the bloody tragedy took place, where every clod of earth is saturated with Jewish blood, the blood of our holiest and dearest to us, fathers and mothers, brothers and sisters, relatives, acquaintances and friends, people like us, with whom we spend the pleasant years of our youth.

Out of generations and generations of Jews and Jewessess, all that remains are silent communal graves, without monuments or memorials that would testify forever about the tragedy that took place to them.

Wild weeds already grow and flourish out of the massive communal graves, covering them completely and removing from them the marks of iniquity and cruelty that was done with them. Along with this, our past lives in Czyzewo are forgotten.

We cannot permit things to reach this situation!

This would be a terrible travesty. This would be a disgrace to the honor of our holy martyrs, who in their last moments, surely thought about us. Can we let it reach this situation?

A holy obligation is placed upon us regarding the community of Czyzewo that was destroyed in such a tragic manner, to that community together with which we lived, suffered, dreamed, struggled, and aspired to better days and a happier life.

We are obligated to erect a memorial monument, an eternal perpetuation, so that we can relate to our children and future generations about the tragedy that once took place. With this, we can perpetuate the memory of our martyrs forever.

We know that a fitting memorial would be to erect a large cultural-communal building on the soil of the holy Land of Israel, that could symbolize the realization of the ideal of all of the natives of Czyzewo, who were imbued with the idea of the love of Zion, but to their ill fate, did not merit to the great miracle of our time – the establishment of the State of Israel. However, due to the great material difficulties involved with such an endeavor, we must abandon this idea at this time.

[Columns 61-62]

We have decided:

To perpetuate the memory of our town with a book-monument, to create a Yizkor Book for the town of Czyzewo.

Our town was small and poor; however a rich, variegated way of life was conducted in it, based on firmly rooted traditional Judaism. Jews lived in Czyzewo for hundreds of years and suffered from tribulations and poverty. Many tribulations, invasions, pogroms, evil decrees and persecutions passed through, and nevertheless, the Jews were able to strike deep roots in their town.

Czyzewo had everything that characterizes Jewish life. Our city had within it interesting personalities of strong members of our people, scholars, Hassidim, and many other lofty personalities. There is much that can be related about them, and a great work is needed to capture all of this.

To accomplish this end, we, the natives of Czyzewo in Israel, have selected a committee to gather material, descriptions, photographs, historical dates, names, testimonies, and sources that are connected to the town of Czyzewo and the Jews that lived there.

All of us together must contribute to this holy endeavor. Everyone who hails from Czyzewo must lend a hand to that idea, whether to register alone or to obtain from others memories, facts, occurrences, episodes, and legends. Everything that relates to Czyzewo, to its life and its Jews must be written in simple, popular language, in language that is comfortable for everyone, without professional or stylistic embellishments. This must be written only in a straightforward, honest style, as befits an ordinary person of Czyzewo. This must be in the holy language that befits each person of Czyzewo.

Along with this, we must gather all of our strength to create a monetary foundation for this joint endeavor. Each of us has a holy duty to participate in this endeavor to the best of our abilities, in order to ensure that this Yizkor book of Czyzewo will be as rich as possible in content, and as beautiful and splendid as possible in its external presentation.

Our organization in Israel is undertaking a major subscription amongst its members to collect the necessary monies for this purpose.

No native of Czyzewo should refuse to give his donation for the benefit of this modest endeavor – a Yizkor book for Czyzewo, which will remain as an eternal memory for our children, and for the entire nation of Israel for generations to come.

Brothers and sisters of Czyzewo émigrés, let us get to work immediately. Let us establish local committees. Please let us know the addresses of these committees very soon.

The deep burden that has burdened our hearts for these many years since we have known about the terrible and frightful tragedy of the murder of our dear ones and family members – is now let loose from the heart with the publication of this Yizkor Book.

We have struggled for all these years with the question of how, and by what means, to perpetuate the memory of the martyrs and to establish a suitable memorial that is befitting of its name. Such a memorial must express in a significant fashion, on the one hand, the magnitude of the tragedy that overtook the natives of Czyzewo with the brutal murder of our fathers, mothers, brothers, sisters, relatives, friends, and the Jews of the entire town; and on the other hand, must serve as our mouth and tongue for future generations to relate about the Jewish community of that town during days gone by, about the simple and humble life of previous generations. It must describe the images and portraits of the townsfolk, as well as various events. In short, it should serve as a faithful lens, as it delves into that bygone era which is no longer. With the passing of that era, all of the people that created and lived their quiet and peaceful lives in that town have disappeared and gone down to the grave.

Therefore, there is a strong desire in our hearts to create a great thing. However, there are restrictions on the possibilities, for natives of Czyzewo in every place aspired to a bold plan, such as: the establishment of a splendid synagogue building or some other public institution in the names of the holy martyrs. We indeed very greatly desired to actualize that which we thought.

This very fact of the lack of any symbolic monument did not let our souls rest. Each year on the memorial day observed on the 8th of Av, the day that the natives of Czyzewo in Israel gather together en masse for a memorial ceremony, this problem was presented to the gathered crowd, and the difficulties were discussed, until a decision was made that the monument would take the form of a Yizkor Book.

We did not reach this decision easily. Many of us who belong to those "of low faith" hesitated due to lack of faith in our physical and spiritual abilities to actualize the publication of a fitting Yizkor Book. This meekness is very typical of people who have only recently been redeemed from the fate of the town, which often depresses the spirit and subdues faith in one's own abilities to some degree. Therefore, the advice to publish a book was pushed off from year to year. After the final decision was taken, a committee was chosen that began to act with great diligence to collect material for the book. It very quickly became clear that the fear of these people was in vain.

Significant abilities and talents were uncovered amongst us. Many of us desired to pour out the bitterness of our hearts by writing our memoirs, stories and various descriptions of the town and the terrible Holocaust that took place in it. They tried and succeeded. Thus was most of the material gathered for the publication of this book. We are now proud and happy to present this book to every man or woman who is a native of Czyzewo, with the purpose of it serving as a symbolic monument for the holy martyrs – a monument that will reside in the house of every one of the natives of our town, in every country that they might reside.

Our community that went up in flames will not arise again, just as the long suffering and highly creative Polish Jewry will not arise again. The new residents of the town have taken the place of the Jews who were murdered; however they have not wiped out their memories from the survivors in our country that has risen to life and in any other country in the Diaspora. Their memories will illuminate the eternal way of life of the Jewish people with a precious light.

[Column 65]

Czyzewo

[Column 67]

Translated from Yiddish by Judie Ostroff Goldstein

The Book Committee would like to extend their gratitude to our comrades, who with their advice and deeds helped create this yizkor book:

ARJE GORZALCZANY, who did not miss an opportunity to remind everyone of their duty to hlep put together and publish the yizkor book. At every gathering and at every meeting he mentioned it, lured and urged people to take up this holy work;

ISACHER OKON, for whom no task was too difficult, whether administrative work or Society activities, especially helping to create this book;

Josef CHELD, for constantly being prepared work for the benefit of the Society and especially for organizing the erection of the matzevah (memorial stone) on Mount Zion in Jerusalem;

Freidel Levinzon, the daughter of our last well-known rabbi and Itsl KIRSZENBOJM (New York), who carried almost the entire burden of procuring the necessary money to publish the yizkor book and helped with advice whenever the book committee in Israel called.

Translator's note:

1. Amalek, Amalekeit – the name of a people that wanted to divide the Jews in the desert. Designation for anti-Semites. [Judy]

The History of the Town

Once, Once…

Translated from Yiddish by Judie Ostroff Goldstein

[Column 69]

It is difficult to know when the first Jews settled in Czyzewo as it was a small community that transformed itself into a village. In Brokhauser's "Jewish Encyclopedia", written in Russian, we are only told that Czyzewo was one of the places where Jews were not limited in their living-rights and that in 1856, 34 Christians and 1457 Jews lived there. According to the census of 1897, the total population amounted to 1785 people of whom 1596 were Jews.

From the same source we also learn that Czyzewo then belonged to the Ostrów District in Lomza Province. According to the general encyclopedia of 1861, Czyzewo belonged to Plock Province and Ostrolenka District.

Old documents from the end of the 18th century, that were in the Provincial archive in Bialystok, show that during the years 1770-1780 Czyzewo – that was the name of shtetl even back then – had 47 houses and 370 inhabitants. Of those, over three hundred were Jews.

Development at that time was very slow, as shown by documents of 1827 stating there were 74 houses and 811 inhabitants.

The mail highway between Warszawa-Petersberg went through the shtetl. The shtetl had no other distinction, except its poverty. The Jews mostly ran small businesses traded among themselves and later with surrounding honorable Polish nobility. With time various artisans arrived, but in general, the craftsmen trades were difficult to develop.

Czyzewo did not have any economic base and therefore, at the time, the Jewish population of the community was not able to grow as in other places.

[Columns 71-72]

In 1854 the railroad line was built between Petersberg and Warszawa and went through Czyzewo. This helped the shtetl flourish.

The Polish Slownik Geograficzny (Geography Dictionary) of 1880 mentions the date of the new railroad line as a turning point in the development of Czyzewo. Then the businesses grew because of the grain industry. There were also new opportunities for artisans.

At the time, new sources of income were being creating. The manufacture of tsitses (the undergarment with four tassels worn by Orthodox Jews), developed and because of the excellent quality of the goods, they were greatly appreciated throughout the country. This product was also exported and was in great demand by American Jews, but the highest demand for tsitses, until 1914 – was from Russian Jews. The trade with Russia was cut off at the outbreak of the First World War in the aforementioned year.

So, life for the Czyzewer Jews alternated between sad and happy, cheerless and sunny days, black and bright spots – two colors that accompanied business and economic life up until the outbreak of the brown plague that led to the complete destruction of the Jewish community in Czyzewo.

[Columns 73-74]

A Tear for a Generous Friend

by Julian Dawidowicz

Translated from Yiddish by Judie Ostroff Goldstein

Julian Dawidowicz, a writer and journalist of Polish radio, warmly responded to our appeal for help in gathering particulars about the past and present in Czyzewo. At the risk of his life, he traveled from Warszawa to Czyzewo several times during 1959, hanging around with Poles who looked at him with suspicion and hatred. He assembled even the smallest trace from the past about the life and destruction of the Jews with great dedication. He gathered them bit by bit and created his finely designed articles about the past and present of the desolate village, where gentiles have taken over the places of the former Jewish residents and since then the village has remained a wasteland. He absorbed the cries that were still carried in the air and described all of it in several articles that are included in various sections of our yizkor book.

Julian Dawidowicz followed our work to perpetuate the memory of the murdered Jews with interest and was prepared to give further help in publishing the book faster. He did not succeed in seeing the fruit of his significant help. A terrible illness interrupted his life.

[Columns 75-76]

An Overview of the Origin and Growth of the Jewish Community in Czyzewo

by Dov Gorzalczany / Tel Aviv

Translated from Yiddish by Judie Ostroff Goldstein

We can and we must with amazement and with satisfaction find the joyous phenomenon in our difficult Jewish lives: ordinary Jews writing history!

It is an amazing, but certain fact that surpasses all dreams. Who would have thought it possible that an ordinary Jew would be able to revive a story from once, once upon a time. To assemble, brick by brick, all that he knows about his shtetl, about past generations, about all the parts and corners of Jewish life and tell this in chronological order. In striving to revive, to create for future generations, the history of a destroyed and obliterated shtetl, I endeavored to comply with the immense will and strength to perpetuate the struggle of generations from our shtetl. This is not an academic article, because nobody in our poor village, myself included, had received the necessary preparation to be a historian. Also there was not any indisputable source about Czyzewo and its Jewish community. The old pinkus (Jewish community book of records) that I remember from Rabbi Boruch Hershman's time, who we all knew so well as Reb Boruch Krajndl's, was given to Jakob Deb Rav's (Plocker) after Reb Boruch's death. Later it was burned along with the village and there were no other books written about our shtetl because it was too small to be included in the general geography or Jewish life in Poland. The only remaining source for my historical "research" was my memory. Therefore, I felt strongly that it was my duty to write and recount everything that I know about our shtetl, about its rise and development. I did this to the best of my ability, embracing everything, exhausting everything, but with the same love that I devoted to helping establish and publishing this yizkor book. With the same persistence, in spite of all the Jewish deaths from hatred, to tell and tell again about the horrifying story of destruction, and the ordinary chapters of daily life.

[Column 77]

With my recounting I was not only delivering, releasing, throwing down the large story of survival and memories, but also felt a clear, distinct and firm mission, an iron duty not to fail, so the life and destruction of all those murdered should not disappear without a trace. I also put demands on myself to collect every detail of our old life in Czyzewo. This is not simply a memorial, not only sitting shiva (observing seven days of mourning for a close relative) and bringing comfort to a mourner, this is a condemnation of the destruction of those murdered. This is our perpetual demand for dues from the world not only for the murdered fathers, mothers and children, but also for the children never born, killed together with their mothers, in their mothers' wombs. And they demand the continuity of their spiritual existence, of their dreams about a beautiful, brotherly, humane life.

The exact date of the establishment of Czyzewo is not clear. But it is certain that it existed for hundreds of years. The old people said that Czyzewo was one of the first Jewish communities in the area, a lot earlier than Ostrów Mazowiecka, but later than our neighbor Zaremby Koscielne[1].

The witnesses to the age of Czyzewo were the gravestones in the old cemetery. They told of hundreds of Czyzewer Jews already at rest under them. In 1820 there were about 800 souls living in Czyzewo and the old cemetery was already, at that time, no longer used. The area of about 4000 square meters was already, at that time, completely used.

[Column 78]

Until the outbreak of the Second World War, the area of Czyzewo took up one square kilometer. It was located on the borders of the following three noble estates. The terrain on the north and southeast belonged to porec (Lord) Sokolowski. On the west the village bordered the fields of the manager's courtyard that belonged to porec Poznanski.

[Columns 79-80]

The southwest portion lay on the border of the land belonging to the Kosker Lord Marzik Godlewski.

We also know that the Jewish community in Czyzewo began to develop along porec Sokolowski's border because all the Jewish institutions were located in the area that had once belonged to his estate. Both bote-midroshim (study and prayer houses), to be precise: both locations on which stand the first and second besmidresh (study and prayer house), both old and new cemeteries, the Jewish slaughter house, in passing, served as the community slaughter house; the steam bath, the almshouse, etc. All of them were built on porec Sokolowski's land.

The public town institutions were also, for the most part, in the same area. Only the new Christian cemetery and the later marketplace were located in the area of the manager's courtyard. Just like all towns and villages[2], Czyzewo was built near a river, the Brok, which did not have an excessively large amount of water during the summer.

No ships sailed this river. But in bygone years, when the village was surrounded with dense forests, in the pre-spring weeks logs we sent from there to the sawmills using the Brok River and then to the Bug River and from there to Danzig using the Wisla (Vistula). Supposedly wood was furnished by Czyzewo to build the capital Warszawa.

Geographical Position

Czyzewo is located on the 107 kilometer-long Warszawa-Bialystok railroad line. One of its closest neighbors was the very ancient village Andrzejewo, 7 kilometers northwest, a small village that existed for many, many years but has only a small population, located off to the side, without any highway connecting it to any neighbors.

Only in the late 1930's, shortly before the outbreak of the Second World War, was a road built through Andrzejewo from Czyzewo to Ostrów Mazowiecka. 14 kilometers to the west was the village of Zaremby Koscielne. Between the two was located the small village Szulborze that later in 1941, played such a shocking role for both towns. Zaremby Koscielne also did not have a highway connecting it with any of its neighboring villages. South of Czyzewo was located the small village Nur through which ran the large Bug River.

From the river Jewish fishermen and in later years the well-known Yehoshua Dojcz, supplied Czyzewo with fish for shabes and yontef.

To the southeast is the town Ciechanowiec, which was connected to the Czyzewo railroad station. Ciechanowiec had strong commercial ties with Czyzewo, particularly through the grain industry.

[Columns 81-82]

To the east was Wysokie Mazowiecki, a village no larger than Czyzewo that served as the District City for many years. To the north of Czyzewo was Zambrów that was also tied to the Czyzewo railroad station. Another neighbor, Tykocin was 40 kilometers away and in the past it had been the seat of the "council of the four lands". 50 kilometers north was the Provincial City of Lomza with its famous yeshiva, where many Czyzewer young men went to study.

Bialystok, the large industrial city, was 67 kilometers away. Before Polish independence it was also a Provincial City.

The First Step on the Road to Development

In earlier times, before the development of Czyzewo, Jews lived in various villages throughout the area. There were Jews in the villages Dombrowa, Godlewo, Rosochate, Przezdziecko, Sutki, Chmielewo, Koski, Brulin, Siedlisk, Zaliesze and many others. The Jews in all the villages were busy trying to make a living as mill lease-holders, distillers, milk lease-holders, etc. It seems that the Czyzewo court attracted the best as tenants. This attracted more Jews from the area to settle on the Czyzewo porec's land.

Among the first Jewish inhabitants besides the water mill tenants, were the windmill owners.

At the eastern border of the village there were four windmills belonging to the old Czyzewo families Glina and Hersh Nata. As the Brok River had little water during the summer, the water mills could not work and they had to use the windmills. The four Jewish families, young and old, stood watch in order to use all the wind. Day and night the large sails turned and ground the grain that brought by the peasants and was processed it into bread and feed for the animals. The shtetl children were allowed to climb and play on the sails on shabes and yontef, because no matter how much wind there was, the mill had to rest and the sails were not allowed to turn.

The blacksmiths were also important to the porec.

Next to the windmills, on rented court land, the Paw, Kowadla and Kon families, stood at their forges from generation to generation.

A strong attraction for Jews to settle in Czyzewo was the fact that the fair took place there.

Jewish traders and artisans were attracted from the surrounding villages to Czyzewo. This is how things went for hundreds of years. Czyzewo grew bit by bit and in 1820 the village had grown to 800 souls.

In the second half of the 19th century, the shtetl began to grow faster when the railroad line connecting Petersberg with Warszawa and with Western Europe (built in 1854) went through the village.

[Column 83]

The fact of why the railroad station was built two kilometers from the town is explained two different ways. One version is that the Tzar's engineers purposely moved the station away from Jewish Czyzewo. Another version said that according to the calculations of the Czyzewer porec, the station would have to be built on his land. Therefore he demanded an extremely high price for his land from the Russian government. Instead, they bought land from the Siedlisker porec at a cheaper price and built the Czyzewo station there.

[Column 84]

The railroad created new sources of income for freight forwarders, guest-houses, etc. From that time on we note a faster growth of the Jewish population in Czyzewo.

In the vicinity of the railroad station, in the villages of Biala and Siedlisk, lived the three brothers Abram Chaim, Shlomo and Judel Lubelczyk as well as Mendel Zysman. They were the owners of the kretchmas (inns) and the milk leases. After the rebellion in 1831, the Russian government forbade Jews from keeping kretchmas. The Jews were advised to take Christian partners who would figure officially as the owners. With time the new partners began to be seen as the only legitimate owners and pushed out the Jewish partners.

[Column 85]

After the Czyzewo station was built, the first of the Lubelczyk brothers settled there and made a living as a freight forwarder. The Zysman family, who held the milk lease, opened a kretchma called "China", a teahouse where also, unofficially, strong drink was sold. Among the first inhabitants at the railroad station was also the Czyzewer family, but from the time of the First World War none of them were left in the village. They had all immigrated to America. The Lubelczyk and Zysman families were also drawn here, as well as the Gromadzyn, Worona and other families who settled at the railroad station. These families, as far as Jewish affairs were concerned, were independent of the Czyzewo rabbi, ritual slaughter, mikvah (ritual bathhouse), cemeteries and the like. But they had built their own besmidresh with Shlomo Lubelczyk and created a miniature community.

[Columns 83-84]

Reb Zajnvel Ajdelsztejn, from the respected old heder. A Gerer Hasid and a distinguished scholar. At the same time he was also the largest manufacturer in town, a generous donor and hospitable man. He was greatly loved by the entire Jewish population, regardless of class.

Reb Aba Rotenberg, born in 5595 (1835) in Suwalk, died - 5690 (1930) in Czyzewo, a sharp mind from the Wolozhin yeshiva, traveled to see the Kock. Along the way he stayed in Czyzewo where he married Szejna-Chai'ke.

[Columns 85-86]

The founders of the Jewish community at the railroad station

Reb Shlomo Lubelczyk, father of the wide-branched Lubelczyk family

The wife of Mendel Siedlisker. The grandmother of the wide-branched Zysman family

[Column 87]

Shlomo Lubelczyk – the father Mendel Sielisker's wife, the of this branch of the Lubelczyk grandmother of this branch family of the Zysman family

Village Jews, Who Belonged to the Czyzewo Community

The Jewish community in Czyzewo also spread its spiritual domination over the individual Jewish families in the neighboring villages. In Rosochate, 7 kilometers from Czyzewo, there were several Jewish families who had lived there for generations. There were several Jewish families also in Dombrowa. They prayed together on shabes and yontef as a minion. These families remained in the villages until the end. There was a score of Jewish families living in the villages Przezdziecko, Sutki, Godlewo and Chmielewo, but under the pressure of anti-Semitism they did not feel that their lives were safe and at the end of 1930 they moved to Czyzewo. The blacksmith Yitzchak Wapniak moved from Brulin to Czyzewo and later moved to Israel where he died a ripe, old age.

[Column 88]

Only the daring Okon family kept their windmill in Kosk until late in the 1930's, until they also in the end could not resist the pressure and left their home where their father and grandfathers had lived for generations.

[Columns 89-90]

The following people paid a heavy price for living in Polish villages. In 1921 the miller, Gedalia from Godlewo was murdered together with his wife.

For having the nerve to be a good settler, the Jewish landowner Moshel Wolfsman and his wife paid with their lives in 1905. After he had already both the estate, he and his wife were murdered at his son's house in Chelenowe village.

About the Community and Immigration

At the end of the 17th century there were about 400 people living in Czyzewo and 150 years later, there were about 2500 people, including all the Jews in the surrounding villages. The Jewish population in Czyzewo remained the same until the end of the 19th century.

In the last 50 years of the town's existence, the young people emigrated and went to the New World, mainly to North America and in the last 20 years, also to Israel.

The Relationship between Jews and their non-Jewish Neighbors

The relationship between Jews and their non-Jewish neighbors, with a small number of exceptions, was good. The entire area was made up of aristocratic courts (estates) and semi-enslaved farm hands and the rest were gentry, the so-called "pans" (squires).

[Column 91]

As the Polish gentry had always found commerce and trade distasteful, they had come to an agreement with the small merchants and traveling peddlers to act as a go-between between those in need of a service and the Jews. They were happy to provide they service and would send Jews from the nearby town. Jewish merchants, butchers and artisans were able to go out freely by day and by night, without fear, and travel around to the near and far villages. Every Christian house was able to serve as an inn. Every peasant cooked, with pleasure, (in the special pot that the Jew had brought with him) a little something for the Jewish artisan, or traveling peddler. The peasant always took the Jew with him to milk the cow, so he would be sure that the milk went right into the special pot and the Jew would be able to drink it. Only during the week of Easter, the Jews did not travel in the villages among the gentiles. For the most part, during the week of Passover, Jews avoided leaving their homes.

[Column 92]

Relations with the Polish population were truly friendly. Every Pole was loyal to his stores and merchants. They never forgot to bring a gift in honor of a Jewish holiday: a fat hen, a basket of eggs or only a sack of apples and pears.

Also, a Jewish storekeeper never forgot before Passover to distribute matzah to all his important clients. Fridays he would honor them with gefilte fish.

Welwel Jabka, the famous droshky driver, at the station in Czyzewo – Leah Zylbersztajn and a tourist

Volunteer fire brigade with Shalom Grynberg (in the center)

[Columns 93-94]

Even the town intelligentsia had Jewish friends. How often for example, the apothecary Paris had theorized about what a pain the Jews generally were, but Leizer-Salte's stood as the master of honesty.

The idyll ended in 1935/36 with the heavy boycott lead by Organinski.

The Town's Christian Intelligentsia

There were about 30 to 40 non-Jewish families living in Czyzewo. They were the community officials, post office, police, teachers, private tutors, 2 or 3 storekeepers, a baker, a wine tavern, priests and their families, an apothecary, 2 doctors, 1 artisan, 2 agents, etc. The officials did not have any competition from the Jews. On the contrary, the Jewish population was necessary for their material needs. Consequently, everything superficially was in order. Those who were forced to earn a living in pursuits similar to those of the Jews exhibited certain hatreds. The professionals belonged to the extreme right in Polish society and were exposed to negative ideas and an attitude of hatred for Jews. One did not expect to be liked by them. However, it must be said that their attitude towards the Jewish population was correct. Naturally they took care that there would never be a Jewish doctor in Czyzewo. During the years when the Jewish doctor Gelbojm lived and practiced, they did everything to make his life difficult. The attitude of the Christian doctors was downright hatred. Even Paris, the apothecary, sabotaged him whenever possible. When Dr. Gelbojm was forced to leave Czyzewo, the Jewish doctors who came after him, without exception, were not able to exist. One after the other they left town.

In General, the Christians lived apart from the Jews, even the youngsters scarcely met together. Once, once, at a ball organized by the firemen, one Christian took part in a Jewish entertainment for a charity.

Economic Structure

The economic structure of Czyzewo was not very complicated. Artisans and merchants – they were at the high end of the economic scale. There was no industry, even in the surrounding area. To reach the nearest industrialized town, Bialystok, one had to travel 67 kilometers.

Stationary and traveling Artisans (Tradesmen)

One encountered a variety of tradesmen among the Jewish artisans: shoemakers, blacksmiths, carpenters, cabinetmakers, tinsmiths, shinglers, roofers, bakers, butchers, hairdressers, watchmakers, wheelwrights, bricklayers, thatchers, turners, cap makers, tanners, etc. There was not a trade in which either the Christian or the Jewish populations were in need of that the Jewish artisans were not able to provide.

[Column 95]

There were stationary and mobile artisans. In the category of mobile or wandering artisans belonged the carpenters who would travel to the villages from Monday to Friday afternoon and build houses for the peasants or stables. They lived in the village the entire week. Friday afternoon the "gospodarz" (landlord) took him home for Shabes. Monday morning he would bring him back. Among those who belonged to the wandering artisans were the tanners and tailors. Monday morning one would see a peasant wagon go to pick up the tailor, his associate and machine and then bringing him back Friday before candle lighting.

Some of the artisans would travel with their merchandise to the fairs in neighboring towns and villages. They were the so-called second class artisans. They would turn out ready-to-wear boots, clothes, furs, hats, various tin bowls, furniture, wagon wheels, spinning wheels and also bakers. There were also blacksmiths would travel around to the markets with a stock of various horseshoes and shoed the horses on the spot. Aside from several Polish shoemakers who made shoes for Jewish businesses and a baker, there were not any Christian artisans in Czyzewo.

Commerce

Jewish commerce encompassed all possible and necessary branches. The economically strong businesses were 2 iron stores, 2-3 wood warehouses, two shoe businesses, 2-3 wholesalers of building materials and also several manufacturing concerns. The rest were small food stores, fancy and dry goods stores, wine taverns, grain traders and horse dealers.

[Column 96]

The butchers were in charge of cattle trading and they would buy up cattle for slaughter. Livestock sales took place only at the fairs and peasants would buy one or two animals, sometimes for milk. Horse dealing was also done at the fairs. But there were stables where horses could be bought on certain days, besides at the fairs. The poorest of the fancy goods manufacturers and shoe merchants would also pack up their little bit of merchandise and leave for the neighboring towns and villages along with the artisans to sell their wares at the fairs.

Small Industry

Except for the specifically Jewish Tzitzis industry, Czyzewo also had a brush factory, that employed 4 to 6 workers and would deliver brushes from Rejz-Wurcel to Grodno, Suwalk, Wolkowisk and even Bialystok. In the Czyzewo area there was a source of soft wood trees and cheap, unorganized labor. Meshal Blajwajs, who was smart, had developed this trade into a respectable scope. Until the First World War there was also a good, firmly established soap factory that belonged to the Rabinowicz family. The factory burned along with the shtetl during the retreat of the Russian military in 1915. Also the four windmills were burned at the same time.

After the doomed windmills, two steam mills came into existence and were able mill all of the flour and feed for the entire area. And in a year when the wheat harvest was good, they were able to export flour to Bialystok and Warszawa. The two mills were able to give employment, along with the owners, to 15 to 20 families.

[Column 97]

Passenger Transportation

About ten families were able to earn a living by passenger transportation and transporting goods. Besides the railroad line, the main connection with the neighboring towns and villages was the horse and wagon. Every morning Shlomo Zelman Hofman would come to the market with his covered wagon, harnessed with three horses (he spoke of them as "eagles"), round up his passengers and at the appointed hour he would get on the road to Lomza, a journey of 50 kilometers.

Shlomo Zelman Hofman went to Zambrów, 22 kilometers away; Leizer Nebach had the concession for Ciechanowiec, 20 kilometers away and his son, Jehuda Mendel, inherited this run.

The only driver to go to Zaremby was Szmuelke Koszleon. The road to Zaremby was difficult, as it was sand. Therefore he never had any competition. His son Michal took over after him.

Andrzejewo, the closest town to Czyzewo, about 8 kilometers distant, was connected with a regular horse and wagon passenger service, but this route belonged to an Andrzejewer, perhaps because he was a Czyzewer son-in-law.

The above-mentioned three passenger services, running on good highways, were at the beginning of the 1930's done away with. Horses and wagons gave way to the newly arrived automobile.

There was not any stable connection with Wysockie Mazowieckie, Nur, Sterdyn and Sokolów. Within the district, people would travel through the Szepetów by train. "Nur" would come with it's wagons. Sterdyn and Sokolów were connected to Czyzewo through family affairs and Hasidim who did not need daily transport.

[Column 98]

Transport

Some of the drivers started passenger traffic to the railroad station. About eight families were employed at this. Others were occupied by transporting goods from the station and back. Some families lived by being porters, loading and unloading heavy cargo.

Religious Personnel and Professionals

At a certain time there lived in Czyzewo a dentist's family that did not stay long, especially when a Polish dentist arrived. A Jewish doctor lived and practiced for a long time. In the late 1930's there were three Jewish teachers in the state school, also 5 to 6 teachers in the Jewish schools such as the modern heder, Beis Yakov, heder, Yesodi haTorah heder. There were two ritual slaughterers, two sextons, 1 bath attendant, two gravestone engravers, a scribe (for religious purposes, i.e. Torahs, phylacteries, etc.), melamdim (heder teachers) for all grades and a rabbi. For the last 36 years until the Second World War, the rabbi was Rabbi Shmuel Dawid Zabludower.

Various Businesses

The following businesses were in Czyzewo: a cotton wadding factory, a wool carder, a small soda water factory, a soap factory. Egg and fowl merchants, lease holders and several families made oil for domestic use. There were freight forwarders and a specialist for sick horses who did not have a university education.

Until Poland's independence, a number of Czyzewer Jews were occupied with illegal emigration. They smuggled emigrants going to America across the border.

[Column 99]

Social Life

Until the end of the 18th century, social life was very limited. During the week Jews were busy earning a living. In the early hours of the morning (from 3 am until they had to work) and evening hours, Jews would go to the kloiz (small prayer room in a person's house or business) and pray as a minion. After Maariv, they would sit for a while in the bes midresh (house of study and synagogue) near the warm oven and talk about various subjects that were of concern to everyone. The scholars were not occupied with this nonsense. They used the early morning hours to study Torah.

At the beginning of the 19th century, the Hasidic wind began to penetrate the town. At that time the ruling of society went over to the Hasidim and dominant among them were the Ger Hasidim and they cooperated in getting Rabbi Boruch Szapira of Stuczyn to settle in town. He was one of the followers of the Kocker court and and a supporter of the later Ger rebbe.

For a short time Rabbi Chaim Lejb Kaliszyner lived in town, also a supporter of the Kocker rebbe and later the founder of the Kaliszyner dynasty.

Playing second fiddle in society life were the followers of the Aleksander rebbe. Both had Hasidic shtiblach (prayer rooms) with rich religious libraries. Besides concentrating on Hasidism, both also concerned themselves with all learning and making sure the town was G_d-fearing. There were also Sokolower and Amszynower Hasidim in town. The latter had a great influence on the common people, on the bes midresh Jews. It was the cause at that time of a sadly, famous "difference of opinion". The Szniadower-Wizners kept the Amszynowers with them and even became leaders of that faction. It is worthy of mention that at the end of the "difference of opinion" in 1903, Czyzewo chose an Amszynower Hasid as rabbi. This shows that there was a compromise as everyone was tired of the "difference of opinion" that had lasted for years, brought insults, anger and worse still disgrace and shame.

[Column 100]

The main faction in the difference of opinion was the Gerer and therefore it is not difficult to understand why the official greeters of the young rabbi were two respected men from the Aleksander shtibl, Yisrael Yitzchak Gorzalczany and Yisrael Tyktin, who had been sent to Ostrolenka to give the rabbinical contract to the young, 23 year-old gaon (genius) Reb Shmuel Dawid Zabludower.

It is worthwhile mentioning that after Reb Shmuel Dawid became the leader, there were no longer any disputes between the Besmidresh Jews and the Hasidim. On the contrary, the shtiblach gave the besmidresh prayer readers, a cantor who was a Ger Hasid, a cantor for the additional service who was an Aleksander Hasid and even a reader of the law who was a shtibl Jew, for the Days of Awe (High Holy Days).

The bes midresh Jews were the so-called "common people", Jewish artisans and workers, hardly scholars. If in the last years pretty gemara melodies were heard coming from the bes midresh, it was the daily page, led by Yisrael Yona Raczkowski, a Ger Hasid. Mainly Hasidic youngsters were learning there.

[Columns 101-102]

In the bes midresh there was a table where a Hasid would constantly study a Mishna (collection of traditional laws) lesson, or something else. There were also half-slumbering bes midresh Jews sitting there. But the study of Torah with enthusiasm, ardor, and the right traditional melody could only be heard in the two Hasidic shtiblach. Therefore it is no wonder that when a young Litvak misnaged (those against Hasidism) groom arrived, who was receiving room and board from his father-in-law, a scholar such as Yisrael-Yitzchak at the beginning against his will had to go to the shtibl. Only there could he find his equals. Besides him, there was the famous "missionary" Wolf Lejb the melamed, who if he cast an eye on a good young misnaged, a good student, or a recently returned students from the yeshiva, had to rescue him and make a Ger Hasid of him.

There was also a small "Khevre Mishnayos" (Mishnah study group) in the bes midresh in which the comfortable Misnagdim Jews, who were not great scholars but also were not ignorant, studied every day a Mishnah chapter with the people. There were "shtibl-Jews". The first lesson giver was Yisrael Tyktin, then later Shlomo Yisrael Gdalja's.

The founders of the "Khevre Mishnayos" were the brothers Mendel and Nuska Gromadzyn, the brothers Moshe and Mendel Niewad, Jekel Wibitker, Avraham Chaim the "zimer", Shmuelja Gaczer, Kelman Zajonc, Judel Orlinsky, Yitzchak Hersh the melamed, etc.

The First Winds of Enlightenment

During all the hundreds of years that Czyzewo existed, in this area virtually nothing changed.

When a boy was three years old, his father wrapped the boy in his talis (prayer shawl) and took him to heder to the grammar melamed. From the grammar melamed he went to the humash-melamed (Bible teacher). Later he went on to Gemara with the Toisefes (additional discussions of the Mishna) melamed. The last stage was undertaken ordinarily only by children from Hasidic families, or sons of rich Misnagdim. Later they traveled the roads to the various Polish yeshivas in Radun, Lomza, Brisk, Warszawa and others. Still later, to the Lublin yeshiva. During the era of Russian rule, there was a law about compulsory schooling, but Jews ignored the decree. It was rare that somebody attended the government school. This was also perhaps because to study with a multitude of gentile boys, meant risking your life.

Those who had the desire to study were self-taught. There were several who received an academic education, i.e., Chaim Shmuel the schochet's son. He had the strength to fight for the title of engineer. There were also private teachers, who gave Russian lessons, or Polish and arithmetic. Of course these lessons were only available to the children of rich parents.

There were also Rebetzin (Rabbi's wives) who taught young women to pray, write and do simple arithmetic. The first public school for Jewish children was founded in 1916 during the German occupation. The principal of the school was Lewi Yitzchak

Rubinsztajn. The boys went to school in the afternoon. At first the school was in a room at the hospital and later in Surowicz's house.

With the coming of Polish independence, the two Jewish professionals, the Jewish Dr. Gelbojm and the Jewish dentist Szachnerowicz (the first dentist in the shtetl during its existence) began to organize a Jewish public school that was run by Mrs. Gelbojm with the help of Miss Blajwajs. The school only had the lower grades. Those who wanted to continue in public school through grades 7 and 8 had to go to a larger town. Only westernized Jews sent their daughters to study in other towns, i.e. Lewi Belczyk, Gorzalczany, Lepak, Prawda and Kejmowicz.

[Column 103]

In the 1930's there was already a government public school for Jewish children that was run according to the government plan. Jewish teachers were Kliar, Chmiel etc and there were also Christian teachers in the Jewish public school.

The winds of enlightenment first began to blow during the German occupation in 1916. The older young people received a taste of knowledge. They wanted to broaden their amateur ideas and then a Jewish public library was founded. The following young people were among he first founders: Alter Szerszyn, Alter Baran, Dov Brukarz, Bucze Jablonka, and Plocker. The first managers were Dr. Gelbojm and H. Szachnerowicz.

Also at that time a Dramatic Circle was created in order to support the library.

During the time of the Japanese-Russian War in 1905, when revolutionary unrest broke out in Russia, the Jewish youth in Czyzewo also revolted. But this was not a class struggle. This was a revolt against the social slavery of their parents.

[Column 104]

With the suppression of the revolution in Russia, the social uprising in Czyzewo also came to an end. Once again daughters were slapped by their fathers for only being suspected of speaking to a young man. Once again, the father waited for evening when he could catch his son or daughter with a Yiddish book. The first enlightenment was suppressed but not extinguished and it awoke ten years later.

The younger generation carried on difficult wars with the older generation for every concession. Only with great difficulty were they able to get a room for the library. Excommunication was the main weapon against the rebels. There were never ending disturbances at the theater.

First at the beginning of the 1930's it stopped. The older generation had to capitulate to the coming generation of middle-class young people who did not have the same politics as the old Hasidic world. On the wings of the Zionist movement they built new cultural institutions in the shtetl.

Besides the government school, during the late 1920's, Agudas Yisrael (Orthodox group) founded the modern girls' school called Beis Yakov. One of the best graduates from Sura Schenirer's Beis Yakow seminary, Professor Tojba, was brought to the shtetl. Also founded through Agudas Yisrael was a school for boys called Heder Yesodi HaTorah. In both schools secular and religious subjects were taught.

Through the Zionist youth, under the leadership of Yechiel Asher Prawda, the "modern heder" was created where boys and girls learned together. Starting with pre-school, Hebrew and other subjects were taught according to modern methods. The directors of the school brought qualified, young, Jewish teachers, graduates of the Tarbut seminary in Wilna and Warszawa. Special buildings were erected for the above mentioned schools.

[Column 105]

Jewish Parties (Political)

There were always sympathizers of the Lovers of Zion movement in Czyzewo, but these sentiments were only strongly expressed after the Balfour Declaration. Then parties of all shades and directions were established. The General Zionist

Organization, Mizrachi, League for a Working Eretz Yisrael, Bet'ar, HaShomer HaLeumi. All had a headquarters where the youth would gather and talk about events, study and broaden their general and political ideas. Also Agudas Yisrael and the Tzeiri Agudas Yisrael carried out substantial activities.

The leftist organizations showed very little life. The Communist Party was outlawed. There were, it seems, no Bundist activities in Czyzewo.

From 1923 to 1926 the left took part in certain activities. These consisted of ransacking the public library and in other demonstrative acts of this nature. The Communists were brought to trial and as a result one young man was sentenced to a year in jail.

Institutions

In Czyzewo there existed government institutions such as the Polish "gmina" (community) and the Jewish Kehilla (community council). There were also religious institutions such as the synagogues and Hasidic prayer room. Additional institutions were the Jewish People's Bank, Free Loan Fund run by the Zionist youth, Agudas Yisrael, Tarbut library, "Centos", (orphanages run by the "Joint"), "Toz" (the "Joint's" health care for children), Bikur Holim (visiting the sick), Linat HaZedek (caring for the sick), Zionist organization clubs, League for a Working Eretz Yisrael, Mizrachi, Tzeiri-Mizrachi and Bet'ar (belonging to the Revisionist Party). There was a modern heder and Beis-Yakov a merchant society and artisans' union.

[Column 106]

All the institutions were partially or totally run by young people who developed these activities and demonstrated that it was possible for young people and also entire families to go to Israel.

The 1st September 1939, the Second World War broke out. The tragic events of this war put an end to all of this. The 7th September 1939, the shtetl was taken over by the Hitlerites.

The 10th October the Hitlerites retreated and the shtetl was occupied by the Soviets.

The 22nd June 1941 – The Hitlerites occupied the town.

The 15th August 1941 (25 Av) – The first round-up, 1750 Jews were murdered in Szulborze.

The 10th September 1941 the ghetto was created in the shtetl.

November 1942 the ghetto was liquidated. All the Jews who were still alive were taken to Zambrów.

January 1943 – The rest of the Czyzewo Jews were sent to the crematorium in Auschwitz.

Those who survived along with who had immigrated to Israel and with the help of the Czyzewo landsmanschaft in New York, Mexico, Buenos Aires and around the world created this memorial book to the memory of Czyzewo that once was, is no more and will never be again.

1. From the poll tax taken in 1765 in Ostrów Mazowiecka, there were 68 Jews (20 families) and a gravestone found in Zaremby Koscielne was dated 1681. (trans. note)
2. Ostrów Mazowiecka was one of the few towns, perhaps the only one, not near a body of water. There is only a small spring and a natural pond created by the spring. (trans. note)

[Column 107]

A Small Detail That Can Serve as an Introduction to the History of the Jews in Czyzewo

by F. Artur H. Szrajer / Brooklyn, N.Y.

Translated from Yiddish by Judie Ostroff Goldstein

Dear Mr. F. Szrajer:

We received your letter with the question about the shtetl Czyzewo that is mentioned in Dr. E. Ringelblum's book.

The book, in which the shtetl is mentioned is The Polish Jews in the Kosciuszko Revolt – 1794 and was published in Warszawa, 1937 as an edition of the History Department of the Institute for Jewish Research YIVO. The book is available at YIVO. The episode about Czyzewo is on page 63-64. Enclosed please find the text that we copied for your Landsmanshaft.

Best regards,
Dina Abramowicz
Librarian

"In the region, in which Jews were not taken to serve in the military, unrest broke out with some of the Christian population." We read about this funny little revolt in a report from Commissar Olszewski. And the story went like this. – When the gentry of Czyzewo **(Czyzew 37)** were called up for military service, they stated that they would not leave as long as the Jews would not go with them. What were the Jews needed for – the cavalry and the experienced storekeepers. What did the Jews have? Maybe the Jews would bring them merit and they would win the battle? But it was something else entirely. They were simply afraid "the Jews who were left at home should not…slaughter their wives and children"… in other words, "they were afraid of a pogrom by the Jews".

The enraged Czyzewo gentry and peasants were not satisfied with threats. "they searched for Jews everywhere (from the shtetl), dragged them to the military exercise grounds and stuck weapons in their hands". Furthermore the stirred up gentry and nobles stated that if the Jews returned home, they would do the same. As this was a critical condition, it was referred to the central government. When they learned of the situation, they advised the commandant to yield "to the will of the people".

37) Arch. Kr. Pol. 388, P.185, 24. Vi.

[Column 109]

The Development and Growth of Czyzewo

By Dov Gorzalczany

Translated from Yiddish to Hebrew by Yosef Avni

Translated from Hebrew by Jerrold Landau

Coordinator's Note: This Hebrew article is equivalent to the Yiddish article that begins on page 76. Because it is the same article, we are not reproducing it again here; but, rather, what follows below are a few of the minor additions found in the Hebrew translation.

In the section on the Economic Structure, the following two sentences are added:

However, for the sake of precision, we should not ignore the existence of the tzitzit (Jewish prayer fringes) factory that marketed its wares to literally half of the Jewish world. Approximately 30 families made their living from this endeavor.

The last Yiddish paragraph is further embellished in the Hebrew, as follows:

Czyzewo Natives in Israel

From among the natives of Czyzewo who arrived at different times, there are also those lone survivors, who put their souls in their palms and fled for their lives from the terrible inferno. They set a goal for themselves of perpetuating the memory of the residents of Czyzewo.

With the assistance of the natives of Czyzewo in New York, Mexico, Argentina and other places, we publish this Yizkor book in order that it might serve as an eternal testimony and monument of witness to the memory of the town of Czyzewo, which once was and is no more.

Community Life

The Beis Midrash. A photo from 1959.
The building now serves as a grain storehouse.

[Column 129]

The Jewish Community - Its Origin and Activity

by Dov Gorzalczany

Translated from Yiddish by Judie Ostroff Goldstein

Just like other Jewish communities in Poland, the Czyzewer Jew's existence was a difficult, bloody struggle. It's true, there were quiet years of calm living with the Christian neighbors. But there were also times when the surrounding world bristled with enemies and evil decrees were also lavished on the Jews in Czyzewo that provided their economic existence. Still the Jews in Czyzewo always had a community life in all its wonderful complexity and living traditions, acts of justice and pursuit of quality.

The Jewish Kehila in Czyzewo was different from others in that the Jews did not feel that they had an imposed government. The members and head of the Kehila (Jewish Community Council) were people from the masses, well liked and esteemed because of their generosity and dear care for the requirements of the needy in the community. So much so that the Kehila remained in our memory, either from our own experience or from experiences told to us by our grandfathers.

Jews in Czyzewo did not wonder or know about individualism. Every Jew was a part of the entire Jewish community in the shtetl. We were raised in the spirit of togetherness, belonging to the people of Israel. We absorbed this feeling with the milk from our mothers' breasts; togetherness was always the way of life for us, in our thoughts and our deeds. For us the concept of community was alive and warm. Accursed are those who disrupted and destroyed it.

[Column 131]

I will try to tell about the things that have always remained in my memory, the things I heard about the Jewish Kehila in our shtetl. I will relate not only what I remember of their activities, but also what I heard as a boy at home, at the rebbe's in the heder, from the gabai in the Chevra Kadisha (Burial Society), in the besmidresh (study house, synagogue) and in the Hasidic shtibl. From wherever Jews gathered and talked about times past and the people of those times.

From these conversations I understood that many years ago when Czyzewo originally became a settlement and began to erect a synagogue, a mikvah, (ritual bath) and a cemetery that it was necessary for someone to appear as an owner of these institutions. Whoever represented these motionless materials had to be worthy in relation to the government. The people at the office where the sale of the places for the synagogue, or the cemetery were registered demanded a name. The only one with a name was the rich man in the shtetl, not an ordinary Jew, a very learned man.

As a result, some years later a conflict occurred. As it happened, the rich man later became poor and the heirs, who searched presumptuously for the father's estate, hit upon this community estate that had been written in his name and did not want to give up believing that it belonged to them.

Such cases happened. They created a lot of bad blood and were the subject of discussions and gossip for many years.

People also told about various other affairs, such as the cost of supporting the rabbi and other religious institutions. In the beginning these costs were borne by the rich Jews

[Column 132]

and the heads of the kehila. Later the "roite faczajle". The religious institutions were supported by the "monopolies" that they had for staples, such as salt, yeast, with help from threats of "prohibitions" and "excommunication".

Some sources of funding were the Jewish slaughtering and the cemetery. The money that was collected was used to support community institutions and people. In this way the administrative body, called the kehilla, raised money in Czyzewo.

Until 1924, the kehilla "dozors" (members of the Jewish community council) were elected in a very primitive manner, exactly as the election for the town council. On a market day, the representative for the community appeared in the street, beating the traditional drum and announced the day when the election would take place for the town council. On that day people from the community came and put up a table, at which sat the bailiff with the secretary, the governor and a representative of the police. They called out the names of the candidates who had been selected to run so that people could vote for the new bailiff and members of the town council. Those gathered raised their hands for one or the other. But the record was written with whatever the "government" wanted. This was how the voting procedure was carried out.

This primitive method was also used for the kehila elections. The meeting took place in the besmedresh. The Gerer and Aleksander Hasidim put forth the names of candidates from their shtiblach. Later, there was also a representative from the Shalomburger shtibl. Amid the racket and commotion from the various factions, the members of the Kehila were elected. The names of members that I remember are Chaim Yudel Wasercug and Yisrael Yitzchak Gorzalczany. Later were Berish Frydman who was head of the kehila, Hershel Malinowicz, Josef Boruch Lepak and Yisrael Yona Raczkowski. Two of them were Ger Hasidim, 1 Aleksander and 1 "Shalomberger".

[Column 133]

The kehila did not have a special meeting place, also they did not have a secretary. The meetings took place at the rabbi's house. Their decisions were given verbally. Only extraordinarily important issues, or laws were written in the large pinkus (record book of the Jewish community) kept by the burial society which was kept in a special place at Boruch melamed's (Hershman), the trustee of the Burial Society.

What Were the Problems That Occupied the Czyzewo Kehila?

One of the most important problems was the price of shehita (ritual slaughter), which in the last years was the only source of income for the Jewish kehila in Czyzewo. The work of the kehila was to fairly divide the income between the rabbi and the slaughterers.

Many times they also had to take over the ritual bath from those who were in charge of it. There was trouble from the Department of Health. They had not adhered to the laws of cleanliness. It happened many times that the head of the Kehila had to sit in jail for a day or two on the charge of "uncleaniness" and other sins.

The Czyzewo mikvah (ritual bath) was a "low one". When one wanted to immerse oneself, one had to go down about forty steps. The Department of Health was of the opinion that this was not hygienic and demanded that the mikvah be raised. The rabbi was against this and was obstinate about it.

The Czyzewo rabbi, Shmuel Dawid Zabludower was not a Ger Hasid and as a matter of course not a keen fanatic, but in the case of the sunken mikvah he maintained a staunch position and stood like steel against raising the ritual bath.

The rabbi had the backing of the Ger members along with the Kehila leader. They were not frightened of the Department of Health that had every time it came to the shtetl searched the mikvah and wrote a protocol about the sunken ritual bath. As a result, a kehila meeting would immediately be called to find ways to fight the enemies who were interfering in Jewish religious affairs…

[Column 134]

There was important business for the kehila to attend to. They had to establish an "eyrev". [1]. This was to let the Jews of the shtetl know where it was possible to carry something on Shabes. Our rabbi was strict about keeping Shabes and did not approve of half measures in regard to the "Eyrev". It was necessary to surround the entire shtetl with a wire, set up on high poles such as the telegraph lines. Inevitably the hooligans would climb the poles and tear the wires. Most of the time they did this on Shabes morning so nobody would be able to fix them. Many times I remember my father standing still in the middle of the street and gaving me his tallis (prayer shawl) to carry. Somebody had suddenly informed his that the "eyrev" was torn and one could not carry anything.

In later years, the dozors realized that they should modernize the eyrev, to use a combination that would be allowed according to the law, and not dependent on the whims of the hooligans.

This did not eliminate the influence of the youth on the activities of the Kehila, it was not the end of their problems or the end of the eyrev being torn. Instead of solutions the gray destruction arrived that so cruelly interrupted the generations of life for the Czyzewer Jews.

Since the feud at the end of the 19th century about a Hasidic and Mitnagid ritual slaughterer, which ended in a victory for the Ger Hasidim, there were not any large fights in the shtetl. The ritual slaughters were Ger Hasidim and even when they were old and their hands shook, nobody bothered them and everything was quiet in the shtetl.

Elections in the Modern Manner

By the end of the 1920's when new election laws were introduced in Poland for small towns, in Czyzewo the elections were held using modern methods, with a list of election rights and a list of candidates, for the town council and the Jewish kehila.

The truth is that in practice the election did not have any relevance for the Jews in the shtetl because the Endekes (Polish anti-Semitic National Democratic Party) hooligans stood at the ballot boxes with sticks and did not allow the Jews to vote. This was the reason, that in Czyzewo where the Jews made up 90 percent of the population, and 50 percent of the entire Dmochy Glinki district, that there was not one Jewish representative on the town council and or on the expanded council.

Due to the same Anti-Jewish motives the effort to end the status of Czyzewo as a settlement in order to have the rights of a town with a mayor did not have a positive result. Czyzewo, until the end, remained with the rights of a settlement (colony).

[Column 137]

The new election law created a fuss for change in the form of the kehila and the compositon of the representatives.

The new law provided Czyzewo with a Jewish community council of eight dozors. With the support of thirty signatures, a list of candidates was put forth. The goal of the elders was to close the door of the kehila to the progressive youth and maintain control. They had close relations with the Sanacja (Polish ruling party) and they collaborated with the government in establishing voting rights. However, they were not entirely successful in barring the road for the young people from having an influence on the activities of the kehila. In 1928, for the first time in Czyzewo, the Zionist parties participated in the kehila elections. My unforgettable comrade and friend Yechiel Asher Prawda was elected as a dozor.

Yechiel Asher Prawda was an interesting person, a fighter for Zionist ideals, a generous and active mizrachist and a strong supporter of the Zionist funds. He worked on behalf of Keren Kayemet and Keren HaYesod (now Jewish National Fund) in our town. He was also religious, prayed in the Aleksander shtibl where he had, by the way, a lot of problems due to his Zionism. He was persecuted and they threatened to throw him out of the shtibl, but he did not give up. He did not stop his work and for him Yisrael came first.

[Column 138]

Not even private business could keep him from his Zionist activities. Business, family – everything was immediately put aside when he was needed to help with elections to a congress, or a celebration for the opening of the University in Jerusalem. He did this openly and boldly, not like other young Hasidim who kept their Zionist sympathies deep in their hearts, but did not express their sentiments openly, so as not to come in conflict with their Hasidic environment.

The elected members of the kehila were:

1. Zebulun Grosbard – Ger Hasid
2. Yisrael Yona Raczkowski – Ger Hasid
3. Lejbusz Frydman – Ger Hasid
4. Alter Wolmer – Aleksander (kehila head)
5. Zindel Lew – Aleksander
6. Yosel Boruch Lepak – Szolemburger
7. Jehiel Asher Prawda – Zionist
8. Majer Moncarz – Besmidresh

As can be seen from the above list, the Zionists had very little influence. This result was caused by the elders who made the voting age 25, did not give women the right to vote and a dozor had to be at least thirty years old. The Zionist movement in Czyzewo was made up of young people.

Officially there was only one Zionist on the kehila, but unofficially – 2, because Lepak who was a Szolemburger candidate was also a member of Mizrahi [2].

[Column 139]

The Kehila Activities Are Modernized

Jehiel Asher Prawda's being elected to the kehila had great relevance in modernizing the activities of the kehila.

The changes were noticeable. They had a secretary who introduced order. The first thing was the kehila taxes and then they organized the ritual slaughters' fees. No slaughterer could be paid in cash – only with a note from the kehila.

The rabbi also had to accept changes. The character of the "roite faczajle" disappeared. The newly organized kehila set a salary for the rabbi that suited the dignity of a spiritual leader. At the shtetl mikvah, a special section was created for bathtubs. It was no longer necessary for people to descend 40 steps to immerse themselves in the public mikvah. For a set fee one was able to order a hot bath from the attendant. Some of the Christian population made use of the bathtubs as well. When taking into consideration the sanitary conditions in our shtetl, one can understand the great significance of these bathtubs.

The kehila also turned their attention to the cemeteries. The old and new cemeteries were enclosed with red brick fences.

The most important event was obtaining a place to build a Zionist People's House where all modern community life in the shtetl was concentrated.

[Column 140]

Obtaining the place for this purpose did not come about easily. Day and night the young Zionist bosses, who were among the top taxpayers and also had influence in various other community activities, did not cease demanding their due. In the end, after a lot of trouble and effort, they were able to get the place to build the house. The modern grade school for boys and girls, with young Hebrew teachers was also located in this house and the Zionist organizations held their meetings there.

In 1935 there was another election for the Kehila. The youth of Czyzewo had grown up and now there were many more Zionists with voting rights. Despite their strength being divided among many factions, through the general influence of the Zionist movement, they were much stronger than in the past. For the first time the monopoly on the office of Kehila head was wrested from the Hasidim. The results of the election even surprised the Zionists.

The members elected to the kehila council were as follows:

1. Zebulun Grosbard – Gerer
2. Eli Rubin Malcman – Aleksander
3. Itche Zylberman – Ger-Aleksander
4. Jehiel Asher Prawda – Mizrahi
5. Chaim Szczupakiewicz – General Zionists
6. Moshe Blajwajs – Revisionists
7. Fejwel Zyglbojm – League for a Working Land of Israel

8. Meyer Moncarz – Besmedresh

[Column 141]

The Zionists had every possibility to elect one of their own as head of the Kehila. – The Hasidic representative evidently appreciated the strength of the Zionists and began exhibiting a willingness to yield. – But he had also, unfortunately, sensed the lack of unity among the Zionist organizations and that led to Zebulun Grosbard, a Ger Hasid, being elected as head of the Kehila.

[Column 142]

For four years the new kehila council led activities with its particular merits and faults. – The Jewish population had a clearer understanding of Zionist idealism. – The Zionist dozors helped spread Zionist consciousness to the Jewish population through their activities. – Zionist speakers, who came from Warszawa, appeared in the bes medresh. – The idea of Zion had become deeply rooted in all classes of the Jewish population in Czyzewo. – Young and old were devoted to the idea with their hearts and souls until the great destruction arrived and wiped out everyone and everything. –

[Column 143]

Dedicated to the memory
of my Uncle Jehiel'ke,
a wise man in Czyzewo,
from whom I inherited his
position in the management
of the bank.

The Cooperative Bank

Translated from Yiddish by Judie Ostroff Goldstein

In 1925/26 after the inflation, when economic life in Poland had become more stable, commercial enterprises needed credit and confidence. Long-term loans were an important part of business. There were not any banks in Czyzewo. The large banks were not interested in opening branches in such a small provincial village.

In Ostrów Mazowiecka there was a "Bank Ludowy" (Populist Bank) and a branch was opened in Czyzewo, but the anti-Semitic wind that blew from this institution and a difficult bureaucracy and in addition the next to incapable Mr. Beker made it impossible to do business with the Bank Ludowy. Therefore a group of Jewish merchants came together: Yeshaya Gorzalczany, Fiszel Lubelczyk, Leibush Frydman, Eli Rubin Malcman, Zebulun Grosbard, Dan Knorpel, Jehiel'ke Gorzalczany, Alter Wolmer, Lepak, Czczupakiewicz and others and they decided to create a Jewish cooperative "People's Fund" in Czyzewo.

It is proper to note that in Czyzewo, that the Societal institutions were not yet controlled by any party, but rather, primarily, by the Hassidic shtibels.

[Column 144]

The first committee was made up of: J. Gorzalczany, Yisrael Yona Raczkowski and Knorpel (an Aleksander, a Ger and a Zionist).

The bank's board had six people: Grosbard, Frydman, Malcman, Gorde, Wolmer, Shaul Hersh Blajwajs (three Ger and three Aleksander Hasidim). The staff was made up of three people: Hebel – secretary, l– cashier and a messenger – Chaim Szapira.

The committee, board and personnel were all either Ger or Aleksander Hasidim. The youth and the Zionists were contemptuously ignored – not one representative.

And so this went on for many years.

The main activity of the bank was to make loans up to three hundred zlotys. These were to be paid back over the period of one year with an interest rate permitted by law. For larger merchants the bank made loans up to 1,200 zlotys and also dealt with currency exchange. The large wholesalers benefited from the banks with loans based on their inventory.

All those who were active in the bank were shareholders and every member had to invest up to 10% of his credit. They invested the money long term at the central.

[Column 145]

The main clients were the small stores and artisans who were desperately in need of help.

At the beginning of the 1930's, Knorpel liquidated his wholesale liquor business, left Czyzewo and returned to his hometown of Ostrowa. There were also changes on the committee. Jeszaja left his position and it was taken over by Jehiel'ke Gorzalczany. Knorpel's position was taken by a Gerer, Leibush Frydman.

There was an economic crisis and our shtetl was not exempt.

Storekeepers and artisans had trouble meeting their payments. Some of the largest merchants had a down turn in their businesses and could not honor their obligations. There was also a psychological crisis. The bank had lost its good reputation. It was no longer a bank. It had become a "homey informal club".

The anxiety level had dropped. "Who should I be afraid of? What, the committee will harm me? They should only try and people would stop reading in the shtibl on Shabes!!"

Afterwards Yechiel'ke Gorzalczany was the head of the committee and when he took over there was a majority with two Gerer – and so they took over the affairs of the bank.

People were afraid of Knorpel and Yechiel Gorzalczany. The threat of shutting down the reading in shtibl on Shabes did not have any effect on them, especially since Yechiel'ke prayed in the Aleksander shtibl. But just as the committee was free of the impartial members, the affairs of the bank went down hill.

[Column 146]

Really, Yisrael Yona Raczkowski was a strong man, but he was not able to take the pressure. Then there arrived an even more important negative factor, the bookkeeper was a "specialist" at his trade, a "clever writer". His handwriting was exact and he was a smart man, but very slow. As is usual when an institution stops growing, it loses momentum and the work increases. There are extra letters, extra messages to debtors and in the end the secretary could not handle the work and a mountain with old, unbearable matters. To the incomplete balances of several years, neglected in the bookkeeping was also added the malevolent unpaid balances. The central, through its controls, was alerted and in the end concluded it had to shut down the line of credit.

About getting help for the bookkeeper, there was no question about it. There was not a Ger Hasid who was an accountant. The only Ger Hasid they could find had already left Czyzewo and was in Israel busy establishing cooperative banks for Poali-Agudas-Yisrael.

Among the Zionists there were accountants. They even offered to help without pay, but they were suspected of wanting to get a foot in the door of the bank, learning the inner workings and then would rebel against the leaders.

[Column 147]

To everybody it was clear that fresh, young strength was needed in order to save the bank. But the Hasidic committee was waiting for a miracle that in the end did not happen. It became more and more difficult. So, at the end of 1936 bank activity had reached the point of stagnation. It was virtually closed. First Yisrael Yona began negotiations with the Zionists.

A meeting was called to elect a new committee and a board. Two representatives for the young people together with Pinya Zysman were elected.

The new committee had to present itself before the central in Warszawa and this would affect the necessary line of credit. Confidence in the town grew, the economy picked up and money began to flow in. Debtors began to pay. There was a complete turn around.

[Column 148]

At the annual meeting in 1938 a workable report was presented. The accountant had put things right. The bookkeeper was put on probation – either he carried out the work or somebody from the committee would do it. There were two people who had the capabilities

A young committee member gave the report. The Zionists' appetite had grown with eating. Having two representatives they wanted more. And if in 1938 they did not manage to do better, then it was sure to happen in 1939. But the bloody bandits of the Nazi beast had settled all the accounts, all the conflicts between the old and new world – were liquidated.

[Column 149]

A candle to the memory
of my friend Yehoshua Lepak,
a faithful public worker.

Gmiles Khsodim Funds

(Charitable Loan Funds)

Translated from Yiddish by Judie Ostroff Goldstein

There are three things people need
Torah, Avoyde (work) and gmiles khsodim.

In the shtetl the third pillar, as you know, that supports the world was missing. That is: a true gmiles-khesed-fund.

Torah, there was in large measure, in various places one heard Torah teaching. At all hours of the morning and in the afternoons and at all times of the year, a page of gemara (commentaries on the Mishnah in Aramaic) was heard from the bes medresh between minha-maariv (afternoon and evening prayers) using a well known gemara melody from the lowest to the highest octaves. Or the different quiet, calm teaching in the small bes medresh of the "Khevre Mishnayes" (Mishnah Society) in the small hours of the morning, or the sweet, ringing, childish voices from the dear heder boys.

Avoyde, Czyzewo was a worker's shtetl. Almost the entire shtetl was involved in manual labor. Everyone worked very hard - not only the artisans, but the storekeepers and peddlers also.

[Column 150]

The women and children were also harnessed to work. Also the second meaning of avoyde – serving the Lord – in this Czyzewo was not lacking.

Gmiles Khsodim, This Jews dealt with amongst themselves. But an organized institution was missing that would give interest free loans, not only to rich merchants, but essentially to those who were financially weak, the needy.

A group of young Zionists activists got together and decide to create a gmiles-khesed fund. Among the founders were Yehoshua Lepak, Dan Knorpel, Noach Edelsztajn, Pinya Sysman, Yechiel Asher Prawda, Avraham'l Grynberg, Yechiel Ahron Serka, Jakob Jablonka, Yosel Litmans hy"d, Motl Szczupakiewicz, Moshe Blajwajs, Yisrael Wengorz, the writer of this article Dov Gorzalczany and Ahron Eibeszyc.

Everybody at the meeting contributed 100 Zlotys and that was the founders' capital. Well-to-do friends loaned large sums on a short-term basis and so it began. Hundreds of loans were given without interest to those in the shtetl the most in need. The maximum loan was 100 zlotys but from time to time exceptions were made and larger loans were given.

[Column 151]

The "Joint"(Joint Distribution Committee) in Warszawa gave a subsidy to the fund – 1 – 1. The administrative work, such as giving out the money, collecting money, accountancy, etc. was done on a voluntary basis by the committee members: Lepak, Jablonka, Grynberg, Edilsztejn hy"d, Blajwajs, Szczupakiewicz, Wengorz and Gorzalczany. Also there were no expenses for rent.

At first the fund was run from Moshe'ke Gorzalczany's store. Later, in the small bes midresh of the so-called Shalombergs and at the end, after it was built, they had they own space in the Bet-Am (People's House).

The fund was busy giving loans, receiving payments. Every Sunday the committee members were on duty by turns. After several months the Zionist Gmiles Khesed fund reigned supreme in the shtetl as the only one in this field. The "Agudat Yisrael" (Orthodox anti-Zionist party) dominated the Czyzewo businesses and did not think that the Zionist G.Kh. Fund would be a success by giving out loans. The only criteria were the borrower's need and a lot of Gerer Hasidim were among the borrowers at the fund. Perhaps therefore, what this was, was a popular necessary public town institution – the Gerer opened a second Gmiles-Khesed- Fund that also rendered a lively activity. They also worked on Sunday evening and their office was at Shlomo Zywieca's.

[Column 152]

The generous volunteers in the Agudas fund were Shlomo Zywieca, Akiva Stuczynski, Jakob Pinchas Fydeto, etc.

Looking at it objectively, both funds sincerely helped the shtetl. But the "Joint" suspended its support. The "Joint" was not able to understand why such a small shtetl had to have two gmiles-khosodim funds.

There were several attempts to unite both funds. Delegates from Central "Joint" negotiated an entire evening and were unable to reach an agreement. At that time, in the large cities, the differences between both camps were enormous and it was the same in the Polish provincial towns.

Neither was able to give up any prestige, each camp wanted to clearly emphasize the positive usefulness of their activities but, in fact, it did not matter, as this did not bother the loan-starved people. In fact, instead of one Gmiles Khesed Fund there were two and they could now get loans from both.

I want to take this opportunity to mention the gratitude that everybody felt for the murdered volunteers of both funds for their tireless volunteer work that was truthfully a blessing for the shtetl.

The survivors should, for a long time to come, be worthy of and devoted to charitable work.

[Column 153]

Linat Hazedek[3] and Bikur Holim

(Overnight Righteous and Visiting the Sick)

by Dov Brukarz / Tel-Aviv

Translated from Yiddish by Judie Ostroff Goldstein

In one of the first years of the 20th century, cholera broke out in Czyzewo. The epidemic hit small and large alike and people were falling like flies. In the botei midrashim (study houses – synagogues) people were saying Psalms all day and all the while people were barging in and running to the holy ark with lamentable sobs, but the cholera that started with one had spread.

Everybody went around gloomy. In the market place small groups of people stood and talked only about "it". People spoke about past cholera outbreaks and what they had done in the past. A grave had to measure and a hupa (marriage canopy) put up in the cemetery and a poor young woman and a poor young man had to be married there. Everyone in the shtetl attended the wedding, which took place Friday afternoon. With white chalk they drew a line around the houses, under the widows. The only Christian doctor and the old-time barber-surgeon prescribed remedies.

This time in Czyzewo they created a Linat HaZedek society. Mendel Tsitses (the four tassels on the Orthodox undergarment) maker (Kanet) was in charge and there were several healthy and robust young people to help him. They were devoted to the work and stood ready to help day and night. As soon as

[Column 154]

somebody became ill, they were sent for. They gave the patient and massage over their entire body, until the entire body had a red glow. It was said that this helped, and that hundreds of people had been saved from dying.

When the epidemic subsided, the mission of Linat HaZedek ended and there was only the Bikur Holim society left whose assignment was to lend cupping glasses, rubber tubes, a hot water bottle and other necessities to the sick.

One person managed the inventory. Money to buy new products came from donations that were collected every week. This was done by specially chosen heder boys who, with a notebook in hand, went around with the gabai (trustee) from the society, who would write the name of the donor and the amount of the donation.

I remember when I was chosen to go around collection donations. The gabai from the Bikur Holim Society was Yehoshua Nisen Tsitsis maker (Kupiec). He was also for many year the officiating cantor at the additional service during the Days of Awe in the bes midresh. After him was Leizer Yosel's, or Leizer Moncarz.

[Column 155]

Yehoshua Nisen, along with most of his family, went to Israel in 1935 where he died 20 years later in Petach-Tikvah. But Leizer stayed and was murdered in the ghetto.

Hakhnasses Orhim (Hospitality)

Until the First World War there existed in Czyzewo a Hakhnasset Orhim. For many years Ahron Shames (sexton) took care of the Hakhnasses Orhim. Several years before the war Hershel Czarne's took over.

The Hakhnasses Orhim has a building with three rooms in the corner of the town. One of the rooms was always busy with a respected overnight guest. In the other two rooms were a couple of beds and straw mattresses. Poor men, strangers who had come to Czyzewo, were able to stay overnight there without asking permission from anybody.

During the First World War the building was burned down together with almost all of the houses in the shtetl. Only the houses on Szmidiszer Street were not burned.

Later when the shtetl was re-built, they erected the botei midrashim and the Hasidic shtiblach but they forgot about the Hakhnasses Orhim. The poor who came had to stay overnight in the botei midrashim or the Hasidic shtiblach. Also the women's section in the bes midresh was used for the poor who had to stay overnight.

Translator's notes:

1. Eyrev – Wire strung on the circumference of a town to classify it as enclosed private property in which objects may be carried on the Sabbath according to Jewish law.
2. Mizrahi – founded in 1916 as a movement for observant Jews who were also Zionists.
3. The volunteers from Linat HaZedek kept a vigil over the sick, to relieve the other members of the household who were tired and could no longer cope with the patient.

[Column 157]

"Centos"[1] – the Organization That Helped Jewish Children

By Dov Abu-Szmuel

Translated from Yiddish by Judie Ostroff Goldstein

In the last several years before the outbreak of the Second World War the economic crisis among the Jewish population in our shtetl became worse. The poverty of the Jewish masses had gone so far that even the shortsighted could see and feel it. It was sharply reflected in the faces of the Jewish children, which were emaciated by the poverty that ruled in their homes. In the morning hungry young boys would run to heder (boys grade school). The girls went to school with smoothly combed heads and nicely twisted braids, but their faces were yellow, pale and without a youthful bloom on them.

There were several reasons for the crisis. First of all it was the direct result of the prevailing crisis in the entire country. The colonels who were then standing at the government helm in Sanehcja Poland were occupied with "humanitarian" problems so as to better the conditions for the animals. The Polish gentry were worried that ritual slaughter was inhumane to the animals. Others organized hunts for Hitler's ministers.

[Column 158]

There were also boycotts in Czyzewo that were organized in Poland and they were persistent. Pickets stood in front of Jewish businesses and workshops on a daily basis and did not allow any customers to enter. The market days and fairs were now taking place on Shabes.

In Jewish homes the hardship became greater with every passing day and it showed on the children's faces.

Then some young, energetic and devoted people created a group that initiated an earnest relief effort.

There already existed a gmiles-khesed-fund and also other funds that lent certain sums without interest to make it possible for artisans and small businesses to get back on their feet. But under the circumstances it was like a weak injection. What was needed was food.

[Column 159]

In these conditions "Centos" was created.

At that time, the "Joint" (Joint Distribution Committee) was very active in Poland. Their help was immensely significant. One of its institutions was "Centos" whose task was to work at bettering the physical health of Jewish children in Poland.

The group was put in touch with the Bialystok district committee and they sent us a representative and a committee was formed, headed by Yehoshua Lepak hy"d[2] and the writer of this article.

The women who were active participants on the committee were Chana'cze Gorzalczany, Rasza Edelsztajn-Bolender, Chmiel (the wife of the Jewish teacher), Dwojra'ke Raczkowski, Shayva Surowicz, Dwojra Raczkowski-Ber.

[Column 160]

These women's lives all ended tragically when the Hitlerites murdered them.

The other members of the committee were Rachel Zysman (today in Cleveland), BatShayva Gorzalczany-Lubelczyk, Malka Malinowicz, etc. They all worked with great devotion.

A people's kitchen was created where every Jewish child, without exception, received a warm glass of milk and a roll every morning.

But we were lucky, Chaya'ke, the widow of Chaim the tailor with two small children, organized the kitchen and began work as the cook.

A group of children having breakfast

[Column 161]

A summer day when the children ate lunch outdoors

The people's kitchen was organized on the premises we rented from Leibush Frydman. Later it moved to Moshe-Lejb Igla's building. The premises were nicely arranged with new tables and benches.

We were very careful to ensure that the lunch would be tasty and also healthy. People gave soup, meat and bread.

All the children in the shtetl came for breakfast and lunch. There were children whose parents were making a living and some were even rich and had the means to feed their children. But we did this in order not to create differences between the children. We did not want the children to be ashamed or think that they were charity cases. Those parents who had the means paid the full value of the meals.

All the work around the institution, except the cooking, was on a voluntary basis by the members of the committee. They helped in the kitchen, purchasing food, serving up food and bringing it to the table.

A lot of work was also done for the health of the children.

[Column 162]

The active Endekes (National Anti-Semitic Party) in Czyzewo never allowed us any Jewish doctors. The Jewish community made great efforts many times in that direction. But every Jewish doctor who came to the shtetl sooner or later had to leave due to anti-Semitism.

And so it was at that time, when the boycott raged and the pickets preached hatred. The only doctor was the old Pole Dombrowski who took care of everyone's illnesses, but we did not have faith in his medical capabilities. And his loyalty was suspect. We were afraid for our children's lives. That forced us to create the "AZA" division of "Centos".

All Jewish children, without exception, we given medical examinations.

Children at lunch

[Column 163]

The beloved Dr. Krau from Sokoly, the "Angel of Salvation" for the Czyzewer Jewish children

Every week Dr. Krau, a Jew, arrived with a nurse and examined the children by turn. The sick children were examined separately.

Besides the regular examinations, house calls were also made for children (in some cases also grown-ups) and these sometimes went on through half the night. The committee members also volunteered their help here as well. Virtually all of this was carried on the shoulders of Bat-Shayva Gorzalczany.

[Column 164]

It happened once that I had to play role of nurse. Old Bezalel-Ber Worona from the railroad station insisted that the doctor had to examine him. We explained that doctor was a pediatrician, but we did not succeed in making him understand this. He insisted that an old man was like a child.

In the end, the doctor determined that it was necessary to drain water from a blister…and I had to be the nurse during the operation which the doctor performed the following Wednesday.

Summer 1938 there was an epidemic of childhood diseases. Dr. Krau decided to give all the children, without exception, blood transfusions.

The only pharmacist in shtetl, Paris, an intelligent man, but an anti-Semite, had a hostile attitude to our work that he showed by raising his prices. Therefore we immediately established contact with the central pharmacy of "AZA-Centos" in Bialystok and through the mediation of Gel Gradus, known by the name Gante, the medications were provided the next day. Gante received 20 groshen for each prescription. But this was more a symbolic payment. He categorically refused to take payment for his trouble.

[Column 166]

Everyday he brought medications to us and the families of the sick were already waiting to take them.

Not all the Jews in Czyzewo understood the importance of the prescriptions. There was a case when negligent parents did not pay attention and the medication was not taken. This negligence lead to the death of Golda's young daughter. From then on I took on the duty of delivering the medications immediately after receiving them.

There was also a case when a child was very sick and local doctor had given up on him. We telephoned a doctor from Bialystok. The young boy recovered. Today he is a respected citizen of Israel along with the other Czyzewers.

For three summers we were also able to send the children to a special cure center that was in Poland: Rabka in Druskenik where "Centos" had a children's sanitarium. A minimum payment was taken only from those who could pay. Also we did not stop caring for the children's health during the winter months. Among other things, they were given cod liver oil every day.

In order not to create differences, rich and poor children, without exception, came for breakfast and lunch

[Column 165]

Volunteers serving lunch from right:
Yehoshua Lepak 2) Shayva Surowicz 3) Rivka Plocker
Across: Chai'ke Zelaznik and Dwojra Keizmacher

The prophylactic was new to us in the shtetl. I think the Polish, Dr. Dombrowski had no idea what it was.

It was impossible to do the transfusions on the regular Wednesday visit and it was overloaded with examinations. So another young doctor was sent and I have him my apartment to him and in a mere six weeks he had done all transfusions for the children who were not sick.

In 1939 we organized a summer camp out the town. The camp was mainly for unfortunate children who were there from eight o'clock in the morning until six o'clock in the evening under the supervision of teachers and educators. All the work in the summer camp was under the direction of the unforgettable, merit earning, social activist, Mr. Yehoshua Lepak, *z"l* (zikhroyne livrokhe, may his memory be blessed), also the women's committee did not spare any effort and with great generosity worked towards the success of the summer camp.

[Column 167]

On the 24th of August, the day of the sudden mobilization, the summer camp ceased to exist.

The End of a Beautiful Activity

The war had not yet broken out, but the situation was strained everywhere at that time. We did not receive the monthly subsidy (a thousand Zlotys) from the Central in Bialystok, but paid the debts from our own pockets; Yehoshua Fiszer for the milk, Yehoshua-Gdiche for baked goods, Nechemja the butcher for meat, etc.

Seven days later, on the 1st of September our shtetl was bombed. Fires broke out and people were killed. About getting the money back that each of us had laid out, there was no point in talking about it. The entire shtetl was plunged into the horror of war. There was hardly a house that had not been touched by misfortune. The hardships were dreadful. The mobilization of the Polish army also hit the young Jewish volunteers. A lot of them would never see each other again. Yehoshua Lepak was also drafted into the Polish army.

Those who escaped the fire unharmed were murdered later in the Holocaust that hit Polish Jewry and did not bypass our shtetl Czyzewo.

Besides my wife and I, who were saved by accident because the Russians arrested me and later sent the entire family to Siberia, the only "*Centos*" (pronounced Tsentos) volunteers left alive were Mrs. Rachel Zysman who at the beginning of 1939 left for America where she still lives today. Also Mrs. Malka Malinowicz was saved and made *aliyah* (immigrated) to Israel.

We are the only survivors of those who with so much love worked to ensure healthy, Jewish children. Their names will forever remain engraved in our memory and hearts.

We have not forgotten those wonderful people who are still alive and feel even today united with the people from our shtetl. These are former Czyzewers in America who supported our "*Centos*" work.

In 1938, Mrs. Heide Kandel visited Czyzewo from America. She saw with her own eyes the work of the "Centos" institution in Czyzewo. She took back greetings to our *landsleit* (compatriots) in America and in response to our message about the epidemic of children's diseases, we immediately received a wire for one hundred dollars.

Besides outstanding support, there was the joy of feeling the solidarity and brotherhood of our *landsleit* in far away America.

[Column 169]

The Merchants' Union in Czyzewo

The Jewish merchants organized a union, as in a lot of other towns in Poland, as a result of the difficult years 1924-25, when Grabski's tax system created a catastrophic situation for the Jewish merchants.

The Jews in Czyzewo calculated that the aim of the tax system was to destroy the weakest Jewish merchants in Poland. They saw it in the law about sales volume taxes. Merchants who were able to prove their sales volume with the help of formal ledgers paid only one-half percent volume taxes. On the other hand, those who could not prove their sales volume, simply because they did not use a bookkeeper, had to pay 2 percent. Officially it was four times more than the large merchant. Factually it came to eight and twelve times more because his sales volume was estimated by a special commission that met twice a year to determine the sales volume and income tax and they estimated whatever amount they wanted.

In Czyzewo this commission brought with it a *Tishebov* (9th day of Ab, a day of fasting and mourning in commemoration of the destruction of the two Temples in Jerusalem, hence a desolate mood) atmosphere. It meant a decline in the last subsistence stronghold. The Jews from the shtetl were in despair. There were discussions about appealing to a higher authority which seldom brought the wished for result. Then they had the idea of organizing a union.

The "merchant class" was made up of a few dozen food stores, two wholesalers of various products, two mill owners, two merchants in the forestry industry, two in the iron industry and several manufacturers. Besides them, there were also more poor storekeepers for whom a large transaction was selling an entire herring to one person. Among these merchants there were also different levels. There were, for example, several where one could buy just a single piece of a herring.

The "Milk Industry"

Mendel Telces, an Aleksander *Hasid* was just such a merchant. He was a tall man with a small blond beard. He never had a store. He stood in the street with a wooden bench on which he placed his entire stock; pieces of white cheese that the children brought on their way to *heder* (religious grade school for Jewish boys).

[Column 171]

He produced the cheese himself from milk that he bought in the Czyzewo yard. Every afternoon one would see him walking with his glossy well-worn boots on Blacksmith Street, where he lived, on the way to the "yard" that was located over a kilometer further from the street. On the way back he carried two large twenty-liter milk cans, one in each hand. Later he came to his senses and carried them with a special yoke like a water carrier. Carrying those cans every day tired him out and in the last years before the war he no longer had the strength to drag the milk such a distance. Besides a Christian dairy had been organized that got milk from the "yard" and there was none left for Mendel, so he lost his livelihood.

Manufacturing, Dry Goods and Grain

The manufacturers, where one could get a meter of white or colored linen, were not much larger; the dry goods stores where the choice was between a spool of thread, a button, a pair of garters and several centimeters of colored ribbon. In the richer stores one could also get colored thread which the peasants bought to mix in weaving they produced. The two shoe merchants belonged to the more fortunate.

A significant number worked in the grain trade which until one year before the war was exclusively in Jewish hands.

During the two market days, Tuesday and Friday, when the peasants brought their sacks of grain in their wagons, the merchants wandered among them, tapped the sacks, untied them, stuck a hand in and knowledgeably looked at the grain and haggled for hours over the price. When they finally came to an agreement, the Jew put the sack on his shoulder and took it away to the "granary". If he had to pay a porter, he would earn nothing.

There were others who had peasants, under contract, who would drive directly to the granary, unload the grain and later, when the price at the market was established, they were paid.

There were very few of those. The majority, which included several dozen families, existed by running around breathless on market days with a sack on the shoulder or with an empty sack.

The children would help and sometimes also the wife.

The artisans were also involved as merchants, such as the baker or the shoemaker who sold his boots at fairs in surrounding villages, the tailor his ready-to-wear clothes; the furrier, hat maker and others for whom being a craftsman and merchant went together. The artisans never felt a need to organize a union. Their taxes were much lower.

The effort by Fejwel Shimon's to organize an artisan's union several years before the war was dictated more by his ambition to become a representative for the craftsmen and a *dozor* (representative) in the *Kehila* (Jewish Community Council, regulated religious institutions).

[Column 173]

Defense Against Economic Failure

The problem of a union therefore existed first of all for the merchants, for whom this was a question of existence, to defend themselves against economic failure.

It began with meetings which took place in the so-called "Shalemberger *shtibl*" (Hasidic prayer-house), near the large *besmedresh* (synagogue, study house and used for large meetings). This was a neutral ground where the Hasidim, Ger and Aleksander, could meet together. These two groups made up the largest and strongest part of the community in the shtetl.

There were no invitations to these meetings. None needed to be sent. Everyone knew immediately and came.

Only men went to the meetings. Only when pressed, the widows, who after the death of their husbands took over his store and out of necessity belonged to the merchant union, also came.

The union chairman was Reb Zebulun Grosbard a quiet, Torah scholar, a Ger *Hasid* with a blond beard and eyeglasses. The main reason he was chosen for the position of director was because he could speak and read Polish. Such people, among the older generation, were rare in Czyzewo.

Reb Zebulun made his living from a tavern, where the kettle with boiled water was never cold. Even *Shabes* (Sabbath, Saturday) people went there from the shtetl with teacups to get hot water to make a glass of tea after the *Shabes cholent* (a baked dish of meat, potatoes and vegetables served for lunch on the Sabbath).

[Column 174]

It boiled particularly fast during the last month of the year, in December, when the license season began. All the merchants, storekeepers and artisans, without exception, had to pay for a license.

Everyone went to Reb Zebulun to write the license request. Reb Zebulun's son and daughter helped their father write the applications. What a tumult there was in the tavern. Zebulun was not able to give advice what with serving hot livers, pouring glasses of tea and giving change.

It became harder for him during the years when it was forbidden to sell liquor and one had to do so in secret in a side room. There were some who took advantage of the opportunity and unnoticed swallowed a hot liver, an egg or a marinated herring. They maintained that the half-*zloty* (Polish money) or *zloty* they paid to have the application written, also paid for liver or…

At the meeting Reb Zebulun volunteered to be the leader and therefore a vote was not needed. Part of the meeting agenda was to select and send delegates to intervene at the provincial tax bureau, the Bialystok merchant union and the central in Warszawa, once also with the Finance Ministry or a district merchants' conference. One of the serious questions was the choice of candidates for the appraisal commission.

There was a terrible din at these meetings and heated discussions. Not only those for whom this was a painful issue were in turmoil, but also those in general who did not pay taxes but without any reason took on others' grievances.

[Column 175]

Almost always the meetings would end with those who had been elected: Zebulun Grosbart, Eli Rubin Malcman, Motl Szczupakiewicz, Fiszel Liubelclzyk and Eli Dimentman.

In later years, when the grown-up youngsters became merchants and could handle Polish well, the mess with the delegations came to an end.

To begin with the Gers and Aleksanders were not able to make peace with the idea that a shaved face Zionist should be their representative. But from year to year the situation became more difficult. The taxes became higher and there were more Christian stores opening. The "farmer" began trading in grain. The tax bureau kept eliminating Jewish competition. The official from the tax bureau arrived in the shtetl with the appraisal commission and was invited to be the guest of the Polish merchants. In order to work against them one had to have new methods, new people, with more boldness and ability to figure out the decisive factors. Some were found among the young merchants, the Zionists who also had the advantage of doing their own bookkeeping for their businesses and were not dependent on the appraisal commission.

All eyes were on these men who with great generosity served the Jewish merchants in Czyzewo.

[Column 176]

I was a part of the delegation together with Motl Szczupakiewicz and Yehoshua Lepak. We went to every appraisal commission and fought against the tendency to ruin Jewish storekeepers. Our work was twofold; at the meetings, in person, to prove and unmask the incorrect attitude of the commission members and have enough knowledge of the system and principles of the tax bureau in order to take advantage of their weak moments to benefit the Jewish tax payers. We wrote the requests and applications and sometimes we were successful.

We were also busy in other areas of community life. We were among the founders of "*Centos*", the library, but in no other field did our work receive unanimous acknowledgment as in defeat.

The library lead to bitterness and fights with the *Hasidim*, the same ones who had with so much impatience waited for us to appear at the meetings of the merchants' union, gifted us with unlimited trust and we made every effort not to disappoint them.

But in this case we were dealing with culture. They immediately saw us as enemies and fought us with great stubbornness.

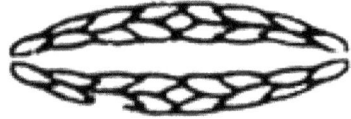

Translator's notes:

1. *Centralne Towjarzystwo Opieki nad Sierotami* or Central Society for the Care of Orphans.
2. Abbreviation used after the name of anyone murdered in the Holocaust. In Hebrew, HaShem Yinkom Domo, meaning May G_D take revenge for them.

[Column 181]

Hasidim

Dov Brukarz

Translated from Yiddish by Judie Ostroff Goldstein

There was no Hasidic rabbi in our shtetl that had followers who would stream from other communities. There was no rabbi's "court" in Czyzewo. But it was a Hasidic city that was tied to great rabbinical courts with their *admo'rim* (plural of admo'r, acronym for adonenu moyrenu v'rabenu. The title of a *Hasidic* rabbi. Literally, our lord, teacher and master), sons of historic dynasties in the Hasidic world and primarily: Ger, Aleksander, Amszynow, Sokolow. There were individual Hasidim who traveled to the pious men of the Rishener dynasty. And the Hasidim traveled to their rabbis for *Shabes* (Sabbath) and *yontoyvim* (High Holidays) and for *yomim neroim* (the Days of Awe, i.e. the High Holidays, the ten days from Rosh Hashanah to Yom Kippur). They would be with their rabbi in prayer, at the "table" and in giving a gift of money.

On his return from the rabbi's table to the *shtibl* (Hasidic prayer house), he would tell long stories about wonderful performances, about the rabbi's *kiddush* (blessing over the wine) and words about the Torah, seasoned with incomprehensible talk about *kabbalah* (Jewish mysticism) and computation of the numerical # value of words. The men would dance and sing the new melodies that were brought back from the rabbi's court. The melodies and chats reflected the peculiarity that made each Hasidic rabbi distinct. They were lyrical, quiet and absorbed in the mystery of all mysteries, in the soul of the world. They were stormy and noisy with feverish ardor, ladders that reach to the heavens, flames that strike at every movement, every turn, burning the footprint of he who turns away to the eternal deceiver and enticer of men's temperament. They girded for the rush of fresh suffering and the need for strength in divine service.

From all of them there remains extinguished ash.

This text must serve as a *matzevah* (memorial) to their great beauty, to the light that was extinguished.

[Column 183]

Hasidic Shtiblakh And Hasidim In Czyzewo

Dov Brukarz

The Czyzewo Jewish population was made up of two classes: Hasidim and *Mitnagdim* (literally, opponents, opposed to Hasidsm). But the Hasidim belonged to various sects: Gerer, Aleksanderer, Sokolower, Amszynower and others. The names came from the cities where the rabbis lived. Each rabbi had his way, his manner of divine service.

Ger, a small town not far from Warszawa after the death of old Kocker, *zts'l* (zeykher tsadek livrokhe means may the memory of a righteous person be blessed) his greatness was revealed. When the Kocker Hasidim split up, they began to search for a leader, someone worthy of succeeding the Kocker. But too well known was the Chidushei Harim and Sfas Emet [1] and the "truthful words" around which were grouped a large number of Hasidim.

The other rabbis: Aleksanderer, Sokolower and Amszynower were also famous and also had their followers in Czyzewo. But just as in the other cities, the Gerer was the strongest and largest group in Czyzewo. The reason for this is a study unto itself. In fact, the Gerer Hasidim in Czyzewo were the most eminent, like in every other city and town.

[Column 184]

Generally the Hasidim and especially the Gerer remained apart from the *Mitnagdim* – in every way; in their clothing, where they prayed and how they prayed. Gerer Hasidim were the "*shtreimel*-Jews". It was said, "under every *shtreimel* (round, fur-trimmed hat) is a Gerer Hasid". Only the very poor wore a "velvet" hat on *Shabes*n (Sabbath, Saturday). But in *shtibl*, one did not see a Hasid without a satin *kapote* (long, black coat worn by Orthodox Jews). One had yet to see a "collar" on a talis (prayer shawl), but always a satin *kapote*. A faint mark still remained on the *kapotes* to show that they had once been "satin". All that remained of the satin was a pair of yellow torn up small stripes, but so long as the lining remained on the shoulders, the "*kapote*" served as a *Shabes-Yontifdike* (Sabbath and holiday) garment.

In general Hasidim used the form of prayers used by the Sephardic Jews. The manner of praying is remarkable. A Hasid, especially a Gerer did not sit at the table or generally sit anywhere while praying. He ran around and rocked in great ecstasy, yelled and clapped his hands – back and forth in the length and the breadth of the prayer house. Once, by accident such a Hasid was invited as the tenth to a *Mitnagid minion* (quorum of ten men needed to conduct certain prayer services). For him this was the worst kind of suffering. One must not refuse and poor thing, he had to pray in the Ashkenazy manner.

[Column 185]

Home and Family

For the Hasidim, home was a temporary lodging, where they stayed between one visit to the rabbi and the next.

The custom of traveling from time to time to the rabbi was for Hasidim, and especially the Gerer, entirely natural.

Mainly they traveled during *Slikhos* (one of the prayers said during the days preceding the High Holidays through Yom Kippur) and lay around in the *"besmedresh"* (synagogue, study house), sleeping on the hard benches with their bundle under their heads or in some cheap inn where one had to pay. The joyous inebriation came from the rabbi, his teaching Torah, and his virtuous example and later, on returning home being able to tell about the great wonders performed by "him". Because of this it was worth the trouble from the several weeks until the end of the *yomim noroim* (Days of Awe, High Holidays) and once until the end of *sukus* (Feast of Tabernacles).

In Czyzewo, the Gerer and Aleksander Hasidim were closest to each other. For many tens of years they had their *shtiblach* together on the floor over the town *besmedresh*, although their demeanor, clothes and character were distinctly different, there were no quarrels between them. In the well known "Wizna-Sniadowo feud, the Aleksander Hasidim undertook a passive position and some even sympathized with the *Mitnagdim* – the Wizna side.

Each young *shtibl* student studied in his own *shtibl* and although the *shtiblach* were neighbors, nobody from either side every crossed the other's threshold. They both had respect for the Sokolower and Amszynower Hasidim.

[Column 186]

There was only a small number of Amszynower Hasidim in Czyzewo, headed by Rabbi, *Reb* Szmuel Dawid Zabludower, who was well liked by everyone. The Sokolower Hasidim had prayed in the *besmedresh* until the beginning of the twentieth century. Then they rented a *shtibl* that was also attended by Amszynowers.

The prayer format used by all the Hasidim was *"Sefard"* nevertheless there were distinct differences in the prayer format, especially by the "Gerer".

Friday night the Gerer Hasidim had an interval between *Kbalas Shabes* (Welcoming the Sabbath) and *Maariv* (evening prayers). During the interval they did not study *gemore* (part of the Talmud which comments on the Mishnah [post-biblical laws and rabbinical discussions of the 2nd century B.C.E.), but that short period was used for reading a book or telling stories about great, pious men.

Shabes morning, winter and summer, the men drank *"khamin"* (warm drink or food) tea, coffee or milk which they would get from the bakery oven where it had been kept warm all night. In contrast, on Friday the *Mitnagdim* would by *"kvitlakh"* (tickets) in the gentile "teahouse" and *Shabes* morning they all went to get a glass of tea that they had already paid for.

After drinking a hot drink, the Gerer Hasidim went to the Hot " *mikvah* " (ritual bath house). Rarely did one notice any other Hasid and especially *Rava Demata* who did not feel the need any *Shabes* and any *Yontif* to immerse himself in the *mikvah* before praying.

Between morning and additional prayers only the Gerer Hasidim had a custom of taking a break of not more than an hour and then they studied *gemore*. They studied alone, by themselves. Others learned in a group, where one of the old men or a young man, a respected scholar, read a lesson.

[Column 187]

In studying, just as in the economic situation, there were differences, but in the *shtibl* everyone was equal there. Still, it was decided that the older Hasidim always took the seat of honor, the eastern wall. But it was remarkable that all the older men were also the richest merchants in the shtetl and as a matter of course the most influential in city affairs.

One of the ones particularly strict about wearing traditional clothing was *Reb* Berish Frydman, a rich grain merchant. Every young man in the *shtibl* had to wear a yarmulke (skullcap) under his hat and a belt. He always had some in reserve, skullcaps and belts, that he would give for free to each young man who did not have a skullcap or a belt or both.

He took care that even outside the *shtibl* walls, in the street or out for a walk, men would wear them. If he, or his assistants, saw a young man or a boy in the street without the two things, *Reb* Berish would warn him with sharp words so that it would not happen a second time. A lot of young men among them the writer of these lines, were expelled from the shtibl as a punishment for disobeying the demands of *Reb* Berish Frydman. He would pretend not to see and looked away, as if not interested in the least, in a cut beard. But he did forgo the "belt and skullcap".

There was one young man in the shtibl who was favored with a special privilege. That was Jesheja the grave stone engraver's son. Even *Shabes* he wore a "cloth hat" without a skull cap, yet to pray he had a silk belt.

[Column 188]

The Aleksander Hasidim had an entirely different appearance. If in the department of "everything being equal" they were not far from the Gerer, but one saw young men sitting and studying even without a *yarmulke* and without a belt.

There were some who wore a white "collar" with "a little necktie" and even "ties". Among the so called "aristocratic" young men, as the Gerer Hasidim called them, were Josef the soap-boiler's (Rubinowicz) Berl, Lejzer the village magistrate's son (Wengorz) Alter, Bine Brucha's son (Garde) and others. The last even wrote for the newspaper "Heint" (Today) which he would freely read and at the Aleksander *shtibl* door, several young men stood and in secret listened to him reading the newspaper and admired his "skill".

Sokolower and Amszynower Hasidim in their entire manner were scarcely any different from the *besmedreshniks*, the *Mitnagdim*, whose clothing was different, but entirely individual.

The only comparison between them and the other Hasidim was only that they prayed in the Sephardic manner. To the third and last meal of *Shabes* they would get together and sing *Shabes* hymns exactly as their neighbors, the *Khevre Mishnayes* (group that studies *Mishnah* which is the collection of post-biblical laws and rabbinical discussion of the 2nd century B.C.E.), the Gerer and Aleksander Hasidim.

Before the First World War, the *besmedresh* and the rabbi's house, all the *shtiblach* with the *Khevre Mishanayes* were on the same street. All week the echo of the *gemore* melodies carried far.

[Column 189]

But *Shabes* the various melodies of those who sang while praying, from all the shtiblach, later the *Shabes* hymns being sung while eating and then at the last meal the Amszynower Hasidim gathered at the *Rava Demata* [the rabbi of the city – i.e. the official rabbi of the city] and there celebrated the last meal "ushering out the queen", scarcely ceased.

Some well to do *Mitnagdim* also went to the rabbi's, good people, like Reb Josef Kanet and Mendel Kanet *z'l* (may his memory be blessed), Reb Avraham Yitzchak Belfer *z'l*, etc.

The bridge that linked the *shtiblach*, Gerer and Aleksander, was Reb Shmulke Fiszel's the grave stone engraver and *tsitsis* (undergarment with four tassels worn by Orthodox Jews) maker. He served both *shtiblach*, he had the tea concession, summer and winter, and …"brandy".

He would furnish 96% proof for each occasion and there were a lot of occasions. A *yahrzeit* (anniversary of a death)– liquor, a graduation – liquor, an agreed upon marriage, a *bris* (circumcision of male baby). An inauguration, even for wearing a new piece of clothing.

If there was no *simcha* (joyous occasion), several "sons-in-law" with future "bridegrooms" got together and had a little brandy.

During the week, in the street, all the Czyzewo Jews seemed like one family. Only the *yarmulke* that the Gerer Hasidim wore told of the existence of two "camps", Hasidim and *Mitnagdim*.

The Hasidim were in the *shtiblach* in Czyzewo and the *Mitnagdim* were in their *besmedresh*.

Hasidic Shtiblach And Botei Midrashim

A Short Summary

Czyzewo was a small shtetl and had several Hasidic *shtiblach* in which respectable Jews, young boys, sons-in-law on *kest* prayed and studied. In the early mornings and long winter nights the *gemore* melodies, and the voices of heated debates over the deep thoughts of the *tanoim* (rabbis whose teachings in the frist two centuries C.E. are included in the *Mishnah*) and *amoraim* (Talmudic rabbis) from *toysefes* (important commentaries on the Talmud), *Maharsh'o* (acronym for morenu harav [our teacher, the scholar] Szmuel Edel, commentator on the Talmud) and other wise commentators carried over the shtetl. The largest and therefore also the most powerful was the Gerer *shtibl*. Among the Gerer Hasidim was a large number of the richest and most respected people in the shtetl, among them: Mordechai Welje, Chaim Dancygier, Moshe Yankel the keeper of a wine house, Berish Frydman, Yoske Grynberg, Zawel Ajdelsztejn and others.

There were Jewish scholars and aristocrats in the Aleksander *shtibl*, but fewer. There were, among others, several respectable young men such as: Josef the soap boiler, (Rabinowicz) Alter Bine-Bracha's Garde, Berl Lejzer Solte's son (Wengorz) Jesheahu Motel Fejga Paja's and others. The Aleksander *shtibl* was much smaller than the Gerer.

The besmedresh was more for "the common people". Zerach the writer (Starkowski) had his group of Jews with whom he studied every day between afternoon and evening prayers – *Ein Yaakov* (title of a well-known collection of the *Agadahs* [stories] from the Talmud). It was from this group that the Shalemberger Hasidim originated later on. Nobody knows where the name came from.

[Column 191]

Jakob Pesze Jute's studied with a second group *shulkhn orekh* (literally prepared table, title of a book containing all Jewish religious laws) and *Chaie Odem* ("The Life of Man" title of a well-known compendium of Jewish religious laws by Reb Avraham Dancyg [1748-1820]). Yitzchak Ahron studied with a group – *gemore*. Studying began between afternoon and evening prayers and went on until late at night.

[Column 192]

There was also a Sokolower *shtibl* where the most respected were Shlomo the baker, Boruch Krejndl's (the *melamed*) (teacher in boys religious grade school) and others. The Amszynower Hasidim went there as well because there was too few of them to have their own *shtibl*.

Translator's note:

1. These are actually names of books, which then were taken on by the authors of the books as pseudonyms. This was a common practice – famous rabbis being named after their magnum opus. Both are the pseudonyms for Chasidic rabbis of the 18th century and are very well known.

[Column 193]

My Great Father –
His Problems, Hasidim and Admirers

Freidel Zabludower-Levinson/New York, NY

Translated from Yiddish by Gloria Berkenstat Freund

Czyzewo was a Hasidic city. There were Gerer Hasidim, Aleksanderer Hasidim, Amshinower Hasidim [Hasidim from Mszczonow, Poland] and others there. All, except the Amshinower, had their own Hasidic *shtiblekh* [small houses of prayer].

They did not put on airs, loved the simple Jews who prayed in the large synagogue and recited psalms in the early morning. These were honest craftsmen, for whom the Hasidim showed reverence and respect. Czyzewo was a Hasidic city. It should be understood that there was a considerable number of *maskilim* [followers of the Enlightenment] – later there were fights between them because of a library, party matters. Simultaneously, the beauty of the pious Jews was understood. They were befriended and boasted about.

[There were] quiet, sincere Jews and life had so much fervor in this dear *shtetl*.

In this *shtetl*, my father, the Rabbi Reb Shmuel Dawid Zabludower, of blessed memory, was on the rabbinical throne for 36 years.

It is very difficult for me, a daughter, to impart the entire greatness of his holy stature, evaluate his great pride as a rabbi, a beloved local rabbi and as a good hearted father. He was equally ready to sacrifice with the deepest love for both, for his children and for the city.

[Column 194]

The Amshinower Rebbe, who was one of the greatest *admorim* [acronym for "our leader, teacher and master," title given to a Hasidic rabbi] in Poland, told me before his death six years ago:

"Your father was one in a thousand among the rabbis and one in a million among ordinary Jews…"

[Column 195]

When I begin to write about my father, I ask God to help me to relate only a portion of his greatness that needs to remain for the generations.

My mother would tell us:

My father arrived in Czyzewo in 5665 (1905) as a young man of 24, as a son-in-law *oyf kest* [support given by a father to his daughter's husband so that he could study Torah] with an Amshinower Hasid and great scholar, Reb Hersh of Ostrolenka [Ostroleka].

The match was actually arranged by the old Amshinower Rebbe, who had a close relationship with my other grandfather. A great scholar from an aristocratic family, he became an in-law of the Amshinower Rebbe.

The rebbe made the match because both of my grandfathers were Amshinower Hasidim.

My mother was then not even 16 years old. My father was two years older.

Everything that I was told by my mother and by other people about my father's young years confirms that he showed great genius even as a child and received rabbinical ordination from the great geniuses of his generation.

After the wedding, my father was supported by his in-laws in Ostrolenka. He sat day and night and studied, and became known as a genius. He had all the characteristics of an outstanding *gaon* [genius].

When the elderly rabbi of Czyzewo, Rabbi Yitzchak HaLevi Epstein, who was also known as a *gaon* of renown, died, the rabbinic seat of Czyzewo remained vacant for a time. There were many candidates, but the Czyzewo community decided to take on the young *gaon* Rabbi Shmuel David Zabludower as rabbi.

[Column 196]

This must have been a great experience in our house because my mother told me with great excitement how it was that day when the three most prominent members of the community of Czyzewo came to Ostrolenka and invited my father to take over the rabbinical seat in their community. Later they sent a written contract in which the city pledged to pay a salary of 25 rubles a week.

Our Family

My mother gave birth to 10 children, of whom only four survived, three daughters and one son.

The oldest daughter was named Tzvia. In 1927 she married a young Hasid from a rich business and Hasidic family. He excelled in his courtesy and goodness and had a good reputation in the business world in Warsaw as one of the most honest merchants.

They had two sons. At the outbreak of the last World War, one was 10 and the other six.

[Columns 197-198]

In 1940 Warsaw was severed and we heard no more from them. We do not even know how they perished.

The first in the group on the left, Chaim, the rabbi's son

My brother, Chaim, was an extraordinarily successful young man with great qualities. His goodness was without end. He studied at the Kletzker *yeshiva*. When he would come home for a *yom*-tov [a religious holiday], he would call me in and confide that he owed many debts. I asked him:

– How can that be? I sent you as much as you asked for each month! If you need to have more, why do you have so many debts?

He answered me:

– I cannot eat alone and watch how the other poor young men cannot buy anything and live only with the allotment they receive in the *yeshiva*. They suffer from need. I have to share with them, therefore, I spend so much money.

It should be understood that we immediately paid all of his debts. Yet, when he came the second time, he again repeated the same thing about the debts.

He was married six months before the war, took a girl from Maladecsze. She was the youngest daughter and her father gave them a large shop and he [my brother] lived in Maladecsze until the outbreak of the war.

When Czyzewo was burned, with great danger he came running and brought warm underwear for everyone and a large valise with various things.

Then when I was in Vilna, he came to see me on a "business trip."

When his business was taken away he became a bookkeeper in a large cooperative. That is how things were organized under the Soviets, when they liquidated all of the private enterprises.

He made arrangements with the other bookkeepers and they substituted for him on *Shabbos*, so that he would not have to desecrate the *Shabbos*.

When our father learned that he had taken a post with the Russians, hot tears began falling from his eyes. When I asked him why he was so sad, he answered:

–Who knows if he will be able to continue to do so? They could force him to come to

work on *Shabbos*. He should not have taken a post with them.

The youngest sister, Gitl, was only a young girl when the war broke out and she perished.

This was our family.

Self Sacrifice During a Great Danger

An episode from the First World War, told by my mother, may she rest in peace

August 1915

This was on the third day when the fighting between the Germans and Russians neared Czyzewo and the Jewish population scattered. Many left for Ciechanowiec and escaped from there to Russia. Others hid in the Jewish cemetery. A large group was hidden with our family in Zawel Edelsztajn's cellar.

[Column 199-200]

It was Thursday night when the German military intelligence office entered our cellar. They saw the civilian population and said:

– Remember, escape from here, because there will be such a battle here in the city tomorrow morning at six o'clock that no stone will remain whole.

Hearing the words, everyone prepared to escape. My mother took the children, prepared something to eat and told my father that we must leave the city quickly in order to save ourselves. Everyone else was ready to go.

When they began to leave it was seen that among those who had hidden themselves were two paralyzed people who could not go along. They said to my father: "What will become of us here? You will leave us here to perish?"

Taking them along was impossible.

My father said:

– Jews, we will not go anywhere! We will not leave the two sick people. We will all remain and leave it to God, blessed by He, and he will in our merit save us.

Although everyone had packed a little food to bring on the way, hearing the fervid talk of my father, they all said that they too would not go and they would stay with the rabbi.

No one went.

My father said Psalms should be recited.

Thus everyone sat and recited Psalms the entire night.

When the battle was to start at daybreak, the Russians began to escape without resistance and the German army entered the city without a battle.

Seeing that the danger of a battle has passed, my mother sent messengers to those who had escaped to the nearby towns that now they could come back. The danger had passed; the battles took place far from Czyzewo.

Pleasures and Severity

When my father, may the memory of a righteous person be blessed, came to Czyzewo as rabbi, the Czyzewer *kehile* [organized religious community] had three ritual slaughterers: Reb Chaim-Shmuel, of blessed memory, Reb Moshe-Hersh, of blessed memory, and Reb Josef-Shlomo, of blessed memory. Later, when Haim-Shmuel died there were only two, and when Reb Josef-Shlomo died, his son, Szolem-Feiwl, of blessed memory, inherited his position.

My father, may he rest in peace, sat for many hours with the slaughterers and worked, making an effort to think of how [the cow] could be made kosher. Their entire existence was bound with the issue of the question. When a cow became unkosher, the butcher became poor. He had to give away the meat half free.

[Column 201]

When there was a question about the butchers, all of their wives would run in with worried faces and breathlessly, barely utter:

– What's up? How do things stand?

This was repeated without end until the ruling came out. When the ruling was "kosher" the joy was without end. If, God forbid, a cow was *treyf* [not kosher] there was despair. My father, may he rest in peace, would go around saddened for days without end.

There were more butchers in Czyzewo than were needed. When a butcher's son grew up there was nothing for him to do and he also became a butcher.

In this way the butcher families grew and there was a surplus of butchers. Great competition arose and they would compete with the prices. The rich butchers sold the meat more cheaply and the poor butchers were forced to lose the last few *groshn* [pennies]. Then they would come running to the rabbi!

– Rebbe, save us, we are sinking!

My father would call all of the butchers together and negotiate with them day and night until there was a settlement; a partnership was made in order that there would not be a conflict over prices. This had to be guaranteed with a "partnership contract" that each would receive a certain percent according to the size of the family and according to the volume of business. There also had to be a safeguard that the city would not suffer, that the prices would not be too high. My father, of blessed memory, was untiring in his work assuring that everyone leave satisfied. He, therefore, applied his great wisdom and diplomacy. Every one had great respect for him.

[Column 202]

The contract was agreed to by everyone at the same time in order to see how it worked and, when the term ended, it was extended or they again went their separate ways until the same problem repeated itself and a second contract for a certain time had to be agreed to again.

Whoever remembers the Czyzewo butchers, who were very smart and sophisticated, understands the great character of my father, may he rest in peace, in reconciling such differences between the 30 families of butchers of which some were very well-off and others were in great poverty. It was necessary to have a deep understanding of their needs in order to carry things out so that no one would feel wronged and that peace would reign among them.

This was the greatest strength of my father, may he rest in peace, who planted only peace, that there not be quarrels anywhere, not in the *beis hamidrash*, not in the city, not among the proprietors.

His goodness was without an end. However, when it was necessary to be strong, when it came to a law, or to *yidishkeit* [a Jewish way of living], he was strong and did not agree to any compromises. However, that he had to act strongly cost him a great deal of his health because this was against his nature.

I myself remember several cases of intense exchanges.

Once there was a question of a Czyzewo matter in which he had a different opinion than the respected proprietors. He came out against everyone and said his final and strongest words. Later, they all came to my father, may he rest in peace, and said that they agreed and begged his pardon for their earlier opposition. They openly declared that everyone consented to what the rabbi had said.

[Column 203]

A second case that I remember was when they came to my father, may he rest in peace, and said that there had been an error made by a certain butcher, one of the richest. My father immediately sent for the butcher. The butcher had a bookkeeper; he sent him to answer. However, my father, may he rest in peace, was not satisfied and said that the butcher himself had to come at once. The butcher was unhappy that his answer by means of his man was not accepted. He did not want to come and said: "I can also live without the butcher's trade." The next morning, my father, may he rest in peace, at once announced that the butcher was banned and no one was permitted to buy any meat until he himself came to explain how the obstacle had occurred.

He was banned for four weeks until he sent the same person asking that the butcher be permitted to come and beg my father's pardon. Many times my father, may he rest in peace, was strict when there was a question of protecting *kashrus* [the laws regarding kosher foods], or other Jewish matters.

In the *Beis-Din* [Rabbinical Court] Room

My father would sit in the rabbinical court room and look into a religious book. He would never study out loud and when someone came in he greeted him with a great deal of goodness and spoke with him with such eagerness as if he had been waiting for him for a long time. He never showed that his studying had been disturbed. He always had a smile and he never said: "Do not disturb me while I study," although he was very zealous.

[Column 204]

A large part of the day was taken with ruling on questions from housewives, who were very observant of *kashrus*, who would come to ask questions about cooking when a dairy item dripped into meat or the opposite.

Mostly there would be questions about poultry. Almost everyone slaughtered poultry for *Shabbos* and there would be a question about almost every second one because the peasants did not pay attention to them and they swallowed nails, pins, etc. when eating.

We children would be busy relaying the questions because the women were not bold enough to come into the rabbinical court room themselves.

Once, *erev Pesakh* [the night before Passover], a certain poor woman came to ask a question. Could she use tea for the four cups of Passover wine? My father, may he rest in peace, asked if the doctor had asked that no wine be consumed. She answered no, only that she did not have any money to buy wine. My father, may he rest in peace, called me in and said that she should be given money for wine.

A great effort was required to provide for the *Talmud-Torah* [school for poor young boys]. It was necessary to pay the teachers of the poor children whose parents could not pay any tuition. This task my father fulfilled with great devotion because it required much effort to be able to cover the expenses of the *Talmud-Torah* and not allow the poor boys to be sent home from school.

Respected guest preachers, couriers, who would come to collect money for *yeshivus*, all came to my father, may he rest in peace, asking that he arrange for men to collect money for their purposes.

[Column 205]

First of all, my father invited everyone to eat. There was no question, whether in the morning or in the afternoon, at whatever time a guest came, they were invited to eat. There would be days when one left and another came in and we were busy preparing the table in the rabbinical court room the entire day.

Ahron the *Shamas* [assistant to the rabbi]

Ahron *Shamas* sat in the rabbinical court room the entire day. He was a Jew, a righteous man, a dear and gentle person. Once he came to my mother and asked:

"*Rebbitzen* [wife of the rabbi], do you know the rabbi?..."

My mother smiled and said:

"What do you mean by this?"

"You do not know anything about who the rabbi is; I sit in the rabbinical court room and wonder at his greatness, his wisdom, his goodness. I feel elevated sitting near him. When the rabbi enters the *beis hamidrash* it becomes so quiet that a fly can be heard flying by and the stillness lasts until the rabbi leaves the *beis hamidrash*; then there is a tumult again. Such respect is seen nowhere else.

My father prayed in the *beis hamidrash* where the simple Jews, craftsmen, came to pray. He gave sermons twice a year: *Shabbos-tshuva* [the Saturday before Yom Kippur] and *Shabbos-hagodl* [the Saturday before Passover]. The entire city gathered in the *beis hamidrash* then to hear sermons which lasted for three or four hours.

The sermon was not only for the learned Jews, but a large part was also for the simple Jews, craftsmen. When my father became weak he had to interrupt the sermon because he spoke with much passion and it affected his health.

[Column 206]

The day when he gave a eulogy after the Kobryn pogrom remains in my memory. He burst into tears and the entire shul cried with him. His every word breathed with love of the Jewish people and he felt each calamity deeply.

Ahron the *shamas* would call everyone to shul on Friday night. Who does not remember his call "*in shul areyn*" [come into the synagogue] with a special melody that no one else could reproduce. When he died at the beginning of 1939 no one was able to continue the tradition of calling everyone to shul as he had done. Jakob Plotsker, who was called Jakob *der dreyer* [Jakob the turner] (by trade a turner of primitive Christian "wheels" for spinning wool and flax) became the *beis-din shamas* in his place and the second *shamas* was Mendel Kuszer. However, neither could reproduce the melody for calling people to *shul*.

When his call was heard all of the women knew that they must bless the *Shabbos* candles. Even the women who came to the market in the city on Friday knew that they must quickly run to buy something because the shops would soon be closed.

He would read the *Megilah* [scroll of the Book of Esther] at our home on Purim. He had his own melody for the *Megilah*. His sweet, extraordinary melody that I never heard from anyone else rings in my ears even today. His reading of the *Megilah* had such a sincere zest.

After Mendel *tzitzis-makher* [Mendel the maker of *tzitzis* – the fringes on garments such a *talis* or prayer shawl] no longer prayed *psukei-dzimra* [*Verses of Song*] on Rosh Hashanah and Yom-Kippur, Ahron took over the praying, and when Fiszel's son, Shmulke, who was the permanent Torah reader, died, Ahron *Shamas* took over as the Torah reader, too.

[Column 207]

In 1938 Ahron *Shamas* became very ill. He was already an old man in his 80's. He died a mere year before the outbreak of the Second World War. My husband eulogized him and the entire city mourned him deeply. He was truly a tzadek [a righteous man]. May his memory be of aid to us! Blessed be his memory.

The Meetings in the *Beis-Din Shtub* [Rabbinical court room]

All of the city problems were dealt with in the rabbinical court room. I remember when Dr. Gelbojm began to take part in the meetings he was surprised to see how simple Jews carried on the communal work with so much responsibility and devotion.

The theme of every meeting was how to alleviate the poverty in the city.

When the *kehile* [organized Jewish community] was more structured there would be eight synagogue wardens with a chairman. Reb Berish Frydman was chairman for a time. Later, Alter Wolmer, who held the office until the outbreak of the Second World War, for as long as communal work was carried on, was elected. He was an active communal worker. He devoted himself to *kehile* matters with warmth.

Itsze Zylberman and Yossel Boruch Lepak also took part in *kehile* matters. Later, Blajwajs, Zyglbojm, Szczupakiewicz and other younger men started to work with them.

All of the problems about city matters were discussed in our house.

[Column 208]

When Passover approached and it was necessary to raise money for *maos khitim* [money to provide for the Passover needs of the poor], my father went out with several businessmen to collect the money. When he received large donations, my father was also sad. Perhaps these people could not give so much money but were doing it because of the rabbi.

Later, when money began to arrive from America before each Passover, my father stopped going to collect money for *maos khitim*. However, the businessmen would continue to collect themselves. When the money would arrive from America, the businessmen came together and made lists of the poor. This poverty grew from year to year and the number of recipients grew larger each year. It grew so much that 120 out of 500 families needed to receive support.

Because there were so many more poor people, the donations became smaller and smaller from year to year. During the last year, my father said that more money had to be collected in the city because the money coming from American would soon not be a solution.

The money would be sent to everyone so that no one would feel bad about coming to obtain a few dollars.

At the meeting, every co-worker would bring a few more names, which were given in secret, that this one and that one had come and asked to be put on the list, only on condition that no one would, God forbid, know. There was surprise on everyone's faces and they nodded their heads with sorrow and added the names.

Everyday life in Czyzewo became more tragic before the Second World War.

[Column 209]

The Exchange of Letters with the Ragoczower *Gaon* [genius]

A short time before the First World War, my father began a correspondence with the Ragoczower Rabbi, who was considered to be the greatest genius of his time.

During the First World War when half of the city was burned including the rabbi's house and the old *beis hamidrash*, my father with the help of several businessmen and Ahron the *shamas* packed his entire library of books in crates and sent them to Yeshayahu Kalinowicz's cellar. Then when the front crept closer and it was necessary to escape, my mother blamed my father that out of all of their possessions he had only grabbed manuscripts of the Ragoczower. He said that they were more valuable to him than everything else. In contrast, my mother grabbed the jewelry and silver and thus saved them.

My mother said that we would have been able to save something more, but the manuscripts were the main thing for my father and wherever we ran he took them with him.

At the time of that war, the correspondence with the Ragoczower *Gaon* was interrupted for several years. It was again renewed until the death of the *gaon*. I think this was in 1936.

This was a correspondence of approximately 25 years. He wrote twice a week and answers came twice a week. This was a world of brilliant material and my father considered it a jewel. He dreamed of publishing it in a book. He said that the brilliance of the Ragoczower was much greater than of our time and it was simply a wonder that our generation had produced such a giant.

[Column 210]

In 1938 my husband visited Lithuania. This was after the death of the Ragoczower *Gaon*. My husband visited the *rebbitzen* and when she heard that he was the son-in-law of the Czyzewer Rabbi, she related how her husband rejoiced, when after the war, letters began to arrive again from the Czyzewer Rabbi. Holding the first letter after the long interruption, he went through the house and said, "Thank God, there is again a letter from the Czyzewer Rabbi." Another time, he suddenly said to the *rebbitzen*:

"Does the world know that there is a rabbi in the small *shtetl* of Czyzewo who does not have an equal of more than five rabbis in Poland?!"

My father, pointing to his large library, would always say to me:

– See, these are my belongings whose worth is incalculable because I possess antique books that can no longer be purchased for any amount of money. They are worth more than the greatest possessions.

All of the walls of the rabbinical court room were covered with books. This was all burned as soon as the Hitlerist airplanes bombed the city on the 8th of September 1939 and the entire city went up in flames. The manuscripts of the Ragoczower *Gaon* also disappeared with the smoke.

This was a Wednesday, two days before the outbreak of the war; I was sitting with my father in the rabbinical court room. [Translator's note: The Second World War began on Friday, September 1, 1939 with the Nazi invasion of Poland.] We saw that the air was filled with gunpowder. However, my father with his great faith still had hope. Perhaps the Most High would have pity and the slaughter would be avoided. He called to me:

[Column 211]

– Freidel, what will happen to my books? Perhaps we should start packing and put them in the cellar?

I looked at the large library and answered:

– How would it be possible to start packing so many books? We will not get any help because everyone is busy with himself.

My father said nothing more about saving his books which were his entire life.

The Rabbi's Grief Over the Poverty of the Czyzewer Merchants During the Boycott

From 1933, when Hitler came to power in Germany, it became worse in Poland from day to day. The *Endekes* [anti-Semitic National Socialists] organized a boycott against the Jewish merchants. In Czyzewo, gentile boys with sticks would stand on both sides of shops and peasants, who went in to buy from a Jew, were beaten and "the pig buys from Jews" was written on his back. The need and desperation among the Czyzewer merchants grew. They turned to the Joint [Joint Distribution Committee] for help and the Joint director, Mr. Guterman, came to us. The merchants were called together and he promised to support them and said they should not lose their bearings and would weather the difficult times. The merchants and the synagogue wardens came together every evening at our house and discussed the situation. My father consoled everyone. They should persevere and the Most High would help; they should not fall into despair.

[Column 212]

New troubles crept in.

Litigation began against the Jews saying that they were insulting the Polish people. There was such a case with us of the merchant Bialystocki. His wife went out and amicably began to plead with the hooligans; why do they not let us live, earn a piece of bread. A witness immediately claimed that she had insulted the Polish people and litigation was started against her that threatened her with years in prison.

The Joint provided a lawyer and she only just escaped the false accusation. All of the troubles played out in my father's rabbinical court room.

This all had an affect on his health. My father became ill with a paralysis at the end of 1935 and, on orders of the Warsaw doctor, had to go to Otwock where he found himself under the supervision of specialists.

My father was not in the city [Czyzewo] for two years and his son-in-law, Rabbi Levinson, took his place.

In 1937, he returned almost healthy, but his right hand and his right foot were a little weak and he walked with a cane. His mind was again as sharp as before. He once told me that his mind worked better than perhaps it had worked before his illness.

He took back the running of the rabbinate with all of the difficult problems that had now arisen. As we lived far from the *beis-hamidrash*, a *minyon* was created in our house.

[Column 213]

My father's prayers were not intense, noisy; they were satisfying without forced religious ecstasy. A suffocating fire smoldered in them, but the quiet, piercing voice, on which the prayers were carried, affected the limbs, elevated the heart and awoke faith.

The Lord is still gracious and merciful!

On *Shabbos* the table was always full, with pious Hasidim surrounding it and seated around it, with a congregation that consumed the Rabbi's teaching.

[Column 214]

My father really wanted the Jews to forget all of their troubles and worries on *Shabbos* and *yom-tov*. When he succeeded in this, his eyes shone as for a lucky one who was saved from a great danger.

I would look at the people and it appeared to me that with every word that my father said, a lament was silenced, with every sparkle of his radiant eyes, a moan was extinguished.

Face after face of all of the Czyzewer Jews, who loved him so much, shone and was brightened.

[Column 215]

The Gerer Shtibl

by Gerszon Góra

Translated by Judie Ostroff Goldstein

If my memory serves, when I was barely five years old I went with my father to pray in the Gerer shtibl, above the Old Synagogue.

I did not have any idea about Hasidism then and yet I always believed in my heart the radiating brightness of the patriarchal figure in that generation.

Reb (honorific, Mr.) Yitzchak Dawid Frydman was the patriarch of the community. He was a short man and his hair, beard and ear-locks were entirely gray. He had a white face and warm black eyes. Uncle Bunem Blajwajs was the opposite of Reb Yitzchak Dawid Frydman. He was very tall and always had a smile on his face. Also the same age was the old man Judele but his small beard was still quite black.

Reb Avraham-Aba Rotenberg, who was called "Aba from Brik" also belonged to the old guard as well as Reb Jakob Szapira and Reb Joske Grynberg. Also the dry-goods merchant Reb Chaim Dancygier who was at that time the shofar (ram's horn) in the shtibl, Hersh-Welwel melamed (teacher in a boys' grade school) and so many more old men of stately appearance. They sat at long tables in the first, large room of the Gerer shtibl and studied from open holy books.

[Column 216]

Time passed and I grew up. I was frequently a guest in the Gerer shtibl, not hanging onto my father's shirt. Just like for dozens of other youngsters the shtibl was my home where I spent the great part of days and nights.

This is how it was for hundreds of Hasidim who spent their entire lives in the shtibl. They struggled to make and living and longed for the hour when the market day would end so they could go straight to the shtibl.

All the shelves were full of holy books. The scholars were deeply immersed in the gemore (part of the Talmud). The weaker students sat with an "Ein Jankew" (folk legends and fables from the Talmud), or a mishnayes (set of mishnah, a collection of traditional laws), or perhaps only a Hasidic holy book. The shelves were full of such holy books that were read by all kinds of people.

From dawn until late at night it was busy with praying minyans and during Talmud (explanation of Jewish law and commentaries) lessons it bustled with sharp opinions. The men's voices drew out the melodies and among them could be heard the high voices of the young and old boys, who were already there in the pre-dawn hours, repeating with fervor what they had learned the previous day.

[Column 217]

And so day became night and wove itself into a new day. Here the differences between rich and poor disappeared.

Everything was discussed in the shtibl from world affairs to problems facing individual Hasidim. No subject was spurned and everything was discussed in a serious manner.

Days and years passed. There was a great fire and the men moved to the second Gerer shtibl that was rebuilt after the First World War. Three shtiblakh were located in this house, the Aleksander, Gerer and Amshynower.

There were three old men who were astonished at the length of their years and I can still see them before my eyes.

The first who comes to mind is my uncle, Bunem Blajwajs. He was the town magistrate, always happy, full of life and ready with a witticism. He felt obliged to attend all the simchas (celebrations) in town, the weddings and bris (circumcision). After he went to Kock and knew the Kocker Rabbi. Because he was not a great scholar he was seldom seen sitting with a Hasidic Holy Book. When the month of Adar arrived, just before Purim, he got up on a table and yell in a loud voice. "Jews, during Adar (Purim is celebrated during Adar) one must rejoice". The second old man was my zeyde (grandfather) Reb Aba Rotenberg, who was among those who moved to the last Gerer shtibl. I see him bent over a holy book, a gemore, a Midrash, or a zohar and even with a tanakh (entire Jewish Bible) - as if he was glued to them. All of his time was dedicated to studying Torah. Every year he read the complete Shas (the six orders of the Talmud), Midrash, zohar and mishnayes. He had very little to do with community business. He was the zealot of the Gerer shtibl. The third was Old Judele who was also a Kocker Hasid. He lived the longest of the three. He studied but also liked to listen to stories or events from the youngsters who talked about secular and Hasidic affairs.

[Column 218]

Now to another generation of old men in the Gerer shtibl, the "Pani" (Polish, gentlemen) who embellished the "mizrakh" (the eastern wall of the shtibl). It was a great honor to be seated at the eastern wall. By this I do not mean the eastern wall because in a shtibl only a simple Jew is able to sit at the eastern wall and at the western wall the greatest scholars. By "embellish the eastern wall" I mean the spiritual eastern wall of the Gerer shtibl.

The first "Pani" group to be considered is the three shoychtim (plural of shoychet, ritual slaughterer) in the shtetl.

The first of the three, who were old distinguished scholars and had become masters of their trade, is Reb Chaim Shmuel Rubinsztajn. He had the appearance of a cabbalist always absorbed in thought. He had a small, grey beard and a high wrinkled forehead. He gave the impression of being a nobleman. If I had not known that he was a shoychet, I would never had believed it. In the shtibl he was one of the "corner" Jews. He liked to sit at the corner of the table and study.

[Column 219]

The second shoychet was Moshe Hersh. His beard never turned grey. He gave the impression that he would have difficulty understanding. He sat day and night studying, always keeping his finger on the gemore as a pointer. Even as a very old man he still went to the slaughterhouse to kill the animals. His hand never trembled. He was also a quiet man who kept to himself.

The third shoychet was the "Shniadaver", the youngest of the three, who took the place of the famous "Wisner Chazan" (cantor), who led the famous contention (division of religious opinion). The Gerer shtibl triumphed and the Shniadaver shoychet was selected. In contrast to the other two, he always sat studying in the shtibl. The Shniadaver was also the bal-tefilah (prayer leader) during the Days of Awe (The ten days of Rosh Hashanah through Yom Kippur, the High Holy Days). He would move the men to tears with his heartfelt prayers.

In the second group of "Pani" were: Reb Zawel Edelstejn, Reb Yeshaya Kalinowicz, Reb Berish Frydman, Reb Alter Szmelkes and Reb Yisrael Yona Raczkowski.

Reb Zawel was the wealthy man in the shtetl, among the respected men in the shtibl and the most hospitable. Visitors in the shtibl were always sent to him and his house was never without guests for a meal. He was always in the shtibl in the evenings and pre-dawn diligently studying a large, long Vilner gemore that he brought from home.

Reb Yeshaya Kalinowicz was also a rich man and had a dry-goods store like Reb Zawel. But he was entirely another sort of man. He was burdened with suffering. His wife was always sick and his only son was a problem. In the end he was entirely abandoned as his son had left for Argentina. Reb Yeshaya was considered the scholar of the shtibl - he always sat with an open gemore studying diligently.

[Column 220]

Berish Frydman, a son of the old Reb Yitzchak Dawid was the mainstay of the shtibl, an important man, responsible for watching out for the younger generation, the young men and boys, so they would remain Hasidim. It is possible, as at other times, that maybe a lot of them argued with him about why he would not allow "neck-ties" around shirt collars or too much dressing. However he did pay attention to any of them because he wanted to maintain the original appearance of the shtibl and he devoted his entire life to this.

Reb Berish was a simple man devoted to Hasidism. He was also one of the most hospitable to guests. Every Yontef (holiday) he traveled to Ger (Góra Kalwarija) where he was always among those who sat at the rabbi's table. Yon Kipper (Yom Kippur) before Kol Nidre (prayer said the eve of Yom Kippur) he was one of three men chosen to say "Al Das HaMakom". He stayed in Ger for the ten days and immersed himself in Hasidism.

Reb Alter Szmelkes quickly became a yoyshev-oyel (Yiddish, a man who stays at home or a man who devotes his whole time to study). During the week he seldom came to the shtibl. He was a scribe and his work kept him away most of the time. On Shabes and the High Holy Days when he came to the shtibl, he was always absorbed in thoughts. He was very knowledgeable in zohar and cabbalah. He took over from Chaim Dancygier as the permanent shofar blower in shtibl. The last of the group was Reb Yisrael Yona Rackowski, a great scholar. He was always the one to read the final prayer on Rosh Hashanah and Yon Kipper in the large besmedresh (synagogue, house of study) and also gave lessons in the shtibl on gemore. He was the first community leader in the shtetl who was sent to represent the Gerer shtibl.

[Column 221]

When all the old men in the shtibl took their special places they became part of the general complexion of the shtibl.

Reb Moshe Dawid Sofer, was always the bal-koyra (reader of the Torah) on Yon Kipper, with the special melody. His reading was masterful, word after word, as if handing out pearls.

Reb Yitzchak Bunem's (son) Bajwajs, one of Old Bunem's sons was a great scholar. In his old age when he became blind, he would sit through every lesson in the shtibl and repeat the gemore. He was very smart and was among the "politically astute" in the shtibl.

Moshe Eliezer, who became the village magistrate after my old Uncle Bunem, was a happy man who always had a sharp mind. He took part in all the celebrations in the shtetl. He had his own remedies and never called a doctor. He always said that for an upset stomach the best remedy was hard, black bread broken up on a little place and spread with clean alcohol. He actually used the remedy and it helped him.

Mendel Yisrael Shlomo's (son) was a tall, skinny man with a wide silk had on his head, that he brought from Russian when he migrated from there during the First World War. Every evening, and especially during the winter nights he already had his circle of listeners at the warm tiled stove where he talk politics or about town news.

[Column 222]

Reb Avraham Szwarc was one of the prominent Hasidim. He had a tavern in town and was the first one allowed to spend money for all community things that the shtibl had to buy as well as the shtibl's large machnisi orchim (hospitable men, society that gave lodging and food to overnight visitors who could not afford a hotel).

Young men were also among those who formed and shaped life in the Gerer shtibl: Reb Zebulun Graubard, Reb Szaul Hersh Blajwajs, Reb Chaim Motl Yisrael-Yona's son-in-law, Reb BenCjon Kitajewicz, Reb Nesanel Stuczynski, Reb Jakob-Pinchas Pedeto, Reb Leibush Frydman, Reb Itche Zylberman, Reb Avraham Yosel Melamed with Yitzchak Tombek, Reb Itchke-Majer Yitzchak-Judel's (son), Reb Itsl Jablonka and Majer Tsitzis-macher (maker of fringes for prayer shawls) and his two sons Yisrael and Moshe'l.

All of the above mentioned were only a small part of the large community who prayed in the shtibl. These were the prominent men who took part in community life and were leaders of Hasidism in the shtibl. There were also young men in the shtibl.

Zelman Shlomo Rziwiec's son-in-law, Benjamin Moshe, Yeshaya Ewri and Michal, Yitzchak Wasermacher's son-in-law. These young men had always been devoted to Hasidism, organized feasts for the start of each new month and the meal "ushering out the Sabbath". They were devoted body and soul to Torah and Hasidism. They attracted other young men such as Chaim Zejgermacher's son-in-law, a Warszewer and the recently married men in town, for example, Akiva Stuszynski, Hershel Zylberman, etc.

[Column 223]

The young single men in the shtibl were: Yehoshua Kotliarek (the last got married), Yeshaya Winograd, Chaim Lejb Kozlowsksi, Natan Szejman (at the end changed to a different camp), Michal Wasercug, Hershel Zylberman, Berl and Moshe Jablonka and the last two Fiszel Kupiec and Gerszon Góra who after the Holocaust made aliyah to Israel.

A group of Hasidic young men from the Gerer Shtibl who were also active members in Zarei Agudas Yisrael

Sitting from right to left: **Celniker, Kardan, Szejman, Zylbersztajn, Jablonka**
Standing: **Winograd, Berl Jablonka, Melcer, Góra, Ahron Jablonka**

[Column 224]

For twenty years I lived the life of the shtibl, twenty years I drank in the atmosphere and lived with the warmth and affection, immersed in a sea of generosity of one for the other, personally and through charitable organizations. I lived with self-sacrifice for Judaism, for Torah and for Hasidism

[Column 225]

My Aleksander Shtibl

by Berl Szajes/Tel Aviv

Translated by Gloria Berkenstat Freund

I spent my most wonderful young years in this *shtibl* [small Hasidic house of prayer; *shtiblekh* is the plural]. Everything I saw there, heard and experienced is deeply etched in my memory. It was a time when it seemed to us that the Aleksander *shtibl* had developed together with the *shtetl* [town], as if it had existed since the origin of the community in Czyzewo. Later it became clear to me that the Jewish settlement in Czyzewo consisted of superb Jews, scholars and craftsmen who studied Torah, and led a warm Jewish life much earlier than the rise of the Hasidic movement.

It was just after the death of the old "Wurker" that the later Aleksander Hasidim began to develop. Around 100 years ago, Reb Yechiel Dancygier, the son of Reb Feywele Gricer, a grandson of the great Warsaw rich man, scholar and *misnagid* [opponent of Hasidism], Reb Tzwi Hersh Dancygier, took over the management and created the first *minyon* [ten men needed for prayer; *minyonim* in the plural] of scholarly young men, who were strong adherents of the new customs and began going in his path, singing the *nigumim* [melodies], keeping to his manner of praying.

At that time Czyzewo began to sense the differences between the Ger and Aleksander Hasidim. Reb Boruch Szapira advised and urged traveling to the *Sfas Emes* [the Ger Rebbe Yehudah Leib Alter].

[Column 226]

Those who were not inclined to the Kotsker style [style of the Hasidim from Kock] created the Aleksander *shtibl*.

Until the great fire in 5638 [1878], the synagogue stood at the location of the *Beis-haMedrash* [house of study and prayer] (which today serves as the grain storehouse for the non-Jews of Czyzewo). The Hasidic *minyonim* developed unexpectedly in rented apartments. After the fire, a large city *Beis-haMedrash* was built at another spot and, in the second story over the *Beis-haMedrash*, the *shtiblekh* of the Hasidim were built. The Aleksander *shtibl* occupied the smallest part, perhaps half the size of the neighboring Gerer.

This was a long, large hall with three windows on the south side that looked out onto the old cemetery. The hall was divided by a large, tiled oven with seats around it that served not only for the old men to take an occasional nap, but also as a *mechitza* [dividing wall] between the students and talkers.

[Column 227]

Every morning, they prayed in a *minyon*. Before praying, from the earliest morning hours, young men, *kest eidems* [sons-in-law who were given financial support by their fathers-in-law], would sit and study a lesson in Talmud. The foremost wood merchant, Reb Zelik Yankel Pszakewicz; Epsztajn's son-in-law, a Litvak arrival from Wisoke, Reb Yisrael Yitzchak Janowski; the *shtibl* regular, Reb Moshe Prawda, a Jew, a scholar and great joker. Sura Ete's Reb Dovid; Shimon Nusan Najmark; Reb Meir Richter, a father-in-law of Reb Yisrael Tyktin and eminent merchant of wool and wheat. Meir Richter was not actually a real Aleksander [Hasid], but after the death of the old Wurker [Rebbe], he became involved with Skierniewice Hasidim. But, as a result of circumstances, after the death of the old Kotsker [Kock] Rebbe, he no longer traveled to a rebbe and he was a worshiper in the Aleksander *shtibl*. As a result, his son and grandson were real Aleksander Hasidim. The prayer in the Aleksander *shtibl* was on time and after the morning prayers the members of the congregation each left for their businesses and to eat breakfast. After breakfast, only the *kest-eidems* returned to study.

At *minkhah*, the group again appeared and each took to his book anew, some to study, some to teach a page of *gemara* with commentaries, and thus it extended until late at night.

Entering the *shtibl* to study was not an obligation, but a right. The majority who took advantage of this had small residences and simply did not have enough space for studying or because their children interrupted them. Those who had good, comfortable apartments came only to pray in public.

The Aleksander path was not to study for the sake of publicity, not to make an impression, but simply because a Jew needs to study, a Jew must learn and mainly because a Jew who can study also savors his learning. As a matter of course, there was no feeling of any kind of organized study in the Aleksander *shtibl*. Some studied orally, others only browsed.

[Column 228]

Prayer in the Aleksander *shtibl* took place with satisfaction, not too much rocking, the *Ekhod* [oneness of God] not shouted out too loud during the *Krishme* [prayer said as part of the morning and evening services and when going to bed], not too much excessive talking at the *Shemoneh Esrei* [18 blessings said at the three daily prayer services].

Naturally, there were also exceptions. Reb Itshe Zylberman, the son of the Prager rabbi and Reb Yisrael Tyktin's son-in-law, would rock robustly during prayer and in the end he left to pray in the Gerer *shtibl*. Naturally, not until after the death of Reb Yisrael Tyktin.

Reb Elihu Ruwin Malcman

Reb Welwele Zylbersztajn was also a strict constructionist. Reb Welwele was the *bel kore* [reader of the Torah during services] in the *shtibl* and God protect us if he caught the tip of a *shin* [letter of the Hebrew alphabet] rubbed off. Then nothing was of help. Experts looked over the Torah scrolls and asserted that it was nothing, other Torah readers said it was kosher [could be used], but Reb Welwele stood by his opinion; he would not read further. Whereas one cannot fast on *Shabbos*, the Torah scroll had to be exchanged for a different one.

[Column 229]

Shabbos in the Shtibl

The melodies for *Lekha Dodi* [*Come my beloved*, a song sung to welcome the arrival of the Sabbath] were sustained by the entire congregation and sung by the young boys in the *shtibl*. A new melody was like a holiday. *Kabbalat Shabbat* [the welcoming of the Sabbath] belonged mainly to those officiating at the morning service. This was Reb Zelik Yankel Psbezokowicz and the younger generation, Reb Yeshayahu Gorzalczany, Reb Botsze Eliasz. Incidentally, his father was a not a Hasid, nor was he a founder of or worshipper with the *Khevre Mishnius* [*Mishnah* Society – the *Mishnah* is the compilation of the "oral laws of the Torah"]. However, he became connected to the Aleksander Hasid, Reb Akiva Zylbersztajn, who was one of those sitting at the rabbi's table in the Aleksander *shtibl* through marriage. He went to the Aleksander *shtibl* with his father-in-law because Reb Botsze (Boruch Yakov) was a learned man, a sociable man and also had a sweet voice; he easily made his way to become the *bel-Shakharis* [person who recites the morning prayer].

There was an agreement with Reb Yeshayahu. He was the main spokesman, not only in *shtibl* matters, but also in civic matters. In addition, he had a deep feel for music. Therefore, he became the *bel-Shakharis* as soon as he began praying in a *talis* [prayer shawl].[1]

Reb Alter Wolmer, one of the very young, newly married men, prayed *Shakharis*. And so did Silka's son-in-law, Reb Moshe'le Blumenkranc. Officiating at the *musaf* service in the *shtibl* was Reb Yisrael-Yitzchak Janowski, with a hoarse voice, but with so much sweetness that it was truly a pleasure to listen to him. His delicious praying was renowned in the *shtetl*. A while later, a Kosower young man arrived, a brother-in-law of Reb Shimon Nusan, who because of his analytical intellect was called *der pikeyekh* [the clever man].

[Column 230]

The person starting prayers and the person who recited the *Minkhah* prayer during the Days of Awe and on holidays and also the daily *Shakharis* also were included in the honored functions in the *shtibl*. Reb Shlomo Yoshi, a quiet, modest Jew, great scholar and very pious, had this title. After his premature death (he received a blow from a soldier during the 1920's during the Polish-Russian War, when he was seized for herding cattle. After his return, he received another great spiritual blow; his beard was cut off by the *Hallertchikes*[2]. He could not bear both the physical and the spiritual blow and died young, leaving a house full of small children and an old father, the above-mentioned Hasid, Reb Moshe Prawda). Reb Mendel, the son-in-law of Reb Mendel Jandzewer the baker, took over his mission. Besides the opening prayers and prayers for *Minkhah*, Reb Mendel also recited the *kiddush* for *Simchas Torah* and he was the clown for the *shtibl* on Purim.

Reb Leyzer Bitner was not only the prayer leader. His praying had the fragrance of cantorial art; he only led the *Musaf* service on *Shabbos* in the *shtibl*. The *shtibl* had to lend him to the Great Synagogue for the Days of Awe. He led the *Musaf* service there until the bitter end.

A separate assignment in the *shtibl* was calling up the men for *aliyahs* [honor of being called up at the Sabbath service to read a portion of the Torah] and *hakofes* [circular procession on *Simchas Torah* marking the completion of the yearly Torah reading] on *Simchas Torah*. Reb Yisroelke Moncarz, who would entertain the congregation at the *melave-malkes* [conclusion of the Sabbath] meals or at regular *kiddushn* [blessings of wine after the Sabbath service] in the *shtibl*, carried this on with great charm and humor. His father was a *misnagid* [opponent of Hasidus], one of the best men in the *shtetl*.

In the *Shabbos* dusk, when the congregation came together in the darkness of the *shtibl*, to end the third *Shabbos* meal, with the *kezayes* of *challah*[3] and a piece of herring, the main attraction was the *Shabbos* melodies. Reb Yeshayahu sang the "Hallelujahs" – Reb Zelik Yankel, *Ki Eshm'rah*[4], later Reb Botsze. The *Y'tzaveh*[4] belonged to Reb Leizer. There were times when Reb Leizer Soltis (Wengorz) would sing the "Hallelujahs." He would also recite the *Shakharis* prayers. However, he resigned when he grew old. He died before the war at a very old age.

[Column 231]

All of the melodies of the various prayers were sung by the young men of the *shtibl*. Only one *Yom Kippur* prayer, the *Avodah*, was sung by Reb Yisrael-Yitzchak Janowski with the assistance of the *beli-Shakharis*, Reb Yeheshua and Reb Botsze. Even when Reb Botsze would recite the *Shakharis* prayers in the synagogue, he came to the *shtibl* for the *Musaf* prayers.

The Aleksander *shtibl* drew to it all of the solid middle class, as for example, Reb Fishl Lubelczyk, who came from the Great Synagogue even though his father was an Otwocker Hasid, Reb Eli Dimentman and so on.

A harmonious, amicable atmosphere always reigned among the congregation of those praying. The entire *shtibl* felt like a large family, each helping the other in their need, with advice and with money… I do not remember any quarrels in the *shtibl*.

When the Aleksander *shtibl* had to present candidates for synagogue warden, the people simply had to be coerced, sometimes with the help of "drawing lots." Thus came Reb Hershel Malinowicz, Reb Zindel Lew, Reb Eli Ruwin Malcman, Reb Alter Wolmer, Reb Fishl Lubelczik and others to the warden room. The people changed from term of office to term of office. There were great scholars among the Aleksanderer. Rabbincal diplomas were a natural phenomenon among those in the *shtibl*, such as Reb Yisrael

[Column 232]

Reb Shmuel Zelik Golombek

Tyktin, Reb Shimon-Nusan, Reb Mordechai-Hersh Surka, etc. However, they did not dream of any rabbinical positions. Reb Yisrael Tyktin was actually the rabbi in Czyzewo for a short time, but soon resigned and took to business.

More guests were seen in the Aleksander *shtibl* on a Friday night than anywhere else. Aleksander Hasidim had a reputation as chartable people. The *gabai* would stand at the door and match a guest for *Shabbos* with each person, according to how he thought it suitable. Reb Yeshayahu had the concession for eminent guests, such as, for example, emissaries from the Aleksander court, from the *yeshivah*, who would stay with him for two or three weeks until they finished their business with the *shtibl*.

The leadership of the *shtibl* was not elected, but arose by itself, as an automatic hierarchy. During the last years it remained in the hands of Reb Shmuel-Zelik Golombek and Reb Mordechai Hersh Surka. The latter would say "*Ahl da'at ha'ma'kom, v'ahl da'at hakahal*[51]," before *Kol Nidre* that was usually recited by the rabbi in the synagogue.

[Column 233]

The Aleksander Hasidim rarely wore a *shtreiml* [fur hat worn by married men in many Hasidic sects]; the majority wore silk caftans in honor of *Shabbos*, not satin, and a velvet cap. Long pressed pants were accepted with polished gaiters, but the innovators, who tried to wear short jackets, could not be endured by Reb Shmuel Zelik. And the followers of modern garb expressed in a direct manner obstinate resistance by leaving the *shtibl*, but not with a light heart. They longed for this embracing communal atmosphere.

[Column 234]

Each Hasidic *shtibl* had its specific holidays. To these belonged the *Suim haSefer*, the conclusion of the writing of *Sefer Torah* and the *yahrzeit* [yearly anniversary of a death] of the rabbis. In about 1912, the Aleksander *shtibl* concluded the writing of a Torah scroll and at this opportunity, a great celebration was arranged in the large apartment and tavern of Reb Shmuel Zelik. There were torches, lanterns of various colored paper, fireworks, *klezmorim* [musicians], a feast with plenty of good things to eat and Hasidic dancing until the grey, early morning.

As a rule, the Aleksander *shtibl* paid more attention to relations between men than to relations between man and God, and they believed in the importance of relating to man and insisted that this was the importance of Hasidus.

Reb Alter Garde

Reb Velvel Zylbersztajn

The Aleksander Hasidim placed great weight on matters in the economic and social realms. They were willing to help with organizing and leading the Zionist interest free loan fund. Reb Ahron Eibeszyc, a son of the Sterdiner Rabbi and Reb Shmuel Zelik's son-in-law, took part in it.

[Column 235]

Tolerance was one of the virtues of the Aleksander Hasidim. They tolerated the different sympathies of various worshippers, for example, Zionists, *Mizrakhists* [religious Zionists], despite the fact that the Aleksander court had a negative attitude toward Zionism. However, many who were spellbound by the idea of returning to Zion and who helped and gave it support could be found among the *shtibl* attendees. Reb Haim Yehoshua Tencza, a *maskhil* [follower of the Enlightenment], with great knowledge of Hebrew and other languages, belonged to this group. Almost everyone of my generation learned modern information from him. He was later the secretary of the *kehile* [religious community]. In general, we met almost no refusals from any Aleksander Hasid when collecting for Zionist funds.

[Column 236]

Dozens of faces, whose names have left my memory, stand before my eyes. However, I will never forget their honesty and sincerity, insight, wise outlook on life.

Translator's notes:

1. A Jewish male usually starts to wear a *talis* at age 13 when he is called up to recite from the Torah at his *Bar-Mitzvah*.

2. *Hallertichikes* were followers of Polish-born General Josef Haller, who organized a legion of Polish volunteers after World War I to help Poland fight the Soviets. *Hallertchikes* were its members and they were rabid anti-Semites.

3. A *kezayes* of *challah* is a piece of *challah*, the traditional egg bread eaten on *Shabbos* and on holidays, which is as large or larger than an olive.

4. *Ki Eshm'rah** and *Y'tzaveh*** are songs sung at the *Shabbos* table:

    **Ki eshm'rah Shabbat El Yishm'reini.*
    Ot hi l'lomei ad beino uveini

    When I observe Shabbat, God watches over me.
    It is a sign forever between God and me.

    ***Y'tzaveh Tzur Chasdo*

    The rock of Israel shall command with kindness.

5. "With the consent of God and the consent of the congregation, we declare it is permissible to pray with those who have transgressed." The prayer recited by the *khazan* (cantor) on Yom Kippur asking for permission to pray on behalf of the entire congregation.

[Column 237]

The Amszynower Congreation in Shtetl

By Pinchas Frydman / Ramat Gan

Translated by Judie Ostroff Goldstein

Everyone depends on luck, even the Hasidim.

Ger and all the others favored large congregations so they could have their own *shtiblach* (small, Hasidic prayer houses) where they would pray daily, study and chat about spiritual and other matters.

The Amszynower Hasidim were not that lucky. Their congregation was small so they did not have a corner of their own. Even though the Rabbi was an Amszynower Hasid, their membership still remained small and even though they dreamed of having their own *shtibl* they could not manage it. They did not want to share with another group because they would have been the minority.

I remember when I was a child that they prayed at Moshe Berkowicz's house. Later the second minion prayed in the large synagogue and the last years they got together with the Sokolker Hasidim, who were also a small group, and created a *shtibl* where every *Shabes* and *Yon Tef* [religious holiday] they prayed together. I would like to tell about the Amszynower Hasidim, their virtues and stories so they can be an example to future generations.

[Column 238]

Josef Mendel Cynamon

Josef Mendel the Baker was a righteous man, his wife Malka was the businesswoman and ran the bakery. She knew how to handle the gentiles, who on market and fair days filled the bakery. She knew when to speak softly and listen, when to reprove with sharp language, or stare someone down. And that is how she ran the business and he, Josef Mendel, would hardly set foot in the bakery.

His day started at "dawn". He was busy most of the day praying, studying and at the *Khevra Kadisha* (voluntary burial society). Later he would wander into the bakery, have a look around and then run to prepare a little for the world to come.

Then one had to collect money for a Jew who fell on hard times, here came a Hassid with a letter from a Rebbe stating that one should help him. What was the address? To Yosef Mendel.

Here comes an author pleading for help to publish his religious book, which will soon appear. But he mentioned to his wife that he still did not have a guest to share his *Shabes* with and cannot go with a guest on *Shabes*.

[Column 239]

So he would run around and sing softly "world do not totter, world, world do not totter" …this was his favorite song that he with a merry melody which would steal into a sad tone. This was how he poured out his cares. For a long time he was a poor man…then he sold butter for a living and he became impoverished.

Yitzchakel the Painter

That was what he was called. I do not remember his surname. It is possible that I never knew it. When called to the Torah he was called Yitzchak ben *Reb* (honorific, Mr.) Eliakim Getzl. If he ever painted – I don't know.

To me he was a short man with a large, grey beard and a huge *tallis* (prayer shawl) bag under his arm. His place was at the rabbi's house or in the synagogue where he would study all morning.

He was a scholar of the old type, simply studied, without getting into debates. He was the *balmusef* (prayer reader for the additional service, *Shabes* and holidays) in the *shtibl*. Well, he was far from being a singer, but everyone knew that he was the appropriate person to lead the community in prayer. When he said, "my all being will recite, Me Kamoha, who is like you", people really felt that every bone in his body trembled.

[Column 240]

He came from the ancient rabbinical authorities of the Hasidim, lived with the motto "Dear are all people, who are created in G_d's image"! Nobody should be wronged, respect is owed to everyone, even children.

Yankel Plocker

This man was known by several names in town. First, Yankel Pesia Ita's. Pesia Ita was his mother's name. Yankel *der dreyer* (the turner) because he was a turner by trade. Yankel *der rov's* (the rabbi's) because he was a rabbi's son. When called to the Torah he was Yakob Ariyah ben *Reb* Chaim Menachem.

He was a capable, bright man and one of the assistants in the Burial Society. Without him the cleansing of the dead would not take place.

He was the sexton in the Amszynower *shtibl* and a prayer leader in the synagogue.

During the First World War he served in the military under Samsonow. When Samsonow was beaten he and a few others made it back to Russia.

During the entire war he never ate *treyf* (unkosher food).

During *Simchas Toyre* (Heb. Simhat Torah, marks completion of the annual cycle of Torah reading) when everyone danced with the Torah, he was in ecstasy. He stood on a bench and yelled, "It should live"! He went after those who had strayed and brought back to the fold.

At a celebration he could not sit in one place. He ran to help prepare, to serve. He was a Hasid without great aspirations, but a dear, simple Jew.

He is gone but not forgotten.

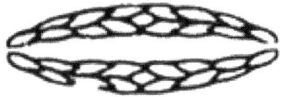

[Column 241]

The Fire Brigade

By Yitzchak Bursztajn/ Montevideo

Translated by Judie Ostroff Goldstein

Reb [Mr.] Jakob prayed in the Sokolower shtibl. People called *Reb* Jakob Yankel *der dreyer* [the turner, (mechanical)], because of his trade. He was something between a turner [lathe operator] and a carpenter. He had a sort of "mechanical thing" in his home for this purpose. It was a combination wheel with rope and tied together pieces of wood in an ingenious manner and all he had to do was press his foot against a plank. The wheel began to turn and with its turning, the entire machine moved. It is with this machine that *Reb* Jakob gnawed the wood and sticks that were needed to make the peasants' spindles. Therefore, men call him Yankel *der dreyer*.

All year Yankel prayed in the Amszynower shtibl, but during the High Holidays he prayed in the large synagogue where he led morning services. Besides he wanted to be closer to the rabbi. He was an ardent Hasid and admirer of the rabbi. Therefore men also called him Yankel *dem rov's* [the rabbi's].

Yankel *der dreyer* was a religious Jew, even a little fanatic. He would become angry at the least little deviation from devoutness. Despite his anxiety over Judaism and making a living, he still had his worldly "hobby". All those years he was always an ardent supporter of the well-organized fire brigade. Especially during a fire in the shtetl, he was always one of the first to arrive at the scene to fight the fire. His work he did with enjoyment. Being a fireman, he considered it a *mitzvah* [doing a good deed].

[Column 242]

Around 1924 the fire brigade in Czyzewo was reorganized to modern standards. The leader, a young Pole, a retired soldier, was very dedicated and well organized. He enrolled Jews and Poles, the majority being young Jews. All of them were issued special uniforms, with brass buttons and caps with lacquered visors. Every Sunday they exercised in the square at the shed. The Commandant drilled the volunteer firemen. From time to time the volunteer firemen also marched, like real soldiers, through the city and out as far as the railroad station. During the exercises several Jews distinguished themselves. But the best was Jakob Epsztajn who was tall young man and swift. He would climb the high ladder quick as a cat and was admired by all the onlookers who would applaud his acrobatics.

[Column 243]

The Daf-Yomi[1] Ended

Hasidim and *Misnagdim* [Opponents of Hasidism]

By Yitzchak Bursztajn/ Montevideo

Translated by Gloria Berkenstat Freund

When they began to study the *Daf-Yomi* in Czyzewo, the Talmud lessons were studied in the large *Beis-haMedrash* [House of Study], although the majority of students were from the Hasidic *shtiblekh* [small houses of prayer]. Later, when the congregation grew smaller, they studied in the Gerer *shtibl*. It must be acknowledged that studying in the *Beis-Medrash*[2] was solemn.

Reb Yisrael Yona's voice during the teaching of the *Daf* had a gorgeous echo in the *Beis-Medrash*. Each word was clearly and distinctly heard, not only by those sitting around the large table studying with him, but also by those who stood and listened. Everywhere that someone stood around the entire *Beis-Medrash*, Reb Yisrael Yona's translations and hypotheses were heard.

[Column 244]

Many modern theaters would have wished to have as good acoustics as the Czyzewo *Beis-Medrash*; the reading rang loudly and was sustained for a long time in the void of the *Beis-haMedrash*.

Reb Yisrael Yona was an earnest scholar; he had a wonderful power of speculation. Since the beginning of the *Daf-Yomi*, he had led it in Czyzewo with other scholars. Not only older Jews were drawn to it, but also the young, who were already able to study a page of *gemara* [commentary on the *Mishnah* (oral law)] with its critical commentary and there was no lack of them in Czyzewo. It was believed that the large *Beis-Medrash* belonged to the *misnagdim* [opponents of Hasidism]. But in reality, it was the *Beis-Medrash* for everyone, without differentiation,

Translator's notes

1. A *daf* is a two-sided page of the Talmud. *Daf-Yomi* is the daily study of such a page. It takes seven and a half years to complete the daily study of the Talmud.

2. *Beis-haMedrash* and *Beis-Medrash* can be used interchangeably.

[Column 245]

A Day in Czyzewo

Shmuel Abarbanel/Tel Aviv

Translated by Gloria Berkenstat Freund

Czyzewo, a *shtetl* [town] like all Jewish *shtetlekh*, a market, Jewish shops, a *beis-medrash* [also known as a *beis-hamedrash* – house of prayer or synagogue], several Hasidic *shtiblekh* [one room houses of prayer] and Jews, Jews who on Sunday morning walk from praying with a *talis* [prayer shawl] and *tefilin* [phylacteries], stop at the market, have a conversation, politics, business, notice a strange young man, approach him [and say], "*Shalom aleichem* [hello], where are you from? Who are you looking for?" That is how I saw the *shtetl* 35 years ago.

However for me the words sound very different; my heart beats with distant memories. I remember my youth, faith, doubts. An entire ball of thread of experiences awakens and I see them alive. Still more, the first time that I heard the name "Czyzewo," it was bound with mystery, secrets.

An actual occurrence:

5685 [1924 or 1925], Sokolow [a shtetl in Poland], in the Rabbi's *yeshiva* [school for older boys], a tired summer day, we sit engrossed in a lesson by Reb Simkha *Rosh Yeshiva* [head of the *yeshiva*], some sort of difficult "school of thought," some sort of small thought constantly ticks and disturbs, "How is a Litvak [someone from Lithuania], a *misnagid* [opponent of Hasidism] the head of the *yeshiva*?..." Suddenly, the door opens a little, quietly, quietly and a strange figure appears, a tall, thin Jew with a long, pointed, gray beard, on his head a sort of compromise of a Jewish hat with a Lithuanian cap, with a sack on his back, and comes in, makes a movement with his hand that we should not be interrupted, sits down for a minute, for the moment on the last bench near the door and is quiet. After the lesson, young boys approach, say hello. He answers with a cold, stiff hand and does not say anything; young boys become uncomfortable. A strange person; who can he be? They look at him intensely. Before nightfall, he prayed *Minkhah* [afternoon prayer]. He stood straight for an entire hour; he did not move. He recited *Al-khet* [first words of the prayer recited on Yom Kippur asking forgiveness for one's sins] on a regular day. Later, he ate bread with onions, drank cold water, all so quietly. Perhaps he is dumb? However, no, someone, somewhere quietly asked a question – When is the rebbe coming? After all, where could he be? He slept at night on a hard bench in the *beis-medrash*, rose at midnight for study and prayer. Perhaps only a penitent? Perhaps only a *lamed vovnik* [one of 36 righteous men upon whom rests the faith of the world]?… This was somehow more plausible to our 14-year old reasoning. We were filled with secret longing…

[Column 246]

He sneaked around so full of mystery, without speaking, for several days. But the same morning when the "rebbe" came back, he tied up his sack and ran away. Where did he run?… The young know – he probably went to "stand watch" in a city where there are no righteous men…

[Column 247]

But…see…he still strides with his sack on his back right to the rebbe's room…

When the *shamas* left, a bold group lunged for the keyhole. They heard some strange words:

"Czyzewer Rabbi… A virgin… Simkha Sanoker – (there was such a person here with us, a somewhat elderly young man with wild, disheveled *peyis* [side curls], blazing, famished, yes, a scholar, a literal child prodigy, an assiduous student, studied the entire night, held his feet in cold water).

– Rabbinical chair, in the future, a small dowry, *kest* [room and board provided to a son-in-law]…

They came to us, a little ashamed, disappointed, explaining that they think it is only a matchmaker, But no! Now we know with certainty it was not so simple that a sort of *lamed vovnik* was here and had brought a woman for Simkha… Very great things can come out of this… Someone even uttered the word "*Mosheikh*" [*messiah* or redeemer]…

But where is he?

Not here! Vanished! Out through the kitchen! And perhaps not out?

Just disappeared?…

The idea lingered that Czyzewo is somehow tied to secret world…

The next year I did not hear more of the cold, subtle argumentation and split hairs of Reb Simkha. My unease chased me through Jewish *shtetlekh* with young Breslover Hasidim. My soul was at ease, *Likutei Moharan* [*Teachings of Rabbi Nachman* of Breslov], stories of rebbes, Hasidic dancing at common meals, oh, how good!… But one still has to study! I was cast-away to Bialystok in the Noworadik *yeshiva*, in a dim, half dark building on the "Khanajkes" [an area of the city].

[Column 248]

Sad, closed off young men who repeat *musar* [ethics – religious study stressing piety], torture themselves and moan. They do not study in all cases. I thought I would find here "a synthesis of learning and manners." I found only sadness and fear, fear of the world, fear of transgressing. No bright ray of light… It was so sorrowful for me and I would simply cry quietly from longing for our style [of study]. Reb Avraham-Yafa, the *mashgiakh* [spiritual supervisor of a Yeshiva], the handsome, majestic Jew with a yellow-blond patriarchal beard, with a mild smile, noticed my mood in my eyes:

– With you, Shmuel, there is no sadness, but melancholy – strengthen yourself.

– Take yourself in hand, he said to me…

I choked… I could not… only when I firmly decided to leave there did I discover that "even a small coin was nowhere to be seen."

I did not have traveling expenses. But this did not frighten me; I knew that Jewish towns would not abandon a young man who was traveling to seek a place of learning.

I arrived in "Lapy" on a Friday (the first train station on the way to Czyzewo). Instinctively, my feet led me to the *beis-hamedrash* and there I experienced one of my greatest disappointments.

I saw him from afar through the open door… My heart began to beat fast… Yes, this is him then… My former *lamed-vovniki;* he was cleaning the *beis–hamedrash* with a large broom in his hand, sweating. Angry, he greeted me with complaints: (Now he did speak, oh, did he speak?!)

– Lapy is not a community cashbox – there is no money for Hasidic young men who are escaping from *yeshivus* [religious schools for young men]…

[Column 249]

Insulted, shamed, I hung around for several hours at the train station and in the evening, at *Minkhah* time, I returned to the *beis-medrash*. Demonstratively, I took a *gemara* and sat down to study aloud. After welcoming the *Shabbos*, a young man invited me for *Shabbos*. Sitting at the table, I asked him a question about the *shamas*. He made a motion of contempt with his hand, "Nonsense, a Jew, a villain, an ignoramus. Every summer he goes from house to house begging, proposing matches, presenting himself as a righteous man, a hermit who studies in order to serve God."

In a bed made of rolls of textiles, I lay late into the night unable to fall asleep. In my head "false righteous men" and *lamed vovnikes* were tangled. Everything became "doubt"… I thought the first crack in the thick wall of my edifice of faith.

My host gave me a *zlote* [Zloty – Polish coin] on *Shabbos* night. He took it from the *gabbai* [assistant to the rabbi] so that I would be able to come again. I arrived in Czyzewo on Sunday, during the week of *Shavous* [holiday celebrating the receiving of the Torah] 5686 [1926].

A quiet town. At the large market stood circles of Jews and they talked, accepted greetings and answered evasively and inquired about the rabbi. I had a small connection to him. Maybe I will meet Simkha Sanoker there; that would be so good. On a side street, on slippery stairs, I entered the *beis-din-shtibl* [small religious court room]. The rabbi welcomed me with a warm smile, questioned, consoled, spoke and taught, served tea (I was ashamed to ask about Simkha). Later, he sent for several young men, told them of my situation, asked that I be helped. They took me to the Gerer *shtibl* with them. We conversed on the way and they were happy with me. We became friendly.

[Column 250]

There was a noise in the Gerer *shtibl*, a tumult, they were praying, they conversed, Hasdisic, joyful. I was again comfortable, so close, so familiar. Little by little, the older group dispersed. Meanwhile, several young men left to go through the *shtetl* to collect money for my expenses, brought me "lunch" and I remained alone. I looked around me and saw strange things – the other door led to the "Aleksander *shtibl*." Was it possible? Ger and Aleksander Hasidim under the same roof? Was it really that way? – Yes! It was! I would have to speak about it everywhere…Useless hatred…I saw young men wearing white collars with neckties, so cleanly dressed. It was a sin in other, deep Polish provinces, strange, they would have to think about it…

Everyone quickly returned to the room; they brought an entire treasure for me. The *gemaras* were not even opened. A conversation occurred about something I did not expect, a conversation that surprised and scared me. It seems that they had gathered thoughts which they had to express to someone new, a stranger. When I told them about Simkha Sanoker, the one who was supposed to be their rabbi's son-in-law – everyone threw themselves into the theme of "purpose." It had already become clear to them that there is no purpose in sitting and studying, waiting for a rabbinate. There were no longer any available *shtetlekh*; in general, there were already 10 *kest-eidems* [sons-in-law supported by their fathers-in-law while they study] waiting in each *shtetl*. Life in the small *shtetlekh* was difficult. Without zest and purpose, one must escape, escape to Warsaw or perhaps even to *Eretz-Yisrael*, do academic study.

[Column 251]

I sat confused by the new themes before me. My attempt to try and carry out a conversation about "Breslover Hasidism," whose "messenger" I was considered, did not help. The group warmed up and became daring; we went out for a stroll, saw the *shtetl*. The conversation continued with each separately and when I sat in the back of the room at night at *Minkhah* time, eating evening bread near a young man whose parents had a restaurant, the young man took out from a box behind the bed several editions of *Literarishe Bleter* [*Literary Pages*], and from there read ideas and poems with enthusiasm, I felt that something was breaking in me. Something new had been revealed for me.

[Column 252]

Late in the evening, when several people came to me – I do not remember their names (the faces stand clearly before my eyes) – and accompanied me to the train station, it became clear to me that "Sokolow is not my place and purpose." I am going home, home to seek a "purpose."

If I did not find a purpose, but only wandered on new paths – Czyzewo, you were the cause of this.

I remember you, Czyzewo, you are a holy loss. I cry at your destruction along with your former inhabitants.

[Column 253]

A *Maskil* [follower of the Enlightenment] Among Hasidim

My brother Arya-Shakhna and his family, may God avenge his blood

Gad Zaklilowski

Translated by Gloria Berkenstat Freund

Arya, such a quiet one, was the quietest in the family. We came from a great distance, my wife and I, to the reception at his wedding in Czyzewo and there we saw our entire family. Hasidim were also there as wedding guests from the bride's side, with *Shabbos-yom-tovidikn* [Sabbath and holidays] charm. Jews with beards and *peyes* [side curls] and Hasidim with satin *kapotes* [long frock coats worn by married men] and *shtreimlekh* [traditional fur hats worn by some Hasidim] like my father. I alone was in European clothing. My father asked me if I had something with which I could change my cap and pointed to my wife, who was wearing a silk shawl on her head that was much prettier than her hair. She was much more practical than I. She knew she was coming among Hasidim.

Father – I said – it is true that there were various customs in various places about bare hair for me, as with women. But mostly, people went with uncovered heads. Our blessed sages also were not fastidious about this and even went to the *Beis haMedrash* [synagogue] with an uncovered head.

[Column 254]

A conversation started on this theme that I will not repeat here, only that my father concluded:

– Listen to what I have to say. My firstborn, I will not examine your learning. But, an observant Jew does not go with an uncovered head. And what does the *Mishnah* [rabbinic commentaries] say: *Notnin alaf khomer makom shehalakh kesham* [A person may have great knowledge, but his behavior can put him in a situation where he does not want to be.] and: "One should not act differently, so as not to cause divisiveness." We need to carry on the way they do where we come from in order to avoid a quarrel.

The bride's relatives also came closer to be able to hear the conversation in which several older Hasidim took part. I listened to the Czyzewo juicy, Hasidic conversation with great enjoyment, until my father, smiling, realized that the conversation was taking up another subject and said:

– What do you say, Gad (strongly stressing the letter "*daled*" [d] in my name, as the "*daled*" in "*ekhad*" is stressed in the *Krishme Shema*,[1] so that it would not come out as an error as with the word God). But Arya the *khazan* [cantor] approached unexpectedly:

[Column 255]

– He said, "Father, just as the "your" from "Honor your father" in the Torah, you should also honor your brother even with your knowledge. Therefore, I must give Gad respect and not carry on any disputes with him." And Dovid, the youngest brother, with the rabbinical diploma in his pocket, said:

"I do have rabbinical ordination, but he [is the one who] studied, not I, so that in matters of *Halakah* I will not interrogate him. But the customs are not according to law but according to compassion."

My mother also listened to the conversation and answered intoxicatedly:

"I also know the law. I am the daughter of a rabbi."

Here I said to her:

"And my father is the son of a rabbi."

Avrahaml Landa, the Sokolower rabbi, a son-in-law of the Czyzewer rabbi, mentioned, pointing to me:

"You see, he is quiet. Soon he will probably have something to say to you." The older Czyzewo people of stately appearance divided themselves. Some spoke favorably about me, because I come from an area where the rabbis even dress in this way. But the others, several strict Kotsker [Kock] Hasidim took even more offense at me because I did not even have any sign of a beard with which they could console themselves:

"Probably it is not with any kind of *ta'ar* (razor), but with a scissors, or a machine."

They intensely wondered how this could happen in a Hasidic house. Such attire?

My father said to me:

[Column 256]

– Do you think they are, God forbid, separate? It is "just like this" – having a conversation with a man from the newspapers. I know them, dear, good Jews.

I understood that my father wanted me to spend them with them.

He said:

– Of course, they must then be answered:

Therefore, I answered and said:

– Gentlemen, two things happened here – one, an error, and the second that we understand our sages of blessed memory. The mistake is that all religious laws and customs about which my respected brother, the ordained rabbi, asks that we obey with a moderate application of the law is only about "bareheadedness," about going with a bare head. But not about with what the head is covered, if with a hat or with a cap? The *Maymer Khazal* [aphorisms of the sages], which we appreciate is the commentary in *Messekhta Shabbat, daf kal* [the tractate dedicated to the laws of *Shabbos*, page 130] which states "*Likha ketuva dela mai b tigra*" – (at every wedding, a quarrel takes place) and thus as it then written how much and about what the quarrel must be, we then fulfill the *mitzvah* [obligation] with the *Maymer Khazal*.

To the veiling of the *kale* [bride]! Then to the *khupah* [wedding canopy – marriage ceremony].

When the *khosan-kale* [groom and bride] were sitting at the table after the *khupah*, they demanded their due from me, a blessing in addition to a *mazel tov* [good luck]. I said to them:

"The letters *kale* [khof, lamed, hey] arranged differently, are read as *hakl* [hey, khof, lamed – "everything"] and the letters of *khosan* [khes, sof, nun] changed in the same manner to *nakhes* [nun, sof, khof – "joy'].

Therefore when *khosan* and *kale* are together, there will be *hakl nakhes* [everything joyful].

[Column 257]

I could record a "world" of Hasidic conversations from that *Shabbos* here, about the *minyon* [*minyonim* in the plural – 10 men required for prayer] at the bride's house, how six *minyonim* of men occupied the two rooms, who sang, with such excitement, a great number of bold Hasidic *Shabbos* songs, with such warm-hearted sincerity.

Where are you Czyzewo, amiable *shtetele*?

Where is your undug grave? What remained of you?

[Column 258]

Where are you, Arya, my quiet, quiet brother? The only *horapashnik* [proletarian], the only manual laborer in the family.

What can I do for you, for your remembrance, more than saying *Kaddish* [memorial prayer] with those from Czyzewo, one of the warmest Jewish *shtetlekh*?

Thus I sit on a stone and cry:

"*Yisgadal veyishkadash*" ["Exalted and hallowed…" – the first words of the *Kaddish*].

Translator's note:

1. Prayer recited when going to sleep and during morning and afternoon prayer – *Shema Yisrael Hashem Eloheinu Hashem Ekhad* – Hear, O Israel: the Lord is our God, the Lord is One.

[Column 259]

The Great Quarrel

Hyman (Anshel) Kowadla

Translated by Gloria Berkenstat Freund

I left Czyzewo for America in 1906 at the age of 20. The events that I will describe took place a mere 10 years before my departure. They are deeply engraved in my memory so that whenever I think about my old home they swim before me as if alive. I see them as if they had just happened, although 60 years have passed since then.

Czyzewo had a population of various classes, as in other neighboring *shtetlekh* [towns], merchants, small traders, artisans, wagon drivers, *dorfs-geyer* [peddlers who went from village to village selling their goods], among them Hasidim from various *shtiblekh* [one room houses of prayer], and *misnagdim* [opponents of Hasidism] who prayed in the *beis-hamedrash* [house of study, also used as a synagogue]. Various quarrels would take place and small disputes over various *kehile* [organized religious community] matters. But it was rare when such a quarrel as I will describe here happened.

In the earlier years when my narrative begins there were two *shoykhetim* [ritual slaughterers]. One of them was Rabbi Josef Leib, of blessed memory, who, already advanced in age, wanted to give up the craft and there was a search for another candidate for his position.

Among all of those who announced their candidacies was a young man from Vizne who in addition to being a good *shoykhet* and *mohel* [circumciser], was also a qualified *khazan* [cantor]. And he showed his mastery on a *Shabbos* at which the new moon is blessed. The *beis-hamedrash* was fully packed with listeners, even the Gerer and Aleksander Hasidim *shtiblekh* that were located on the second story over the *beis-hamedrash*, also came to hear him. The women's section was also full. They could not rave enough about the *khazan* with his choral singing, the sweetness of his prayer and blessing of the new month captivating the entire congregation.

[Column 260]

After the rabbi of the city at that time, Reb Moshe Yoal, blessed be the memory of a righteous man, saw the Vizner's *khalef* [slaughtering knife] and the writings from many prominent rabbis and *shoykhetim* who had provided witness to his *kashrut* [observance of the kosher dietary laws] and abilities as a *shoykhet* and *mohel*, he was hired as the *khazan* in the *beis-hamedrash* and it was demanded of the city *dozores* [synagogue wardens] that they hire him as the *shoykhet*. At that time he also had the opportunity to show his abilities as a *mohel* specialist.

And here the quarrels began. The Hasidic group, particularly the Gerer *shtibl*, left in a great tumult, against the nomination of the Vizner as *shoykhet*. In no way would they permit a *khazan* in Czyzewo to be employed as *shoykhet* who while praying sings with notes just like a *klezmer* and cuts his beard with a scissors. They immediately found a young man from Śniadowo was a good *shoykhet* and *mohel* and also a good *bel-tefila*h [person who recites the prayers in the synagogue]. But after the people in the *beis-hamedrash* heard the Vizner, by no means did they want to change from him to another one. And little by little a quarrel flared that was transformed from cursing to fighting and reaching the spilling of blood. The *shtetl* was divided into two camps. And in the course of two years not one day passed that some bloody fighting did not take place between the Hasidim, followers of the Śniadower side, and the opponents of Hasidism, followers of the Vizner.

[Column 261]

It quickly led to police involvement because of the frequent fights and the denunciations that were made to the police by both sides and this led to frequent arrests and trials.

The fight would often take place on Friday night when the Hasidic *shtiblekh* would place young people, and even older people, under the window of the *beis-hamedrash* in order to listen to the Vizner prayers. They would be attacked by people from the *beis-hamedrash* and it became a bloody fight until the police intervened and arrested several of those fighting.

The butchers attended the *beis-hamedrash* and belonged to the Vizner side. The opponents would only employ the other *shoykhetim* [ritual slaughterers] to slaughter the chickens, although the rabbi of the city, may the name of a righteous man be blessed, did not forbid slaughtering by the Vizner.

[Column 262]

The fires of the quarrel flared to the highest level on a *Simchas-Torah* [the celebration of the conclusion of the yearly reading of the Torah] during the *hakofes* [circular procession with the Torah scrolls] in the *beis-hamedrash*, led by the Vizner *khazan* and his choir. Several young people from the Gerer and Aleksander *shtiblekh* stopped in the antechamber, perhaps without bad intentions, but *beis-hamedrash* attendees suspected that they would rush into the *beis-hamedrash* in order to disturb the *hakofes*. Terrible fights broke out and a tumult began in the entire *shtetl*. The shouting from the beaten to bloody and the cursing of the crowd actually reached to the very heavens and while the local police were powerless and could return order to the *shtetl*, the head of the post office telegraphed the district police chief in Ostrowa and gendarmes and police arrive from there and carried out many arrests. Several dozen people were arrested on *yom-tov* [religious holiday] and were placed in Christian wagons and immediately taken to jail in Lomza.

Mass beatings ceased, but because of various secret police agents and informers from one side or the other, there were always more arrests.

Many of the arrestees were freed after a short time, some of them because of a lack of evidence showing their guilt and others who were successful in establishing their innocence.

It appeared as a calming of the mood had begun and life in the *shtetl* welcomed a more normal character. But as a result of an accident that occurred, the almost muffled ardor of the quarrel again broke out. A fire happened at the house of Zanwil Edelsztajn and several of the men from the *beis-hamedrash* were arrested on the charge of setting Zanwil's house on fire. It was said: those from the Hasidic side had pointed out the *misnagdim* to the police, that they had a hand in the fire. In the course of almost an entire year, the arrested were investigated. The examining magistrate came to Czyzewo often in connection with the investigation. However, he could not get any direct proof and everyone was freed.

[Column 263]

In time a tragic event happened:

When Tuvya, of blessed memory, was freed from suspicion of taking part in setting fire to Zanwil's house, he wanted to show that the suspicion was groundless. He was afraid that this would disturb his earning a living as a butcher. Before the reading [of the Torah] on a *Shabbos*, he went up to the *bimah* [elevated area from which the Torah is read] in the *beis-medrash* and swore on the *Sefer Torah* [Torah scroll] that he had no connection with the fire. But he died the same year. Some of the people saw in this a punishment from heaven for swearing falsely. Others said that he had a heart attack because he could not bear the heartache of the shame because of the false accusation.

[Column 264]

The quarrel ended when the Vizner *khazan* received a contract from an American town, where he became the *khazan*, *shoykhet* and the *mohel*.

[Column 265]

The Great Peace

(A folk tale about Czyzewo in the past)

A. Wiewiurka

Translated by Gloria Berkenstat Freund

It really has only one name. Czyzewo, but it is really two Jewish *shtetlekh* [towns]; and not because a river, a bridge or a forest divides this tightly compressed *shtetl* [town]. It is two *shtetlekh* because two Hasidic sects, Gerer and Aleksanderer, carried out sharp arguments that ended with this: there were two rabbis, two *shoykhetim* [ritual slaughterers] and two *shamosim* [synagogue officials who assist the rabbi] in the *shtetl*.

This happened when the old Aleksanderer Rebbe [the head of the Aleksanderer dynasty] died and a large group of his Hasidim, not strongly approving of his son, conferred and began "traveling" to Ger.[1] Earlier, most of the Czyzewo scholars and rich Jews, also including the Rabbi, Reb Yonale, were from the Aleksanderer group. The Gerer was the smaller party. Now, however, both parties were equally large. As the rabbi was also among those who had gone over [to the Gerer], this greatly irked the remaining Aleksanderer. It had been their right for so many years to choose the rabbi and the *shoykehtim* in the *shtetl* – they decided to bring a separate rabbi, an Aleksanderer Hasid.

Said is done; on a beautiful night, another rabbi was brought into the *shtetl*.

[Column 266]

Six wagons traveled with him. Moshe-Josef *Melamed* [religious school teacher], with a torch (flare-sticks) in his hand and a lot of cheap whiskey in his head, danced in front of the wagon on which the new rabbi sat, and, with his hoarse voice, grated, "Long live the king." A group of Hasidim drank and sang Aleksanderer melodies the entire night, "to the great displeasure of the Gerer," so that the entire *shtetl* shook and, in the morning, the *shtetl* had two "men of great distinction."

The Gerer were insulted by this: is it possible to "Encroach upon the rights!"… Bring in another rabbi, when Reb Yonale has been the rabbi in the city for 30 years and what kind of a rabbi! A gentle Jew who would give away his soul for a Jew… They were furious and three days later there remained no panes of glass in the windows of the *Shniek* [second one] (that is how they referred to the new rabbi)… Who knocked them out we do not know to this day; suddenly a stick had knocked on the panes, the glass shattered and the stick vanished.

It should be understood that on the same night, the windowpanes of the Rabbi, Reb Yonale were knocked out. Moshe-Josef *Melamed* had knocked out the windows here; he actually did it gracefully, not hurrying and after each blow, he stuck his drunk red face in the windowpane hole and looking right in the rabbi's face hoarsely shouted:

[Column 267]

– Old drunk, I have excommunicated you!

The *shamas* and two Gerer Hasidim chased him. In the middle of the market a large crowd came running from both parties. Hands crawled into beards, fingers entangled in *peyes* [side curls], slaps reverberated and flew from cheek to cheek and when the battle ended, the crowd saw that a *minyon* [10 men necessary for organized praying] of hats lay trampled in the mud. Quietly and ashamed, they bent over, each taking his hat, and went home.

From then on, Czyzewo became two *shtetlekh*. The "Gerer" realized that the two *shoykhetim* were "Aleksanderer." They decided to appoint their own *shoykhet*. The deed did not please the *shoykhetim*; one of them, Simcha Bunim, thought about it and went over to the Gerer. The two same *shokhetim* remained, but divided – one showed the slaughtering knife to the old rabbi and one to the new. The butchers were also divided – the Gerer bought meat from theirs and the Aleksanderer from theirs. And when all of these matters were arranged, the true quarrels really began.

Moshe-Josef *Melamed* went around and swore on his word that the old "senile one" could not decide any question and Chaim-Moshe, the *melamed* from the Gerer "congregation," simply argued that the *Shniek* is a *sheygets* [pejorative word meaning non-Jewish boy or man, also used when referring to someone whose piety is being questioned], a transgressor.

The rabbis themselves said nothing. Reb Yonale was a Jew, a naïve person and continually admonished that quarreling was an ugly thing and he would say, smiling into his beard, that if one rabbi is good, then two rabbis are certainly good! Why in Warsaw, not to give an evil eye, are there so many rabbis… It is tolerable; Czyzewo, a very considerable *kehile*, does not have to be ashamed…

[Column 268]

The new rabbi, too, was a Jew, a quiet one. He would circle up and down across his *beis-din-shtub* [religious courtroom] in his flowery robe, listening to all that was told to him and quietly shake his head with his long, black beard, then go to his *seforim* [religious books] cabinet, take out a book and look and it always appeared that he did not know what he had been told…

The Aleksanderer stopped persecuting the old rabbi as a result of an actual occurrence.

A poor Jew, the wife of a wagon driver went to the new rabbi to ask a question about a chicken that had a broken wing. The chicken was *treyf* [unkosher]. There probably was bitterness in her heart. Incidentally, she was afraid of her husband, who shouted that he did not need a chicken for *Shabbos*. She thought about it and went to the old rabbi with the chicken. He examined it: *treyf*. However, the rabbi saw her tears. He said to the woman: Show me the chicken again. I will look again. Perhaps I will find a rabbinic approval. He took the chicken and went into the kitchen with it. In a second, he came back with a chicken in his hand. He gave it to the woman and said with joy: yes, the chicken is kosher.

The Jewish woman ran away happy and in two hours the entire Aleksanderer public cooked like a kettle: the "old one" had made fit a *treyf* chicken!

Moshe-Josef *Melamed* and an entire gang rushed into the rabbi's house with tumult and screaming. The rabbi saw such a large group.

[Column 269]

He sat on an armchair and calmly asked:

– Jews, what do you want?

However, the clamor grew larger: Unpure chicken … chicken … unpure deciding religious questions.

The rabbi became angry and cried out:

– You are yourselves unpure!…

It was lucky that the rebbitzen entered and the crowd learned from her that the rabbi had given his own slaughtered chicken to the woman…

The Aleksanderer left the "old one" alone after this deed. But then the parties themselves became even greater enemies. They did not intermarry; as far as possible they did not do business with each other and fathers-in-law became angry with their own sons-in-law who belonged to the opposite side.

* * *

The commandant, who had reigned over Czyzewo for three days, did not want to permit speculation about which of the two sides was correct and who was the true rabbi – he sent for both rabbis and informed them that in the morning, no Jewish soul should remain in the *shtetl*.

Just as the old rabbi and his *shamas* left the commandant's house, the new rabbi arrived with his *shamas*. For a moment, both rabbis looked into the others eyes and each went his way.

This was the first time that both rabbis had seen each other and understood each other.

In time an entire Gerer group was assembled in the small Gerer synagogue and, also, a number from the other side. The rabbi stood on the *bimah* [elevated area on which the Torah is read], his hands trembled and his voice also shook.

[Column 270]

– It is a temptation… A dark time… as a verse states… I ask you, Jews, to stop wringing your hands… and I ask the women not to cry… do not let enemies think that we have, God forbid, lost our faith in our God… thus is His will… Let everyone take what he can and, in the morning, we will leave the city.

But now there was a great lament from the women who stood on the chairs, their faces wrapped in shawls and the rabbi had to interrupt his prayer. The *shamas* banged twice on the table. Women suppressed their sobs. The rabbi spoke further with anger:

– I decree that there should be no crying… Where Jews go, the Divine Providence goes with them… God does not leave, God forbid, his people… Everyone should calmly pack what they can and when the day begins we will leave… Until God will take pity…

The crowd quickly approached, each ran to see what he could do. Moshe-Josef *Melamed* ran around to his businessmen and asked for at least a half month. Jewish women quietly pinched their cheeks to hold in their crying as the rabbi had requested.

Although the entire *shtetl* knew the sad news, the Aleksanderer group, however, was in its small synagogue and again heard the news from their rabbi. The new rabbi already knew that the old rabbi had decreed not to cry; he agreed and also issued the same edict.

And in the morning, both Czyzewos gathered at the bridge. The Aleksanderer with their rabbi, *shamas* and *shoykhet* at the head and the Gerer with their rabbi, *shamas* and *shoykhet* at the head. There were no wagons and horses in the entire area. They were forbidden to stop in any *shtetl*; the crowds went with children in their arms and packs on their backs. Both rabbis and *shamosim* carried *Sefer Torahs* [Torah scrolls]. A Jewish woman could not restrain herself from crying; she stopped, remained behind the crowd and sobbed into her shawl.

[Column 271]

The neighboring *shtetlekh* which they passed through were already empty of Jews. Several gentile girls called after them: "*Zydi do Palestini*. [Jews to Palestine]." Gentile boys twirled a pig ear from their waists, but the crowd went farther, farther silently, each group with its rabbi. Their eyes did not look with hate, but one did not speak to the other – angry is angry!

They were in the Przerewer forest at night and it was here they were to remain overnight and to go farther in the morning.

Several men with the rabbis remained to stand on guard and the remaining spread out silently on the ground, among the trees whose branches shook.

[Column 272]

The old rabbi, Reb Yonale, stood and looked at the sleeping crowd. He saw the children huddled to their mothers' bosoms because of the cold; he heard the uneasy, sighing breathing of those sleeping. He saw God's children strewn in the forest like lonely, wandering, homeless animals. It strongly tugged at his heart.

He turned away from the remaining guards to the side, fell to a tree, clung to it and began to sob: the Almighty… The…Almighty…

Something touched him. He looked around – the new rabbi stood near him, his head sunken on his chest like a tree that bends in falling.

– "Excuse me, Rabbi," – he murmured quietly and stuck out his hairy hand to Reb Yonale.

And in the morning, as the crowd awoke to wander again, there was one Czyzewo. At the head went both rabbis and behind them an exhausted congregation and in their mournful eyes shone a new light of hope.

(From the book, *Extinguished Light*)

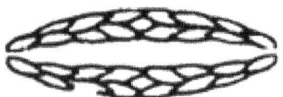

Translator's note:

1. Ger [Gora Kalwaria] was the home of the Gerer Rebbe. "Traveling" to Ger traditionally means traveling to the court of the Gerer Rebbe. Here it means praying in the Gerer synagogue.

[Columns 273-274]

Hassidim in the Town

by Ahron Tapuchi (Jablonka) of Tel Aviv

Translated from Hebrew by Jerrold Landau

The Hassidic movement, that begin its sweep from the areas of Ukraine, Podolia, Volhynia and Polsia[1], forged a path for itself into central Poland. It penetrated the large, central cities that were fortresses of Torah and Halacha (Jewish law), and also did not pass over the hundreds of towns that were scattered throughout its borders and the numerous villages that were far from the large gatherings of Jews and the centers of Torah, and for the large part were bastions of boorishness and ignorance.

The gloomy and penetrating reality was that Polish Jewry always was a fruitful ground for the rooting and spreading of various variegated revolutionary movements.

The Hassidic movement was received by the Orthodox masses as a comforting and redeeming messianic movement. Therefore, the masses were drawn towards it. In it, they saw an endless "wellspring" of joy and enthusiasm, a non-failing source of exaltation, loftiness, hope and faith, a gateway to ultimate redemption.

The influence of the Admorim[2] and their courts on the masses of Polish Jewry strengthened from day to day. They spread their protection upon the masses, and imprinted their spiritual stamp upon the way of life of the masses.

The elderly, youths and young men, including large scale merchants, craftsmen, men of deeds as well as poor folk who lacked a livelihood – all of them would be enchanted by the magical personality of the holy Admor. They would travel to the Rebbe in order to grasp his hand, receive a greeting, ask his advice, and to hear words of Torah from his mouth. From near and far, they would gather in the Rebbe's courtyard in order to live for a short period in his precincts. They would cleave to the Tzadik more than to their own families.

They would stream in from all corners of the country. Some were broken and weakened from the tribulations of the journey. Many had swollen and wounded feet from so much walking by foot (dozens of kilometers), and other bodily afflictions. Nevertheless, as soon as they would reach their destination, they would immerse in a kosher mikva (ritual bath) in order to purify themselves from all the filth of body and spirit. Refreshed and purified, they would make haste to greet the festival in the precincts of the Tzadik. They would hurry to find places in the synagogue, and they would stand for long hours in order to merit to see the countenance of the Rebbe, and to bask in his radiant splendor and spiritual nobility.

For dozens of years during the end of the previous century and the beginning of the current century (until the Second World War), Polish Hassidism was considered to be in the era of two Hassidic courts – the two most famous Admorim in the entire Jewish world – Ger and Aleksander.

[Column 275]

The shining illumination of Hassidism had great influence. It broke out from the Hassidic courts, affected all that passed by, and shone its holy glow upon the length and breadth of all Poland. It brightened and illuminated the skies of the dark, gloomy exile that covered our people in those days.

Ger, a tiny town near the capital city of Warszawa, turned in to a metropolis of Hassidism. On festivals, it was like the Jerusalem of below[3]. The Rebbe's synagogue was like a miniature Holy Temple, and the large courtyard surrounding it, filled with Hassidim who made the pilgrimage for the festival – was like the courtyard of the Miniature Presence[4]. The Polish capital of Warszawa served as the center of business and secular pursuits for the Hassidic world during the days of the weeks. Tiny Ger – the capital of Hassidism and holiness – served as their spiritual capital for the Sabbath and festival Jews.

A special small train (Kolika in Polish) was provided by the government to transport Hassidim from Warszawa to Ger. It was always filled to the brim with Hassidism who were making the pilgrimage.

Our town of Czyzewo was non-Hassidic from a geographical perspective, for it was surrounded by a ring of towns of zealous Misnagdim[5], who were a consecutive and natural continuation of the Lithuanian region. Nevertheless, this fact did not change one iota the way of life and thought of the Hassidim in our town, most of whom were faithful to the courts of Ger and Aleksander. From this perspective, they served as the "border guards" who faithfully protected and guarded the Hassidic movement on the frontier of the Lithuanian influence.

In 1915, at the time of the First World War, the large synagogue that served also as the home of the prayer rooms (shtibels) of Ger and Aleksander Hassidic groups was destroyed. Then, small prayer quorums and prayer rooms in private homes were organized on a provisional basis. The situation continued in that manner until the end of the war.

In 1918, the large synagogue was rebuilt, along with a large, splendid women's gallery. This renovation did not leave any room for the Hassidic prayer rooms, and they were forced to find new accommodations for themselves.

At that time, at the outset of the era of independent Poland, bands of murderous Polish robbers and murderers roved around our region, and instilled their fright upon the travelers along the roads and upon the affluent Jews who lived in villages. In the village of Godlowa, which was next to the Czyzewo train station, lived a Jewish family consisting of a childless husband and wife. Gedalja the grinder, as he was called, owned a large windmill and a well-ordered village farm. One night, the Polish pillagers murdered both of them, Gedalja and his wife.

[Column 276]

The relatives of the murdered family donated their house (a wooden house, which was taken down and transferred to the town) to establish a Talmud Torah in their memory. The two Hassidic prayer halls of Ger and Aleksander found their homes in this house. At a later time, the Hassidic followers of Amszynow and Sokolow set up their places in a small room in the attic.

While we are discussing the Hassidim of Czyzewo, we should step back a bit and discuss the differences in approach and style between the Ger and Aleksander Hassidic factions, as they appeared before our eyes at that time, and as they continue to live in our memories until this day.

The Hassidim of Ger were extreme by nature. For the most part they were scholars, and they were accustomed to leaving their homes and families prior to the festivals in order to travel to the Rebbe. On the other hand, the Hassidim of Aleksander were also knowledgeable in Torah, but did not particularly stand out in scholarship, and bore no complaint about that. They would suffice themselves with a trip to the Rebbe on occasion for a regular Sabbath. The Hassidim of Ger were very particular about the traditional garb, with shriveled pant legs rolled up into their stockings, collars without ties, etc.

[Column 277]

Their exactitude in this area knew no bounds. Young people who desired a white collar with a tie would be forced to remove the tie before entering the shtibel. Zealots such as Reb Berish Frydman, Reb Avrahamel Szwarc, Reb Sane Stuczynski and others, wearing their shtreimels[6] stood on guard to insure that nobody would break the conventions. If, despite all these efforts, someone managed to enter the shtibel wearing a tie, they would stop the Torah reading, and the violator would be forced to immediately remove it. If he would not, he would be forced to "leave the shtibel immediately and forever", for there was no compromise among the Hassidim of Ger! It was impossible for there to be. On the other hand, the Hassidim of Aleksander dressed each in according to his desire, without concern for such Hassidic conventions. There were even those who strutted along in white-heeled shoes, as was the fashion at that time. Hassidic elders such as Reb Szmuel Zelig and Reb Mordechai Hersh did not pay attention to this type of thing. Indeed, the son of the latter was known as the chief "dandy" of the Hassidim in the shtibel…

This tendency toward extremism and separateness also characterized the Ger Hassidim in the communal and social realms. Here are a few illustrative examples:

When the law of compulsory education was passed in Poland, and there was a danger the Jewish girls would be forced to study in mixed public schools (boys and girls together), and would also have to study secular subjects, the Hassidim of Ger in our town found ways to circumvent the law. To protect against this, they established a "Beis Yaakov" girl's school. They acted similarly in their struggle for the education of the boys. When a progressive school called "Cheder Metukan" was established in Czyzewo where secular studies were also taught, the Hassidim of Ger arose and established their own school by the name of "Yesodei Hatorah", where a small amount of secular studies were also taught. They did this in order to distance the children from the Cheder "Mesukan"[7] (Metukan, in Ashkenazic pronunciation), as they nicknamed to the "Cheder Metukan". They behaved similarly in their relationship to the activities of the communal institutions. Hassidim of Aleksander would be able to sit under one roof with members of Mizrachi[8] and general Zionists in the running of the charitable fund, and were able to act in a unified fashion for the benefit of the residents of the city. On the other hand, the Hassidim of Ger would not agree to such joint activity, and they founded their own, separate, fund. All arguments made by representatives of the Joint[9] did not succeed in convincing them from refraining from taking such a step, which threatened the existence of the funds, since the Joint would not be able to support the two funds simultaneously. No! They had to act on their own. There was to be no joint activity with others, that's that!

[Column 278]

In truth, it should be noted that the Hassidim of Aleksander agreed in their thoughts with the deeds of the Ger Hassidim, but they would never be so brazen as to do such acts of disunity, as the Ger Hassidim often did. Apparently, the Hassidim of Aleksander realized that they had whom to depend upon…

As is known, the power of the Hassidim of Ger was great even in the political realm. The Agudas Yisrael movement was the work of their hands. They founded it and reared it throughout all the years.

In our town, there was Reb Shlomo Calkes (the son-in-law of Reb Yitzchak Hersh Melamed), who was the founder of a branch of "Shlomei Emunei Yisrael"[110], the first incarnation of the Agudas Yisrael faction. He was one of the young zealots of the Ger Hassidim. He was G-d fearing, an accomplished scholar, extremely erudite. Having received his rabbinical ordination, he at times assisted the rabbi of the city.

The Hassidim of Aleksander did not participate with him. They stood at the side, and even opposed this political organization. These two Hassidic factions were very different in their activities. Ger symbolized might, brazenness[111], short-temperedness, and negating the fellowman. On the other hand, the Hassidim of Aleksander were quite the opposite – they were even tempered, patient, and solidly bourgeois from the perspective of Torah merged with the ways of the world[112]. The points of commonality between the two Hassidic camps were that both worshipped according to the Sephardic rite[113], and both of them loved melodies, despite their differences in styles of singing.

With regard to melodies, there were on occasion "thefts", and there were conflicts between the musicians[114] of Ger: Reb Szaul Hersh, Reb Yehoshua Nissan, Reb Chaim Yudel and Matel-Chaim; and the musicians of Aleksander: Reb Zelig Yankel, Reb Yisrael Yitzchak Janowski, Reb Jeszaja Gorzlaczani, Reb Botsze Eliasz, and Reb Lejzer Bitner.

The two groups both felt themselves as the spiritual guardians of the worshippers of the large Beis Midrash, and both expended their energies on their behalf. That is to say, they served as cantors on the High Holy days in the Beis Midrash. Reb Szmeulke Fiszels served as the prayer leader for Shacharit (the morning service) on the High Holy Days, and after his passing, his place was inherited by Reb Yehoshua Nissan of the Ger Hassidim, and later on by Reb Lejzer Bitner of the Aleksander Hassidim.

[Column 279]

They similarly helped out with Torah study: Reb Yisrael Yona Raczkowski of the Ger Hassidim taught the daily page of Talmud in the synagogue. In the Chevra Mishnayos group, Reb Yisrael Tyktyn of the Aleksander Hassidim taught Mishna publicly. Both of them, the Hassidim of Ger and the Hassidim of Aleksander, attempted to bestow of their spirit and their erudition upon the worshippers of the synagogue, who were Misnagdim, simple Jews, men of labor and toil.

In portraying the spiritual portrait of the lofty people of the Ger, it is fitting to add a few general points. In contrast to other Hassidim who were particular about the splendor of their clothes and their outward appearance[115] they did not pay attention to such meaningless details at all. Rather, their thoughts were focused on the celestial spheres, as if they were always searching for rectification of their souls from the internal unease that was always afflicting them. Love of G-d from the perspective of "with all your heart and with all your soul"[116] was actualized with them. They dedicated much of their time to the purity of the body and soul. Reb Berish Frydman often repeated the adage of the Kotzker Rebbe, that is to say: "The I[117] is a silent thief, stealing from the person and poisoning him without them knowing. The poisoned person does not know that he was affected.

[Column 280]

A person has to look in deeply to himself in order to search out and find this hidden thief, the 'I', and to uproot it from his heart." In the language of the Kotzker, "expelling it from himself in order to be free from all influences and motives."

For the most part, the Hassidim of Ger did not travel to the Rebbe to request healing for the body, but rather for ascendancy of the soul… The pure young man Reb Binjamin Jeszaja or the lovely pair, Reb Yitzchak Tombek and his friend Reb Avraham Yossel the teacher and others like them always felt that a layer of dust was accumulating on their souls and impeding their spiritual improvement. Therefore, they set out on a journey to the Rebbe to shake themselves out, to renew themselves, and to investigate the imperfections and cracks that came upon them since they were last at the Rebbe. Without stop, they always were engaged in self-examination, and the adage "Do not be righteous in your own eyes…" was always upon their mouths.

Thus were the Hassidim, and thus were the shtibels in our small town of Czyzewo where we children absorbed our first influences. We are still sustained to this day.

Indeed! The chain has not been severed.

[Column 281]

The Gaon Reb Szmuel Dawid of Holy Blessed Memory

The Last Rabbi of Czyzewo

By Rabbi Yosef Pinchas HaLevi of New York

Translated from Hebrew by Jerrold Landau

Czyzewo was situated on the border area of Lithuania and Poland, between the vibrant Hassidic centers of Poland on the one side, and the fortresses of the Lithuanian Misnagdim on the other side. Nevertheless, Czyzewo itself was a bastion of Hassidism. It had many Hassidim of Ger, Aleksander, Amszynow, and others. At an earlier time, it was also the honorable dwelling place of the Admor Rabbi Baruch Szapira of holy blessed memory, the student of Rabbi Mendele of Kotzk of holy blessed memory. He led a Hassidic community there. The influence of the Hassidim upon the town was great. They spread Torah and awe of G-d in the town, and they played a very prominent role in communal life. In reality, they were the hewers of the image of Czyzewo in the full sense of the word, until such time as the representatives of other organizations and movements appeared, and the town turned into a town with both religious and secular factions together. There were branches of Agudas Yisrael, Mizrachi, Zionists, Beitar, Poale Zion, and others. Each one of these groups attracted a different circle and faction, and tended to its own needs.

The agitation, deceit and struggle between the factions would break out with greater frequency and might as the elections to the Polish Sejm (parliament) or the local community neared. More than 100 kilometers separated Czyzewo from the Polish capital of Warszawa; however, for some reason, it was as if Czyzewo was some sort of suburb of Warszawa, and it was influenced by the spirit of Warszawa, as if it too was the nerve center of Polish Jewry. The city served as a mixing pot for any question that had to do with Jewish life, whether in the world at large, Poland, or Czyzewo in particular. Every faction and group took its side in the debate and defended their position strongly, for truth and justice could only be with their own side. No small number of debates broke out in this manner.

[Column 282]

A stormy conflict broke out in Czyzewo at a certain time in the previous century, when the question of the appointment of a shochet (ritual slaughterer) arose in the community. Two factions formed in town: "Wizner", those that wished to appoint Wizna since he was also a cantor, and "Szniadower", who wished to appoint the shochet from the city of Szniadowo. The controversy and provocation in town reached such a point that the police had to become involved in the matter. A few of those involved were arrested, and a black cloud of conflict, vain hatred, and factionalism darkened the skies of peaceful Czyzewo and its Jewish community. The crisis lasted for a long time, until…

Until something took place that seemed as if it was a miracle from heaven. A new rabbi appeared in the city, who was revered, opposed by nobody, and appointed by complete consensus. He was my teacher, my rabbi, my father-in-law the Gaon and Tzadik Rabbi Szmuel Dawid of holy blessed memory (may G-d avenge his blood), who loved peace, and pursued peace in the most sublime fashion, hated reward and honor, and immersed himself completely in Torah, wisdom, and fear of Heaven. On account of his noble personality and even temperament, he was able to set himself up as the skipper of the storm-tossed ship, calm the rough winds that were still blowing, and placate the town.

[Column 283]

The Jewish community of Czyzewo considered itself fortunate at that time, in that it merited choosing as a rabbi in such a successful manner a man who was like a savior angel. He was able to restore Jewish life in the town to its normal path as it was previously. He knew how to endear himself to all of the groups and factions in town. He loved people, and brought them near to Torah.

His Origins

Rabbi Szmuel Dawid Zabludower was a native of Warszawa. He was a scion of a wonderful family, and was the ninth generation from the Gaon Rabbi Yom-Tov Lipman Heller, the author of "Tosfos Yom Tov".

He grew up in Warszawa, where he ascended the ladder of Torah. He did not study in the Lithuanian Yeshivas, but nevertheless, he acquired the Lithuanian style of study, which was not customary in Poland. He was taught the secrets of this style of study from one of the famous Rabbis of Warszawa, Rabbi Pesachya, who was a student of the famous Gaon Rabbi Yosef Dov Soloveitchik of Brisk, of holy blessed memory.

The Gaon Rabbi Yosef Dov lived for a blessed period of years in Warszawa, after he was exiled by the Czarist government from the city in which he served as a rabbi – Slutzk, for the crime of denigrating the honor of Czar Nikolai I regarding the decree of "Cantonistim" (the conscription of Jewish youths for army service and for renouncing their faith). During those years when he was in exile in Warszawa, rabbis who were very great in Torah would gather in his home and study Torah from his mouth. Rabbi Pesachya of holy blessed memory was among these rabbis, and he learned the Lithuanian style from Rabbi Yosef Dov, and he educated his young student Rabbi Szmuel Dawid in that style as well.

He married my mother-in-law Rebbetzin Yocheved at a young age. She was the daughter of a well-placed family, that of the Nagid[18] Rabbi Zwi Srkowicz of Ostrolanka. When he was only 24 years old, he was called to the honorable service as the rabbi of Czyzewo, and he was received there with honor and appreciation. He occupied himself with Torah and service diligently, day and night. His great diligence astonished even great and well-placed people, and his breadth of knowledge and memory were like a "pitched well that does not lose a drop"[19]. He was expert in all of the many books that enriched his library – by heart, for every word that had once passed through his brain would never be forgotten. His sharpness was well known, and his deep penetration into the minutiae of Jewish law granted him great fame, and surrounded him with a splendorous halo. All of the greats of the generation revered him, and enjoyed engaging him in Halachic debates. They asked questions of him. The numerous writings of the Gaon Rabbi Szmuel Dawid, and the hundreds of Halachic letters that he sent out were a veritable treasury of interesting

Torah novellae[20] that lit up the eyes of scholars. These writings were hidden away at the outbreak of the First World War in a pit, and to our sorrow, were lost in the Holocaust.

[Column 284]

Among others, Rabbi Szmuel Dawid was in contact with the genius of Rogaczow, the Gaon Rabbi Yosef Rozen, the author of "Tzafnat Paneach", the person who turned into a living legend during his life, and who was known as the "Living Talmud". My father-in-law of holy blessed memory said of him that "From the days of the Shach (Rabbi Shabtai Cohen, the author of the commentary Siftei Kohen – forming the acronym of Shach – upon the Choshen Mishpat section of the Code of Jewish law, who lived more than three hundred years previously)[21], there was nobody as expert as him in all the treasuries of Torah." All of the rabbis of his generation would sent to him their Torah novellae and questions, and even though he denigrated most of the letters, claiming that they were of no worth – he would answer each one appropriately – nevertheless, he related to my father-in-law's questions with honor and seriousness. When this Gaon received a letter from Rabbi Szmuel Dawid, the rabbi of Czyzewo, he treated it seriously, read it carefully, and answered it in an appropriate fashion. Rebbetzin Rozen related one incident: "Once, a month passed without him receiving a letter from Rabbi Szmuel Dawid[22], and this bothered the Gaon greatly. When he finally received a letter, he said with satisfaction: Thank G-d that I received a letter from the Czyzewo Rabbi". The Rebbetzin pointed out that there were only three rabbis of renown that merited the esteem and reverence of the Gaon, and Rabbi Szmuel Dawid was one of them…

The Complete Person

[Columns 285-286]

The rabbi of Czyzewo was a lofty individual. He was a righteous in all of his ways, and pious in all of his deeds[23]. Those close to him were able to tell about his wondrous deeds, and his holy and noble behavior. He literally distributed a fortune in charity, his home was open wide to any visitor, anyone in need, or any poor or troubled Jew who would turn to the rabbi of holy blessed memory. He excelled in the attribute of entertaining guests (Hachnasas Orchim) in a splendid fashion, and he received every Jew pleasantly. His refined behavior characterized his noble character. He was pleasant to his fellow man. He never had an argument with anyone, and he never imposed his will upon his fellow. He was able to carry on a pleasant and enthusiastic conversation, and every word that issued from his mouth was weighted with gold. He scrupulously avoided idle chatter or any trace of gossip. He had certain expressions and adages that were unique to him, which flowed with excellence and purity.

[Column 287]

During Times of Difficulty

On Rosh Chodesh Tammuz of the year 5695 (1935), my father-in-law fell seriously ill. According to the advice of the physicians who were called from Warszawa, he had to leave Czyzewo and move to Otwock. Leaving the community and the town where he served as rabbi for dozens of years caused him great anguish of the soul. He continued to maintain a strong connection with the residents, and he took interest from afar in the affairs Czyzewo, even when his son-in-law, the writer of these lines, took his place.

At that time, black clouds began to darken the skies of Jewish Poland, including Czyzewo. The general embargo and the pogroms led to a general economic crisis and even the well to do were hungry for bread. After some time, my father-in-law returned to Czyzewo, and encouraged the spirits of the downtrodden local Jews.

When the German invasion of Poland began in the year 5699, Czyzewo was among the first towns that were damaged by the German bombardment. Only the building of the Beis Midrash was not destroyed. On the eve of Rosh Hashanah, the Nazis streamed into Czyzewo. Prior to igniting the Beis Midrash, they removed all of the Torah scrolls, poured kerosene upon them, and ignited them. When he heard of this terrible deed, the rabbi's eyes filled with tears, and he rent his garments[24].

The 8th day of the month of Av was the bitter day when the rabbi of Czyzewo, Rabbi Szmuel Dawid, was murdered in sanctification of the Divine name along with his wife Rebbetzin Yocheved, their daughter, and all the Jews of Czyzewo, may G-d avenge their blood, by the accursed Nazis, may their names be blotted out.

His Family Members

The eldest daughter of my father-in-law was Czwia (Tzvia) who married Reb Dawid Szniad of Warszawa. He was blessed with wealth, and was a large-scale fur merchant. His home was a gathering place for scholars, and all of the great Admorim who visited Warszawa would be put up at his home. They perished in the Holocaust along with their children.

The son of the rabbi, Reb Chaim, was known as a great scholar who followed in his father's footsteps. He married in the city of Mlodocin, where he lived until the outbreak of the war. He perished in the Holocaust along with his family.

His daughter Rebbetzin Freidel, and his son-in-law, the writer of these lines, were saved along with their only son Hershel. Today, they live in New York, America. They got established there with the great help of the natives of Czyzewo.

Written with tears.

By Yosef Menachem HaLevi Levinson[25]

[Column 285]

Rabbi Szmuel Dawid Zabludower
of Holy Blessed Memory

By Gerszon Gora of Tel Aviv

Lines regarding his character:

For the past approximately thirty years, each Passover, year after year, the noble personality lights up in front of me, the holy, refined, and splendorous image who, prior to each Passover, would summon up all of his resources and discourse for hours upon hours about Torah, holiness, Jewish law (Halacha) and homiletics (Aggadah).

I knew him throughout the entire year. He walked in measured steps to the synagogue of the town for prayer, being accompanied by Ahron the Shamash (sexton).

I saw him at various occasions in the town, at joyous occasions, sacramental meals[26], observances of mourning, funerals, marriage ceremonies, and circumcisions. He was always the same refined personality. He walked upright and erect, with a heartfelt smile on his face, and with loving glances to everyone.

[Column 287]

He was the rabbi of the town. He served his community for approximately forty years. These were four decades, variegated and with many changes.

He came to town when all of the residents were hewn out of a single mold. Even though they were divided into Hassidim, Misnagim, shtibels, synagogues, the common factor among them all was that the Beis Midrash, shtibel, prayer, study of Torah, the cheder, and men of the shtibel comfortably ruled over the town. Any edict issued by the rabbi of the city was accepted without complaint or debate. The rabbi would always decide all communal matters.

He came to town as the rabbi of all of the townsfolk. He worshiped with the shoemakers, tailors, wagon drivers, and porters – all of the members of the "masses" of the town. He recited his prayers together with them all in accordance with the

Ashkenazic rite[27]. However, deep inside burned the flame of Amszynower Hassidism. That flame was never extinguished in him. As he stood at the eastern wall next to the Holy Ark with his face towards the wall, it was possible to discern that he was not merely praying. Rather, all of his limbs were trembling – in accordance with the adage "All of my limbs state the glories of G-d".

I saw him for many years. I knew him for a long time, from the time that I began to be aware of my surrounding until I left the town. However, for most of the town, I knew him in only a casual manner. For who in the town did not know the rabbi of the city? Who did not see him in the street and in the synagogue, in the mornings or evenings? To delve into his mysteries, to know him more closely, to penetrate into his soul and obtain a clear picture of his deep spiritual personality, this was a very difficult task, and it is possible to honestly state that most of the townsfolk, whether Hassidim or Misnagdim, did not really know him and did not understand his spirit.

[Column 288]

Therefore, when Passover approached, and I remember that in those days, several decades ago, the rabbi of holy blessed memory would invite me to his home to the "room of the Beis Din[28]", to assist him for the approximately ten days prior to Passover in registering the sale of chometz[29]. I would assist him in dealing with all of the details, in clarifying to everyone that they must list in precise detail all of the leavened products in his possession, and even any mixture that might contain leaven, or any questionable leavened product. After everything, the rabbi himself would inspect the list, and, prior to accepting authority for conducting the sale, he would ask the seller if perchance he forgot to list one type of chometz. He would even mention various cosmetics and paints that might have chometz components. Each person's list would almost double after the examination of the rabbi. As I remember those days, I once again see before my eyes the sublime image of the rabbi, but the image is completely different. It was not the image that I knew before I became closer to him. It was not the rabbi that answered questions of Jewish law, and adjudicated halachic questions. It was a different personality, sublime, immersed for the entire day in the great sea of Torah and halacha.

Slowly, slowly, small cracks opened before me, tiny windows into his hidden essence. These were windows into his modest life, which was secluded within the four ells of that narrow "Beis Din room".

When he entered the "Beis Din room" after eating breakfast, his order of the day was already planned out. First, he began to remove books, one after another, from the tall bookcases, which were packed with books. (The entire area behind the desk was filled with books.) He sat in the armchair and began to study the books, with exceptional concentration. Most of the books were books of halacha, as well as both old and new responsa literature[30], written by the great adjudicators of Jewish law from the current generation, and previous generations.

His entire life was dedicated to issues of halacha. When a halachic question, or any other difficult question, came before him, he could dwell for weeks or months upon it. He would spend days and nights clarifying it and researching it until he arrived at the true answer, in accordance with Jewish law.

He would study Torah in an orderly and set fashion. He would start with Talmud, along with all of its commentaries, and follow that with books of responsa regarding the questions and answers from our own era.

[Column 289]

He never tired of delving into his books, which continued until late in the night.

He was very logical, and he fulfilled the verse "do not be afraid of the face of any man"[31] in the true sense of the term. There were isolated incidents, of which anyone in the town can relate, where one of the Hassidic residents of the town would visit him and begin to complain about the situation in the town, and about the tasks that the "rabbi of the city" is supposed to fulfill in a given situation, with out sitting with his arms folded. When he realized that the person standing before him, even though he was a respected Hassid, was exaggerating and going to far, not with respect to his own honor, for he was willing to forgo his own honor, but with respect to the honor of the Torah and the rabbi of the city he acted according to the law of "the zealous should attack him"[32] and give the complainer "a slap on the cheek"[33] on account of his brazenness and nerve in speaking against the rabbi.

Such "slaps on the cheek", occurred very rarely during his forty years of service. Once it occurred to a certain butcher, and another time to a certain communal administrator (parnas). However, the reason was always one of honor of the Torah or the rabbinate.

There was one matter that he struggled against for many years, almost until the day of his death. This was with regards to a halachic question that many of the rabbis of Poland, even great ones, struggled with.

This was a question with regards to tzitzit (ritual fringes), which came before him in his town of Czyzewo. Czyzewo was almost the only town in the entire world where there were several dozen small factories that made tzitzit and exported them to Jewish communities all around the world.

At first, all of the labors regarding tzitzit were done by people in accordance with the law, and with the intention of the fulfillment of the commandment of tzitzit, from the first moment when the raw wool was converted into combed wool in preparation for spinning, and later when the strands were twisted simple, not interwoven, strings. This work was very difficult on the manufacturers, who made tzitzit with great speed. Once, a few of the larger manufacturers went to a rabbi of Zambrów, near Czyzewo, where the rabbi was elderly and expert in adjudicating Jewish law, and requested that he permit them to perform the work on the strings prior to intertwining them by means of an electric machine, without the power of a human.

[Column 290]

They claimed that the main act of making of tzitzit takes place from the time of the interweaving, and thereafter[34]. After studying the situation in great detail, the rabbi of Zambrów permitted them to do this.

This news of the permission that was received by the large tzitzit manufacturers to perform the first works on the threads, prior to intertwining (as it was called in Yiddish, far shpin[35]), by machine, without human power, reached the ears of the rabbi. He found out that these manufacturers actually started making tzitzit in this fashion. He then aroused himself as a lion, and invited in all of the owners who began making tzitzit in accordance with this new leniency. He warned them that he would publicize in all of the newspapers that their tzitzit are ritually invalid.

His efforts to put a stop to this did not fully succeed, since he could not come out in public and invalidate their tzitzit, for they had a legitimate permit to do make them in such a fashion. However, on occasion, notices were published in newspapers directed to the purchasers of tzitzit of Czyzewo that they should make sure that the ritual certification (hechsher) of the tzitzit was issued by the rabbi of the city, and not by any other rabbi. This was more than sufficient.

Such letters were published in the "Darcheinu" periodical of the Agudas Yisrael organization of Warszawa, in issue 1 and issue 2.

This question took up much of his time, and not a day passed when he did not deal with it. I remember that he once called me to his house and requested that I make many copies of a letter that he gave me. This was a long letter to the Torah leaders of Poland, Hungary, etc. that requested them to express their opinion regarding this question. In his letter to them, he brought down all of the sources and proofs, both to permit and to forbid, and he expressed his own opinion that the situation was forbidden. These letters was sent to the Gaon of Dvinsk of holy blessed memory[36], to the Gaon Rabbi R. L. Cyrelson of holy blessed memory, and to Rabbi Chaim Ozer Grodzinski of holy blessed memory, as well as many other rabbis of Poland. From among the responses that he received, the response of the Gaon of Dvinsk was quite interesting. On his postcard, he only included source references, i.e. look here, look there, look there. The rabbi spent several days in analyzing the postcard of the Gaon of Dvinsk, which included references to several dozen books. His opinion went along with the majority to prohibit the "far shpin" by machine. There were also some Torah giants who did not have a clear view on the matter, and others who permitted it.

[Column 291]

New winds began to steal upon the life of the town. The community began to change. A few members of Mizrachi and the Zionist Council began to become members of the communal council and became parnassim (administrators) in the town.

The town began to change somewhat from the set patters of hundreds of years. Over and above the established cheders of the town, the Yesodei Hatorah Talmud Torah and the Beis Yaakov school, a new school opened, called "Cheder Metukan", with a Zionist Mizrachi outlook. Various youth groups were founded, as well as a secular library. The purpose of all of these organizations was to sway from the general custom and traditions.

These matters deeply affected the rabbi, and his soul wept in private. He had come to town when the city was 100% Jewishly traditional. He had never imagined that these pillars of Judaism would, Heaven forbid, begin to waver.

He loved peace by his nature. During the time of his tenure, there was barely any controversy in town. He always would strike a compromise among disputants, and also within the communal council. With the sweetness of his words and his influence, he would always succeed in tipping the scale toward the benefit of religious matters.

[Column 292]

As I have stated, not everyone knew him truly, for he was always taciturn. He was always enclosed within his four ells of halacha, in the room of his Beis Din. However, all of the rabbis of Poland knew a great deal about him. Many questions were sent to him, soliciting his halachic opinion.

During his last years, prior to the Holocaust, he was confined to his bed due to a paralytic illness that affected him. Even then, he did not desist from his study, and he was completely immersed in halacha and Torah.

When the bitter day came upon the town, the day when more than 1,500 people were marched on foot by German officers to the village of Szulborze, where gigantic pits were already prepared for the Jews of Czyzewo – they placed the paralyzed Rabbi Szmuel Dawid Zabludower into a wagon, and transported him along with the townsfolk, and his entire community. The Germans murdered him by machine gun, and he rests in the large communal grave in the village of Szulborze.

May his memory be blessed, and may G-d avenge his blood.

Translator's notes:

1. I am not sure of the identity of this area.
2. Admor (short for Adoneinu Umoreinu) is a term for a Hassidic leader.
3. In Jewish lore there is an earthly Jerusalem (the Jerusalem of below), and a celestial, mystical, spiritual Jerusalem in the heavens (the Jerusalem of above).
4. The 'Miniature Presence' ('Zeer Anpin') is a Kabbalistic term for a manifestation of G-d.
5. Misnagdim (literally 'opposers') are Jews who oppose Hassidism. The spiritual center of the Misnagdim was Lithuania.
6. A shtreimel is a Hassidic fur hat.
7. Mesukan is dangerous in Hebrew. In Ashkenazic Hebrew pronunciation, it would sound the same as "Metukan", as the spelling of the 't' in that word would be pronounced with an 's' sound.
8. The religious Zionist organization.

9. The Joint Distribution Committee, a worldwide Jewish assistance organization.

10. The Full Believers of Israel

11. The Hebrew word here is 'chutzpa', which is known in English as well.

12. i.e., they believed in intermingling the observance of Torah with the ways of the world (i.e. business, professionalism, etc.). The conflict of Torah only vs. Torah with the ways of the world is still prevalent within Orthodox Judaism of today.

13. There are several styles of prayer formats within Judaism. The true Sephardim (Jews of North African origin) as well of Middle Eastern Jews (e.g. from Iran, Yemen, etc.) use various forms of the Sephardic form. European Jews generally use the Ashkenazic form. Ashkenazic Jews who are influenced by Hassidim used a modified form of the Sephardic rite, called "Nusach Sephard". This is not the true Sephardic rite of the Sephardic Jews – it can better be termed as the Hassidic rite. It has some Sephardic influences due to it being based on the opinions of Rabbi Yitzchak Luria of Safed, whose Kabbalistic ideas influenced the early Hassidim. There is much to write about the topic of prayer rites, but here is not the place.

14. The term here most probably refers to laymen who serve as cantors in the synagogue.

15. The Sadigora and Rizhin Hassidim are known for this.

16. A quote from the Shema prayer, describing how a Jew should love G-d.

17. The 'I' here might be better termed as 'ego'.

18. A Hebrew term for a leader, rector, or nobleman, quite common in the middle ages but less common in the era that is under consideration here. It would be used for a very honorable and revered rabbi.

19. A quote from the Mishnaic tractate of Pirke Avot, describing a scholar with a phenomenal memory, who never forgets anything that he learned.

20. A Torah novella (chidush – innovation) is an innovative Torah or halachic thought or derivation.

21. The Shulchan Aruch, or the Code of Jewish Law, compiled by Rabbi Yosef Karo during the 16th century, has several commentaries on its folios. The two main ones are the above mentioned Shach, and the Taz.

22. The original text says "my teacher, my father-in-law", the author speaking about Rabbi Szmuel Dawid in the midst of the quote, but for clarity I inserted the name.

23. A play on words from Psalm 145 (the well-known Ashrei prayer recited 3 times daily): "G-d is righteous in all of His Ways, and pious in all of His deeds".

24. Rending of one's garments is a traditional Jewish expression of mourning.

25. This author's name is different from the name given at the beginning of the article. This difference is hard to resolve, but the fact that the first name is the same, and the Levi status is given in both, it is possible they are the same people. The name at the beginning does not give a last name, and the one at the end does -- so there is no contradiction there. The only contradiction is in the middle name -- Pinchas at the beginning and Menachem at the end.

26. Meals that follow circumcision, the redemption of the firstborn, weddings ceremonies, the week following wedding ceremonies (Sheva Brachos), etc.

27. Specific references to prayers are given here. The reference is to the prayer of "Mizmor Shir Chanukat" being recited prior to "Hodu". This is in accordance with the Ashkenazic rite. The Hassidic or "Nusach Sefard" rite would recite these prayers in the opposite order. See note 13 for further details.

28. The Beis Din is the rabbinical court.

29. On Passover, it is forbidden to eat, and even to own, leavened products (chometz). Prior to Passover, all of the leavened products in one's home are sold to a gentile, so that it is not owned by a Jew for the duration of Passover. The technicalities of this sale of chometz are quite complex, and it is generally arranged by a rabbi. The halachic (Jewish legalistic) details mentioned in the next few lines are complicated, and it is not possible to elaborate on them fully here.

30. Responsa are questions and answers regarding points of Jewish law.

31. This verse is from the beginning of the book of Deuteronomy.

32. There are certain specific areas of Jewish law, where it is recommended that zealous people take the law into their own hands in order to prevent an abomination.

33. By the quotes, it seems clear that this is not meant to be taken literally.

34. In accordance with Jewish law, it is preferable, and often mandated, that ritual objects be made with the specific intent of fulfilling the commandment (mitzvah). This would preclude these objects being made by machine. The question being dealt with here is how far does this apply with respect to tzitzit.

35. Literally – pre spinning.

36. Dvinsk is the city of Daugavpils in Latvia. Rabbi Meir Simcha of Dvinsk, often known as the Ohr Sameach, was one of the Torah leaders of that era. The rabbi mentioned in the next sentence, Rabbi Chaim Ozer Grodzinski, was one of the leading rabbis of the pre-Holocaust era.

[Column 293]

The Rabbinate of Czyzewo

By Gerszon Gora

Translated from Hebrew by Jerrold Landau

The scanty facts that remain for us and merge together for the chapter "The Rabbinate of Czyzewo" are scattered about, a bit here and a bit there. Indeed, nobody ever would have imagined that a time would come when this type of information would be needed to erect a memorial monument to a splendid past. Indeed, our town did maintain an exacting ledger of the Chevra Kadisha (Burial Society), in which all of the special events and experiences in the life of the town were recorded. This ledger served as a source for a great deal of historical material, spanning centuries. The chapter on the rabbinate was significant. However, to our sorrow, even this ledger has passed into oblivion with the terrible devastation of Czyzewo.

Without this, when we come now to record some scanty lines for the chapter "The Rabbinate of Czyzewo", we are forced to utilize scattered lists and data from various sources of rabbinical literature or Jewish newspapers from many years ago. From them we can put together a clear picture of the history of the rabbinate in our town.

The following can be clearly established: Czyzewo excelled in its rabbis from way back; and throughout all of the eras was considered to be one of the small number of towns in all of Poland where rabbis who were great in Torah lived even in the earlier times. These were famous Gaonim, who bound the crown of the rabbinate of Czyzewo to their heads, and made it into something splendorous. The reason that these renowned rabbis streamed there was because the populace of the town comprised of excellent, choice people, men of deeds, Hassidim and G-d fearing people. The geographic position of Czyzewo also characterized it and set it apart from all other towns of Poland. It was a border town on the boundary of the realms of Hassidim and Misnagdim in Poland and Lithuania. The town was nestled in an area between the fortresses of the Gaonim and Torah greats, as well as the founders of Hassidism. This fact explains well the phenomenon that both Hassidim and Misnagdim occupied the rabbinical seat at times. These rabbis included those educated in the Lithuanian Yeshivas and students of the Gaon of Vilna, as well as natives of Poland who were brought up on the courts of the famous Admorim of Pszyscha and Kock (Kotzk), or other Rebbes.

[Column 294]

As I have stated, we do not have a unified body of material on the rabbinate of our city. Therefore, we will utilize the material that was found for us by the writer Rabbi Moshe Czinowitz. He collected information from the literary sources of the bygone era, starting from the year 5599 (1839). We have no information about the time prior to this. It will be the task of a future historian to produce a book about the entire rabbinate of Poland, from its beginning until its bitter end in the terrible Holocaust.

Rabbi Chaim Leib Epsztajn of holy blessed memory

He was the rabbi and head of the rabbinical court of Czyzewo from the year 5599, and for a blessed number of years following. At the same period of time, his signature appears among the signatories from Czyzewo upon the book "Shvil Hayashar" ("The Straight Path") (a commentary on the book of the Rif [1]) by the Gaon Rabbi Shmuel Shuskes of Vilna, that was printed in 5599. He served as the head of the rabbinical court of Chorzel prior to that (5595). From Czyzewo, he moved to Sokolow, and in his latter years he served as the rabbi of Kolszyn, where he died.

The book of responsa of Rabbi Epsztajn [2], called "Pri Chaim", was published posthumously in the year 5673 (1813). From between the lines of this book, we learn that the author was the expert student of the famous rabbi of Kock, Rabbi Menachem Mendel of holy blessed memory. It is quite possible that he was the first spiritual influence of Hassidim in our town. Perhaps thanks to his influence, this small town on the Lithuanian border became a fortress of Hassidism.

[Column 295]

From the year 5599, when he began to occupy the rabbinical chair of Czyzewo, we find a response by him to a question of permitting an aguna [3]. This response was written to the first rabbi of Lomza, Rabbi Shlomo Zalman the son of Mo"haran, and his two judges, Yechiel Aryeh the son of Reb Josef, and Shlomo Zalman the son of the rabbi and Gaon of Wroblowa. He maintained a Torah oriented correspondence during that era with the greatest rabbis of the generation, included Rabbi Feivel of Gorysze [4], the head of the dynasty of Admorim of Aleksander.

In the section on sermons in his book "Pri Chayim", we find, among other things, his eulogies for the famous Admor Rabbi Yitzchak of Warka (died in 5608 – 1848); the rabbi of Parczew and the rabbi of Wyszogrod Rabbi Jakob Dawid of Mezeritch, who both died in the year 5623 – 1863, when rabbi Epsztajn was serving in the rabbinate of Kolszyn.

His son Rabbi Simcha Epsztajn served as a rabbi in a variety of communities. In his final years, he served in Pultusk. He spent his youth and was educated in Czyzewo.

The following householders of Czyzewo are appear as signatories [5] of his book "Shvil Hayashar", along with others: Reb Chaim the son of Reb Josef Jozel, Reb Szmuel Meir the son of Reb Jehuda Lejb, Reb Ahron the son of Reb Zeev, Reb Shlomo Zalman the son of Reb Yitzchak Zelig of the village of Sudek, and Reb Moshe Arje the son of Reb Yitzchak Eizek Meizelzon.

Rabbi Eliezer Szmuel of holy blessed memory

He was born in Krottingen, in the region of Kovno in the Zamot area of Lithuania. He was born in approximately the year 5585 (1825). During his youth, he was a student at the famous Yeshiva of Volozhin. At that time, Rabbi Yitzchak, the son of the founder of the Yeshiva Rabbi Chaim of Volozhin, served as a head of the Yeshiva. He was appointed as a rabbi in a town near to his native city at the age of 20, and after some time, he was appointed as the rabbi of Czyzewo. There is evidence that he served as the rabbi in Czyzewo until the year 5628 (1868).

[Column 296]

We can assume that he was an educated rabbi [6] in accordance with the ways of the time. His brother-in-law was Eliezer Zylberman, the founder and editor of the first Hebrew weekly "Hamagid", and also a native of Krottingen.

In the year 5628, Sir Moses Montefiore decided to set up a Talmudic Academy in his native town of Ramsgate England. He wished to bring there rabbis who were learned in Torah, who would receive all of their livelihood and sustenance from him. The rabbi of Czyzewo, Rabbi Eliezer Szmuel was among the three rabbis who were chosen for this position, and bestowed of their glory upon the Talmudic Academy that was called by the name "Yeshivat Ohel Moshe Veyehudit". It is probably that his brother-in-law, the editor of Hamagid, had a hand in his appointment. This institution survived for a long time, until the year 5648 (1888), about three years after the death of the knight. At that time, the directors of that institution decided to liquidate the Yeshiva, and from the monies received in the liquidation, they would pay compensation to the rabbis who taught at the Yeshiva, supporting them for life in any place that they would choose to settle. Rabbi Eliezer Szmuel of holy blessed memory moved to Montstar, near the hospital. He died there in the year 5654 (1894).

He published several works during his life. These included "Toldot HaLevi", that is Eliezer the Levite, who was the assistant and translator for Montefiore, who accompanied him throughout all the years of his long life. This work was in Hebrew. He also translated "Sefer Yehudit", which was written about the wife of the esteemed knight. It includes her diary and travel log from the year 5599 (1839). In his long introduction to this book, the translator describes the activities and life history of Lady Judith Montefiore. He includes many rabbinical statements that deal with the honor of women, which was great in the eyes of the rabbis of the Talmud. In these books, the name of the rabbi who was the translator is not mentioned, in the same manner as he appears anonymously in his many articles in various issues of Hamagid. In the year 5650 (1890), the rabbi published a sample pamphlet containing selections from his large book "Baalei Asifot" – a book that anthologizes statements of Talmudic rabbis from both Talmuds[7], and organizes them in alphabetical order. He was not able to complete that work on account of his old age.

Incidentally, it is worthwhile to point out that in his article on the Yeshiva of Sir Montefiore in Hamagid of 1869 (37), the rabbi mentions his Czyzewo, the locale of his former rabbinical service, as a city "full of scholars and scribes".

[Column 297]

In Hamelitz of 1894 (3), there is a long article about Rabbi Eliezer Szmuel of blessed memory, by Yitzchak Yaakov Hirshborn of London.

Rabbi Yisrael Tyktin of holy blessed memory

According to Reb Zalman Stolowicz (now in Israel) Rabbi Tyktin conducted the rabbinate in Czyzewo for a brief period of time "between two kings", that is between one rabbi and the appointment of his successor. He took over the rabbinate after the death of Rabbi Eliezer Szmuel of holy blessed memory. He was a great scholar as well as wealthy. Torah and greatness merged together with him. He ran a large store off iron implements. He was ordained by the "Chidushei Harim" of Ger[8]. Since he was quite occupied with his multi-branched business, he transferred issues requiring rabbinic decisions to Rabbi Ahron Hirsz Grodus of holy blessed memory, a resident of the city who was a scholar, and knew how to make rabbinical decisions. The two of them together conducted the rabbinate of Czyzewo until a new rabbi was chosen, Rabbi Moshe Joel Hagerman.

Rabbi Moshe Joel Hagerman of holy blessed memory

He was an expert student of the Chidushei Harim, who was the father of the Ger Hassidic dynasty. He was the scion of a family of rabbis and Hassidim. His maternal grandmother was the Gaon and Kabbalist Rabbi Dawid HaLevi Horowicz of Olkusz (in the area of Kielce). His father, Rabbi Jakob Shlomo, was related to the Bach, Taz, and Tosfos Yom Tov[9].

We learn of his greatness in Torah from his book of responsa, dealing with all sections of the Code of Jewish Law (Shulchan Aruch), titled "Shai Lamorah". It was published a long time after his death (Piotrkow, 5672 – 1912), with the approbation of all of the Gaonim and Tzadikim of the generation.

[Column 298]

The Admor Rabbi Avraham Mordechai Alter of Ger of holy blessed memory wrote about the author of this book as follows: "The Rabbi, the Gaon, the veteran Hassid". The Gaon Rabbi Yitzchak Feigenbaum, one of the chief teachers of Warsaw, honors him with the title "The Gaon, the Hassid, who is famous for his holiness and asceticism… who was his friend and cleaved to him like a brother". The Gaon Rabbi Szaul Moshe of Wierszow (died in Tel Aviv) testifies regarding him that "still in his youth, this rabbi who authored this book was famous, and he was publicly praised as a sharp Gaon and great Hassid". Other rabbis who granted their approbation were: Rabbi Isuchar Berish Graubard, the rabbi of Bendin; his brother Rabbi Jehuda Lejb Graubard, the rabbi of Staszow; Rabbi Jakob Orner the rabbi of Sochaczew; Rabbi Moshe Noachum Jeruzalimski, the rabbi of Kielce; and

Rabbi Aleksander Ziskind Lipszic, the rabbi of Ozorkow, who was the in-law of the author. He waxes great in his praise, and writes that "he was a great and broad in his Torah knowledge; both in the hidden and revealed Torah[110] were with him in full measure; he also conducted himself in the ways of Hassidism and great asceticism; during his youth, he poured water on the hands[111] of the rabbi of all Yisrael, the prince of Torah, our rabbi the Rim; he was one of his greatest students, and esteemed him very greatly." It is especially important to point out the approbation of the Lithuanian Gaon Rabbi Chaim Soloveitchik of Brisk, who also testifies that the author was "a famous Gaon".

In the words of rabbi Josef Levinsztejn, the rabbi of Sirock, that are brought down near the beginning of the book, Rabbi Hagerman composed an orderly essay on the "Choshen Mishpat" section of the Shulchan Aruch[112] and on several tractates and Talmudic discussions. However, these were burnt, and are lost.

In his Halachic responsa, Rabbi Hagerman discourses with the great rabbis of the generation, including: Rabbi Baruch Zwi Rozenblum, the rabbi of Piotrkow; the Gaon of Kutna Rabbi Yehoshua Tronk, the Gaon of Kalusz Rabbi Chaim Elazar Wachs; and the Gaon Rabbi Avraham Borensztejn, the rabbi of Krasznowice (later the rabbi and Admor of Sochaczew, the son-in-law of Rabbi Mendele of Kotzk). Rabbi Hagerman writes the following to this Gaon: "I remember in days gone by, when I stood before him and suckled honey from the rock, with milk under my tongue, as he led me through the circles of righteousness and the paths of study, I still had many days to lean upon him and be supported. He was a foundation rock when I saw the splendor of his face, as he assisted me with everything that my soul requested in the paths of study."

There is evidence that Rabbi Moshe Joel Hagerman was a confidante and friend of the Gaon Rabbi Avraham Borensztejn, or as he was better known, Reb Avrahamele Sochaczewer, the author of the "Avnei Nezer" during the time that he was supported at the table of his father-in-law the Rebbe of Kock, where the first Rebbe of Ger, the Chidushei Harim also found shelter. According to a story that is told by natives of Olkusz who are now in Israel, Rabbi Moshe Joel Hagerman studied together with the Gaon of Sochaczew in the same cheder during their childhood, and continued to study together in the Beis Midrash of Olkusz, their hometown. This was prior to their being coronated as rabbis in the Jewish world. Every morning, Reb Avrahamele would wake up his friend Moshe Joel, and the two of them would walk together to the Beis Midrash to study their regular lesson.

[Column 299]

As is pointed out in his book "Shai Lamorah", Rabbi Hagerman served as the rabbi of Jezew from the year 5617 (1857); and in the years of 5635-5647 (1875-1887) as the rabbi and head of the rabbinical court of Czyzewo. From there he moved to Zarnowka (in the region of Kielce). He was brought to rest there after he died around the year 5654 (1894).

During the years that he occupied the rabbinical seat of Czyzewo, we find that Rabbi Moshe Joel issued responsa in Halachic matters to rabbis of the area, such as: Rabbi Yitzchak of Zaromew; Rabbi Jechezkel of Nur; Rabbi Josef Levinsztejn of Sirock; the rabbi of Szniadowo (near Lomza); and Rabbi Yehoshua Jechezkel the rabbi of Ostrowo. In a letter from the year 5638 (1878), he turns to the author of "Nefesh Chaya" with a question regarding a fire that broke out on the Holy Sabbath in Czyzewo. Several kosher and passul Torah scrolls[113] were burnt in the fire, and a number of pieces of parchment were left. He asked a question with regard to the halacha regarding the proper burial of the remains.

A few of his Halachic responsa were directed to the relative of the Admor of Ger, the Gaon and Hassid Rabbi Pinchas Eliahu Rotenberg, the rabbi of Pilce. He also maintained a Torah oriented correspondence with his brother Rabbi Yitzchak Paltiel, the rabbi of Olkusz, and with Rabbi Jehuda Lejb Graubard, the rabbi of Staszow. The latter, in his approbation of the book, testifies that the author was "a great and renowned Gaon, a lion amongst his colleagues, an overflowing well, who spend all of his days in the valley of Jewish law".

His book "Shai Lamorah" was published by his son and student, Rabbi Yitzchak Jehuda Hagerman, the son-in-law of the rabbi of Ozorkow, Rabbi Aleksander Ziskind HaKohen Lipszic, and his successor in the rabbinate of Zarnowka. Incidentally, in the long introduction that the author wrote for his book, his splendid image of a great innovator in the area of Aggada (Jewish lore) and exegesis also stands out. He is expert on the Midrashim (exegetical lore) of the sages, and in investigation to the theory of Hassidism, in accordance with its founder the Besht[114], to whom he cleaved all of his days, and with all stands of his heart and soul.

[Column 300]

Rabbi Jakob Yitzchak HaLevi Epsztajn of holy blessed memory

He occupied the rabbinic seat of Czyzewo for fourteen years, between 5649-5663 (1889-1903). He died on the 27th of Adar of that year. An announcement of his death appears in Hatzefirah of that year (number 71). The announcement states that the rabbi died at the young age of 42, and left behind a young wife and five young children. (Hamodiah, Reb Zerach Starkowski).

He came from Lithuania, and was a relative of Rabbi Yechiel Michel Epstein, the rabbi of Novhorodok and the author of the "Aruch Hashulchan"[115]. He was a student of the famous Gaonim the Netziv of Volozhin and Rabbi Chaim Soloveitchik of Brisk. He studied in the famous yeshiva of Volozhin.

During his tenure, the "famous controversy" between the Chazan-Shochet of Wyzne and the Shochet of Szniadowo took place, which shook up the entire area and whose echoes reached the governing authorities. This controversy that spread in its time divided the city into two camps of disputants who hated each other with a strong hatred.

The background of the controversy was as follows: our city was a bastion of Hassidism. In particular, the Hassidism of Rabbi Moshe Joel of holy blessed memory, who was one of the first students of the Chidushei Harim of Ger, as well as one of the frequenters of the home of the elder Rebbe of Kock, took root. At that period of time, the community of Czyzewo was searching for an experienced shochet who would serve the role in a permanent fashion. The community divided as follows: the masses, simple householders who worshiped in the Beis Midrash as well as artisans wished to seek a shochet who could also serve as a chazzan (cantor) and would be able to lead the services on the High Holy Days. However, most of the worshippers of the shtibels, the Hassidim of Gur, Aleksander and Kock (excluding the Hassidim of Mszczonow (Amshinov) who sided with the householders) opposed this, claiming that the shochet should be a great fearer of Heaven and not an experienced chazzan, but rather an ordinary Hassidic prayer leader.

[Column 301]

During the heat of the controversy, a young man from Wyzne appeared in town, splendid in countenance with a well-kept beard, trimmed with scissors. He had no peer in the whole region of Lithuania, and he did not, Heaven forbid, impinge upon the kashruth of shechita. In addition to this, he was a wonderful chazzan who knew how to sing, and was able to read musical notes. On the first Sabbath that he officiated, he enchanted his audience with his strength in singing and melodies. The rabbi of the city examined him carefully to see if he knew all of the laws regarding the slaughter and ritual examination of animals, as well as if he knew how to properly check the shechita knife (chalaf). He passed the test properly, and the rabbi informed the community that there is no problem or lack with his knowledge of the laws of shechita, and he gave him the approbation to practice shechita. Based on this approbation, the householders appointed him as a chazzan and shochet. However, when the Hassidim of the shtibels, who guarded each dot and tittle of the traditional Hassidic way of life, heard that in Czyzewo they were about to appoint a shochet who was also a chazzan and knew how to sing and read musical notes, and whose bread was trimmed and well-kept – they immediately raised a great tumult and declared open warfare.

This battle brought Rabbi Epsztajn into an extremely difficult situation. He was no longer able to become involved in the matter, since the events developed rapidly, and the controversy deteriorated from the usual style and reached the point of provocation, bloodshed, and slander, etc. From his perspective, he had no issue with the chazzan of Wyzne. His dress, his cantorial style, and his trimmed beard were not issues for him, for he himself was a native of Lithuania, where they were used to this style. One the other hand, he understood the spirit of the Hassidim very well; that it might not be fitting and proper in a Hassidic town such as Czyzewo to appoint such a chazzan-shochet.

This controversy (described in this book in a different place) was one of the factors that shortened his life. He died, as has been mentioned, at the very young age of 42.

Rabbi Szmuel Dawid Zabludower of holy blessed memory

From Ostrolenka, where he was supported by his father-in-law, the rabbinical leader Rabbi Zwi Srkowicz as he studied Torah and served G-d, Rabbi Szmuel Dawid Zabludower was called to serve honorable in the rabbinate of Czyzewo a few years after his wedding. He was an enthusiastic Hassid of Mszczonow (Amshinov), and thanks to that, he was accepted willingly and joyously by the entire Jewish community of Czyzewo. This was satisfactory to the Hassidim, and also served as an appeasement to the supporters of the Wyzne shochet, who included the Mszczonow (Amshinov) Hassidim, headed by the elder renowned Hassid Rabbi Moshe Ber Kackowicz of blessed memory (His son Yaakov David and daughter Yocheved are today in Israel).

[Column 302]

This chapter of the rabbinate of Czyzewo was one of the most splendid and interesting in the life of the city, for Rabbi Szmuel Dawid was one of the Torah giants of his generation, who raised the level of the banner of his rabbinate to lofty heights, and who was acceptable to all members of his community for a blessed period of close to fifty years. The era of his rabbinate was one of the most difficult and stormy in all of Jewish history. There were two world wars during this period, and at the end came the Holocaust of Europe that destroyed the majority of the people and the structure of the large Jewish community of Europe, including our town of Czyzewo.

The chapter of his life added a radiant page in the annals of the life of our town. During his tenure, our town knew a peaceful life, and no sound of strife and controversy could be heard. Despite the fact that in the latter part of this era, the winds of the times blew into the town, in the form of political factions and parties that divided the town, such as: Agudas Yisrael, Mizrachi, Zionists, Beitar, Poale Zion, Bund, etc., factions that were born due to the massive changes in communal life in Poland – despite all this, the rabbi, with his great wisdom, knew how to repair any breach that would come up at any time, and to set the course of communal matters in the paths of peace and brotherhood.. In a separate section of the book, we will describe his family, his personality, and his death.

Rabbi Szmuel Dawid Zabludower of holy blessed memory was the last rabbi of Czyzewo. He fell as a brave martyr in sanctification of the name of G-d, along with his flock, on that bitter day, the 28th of Av 5701 (1941), at the hands of the Nazi enemy, may their names be blotted out.

Thus was covered the grave of Czyzewo, the holy town.

[Column 303]

My Grandfather ...

By Gerszon Gora

Translated from Hebrew by Jerrold Landau

From my early childhood, my soul was bound with his soul. An internal love was kindled inside of me, and drew me to him. I felt that I had some sort of natural affinity to him. My entire self was devoted to him, as a child is devoted to his caregivers and those who embrace him.

He bore my thoughts and my dreams. I wove the visions of my childhood around him.

From him, I drew my youth; true youth, pure and sublime, filled with lofty, holy dreams.

The splendor of his face and the flame of his eyes sustained my thirsty, yearning soul.

I remember when I was still a young child and was interested in stories and tales, that would bestow sublime spiritual content to a child and envelop his soul with pleasant dreams – he would always take me upon his knees, caress me with soft, loving caresses, as he told me stories of Rebbes, Tzadikim, and sages. I thirstily swallowed up every word and expression that came from his mouth, his heart and his soul.

Then, I would feel as if all of the chambers of my heart had opened, and wide vistas were exposed to me. He ignited my soul and bestowed refinement and softness upon me.

Thus were the sublime paths of Judaism implanted into my soul. With his stories of the lives of Tzadikim, he crystallized concepts of spiritual life into my frail brain[116].

Desire and longing, pining and impatience – this is how his soul expressed itself towards the Land of Israel. All the days of his life were filled with longing and pining for the Land of Israel. This was the axis around which revolved all the events of his life.

"The Land of Israel" – this was the only word that filled his entire soul. He sprinkled upon it the dew of hope and comfort, of revival and redemption.

[Column 304]

His soul went out towards the Land of Israel; to see it with his own eyes and to breathe its air, the air of souls, with his own nose.

He always nurtured the longing to see the Land of Israel. From his early childhood, this hope strengthened his spirit. He thought about this day and night, when he went to sleep and got up, when he was awake and during his dreams.

Sometimes, when he was immersed in his studies, he would stop for a brief moment, approach me and say: "Yes, yes, go, go quickly, with the help of the Blessed G-d…"

"To where?", I asked.

"To the Land of Israel".

"But when?"

"Speedily, speedily. We will soon all merit to see the face of the Messiah, for he is already about to come."

His emotions overflowed as he said these words, until his entire body was trembling and shaking.

Any time that mention of the "Land of Israel" came upon his lips, his eyes would fill with tears. These were tears of happiness, full of hope and comfort. Tears that almost satisfied his spiritual thirst and burning love. Tears of longing, of pining…

He was a straightforward man who sat in the tents of study[117]. The wide world was strange to him. The sound of the turning of the wheel of life in the world did not reach his ears. He was a straightforward person. He never had a moment of emptiness, of vanity. I always saw him poring over a book, whether it was a Gemara, Midrash, or Zohar[118]. He was always immersed in his studies. He would finish the entire Talmud yearly. If he felt that he would not be able to finish on time, he would remain awake for entire nights catching up.

Even during his final days, as his strength waned and his power dwindled, he attempted with all his might to continue his study sessions as previously, without missing even a small amount. He studies his lessons as previously, with great diligence.

[Column 305]

Even as he lay seriously ill on his sickbed, he always held a volume of Talmud in his wrinkled, sinewed hand, and his mouth never desisted from study. He studied with a pleasant melody, even though every word that he uttered sapped some of his remaining blood and vigor.

"On the contrary", he would suddenly say, "When I am learning, I feel as if waves of vitality and joy wash over me, causing me to forget my weakness and pain. And during a time that I am not able to study Torah, I see myself as if sitting in a narrow, choking prison cell, without air to breathe."

The study of Torah was literally his breath of air.

He sat in tents.

He drew waters as clear as crystals from the wells of Hassidism. When he spoke about the Rebbe of Kock of holy blessed memory, an agonizing sigh would issue from the depths of his heart, along with the hushed painful words: "Indeed, I did not merit… I did not merit…"

With a voice suffused with grief and longing, he told me the story, how during his youth he made preparations, along with a group of Hassidim, to go to Kock (in those days, they would go there for the festivals), and to his great sorrow, he was too late to join the journey, and in that year the Rebbe of Kock of blessed memory died.

"I did not merit to see him alive", he would always tell me. He was sorry about this for his entire life, and his soul was not settled.

He rectified this omission with regards to the author of the Chidushei Harim of blessed memory, and the author of the Sfat Emet of blessed memory[8]. Throughout the days of their life – from the time that Hassidim began to travel to the Rabbi Rim of blessed memory, until the time of the death of the Sfat Emet of blessed memory – he would travel there times a year to them, without even missing once. There were no obstacles to him to prevent him from travelling to the Rebbe.

The journeys to the Rebbe for the festivals were to him the essence of his life. Those days were the happiest and best of all the days of the year for him; those days when he was able to bring to fruition his connection and cleaving to the Rebbe. During those days, he expressed his true Hassidic essence.

[Column 306]

It is worthwhile to mention an interesting fact, which demonstrates to use the extent of his dedication to his journeys to the Rebbe.

On one occasion prior to a festival, when my grandmother was giving birth, everyone requested of him not to travel to the Rebbe. In order to ensure that he would not travel, they hid his boots on the night before the journey. The next day, he rose early. When he saw that his boots had disappeared, he did not hesitate at all, but put on my grandmother's shoes and thus traveled to the Rebbe.

From the waters of this well, the pure well of Hassidism, he gave drink to his children and grandchildren. He always attempted to instill in the hearts of the young and old ones the Hassidic idea, and the full extent of the Hassidic essence. He attempted to instill in the hearts of his young grandchildren an Orthodox education, which would appeal to their youthful vigor, in order that it would remain forever in their hearts. He saw all of this in Hassidism.

He immersed himself in the waters of Hassidism for his entire life…

On his final day, Rosh Chodesh (New Moon) Tammuz that occurred on the holy Sabbath, he arose early as was his custom, and he studied his lesson in Talmud for two or three hours. Then he went to the synagogue to worship, and, arriving there before the time of prayer, he took a book of Midrash and studied the weekly Torah portion. He did not know at all at that moment that his minutes were numbered, and that very shortly, his pure soul would ascend on High. He only knew that every moment that he lived, he was able to collect and acquire many treasures for the eternal world, where all of the pure souls bask in the splendor of the Divine Presence. Indeed, this idea was always before his eyes, and I never saw him sitting idle, without engaging in spiritual endeavors, even for a brief moment.

When the prayer leader started "Hodu"[19], he closed the Midrash, wrapped himself in his Tallis, and began to recite the prayers. However, a moment after wrapping himself in his Tallis, a groan broke forth from his heart, a hushed groan, the groan of the soul as it separates itself from the body. His soul ascended Heavenward on the holy Sabbath, as he was wrapped in his Tallis.

[Column 307]

One of the Five

Translated from Hebrew by Jerrold Landau

In the list of natives of my town in my notebook prior to my travel to the Land of Israel, I read the first entry in the list:

"Benjamin Moshe Jeszaja the son of Rivka Rachel, etc.", with a first request to leave a note for him in the Western Wall. The second request was to go to the Tomb of Rachel our Matriarch, and send him a thread that surrounds the grave[20] … Remember to make mention of my name in all of the holy places… Benjamin Moshe Jeszaja the son of Rivka Rachel…

The entry in my notebook was written in his handwriting. I still remember those moments when he wrote those words "with trembling and solemnity", as two teardrops fell down and wet the name, one on the word Benjamin, and the second on the word Rachel.

He lifted his eyes and grabbed my hands silently, without uttering anything, as if he lost his power of speech. It was if he was like one of the mutes in the courtyards of the Admorim, or one of the unique spiritual people who guard their tongues from speech.

I looked at him for some moment – I was also dumbstruck like him. I waited for him to open up his wellspring, as he was wont to do at all times, up until the final day before my travels. I waited for words of parting and support, however it was in vain. He stood silently, and looked at me with two wet eyes and choked words. He strengthened himself until finally he uttered his numbered words:

"Know Gerszon, the Land of Israel requires fortitude. Anytime the holiness is greater, the external shells are also greater, Heaven forbid[21]. Therefore go, succeed, and first and foremost, gird yourself!"

There was silence again. The two hearts separated. The notebook went from hand to hand, and everyone inscribed it. Everyone wrote their requests and hopes, and I remained standing by the side of Benjamin Moshe Jeszaja. I clasped his hands, and the words: ""the Land of Israel requires fortitude" burned in my heart like a scalding flame.

[Column 308]

He removed his hand from mine, and caused my heart to shudder once again with the following words:

"But remember! Fortitude, fortitude! And as for me at that time – I am no longer"… I always maintained the thought that I would merit to see him again myself, as he wraps his hands with the thread of the Tomb of Rachel for a god omen. The thought remained with me that we would once again be able to continue with those spiritual journeys here in the Land. However, he wishes came to naught. For a letter arrived, saying: "Everything was destroyed!"

* * *

In the first days after his arrival, the elder Hassidim and men of deeds whispered among themselves that Moshe Zwi the shochet had brought a precious gem into his home. They had never seen a young man such as this before.

He was still in the midst of the seven days of celebration following his wedding, and his dwelling had turned into a shtibel.

Early in the morning prior to dawn, in noon, and in the middle of the night, Benjamin Moshe Jeszaja would sit, wearing his groom's clothing, poring over a volume of Talmud, Zohar, or other Hassidic work.

He was very quiet during the first days. He was modest, he did not know the area, and he was testing out the shtibel with its young men and elders. It was as if he was tracing his way through the new world that he was brought into on account of his marriage – checking to see if it was fitting for his spiritual work, and whether he would be able to continue with it, which he had placed as the goal of his entire youth? It was the purpose of his life. Hassidism, belief in Tzadikim, cleaving to their ways – these were the main ideas that led him. This was not only for himself, for his 248 organs and 365 sinews[22], for all of Israel are interconnected with each other, and it is incumbent to show the correct path to everyone, to all who are struggling and perplexed with their spiritual life. On account of this, he examined his new surrounding very carefully[23]; he looked at each young man, every youth, and even every child who appeared in the shtibel, with his penetrating gaze. He searched, and he finally realized that in the shtibel, a large field of activity lay before him.

[Column 309]

He began to become acquainted with the people of the shtibel. He examined them carefully, he learned the character of everyone, and he finally established his own group – of five people.

Five young men, "the pride of the shtibel", headed by Benjamin Moshe Jeszaja, became very quickly the "central beam", the "living artery" of the shtibel.

Matters of charity, good deeds, assistance to the poor, accommodations for an honored guest, a fitting place to sleep – all of these were organized by the "group of five" through the efforts of Benjamin Moshe Jeszaja.

If a rumor reached Benjamin Moshe Jeszaja that in the home of one of the men of the shtibel the "furniture" was not in order[24]… that the wife of someone was at one point not careful with regards to covering the hair, or if there was a reliable witness that "modern fashion" entered into the home of someone, Heaven save us – his personal response would immediately be forthcoming. That very day, he would enter into a conversation with that individual about some matter, and even invite him for a stroll outside the town.

During his conversation, he would not get to the crux of the matter immediately, but would talk around the issue, discussing Hassidism, Judaism, stories of Admorim and people of renown, and various customs that have penetrated into Hassidic homes due to our great sin. However, during the conversation, he was very careful that nobody should feel that the words were directed to him. His style of conversation was not to speak about the "darkness" but rather to instill rays of light into the heart, a spark of fire into the soul, and the darkness would disappear on its own.

[Column 310]

Thus did he instill droplets of Hassidism into those damaged and cloudy hearts; into those souls to which the winds of the time had begun to penetrate – until the hearts began to purify themselves.

"If there are no kids, there are no billy-goats" he used to say. He was concerned about this – if five young men sit and occupy themselves with Hassidism, study Torah, walk in the paths of their fathers and people of like mind, what would be with the children? How can they be directed into the right path, so that Heaven forbid they will not be affected by the vicissitudes of the time, and the spirit of impurity that has descended, Heaven save us, onto the world of late? -- He would gather together sheaves, of those who already had reached the age of Bar Mitzvah, of those whose "good inclination" had already begun to struggle and wrestle with the "evil inclination" in their hearts. He would begin to inspire them with his discussions and beloved stories about the Hassidic greats. Slowly, he would take them under his wings, and guard them as something more precious than anything.

The Land of Israel was especially important to him. He did not read papers. He satisfied himself with a brief glance at the newspaper headlines. Nevertheless, he knew everything that transpired. He knew of the enthusiasm in the hearts of the Orthodox youth as they prepared for aliya.

He understood the spirit of the youth. His heart and spirit were with him. He himself registered for aliya, even though he felt that he was not yet prepared, for he was still lacking the spiritual preparation necessary for the Land of Israel. He would always remind us youths of this sentence in "Sefer Chareidim".

"Every Jewish person is required to love the Land of Israel, and to come to it from the ends of the earth with a great desire, as a child comes to the bosom of his mother". To his friends who began to prepare for aliya, he advised them to look in the book of the Shela[25], in order to become acquainted with the preparations that a Jew must make for aliya, and what is the order of life there – in the Land of Israel.

The sages state that "The Land of Israel is the palace of the King". How can one live a simple life in the Land of Israel? – he would always remind us. I will not forget these reminders. I will not forget those hours when Benjamin Moshe Jeszaja strolled with me, once he discovered that my lot fell to be among the first of the young Orthodox people of our town to make aliya. We walked among the thick, old trees on the path that was known to everybody as "the Hassidic Path". During winter nights, in the latter half of the month of Shvat 5684 (1924), when the cold was at the height of its power, when the frozen snow echoed under our steps, everything was white, the fields were white, as were the strong trees, the branches waved over our heads along both sides of the path as a canopy, through the valley in which the Warsaw-Bialystock train passed a distance of several kilometers – and we, two individuals walking arm in arm, covered in winter furs, were the only ones disturbing the idyllic winter "white" before us, to the light of a full moon, two long shadows.

[Column 311]

We were alone on our stroll. He would talk, lecture, and wax with enthusiasm about his streaming ideas on the Land of Israel and life there. I was silent as I followed after his footsteps. I listened very carefully to every word and expression that issued from his mouth, as he described the holiness of the Land of Israel to me.

***

Approximately fifteen years ago, a young man slightly older than twenty came to our town. He was short, with red cheeks, refined and thin, with signs of a small beard under his chin. His long peyos (earlocks) were not curled, but dropped straight down over his face as if to cover over his lack of a beard in the center of his face. He had a large, wide forehead, with a number of furrows and wrinkles in accordance with the books of the Kabbalah and the Zohar[26]. He had eyes blue as the sky, which always gazed and looked at everything. He had a constant smile. Every conversation of his was accompanied by this charming, enthusiastic smile.

[Column 312]

– About fifteen years ago…

Now I look over the letter, look for signs of life, read between the lines. Perhaps, perhaps, I can find at least some of those special people who graced our city, who bestowed it with a spiritual life. But for naught…

Everything was destroyed –

In the large cemetery, in the gigantic communal grave that was erected in my heart regarding my native town, I tearfully pass by the pleasant grave of one of the splendid personalities of our town. It is without a name and inscription, but nevertheless a sublime and important personality, whose image will never be erased from my memory.

This is the noble image of the young man, one of the five: Benjamin Moshe Jeszaja the son of Rivka Rachel.

[Column 313]

Reb Zebulun Grosbard

By Ahron Tapuchi (Jablonka) of Tel Aviv

Translated from Hebrew by Jerrold Landau

When Hillel died, they said regarding him, Oh the modest one, Oh the pious one. Tosefta, Sota 13[27].

He had a straight, upright posture; wise, quiet eyes; and a branched beard. He had an adorned face that exuded clarification; splendid, that expressed refinement and seriousness. His entire personality exuded honor and nobility. His clothes were always clean and orderly, without any stains, fulfilling the adage: "A scholar should not have a stain upon his clothing".

***

He was from among the old-time Gerrer Hassidim. He would travel to the Rebbe with pining and heartfelt appreciation. This was not so that he would be able to be "honored and well-received", "close to the table". He was a serious person, upright and complete with himself, wit his fellowman, and with G-d. He was honest in all of his ways, paths, dealings, and steps.

It was thus that he was created and entered to the light of the world. No common or uncommon wind was able to influence his personality, his level-headedness, and the calm foundations of his soul. He was a member of Agudas Yisrael. Every newspaper and manuscript of the Aguda found its way to his table. He obeyed all decisions of the party, and nevertheless, he placed himself above all factionalism. Not even a trace of deviousness and jealousy cleaved to him. He was never exuberant or angry, but he was always ready to listen to his fellow man with patience and pleasantness until the end. He never departed from his element; he never mocked or mimicked during his friendly conversations, or in his inner heart.

***

He was a special, rare personality, as if he was created to serve as an example, in the tradition of "see one like this, and sanctify". He was a faithful prayer leader, acceptable to his fellowman, always surrounded by a group, though he stood shoulders above them. All of his deeds were measured and thought through in a serious manner. Despite all of this, he was always willing to lend an ear to anyone who was struggling and opposing, to anyone full of bitterness of the heart and anger. He would always listen, and offer explanations quietly and peacefully, as he convinced and won over the heart of the disputant.

[Column 314]

***

I saw him on many occasions, during public appearances and stormy debates. As the chairman, he always knew how to exert control, not only over the gathering and the order, but also, first and foremost, over himself. He never made himself appear as the victor, but rather he remained quiet and discreet. He regarded himself as the man dedicated to the mission, the servant to all segments of the community, the learned person and man of the book; nevertheless distant from didactics, not an uprooter of mountains[28]. His strength was in his straightforward intellect, his diligence and his breadth of knowledge. He knew how to work with the pen, and he was fluent in three languages – Hebrew, Russian and Polish – both written and oral. Nevertheless, he never made use of his vast knowledge as "a spade to dig with"[29].

[Column 315]

He owned an inn and a coffeehouse in the town. His coffeehouse served as an inn. The wagon drivers and porters of the city could be found there at all hours of the day and evening, whether they waited for passengers, orders, work; or simply passed the time during a break in their work, between an arriving and departing train. They did not leave the place until the inn was closed, that is to say, after midnight. For the most part, they sat and chattered, as was the manner of porters and wagon drivers. Nevertheless, they did not bother Reb Zebulun during his work. He would stand up to deal with a customer, he would pour a cut of tea and bring a slice of bread or cake, and he would even glance at the daily newspaper and manuscripts. He would write requests for various people to the authorities, since he was familiar with the laws of the state.

∗ ∗ ∗

He served as a communal administrator in town for many years, and as the head of the community during the final years before the outbreak of the Second World War. With the conquest of the town by the Nazis, he was appointed as the head of the first Judenrat in town, however within a few short weeks, Reb Zebulun submitted his resignation.

He said: "I am not capable of continuing on".

The face of the community darkened when news of his resignation spread.

[Column 316]

They attempted to speak to his heart, to support and strengthen him. He listened silently, and lamented, "I cannot continue in this manner". He put his hand to his heart, and everyone understood him.

He was not able to serve as the head of the community, while simultaneously keeping secret the sinister intentions of the enemy towards the community.

He could not impose the will of the conquerors upon them.

He cannot falsify his task, and he would not serve as a tool for the executioners.

With his great understanding, he very early on realized the full extent of their evil intentions, with their diabolical demands. With decisiveness, he left the Judenrat.

He the multi-faceted activist, of refined heart and upright, who looked into the vale of destruction and did not fall into the trap – he was one of a kind, one of the most splendid of the natives of our town. May G-d avenge his blood.

Translator's notes:

1. Rabbi Yitzchak Al-Fasi of Morocco, the author of one of the treatises of Jewish law that served as a precursor to the formal Code of Jewish Law (Shulchan Aruch).

2. A book of responsa is a book about a rabbi's responses to queries on Jewish law. The answers to these queries that would be of public interest would be published into a book of responsa, in question and answer form.

3. An aguna is a 'bound wife', who is not permitted to remarry on account of the disappearance of her husband, perhaps through war, or on a long journey. Until the husband's death can be proven with certainty, the woman is not permitted to remarry. A large body of rabbinical responsa literature deals with the application of this in specific cases, and tries to find 'openings' to ascertain the death of the husband, and thereby allow the woman to remarry. In modern times, this term is also used to describe a woman who is 'bound' and not allowed to marry due to her husband's refusal to grant a religious divorce (get).

4. I was not able to identify some of the town names in this paragraph and the following one. The versions that I used do reflect actual towns in Poland, but there were several towns with similar spellings that might have matched. The following are the ones I could not identify definitively: Gorysze, Warka, Parczew, Kolszyn.

5. The list of signatories most probably refers to those whose names are inscribed in the book as having assisted financially with the publication.

6. The term Maskil here refers to familiarity with secular education. It does not refer to the implication, which often accompanies the term, of abandoning orthodoxy.

7. The Talmud exists in two editions, the more common, later, Babylonian Talmud, and the less common, earlier Jerusalem or Palestinian Talmud.

8. The name given to one of the Gerrer Rebbes. The Sfat Emet, mentioned later in this section is the son of the Chidushei Harim.

9. The literary names of three well-known rabbis. The Bach and Taz wrote commentaries on the Shulchan Aruch (Code of Jewish Law). These commentaries appear on the folios of the standard edition of the Shulchan Aruch.

10. The revealed Torah is considered to be the written and oral law, whereas the hidden Torah is considered to be the realm of mysticism and Kabbalah.

11. A euphemism referring to someone being in close contact with a teacher as a disciple.

12. The Shulchan Aruch has four sections. The Choshen Mishpat section deals with the laws of jurisprudence – civil law, damages, and court cases.

13. A kosher Torah scroll is one with unbroken letters and various other features that make it fit for ritual synagogue use. A passul (invalid) Torah scroll has broken letters, missing words, errors, or other such problems that render it invalid for ritual synagogue use.

14. The acronym for Rabbi Yisrael Baal Shem Tov, the founder of Hassidism.

15. A major work on Jewish law from the 1800s.

16. An enigmatic phrase follows here, which reads roughly as follows: "which, in comparison to military booty, smite and dim the physical life." I did not include this phrase in the translation.

17. A phrase from the book of Genesis "A simple man who sits in tents", used to refer to the Patriarch Jacob. This phrase is often used to describe an honest, upright person who enjoys studying (i.e. sitting in the tents of the study hall).

18. Gemara is a book of Talmud. Midrash is a book of ancient rabbinical lore. Zohar is the main book of the Kabbalah (Jewish mystical works).

19. The beginning of the prayers on the Sabbath morning (in accordance with some opinions, that recite some of the earlier blessings in silence).

20. Rachel's Tomb is located just outside of Bethlehem. It is a mystical custom to wrap scarlet thread around the tomb, and then to keep the thread on one's self as a good omen.

21. The external shells refer to the antithesis of spirituality. It is said that where there is greater spirituality, there is greater potential for the antithesis of spirituality as well. For example, a pious person who falls into sin is in a much worse state than an impious person who commits the same sin.

22. According to Jewish lore, a human body has 248 organs and 365 sinews.

23. Literally 'with seven examinations' – a term used to define a very careful examination. It is based on the Jewish law that there are seven main questions that one asks witnesses in a legal case to ascertain their validity.

24. A euphemism for a household problem.

25. A medieval sage, known by his acronym Shnei Luchot HaBrit "Shela".

26. I am not sure of the meaning of this.

27. The Tosefta is an addendum to the books of the Mishna, consisting of Mishnaic style statements that were not incorporated into the text of the Mishna itself – but which nevertheless are regarded as authoritative. Sota is one of the tractates of the Mishna and Talmud.

28. A term used for someone who delves into the depths of a subject, perhaps at the expense of breadth.

29. A reference from Pirke Avot (The Mishnaic tractate of Ethics of the Fathers), which warns one not to make use of Torah "as a spade to dig with", i.e. for the means of obtaining a livelihood.

[Column 317]

The Admor Rabbi Baruch of Czyzewo[1]

by Rabbi Tanchum Rubinsztajn

Translated from Hebrew by Jerrold Landau

He was born in Szczuczyn [Grajewo County, Podlaski Voivodeship], a Lithuanian town filled with Misnagdim (opponents of Hassidism) who were sworn against Hassidism, in approximately the year 5557 (1787). His father was a Misnaged, the wealthy scholar Reb Yaakov Yosha Szapira. He was the grandson of the great Gaon Rabbi Yaakov Yosha, the author of "Pnei Yehoshua"[2], of blessed memory.

He studied Talmud diligently until his marriage. He received his Torah training from the Gaon of the generation, Rabbi Akiva Eiger[3] of holy blessed memory, after his marriage, when he had attained great heights in Torah and continued to study with diligence, he suffered headaches because of his great effort. The doctors advised his wealthy father that he should cease his studies in order to take a break from the depth of his concentration.

To this end, his father sent him out with a wagon laden with textiles, along with a staff of officials who would be responsible for the sales, so that Reb Baruch would be able to serve as the director and treasurer. On their return trip, Reb Baruch heard about the Tzadik Reb Yitzchak (Itzikl) of Vengrova, the student of the Chozeh (Seer) of Lublin, and about his holy work. Reb Baruch immediately gave the money of the proceeds of the sales to his father's officials, and commanded them to travel to Staciunai. He himself turned towards Vengrova.

That Sabbath eve, the Tzadik of Vengrova told his wife the rebbetzin: prepare good delicacies for an honorable guest who will be coming to spend the Sabbath with us.

On Friday afternoon, the Tzadik stood on the porch of his home and waited for the arrival of the guest. When he did not appear, he sent all of the people of his household to wait for him along the way, to show the guest the way to his house. Approximately two hours before the onset of the Sabbath, they saw the honorable wagon plodding along the way, and inside there was a fine young man wearing the clothing of wealthy people. His appearance exuded honor and glory. This was Reb Baruch, who was looking for the Beis Midrash of the Tzadik.

[Column 318]

That entire Sabbath, the guest did not move from the side of the Tzadik. He was drawn to him with bonds of love and enchantment. On Sunday Reb Baruch wrote a letter to his parents informing them that he was very happy that he found the true means of service of the Creator, and that he intended to spend several weeks in the home of his new rabbi, in order to investigate the ways of service, and to study from his generous character traits that were imparted to him by his Rebbe the Chozeh of Lublin[4] of holy blessed memory.

Upon reading this letter, Reb Yaakov Yosha arose and said to his wife: "Sura, we should certainly sit in mourning for our son Baruch, who has gone out into a bad crowd and has become attracted to the Hassidic sect."

As time went on, the home of the Tzadik became more and more endearing to the young man. He sent letters to his parents, waxing in great praise of his Rebbe, until he succeeded in convincing his father that this was the true path that G-d has chosen. Not only this, but he also spoke in an honorable fashion regarding the son of his Rebbe, Tovia Yechiel, and his younger sister Gitka Szapira. The matter had come from G-d[5], and the match was completed successfully. From that time, the Szapira family became a venerable Hassidic family.

At the urging of his Rebbe, Reb Baruch traveled to dwell under the shadow of the Tzadik Reb Yosef of Zhidachov, the son of the Chozeh. After the death of Reb Yosef in the year 5558 (1788), Reb Baruch moved along with his friend Reb Hirsch of Parchowo (who was the prayer leader and the student of the Zhidachover) to the Beis Midrash of Reb Simcha Bunim of Przysucha (Pshischa).

[Column 319]

As they entered the anteroom next to the inside chamber of the Rebbe, the two young men were first examined by the group of students of the Rebbe, Reb Bunim, to see if they are fitting to enter into the internal holy chamber.

As they began to pEsther them with challenges in order to examine them and determine their worth, the Rebbe sensed this, went out to his students, and called out: "Leave them and do not bother them, for they come from a good cheder, and there is no need to examine them." (Ohr Simcha, page 12, paragraph 18.)

In the Beis Midrash of Przysucha, Rabbi Baruch found his fitting place. He continued studying with great diligence and energy, with asceticism and holiness. His Rebbe loved him very much.

When his Rebbe asked him if he has a good place to stay, Reb Baruch answered: "Whoever does not take up any place is not short of a place, and any place is a good place for him." (Siach Sarfei Kodesh, part one, paragraph 207.)

As has been pointed out, Rev Baruch was the son of wealthy parents, and he supported several of the students of the Przysucha Beis Midrash from his own pocket. He even provided three rubles per week to his friend Rev Mordechai Yosef of Izbica.

The Hassidim related: Once, Rev Baruch went to immerse himself in the river. His friends took his shoes and silk socks, and sold them in order to purchase drinks. Reb Baruch was forced to return from the river barefoot, and he was very distraught about his pitiful walk. When the rebbetzin found out about this, she went to her husband the Rebbe Reb Bunim and said to him: "We have such an honorable and noble young man with us, why did they disgrace him so that he had to walk barefoot through the streets of the city?" Reb Bunim asked: "Who is it that played this trick on him?" She answered: "The Izbicer". He immediately decreed upon him that he must leave the Beis Midrash. After a little while, the veteran students entered, headed by Reb Menachem Mendel of Tomaszow, in order to assuage their Rebbe and intercede with him to permit the Izbicer back in the Beis Midrash. The Rebbe answered them: "Go and see if he has already passed the tax checkpoint outside the city, and if he did, do not bring him back.

[Column 320]

If he did not, bring him back, for he is one of us."

It is said that Reb Mordechai Yosef had already passed the tax checkpoint, but his friends, headed by Reb Menachem Mendel, brought him back and did not say anything.

Much later, when Reb Mordechai Yosef rebelled against his Rebbe, set up his own pulpit in his Beis Midrash in Izbica, and attracted several hundred Hassidim of Kock to him, Reb Mendel's friends said to him: "This happened because we did not listen to the recommendation of the Rebbe of Przysucha. (Heard orally.)

Reb Baruch was very exacting in the observance of the commandments, and he was very careful about fulfilling each and every paragraph in the Code of Jewish Law (Shulchan Aruch). Because of this, they used to call him "The pious one" ("Der Frumer"). In Reb Bunim's old age, when he was ill and had to eat soaked matzo on Passover[6], he commanded to distribute his leftovers to Reb Baruch [7]. Because he was so "pious", he would stumble with the leftovers of soaked matzo.

Reb Baruch used to say in a clear fashion: "All types of ill luck are attributed to a 'pious one'. We find in the Torah regarding the law of the Nazirite (Numbers 6, 9): 'If a person dies in his presence in a sudden fashion, and renders his naziriteship unclean", it cancels all of the time that he has spent in his period of naziriteship, and he must start from the beginning again. Why does the Torah not hint at such a sudden death with regards to the Cohanim (priests), who also have to guard themselves from ritual impurity (Leviticus, 21, 1)? That is because the Cohen is intelligent, and he is careful about impurity due to his holiness that stemmed from the virtue of his birth, and therefore no mishap would come upon him. But since the Nazirite accepted upon himself additional restrictions, and forbade for himself things that are permitted due to excess piety, ill luck comes upon such a 'pious person', and sudden impurity happens upon him. (Siach Sarfei Kodesh Section 2, paragraph 17).

As a Hassid of Przysucha, who absorbed to himself all of the purity of this sharp witted Hassidism, Reb Baruch returned to his parents' home in Staciunai and conducted himself there in accordance with the Hassidism of Przysucha. He used to delay the times of prayer, and he would recite the Kiddush on the Sabbath at a late hour, after studying Zohar[8] prior to Kiddush. On one winter Sabbath, when Reb Baruch delayed the Kiddush, his father Reb Yaakov Yosha decided to go to the second floor where his son lived, in order to find out what he was occupying himself with at such a later hour, and why he was delaying the Sabbath meal. He stood behind the door and listened to his son reciting with trembling the verse: "She is dressed in strength and splendor, and laughs at the time to come"[9]. These words were recited with enthusiasm and holy awe, as he repeated and stressed to himself the words "and laughs at the time to come"[10]. The father trembled from the soulful devotion of his son the Hassid. He returned, and told his wife: "To a Shalom Aleichem prayer such as this, the Ministering Angels are content to wait even until midnight… (From the elderly Hassid Reb Mordechai Bialistocki of blessed memory, the son-in-law of Reb Zusha Szapira, the son of Reb Baruch).

[Column 321]

Reb Baruch was numbered among the most important and faithful of the students of the Beis Midrash of the Rebbe of Kock. When he took leave of Kock to return to Staciunai, the Rebbe said to him: "The Besht[11] came to instill service of the heart in the Jewish people, so that fear of Heaven should not be 'like the commandments of men, performed by rote' (Isaiah 29,13). This style of service spread out rapidly in the areas of Podolia and Volhyn. Rebbe Elimelech of Lizhensk (Lezajsk), by means of your grandfather[12], succeeded in turning the hearts of the people of Galicia to holy service with us here in the country of Poland. Now it is fitting to bring the people of Lithuania to this way. Turn your heart to your task and your role. (Siach Sarfei Kodesh Section 1, paragraph 89.)"

Despite all of his subordination to the Rebbe of Kock, he also had an independent stance. When the Rebbe asked him why he does not ask his advice regarding marriage matches for his children, Reb Baruch answered that he realizes that the Rebbe does not have knowledge in matters of matchmaking. The Rebbe of Kock pointed out to him: "The Rebbe can still offer good advice." (Siach Sarfei Kodesh Section 4, page 18.)

After the death of the Rebbe of Kock, when Rabbi Yitzchak Meir the author of the Chidushei HaRim[13] returned from the funeral and traveled to Warszawa along with hundreds of Hassidim, including veteran Hassidim of Kock such as Reb Baruch and Rabbi Avraham of Pieryszew – the Tzadik Reb Yitzchak Meir turned to Reb Baruch and said to him: "You are a man of understanding, perhaps it is worthwhile to travel to Libavitch to see if there is a place for us there?" Reb Baruch answered: "Why should I travel to another place, since I have a Rebbe here, and we can all go to him." When the Rim continued to speak about the greatness of the rabbi from Pranszice[14] (Rabbi Chanoch of Aleksander) and pointed out that it is possible to send 20,000

Hassidim to him, and he would lead them faithfully – Rabbi Baruch shouted: "Now is not a time of modesty. The crowd is streaming to you, and there is no other option than to receive us under your leadership. (Meir Einey Hagolah", paragraph 473, and see also paragraph 291.)

[Column 322]

When Reb Baruch took ill and consulted doctors, they told him to drink of the waters of Carlsbad[15] for healing. He asked the advice of the Rebbe of Gur, who opposed the drinking of the water. Rabbi Baruch asked him: "Did not you take ill with this illness many years back, and you asked the Rebbe of Kock, who agreed to the drinking of the water, and it was indeed good for you?" The Rebbe of Gur answered: "Today I am the leader, and I set the order." Rabbi Baruch listened to the advice of the Rebbe, and it was good for him. Later, after the death of the Rim, his illness returned, and his friend Reb Ben-Zion of Ostrowa said to him that, apparently, now that the Rebbe of Gur has died, you can follow the advice of the doctors with the approval of the Rebbe of Kock. (Ibid. 524, and in Siach Sarfei Kodesh Section 3, paragraph 259.)

Reb Baruch was almost seventy years old when the Rebbe of Gur died. Nevertheless, he did not hesitate to travel to the Tzadik[16] and accept his authority, even though many turned to him and asked him to lead a flock, for he was worthy to do so. In this matter, he used to conduct himself in the manner of his Rebbe, the Rebbe of Gur of holy blessed memory, who used to say the following regarding the verse (Proverbs 23, 23) "Obtain truth and do not sell it.". Is it not obvious that if one indeed desires to acquire truth, he should not sell it? Rather, the intention is that at all times when one succeeds in acquiring truth, one should not join the sellers, but rather one should attempt to attain even more than one has ("Pillar of Truth", 101). Already in that same year, on the 19th of Elul 5627 (1867), we find Rabbi Baruch participating in the dedication of a new synagogue in Nesvizh, and standing bowed over before the elder rabbi, Reb Yitzchak of Nesvizh, repeating over to the crowd the Torah that the rabbi said during the synagogue dedication, for on account of the great crowding, the congregation could not hear the words of the weak rabbi. ("Karon Tov", 12, page 1).

Rabbi Baruch was deeply influenced by the holy splendor of the Tzadik of Nesvizh, and he hastened to send a letter to Rabbi Leibele of Gur (the author of the "Sfat Emet" of holy blessed memory), of what his eyes witnessed in Nesvizh. This is the text of the letter[17]:

[Column 323]

"Peace to my friend, sharp and brilliant, a Hassid of a precious spirit, a man of wisdom, our teacher and rabbi Leibele, may his light shine.

My lips wish to inform you of the honorable rabbi who should live. It is impossible with human power to fathom the rabbi… For he is a wondrous man, complete, and one cannot describe him.

Aside from this, I have found no end to the wondrous Torah that I have heard from his mouth, which need not be rectified, for he is holy from the womb, for his holy father of holy blessed memory brought for him a holy garment, which did not need any effort to complete. His work is the holy work to unite unities, and to ensure good influence for the entire House of Israel, as a Tzadik who is the foundation of the world, with all its meaning.

I set my heart to find out the motivation of those who come to him, and I realize that they all found an advantage, whether because of the man whose name was renowned due to his natural manner in approaching the holy, or because of his great influence of holiness upon the masses.

People who are known by the term of Hassidim draw influence from him with love and awe, to turn away from bad and to do good, simply without any trickery.

Masses of men and women, when they saw the signs that were done by the rabbi may he live, understood and knew that G-d is sitting in judgment in the world, and the honor of Heaven is growing. Is this not the hope of Israel to enlarge the honor of the kingdom of the Blessed One upon us.

I instilled all this into my heart; I investigated and searched out during all my time there. My soul yearns to cleave to him. I will follow him, and never abandon him, with the help of the Blessed G-d. Behold you, as my friend, on behalf of the love of our elder master, the Admor of holy blessed memory, I have written these words to you, and it is worthy for you to keep this letter of mine.

The eyes of the wise are full of understanding, and they will not understand a matter and then pervert its meaning, and come to sin with their souls even with respect to the proud Tzadik.

From your friend who loves you,

Baruch Szapira"

("Zicharon Tov", 15, page 2).

However, he did not spend too long in Nesvizh, for the elder holy man died on the 21st of Shvat, 5628 (1868). He then returned to his home in Staciunai, and continued to stand on his guard in Torah and the worship of G-d. He did not take any benefit for himself, for he was very discreet. His wife Rasha Mirl took care of the home and the business. She was a woman of valor, and was very wealthy for her entire life.

[Column 324]

Friendly relations pervaded between Rabbi Baruch and the Tzadik Reb Leibele of Gur. When his holy grandfather the Rim of Gur died, and the community turned it attention to Rebbe Henech of Aleksander who was a leader, Reb Leibele turned to Rabbi Baruch in a letter, and requested his advice: "I hereby request from your honorable holiness to give me advice, for I am left bereft of everything, and the crown of my head, my parent, teacher and Rebbe has been taken from above my head, and I am a boor who does not know what to do… I therefore turn my heart to Your Holiness that you should comfort me in a letter with appropriate advice, for you are a man of truth… Many of our associates travel to the rabbi Reb H., may his light shine (this refers to rabbi Henech), and I do not know the man and his words. He is an honorable man and a Hassid in our eyes, but we do not know of him nor have heard of him as a Rebbe or a leader of our generation, and we have also not heard the opposite…" (from "Hassidic Greats" by Rabbi Bromberg, volume 20, page 22.)

As has been stated, Rabbi Baruch returned from Nesvizh to his home, and his righteousness and holiness were declared in public. Hundreds of Hassidim of the elders of Aleksander turned to him for advice. He pushed them aside and refused to lead a community. When the venerable elder Reb Yaakov Aryeh of Radzymin died suddenly (on the 18th of Tammuz 5635 – 1875), hundreds of Hassidim of the elders of Kock appeared in Staciunai of Lithuania, and did not let up until he was forced to accept the mantle of leadership of the flock. They appeared in Staciunai prior to Rosh Hashanah and filled the entire city with Hassidim, much to the surprise of the residents, who were sworn Misnagdim. Immediately after Sukkot, the rabbi and all of his family moved to the city of Czyzewo, where the means of communication were better. There, they set up a large Hassidic courtyard, as was fitting for a Rebbe and leader of a flock. Many were saved by him, for he was a worker of omens, and known as performing acts of deliverance.

One evening, while the old rabbi was reciting the evening service in his Beis Midrash that was next to his room, his sister Gitka laid her granddaughter on the bed of the Tzadik. After the Tzadik had finished his prayers, eaten dinner, and concluded the order of his day, he approached his bed to lie down. When he noticed the girl sleeping in his bed, he shouted loudly: "Descend from my bed immediately!"

[Column 325]

The girl immediately arose from the bed, and ran to her mother in tears. From that time, she was no longer paralyzed in her legs.

Rabbi Baruch took in Sivan 5637 (1877) and moved to Warszawa. There, his friends from Przysucha, the remnants of the holy comrades, came to visit him. They all expressed their reverence to him and said that they could smell the Hassidism of Przysucha, sharp and stubborn, from his entire body and soul, as it had been received from their Rebbe, Rabbi Simcha Bunim.

Rabbi Baruch returned his soul to his Creator on the 22nd of Av, 5637. He was buried in Warszawa, near the grave canopy of his friend, the Tzadik Rabbi Yaakov of Radzymin. This writer used to light an honorary candle at his candle every Friday, which would remain lit all week. The Hassidim relate that the "Sfat Emet" of holy blessed memory said: "A great merit came upon the city of Warszawa, in that the Tzadik of Czyzewo was buried there, for very few people knew his essence, and were able to appreciate the magnitude of his piety."

Rabbi Baruch, the son of Misnagdim, left behind a righteous generation of wonderful Tzadikim and Hassidim. His eldest son Reb Natan was known as Reb Notka Pilcer, on account of the name of his father-in-law Rabbi Aryeh of Pilce (the son-in-law of Rabbi David Birenbaum, who was related by marriage to Rabbi Akiva Eiger. Siach Sarfei Kodesh section 5, page 92). He was counted among the prominent Hassidim of the Rim of Gur, and the honorable Hassidim of the Sfat Emet. After his father died, his Hassidim asked him to take over the running of the community, but he refused. He answered sharply: "What would be if I was a Rebbe, they would erect a canopy over my grave…" When they did not let up, and urged him greatly, he fled to a pharmacy, lifted his hat off his head and groaned: "A bareheaded Rebbe such as this you desire for yourselves?" Then they let him be.

[Column 326]

His son Reb Zisha of Stawiski was also known as a great scholar and a wealthy merchant. All of the people around him took honor in his name. He was revered by all on account of his intelligence and righteousness.

My elder father-in-law, the Hassid and scholar Reb Yaakov Yitzchak, the grandson of Reb Chaim of Czyzewo, known as Reb Yaakov Czyzower, was known as a great Hassid. He had merited traveling with his grandfather Rabbi Baruch to Kock, and was also numbered among honorable Hassidim of the Sfat Emet of holy blessed memory. He was the scholar of the family, and his pious grandfather took great pride in him.

Rabbi Baruch left behind six sons, and all of them were Hassidim and men of deeds. This should not be surprising in our eyes, for Reb Yaakov, the pious father Reb Yaakov from Czyzewo, who was known as a veteran Misnaged; the maternal grandmother of Reb Baruch the pious woman Chava, was the sister of the holy brothers Elimelech of Lizhensk (Lezajsk) and Reb Zisha of Anipoli (Annopol), may their merit protect us.

Translator's notes:

1. The footnote at the bottom of the page reads: Copied from the book "The Rabbi of Kotzk (Kock) and the Sixty Mighty Men Surrounding him."

2. Yaakov Yehoshua Falk (1680-1756), a famous rabbi who wrote a Talmudic commentary called Pnei Yehoshua. Like many famous rabbis, he became known by the name of his work.

3. Rabbi Akiva Eiger (1768-1838), a famous rabbi who wrote many commentaries on the Talmud and Code of Jewish Law.

4. Rabbi Yaakov Yitzchak, known as the Chozeh (Seer or Visionary) of Lublin (1745-1815), was a great Hassidic leader during the early period of Hassidism.

5. A quote from the book of Genesis, which Bethuel said when confirming his agreement to the marriage of his daughter Rebecca to the Isaac (i.e. the match was made in Heaven).

6. Many people have the custom on Passover of not eating matzo that is soaked in a liquid. This is not forbidden by law, but is an extra stringency observed by some.

7. It was the custom of Hassidic Rebbes to distribute their leftover food to their disciples (as it has been blessed by the Rebbe).

8. A section of the Kabbalah.

9. Proverbs 31, 25, a verse from the "Aishet Chail" song chanted at the outset of the Sabbath eve meal, after the "Shalom Aleichem" song that welcomes the angels into the home.

10. A reference to greeting the future (the World to Come or life after death) with confidence if one lives one's life properly.

11. The acronym of the Baal Shem Tov, the founder of Hassidism.

12. I am not sure to whom the grandfather refers here.

13. The Chidushei Harim became the Rebbe of Gur (often known Ger). The official Polish name of the city is Gora Kalwaria. Gur / Ger is a major Hassidic dynasty, still prominent today.

14. I was not able to identify the town of Prazniche. Aleksander is a Polish town, the Rebbe of which became the leader of a Hassidic dynasty.

15. Now Karlovy-Vary in the Czech Republic.

16. Apparently, the successor of the Rebbe of Gur.

17. Parts of this letter are not translated literally, due to the poetic style of the letter.

[Column 327-8]

Youth Movements and Political Parties

[Column 329]

Youth Movements and Zionist Activities in our City of Czyzewo

by Yitzchak Szlaski of Tel Aviv

Translated by Jerrold Landau

Within the socio-cultural excitement that was appropriate to the restricted conditions of a small provincial town such as our Czyzewo, and within the general realm of multifaceted activity in the field of Zionism with which our town also excelled during the proud era of Zionist pioneering, the Zionist youth groups stood out and prominently in great glory and successful activity, each according to its own faction. These activities brightened the gray skies of this typical Diaspora town. They blew a spirit of enthusiastic life into its Jewish residents, awakened in them the somnolent national feeling, strengthened their social standing, and raised their honor in their own eyes and in the eyes of the gentiles around them.

During its first steps, this positive phenomenon did not find the required echo in the midst of the Jews of the town. Many opposed it and placed obstacles in the path of its development, based on the realities of the Jews of the town. However, the small group of idealists who toiled with dedication and faithfulness for the Zionist idea succeeded in overcoming any obstacle placed in their path.

Indeed, not much time passed before various youth organizations, all with a pioneering Zionist inclination, began to arise. The youth were drawn to them in their masses with youthful enthusiasm. In them, they received their first social, nationalist and pioneering education. The Zionist doctrine exuded from them, permeating the town and spreading its influence upon Jewish life in the town, from both a national economic and practical Zionist perspective. In these youth groups, the first of the pioneers were trained for aliya and realizing the goal of the upbuilding of the homeland in the Land of Israel.

As I now cast a backward glance and come to survey briefly, from a historical perspective, the history of the development of these youth groups, their activities and achievements, I am proud to state with satisfaction and pleasure – that was indeed the way it was. We were correct at that time in our activities for the benefit of the youth of our town! All of the ideals that we preached to them have been realized! Our vision turned out for us and for many of them to be a pleasant and good reality. It is unfortunate that only a portion of us merited this!

[Column 330]

We were a small group of young people. Most of us Beis Midrash students became enamored with the Zionist idea with great enthusiasm and pure belief. We searched for freedom and salvation for the forces of youth and the tensions of thought, and the possibilities of concrete expression in day to day activities for a specific sublime idea. For us young people, educated in Yeshivas, the children of good families from circles of those faithful to the faith of Israel – what could be a more sublime idea than the return to Zion and the education of the youth towards aliya and the building of the Land? Therefore, we thrust our souls forward; we exerted our power, and made this seminal jump[1]. We went out against the boorishness and boring innocence that ravenously consumed the youth of our town. We stood up against the idle notions of Agudas Yisrael, which was inimical to the Zionist spirit. However, above everything, we saw it as a holy obligation upon ourselves to wage an energetic war against the Communist venom that attracted the pure souls of the neglected youth with its secret charm, and planted in them nationalistic ruin and destruction by negating all that was holy to our people.

[Column 331]

We began this activity with great effort. We performed our tasks with dedication and faithfulness, with the faith and trust that our toil would not be for naught. Indeed, not much time passed before all of the youth was conquered by us and was taken over by the pioneering Zionist idea.

"Hashomer Haleumi" was the first Zionist organization that arose and began its activities in Czyzewo. Other organizations stemmed from it as time went on. However, the common denominator among all of them was that they all raised the horn of nationalistic Judaism in our town, and played a great role in the education of the youth towards a social life filled with a practical Zionist spirit. We merit the fact that today in Israel there are more than 120 families of Czyzewo natives, and indeed the majority of them were educated in these youth groups.

[Column 332]

Thanks to the practical care of the counselors, people made aliya to the Land, laid down roots there, and assisted in its upbuilding and its defense during the War of Independence. They established their families and their lives, which is now a life as an independent citizen in the homeland of the State of Israel.

B.

Hashomer-Haleumi Hanoar-Hatzioni

A schism took place in the Hashomer Hatzair youth movement in Poland at the end of the 1920s. On account of the leftward turn of this movement, some of its leaders who remained faithful to the pure Zionist idea left and founded a new nationalist Zionist youth movement called Hashomer Haleumi. With the passage of time, it changed its name to Hanoar Hatzioni.

[Column 333]

This movement was established under the auspices of the central committee of the Zionist organization in Poland, and was received with great support by the masses of general Zionists in each and every place. A chapter of this movement was established in Wysokie Mazowieckie that was close to Czyzewo. The founders and counselors of this chapter decided to also found such a chapter in its neighboring town Czyzewo.

One summer evening in 1929, a group of us youths gathered together in the cheder room of the teacher Reb Ahron Wajntraub. We listened to the publicity speeches of two of the heads of the chapter of Wysokie regarding the founding of a chapter, or as it is called a "nest" [2] of Hashomer Haleumi in Czyzewo. Prominent among the members were Arjeh Gorzalczany, Yankel Gromadzyn and the writer of these lines.

The words of the speakers, spoken with extra enthusiasm, inspired us. The words fell upon fruitful soil and took root well in our minds. The internal push and deep desire for some sort of public activity went into action. The Zionist spirit that imbued us all also did its work. We found a fitting field of endeavor for the drive and youthful spirit that was living and fermenting in us. Therefore, that very evening, we decided to establish a branch of Hashomer Haleumi in Czyzewo. This youth group was indeed established within a few days, and maintained its activities in our town for all the time until the destruction.

Hashomer Haleumi

The three aforementioned members were chosen as heads of the 'nest', and they approached their duties with the full sense of the responsibility that was placed upon them. These duties began with the technical arrangements for a meeting place, and continued with the spreading of Zionist doctrine and instilling elementary knowledge in matters of culture and societal life.

When they heard this great news of the founding of a youth organization and the opening of a meeting place, many youths from all strata of life began to stream to us. A significant portion of the boys and girls were from poor families, and many were forsaken youth who had no Torah or manners. A new world suddenly opened up for these young people; a world filled with content, a world that was full of joy and happiness, a world that educated and prepared the youth for a life of freedom, building and creativity on the land of the homeland, that had been yearned for from generation to generation.

[Column 334]

The first meeting place that was opened was in the home of Jakob Goldberg, who was known as "Yankel Goldberg". The members of the leadership committee prepared all of the necessary improvements and renovations with their own hands. They decorated the hall with pictures of the leaders of the Zionist movement and scouting symbols. They immediately began to plan educational programs, in accordance with the directions from the national leadership in Warszawa.

A significant portion of the program of the youth movement was involved with scouting. This was actualized with drills, hikes, summer camps, the study of signal code, etc. The member J. Gromadzyn at first worked in this area. Since at the time he was a student at the seminary for Hebrew teachers in Vilna, he had gained a great deal of knowledge in that area, and he dedicated himself enthusiastically to imparting that knowledge to the campers. Groups of Shomrim and Shomrot [2] went out each evening to the fields around the town in order to play various sports and conduct drill exercises.

The members Yitzchak Szlaski and Arjeh Gorzalczany conducted the cultural activities. Each evening, they would conduct friendly discussions in groups on various topics, such as "Judaism and Zionism", "Jewish and General History", and "The History of the New Settlement in the Land of Israel". Presentations and events on various current topics would take place. These topics included: "The Nation of Israel in the Present", "The Political Situation in the World", "British Politics in the Land of Israel", etc. Classes were organized for the study of Hebrew, and participation in these classes was mandatory for all Shomrim and Shomrot.

They thirstily absorbed our words. They listened to our discussions and presentations with honorable awe. The paid attention, and fulfilled our orders and directions completely. Thus, they slowly became accustomed to the new life. The knowledge that they gained enabled them to participate in a lively fashion in the interfactional discussions and debates. On account of this, they became more interested in what was transpiring in the world.

[Column 335]

Two commanders of the Shomer Haleumi
Seated Yitzchak Szlaski and standing Arjeh Gorzalczany.

(Translator's note: the banner at the top reads:
"Long Live Hashomer Haleumi".
The banner at the bottom reads:
"Strong" – i.e., "Let it be strong").

The songs and dances are a chapter unto themselves. They played an important role in the educational curriculum and the activities of the "nest". Each evening, at the time that the Shomrim and Shomrot gathered, the voices of song and dance would literally pierce the heavens. Their echo would be heard from afar outside the city. This became the daily bread of the youth. It supported them and awakened in them an intensive feeling of a full life, filled with interest and content. New songs were added daily, some of which came to us in writing from the material that was prepared by the central leadership in Warszawa, and others were learned from the Shomrim and Shomrot who came to us from other cities, as they were travelling to Hachsharah[4] centers. These songs in no small manner helped in the learning of the Hebrew language, and in making it relevant to daily life.

The movement breathed a new spirit into the life of the youth. Even the external appearance changed.

[Column 336]

The gray and khaki uniform, decorated with scouting symbols, imparted splendor and glory to the boys and girls. The increased their pride and stood up straight. The sadness and oppression that were so typical in the appearance of the youth in the small towns of Poland disappeared form their faces. They wore the look of self-assurance influenced with Jewish national pride.

The good, simple mothers and fathers were filled with contentment at the appearance of their clean and polished sons and daughters, who filled the homes with light and joy. They also became attached the great Zionist vision that filled the hearts of their children. In the privacy of their hearts, it seemed perhaps as if they themselves also hoped that they would attain the merit of perhaps following in their children's footsteps, making aliya to the Land and inheriting it…

A chapter of the General Zionist faction existed in Czyzewo. This primarily attracted young adults who had studied, and who had succeeded in their private lives in becoming established in business or small-scale manufacturing. The vast majority of them were the most honorable of the younger generation. By their nature, they were people of status who were more satisfied with factional activity than practical activity, with the exception of course of work on behalf of the funds, primarily the "Keren HaYesod". Most of the canvassers for this fund in town came from that group.

Factional liveliness appeared mainly at the time of elections for the Congress or some other special vote of the Zionist movement. This dynamism that was missing among the adults was made up by the youth through the intensive activities that were brought into the meeting hall of the adult Zionists. Thus, bonds of support were formed that resulted in mutually supportive activities between the adults and the youth. Hashomer Haleumi found enthusiastic supporters among these Zionists, who were faithful and dedicates patrons of their organization. On the other hand, the adult Zionists found in the youth strength and support, and a sure guarantee that the existence of the chapter will continue into the future. Indeed, this mutual support and close, beneficial interrelationship continued among them for all the years.

[Column 337]

Specific interest in the problems of the youth, that was were expressed in various forms both material and moral, was shown by the members: Shalom Grynberg, Yehoshua Lepak, Chajim Sztatchopakowicz, the Grynberg brothers, and Noach Edelsztajn of blessed memory; as well as by the following people who are still alive, may they live long: Motel Sztachopakowicz (today in America), Dov Gorzalczany (today in Israel), Moshel Blejwas (today in Canada), and others. The important women activists were: Fejgel Wasercug, Golda Bolender, Dwora Edelsztajn of blessed memory; and the following woman who is alive, may she live long: Freidel Zabludower the daughter of the rabbi (today in America). I still remember the meetings and assemblies that took place on Sabbath and festival evenings. We would go together for a friendly discussion or a guest presentation. The atmosphere was pleasant. It was imbued with the spirit of the Land of Israel. The youth excited the adults with their song and dance, and they too entered into the circle. We sang and danced until our energy was spent. On the national holidays such as Lag Baomer [5] or the 20th of Tammuz, as well as on the occasion of special activities on behalf of Zionism, celebrations, presentations, and parades through the streets of the town were arranged. These were all arranged with the active assistance of the adult Zionists, whose protection enabled us to overcome all obstacles that the various opponents laid in our path.

[Column 338]

This idealism in the Zionist movement did not last for a long time, only for a year and a half. The family feud that broke out in that era within the Zionist movement, between the followers of Jabotinsky and the general Zionists, spread out and permeated the entire Jewish population of Poland. Our Czyzewo was affected by this in no small fashion.

Beitar

Yankel Gromadzyn was the first to disturb this idealism and foment the first schism within Hashomer Haleumi. He, along with a large group of people who had been educated by the movement, left Hashomer Haleumi and established a Beitar chapter (the revisionist youth, based upon the Jabotinsky movement). The influence of the first schism was recognizable, for it laid the foundation for additional schisms that came in its wake. The establishment of a chapter of Beitar, that stood at the extreme right of the Zionist movement, provided the impetus and forced the side that opposed the right leaning Poale Zion movement and the "League for the Working Land of Israel" to organize their own youth, as a counterbalance to Beitar. The formed the "Jugentskaut" youth movement. A little while later, the religious circles within Zionism, "Mizrachi", did the same thing. They organized the religious youth and formed a "nest" of Hashomer Hadati.

[Column 339]

The increase in the number of youth groups in the town weakened Hashomer Haleumi. We must take into account that the number of boys and girls in the town was small, and most of them were already previously organized into that movement.

As a result of this, factional competition broke out between the various youth groups. They began to pursue each and every boy and girl. Each group tried to attract them. This competition took place along the entire front of Zionist activity and expression, and included stormy debates between the factions that did not reach conclusion.

As is known, at that time all of Polish Jewry was caught up in this turmoil of interfactional dispute, and our small Czyzewo was no exception. This factional vortex did not add health and honor to the Zionist movement, despite the fact that practical activity increased on the heels of the competition for hegemony in the various fields of action.

The succeeding years in the annals of Hanoar Hatzioni in Czyzewo form one long chain of intensive Zionist activity. After various schisms and the splintering off of parts of it into other Zionist youth groups that arose and organized themselves on the basis of extremist Zionist doctrine to the right and the left, and operated in accordance with noisy and explosive mottoes – the Hanoar Hatzioni movement, which remained faithful to original Zionism, continued to operate discreetly and on a small scale, yet with dedication and commitment to the ideals of general Zionism. It educated people towards Zionism, aliya, and actualization. All of the other Zionist factions and youth groups that were found in the city also increased their Zionist activity, in accordance with their specific ideological and factional bent.

As the year went on, Arjeh Gorzalczany also left Hanoar Hatzioni and transferred to Hashomer Hadati, which conducted widespread activities amongst the "nationalist religious" youth of Czyzewo.

Only one person remained from among the original founders of Hanoar Hatzioni, the last of the group, Yitzchak Szlaski. He continued to direct Hanoar Hatzioni until he made aliya to the Land in October 1935.

[Column 340]

Translator's notes:

1. This is literally: "this Nachshonite jump", referring to the Midrash (exegetical commentary on the Torah) that the Red Sea did not split until Nachshon the son of Amminadab (the prince of the tribe of Judah) jumped into the sea.

2. The Hebrew word 'ken', meaning nest (for those who know Hebrew, it is spelled with a 'kuf' rather than a 'kaf' – for when spelled with a 'kaf' it means 'yes') is often used as a term for a chapter of a Zionist youth group.

3. From the name of the group 'Hashomer". Shomer literally means guard. The form Shomrim is the masculine plural, and Shomrot is feminine plural.

4. Hachsharah (literally: preparation) is a program for preparing people for eventual aliya. Hachsharah activities would often take place in a rural setting, as people learned the agricultural skills that would be helpful in the building up of the Land after they make aliya.

5. A minor holiday that usually falls in May, one month after Passover. Bonfires are often made on that day.

D.

We cannot conclude the story of Hanoar Hatzioni without describing in a general fashion a few characters and events that took place during the period of existence and activity of this youth group.

There were four girlfriends.

They were young girls when they joined Hashomer Haleumi at its founding. These were Esther Eliasz, Lea Szinman, Malka Muncarsz, all of blessed memory, and, may she live long, Sura Dina Bolender. The common characteristics of all of them were their noble intentions, simplicity, modesty, and strong desire to learn, to know about the life of the nation in general and the Land of Israel in particular.

They joined Hashomer Haleumi along with the rest of the youth that streamed to this movement at its inception. However, they stood out immediately on account of their dedication to the ideas and ideals that they gleaned from the friendly discussions and classes, as well as on account of their boundless faithfulness to the both the counselors and the campers.

The first of them who went to Hachsharah, and merited to be the first one to make aliya from the "nest" in Czyzewo was the member Sura Bolender (today Mrs. Gafni in Israel).

Malka Muncarsz was a sickly girl. She was always serious and imaginative. She had a deep understanding, and she wrote songs and stories. She died in her prime. (We will devote a number of lines later to her funeral, a true Zionist funeral.)

Esther Eliasz also made aliya to the Land of Israel. She went through some difficult years during her period of absorption. Later, she married and established a family. However, a bitter fate cruelly overtook her. She contracted a serious illness and returned her pure soul to the Heavens at a young age. She left behind two young children, a son and a daughter.

The last of them was Lea Szinman.

This pure and refined soul was stubbornly and enthusiastically dedicated to the ideas and ideals, and this was very typical of children of the Szinman family. She was the only one of the group of friends to remain in Czyzewo. She later became the head of the "nest", and served in this position until the outbreak of the Second World War.

[Column 341]

To our great sorrow and anguish, she did not merit realizing the desire of her life – to make aliya. She perished in the Holocaust along with the rest of the House of Israel, may G-d avenge her death.

Her image stands before my eyes at the time of writing these lines. Lea Szinman, the tall, thin girl with red cheeks and a stubborn penetrating glance that elicits pity, the daughter of good people whose short life passed in pain, agony, and anguish, displayed faithful and friendly dedication to me as a camper and a student.

As I remember you, Lea, my eyes fill with tears. May these isolated tears take the place of flowers atop the giant communal grave where you also have found your eternal rest.

E.

A unique personality who is worthy of being remembered is Shalom Grynberg. He was an older man, a merchant and a professional, as well as an activist and a man of deeds who loved to express his personality and actions. He occupied himself with communal matters, whether as the gabbai (trustee) of the Beis Midrash, the fire chief, conducting Zionist activity, work for the charitable fund, or other matters. This man found some reason to dedicate a significant portion of his Zionist activity for the benefit of Hanoar Hatzioni. Many of the older Zionists supported and assisted this youth group, however the dedication and assistance of Shalom Grynberg was boundless. He participated in almost all of the meetings as if he was one of the youth. He listened and paid attention to every detail, large or small, including matters of education and Zionist problems. He primarily dedicated his time to technical matters concerned with administration, running the business of the hall, etc.

He concerned himself with the campers of the "nest" like a dedicated father. He concerned himself with their dress and cleanliness. Organizing any activity in the hall was not difficult for him; whether it was in the day, which involved pushing aside his personal business, or even late at night, so long as it was for the benefit of the youth. I often thought: "What moves such a man to dedicate so much time, effort, energy and money to the education of the youth to the Zionist idea?" I knew the secret places and struggles of his soul. At times, it seemed as if the paths of his life were doubled over, and his deeds were not always consistent. However, regarding his activities for the youth, I can testify regarding him to the Heaven and earth that he was pure and clean, without any trace of fraud or wrongdoing. He was completely dedicated to the youth with the Zionist idea, he was all for the Land of Israel.

[Column 342]

As one of us, he was always concerned about finding ways to strengthen and enlarge the ranks of this youth. He would speak to the hearts of the youth, convincing them to remain true to the movement. He would influence the parents to direct their children to this movement. He would participate in the hikes to the villages on vacation days, and even in trips farther afield. He would appear at the regional conventions, and once even at the national convention of the movement in Warszawa.

They would frequently mock the "Shomernik" Shalom Grynberg in the adult Zionist circles. He was a person unto himself. Until the day that I left Czyzewo, and even afterward, he was the living spirit of the movement. With his dedication to the youth, he earned our faith and friendship. The youth saw him as one of themselves in every matter. They consulted him for advice. Many educational and pioneering activities took place with his active assistance. He was imprisoned by the local Communists along with other Zionist activists when the Russians conquered Czyzewo after the outbreak of the war. At first, he was sent to Siberia alone, and after a short time, his wife and children were sent to follow him. His wife and children succeeded in escaping the Nazi Holocaust, and they merited making aliya to Israel. However, he disappeared without a trace. According to what we heard, he was murdered along the route to Siberia in accordance with a special order of the Czyzewo Soviet [1]. May G-d avenge his blood.

F.

The Zionist Funeral

It is unnecessary to point out that this concept was strange to the atmosphere of our town, even in the time period that we are now dealing with. This realm of activity was, as is known, entirely holy, and was given over to the sole good graces of the Chevra Kadisha (Burial Society) and its trustees. In truth, nobody from among us would try to contradict this. Our plans regarding this funeral did not touch upon Jewish law at all, nor did they affect at all the authority of the Chevra Kadisha. All that we wanted was to give the funeral a Zionist character that would be expressed in a mourning procession, carrying the blue and white flags at half mast as a token of mourning, and with eulogies at the time of the closing of the grave. However, they did not wish to agree even to this, and they enlisted the rabbi of the town, Rabbi Shmuel David Zabludower of holy blessed memory, and the chief trustee Reb Yisrael Yonah Raczkowski of blessed memory to stand up against he breech of the Zionists and their follies.

[Column 343]

The events as they were are described as follows:

Malka Moncarz, the daughter of the furniture maker Reb Yosel Moncarz, had a chronic heart ailment. Despite her illness, she was among the first to join the "Shomer Leumi". Due to her natural talents, and her deep understanding and widespread knowledge, she excelled in her dedication to the ideas that she learned during the time that she was part of the movement. However, fate was cruel to her. Her illness became more serious day by day, and on the eve of Yom Kippur, 5694 (1934) [1], she gave up her pure soul.

The news reached us during the Kol Nidre service in the synagogue of the Zionist minyan that convened in the building of the Hebrew School (next to the house of Yehoshua Lepak of blessed memory). After the conclusion of the service, most of the worshippers went to the house of the deceased to recite Psalms in unison. Afterwards, a rotation was set up, day and night, until the time of the funeral. The next day, Yom Kippur, during the time of the recess in the services [2], the scene was repeated. All of the worshippers of the "minyan" went to the house of the deceased to recite Psalms for the uplifting of her soul. At the conclusion of Yom Kippur, we gathered in the meeting place for a mourning gathering, to which were invited representatives of all the Zionist groups in the town.

This gathering was honored by the presence of the elder of the Zionist movement in our town, the educator of a generation of Zionists, the man of deeds, the enthusiastic and dedicated activist Reb Yechiel Asher Prawda of blessed memory. He was a wonderful well-rounded personality, and it is fitting at this time to perpetuate him in a special manner in this Yizkor Book.

He was an Orthodox man from the Hassidim of Aleksander. He suffered all his days from persecutions by the extremist Hassidim due to his Zionism. They, despite all their efforts, did not succeed in changing his mind regarding Zionism. Furthermore, as much the persecutions intensified, so did his efforts on behalf of Zionism. He did not hide his opinions, and he spread them publicly. He attempted to influence and attract the masses more and more toward Zionism. He was especially active among the Orthodox youth.

[Column 344]

As a Mizrachi member, he headed that faction. He founded and organized the religious youth in the ideals of the Mizrachi pioneers, and he assisted in the founding of the "Shomer Hadati" youth movement. He was among the prime founders and pillars of support of the "Yavneh" Hebrew School, which was directed by the writer of these lines.

During his free time, one could see him in the marketplace with a child in his arms, discussing and debating. About what? – Obviously about Zionism. His expertise in all the events that were taking place in the renovated Land of Yisrael was wondrous. He was wont to express with a sweet flavor and special joy the names of all new settlements that were founded by the builder pioneers on the lands of the Jewish National Fund. As a practical Zionist, he had a special feeling towards this fund. He made his nights like days in collecting money for the national funds. Just like a merchant, he would count and enumerate each dunam of land that was redeemed and reclaimed in the Land of Israel on behalf of the nation.

As I recall this enthusiastic and faithful activist, my entire being is filled with honor and reverence for him. How wonderful are the ways of G-d and the fate of the person that places himself in His hand! Reb Yechiel Asher Prawda, the man of much action who preached Zionism all of his days, did not merit in making aliya to the Land and living there. He was killed by the Nazi beasts and their accursed Polish accomplices during the time of the Holocaust, may G-d avenge his blood. His name shall be remembered by the natives of our town forever and ever.

By virtue of his participation in the mourning meeting, Reb Yechiel Asher wished to prove his dedication and love for all streams of the Zionist youth. Therefore, he also joined the funeral committee that was chosen that night. The committee declared three days of mourning in all of the Zionist organizations, and decided to pay their last respects to the deceased by arranging a Zionist funeral. The program would be: a mourning procession by the youth carrying the national flags covered with symbols of mourning, as is customary in the world of progressive culture. Preparations for actualizing this decision in full began immediately.

This news traveled very quickly through the city, and reached the circles of the extremist Hassidim who immediately girded themselves for battle against this Zionist "iniquity". To this end, they enlisted the trustees of the Chevra Kadisha, and requested that they not permit this disgrace of the deceased by the Zionists. They claimed as follows:

[Column 345]

Such a ceremony was never conducted during a funeral in this town, and there is no reason to permit such on this day. It must be opposed with all energies.

On the day of the funeral:

In the morning, one only had to go out on the street to realize that the entire town was astir. Rumor after rumor was spread in public, each one more terrible than the previous. – The Zionists are prepared, as it were, to perpetrate deeds that should not be done. Such as: they were not willing to permit the members of the Chevra Kadisha to conduct the tahara [10], but they rather wished to do it themselves. – They were going to dress her in blue and white shrouds. – They were going to fill the grave with flags and emblems of the movement, – they were going to sing songs during the funeral, and pass her coffin by all of the headquarters of the Zionist factions for eulogies at each one, etc., etc.

[Column 346]

Rumor chased rumor. As the rumors were transmitted from mouth to mouth, they became frighteningly confused. There is no need to add that there was not one scintilla of truth in all of these rumors. They were all spread deliberately at first by those who took offence to the actions, in order to fill the pure youth with fear and terror, and to deter them. They wished to demonstrate general opposition by the masses of the Jews in the town towards the Zionists, on account of this abominable deed.

A few hours prior to the time of the funeral, there was a gathering of the masses on the streets of the city. Groups of people were accusing, opposing, discussing and debating among themselves.

Standing from the right: **Berl Cukrowicz, Yitzchak Blumsztejn, Gedalya Sorowicz, Yitzchak Szlaski**
Seated: **Chuka Akselrod, Sheina Gromadzyn, Shalom Grynberg, Szviva Lubelczyk, Peshke Fenster**
Kneeling: **Avraham Cukrowicz, Moshe Nitabach**

The debates were very stormy and emotional, and there was a fear of serious disruptions from the extremist opponents. The funeral committee, wishing to prevent scandals and clashes among the gathered crowed, decide to send a delegation to the rabbi of the town and to clarify to him full details of the program of the funeral, in order to contradict all of the false rumors that had been spread in public in order to discredit us.

[Column 347]

To the credit of the rabbi of holy blessed memory, I will recall here that he, as a pure righteous man, upright without any factional tendencies, understood our spirit and believed our words. However, due to the pressure of the zealots that surrounded him, he requested that we prevent this.

Due to the awe and reverence we had for our esteemed rabbi of holy blessed memory, and also due to logistical reasons (it was a market day and it would be difficult to arrange a procession through the streets of the town) we decided to forego the procession through the streets of the town, and the entire ceremony was to be moved outside of town.

The youth gathered with their uniforms and flags in the Hebrew school building that stood on the edge of town, on the way to the cemetery. They wore emblems of mourning and waited for the arrival of the coffin, in order to give honor to their deceased comrade.

In the cemetery after the closing of the grave, we remained near the fresh grave in order to unite ourselves with the memory of the young woman who earned a name for herself as a faithful daughter of Jewish values and Zionism during her short, tragic life. Fate was bitter for her, and she did not merit realizing her life's dream – to make aliya to the land of Israel. With the singing of Hatikva [112] and a moment of silence as a token of mourning, we parted from her forever. May her memory be blessed.

The Bazaar for the Jewish National Fund

"There is a precious stone in the treasuries of the Holy One Blessed Be He, and Sabbath was its name."

This paraphrasing will faithfully survey and accurately define the great and important task that the Jewish National Fund filled in the annals of national life in general and in the Zionist movement in its factions in particular. The early years of the 1930s are considered to be, as is known, the pinnacle of the pride in the Zionist movement. At that time, the Zionist idea celebrated its great victories in all areas of life. The Jews of Poland in their masses joined the various factions of the Zionist movement that were increasing and strengthening. These factions made their inroads in every home and every Jewish settlement in the nation of Poland.

Slowly but surely, as the stature of Zionism and its factions rose, so did the factional antagonism. The ideological divisions widened, and, with the passage of time, turned into literal internecine hatred, causing endless controversy and disputes.

[Column 348]

We would often read on the pages of the newspapers news about Zionist meetings that ended with the outbreak of internecine, interfactional controversy that was filled with physical violence, on occasion even coming to the point of bloodshed.

Similar fistfights, albeit in a more limited and modest fashion, were a common occurrence in our town. The factional divisiveness held sway over us as well, and ideological clashes during stormy debates at public gatherings and other events were considered at the time as intensive Zionist activity, and the more that one engaged in such, the more praiseworthy it is [113].

In light of this reality, it is easy to understand the great and very important role that the Jewish National Fund played in promoting peace in the midst of the large Zionist camp among the Jews. The Jewish National Fund bestowed its own splendor and the sprit of the Land of Israel upon the entire Zionist movement. It shone its great light upon our activities even in the group itself. The splendor of its deeds influenced us all in a calming fashion, which quieted the spirit. Despite the differences in ideology, it succeeded in uniting everyone to this holy task of redeeming the land of the homeland.

A committee that was composed of representatives of all the Zionist factions stood at the helm of the Jewish National Fund in our town. Only with regard to the election of a chairman (known as Morasha) did an interfactional competition take place, through accepted democratic means.

All public gatherings of the Jewish National Fund, which for the most part included the participation of representatives of the central organization and guests from the Land of Israel, turned into large-scale gatherings that drew people close and enhanced mutual understanding. Many activities took place with close cooperation between all factions, and were conducted with great success.

The bazaar on behalf of the Jewish National fund, that will now be described, took place on Purim of the year 1934, during the period of the tenure of this writer as Morasha of the Jewish National Fund in the town. This was the first event of its kind in Czyzewo.

[Column 349]

During one of the regular meetings of the committee at the time of the special deliberations regarding increasing the income of the Jewish National Fund, the idea arose to organize a bazaar, that is: an exhibit of various items that would be gathered by the activists through public donation. These items would be sold, and the income would be dedicated to the Jewish National Fund.

Various other suggestions arose regarding the main idea of the bazaar. These included the setting up of cultural celebrations, performances, and entertainment evenings with a Zionist character during the period of the bazaar, in order to attract and interest the community that would visit the bazaar.

This idea greatly enchanted us, and was accepted with unanimous agreement. In order to actualize the idea, a special committee was set up of women active in the head committee. This was called the "Bazaar Committee", and was responsible for the honorable and difficult task of preparing a full program for the actualization, enlisting the needed people and means to conduct the bazaar from its inception until its end.

[Column 350]

The members on this committee were: F. Wasercug, G. Bolender, Litmans, Wengorz, Yocheved Held, Jelin, Frydman, Lubelczyk, G. Bolender [114], F. Plocker

It is simply impossible to describe the enthusiasm that was awakened for this event. Our town, which was experienced with various communal activities, did not know of such enthusiasm previously. The women of the community infected all of the women of the town with their dedication and blessed work. An atmosphere of preparation for the bazaar took was created. In every home, they sowed, wove, and knitted various creations. Competitions for the preparation of fine and ample exhibits for the bazaar took place.

Standing: **Dovka Jelin, Bat-Sheva Lubelczyk (Gorzalczany)**
Seated: **Feigel Wasercug, Rachel Litmans, Frumcha Gromadzyn, Yitzchak Szlaski, Golda Bolender, Yocheved Kackowicz, Feigel Plocker, Miriam Frydman**

All of the necessary preparations took place during the course of two months. Plentiful exhibits were collected. Aside from knitted and woven items that possessed artistic value, we collected many ordinary items of various types. We turned to large, well-known manufacturers in Poland with whom the merchants of Czyzewo maintained business connections, and requested donations of goods for the bazaar. They responded to our requests generously, and the items that were received were of significant monetary value.

[Column 351]

At the designated time for the program, we rented the largest and finest hall in the town, which was the "Rolnyk" of the Polish agricultural society, along with all of its adjoining rooms. The exhibits were arranged in an appropriate fashion, in good taste.

The women did not begrudge their time and energy in order to beautify and decorate the exhibition, so long that it would be successful. For we said: if the exhibition makes a good impression on the visitors, it would attract a larger crowd, and then its success would be assured. Indeed, this aim was realized to its fullest extent. The evening of the opening of the bazaar, the first in Czyzewo, can be registered as "a unique event" in the annals of Zionist activity in our town.

This large hall was too small to accommodate all of those who came. Youth and adults together came to be present at the festive opening, which was planned with great detail, and included a rich, multi-faceted program. The speakers and blessings that were heard from the stage at this historic event served as a faithful expression to the heartfelt feelings and sublime spirit of the speakers and audience together.

[Column 352]

After the cutting or the ribbon, accompanied by the playing of the firefighter's band, the curtain was opened. The spectacular "Impozantit Exhitibion" [15] that had become a reality was opened before the eyes of the community. Joy and gladness pervaded among all of the gathered. The eyes of the organizers beamed with happiness and joy. Indeed, they had accomplished what they desired. The hard work and many efforts paid off and were crowned with success, as we had figured would have happened from the outset.

The bazaar lasted for eight days. The hall was full on each of those days with people who came from all strata of the community in the town.

Various meetings, parties, presentations on interesting topics, etc. were arranged each evening. Everything went according to the plan that was set out from the beginning. The hall of the bazaar and the additional rooms that were adjacent were turned during this time period into a *lovely* communal hall to which people came daily to enjoy several pleasant hours together, to chat amongst friends, and to listen to the tunes of the firefighter's band.

[Column 353]

The items on display diminished day by day. They were sold, or more accurately, they were literally grabbed up one by one. Significant sums of money accrued to the coffers of the Jewish National Fund. This was not only from the sale of merchandise, but also from the other events that accompanied the bazaar, and took place with great success. There was joy amongst us.

Even the closing evening event that was conducted in good taste was greatly successful. The discussions regarding the great success instilled satisfaction on all of the participants. They joy of the bazaar committee was especially great.

The second and final bazaar, similar in form and content to the first bazaar, took place the following year, and it was also successful.

Seated from right: **Dovka Jelin, Yocheved, Kacowicz, Feigel Plocker, Rachel Litmans, Frumcha Gromadzyn, Feigel Wasercug**
In the second row: **Bat Sheva Lubelczyk, Yitzchak Szlaski, Golda Bolender, Miriam Frydman**

Translator's note: the inscription on the photo itself reads:
"Second Keren Kayamet Bazaar, Czyzewo, March 20, 1935."

That year, 1935, the large-scale exodus of activists of all the factions in town began. Most of them made aliya. Their aliya left a great void in all areas of cultural and Zionist activity in town. Thus, the two bazaars that took place one after the other in consecutive years remain as isolated events; however their pleasantness is etched in our memories of our town of Czyzewo until this day.

Summary

In this survey, I attempted to portray with my modest pen and to briefly describe the Zionist activity in our town, in its various factions, and the youth organizations that arose within this one short timeframe. I am not oblivious to the fact that Zionist activity of various forms existed in great measure for many years before this timeframe.

Our Czyzewo was not noted for outstanding, famous personalities, known in the realms of culture and the various sciences. However, it was always alert to what was taken place in the wide world, and in particular in our Jewish world. The alert, effervescent youth in it always took an active role in the various events of every era. We heard about this in great measure from the stories of our parents and grandparents when we were still young children in the town.

[Column 354]

Our town knew variegated and intensive Zionist activity, appropriate to the spirit of the times, throughout all the years subsequent until the end of the First World War. Rather than me describing this, it would be more appropriate for our senior fellow natives who are living amongst us today, who themselves worked and carried the yoke of Zionist activity in our town upon their shoulders.

With the passage of years, as the strength of the Zionist idea grew in the Jewish street, the practical activity also expanded. There was already a new, younger generation, the generation of youth coming of age, alert and excited, who lived the life of the era in all of its ramifications. An important and difficult historic task was placed in the hands of this youth. This task was to win over the town for Zionism from educational, cultural and practical perspectives during this historic time. In summary, we must point out that they stood up to their task with great success.

The activities for Zionist realization reached the pinnacle of our ideals, and thanks to this, we succeeded in a significant fashion to flow with all of the historical events of this latest period in the annals of our people. We left the slavery and decline of exile for the redemption of national and cultural freedom in our renewed country. We were saved from the terrible Holocaust that brought with it the annihilation of our families in the towns of the exile of Poland, to a life of future and eternity as citizens with full rights in the land of Israel.

As one of these fortunate people, I fulfilled a modest, traditional and pleasant duty in this survey. I described some of the activities and events in the field of Zionism in this exciting time in our small town of Czyzewo, with the clear aim to erect in this Yizkor Book a memorial to the bygone era, of a Jewish town that once was and is no more, to its holy sons and daughters whose thread of life was cut off in the middle with evil cruelty by the Nazi murderers and the cursed Poles, may their names and memories be blotted out.

The memories of the martyrs will be preserved in our hearts forever and ever.

Translator's notes:

6. The C. heading is missing from the text. I suspect it was inadvertently omitted.

7. Here, the term 'Soviet' would mean Communist Committee.

8. There is an error in the year here, as Yom Kippur 5694 would correspond to the year 1933.

9. The Yom Kippur services occupy most of the day, but in many synagogues, there is a break of 2-3 hours in the mid-afternoon, between Musaf and Mincha.

10. The ritual washing and cleansing of the body prior to burial. The details of the tahara complex.

11. The term used here for 'discredit us', is literally to 'make us stink'. This is the term used near the beginning of Exodus (5:21) when the Jewish people are describing the situation that they found themselves in with reference to Pharaoh after Moses first tried to intercede with Pharaoh.

12. The Zionist national anthem, later to become the national anthem of the State of Israel.

13. A quote from the Passover Haggadah, indicating that the more one tells of the story of the Exodus on Passover night, the more praiseworthy it is.

14. Either this name was repeated a second time in error, or two people bore the same initial and same last name.

15. The word 'impozantit' is seemingly an 'Anglicism' (i.e., an English word Hebraised). It seems to mean 'imposing', but probably more accurately translated here as 'impressive'.

[Column 355]

The Mizrachi Organization of Czyzewo

By Eliahu Gora of Tel Aviv

Translated by Jerrold Landau

At this time, we do not have in our hands the exact date of the founding of the Mizrachi organization in Czyzewo. To our great sorrow, none of the elder founders who stood by the cradle of its foundation are still alive. As far as we can estimate, this was at the beginning of the 20th century. However, what we do know from the handful of survivors of the Mizrachi organization who live with us today in our Land, and were active among the religious youth in our town – that the annals of the existence of

Mizrachi in Czyzewo can be considered to have started from the first appearance of the idea of that movement in the general Jewish world: that is during the last decades of the 1800s.

Our small town was always attuned to every new movement in the life of our people, whether social, cultural, communal or general. The fundamental idea of national renewal in its variegated manifestation, whether from the founding of Chibat Zion[1] or afterward, as well as the national Zionist movement founded by Dr. Herzl of blessed memory that spread in the Jewish street, penetrated our town as well and conquered strong fortresses in the hearts of the young generation – most of them fine young men, the children of Hassidim immersed in Torah and people of good deeds. Czyzewo, as a fortress of Hassidism, was blessed with many such people.

With the crystallization of the national religious idea in the framework of the world Zionist movement that resulted in the founding of the Mizrachi movement; a group of young men found in it a suitable domain for their national spirit and their religious foundation. They went ahead and founded the first group of the national religious movement, and with this they established the foundation for the Mizrachi organization in all its manifestations, which was organized later and existed in Czyzewo for all the years until its destruction.

[Column 356]

The spiritual resource from which the pioneers of the national idea received their sustenance was, among others, the Hatzefira newspaper, which was published by Reb Zerach Starkowski of blessed memory. He was also known therein as the correspondent regarding life in the town. This activity was obviously conducted underground, and was hidden from the Hassidic parents, who saw this newspaper as "treif and passul" [2] and would be prohibited as "bal yiraeh and bal yimatzeh" [3] in a Jewish home. Indeed, the influence of the Hatzefira newspaper was significant. People would enter secretly into the women's hall of the great Beit Midrash in order to read the newspaper in unison. They would exchange impressions and enjoy the aroma of the national spirit that this newspaper imparted to them. They would also arrange meetings and gatherings of youth in order to instill the idea of the religious national renaissance to them.

Reb Chaim Yehoshua Tancze, particularly excelled in this holy work. He was one of the unique people in our town given that he was a Jew imbued with Torah, a Hassid and a Maskil all in one. He served for all these years in the task of the secretary of the Jewish communal council. The following were his friends who gathered around him and helped him with this factional work: Reb Moshe Najmark, Reb Yaakov Landau, Reb Yechiel Gorzalczany, Reb Fishel Bronsztajn, Reb Fishel Lubelczyk, Reb Moshe Ahron Belfer, Reb Shalom Kitaj, Reb Meir Shimon Ribak, the brothers Avraham Yosel and Binyamin Slucki, Avraham Lamport, and Reb Yechiel Asher Prawda of blessed memory. There were also those who worshipped in the Great Synagogue: Reb Yosel Baruch Lepak and Reb Shmuel Velvel Kandel of blessed memory. Their efforts were expressed not only in the conducting of publicity meetings, but also in collections for the Jewish National Fund and other Zionist activity.

[Column 357]

The following story, which I heard in Israel from Reb Moshe Najmark of blessed memory, will testify to the level of holiness to which they related to the Zionist movement and its leaders.

On the day of the passing of Dr. Herzl of blessed memory, they gathered for a memorial evening in the women's hall in the Great Synagogue, where they eulogized him appropriately and studied chapters of Mishna for the elevation of his soul. This fact proves clearly the level of feelings of awe and honor to which they related to the founder of the Zionist movement, even at the first steps of nationalistic religious activity. This organizational and ideological activity continued on throughout all the years until the end of the First World War.

Hashomer Hadati and Young Mizrachi

The activities of the Zionist movement moved to a very different level in the year 1918, after the Balfour Declaration. The era of intensive activity for the building of the Land started, as did the period of the Third Aliya.

[Column 358]

The Mizrachi organization was reconstituted in Czyzewo. Reb Yechiel Asher Prawda of blessed memory stood at the head of the movement. The following members joined efforts with him: Simcha Lew, Yaakov Astranzanski, Yudel Richter, and, may he live, Reb Yechiel Eliasz, who was among the first of the Chalutzim (Zionist pioneers) who made aliya. During a later period, the following members excelled in their faithful efforts: Moshe David Litwak, Yisrael Yitzchak Lew, and may they live, Eliahu Zylbersztajn, Pinchas Frydman, Eliahu Gora, Yaakov Kandel, who are today in Israel. The son of the rabbi, Reb Chaim Zabludower of blessed memory was also active. All of them were the children of Hassidic parents, who were themselves frequenters of the Beis Midrash. They gazed and were affected by the national spirit that began to express itself with greater energy among Polish Jewry.

As a result of this blessed activity, factional institutions were founded, such as the Yavneh School, and the Hashomer Hadati youth movement. The movement also supplied appropriate representation to all the communal bodies and institutions that were in existence, such as the communal council, the fund committees, and election committees for the congresses, etc.

[Column 359]

A new era of vibrant activity began with the organization of the Hashomer Hadati youth movement. The establishment of the chapter of Hashomer Hadati stemmed the tide of the migration of the religious youth to the liberal youth movements. The sons and daughters of Orthodox homes who joined us took upon themselves the yoke of Zionist doctrine blended in a fine fashion with the love of the people of Israel, the Torah of Israel, and the Land of Israel. These youths were blessed with the values of the nationalist Zionist movement, and bore the flag of Mizrachi in our town with pride.

Through the efforts of the religious youth, a Kibbutz Hachsharah [1] of "Hechalutz Hamizrachi" was established. It only existed for a brief period, but the pioneering influence of the youth was quite recognizable. The following martyrs were among the active counselors in the Hashomer Hadati organization: Baruch Grossbard, Dov Lubelczyk, and the girls Tova Zylbersztajn, Yehudit Rotman, Moncarsz, and the Szwarc sisters, may G-d avenge their blood. As well, there were the following people, may they live long, Yehoshua Wolmer (in Nicaragua), Chaim Belfer, Eliahu Zylbersztajn, and Avraham Kandel (the latter three in Israel).

[Column 360]

A significant number of these boys and girls came from homes of Hassidim of Gur, who were opposed to any movement that had even a scent of Zionism, even if religiously based. However, they became enthralled with the religious Zionist idea with the entire flame of their hearts, and their young souls worked with enthusiasm and love for Zion and Zionism together. They were infused with faith and hope that the day would come when they would be able to make aliya to the Land of Israel, to build it and be built by it. However, to our sorrow, fate was cruel to them, and they did not merit to do so. Most of them went to the stake and perished together with all the Jews of Czyzewo in the terrible Holocaust that was perpetrated against the splendid Jewry of Poland. May G-d avenge their blood.

Their holy memory will never depart from us!

[Column 361]

Memories from the Hachsharah Kibbutz in Czyzewo

By Aryeh Porat of Tel Aviv

Translated by Jerrold Landau

Holy and blessed is your memory, my town of Czyzewo, regarding your Jewish residents who perished at the hands of the murderers, may G-d avenge their blood; and regarding those, may they live long, who found refuge in all lands of the earth, especially those who are living with us today in our Land.

Czyzewo is the second town in the annals of my life that my soul became attached to with bonds of blood and love, and that became an inseparable part of me.

I arrived in Czyzewo in 1934 and was appointed as the director of one of the Hachsharah depots that had already existed there for about a year previously. I stood at the helm of this Hachsharah kibbutz for two years. It consisted of approximately 40 boys and girls, who regarded themselves as strangers in the exile of Poland. Their entire desire, longing and purpose was to make aliyah to the Land of Israel. As was needed in the previous era, they had to become used to a difficult life and to hard work in particular – pioneering work.

During this period of time, I was able to get to know a significant portion of the residents of the town. Their memories from that time are etched in my heart, and I remember them with love.

Prior to my arrival in Czyzewo, I imagined that town as a place of manufacturing and industry that was short of working hands, and I thought that the hands of these "kibbutzniks" would be a blessing for the residents, and that the large amount of work in the town would be a blessing to the kibbutz, that would enable it to maintain itself in an honorable fashion. How great was my disappointment when I saw before me a remote town, like all other forlorn towns in Poland prior to the war, infused with the exilic reality that prevailed at the time. Then, I feared greatly for the future and continuation of the Hachsharah Kibbutz in such a place such as that were there was a dearth of work. However, when I got to know the Jews of Czyzewo from close up, the fear dissipated. A new feeling replaced the disappointment, a feeling that I still carry with me as a duty until this day. That is: the Jewish objective.

[Column 362]

Immediately upon my arrival, the Committee of Friends of the Kibbutz was founded, which called itself "Patront". It took upon itself the task of concerning itself with places of work to create something from nothing for the Kibbutz, so that it would not know hunger and want.

The members of this Patront were of varying ideologies. However, this "Jewish objective" united all of them – and they were one. The following are the names of the people who were members of the Patront:

Shalom Grynberg, Berish Grade, Yehoshua Lepak, and Noach Edelsztajn of blessed memory. Dov Gorzalczany, and Mottel Szczupakiewicz, may they live long.

We had permanent and temporary workplaces. There were those people of means who were able to permit themselves to give set places of work. These included Dov Gorzalczany, who provided work in loading and unloading fertilizer, chemicals, naphtha, and other such tasks. There were others who, even though they did not have an excess of work, nevertheless took the duty upon themselves to give permanent work to the members of the Kibbutz.

This is in praise of those dedicated people who provided work, such as:

"Mendel the Aliar". He was the owner of an oil refinery [5]. This Mendel was old, tall, thin, and hard of hearing, with a constant smile on his face.

[Column 363]

He employed two members of the Kibbutz on a permanent basis. On days when there was a dearth of work, or when he did not have anything with which to keep them busy, he would sit with them and tell them stories of the past. He did not reduce their pay.

Yitzchak Wasercug. He was a handsome Jew. It was said that he was wealthy. However, the wheel of fortune turned away from him, and his fortunes declined. However, the good, warm Jewish heart remained with him forever. He employed a few of us to change the water in the city mikva (ritual bath). He would say, "indeed we may or may not need the mikva for today, but you certainly need work. 'If there is no grain, there is no Torah [6]'. Work and receive your payment."

Saneh Stuczynski. He was a member of Aguda [7]. He was not so taken with "Zionism". He waited day by day for the footsteps of the Messiah to be heard on the streets of Czyzewo. Nevertheless, he was a splendid Jew, and he relations with us were good and dedicated. During the time that we worked in preparing the crates for packing the fruit, he would warn us: "Workers, protect your shoulders from the gusts of wind, so that the nails will not twist you!"

Shimon the tailor. He had thick, black eyebrows. He was approximately fifty years old, and he had some white hair. He had a thick, rough voice, but a warm, soft heart. He would say: "Send one of you to me to work, send him, it does not matter, so long as he knows how to at least sew a button. Why should my lot be wanting in providing work for the Kibbutz members?"

Noach Edelsztajn. His yard was full of twigs organized lengthwise and widthwise. He would purchase more on a daily basis. He would call over the woodchoppers from the Kibbutz to come to work, and treat us casually. He would say. "Sing children, for 'work is our life, and will save us from all tribulation'!"

Chaim Szczupakiewicz owned a building materials warehouse. This was our permanent workplace. It was a place of refuge for us. He would say: "If one of you remains without a day of work, send him to me, and I will keep him busy with something."

[Column 364]

Yankel and Rishka Kitaj were not specifically among those who gave work, but were numbered among the Kibbutz members. They actively participated with us, both in our joys and our worries. In one word, we prepared ourselves and bound ourselves together. Yankel's pockets were always filled with sweets, and each of us knew about this. He did not give, but whoever wished any would have to place his hands in his pockets and take out "whatever came onto the fork". During such a "pickpocketing" effort, it was evident from Yankel's face that he was deriving a great deal of pleasure. When a Kibbutz member would take ill and have to remain in bed, we knew for certain that the merciful hand of Rishka, Yankel Kitaj's wife, would take care of him and assist him with all his needs, including giving medicine on time or a glass of tea.

Oh, Would It Be That I Were Able!

I will never forget the words of Leizerke the son of Yankel and Rishka on the day that I packed my suitcases on the eve of my making aliyah to the Land, and it is as if I can hear them still today. He turned to me and said: "Throw out all of these shmates [8] in your suitcases and take me in their place…" Oh, how I wish I could have… Similarly, I remember one boy whose name was Kocmacher, who came to us at the Kibbutz. He was the son of poor people, and his entire desire was to make aliyah to the Land of Israel. However, he was lacking the necessary means in order to actualize this desire. His many pleas and requests for me to help him cut through my heart. I stood before him helplessly and thought: "I desire with my heart to help you, but… Oh would it be that I were able."

How can I conclude without mentioning Moshele Gromadzyn? He owned a grocery store on the Street of the Smiths (Szmydisza Gasse). He gave us an open credit for anything we need from his merchandise. He never came to us with requests and demands for payment.

How can I forget and not mention Chanale the milker, the "mother of the Kibbutz" whose route to distribute milk took her first of all to the Kibbutz. During her free time, she would come to teach the girls the manners of "the woman of the house" regarding cooking, laundry, and other housework. If someone took ill, she would immediately wish to summon the (Christian) doctor. This doctor would come even at midnight, and if we tried to pay him for his services, he would literally become offended. May his memory also be blessed.

Thus did the Kibbutz intermingle with the life in the town, and become a unified family among all the families. Among other things, it participated in the cultural life of the town with various performances and celebrations. It also as counted among the local dramatic circle, whose members included Plocker, and David Moncarz, as well as, may she live Mrs. Sheva Gorzalczany and others.

[Column 365]

Finally, I will eulogize with a few lines my father-in-law Reb Alter Berish Grade of blessed memory and my mother-in-law.

I loved this man even prior to giving the official imprimatur upon the regarding the relations between the bride and groom. We would spend hour upon hour engaged in mutual conversation. He was an Orthodox man with a Hassidic outlook on the one hand, and with a realistic outlook upon life on the other hand. With enthusiastic words, he would awaken and encourage the endless struggle for an independent state in the homeland. He would say: "It is better to stand in fear next to a drawn knife of an Arab than to stand daily before the insults and denigration of the exile". He would add: "You desire something ideal – you have a purpose in life, but we here are like 'sheep to the bountiful slaughter'…" I did not understand then how right he was. Our first concern was, how would the train rest in a Jewish state on the Sabbath?

It is most unfortunate, regarding him and the many others like him, that they did not merit to see with their own eyes that the Israeli train does rest on the Sabbath in the State of Israel. It is most unfortunate for those who have been lost and will never be forgotten!…

[Column 366]

I also engaged in private teaching along with my task of running the Kibbutz. That is to say, I gave lessons. My students included children from Orthodox homes, whose parents opposed from the outset any secular learning, or that their children should study along with the children of the gentiles. However, slowly but surely, their eyes became opened to see in the footsteps of the catastrophic situation that prevailed in Poland at the time, that there is no other choice. The day would come when their children would have to uproot themselves from their homes and wander to different countries. Then they would encourage them to rectify what they had rejected.

When I remember my students now, I wish to make note of two of them whose talents and excellence in studies astounded me. One was the grandson of Reb Yisrael Yonah Raczkowski. His accomplishments in his studies, especially in mathematics, were so great that in a short period he accomplished what would have taken others twice as long. The second is Berele Lubelczyk. How astonished was I at his phenomenal memory. He had a quick grasp, and the understanding of an elder, settled man.

It is too bad! How unfortunate is it that such talented people with fine memories were cut off without mercy in an untimely fashion.

May their memories be blessed forever!

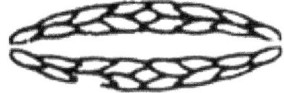

Translator's notes:

1. Chibat Zion was a precursor to the formal Zionist movement.
2. These two words have halachic import. Treif (literally 'torn', from the Jewish law prohibiting meat from an animal that died due to a violent injury or an illness that punctured various internal organs), is colloquially used to describe any non-kosher meat; and 'passul' (literally 'invalid'), refers to a ritual object (e.g. Torah scroll, sukka, shofar, lulav, etc.) that is unfit for ritual use.
3. Literally "it shall not be seen and shall not be found" referring to the prohibition of owning chometz (leavened bread) during Passover.
4. A farm set up for practical Zionist training (i.e. learning farming for eventual use in Israel).
5. Oil here has the edible connotation ('shemen') rather than the fuel connotation.
6. A phrase from Pirke Avot (the Mishnaic tractate dealing with moral adages) indicating that Torah can only exist if there is physical sustenance to go along with it.
7. The non-Zionist Orthodox movement.
8. The Yiddish word that roughly translates as 'rags'.

[Column 367]

The Zionist Organizations in Czyzewo

by Yitzchak Szlaski

Translated by Gloria Berkenstat Freund

We were a small group of young men who mainly came from *yeshivus* [religious secondary schools], houses of prayer and Hasidic *shtiblekh* [small one-room synagogues], wherever the Zionist idea reached us. We saw the most elevated manifestation of Jewish life in exile in this idea of the return to Zion and we devoted ourselves to this idea with all of the fervor in our souls.

This was at the end of 1920. A split took place then in the youth movement *Hashomer HaTzair* [the Young Guard – Socialist-Zionists] in Poland. Several of its leaders emerged who did agree with the leftist ideological direction of this movement and [they] founded a new Zionist youth movement named *Hashomer HaLeumi* [the National Guard], which later changed its name to *Hashomer HaZioni* [The Zionist Guard].

On an end-of-summer evening in 1920 we came together at the residence of the teacher, Reb Ahron Wajntraub. In addition to me, the most active comrades in the group were Arya Gorzalczany and Yankel Gromadzyn. Two comrades who led the branch in nearby Wysokie Mazowieckie gave informational speeches.

That evening it was decided to create a branch of *Hashomer HaLeumi* in Czyzewo. The was the first youth organization that was active in Czyzewo as well as later, until the final destruction.

[Column 368]

Arya Gorzalczany, Yankel Gromadzyn and I were elected as the leaders of the "nest" and we immediately went to work on publicity and technical organization.

The club, which we opened, drew more young people from all classes with each day. Poor children in whose homes the poverty took away every possibility to study also came. We welcomed them with the greatest warmth, taught them the most elementary information about the world and life, about *Yidishkeit* [Jewish way of life] and Zionism.

The club, which was located in a shabby, rented apartment, became full of youthful life. We, the members of the leadership, carried out the needed remodeling ourselves, adorned the walls with pictures of Zionist leaders and thinkers, with scouting symbols and pictures of the *Eretz-Yisrael* population.

The scouts, who organized outings, summer camps and various sports competitions, occupied an esteemed place in the activities of our young organization.

[Column 369]

This section was led by Yankel Gromadzyn. He was a student in the Hebrew Teachers' Seminar in Vilna for a time and was skilled in his field.

Arya Gorzalczany and I took the cultural work upon ourselves. Every evening we led special groups and circles conversing on the subjects of "*Yidishkeit* and Zionism," "General and Jewish history," "Concerning the current period for the Jewish people," "The political situation in the world," "English politics and the fight of the new Jewish resident in *Eretz-Yisrael*." Lectures in the Hebrew language were organized, which were obligatory for all of the members.

These activities of ours changed the face of the young people in the *shtetl* who showed ever more alertness and interest both for political and general communal and Jewish national problems. Their backs straightened with pride and self-confidence.

Songs and dance had an important place in the program of our activities and truly were the daily bread for our young people.

Our activities also brought life into our division of the general Zionists, which lasted for a long time, but their activity was feeble and it was hardly felt. The older Zionists began to show an interest in tangible work with the rise of dynamic activity by the young. Shalom Grynberg, Yehoshua Lepak, Fejgel Wasercug and Golda Bolender, who perished in the cruel Hitler catastrophe, particularly emerged.

[Column 370]

Our dear Motl Szczupakiewicz, who today is in America, Moshel Blajwajs, today in Canada, Dov Gorzalczany, today in Israel and the rabbi's daughter, Freidel Zabludower, today in America, particularly excelled with their unlimited activities.

Encounters and gatherings and the *Shabbos* [Sabbath] at night and holidays remain in my memory; the comradely conversations and readings, the songs and dancing that with their enthusiasm carried away even the older Zionists.

On *Lag B'Omer*, the 20th of Tammuz we organized meetings, presentations and marches through the streets of the *shtetl*. [1] The comrades mentioned helped us overcome the difficulties placed in our way by various opponents.

This ideal coexistence existed for a year and a half until [Ze'ev] Jabotinsky's supporters also obtained influence in our *shtetl* and Yankel Gromadzyn and a larger group of young people left *Hashomer HaLeumi* and created the Revisionist youth organization *Betar*. The right *Poalei-Zion* [Workers of Zion – Marxist Zionists], the League for Working *Eretz-Yisrael* arose right after that. Slightly later, the *Mizrakhi* [religious Zionists] organized the religious young people and created *Hashomer HaDati* [religious Zionist youth group].

This party competition carried on tempestuous discussions and fights. In time, Arya Gorzalczany also left our organization and joined *Hashomer HaDati*. I, alone, of the first founders, remained and I continued my work among the Zionist young people until 1935 when I emigrated to *Eretz-Yisrael*.

Translator's note:

1. *Lag B'Omer* is the 18th of Iyar – a holiday celebrated in the spring during which it is customary to go on outings and to light bonfires; Theodor Herzl, the founder of modern Zionism, died on the 20th of Tammuz – the 3rd of July 1904. The author of this article may have confused the two dates.

[Column 371]

The Movement for "A Working Eretz–Yisrael"

By Malka Szejman – Tel Aviv

Translated by Gloria Berkenstat Freund

In addition to the cultural life in Czyzewo, the young people also had political instincts and in 1927 a group of students created the youth library, which later joined the city library, which was invigorated by the strength of the young people.

Poalei–Zion Committee
Standing: **Rotman and Rochel Garde**
Sitting: **Ruchele Kalan, Dovid Moncarz, Liba Rotman, Malka Szejman, Avraham Cukrowicz, Shmulke Okon**

The group around the youth library later were those who created the *Poalei–Zion* [Workers of Zion – Marxist Zionists] movement, the League for a Working *Eretz–Yisrael*, *Freiheit* [Freedom] and *Hahalutz* [Zionist pioneer movement] in Czyzewo in 1928 with the help of several older comrades ([who were] the nucleus of *Poalei–Zion* from the years 1917, 1922, 1925). Included in their ranks were a large number of the students, young workers, young men from the *yeshivus* [religious secondary schools] and Hasidic *shtiblekh* [small one–room synagogues].

[Column 372]

In a short time, the movement for A Working *Eretz–Yisrael* grew to be one of the largest party organizations in Czyzewo and in the entire surrounding area. The organization became stronger in quantity and quality every day despite the persecutions that we endured from the pious and Hasidic elements in Czyzewo.

I will only tell about one of the many incidents and conversations that took place between us and the pious ones.

It was right after the events in *Eretz–Yisrael* in 1929. When the activists from the party consisting of the Comrades Avraham Cur (Cukrowicz), Nidbach (Nitabach) and the writer of these lines (today all in Israel), Feigel Cukrowicz (today in America), Yisrael Yitzchak Bursztajn (today in Uruguay) and other comrades, who did not live to come to Israel and bring about their ideals, held a meeting and considered the question of honoring the fallen heroes who had defended the Jewish population in *Eretz–Yisrael* as well as the question of the Congress of A Working *Eretz–Yisrael* that was supposed to take place then in Berlin, several Gerer Hasidim and others unexpectedly arrived and began to demolish the meeting premises. They had come to rescue their children. Fights broke out. The police came, then trials. Then, as it happens, they were finally persuaded that our struggle for "Zionism" was correct. Their children, who later joined our ranks, then became the activists in the Zionist organizations in Czyzewo. After the departure for Yisrael of the activists, my brother, Nuska Szejman, a former *yeshiva* [religious secondary school] student, became the political and spiritual leader, teacher and activist for A Working *Eretz–Yisrael* in Czyzewo as well as in the surrounding area.

[Column 373]

Standing: **Mnakusa (brother and sister), Mordechai Moncarz, Rochel Hofman, Shayna Kandel, Feigel Plocker, Fayga Feldsztajn, Rochel Garde**
Sitting: **Sura Minc, Rivka Zysman, Rosman, Chaim Slucki, Rochela Kachan, Avraham Cukrowicz, Liba Rosman, Leibel Eides, Rochel Zysman, Shalom Kirszenbojm, Avraham Eli Bursztajn, Gitka Szejman**

[Column 374]

I emphasize that thanks to our political instincts and initiatives during that era, thanks to our devoted adherence to the Zionist ideal and calling the young to join our ranks, a number succeeded in emigrating to *Eretz–Yisrael* and remained alive. These were individuals from large families in Czyzewo, which perished in 1941 at the hands of the Hitler murderers and their collaborators.

Our widespread work was in every area. We divided the young people into groups. The groups were led by the comrades Yitzchak Gora, Avraham Cur (Cukrowicz), Gedalia Surowicz, and by me. (Today all are in Israel) and later by my brother, Nuska, may his memory be blessed.

[Column 375]

**Sirkin Group in 1932
at the departure of Comrade Leah Bursztajn**

The groups were led with various themes: "History of the worker movement in *Eretz-Yisrael*," "Borochovism," "Marx and Engles," "Natural science," "Historical Materialism," "Cultural history," as well as various Zionist themes such as: "Herzl," "Nardau," "*Ahad Ha'am*" ["one of the people" – the pen name of essayist, Asher Zvi Hirsch Ginsberg] and of various leaders of social–democracy in the world.

[Column 376]

The groups trained the younger comrades who later led the groups. One of them is Mordechai Moncarz, a well–known partisan in the Bialystok area (today in America) and [there are many] others. Evening events about various themes, excursions, fraternal conversations and so on were arranged.

Our comrades were active in all institutions in Czyzewo such as: *K.K.L.* [*Keren Kayemeth LeYisrael*– The Jewish National Fund], the library and later in the kehile [organized Jewish community], the fortress of *Agudas-Yisrael* [Union of Israel – Orthodox political movement]. Our words were heard everywhere. We built a majority everywhere, in the dramatic circle and in other institutions. We later created the [organization] Oved [Worker], which brought most of the artisans in Czyzewo into our ranks. A large number of them succeeded in emigrating to *Eretz-Yisrael*.

[Column 377]

We always received the appropriate number of votes and often a majority in the election to the [Zionist] Congresses. We had what the masses wanted, firstly, the active work for the Zionist organizations in Czyzewo and also for the Histadrut [General Organization of Workers] with its branches in *Eretz–Yisrael*.

The League for Working *Eretz–Yisrael*, at which I held the office of chairwoman and Avraham Cur (Cukrowicz) was *maskir* (secretary), enrolled many sympathizers in addition to the comrades from *Poalei–Zion*, Socialist Zionists and *Freiheit*. We would send a great deal of money from the League to *Histadrut*. Our comrades who left for the *hakshore kibbutizim* [pioneer communal settlements] such as the detachments from "Borochov," "Klarow Shmarja" and "Tel Hai" were the most active ones.

**Sirkin Group in 1932
at the departure of Comrade Leah Bursztajn**

[Column 378]

We would often have visits from the comrades Bialopolski, Morgnsztern, Szpizman and others from the *Poalei–Zion* central committee. The central committee gave great recognition to our extensive work.

We would all take excursions together with the organizations from the surrounding *shtetlekh* [towns] Ciechanowiec, Zaromb [Zaręby], Wisoki Mazowieckie and others. We would arrange reciprocal visits and joint gatherings.

[Column 379]

We were connected to Zaromb as if we were one organization. Comrade Shmuel Leib Ruskalonker, of blessed memory, helped us a great deal. Comrade Betsalel (Tsalka) Rozenblum (today in Israel) was like a part of our young people. We would also send delegates to congresses in Warsaw, Bialystok and to seminars. Here, too, in Israel our comrades are esteemed. They were active in the *Haganah* and *Palmach*.[1] Today comrades are found on *kibbutzim* [collective communities] and in esteemed positions in *Histadrut* and its branches.

[Column 380]

Translator's note:

1. The *Haganah* was the underground Jewish army during the British Mandate; *Palmach* was its elite fighting force.

Freiheit excursion

[Column 379]

Freiheit

By Leah Dimentman (Bursztajn)/ Tel Aviv

Translated by Gloria Berkenstat Freund

The events in *Eretz–Yisrael* in 1929 shook the Jewish young people in Czyzewo. The wish to emigrate [to *Eretz–Yisrael*] and help to build a national home grew every day and the creation began of pioneer administrative bodies to find a way to *Eretz–Yisrael* with collective strength.

[Column 380]

An intensive movement for organizing arose in Czyzewo. The *Poalei–Zion* Zionist Socialists and *Freiheit* [Freedom], *Hashomer HaLeumi* [the National Guard], *Betar* [Revisionist youth organization] and others were founded. Almost all of the young people were organized in rightist and leftist Zionist groups.

Naturally, the organizing was not easy. The older people looked at it as if they [the young organizers] were involved with heretical deeds. But the question of money was the most difficult of all. The young people did not work and they actually never had the money with which to rent even a small meeting hall. The first meetings actually took place in the open air.

Freiheit developed very quickly. New comrades joined every day; vigorous cultural activity was carried out. The young people avidly devoured the daily and weekly newspapers such as *Befreiung* [*Liberation*], *Arbeter–Shtime* [*Worker's Voice*] and *Yugnt Freiheit* [*Young Freedom*], the monthly journal, as well as *HaHalutz* [*The Pioneer*], the Hebrew newspaper.

The organization *Freint far Eretz–Yisrael* [Friends of *Eretz–Yisrael*] also was created the same year. This was support for *Kapai* [*Kupat Poalei Eretz–Yisrael* – Palestine Workers' Fund].

Freiheit was divided into three groups: twice a week, social and timely political problems [were discussed].

[Column 382]

A choir and a dramatic circle and a group for sports exercise were created. During the summer, exercise took place in the Czyzewo or Sutker Woods and on the ice during the winter. In addition, *Freiheit* created a group of scouts. Children aged 10 to 14 were accepted there.

A strong revival brought close contact by *Freiheit* with the *Freiheit* groups in the surrounding nearby and distant shtetlekh [towns], such as Zambrów, Ciechanowiec, Zaromb [Zaręby] and even with Ostrowa.

Freiheit

[Column 381]

A group of *Poalei–Zion* [Workers of Zion] comrades

We were most strongly connected to the Zaromber comrades who later, during the Holocaust, also shared the bitter fate of annihilation and were united in one mass grave in Szulbacz.

The second *Freiheit* conference took place in Warsaw in 1931. Czyzewo sent three delegates to the conference. Czyzewo comrades also took part in the summer colonies in the village of Zani (near Zambrów) and the next year in the colony in the village of Szcakow (near Ciechanowiec). Many Czyzewer comrades also took part. It cost 20 *zlotes* for each comrade to spend a month in the colony and they collected *groshn* by *groshn* and even food items during the year to cover the expenses.

Freiheit Committee 1932
Leah Bursztajn, Malka Szejman, Dovid Malkarcz, Shayndl Kandel and Mordechai Frydman

[Column 383]

In 1932 a place for a *hakshore* [agricultural training settlement] was created in Czyzewo for *halutzim* [pioneers] and also *Oved* [Worker] for family members and that year a group of *halutzim* and their families actually emigrated to *Eretz-Yisrael*.

[Column 384]

The thirst for emigration with the help of certificates was very strong even among those who were waiting for the redemption and the coming of *Moshiakh* [the Redeemer], particularly after the anti–Semitism became wilder and more brutal in Poland.

[Column 383]

My Father's Agony and Ecstasy
When Organizing the Mizrakhi

by Matisyahu Prawda

Translated by Chana Pollack and Myra Mniewski

In my memory, Czyzewo remains a shtetl of hasidic *shtiblekh* (small prayer houses) and Zionist organizations. The youth were brought up with a life purpose, with ideas to campaign for a better tomorrow for the Jewish nation.

The youth organization, which after 1929 was extremely active, was not created with ease, because most of the Jews of Czyzewo were hasidim and simple religious folk, who held that one had to wait for the arrival of the Moshiach before emigrating to Eretz Yisrael. Yet, the Zionist cause was nonetheless being instilled in many young Jewish minds and partly amongst the older generation as well.

My father, Yekhiel Asher Prawda, from the Aleksander hasidic sect, was one of the first to create the religious Zionist party "Mizrakhi." By doing this he induced the wrath of the hasidim. Their anger was so strong that he was forced to stop praying in the Aleksander *shtibl*. This was harsh punishment for my father, similar to a *kheyrem* [being shunned]. Yet, all of this did not scare him away from his Zionist activism. With even greater fervor, he delved into the work of proponing the Zionist cause to religious youth.

[Column 384]

The greatest satisfaction of his work was his opponents' slow transformation into the Mizrakhi camp. He saw this as a manifestation of recognition and comprehension of the Zionist cause, which was the purpose of his life.

When it came to the *Sejm* [parliamentary elections], he was tirelessly active. On *shabes*, in the big *besmedresh*, before the Torah reading, he got up and delivered a sermon in which he attacked the Agudas Yisrael[1] for supporting Pilsudski's list # 1.

[Column 385]

He and the Zionist Berl Gorzalczany, a merchant, stubbornly fought the tendency of endorsing the government party.

The Rabbi held with the Agudas Yisrael, who also called upon the Czyzewo Jews to vote for the Pilsudiski slate. The Rabbi was against the idea of religious Jews going against the government. On that same *shabes*, someone reported to the police commissioner that my father spoke against the government.

In the midst of the heated fight, the commissioner entered the *besmedresh* searching for my father. The Jews standing near my father, threw a *talis* (prayer shawl) over him so the commissioner wouldn't find him.

Afterwards, he was forced to go into hiding for an entire week because the commissioner threatened him with severe punishment. We were very frightened then, knowing that the commissioner was a very strict and brutal man. Once, during a wild holiday celebration, he cut someone's hand off with his sword.

Four rows of young Mizrakhi members

First row: **Melcer, Rabinowicz, Raczkowski, 2 brothers, Chaim Grade, Wolmer, Grosbard, Belfer.**
2nd row: **Eybishets, Eliahu Gora, Eliahu Zylbersztajn, Yisrael Yitzchak Lew, Avrom Berl Lubelczyk, Bolender, Kitaj.**
3rd row: **Celniker, unknown, Bolender, Starkowski, Kitaj, Zysman.**
Last row: **Kahan, Malcman, Belfer, and a boy fun Staker shoemaker**

[Column 386]

The following week when his wrath calmed he ceased searching for my father, who again delved into his work of proponing Zionist ideology to young and old.

In 1933, the youth organization Hashomer Hadati was created in Czyzewo. In 1938, as a member of the Hashomer Hadati, I made *aliya* to Israel. The words of Zalman Belfer, "Hold a plowshare in one hand and a gun in the other; fight for your own country," accompanied me.

Translator's note:

1. Ultra Orthodox political party.

[Column 387]

Agudas Yisrael

by Gershon Gora

Translated by Gloria Berkenstat Freund

I think *Agudas Yisrael* [Union of Israel] was the first organization in Czyzewo because until its founding there were no communal organizations with as much of a scope as it later developed.

There were all kinds of Hasidic *shtiblekh* [small, one-room prayer houses] with the Gerer and Aleksanderer [Hasidim] at the head. In addition to the *Khevra Mishnius* [group that studies Talmudic commentaries], there also were communal groupings such as *Bikur Holim* [society for visiting the sick], *Gmiles Khesedim* [interest-free loan] funds and so on.

The young people were divided into two strata: the religious, who were concentrated with their parents at the various Hasidic *shtiblekh*, and those who were called "progressive." They were found under the influence of the wave of the Enlightenment, which also reached Czyzewo.

The original founding of *Agudas Yisrael* in our *shtetl* [town] took place during the time of the First World War when Poland was occupied by the Germans. The actual date of the founding of *Agudas Yisrael* in Poland was 1914 when the first conference took place in Katowice, but the actual organizing of the Orthodox Jews in Poland first took place in 1918-19.

[Column 388]

The two main organizers of *Agudas Yisrael* in Germany, Dr. Pinkhas Kahn and Dr. Karlbach, may his memory be a blessing, whose appearance created an animated stir among the religious masses, then came to Warsaw.

The central [office] of *Agudas Shlomi Emuni Yisrael* [Union of the Faithful in Israel] was then created in Warsaw. This change in name was made especially for Poland. This central [office] encompassed more than 600 cities and *shtetlekh* [towns] to which directives about the creation of divisions of the Orthodox organization, *Shlomi Emuni Yisrael*, were sent.

We can assert with complete certainty that our *shtetl* was one of the first to accept with great enthusiasm the proposal to found an organization of Orthodox Jews. Over a short time, the organization, *Shlomi Emuni Yisrael*, was an actual fact in Czyzewo.

During the later years members of this organization left who became leaders of the various Zionist, Mizrakhi and even leftist parties.

Belonging to the leadership and active workers of this organization of Orthodox Jews were:

[Column 389]

Yisrael Yona Raczkowski, Natanal (Saneh) Stuczynski, Motl-Chaim, Yisrael Yona's son-in-law, Shaul Hersh Blajwajs, Zebulun Grosbard, Avraham Szwarc, Berish Frydman and his son, Leibush.

Yehoshua Katliarek, Hershel Zylberman, Chaim-Leib Kazlowski belonged to the leaders of the young.[1]

Czyzewo in time became a stronghold of *Agudas Yisrael*. Every action that was undertaken by the central office of *Agudas Yisrael* in Warsaw had a warm echo in Czyzewo.

The most esteemed scholars in the *shtetl* were members of *Agudas Yisrael* and gave the organization importance and authority.

A group of *Tseiri Agudas Yisrael* [*Agudas Yisrael* Youth]

Among others: **Gershon Gora, Yehoshua Katliarek, Eli Velvel Kerdan, Akiva Stuczynski, Yeshai Winograd and Chaim the rabbi's son)**

[Column 390]

The first office of *Agudas Yisrael* was in [the home of] Natanal Stuczinski, a Gerer Hasid and wood merchant.

At that time Reb Shlomo Tsalka lived in Czyzewo. He was a son-in-law of Reb Yitzchak-Hersh, the *melamed* [religious school teacher]. [He] was short in stature with a long black beard and constant smile on his genteel face. He, in time, became the person at *Agudas* who was relied upon and busied himself with organizational work with much enthusiasm, not sparing any effort or energy for the growth of the organization.

Reb Yisrael-Yona Raczkowski and Reb Shaul Hersh Blajwajs were Gerer Hasidim. Almost all of the young people at the Gerer *shtibl* [small one-room synagogue] were members of *Agudas Yisrael*. Other *shtiblekh* and the house of prayer also were represented in the leadership of *Agudas Yisrael*.

The older young men such as Chaim-Boruch, the son of Shmuelka the tailor, Izak Krystal, Eliezer, the son of the bricklayer (today in Israel), both brothers, Yeshaya and Moshe, the *tsitsis* [fringed undergarment worn by pious men] makers were in the main ranks of the young.

The first activity of the *Agudas* in Czyzewo was the founding of Jewish educational institutions. This brought with it the first crisis in the structure of religious education of that time. All of the old *khederim* [primary religious schools] were liquidated and were replaced by a universal *Talmud-Torah* [primary school usually for poor boys] that carried the name *Yesodei-haTorah* [*The Foundations of the Torah*]. There were six grades there in which teaching was from the *alef-bet* [alphabet] to the *Gemara* [Talmud] with commentary.

The creation of *Yesodei-haTorah* was a great event in the *shtetl*. The new manner of teaching and education astounded everyone.

News about the *Beis-Yakov* schools [religious primary and secondary schools for girls], which had been founded in various cities and *shtetlekh* [towns], began to arrive in the *shtetl* at that time. The name of the founder, Mrs. Surah Schenirer, became well-known everywhere. This idea also received supporters in Czyzewo and the leader of *Agudas* wrote a request to Mrs. Surah Schenirer, who lived in Krakow, asking that she come to Czyzewo to organize the founding of a *Bais Yaakov* school.

[Column 391]

A group from *Tseiri Agudas Yisrael*
In the center: **Wisenrad, Gershon Gora, Yehoshua Katliarek**

Mrs. Surah Schenirer responded to this request and came to the *shtetl*. She stayed with Reb Natanal Stuczinski.

A meeting of women was called at which Surah Schenirer presented the idea and purpose of the *Beis-Yakov* schools. An organizing committee was created on the spot.

[Column 392]

The resolve and effort with which the activists on the committee worked must be underlined. In a short time, a female teacher named Troyba was brought to the *shtetl*.

A group of *Bais Yaakov* girls

[Column 393]

The first *Bais Yaakov* school was located in a rented location at Szmidisher Street. Later it moved into its own building.

This school brought warm life into the *shtetl*. Even *Mizrakhi* [religious Zionists] and Zionist parents sent their children here.

It opened new worlds for the religious girls. It widened their horizons in Jewish thought and Jewish knowledge, about which they then did not have any idea. The *Bais Yaakov* school brought the young Jewish girls to the sources of *Yidishkeit* [Jewish way of life], to *Tanakh* [Hebrew Bible], to the Jewish laws, to understand the essence of the Jewish prayers. The female teachers made an effort to insure that the meaning and the beauty of every word were absorbed into the children's hearts.

A group of girls from the *Bais-Yaakov* School

[Column 394]

The first teachers were: Troyba, Krawiec and Rotenberg (the last two live in Israel now). At the same time, the *Batya Farband* [association] was founded in our *shtetl* [town] to which the adult, female students belonged. The *Bais-Yaakov* teachers, who led the activities of the students in the association, always were at the head of the *Batya Farband*. Gatherings were arranged from time to time, which had a great success with the orthodox women in the *shtetl*. It is a fact that this movement was very beloved by all strata of the Jewish population.

[Column 395]

A group of *Bnos Agudas Yisrael* [girls division of *Tseiri Agudas Yisrael* – *Agudas Yisrael* Youth] with Miss Rotenberg in the center

The *Agudas* circle in the *shtetl* systematically widened. The adult generation created a strong youth organization, *Tseiri Agudas Yisrael*.

The activities of *Agudas* grew more lively and creative with each day. It began to publish an orthodox daily newspaper, *Der Yid* [*The Jew*], a monthly Hebrew journal, *Digleinu* [*Our Banner*], *Orthodokishe Yungt Bleter* [*Orthodox Youth Newspaper*] and *Beis-Yakov Zurnal* [*Bais-Yaakov Journal*] in Yiddish. The newspapers made the activities of *Agudas* in the *shtetl* more colorful, effervescent, infused with the religious idea and aroused and encouraged the fight for a religious, Jewish life.

* * *

The sad destruction of Polish Jewry arrived. Czyzewo, our *shtetl*, was entirely destroyed and the most beautiful and clean flower that was called *Agudas Yisrael* was erased in Czyzewo and along with it the heroic and romance of that effervescent time.

Translator's note:
1. The surname Kaliarek is spelled Katliarek below.

I Say Goodbye to the Shtetl
(On the day of my departure to Eretz-Yisrael)

by Gerszon Gora / Czyzewo

Translated by Gloria Berkenstat Freund

…And all went. In that gray dawn, everyone got up, sneaked on foot, step after step, with only one thought - to accompany the first emigrant sent out from the *shtetl* [town] to *Eretz-Yisrael*.

[Column 396]

Jews with great silver beards went who had soaked *Eretz-Yisrael* with their tears for dozens of years and were transformed into an eternal source of longing. Middle-aged Jews, preoccupied Jews, apprehensive Jews went whose every bite of bread was dunked in tears. Every day for them was a day to create the world. In the very early dawn, they also sneaked onto the highway that led to the train station with beating *Eretz-Yisrael* hearts, accompanying their first son, their first pioneer to *Eretz-Yisrael*. And the young went, stormed, those who had waited for such a long time with beaming faces in the moment, those who always had a very spirited ardor and fervor for *Eretz-Yisrael*, had to hide in the deepest recesses, not even being able to dream, to quiet their thirst, they had to watch how others who craved *Eretz-Yisrael* emigrated in groups, hordes. They also stood at the train station.

[Column 397]

All, all came along, giving their last respects, their fervent feelings, with the first [migration of the] swallow, with the first Orthodox emigrant who had the honor of going with the flag of the Torah in his hand to their deeply beloved *Eretz-Yisrael*.

And the train station had a new appearance. The first time in the *shtetl*, such solemnity, such a crowd. So the young celebrate, demonstrate and the older ones stand calmly, hiding their joy inside; everyone together clings to their "only one" from whom they need to separate within a few minutes.

And I confess in full that never, never would I have known that such a hidden thirst of the soul for *Eretz-Yisrael* had nested in all of the assembled escorts in the train station as I saw and felt in the last minutes before my parting from them, from my birthplace on the road to *Eretz-Yisrael*.

An old ancient Hasid, the most respected one in the *shtetl*, stood next to me. He pressed my hand at the last minute before my departure. However, he quietly whispered with his dried up lips and two streams of tears flowed from his mild eyes - his last parting words:

- Remember! *Eretz-Yisrael* is holiness; you have to accept the idea of becoming a worker in Palestine - remember, it should, God forbid, not be the opposite. "One who sins in the king's palace is not equal to one who sins from afar."

He immediately became quiet. However, he continued to firmly press my hand. And in the noise of the over-crowded train station I heard the beating of his heart. Here [also] stood near me a young man who for all his life had engaged in prayer, in Hasidism. He pressed my hand firmly and asked me like a child:

[Column 398]

- For the sake of God, you should mention me at all of the graves of the righteous, give *kvitlekh* [notes to Hasidic rebbes asking for Godly intervention] for me and give charity for me.

Thus they said goodbye to me one after the other, heart after heart, soul after soul and each one of them a flowing spring of love and longing. Joy bubbled in each heart that they had lived to send the first comrade from their *shtetl* to the Holy Land, to *Eretz-Yisrael*.

The chairman of the young men, who had gone through all of the birth pangs of the organization and had been able to see its intense blossoming and the joyful harvest, drew near to me. He also pressed my hand. He also said goodbye to me sincerely. He also had something to remind me and tell me:

- Remember! You are traveling to our holy land, to build, to create. Remember to build up the ruin of the Jewish spirit, to create more of a "paradise" there and "Vineyards of the Law," increase the ranks of the young and, mainly with self-sacrifice for our idea, to strengthen the faction of workers.

And the emotion in my heart bubbled up like an ocean.

These were the last minutes of my parting with such a warm incandescent environment. Now, I needed to become a community spokesman for my comrades, carry with me all of their requests and strivings, begin to fulfill my task, my mission as the first one from the entire *shtetl* who had the honor to emigrate.

[Column 399]

I am weighed down with feelings. All of the parting words of the best ones in the *shtetl* always swim in my memory. "Remember, *Eretz-Yisrael* is holiness; you have to accept the idea of becoming a worker…" "One who sins in the king's palace is not equal to one who sins from afar…" "With self sacrifice for our idea…"

I was overburdened; how difficult it was to leave all of the dozens, dozens of stormy hearts and alone, alone take their requests and fill them! How difficult it was to part with all of those who were warm, closest and in a minute leave them.

However, time does not know of sentiments. The large railroad clock struck the dawn hour:

Seven.

In minutes, the engine will pull you, [shoot] a slingshot for hundreds of miles.

Spontaneously, an echoing song tore out of everyone's throat.

[Column 400]

A dance.

Hand on shoulder with "Purify Our Hearts" ringing as in the most solemn days of the *shtetl*.

The train stopped for only two minutes.

One minute.

We were still dancing.

Tears immediately started to flow from dozens of eyes: that enthusiastic young Hasidic man cried; every old, grey Hasid cried. All of the escorts, young and old, cried and, there at the train-wagon Window, hot tears also trickled. Fathers, mothers and sons cried.

The train was already on its way. However, the last words of the old, grey Hasid still rang in my ears:

"Remember, *Eretz-Yisrael* is holiness; you have to accept the idea of becoming a worker."

Gerszon Gora
Czyzewo - Warsaw Adar 5694 [February or March 1934]

The First Buds of Communism

by Yitzchak Gora/Tel Aviv

Translated by Gloria Berkenstat Freund

This was at the end of 1918. At that time a change occurred in my life that marked the beginning of a new road: together with other Hasidic young men of the Gerer *shtibl* [one room synagogue], I joined the *Paolei-Zion* [Workers of Zion – a Marxist Zionist political party] that began to organize in Czyzewo a year before.

[Column 400]

In the leadership were then found: Dovid Jabka, Nisl Ratman (Rimacz), Itshe-Meir Kszeckower, Avraham-Hershel, the son of the furrier, who the Poles later shot because of the ostensible accusation that he had deserted from the front.

I was 16 when I was drawn into political activity for the first time. We rented a room for our premises from Yisroelik Milner for the *Paolei-Zion* organization where we were located for two whole years.

[Column 401]

Those years have materials to fill a many-paged volume. For me, as for dozens of other Hasidic young men, new worlds, new needs and new dreams were opened. The greatest dream was to travel to *Eretz-Yisrael*.

At the same time, we were fully aware of the need to personally arrange our own futures. I traveled to Warsaw where I found work in a chocolate factory. I did not have the chance to become a great craftsman, so the earnings were small and finally I let a cousin who wrote from *Eretz-Yisrael* convince me that this was a bad trade there and I succeeded in learning the building trade. I then threw myself into carpentry.

Forty years have passed since I traveled a long, difficult road. I have been in many countries, met thousands of people, lived through painful and joyful times. When I remember my past, my life, my work, I come to the painful conclusion that I have forgotten many important moments. It is as if an invisible power has covered everything with an impenetrable veil. However, the encounter with the communist leader Amsterdam has been preserved in my memory. He possessed a wonderful power to convince and transport the youth of that time who yearned for action to mutiny and revolt.

[Column 402]

It seemed that we were joining a new era – an era of active revolutionary struggle that would solve the Jewish problem in anti-Semitic Poland. There awoke in me the will to struggle for respect and the Jewish national rights of the Jewish people on one side and for the victory of socialism on the other.

I became a communist.

In the beginning of 1923 I traveled back to Czyzewo.

Dovid Jabka was then the only person with whom I spoke and I told him about my communist beliefs. Dovid Jabka was already an intelligent young man and understood that the worker needed to struggle for his interests. However, he did not want to give up his Zionist ideals to which all of the Czyzewo young clung.

I poured out everything I had heard, and I heard a lot from Amsterdam and from other leaders in the then communist movement. I described for him the great scope of the movement that would conquer the world and solve the Jewish question, just as it was being solved in the Soviet Union, where Jews were in the regime and all over, as equals.

This had the effect of captivating and intriguing him. The illegality, the daring impressed us and Dovid was persuaded and began to help me stir up others.

[Column 403]

The Jewish youth in Czyzewo then had an inclination to theorizing; they were open-minded in their ideological opinions and had a wide choice in setting off in the direction of Zionism and socialism. The Zionist organizations were splintered and, therefore, over the course of two months, it was easy for us to organize 120 young people and convince them about the truth of the communist idea.

We came with something new that resonated with the storms of the wider world and it showed that we understood them better than others. However, the conspiracy, the danger stirred up everyone, which gave us the halo of martyrs for a great thing.

I stayed in contact with Warsaw and Bialystok and received the illegal literature, appeals, brochures and circulars that were sent from the central committee of the party.

The 120 young people among whom also were found Hasidic young men and daughters from esteemed members of the middleclass were organized into 12 circles, secret, conspiratorial.

In the circles we would read the illegal brochures about the concentration of capital that accelerated our own death, about the tax system and the development of technology. The boys and girls understood very little of this, but in spite of this, they listened with anticipation and swallowed the words and concepts, which took root in their brains.

Moshe-Leib Blajwajs and Ahron Weter belonged then to the lively activists. However, there was a shortage of leadership elements.

How We Celebrated the First of May

A great demonstration took place earlier in the forest. The mood was earnest, a holiday [mood]. There were discussions and songs were sung. It was our first celebration of the 1st of May.

[Column 404]

Later, one by one, we went to the market, moved among the peasant wagons and unnoticed laid the cigarette paper appeals and brochures among the sacks. The peasants could not understand very much from those papers. Yet, among them there were those who were impressed by the rise of the young in the struggle against injustice. They also were embittered by poverty and this was expressed through us. It grew. However, later others came and made use of the same bitterness against us, against the Jews in the *shtetl*. The result was that later the famous pogrom came.

I sobered up a lot earlier. I was infected by Trotskyism, felt Stalin's pettiness and saw signs of anti-Semitism in the party. At a meeting in the forest I gave a speech in which I said that I was disconnecting myself from a communist movement that lets itself be led by Stalin. I urged sympathy for Trotsky.

Many applauded when I finished speaking. Sixty young men stood up and announced that they were going with me.

At that time, I did not let myself be carried away. The disappointments cooled my revolutionary enthusiasm and, therefore, I did not rush to run carelessly on the ice of the illegal work. I looked for the goal and saw that it was still far away and, meanwhile, it was being used by charlatans. In my respect for the honest revolutionaries, however, I saw how they were tools in the hands of those who aspired to power and a career.

[Column 405]

The other communists who went with me also understood it this way and little by little sobered up until we finally became active members of the *halutz* [pioneers preparing for emigration to *Eretz-Yisrael*] movement in all its shades, with more effort and faith that here we would complete our down payment. We saw everything more clearly, what was happening in the world, looked at the Jewish wounds and felt the new responsibility for our people.

[Column 406]

Later, the sobered up communists gave a great deal of youthful energy and youthful fervor to various Zionist organizations.

Communists

by Dov Gorzalczany

Translated by Gloria Berkenstat Freund

No one remains among us of the former communists in Czyzewo who could feel able to write the history of this movement in our *shtetl* [town]. Although we struggled against this movement and many of us suffered physically at the hands of the communists when the Soviet regime arrived, which did not cease persecuting every active Zionist, we will not close our eyes in this yizkor book [memorial book] to the communist activity among the young Jews in Czyzewo. We will describe with great objectivity everything we can extract from memory about every corner of communal life in our *shtetl*.

The reverberation from the October Revolution in Russia also reached the young in our *shtetl*. It was the time of *sturm un drang* [storm and drive or stress] and it also found several intelligent boys and girls in Czyzewo who took the new belief in the redemption of humanity and took upon themselves the mission of creating an organizational framework for their revolutionary activity. They saw redemption of the Jewish problem in the ascending communist idea. In my memory has remained as the most active communist workers the names:

[Column 406]

Dovid Jabka, Yitzchak Gora, Blejwajz, Wisznia and Rivka Prawda.

Their entire work consisted of meeting in secret circles of the young and teaching them the principles of historical materialism, the doctrine of Marxist–Leninism. We did not know who the secretary was. However, we heard about presentations and lectures on political themes, which they organized. Our discussions with them would extend until late at night.

[Column 407]

We also knew that they collected money on behalf of the illegal International Red Aid Fund, which helped the victims of the reactionary Polish regime.

There were times when the activities of the communists were really felt. The number of their followers grew and they did everything to infiltrate the apolitical Jewish youth organizations, the *Folks–Bibliotek* [People's Library], the dramatic circle. They arrived with much fervor and fanaticism. True, they spoke a great deal about the ideals of equality and brotherhood, about love of the oppressed person and the fight for his liberation. But more than anything, their spirits flared up when it came to the question of *Eretz–Yisrael* and Zionism, to the problems of Jewish tradition and the Hebrew language. The communists saw in all of this the manifestation of dark reaction and capitalism. Everything that was national was backward for them and led to dulling the minds of the Jewish masses and drew them away from the struggle against the capitalist enemy.

Thanks to this enemy, in 1925–6 the communists precipitated the crushing of the Jewish *Folks–Bibliotek*, which had been created with so much effort in Czyzewo and was the only progressive cultural institution in the *shtetl*.

The Jewish *Folks–Bibliotek* was a thoroughly progressive institution. Young people from every political organization benefitted from it and not only the Jewish ones, but also the Christian population began to come there to read books and to borrow them to take home.

[Column 408]

The red flag was hung in Czyzewo for the first time in 1926.

The entire *shtetl* became agitated on a beautiful morning. A red flag was seen fluttering on a telegraph pole and everyone knew that this was the work of the communists. However, until today, no one knows if this was done by Czyzewo communists or special emissaries from somewhere else who had been designated [to do so] by the central committee.

Great turmoil arose among the regime publications in the *shtetl*. This little piece of red linen had simply been brought out by the people just as if they had carried out a giant conspiracy in secrecy.

A series of arrests began that underlined even more the panic of the police. The guilty and the innocent who had never had any connection to the communists were arrested. Among those arrested was Motl Szczupakiewicz, who was quickly freed "because of lack of proof"…

On the contrary, Jabka, Gora, Blajwajz, and Rivka Prawda remained in jail for many years.

The hanging of the red flag and the chain of arrests actually were transformed into a great event in the *shtetl*. It was talked about for a long time in all houses. It also was said that the entire story of the flag smelled like a provocation; there was a provocateur in the ranks of the party who provided secrets to the police and did things that were instigated by the Polish secret police.

[Column 409]

In 1927 an all encompassing communist trial took place in Lomza that echoed through the entire nation and very strongly in the nearby *shtetlekh* [towns], among which was Czyzewo. This brought new discussions.

At that time Yitzchak Gora, who had broken with the Communist Party before the incident with the red flag, was freed and began to move closer to the Socialist–Zionists.

Jabka, Blajwajs and Prawda were sentenced to long years in prison. Several years passed until their appeals took place, which freed them after serving a shortened sentence.

Dovid Jabka left jail a sick person with severe stomach problems and could not arrange any work for himself. He also could not find his place in the community because his closest comrades already had left the *shtetl*, some to *Eretz–Yisrael*, some to Argentina. Despondent and resigned [to his fate], he committed suicide.

Dovid Jabka was an interesting person; he possessed a deep analytic sense and stubborn belief in justice, in man. He read a great deal and studied and was prepared to sacrifice for his ideals.

Yitzchak Gora has lived among us in Israel and is active in our *landsmanschaft* [organization of people from the same town] and is beloved by everyone who comes in contact with him.

Blajwajs lives in Argentina, isolated from the Czyzewo *landsleit* [people from the same town], and we do not know if he still has the same beliefs he had or if he has sobered up from his young inebriation.

[Column 410]

Rivka Prawda, who [found] disappointment in the ideals in which she had so strongly believed, died with the thousands of Czyzewo Jews. She possessed a great deal of enthusiasm for the fight to which she gave herself with the entire fervor of her exalted soul. She believed straight forwardly in the illusion of communist freedom, even at the time when the staged trials against the leaders of the Russian Revolution took place in Moscow. She fervidly defended the Moscow line. Her naïve belief in Stalin had in her the piety of her grandfather. In addition, she was smart and intelligent enough to find the logically strong arguments with which she defended the zig–zagging ways of Soviet communism during discussions which were carried out among the young in the *shtetl*. She had in herself the way of a romantically ennobled figure.

Another but tragic fate remained for Mr. Wisznia, who had traveled to America before the war. He had traveled to his girlfriend, but he became a young widower and remained so lonely that to this day he lives separated from his former *landsleit* [people from the same town].

A number of other communists from Czyzewo emigrated to Argentina and Uruguay where they remain today. All of our attempts to contact them have not succeeded. We do not know the reason for the embittered separation: are they embittered because of the disappearance of their dream of a free community without difference between people and nations?

[Column 411]

A teacher named Klar lived in Czyzewo for a time. He came from the Galiciander *shtetl* of Zaleszcziki [Zalishchyky, Ukraine] and he taught in the Czyzewo *Folks–Shul* [public school] until the [Second World] war. He was a fanatical communist.

In October 1939, when the Soviet Army occupied Czyzewo, this Klar was a frequent visitor of the Russian commissar and worked with the *NKVD* [*Narodnyi Komissariat Vnutrennikh Del* – People's Commissariat for Internal Affairs] to turn over into their hands all of their political opponents, among whom were people who were his close friends. His stubborn cruelty, his hypocrisy evoked a horrible disgust. He betrayed the Jews with whom he had spent long hours in conversation, eating at their *Shabbos* [Sabbath] table and at holiday meals.

After the Hitlerists marched in, he was one of their first victims.

Such behavior characterized several other communists in our *shtetl*, in contrast with honest communists, such as Rivka Prawda, her husband, Binyamin Plocker, and so on, who, immediately upon meeting the complicated dream face to face, saw the great lie and were deeply shocked, not wanting to discount their actions, but remained standing from afar.

[Column 412]

During the same frightening time, others, those narrow–minded communists, undertook becoming the leaders of the burned and destroyed *shtetl*. They wanted to make a career at the expense of their early political opponents. They frolicked in a wild devil's dance, denounced and sentenced the best people to jail and exile.

At the same time, Rivka Prawda and her husband, Binyamin Plocker, and other former honest communists helped; they warned everyone they knew that there was a threat of arrest. They risked their own lives; they thus remained honest defenders of the free person until they perished with all of the Jews of Czyzewo.

Bundists

by Dov Gorzalczany

Translated by Gloria Berkenstat Freund

The great majority of the young Jews in Czyzewo, were permeated with the ideals of Zion and Jewish revival in *Eretz-Yisrael*. They did not see any future for themselves living their lives in the land where they were born, not in their home cities, not in the nearer and more distant cities and *shtetlekh* [towns], where need would often drive them away. Therefore, the ideals of both the Bund and of the communists did not have any wide reverberation among the Jewish young in Czyzewo, who expressed their strivings to *Shives Tsion* [return of the Jews to Zion] in all kinds of organizations.

[Column 412]

Yet there were several young people in the shtetl who considered themselves Bundists. They were readers of the Bundist *Folks–Zeitung* [People's Newspaper], which was published in Warsaw. The reading of the *Folks–Zeitung* actually was the main sign according to which one was considered a Bundist.

[Column 413]

It was not always a certain sign, because there were also communists who would rather have read a Bundist newspaper than a Zionist one, because according to their interpretation, it [the Bundist newspaper] represented the interests of the working class.

Socialist ideas invaded Czyzewo during the years 1904–5. In contrast with the large cities and the enthusiasm for [the ideas in the cities], it was clearly theoretical, with a naïve, simple provinciality. It could not be a question of any broadly led fight and awakened class–consciousness because the differences between the artisans and the employers were negligible. Both, equally, worked very hard for a livelihood.

Yet the revolutionary winds, which blew across the cities and countries under the former tsarist rule, also left traces in our *shtetl*.

The young ones who believed in the revolution were idealists. Among them were found middle class boys and girls. Individual *Beis–Medrash* [house of study] young men and students were drawn in.

They came together in secret, organized illegal gatherings and discussed the principles of social democracy. The gatherings took place in the forest where guards stood, who protected against intrusions by the gendarmes. They sang revolutionary songs and spoke about great strikes and giant demonstrations that were taking place in the wide world in the struggle "against tsarism and his rotten, despotic government."

[Column 414]

Contact with the centers of revolutionary activity was very weak in Czyzewo and did not find any expression in daily life. Therefore, revolutionary enthusiasm was quickly extinguished.

There were those who emigrated to America and remained socialists their entire lives, despite the fact that they became rich from the exploitation of their workers. However, this did not hinder their continued membership in the Bund and their speaking about social justice and brotherhood.

Sympathizers of the Bund also remained in Czyzewo, but they were not organized, they did not carry on any political or cultural activity, even during the times when the Bund was legal. No one understood what its beliefs were; it appeared that their only purpose consisted of hatred of Zionism and intolerance of the Hebrew language, to which the Czyzewo young people showed a great deal of love.

During my childhood years I heard that Shmuel Rozenberg (the football player) was a Bundist and during the First World War created a cooperative store which existed for a time on Nurer Street in the house of Chaim Shmuel, the ritual slaughterer.

Fejwel Zigelbaun also was considered a Bundist for a time, but he later joined the League for Working *Eretz–Yisrael*. Angry tongues in the shtetl saw in this step a calculation to become a *parnes* [elected head of the community] at the kehile [organized Jewish community]. He actually did become one.

[Column 415]

Shmuel Rozenberg, who went from being a Bundist to a sympathizer of *Agudas Yisrael* [Union of Israel – ultra Orthodox religious party], went further. On the other hand, his career consisted only in that he became the *gabbai* [assistant to the rabbi] at a house of prayer.

Another active Bundist from Czyzewo emigrated to *Eretz–Yisrael* and lives today in Jerusalem as a very pious Jew. He belonged to the very extreme Orthodox who verged on [being] *Neturei Karta* [Aramaic term, Guardians of the City – an Orthodox Jewish sect that rejects Zionism]. Did his ideological transformation come through a type of ideological struggle by a repentant sinner? What were the reasons that persuaded him to break with his past and from being an atheist to become a fervid believer in Providence? This is not known; every attempt to communicate with him has been met with his categorical refusal. He lives separated and does not want to talk with anyone about those romantic times.

[Column 416]

A group of *Tseiri Agudas Yisrael* [*Agudas Yisrael*] Youth

1st row: **Yisrael Yitzchak Celniker, Eli Velvel Berdan, Nuska Szejman, Moshele Zylbersztajn and Moshele Jablonka**
2nd row from the right: **Yeshayu Winograd, Berl Jablonka, Ahron Melcer, Gershon Gora and Ahron Jablonka**

[Column 420]

Theater

The First Flash of the Yiddish Theater in Czyzewo

by Dov Brukarz

Translated by Gloria Berkenstat Freund

What is meant by the concept of Yiddish theater in Czyzewo? Competition from a professional collective, actors and directors? God forbid! The song that caressed the ears, sneaked into the heart, woke a sorrowful feeling and the song that echoed cheerfully, lively and happily with hundreds of voices in the room, carried from mouth to mouth. And the plays? Did they intend to create a new style of dramaturgy in Czyzewo? No one then thought of this. There were intimate figures, rooted in the depth of the soul of the people who always yearned for a simple, healthy entertainment and loved to ridicule the ridiculous person, *Kuni Lemls* and *Binkes-Pinkes* and together all drew their inspiration from the old Jewish *Purim-shpiler* [Purim actors], who during the dark days of the bleak persecutions and vexations, entertained the Jew in the ghetto.[1]

This was also the strength with which we conquered all difficulties in putting together our theater collective. This also was the secret of their success. The fullest harmony always reigned between the Czyzewo audience and the amateur theater collective.

[Column 421]

A theatrical performance was carried out for the first time at the beginning of 1916, under the German occupation.

A young man, Goldsztajn, a photographer from Ostrow (the only photographer in the *shtetl*) was staying in Czyzewo. He began to organize a dramatic section.

A commission of 10 people was chosen at one of the library meetings:

[Column 422]

Goldsztajn, Ungresbard, Plocker, Badaczker, Szerszyn, Mordechai Brukarz, Moshel Lubelczyk, Shalom Czelianogora. All of these are no longer among the living and, *yibodl lekhaim*,[2] Berl Brukarz and Avraham-Josef Ritholc, who became the director.

Avraham-Josef Ritholc undertook to put together an ensemble and lead the first performances: *Der Restauran* [*The Restaurant*], *Der Shadkhan* [*The Matchmaker*], *Beym Fotografist* [*At the Photographer*]. However, the question arose of a suitable hall. It was decided to make use of the train station for this purpose. No trains functioned then for civilians, only for the military. The large hall was not in use yet.

[Column 423]

It was discussed with the head of the train station who agreed without difficulty to make the building available for this purpose. He also placed boards for us for a stage. The first performance took place during Chanukah.

Before the start of the performance, a children's choir sang the German song, *Heil dir im Siegerkranz* [*Hail to Thee in Victor's Crown*]. After the three one-act plays, a dance and a gossip game, flying post [a relay race in which a letter is passed from person to person for delivery] took place.

Avraham Josef Ritholc directed all of the work. He adapted the music, put together an orchestra in which Simkha Litman's son, who is now in America, Moshel Litman's son, shot by the Poles, Itshe Lubelczyk, died in Syria, played fiddles. He himself adapted the melodies, created, directed and led the dances. In addition, he played a role in each one-act play.

[Column 424]

The initial members of the dramatic circle were: Hershel Baraczker, died in America, Moshel Lubelczyk, died in America, Shalom Grynberg, went missing after his arrest by the Russians, Shmulke Wengorz and Moshel Zysman, victims of German violence, Berl Brukarz and Dwashke Kanet, today Dvora Brukarz – both are in Israel, Starkowski Fishl, Chaya-Rivka Gromadzyn-Kirszenbojm, Nekha Glina-Zysman, all are in America today, in the orchestra.

The success of this evening was very great and we immediately began to prepare the performance, *Der Wilde Mentsch* [*The Wild Man*], for Purim. All of the income was designated for the *Maos Khitim* [society providing matzoh and other foods to the poor for Passover]. We baked matzohs in the bakeries of Dovid the *malamed* [religious school teacher] and Sura Ete's son Yisroelke for an entire week and sent them to poor families. We did the same with potatoes, wood and coal. Almost all of the young people in the *shtetl* helped with this work.

In time the drama circle was enlarged. Those who joined were: Belitshe Bolender, Sheva Surowitz, Esther Boran (perished in Poland), *yibodl lekhaim*, Hendl Glina-Ginsberg (today in Israel), Itsl Kirszenbojm (today in America) and others. During its existence, the dramatic circle performed the following plays: *Der Yidishe Harts* [*The Jewish Heart*], *Hertsele Meyukhes* [*Hertsele, the Man of Aristocratic Descent*, an operetta by Mojzesz Richter] and *Sura Sheyndl fun Yehupets* [*Sura Sheyndl from Yehupets*]. The income was donated to the Folks [People's] Library, which was enriched with hundreds of books.

From the right: **Moshel Lubelczyk, Shmulke Wengorz, Shalom Grynberg**

This lively activity continued until 1918 when the Poles took over the government. The *Hallerczyks* [followers of the anti-Semitic Polish General Josef Haller] arrived and the persecutions of the Jews began. Beards were cut, beatings, torture. Czyzewer young people came together in the Polish military. The war with the Bolsheviks began. In these conditions there could no longer be any talk about communal work.

[Column 425]

In 1922, this was several months after I was freed from military service, my wife's entire family and I, which then numbered nine people, left for Yisrael.

The Rubinowitz family, or as they were known, Meitshke Binyamin Sender's [family], also left with us for *Eretz-Yisrael*. These were the first pioneer families in Czyzewo.

Translator's notes:

1. A *Kuni Leml* is a fool. The name is derived from the name of a character in a play, *Shnei Kuni Leml – Two Kuni Lemls* – by Avraham Goldfaden.
2. May they be separated for life – said before or after mentioning a living person among those who are dead.

Days and Nights on the Magic Stage

by Simkha Gromadzyn/New York

Translated by Gloria Berkenstat Freund

I do not intend to cover everything that was done in the area of Yiddish theater in Czyzewo. I left for America at the end of 1925. Others will probably write about the later years.

The pioneer, Avraham Yosef Ritholc, the father of Yiddish theater in Czyzewo, and Berl Brukarz should tell about the rise of the Yiddish theater. He [Berl Brukarz] is perhaps the only one living today of those who took part in opening the Yiddish stage in Czyzewo in 1916. First near the train station, later in the storeroom of the firemen, which remained the Yiddish theater building until the end.

I will provide only some characteristics of the time when the theater was led by me.

Traveling Troupes

In the course of time, various traveling troupes came to the *shtetl* [town]. There were those that would integrate the local forces into their performances; others performed alone, with their own strengths.

[Column 426]

Two traveling troupes particularly remain in my memory. Meir Winder led one of them. Maks Pokoj [Pozkowski] led the other one. They produced operettas and dramas. The audience, particularly the young, went en masse to their performances.

I remember an episode:

Meir Winder's wife, who also performed in his troupe, was then already in the later months [of her pregnancy]. Returning home to the inn of Yitzchak Chaim, Yudel's son, after a performance in a cold, unheated room, she felt ill and they had to send for a midwife.

Very early in the morning, the entire *shtetl* knew that the actress Winder had given birth to a son at the inn of Yitzchak Chaim, Yudel's son, where a *bris* [ritual circumcision] took place on the eighth day.

Later, Winter was one of the most distinguished actors in the Warsaw Yiddish theater. He was warmly welcomed by the Yiddish press when he came to America in a guest role.

[Column 427]

Several words about the leader of the other local troupe, Maks Pokoj.

No wife traveled with him, but a bride, also an actor; we called her Miss Perlman the Soubrette [a female character in plays and operas, who is flirtatious]. She really was talented, pretty and sang with a touchingly sincere voice. She often did not eat enough in the great frost, in the unheated room.

All of these actors loved our *shtetl*. The enthusiastic young people also showed a love and sincere respect.

In 1920-1921, right after the Bolshevik invasion after a short pause, an amateur theater group organized itself in which I was very active and to which I gave a great deal of time and effort.

Among the best plays performed were:

Jakob Gordin's *Di Shkite* [*The Slaughter*] and *Khasie di Yesoyme* [*Khasie the Orphan*], Leon Kobrin's *Der Dorfs-Yung* [*The Village Youth*] and *Tsebrokhene Hertser* [*Broken Hearts*] by Lateiner, which actually was our first play.

We rehearsed it [our first play] the entire winter. We performed it for the first time on Purim. It was an enormous success. Many people had to leave because of a lack of seats. The firemen's barn was fully packed.

The performances were a success not only among the "common people" but also among the intelligentsia. After the performance Doctor Gelbojm went onto the stage and shook my hand, expressing his satisfaction with my direction and with the good acting by those taking part.

[Column 428]

The next *Shabbos* night we again presented the same performance, again with great success.

A short time later we produced *Di Shkite*. This time, it was directed by Meir Ribak. Immediately afterwards, we presented *Dem Fotografist* [*The Photographer*].

Meir and Yosef Moncarz and Yakov Jablonka, guests from America, came to one of the presentations. They sat, understandably, in the first row and applauded with great enthusiasm, saying aloud: "They are acting like true actors."

The *Dorfs-Yung* and *Khasie di Yesoyme* were directed by Avraham Yosef Ritholc. Taking part were:

Rochel Zajonc, Perl Perlmuter, Brayna Glina, Sura Mankuta, Shayna Zysman, Khantshe Gromadzyn, Yenta Baran, Liba Szerszyn, Chaya-Sura Kirszenbojm, Chawtsha Gromadzyn, Shmulke Janowski, Yehoshua Lepak, Simcha Gromadzyn, Yosef Wiszniak, Yitzchak Hersh Gora, Itsl Kirszenbojm, Yosl Cymes, Yakob Ciranke, Isser Litmans, Simcha Prawda, Mordechai Brukarz. Our make-up artists were: Avraham Yosef Ritholc and Hershel Moncarz. Leibel Akselrod was both cashier and bookkeeper.

Moshel Blajwajs is worth a separate description. He was the engine of the amateur dramatic group. There were no difficulties he could not vanquish. [He was] a dynamic type with a great deal of initiative. It often happened that someone in the amateur dramatic group did not come to a rehearsal. Moshel Blajwajs disregarded any frost, any darkness, any mud and ran to the member to track him down and bring him to the rehearsal.

[Column 429]

Mordechai Brukarz

His creative spirit encouraged us in our work.

He carried around a great plan that our troupe should go to the provinces as guest performers in the *shtetlekh*: Andrzejewo, Zaromb [Zaręby Koscielne], Nur and a whole series of others. His dedication to the amateur dramatic group was limitless.

Prompting was among the most difficult and responsible work in the amateur dramatic group. Mordechai Brukarz, the prompter, had to labor with each actor separately, at the rehearsals and on the stage, from behind the cabinet. He would nimbly help in every confused situation when something ceased to work for a minute because of this or that fault.

[Column 430]

Directing the first presentation, I gave the matter of [obtaining] props over to several members of the group and [listed] for them exactly how each act was to look. For the first act, which represented a hospital, it was necessary to have several small beds and clothing for a nurse. Another scene was to take place in a rich salon. There was no electric lighting yet in Czyzewo then. We had to create the impression of wealth through the presence of various objects. I myself had to wear an elegant tailcoat that I borrowed from Yudel the *badkhen* [wedding entertainer]. No one else in Czyzewo would have such clothing.

It occurred one evening that I walked into the theater with my pack of clothing, barely pushing through the thick rows of people who were waiting at the box office for tickets; armed policemen maintained order; firemen guarded against a fire. *Shtarke yungen* made sure that no one entered without a ticket. Then I was in the room; I asked that the curtain be opened and I wanted to see how the scene in the rich salon had been prepared. I became dejected. The table and the chairs, the short, small curtain on the window, the small wall lamps – everything was drenched in poverty.

There were still three hours until the start. We would not start earlier than 11 o'clock at night and the performance lasted until four o'clock in the morning. With Yosef's help (his name was Yosef-Aba. Jokers called him Abtshe and added Abtshe the cat), I succeeded in saving the situation. He immediately ran to the *Beis haMedresh* [house of study or prayer] and brought the extra bright oil lamp from there. Others left to bring six "Viennese" chairs, vases of flowers, beautiful, framed pictures on the walls. I ran home and took the drapes that my sister had washed and pressed in honor of Passover.

[Column 431]

Just that day my sister looked into the theater and probably immediately recognized the drapes. I trembled; I expected that she would attack me, shout, curse.

I was so surprised when my sister came on the stage after the performance and with a smile helped me take down the drapes. Everyone in the room laughed.

– A young person's idea…

It seems that the success of the performance had an effect on them.

The rehearsals would take place in the theater office. There was no lack of curious people who came to watch. Understand that such curiosity greatly interfered and we had to carry out a ban on strangers being present during the rehearsals; one of the members stood at the door and did not let anyone in.

It once happened that at a rehearsal of the *Shkite* they came saying that three members were standing in front of the entrance asking to be allowed to come in. This was: Shaya's daughter Perl with her friend and one stranger, who had just arrived from Mlawa. All three were beautiful girls and I did not have the heart to refuse them. After the performance, I even accompanied them home. The girls were enthusiastic about our performance, particularly the stranger from Mlawa, who was named Leah Zilberstzajn, and now she is my wife.

[Column 432]

The Road Becomes More Difficult

We prepared for Kobrin's *Dorfs-Yung* in a serious mood. We took to studying the roles with great seriousness. Everyone rewrote their role and tried to make it come out even better, more honest. The rehearsals proceeded with a great deal of fervor; there was help, a gesture was corrected, modulation of the voice. Little by little the atmosphere of a school began to be created, an intimate, but a serious one. Everyone came to learn that for which he had yearned.

Everyone in the group had their little bit of theater experience, but the types that we presented were true, folksy, authentic ones. We felt familiar with them. This helped us to give them form, the expression we wished.

The more rehearsals we had, the more complicated the matter of theater and the laws of acting became. Each day we understood even more the colossal difference between wanting to be an actor and the actual, real demands of the stage.

Therefore, we really worked, studied the text together, then the gestures, moving with our heads, with our eyes, with our eyebrows. Each performance was an experiment at which we learned. Everyone felt that something already had been achieved. But with each further performance the road became more difficult. Everyone placed greater demands on themselves.

[Column 433]

Simkha Prawda played the role of Khatse the preacher, the *muser zoger* [moralist] in *Dorfs-Yung*. He wanted to embody his role and whenever he had a free minute he used it to learn the mimicry, the gesticulation and the particular melody of a preacher.

Once he entered our oil manufacturing shop on a Friday market day, did not look around at anyone and again walked to the large room and closed the door behind him.

No one rushed. There were many customers and, truly, we had an open door. An hour later, when it was a little quieter, my father heard some sort of voice from the large room, the voice of a preacher who was giving an admonishing and heart-rending sermon. He slowly opened the door and saw Simkha, rocking and speaking to an empty room, entirely removed from the outside world. He did not see and did not hear what was going on around him.

My father called loudly to my mother:

– Chaya-Rayzl, come here, you will see a theater…

Simkha did not hear and continued to play his role.

Translator's note:

1. Literally, "strong youth" – a phrase that refers to strong, young men who would defend the Jewish population of a city or *shtetl* from any threats from the non-Jewish population. The *shtarke jungen* usually included butchers, because they were already "armed" with the knives of their trade.

The Third and Last Period of Yiddish Theater in Czyzewo

by Dov Gorzalczany

Translated by Gloria Berkenstat Freund

As has already been said, under the leadership of Avraham Yosef Ritholc at the beginning of 1916, a dramatic section was organized at the Yiddish *Folks* [People's] Library with the purpose of supporting the library with its earnings and a portion also would be used for social help.

Everything was paralyzed during the years of the Polish-Bolshevik War; there was no possibility to continue with any communal activity and until 1922, the majority of those most involved with the theater section and many leaders and activists at the library emigrated from Czyzewo. Among others were: Hershel Baraczker (died in America), Moshele Lubelczik (died in America), Alter Szerszyn (died in Israel), Yohanan Angres-Bard (perished in the ghetto) and, *eybodi lekhaim*,[1] Berl Brukarz (now in Israel), and Avraham Yosef Ritholc (in America).

[Column 434]

After the emigration of the founder, conductor and director of the Jewish theater in Czyzewo, Avraham Yosef Ritholc, the leadership of the music ensemble and dramatic circle was taken over by his student, Simkha Gromadzyn, who later also emigrated to America.

[Column 435]

Simkha left no students after him who could take over the leadership and it must be said in truth that because of his departure from the *shtetl* [town], the amateurs and the entire dramatic circle actually was orphaned because, in addition to Simkha, Mordechai Brukarz, Leibel Akselrod, Chana Glina, Nekha Zysman (Glina), Sura Mankuta (Berkowicz), Itsl Kirszenbojm, Chaya-Rivka Gromadzyn (Kirszenbojm), Shayna Baran, Shayna Zysman and Shifra Ritholc also emigrated.

The chaos became even greater when a political split began among the Czyzewo young people and in 1926, the library split – right and left. It was as, if in a way, both sides had nothing.

Column 436]

The main pillar that supported the library, where all of the modern young people in the *shtetl* were concentrated, was the income from the dramatic section and if it mainly ceased to exist, it was evident that everything fell, everything ended.

In 1927 the Zionist young people again organized the *Folks*-Library, as well as the dramatic circle that produced various Yiddish plays with their own strength and often with the help of foreign traveling troupes or directors.

The following people participated in the drama circle:

Avraham Cukrowicz, (now in Israel, Cur), Gedalia Surowicz (in Israel), Peshke Fenster (in America), Chuka Akselrod (in Honduras), Pesha Lepak (Markowski, in Israel), Chaya Sura Kirszenbojm (in Israel), Sheva Lubelczik (Gorzalczany, in Israel), Yehuda Mankuta (Brazil), Dovid Riba (in America), Shayna Riba.

Yohanan Angres-Bard
(Perished in the Warsaw Ghetto)

Alter Szerszyn
(Died in Israel)

[Column 437]

Yechiel Ahron Serka, Dovid Moncarz perished, may God avenge their blood. The plays that they presented were:

Karbin's *Der Dorfs-Yung* [*The Village Youth*], *Der Rumenisher Khasane* [*The Romanian Wedding*], *Mit Fremde Hilf* [*With Foreign Help*], *Der Karger* [*The MIsser*] by Moliere, *Vi Zenen Meine Kinder?* [*Where Are My Children?*] *Dos Groyse Gevins* [*The Lottery*] by Shalom Aleichem, *Kaptsnzon et Hungerman* [*Pauper's Son and Hungry Man* by Avraham Goldfaden, also known as *Di Kaprizne Kale-Moyd – The Capricious Bride*] and so on.

[Column 438]

From time to time, the older amateurs, Shmuelka Wengorz, Shalom Grynberg took part in the presentations; both are no longer here.

In the course of time, new strength replaced those participants who emigrated.

On the 1st of September 1939 everything came to an end…

Translator's note:

1. *Eybodil lekhaim* is a traditional phrase meaning "may they be separated for life" – it is used to separate the names of the dead and the living when they appear in the same sentence.

Our Drama Circle

From right to left, standing: **Dovid Moncarz, Leibeleides, Sheva Lubelczik, Dov Gorzalczany, Sura Kirszenbojm, Gedalia Surowicz, Pesha Lepak, Yakov Gromadzyn.** Sitting: **Moncarz, Ceranka, Gora, Cukrowicz, Chana Gorzalczany, the director Chana Akselrad and Mirka Riba** In the second row, sitting: **Binyamin Plocker, Rivka Gromadzyn, Berl Cukrowicz and Shayna Riba**

[Column 437]

The Library – The Center of Cultural Life

by Dov Gorzalczany

Translated by Gloria Berkenstat Freund

The beginning. The reader will find the history of the founding of the library in Czyzewo in the memoir written by Dov Brukarz. Looking back, my memories reach only to the year 1925.

[Column 438]

After wandering through various premises, the Jewish library finally came to rest in the house of the Szczupakiewicz brothers. This house was located on the train road almost outside of the city. There, on Friday nights, the kerosene lamp could be extinguished without fear and there also could be help from a *Shabbos-goy* [a non-Jew who performs the tasks forbidden to Jews on the Sabbath].

[Column 439]

In this premises, I began to take my first steps into the modern world.

The library in Czyzewo, just as in many *shtetlekh* [towns] in the larger Polish provinces, served not only as an institution to receive a book and to exchange a book that had been read; it also served as a reading room, as a meeting place for the young, a place for readings, conversations, theater rehearsals, a communal club. This was a substitute in miniature for all kinds of communal, modern places and institutions.

The library room was open all seven evenings of the week from the early evening hours until 11-12 at night. Books could be exchanged three times a week. The other evenings were spent reading newspapers and other periodicals, playing chess and checkers.

The Friday nights and *Shabbos* nights were for various so-called cultural undertakings, such as readings, evening courses, judgments of books, and so on.

The library was supported by the weekly member dues, by the income from readings and by theater presentations that the dramatic circle gave several times a year.

All work, both office and administrative, was done voluntarily by the managing committee members, so that the expenses consisted of rent, lights, heat and small office expenses.

[Column 440]

Newly published books were always purchased with the money remaining after covering all of the expenses. In 1925, the treasure of books numbered 800 copies.

The number of members and readers did not exceed 120.

In addition to all of the concerns and tasks was the problem of "authorization" [because] a public institution at that time in Poland needed to have the permission of the regime. Many difficulties and great expenditures were connected with obtaining this for an independent local institution, so the organization had the idea of creating a division of the Zionist organization.

Such an institution, which was a political organization, could carry on unlimited cultural activities. The library actually was called the Library at the Zionist Organization in Czyzewo.

There being no other choice, all of those who were leftists and opponents of Zion agreed to this legal status. Some were members with active or passive voting rights and the majority consisted of readers. The difference between a reader and a member was only that one [a member] could vote and be elected to the managing committee and the other [a reader] could not. No one ever had their right abridged to read and exchange as many books as they wished abridged.

In 1925 the central office of the Zionist organization in Warsaw increased its activity and sent emissaries to the provinces for an inspection.

That was a [Zionist] Congress year. They were interested in increasing the memberships in the Zionist movement.

[Column 441]

Therefore, such a delegate came to the *shtetl* and turned to the managing committee and asked for a meeting to be called where he would speak to the comrades about memberships in the Zionist organization.

An active comrade from the far left, Comrade Jabka, was then a member of the library managing committee. Naturally, he was against calling such a meeting in the library premises. They tried to persuade him. It was a timely issue; the delegate was leaving in the morning and memberships were increasing in any case. Whoever did not want to come to the meeting did not have to; it was a voluntary matter, nothing more. It would be an evening of "distain for Torah."

However, nothing succeeded. They could not persuade him and the antagonism began.

The meeting took place. The delegate left and it appeared as if everything would return to normal, but the opponents, whose blind hatred to everything that smelled of Zionism was so stubborn, did not think so and they did not give up the further fight.

On a beautiful morning it was learned that the library had been robbed. All of the books were taken; only those that could not be carried were left. Even the tables and chairs were taken. No search was successful, police and not police; the library ceased to exist.

A transition period passed. The best and oldest comrades emigrated during the years 1924-26. Among them: Leibel Akselrod, chairman of the managing committee (today in America), Shmulke Janowski, secretary (today in Uruguay), Simkha Gromadzyn (today in America), Kirszenbojm and others. Mordechai Brukarz, of blessed memory, also emigrated. Only the young ones with little experience remained. Therefore, it took two years until a new library began to sprout.

[Column 442]

A founders meeting for the organization of a new library was called on a *Shabbos* during the winter months of 1926.

The Messrs Meir Leibel Zysman (today in Mexico), Chava Akselrod (today in Honduras), Yitzchak Hersh Gora, Avraham Cur (Cukrowicz), Gedalya Surowicz, the writer of these line (all in Israel), Shayna Riba, may God avenge her blood, were the organizers.

About 50 young people took part in the managing committee. It was decided to found a library; the legal name of the institution was "A Division of the *Tarbut*[11] Central Committee in Warsaw."

A self-taxation was carried out and a fundraising collection. We rented premises from Nechemia Perlsztain. In the mean time, the few books saved from the thief in 1925, brought by the readers, served as a foundation.

These were young people who came to us from the farthest left.

And the activities of reading and exchanging books, literary talks and events connected with them began again. Later, the library moved to a larger premises on the first floor of Alka the *shusterke* [either a female shoemaker or wife of a shoemaker].

Groups of opponents again were created. This time, from the far right, a group of Revisionists. The *Betar* [Revisionist Zionist youth movement] young people began to revolt. However, the managing committee strengthened itself and overcame the new revolt.

[Column 443]

At that time, this was during the years 1930-33, the young, particularly in the national camp, became strong members of the proletariat. A new power, the League for Working *Eretz-Yisrael*, arose then.

The young leaders of this movement saw the library as a bit of competition. They made attempts at taking control of the library managing committee and thought perhaps of cooperation with the party.

A bit of friction took place that damaged the dramatic circle and as a result decreased the income for the library.

The splits also led to a decrease of the level of the theater repertoire and of the technical and artistic organization of the performances.

Almost every political movement created its own dramatic circle; each organized theater performances just for practical reasons (income). So the level [of the performances] fell, as has been mentioned, particularly after the emigration of a number of comrades.

However, despite all of the difficulties the library had, it existed and developed. Those who carried the responsibility for the existence of the institution, remember well the discord of the year 1925.

The number of Yiddish, Polish and a small number of Hebrew books slowly grew and in 1929 it reached 1,500 copies.

[Column 444]

Although the institution was purely Jewish, the doors also were open for the Christian population. During the last years before the [Second World] war, Christian readers began to come in. Almost the entire intelligentsia in the *shtetl* borrowed books from us and were official readers [paying] monthly dues.

The library bought a large radio apparatus (almost the only one in the *shtetl*) when electricity came to the *shtetl* (only at night) through the Messrs. Lepak and Szczupakiewicz. Every evening, when the electrical power began to function, the radio apparatus began to increase the interest of visitors.

In May 1939, during the well-known speech of reply by the Polish Foreign Minister, *Pulkownik* [Colonel Josef] Beck, may his name be cursed, the electricity gave a special power to this broadcast and the library premises was packed with people from every strata and class. Jews with beards, Hasidim, for whom this was the first visit to the premises, came to hear the speech on the radio.

The entire street was packed, like at the greatest event and we placed the radio apparatus near the window so those who could not come inside could also hear.

The library activists then received their satisfaction in official recognition from the *shtetl* that their work was important. The older generation realized that it was not worthwhile to carry on a conflict and go against the storm. But…

On the 6th of September 1939, the library house along with a third of the *shtetl* disappeared in the fire of the Hitlerist incendiary bombs and the most important institution, which had so helped the spiritual development of the young in Czyzewo and had so much promise for the future, had its existence ended forever.

[Column 445]

At this opportunity, may we remember the names of the young people, just child community workers, who are no longer alive and who voluntarily gave so much energy and devotion to the library:

[Column 446]

Shayna Riba, Dovid Moncarz, Kirszenbojm and Rotman.

Translator's note:

1. The *Tarbut* schools were secular Zionist Hebrew language schools that prepared their students for life in Palestine.

[Column 445]

We Build a Beis Am[1]

Translated by Gloria Berkenstat Freund

The Building Committee:

Moshe Blajwajz – Canada, Motl Szczupakiewicz – America, Yisrael Wengorz – Argentina, Dov Gorzalczany – Yisrael.

Yehoshua Lepak, Noakh Edelsztajn, Pinya Zysman, Yechiel Asher Prawda, the last one – all perished. May their blood be avenged!

It could not go further!

Komets alef o. Komets beys bo.[2] The teacher of the children, naturally only of the boys, was the jailer. (I do not know even now why my first teacher was called the jailer). Possibly, he once was a locksmith by trade and had no luck [as a locksmith] and became a teacher of the youngest students.

It also was impossible to accept as a fact that the "*kheder*" [religious primary school], where our future children would someday study Torah, would be a "kitchen" in which the boys absorbed the smells of the "meager cooked foods," as well as the abuses shouting and very often, also, curses, with which the "rebbe"[3] would treat his "*rebbitzin*" (his wife[4]).

In addition to the unsanitary conditions and their bad technical comforts, children sat on high chairs with their feet hanging in the air for the entire day and still other things.

[Column 446]

There was a group of young people, future fathers, who came together and decided to build a house for a modern *kheder*, a *Kheder Metukan*[5].

Finding an apartment was once the main problem for every modern institution. Various attempts already had been made to organize a modern *kheder*. Several fathers, such as the unforgettable Yechiel Asher Prawda, Shmuel Velvel Kandel and so on, brought a modern teacher, a certain Portnoy, to Czyzewo, who taught the children according to system of the *Kheder Metukan*.

However, a suitable place that would be appropriate for the conditions of a modern *kheder* was not even available sometimes. They again had to use private apartments. So the above–mentioned eight friends also took to this problem.

First of all, at the first deliberations the comrades taxed themselves with sums of 100 *zlotes* and less, each according to their ability. A collection action was carried out among the fathers of the future students and they began the work [of building the *kheder*].

[Column 447]

The first question was: obtaining a spot on which to be able to build. There could be no talk about buying a plot. In addition, there were no financial opportunities. The only way out was to obtain a spot from the *kehile*[6] as was appropriate for a communal institution.

There were enough spots that belonged to the *kehile*. The difficulty was only how to obtain the permission from the *kehile* managing committee. Of the eight *dozors* [members of the synagogue council], two were with us. This was Reb Yosl Boruch Lepak and Yechiel Asher Prawda, but this was not enough.

This was in the era when Reb Alter Wolmer, an Aleksander Hasid, was at the head of the *kehile*. The other one who represented the Aleksander Hasidim was Reb Zindel Lew. That the Gerer *dozors* would have any influence was unthinkable. We, therefore, had to find the means to neutralize the Aleksander [Hasidim]. This meant that they would be "*pareve*" [neutral] during the vote about giving a plot to build a Zionist *kheder*.

A number of members of the building committee were really very young people, but they belonged to the so–called "rich men," people who were prosperous in their businesses, activists in the merchants' union, city wholesalers and so on.

One of them was given the mission to go to Reb Zindel Lew and prevail upon him that if he did not agree with giving a plot, at least he would not be against it, would be neutral. It was clear to us that after Reb Zindel's agreement, the chairman, Reb Alter, would not be opposed. Reb Zindel stood higher in the Hasidic hierarchy of small prayer house chairmen.

[Column 448]

Our comrade applied all arguments and, finally, the strongest argument was:

That, finally, nothing would help you, nothing, if we did not get the plot in a good way, we would obtain the plot in a bad way and we would see that there would be impediments for our Hasidic fathers.

The answer given then by Reb Zindel Lew is still not clear to us today. He gave an incomprehensible rumble into his gray–black beard, his thick black eyebrows covered his lowered eyes and in no way could we know if he had smiled then or had looked angrily over the entire matter.

After this conversation with Reb Zindel, the group decided to start to build!

Comrade Motl Szczupakiewicz received the task of taking care of the plan, the community–certificate for building.

He took care of everything without any difficulty.

The plot that we had chosen for this purpose was on Nuder Road near the small well, right near the Striga [River].

The earth was very swampy there and in order to dry it out, we needed a great deal of *żwir* [gravel] (rocky sand). This was arranged by Comrade Kepak. The Sudker nobleman permitted us to take as much material as we needed from the Sudker gravel pits free of charge.

[Column 449]

A mobilization took place of "men and horses" and all of the committee members appeared armed with shovels in their hands on a bright morning right at sunrise and [worked] until close to noon and a giant gravel mountain grew on the swampy land.

The Kitaj brothers and Lepak provided their horses and wagons for us. The building began.

A wooden house with four rooms was built on this spot that could be transformed into two large rooms according to what was needed.

Later, not only the *Kheder Metukan*, led by Mr. Yitzchak Szliaski, Yankel Tencza and others, but the Zionist organization with all its small offices was also located there.

[Column 450]

The meetings and gatherings of *Keren–Kayemet*[7], *Keren–Hayesod* [United Yisrael Appeal], *Shkolim*[8], elections to the [Zionist] congresses, as well as a Zionist *minyon*[9], where prayers took place every *Shabbos*[10] and holiday and during the Days of Awe, took place here.

Every *Shabbos* before the reading of the Torah, members spoke there about the subjects of the day. Members of *Haoved HaZioni*[11] were concentrated here; the comrades would explain matters to the "ordinary people" with regard to *Eretz–Yisrael* and which had a connection with municipal work.

All of this blossomed, bloomed – until the 1st of September 1939.

Everything was destroyed!!!

Translator's notes:

1. Community Center
2. Children were taught the Hebrew alphabet using vocalizations of the letters. A *komets alef* has an "o" sound; the *komets beys* has a "bo" sound.
3. Hasidic rabbi, here used as an honorary title given to a teacher.
4. Rabbi's wife, here used as an honorary title given to the wife of a teacher.
5. Modern religious school
6. Organized Jewish community
7. Jewish National Fund
8. Membership dues collections for the Zionist organizations
9. 10 men required for prayer

10. Sabbath
11. The Zionist Worker

[Column 453-454]

Way of Life and Characters

An Ordinary Market Day

[Column 457-458]

Jewish *shtetlekh* in Poland

by Chaim Grade

Translated by Gloria Berkenstat Freund

Jewish *shtetlekh*[1] in Poland, were you only of straw and of moss
That the wind could carry you away without a trace?
My poor praise, my holy, ecstatic vigil,
Have you left only the church so that its peal would say *Kaddish*[2] for you?
The marketplace is full of traders and village wagons,
The fairs still clamor with cheerful bustling.
The village virgins kneel at the stones near Jesus.
As if they want to thank him for there no longer being any Jews.

Jewish *shtetlekh* in Poland, a *talis*[3] was woven in the heavens from your prayers,
But your moans caused a tear in the fabric of the quiet melodies;
You lived in a reflection of untold dreams,
As a reflection of day in a well at night
The sadness followed you like a shadow.
The thresholds of your houses hid themselves – demarcations;
You sold herring to the peasants… but the 10 Sinai commandments
Gave light to your shops.

Dreamy fathers, your stringy beards
Are now the autumn spider webs that hang in the air,
They hang like rusted harps at the river's edge in Babylonia…
On deformed willows on Polish earth.
We stopped in the *shtetl* Czyzewo. The vehicle reached a tavern.
The passengers hungrily, cheerfully besieged the table.
They took a drink of whiskey and their eyes sparkled with joy,
That there no longer were any bearded Jews at the market stands,
The market place is like a peasant's face sprinkled with gold freckles.

[Column 459-460]

And fleshy [female] peasants stand on Jewish thresholds.
A fall of flooding water leaves more signs,
Which were left here by our community.
Only I see the porches of the occupied houses –
A shadow with *peyes*[4] that shouts into a blowing storm.

Jewish *shtetlekh* in Poland, you shone in my heart and memory,
Just as the places in the Holy Land shone for me in the *Khumash*[5].
My childhood crossed my home river barefooted – and it became my Jordan.
Therefore, now the Western Wall is a ruin – my several walls.

Jewish *shtetlekh* in Poland, your wealth
Which your neighbors robbed – I have already refused.
I have mourned your death with burning tears

But I will constantly follow you, disappeared shadows, and ask
Why did you entrust your holiday to exile,
And Polish *shtetlekh* , like rich gems woven into the *keser*[6]
Of the Torah? Why, blinded by faith, did you build
The Temple of Hasidus[7] in opposition to the princely castles?
Why brothers, did you plant the orchard of wisdom
In the void, on squat, green roofs of *kloyzn*[8]
Why did you, Hasidim, dance ecstatically on gentile meadows –
And ask for the Divine Presence to house you here?

Here calm *soyfrim*[9] would write *mezuzus*[10] on parchment
With goose feathers and oak gall ink.
And we would place them on our doors – to protect us from being driven from this land.
The autumn wind roared in our music.
We twisted on the fields like a golden chain,
And towns and crosses on the road also wrapped in the dance circle;
We planted trees for our grandchildren,
As if the land had been our own –
But the neighbors decided: that they should repair the bridge over the river [with the wood from] the wooden synagogue,
And lay a sidewalk from the headstones.

The ancestors firmly established a stone synagogue.
The naked walls decorated with God's name, –
And for hundreds of years we preserved the seats
Of those leaders who led us here

[Column 461-462]

Lived in cellars. – But carved an oaken *omed*[11] in the small synagogue.
Clad in rags, but velvet and silk for the curtain for the Torah ark.
For generations warmed their bodies, which were without strength from crying, On cold mornings with the songs of *Tilim*[12]

I search the roads for the *talis* that I have woven
From *shtetl* stories, cemetery legends and work songs. If I would only find a piece of my torn *talis* –
Then I would weave it again.

I walk the roads of Poland. The winds murmur
Like groups of Hasidim who are traveling to their rebbe for *yom–tov*[13].
They sing and dance, they stride in front and back, their arms entwined
And push me forward to live.

Translator's notes

1. Towns
2. Memorial prayer for the dead.
3. Prayer shawl
4. Sidecurls
5. Five Books of Moses
6. Ornamental crown for the Torah scrolls
7. Hasidic philosophy

8. Small synagogue
9. Scribes
10. An ornamental box placed on a doorpost containing a parchment on which is written the *Shema Yisrael* – Hear O Israel – prayer
11. Synagogue lectern
12. *Psalms*
13. Religious holiday

[Column 461]

Our Guardians

by Ahron Jablonka

Translated by Gloria Berkenstat Freund

In quiet rest.
I hear their tremble –
Tortured, they float
And quietly whisper:
"We are your guard
We are your guardian"…

Wrapped in grey clouds,
They float – a community.
The sadness of the night in their hands
And they guard in deadly silence
The walk to the *Akedah* [1]
In the dark.
And Father Yitzchak cries
For the grandchildren
His dear loss.

[Columns 463-464]

They come from Szulbacz
And come to me.
I hear their murmur:
"The distance is far,
We come from afar to protect you
As the angel protected Yakov.
Our clothing is grey
Sewn from the clouds.
No one prepared shrouds for us,
We float around with the clouds
And become slaves to your trembling
And become your guard, your guardian."

Translator's note

1. The Binding of Yitzchak – Isaac – as a sacrifice.

[Column 465]

They Come and Demand Their Due

by Ahron Jablonka

Translated by Gloria Berkenstat Freund

And so night after night
They arrive.
In stillness I hear their pacing
In their hands, the frozen, suppressed sobs,
In their mouths, cold, dark teeth,
[They come] on Auschwitz trains.

They knock on the walls with burned hands,
Their clothes burn like *yahrzeit* candles.[1]
From the walls they come, dispersed by silence
In a heart that burns
And is not burned.
They come to remind [us] of the vow…

They sing their song of death
As a collective prayer:
Take our task
Take our song
And give it to your son.

[Columns 465-466]

We are the community from your *shtetl*.[2]
Your five brothers are with us.
And your mother
Does not extinguish your pain,
Let it be like a flame
That lights the frozen community.

Make a cloth for him,
The royal figure – *Mara de–atra*[3]
The *tzadek*[4] and genius –
Reb Shmuel Dovid Zabludower,
With hands spread.
Enveloped by his *talis*[5]
He brings to the synagogue his blessing for those praying.

Walking here are the Brainsker wiseman, Ben–Tzion,
Shaul–Hersh the apprehensive one, the sharp mind,
Avrahaml Szwarc, the community worker and philanthropist.
The community comes and like a powerful intercessor
Burns the names on the stars with a burning fire.
They come to demand of us,
They come to remind [us]
From world to world – our cries are heard.
We search for the calm in our hearts.
[It] cools our fire, the day–long fire,

So we will not forget,
So we will not forget.

See our body; it has no grave.
It is naked and night has not welcomed
Each of our limbs into the bosom of the earth,
So we have now come here to you.
Take a shovel of earth of memories and guard [them].
In your heart dig a grave, you will cover it yourself.
A community of fathers and children arrives
Liberated for an eternity from knives and butchers.
The burned community stands at your window
Tortured in life, defiled at death.
Take your *talis* and spread it over everyone
On your babies and young brides.

[Columns 467-468]

How can a person die who is already dead?
How then can a person live who has no life?
They come and carry death like a hump,
That the murderer gave them in agony,
The martyrs of Czyzewo, of Zaromb and Sambor.
They come to me and demand a grave,
And I kneel in reverence in *khtsos*[4] at the *shtender*[7]
And breathe with them with my every limb,
Until the morning begins to dawn
And they will leave for the land of forgetting,
And I will roar like a wounded lion
And feel the pain in my sleeping and eating…

Translator's notes:

1. Memorial candle.

2. Town.

3. Aramaic – "master of the house" – the local authority for rabbinical law.

4. Righteous man.

5. Prayer shawl.

6. Custom of midnight study and prayer in memory of the destruction of the Temples.

7. Reading desk.

[Column 471]

The First Strike

by Dov Brukarz

Translated by Gloria Berkenstat Freund

It was in 1905.

I was then a *kheder-yingl* [religious primary school student]. Because the teacher did not have permission to run a *kheder* [religious primary school], because his residence did not maintain the sanitary conditions demanded by the police for a school, the teacher had moved his school to the house of prayer. However, on this day there was turmoil and upheaval with a "pogrom" in the house of prayer and the rabbi freed us from learning and sent us home.

It was the Jewish strikers [working] for Shmulke the tailor, who had his tailor shop across from the house of prayer, who created the "pogrom." He had four sewing machines and hired men. The workers demanded a 12-hour workday and Shmulke did not want by any means to give in. So they entered his shop and broke the machines and the furniture and knocked out the windowpanes and a little blood was spilled. There was a bitter fight because Shmulke's son Isser and his son-in-law resisted.

Dovid Czimbam (Goldberg), a shoemaker by trade, stood at the head of the strikers. Under his leadership were: Meir Karesz, an egg trader, who would buy eggs with his mother on market days, which they took to Warsaw; Faydekhe's son and two daughters who sold fruit that they bought from the orchards and took to Warsaw and Bialystok; Yosef Shmerl's [son] (Czeliasniak), a worker at *tsitsis* [fringed undergarment worn by pious men] and carpentry, and so on.

[Column 472]

They were the leaders of the strike, but the socialist group also included many others. The majority of them were children of esteemed members of the middle class and even of rich men. [They included] the daughters and a son of the Zajfnzider [family], a son of Yosef Szepke, Motl Bolender, Shayva Surowicz, Sura Szczigel, Berl, the daughter of the *melamed* [religious teacher], Sura-Misha's daughter Altke, Tyktin, Mordechai Welje's daughter Fraydke and many others.

A similar strike also took place against Yosl Baczan the shoemaker. He lived on Modlin [Street]; this was in a part of the *shtetl* [town], on the southeast side right near the river. This Yosl Baczan would not agree that his only journeyman should not work more than 12 hours a day. The strikers burst in on a Friday and beat him severely. He later walked around with a bandaged head for a long time. When the police came there were no longer any strikers to be found.

[Column 473]

Morozow, an embittered enemy of the Jews, was then at the head of the Czyzewo police. Early in the morning of *Shabbos* [Sabbath], he encountered Dovid Czimbam at the entrance to the teahouse located in Berish Frydman's house. With the help of several policemen, Morozow attacked Dovid and wanted to arrest him as the one responsible for the bit of work at [the workshop of] Yosl Baczan. Dovid did not allow himself to be arrested, holding on to the wooden steps of the entrance. The policemen could not tear him away in any way from the spot. Morozow barged in with wild fury and with the sword that he carried at his side. He gave Dovid a blow over his arm and broke the bone. The policemen carried him away in this condition.

[Column 473]

Khederim, Schools, Teachers and *Melamdim*

by Dov Brukarz

Translated by Gloria Berkenstat Freund

There were many *khederim* [religious primary schools] in Czyzewo, but for many years only one *folkshul* [public school] existed with only one Christian teacher. The students then consisted of only Christian children who came from the surrounding villages. The languages of education were Russian and Polish.

The Jews in Czyzewo looked at the school as at an evil plague that causes mIssery.

According to Russian law, the *melamdim* [teachers at religious schools] had to send the children to the *folkshul* every day for at least two hours. Well, what parents or teachers wanted their child to interrupt their Torah study because of some sort of gentile school? In general, the majority of *khederim* were *trayfe* [nonkosher, illegal in this sense]; they did not have any permission to run a *kheder* and, therefore, were afraid of an evil eye from the police. They did everything they could to be able to avoid the school edict.

First of all, until 1910, Jewish children, particularly girls, learned to write in Yiddish and Russian with the two Jewish teachers, also illegal, Yankel the *lerer* [teacher] and Zerach Starkowski, whom we called the writer because he would write administrative requests and petitions and applications for the Jews to the various government institutions, even to the highest court and to the tsarist tribunal. Later, he was only involved with travel matters, was in contact with the German travel bureaus and, because of this, actually was arrested at the outbreak of the First World War. He was threatened with exile. From jail he sent out a declaration to the Warsaw governor who ordered that he be freed. He died in America years later.

[Column 474]

The two teachers also would write letters for *Amerikankes*. That is what we called the women whose husbands were in America. For 10 *kopekes* [coin of small denomination] they wrote a short letter that spoke to the heart and could move even a stone.

Another teacher, Chaim-Shaya, arrived in 1910. In a short time he remained the only teacher in the *shtetl* because the two previous [teachers] were involved with something else. Boys and girls studied together with Chaim-Shaya. They learned Russian, Polish, Yiddish and Hebrew with the *Ashkenazi* dialect.

[The children] studied in all of the *khederim*, beginning with the teacher of the youngest children and ending with a teacher of the *Gemara* [Talmud], from *Shabbos Bereishis* [the first Torah portion of the yearly reading cycle] and through the entire winter, from seven in the morning until around nine o'clock at night with a break for the lunch hour.

[Column 475]

Diligent *Gemara* students [boys] then went to a Hasid's *shtibl* [one room house of prayer] after eating at night and studied until late [at night].

On the first Sunday after *Sukkos* [The Feast of Tabernacles, which takes place in September or October], the teacher reminded the children as they left for lunch:

– Do not forget to bring a *kopeke* for kerosene.

There was no electrical lighting then in Czyzewo.

When I visited Czyzewo in 1935, the *shtetl* already was lit by electricity, which was provided by the "Parowa Mill," which belonged to Yosl-Boruch Lepak and partners.

All of the houses and, as a matter of course, also the *khederim* were lit by kerosene. Each *kheder* boy had to contribute to the cost of kerosene in the amount of one *kopeke* a week.

The nighttime study in the *kheder* evoked very great interest among the *kheder* boys, not because of studying *Gemara*, but because of the art of creating paper lanterns in various forms, size and color.

A strong competition in creating the lanterns among the *kheder* boys continued for the entire winter. Each boy tried to out-do the other. The lantern was smeared with oil so the light from the tallow candle would clearly shine. There also were tin lanterns, but only the rich boys were able to have one of those.

Coming home at night after studying with the lantern with flowered paper one had created himself[gave the boy] the feeling of childish pride. However, the lantern often would meet an *ein-hora* [evil eye, something bad] and always, of course, the prettiest one and as soon as one left the *kheder* the lantern caught fire as if by a magical hand and… in one blink of the eye, all of the toil was transformed into smoke and a bit of ash that the wind immediately dissipated everywhere.

[Column 476]

No more lantern. No longer a privileged person! As if done deliberately!

Regret over the burned lantern did not last long. As soon as the boy crossed the threshold he went to the usual, prepared material and in the morning he came to the *kheder* with a brand new and modern lantern that would cause wonder and envy among his friends.

A childish fantasy could not imagine a greater pleasure.

Coming from *kheder* with a round, beautiful lantern that illuminated the trodden paths in the deep snow that meandered up to the home where the mother's mild eyes and lips were waiting, the boy felt pride in his own work.

I was a fortunate one; my mother greeted me, her successful young son and a good student whose small face was reddened by the cold and childish joy. She did not cease dreaming that perhaps her efforts, her exertions to help her young son with the best teachers, not sparing the money needed for tuition, saving more than she could from the money his father sent on which they were to live in order to be able to educate her small son to send him on the path of righteousness. Perhaps God would help and he would grow up to be a rabbi or just a great scholar and he would be good to God and to people. Mothers would be envious. She, therefore, was fortunate, extremely happy.

[Column 477]

Every *Shabbos* [Sabbath] afternoon, one prepared to be questioned [examined] to see how far along he was in his studies.

The examination was prepared earlier by the *melamed*. Rarely was the *melamed* at the examination. The examiners were almost always Yoske Szapira's son Boruch, Berish Frydman, Yisrael-Yona Raczkowski, Moshe Yankel the Winszenker and others.

[Column 478]

The boys later notified the rabbi, the father or the mother of their success at the examination and in return they received good sweets.

> "Oh that my head were water and my eyes a spring of tears, that I might weep all day and night for the slain of the daughter of my people!"
>
> Jeremiah 9:1

[Column 477]

A Ray of Light from Past Years

Dov Brukarz

Translated by Gloria Berkenstat Freund

Imparting my memories of life in Czyzewo, I have the feeling that I am uttering laments over my birthplace in which I spent some 20 plus years of my childhood and youth, years of dreams and aspirations. I still feel bound to it and to my close relatives, comrades and friends, years after leaving the *shtetl*, with its small wooden houses, covered with shingle roofs, with the large market and its two rows of shops. There were three two-story houses found here, with brick walls. Only Shimon-Nusan the *melamed*'s [religious elementary school teacher] two-story house was wooden. A little farther, where Zambrówer Road began, right near the Brak River, stood the Catholic Church with its two large tower windows looking out on the city market, from which the three main street spread out – Szmidisze Street on the west side, Kalje Street from the east side and Ciechanowiecer or Nurer Road on the south side.

[Column 478]

Everything I describe is only perhaps a thousandth of the many generations of Jewish life in Czyzewo that was so mercilessly destroyed, just as in hundreds of other Jewish cities and *shtetlekh* [towns] where our savage enemy did not leave any scent of Jewish life.

The Time of Transition

I begin in 1913 because this year was a time of transition in my life.

[Column 479]

I left the *yeshiva* [religious school] and remained standing at the crossroads, without a definite direction for my future, a period that was so characteristic for Jewish young people at that time.

It is clear to me that in my descriptions I will also weave in episodes and events that I experienced in my earlier childhood years or I will retell stories from my parents and other people. I will not avoid them. Let it remain a memorial and enrich the picture of Jewish life in Czyzewo before the Holocaust.

For such young men as I at that time, Czyzewo was a place to come together to spend time. We established certain places where we would meet for a conversation. Such meeting points were the brush factories, one of them belonging to Shalom, Miriam's son, who was at first called Czeliangura and later Grynberg. The second brush factory belonged to Yitzchak-Benimin's son, Moshel Blajwajs. They were brothers-in-law years later.

At this opportunity I want to mention that just as in other *shtetlekh*, in Czyzewo it was not customary to call someone by their family name. Everyone had his nickname, particularly when there were many people with the same name, such as for example, Itshes, of which there were very many in Czyzewo. Therefore, I will also call these people about whom I will speak by the names with which they were known in Czyzewo because there are many people there whose family names are not known even today. These people carried their nicknames with the greatest naturalness. No one made an effort to find out the origin of the nickname.

[Column 480]

The young men who would come to these "small factories" would include those whose concerns centered around earning money for cigarettes, or for buying a young girl chocolates and soda water, fruits in Fladeszczike's orchard, or only for a quiet stroll in a splendid moonlit night.

It should be understood that the category "*fardiner*" [one who earns much money] could not be applied to the "working class." There were not yet any parties then in Czyzewo. However, there were sympathizers toward various parties that existed then in Poland. There also existed class differences in Czyzewo, such as, for example: wagon drivers and porters, on one side and retailers, wealthy children, half and entirely idle on the other side. There were also sharp differences between Hasidim and *misnagdim* [opponents of Hasidism].

There were also two Alters among my friends who entered the small factories, Aizik Baran's Alter and Fayge-Brocha's Alter, to whom I was strongly attached and because we were always seen together, we were called "the triplets." They had a great influence on the course of my life. We took the initiative upon ourselves to found the "people's library." Others later also helped in running it, my brother, Mordechai, may he rest in peace, among them.

This was later and I will return to it because this is an interesting chapter in the life of Czyzewo. Alter Baran played an important role here. Alas, he died in 1917 at the age of 21. Fayge-Brocha's Alter Szerszyn died in Petah Tikvah in 1938 at the age of 42.

[Column 481]

There was another place where young people would meet. This was the barbershop of Avraham Josef Itsl, the son of the *klezmer* [musician] (Ritholc) where young men[1] and young men already married, who found it difficult to part with the life of an unmarried young man, would come. A "dramatic section," as well as an orchestra, was founded in this barbershop through the initiative and leadership of Avraham Josef.

At all of these meeting places only young men would come together. Young women would meet separately in a residence of either this or that friend. If there was a brother there, young men would visit briefly. They said that they were coming to see the brother and if the parents were not in the home, there were found circumspect young men who danced a waltz, a polka, a *sherele*, a *fadisfan* or a *Krakowiak* (dances popular at the time) with the young women. The dances were done according to the cadence of the songs that were sung by the dancers themselves.

Fantn-shpiel [guessing games] were also included in the entertainments. And also "rumors" during which anonymous complimentary letters were sent with trusting young men and young women specifically chosen for this purpose. The best letters were later given a prize by a jury. For the *fantn-spiel*, a committee presented riddles to each participant and those who could not answer would be punished by the jury and after carrying out the verdict they would get back their *fant* (deposit). The most severe punishment was to kiss a young woman…

During the summertime we came together in the orchards and forests around the city and on the roads outside the *shtetl*. Mostly we would stroll on Zembower Road where meadows with wide many-branched trees stretched on both sides and we could rest. The road was full of people strolling. Here could be seen young men arm in arm with young women, couples in love. There were no automobiles parking then and because it was *Shabbos* [Sabbath] it was rare to see a peasant wagon…

[Column 482]

The Torn-Out Poplars

A beloved stroll was also on Ciechanowiecer Road with its tall and thick poplar trees that stretched like a beautiful boulevard to the train station. In 1907, 49 poplars were torn out by the roots and in their place stood deep holes.

This happened on the day when a pogrom was being prepared against the Jews in Czyzewo. Several days before *Yosef's-hoga* [the holiday of Jesus – Easter], the police learned about it and called for reinforcements from the *powiat* [county]. A company of soldiers also arrived. No Jews were seen outside. Everything was closed and they sat with beating hearts even in the special hiding places. But when a giant procession accompanied by echoing bell-ringing began, everyone experienced suffocating breathing. All of the streets were packed with peasant wagons, ready to be loaded with the possession of the *Zydes* [derogatory Polish word for Jews] that would need to be taken after the slaughter and murder.

Suddenly the sky became very cloudy and a downpour began. There was thunder and lightning. A fearful gale tore trees and roofs. Fear and great turmoil engulfed the peasants everywhere.

[Column 483]

Then, the 49 poplars on Ciechanowiecer Road fell. Four such poplars stood not far from the Jewish cemetery near the furrier Moshe-Khatskl's garden. Two fell and two were broken in half. The two remaining tree trunks were used by the *tsitsis* [fringe found on a *talis* or prayer shawl; fringed garment worn under clothing by Orthodox Jewish males] makers during the summer to stretch the *tsitsis* threads for drying.

[Column 484]

The fear of the non-Jews after these events lasted for a very long time. The Jews saw in this a miracle from heaven.

Translator's note

1. The Yiddish word *bokhur* - *bokhurim* in the plural - is used for unmarried young men.

[Column 483]

New Winds

by Dov Brukarz

Translated by Gloria Berkenstat Freund

With the outbreak of the First World War in 1914 new winds began to blow among the Czyzewo young. Groups were formed that carried on fervent political discussions. The meetings in the brush factories and in Avraham Yosef's barbershop were still more heated with discussion of world question. The young showed a strong drive to read books, newspapers. But we had to refrain from opening a library because of the dangers that lurked for every Jew as a result of the Russian defeats at the front.

Old Khanina Szerszyn had a few of his own books and lent them out among the thirsty young who contributed with a small payment so the money could be used to buy new books. All of the discussions were fiery and took place in the middle of the market and drew larger groups of people who would scatter when a Russian policeman appeared.

When the Front Neared

The Warsaw–Petersburg (which was called Petrograd during the war and now Leningrad) train line ran through Czyzewo. The passing military [troops] would stop in Czyzewo for a short time. The soldiers were quartered in private houses. Several small incidents of theft and robbery took place. However, in general, they brought in a revival in retail [commerce]. Simultaneously, Czyzewo Jews began to provide military boots, uniforms and military great coats as well as meat and bread.

[Column 484]

Life became more difficult when the front neared Czyzewo. Great masses of the military that began to give a difficult time to the Jewish population arrived. During the last two days of Russian rule, Cossack murderers began to rampage.

At night, the sky was red from the flames that approached from the villages that the Russians had burned during their withdrawal. Along with the heavy cannon fire, desperate screaming was heard moving from among the shops, to the market, to the neighboring alley that the soldiers had begun to loot. An individual case was when an officer drove away a band of soldiers who had looted the shop of Yoske (Grynberg), the son of Nisle.

[Column 485]

On the last day in the afternoon all of the Jews in the *shtetl* went out onto the field in front of the slaughterhouse, near the new cemetery. It was announced from the [Russian] military headquarters that the *shtetl* would soon be set on fire. A small number of the population withdrew to the cellars of the Zawel Yudelszten's and Pesakh Surowicz's brick houses.

Suddenly we saw from the distance that the wings had begun to turn on one of the four windmills that were located on Kalja Road. This curdled everyone's blood from fear. This could only mean a sealed death sentence, not only for the owner of the mill but also for the entire *shtetl*. The Russians could see secret signals in this that the Jews were giving to the Germans. Such rumors had been going around for a long time.

It did not take long and the soldiers began to search for Simkha Glina, the son of Mendel–Yisrael Shlomo. Someone pointed him out and he was taken away. I do not know what happened and Simkha returned a few hours later. Several minutes later all four windmills were in flames, which engulfed the surrounding houses.

The shooting became thicker. Bullets and shrapnel passed over our heads. The Germans shelled the train station. Shrapnel exploded in the middle of the city and the sad news immediately was carried that Berl–Dovid's wife, Chaya, was killed. Right after her, the wheelwright, Yitzchak. Avrahaml, Sura Malka's son–in–law, was wounded. These were the first victims. Later, there were others.

The shooting got even heavier at night. Frightening shouts of hoorah were heard.

[Column 486]

The Russians had attacked; everyone in the field was seized by a horrible fear. People ran to the cemetery in great confusion, hid behind the fence, behind the headstones. Others ran into the brick building of the slaughterhouse. They ran back and forth under the hail of bullets. The child of Hersh Velvel's daughter–in–law, whom she was holding in her arms, was shot. We hid under the wagons that were fully packed with furniture and bedding. Avrahaml Moshe, the bookbinder's son, lay near me shoulder to shoulder.

Suddenly it became still. The Germans withdrew to the river. The Russians chased them. Cossacks ran past us with wild, distorted faces and outstretched rifles with sparkling bayonets. An infuriated Cossack bent to our side and stuck the bayonet into Avrahaml's heart. He was still alive. I helped carry him into the slaughterhouse. He looked at me with sad eyes and asked me to sit near him. We could not help him at all and he quietly breathed out his soul.

Meanwhile, another young man was stabbed in the same manner outside. We did not know him. He came running here from Januszkowo, thinking that it was quiet here and found death here. Yossel Katliarek's wife began birth pains at the same time and gave birth to a boy who died during his childhood.

When night fell, it suddenly became light from the flames that engulfed the entire *shtetl*. We did not see any Russian or German military. Everyone left on foot, running on the Ciechanowiecer road, on the road to Russia. A large number had wagons. It lasted several days until we arrived on the Russian side of Ciechanowiec in the forest. We were seized there by Germans, who told us to return to Czyzewo.

[Column 487]

On the way, the German soldiers distributed bread, jams and chocolate to us. It was worse in the *shtetl*. German soldiers came into Yakov–Arya's [shop] to buy sugar. It was *Shabbos* and Sima–Leah led them into the shop; in several minutes they stole everything, left it empty shelved and escaped.

My partner Shmulke, Malka the baker's adopted son, and I left on foot for Ostrowa. There we bought cigarettes, cigars and matches and returned to Czyzewo with full sacks on our backs. We did very well on the transport and again returned to Ostrowa. Returning loaded with full sacks, we were very close to the *shtetl*. We met German soldiers who asked us to give them cigarettes, cigars. We quickly emptied our sacks. We considered it good luck – [they] quickly took the goods; the soldiers immediately were back in their wagons and without a word quickly departed. We thus lost all of our possessions [and] foreign money. We no longer had anything with which to trade.

Life began to become normal again little by little. The German commandant put together a militia and I was appointed as an interpreter at the headquarters. The Jews, local and foreign benefited from many favors. The Christian population tried to agitate with the German commandant against the Jews, denounced the Jews as smugglers of city wheat, kerosene, horses and other things. I was successful everywhere – with the help of Itshe Mankuta – at influencing the commandant on behalf of the Jews.

[Column 488]

My Activity in the Library

At that time the provisional committee to found a library came together. All of the very young men and girls from Czyzewo were invited to the meeting where on the agenda were the questions:

1. Approve the founding of a library,
2. Determine the level of the enrollment cost and member's dues,
3. Elect a managing committee and a review committee,
4. Discussion, questions and answers.
5. Signing the invitation were: Baran, Brukarz and Szerszyn.

At first the library was in the residence of the Plocker family, a brother–in–law of Itshe Mankuta, who voluntarily provided a place where books brought by Alter Szerszyn were distributed. A short time later, an apartment of two rooms was rented from Leibel Benyimin Senders where the first founding meeting took place.

The following people were elected to the managing committee: Baran, Brukarz, Dr. Gelbojm, Jablonka Butsza, Szachnerowicz and Mordechai Brukarz as librarian.

[Column 489]

The library received the name "Jewish *Folks* [People's] Library in Czyzewo." The premises were fully packed every evening. A division for chess and checkers also was created under the leadership of Dr. Gelbojm. Readings on various themes were given by Dr. Gelbojm, Dentist Szachnerowicz.

A stir began in the *shtetl*. The Hasidic parents learned that their children were going to the "Jewish *kosciol* [Catholic house of worship]" (that is how they referred to the library) and reading the secular books there. They began to demand of Leibel that he throw out the unclean books. Otherwise, they threatened to not permit him to offer the priestly blessing on the holidays (he was a *kohan*). Leibel was actually very frightened and put a lock on the door of the library.

The German commandant (he was Jew with the name Rozenbaum) sent two soldiers to rip off the lock. When Leibel tried to resist, they served him with several blows. This made an even stronger impression than the threat about the priestly blessing. In addition, we gave him an increase in rent money. The incident ended with this.

[Column 490]

At the demand of the then Rabbi, Reb Shmuel Dovid Zabludower, may the name of a righteous man be blessed, we gave him our word of honor that the library would be closed from Friday at night to *Shabbos* after *havdalah* [the concluding *Shabbos* prayers]. The pious group did not stop making a fuss, until finally they became accustomed [to the library]. Their children contrived to take book from the library.

My activity in the library lasted until 1918. I became ill and was operated on in the Warsaw Hospital. Immediately afterwards I was mobilized into the Polish military. Therefore, I had to give up all communal work.

Returning after several months of active military service, I still helped to liquidate the cooperative store that was founded in 1917 with the help of Lew Yitzchak Rubinsztajn, Szachnerowicz and me. There were various unsuccessful attempts to strengthen the cooperative. However, it could not be supported in any way and it had to be liquidated against our will.

[Column 489]

A Regular Market Day

By Dov Brukarz

Translated by Gloria Berkenstat Freund

Dawn. It is quiet in the *shtetl* [town], the streets and alleys are empty. The butcher blocks made from tree trunks lie strewn about in the market. A whinny is heard somewhere from a wagon driver's horse that is resting from his short trip to the train station two kilometers to the east of the *shtetl* where its master drove it hitched to a half-covered carriage for passengers who needed to travel to Warsaw or to Bialystok and back.

[Column 490]

It is becoming a little bright on the east side; the day is beginning to dawn. Somewhere is heard the creaking of doors. Here and there silhouettes appear that are not hard to recognize in the dark blueness of the coming morning. I see them now, as if alive before my eyes. Here goes Motl Fertl, cabinet maker. Aizik the shoemaker, Kalman the furrier, Elya the blacksmith, Shmulye the tailor, Berl *Malamed* [teacher in *kheder* – religious primary school] and others. Each with a *talis* [prayer shawl] under his arms going in the same direction. To the *Beis-haMedresh* [house of study and prayer], to pray with the first *minyon* [quorum of 10 men needed for prayer]. The *Beis-haMedresh* was opened earlier, the extra-bright lights lit. Cleaned, and water has been poured into the hand cask, the lights lit near the lectern. Ahron *Shamas* [*shamas* – rabbi's assistant] had prepared everything with his assistant, Yisroelke, the gray-haired assistant *Shamas*.

[Column 491]

They did not only do all of the work in the *Beis-haMedresh*, but also other city requirements, such as going to inspect the *eruv* [wire boundary within which things can be carried on *Shabbos*] every Friday and, when it was necessary, they also fixed it, so that it would be possible to carry things on *Shabbos*. And they were also the *Shamasim* of the *Khevre-Kadishe* [burial society]. They each did separate work for weddings and *brisn* [religious circumcisions]. Ahron needed to invite the guests on the day of each celebration. And Yisroelke helped the men prepare the tables. And for women, Heike, the *beterke* [woman who invites wedding guests] helped to serve the food. Heike was *shamaste* [the wife of the *shamas*] in the woman's section of the synagogue and a volunteer with the *Khevre-Kadishe*. She died in her old age before the First World War. Only Ahron *Shamas* always accompanied the *rav-damta* [Aramaic word – rabbi of the city] to and from the *Beis-haMedresh* every day.

Ahron went to repair the *eruv* during the first week after the Bolsheviks entered the *shtetl* and was arrested as a spy. But he was freed with the help of a Jewish officer who was in the *tcherezveitcheike* [reconnaissance office], who clarified the matter of the *eruv* among Jews.

[Column 492]

The *Kherve-Mishnius-Beis-haMedresh* [synagogue of the *Mishnah* group] was in the same nameless street. Three Hasidic houses of prayers were also concentrated in this street. The Gerer and Aleksander were past the city synagogue and the Sokolower *shteibl* [Hasidic house of study] at Arke Lung.

It was already light.

Here the baskets and boxes of greens and fruits are being carried out into the market and from Shashe and Chava, the potter, and from the blond Moshe and Moshe Wolfczikhe. These are the usual stall-keepers. Each one sits in her spot, which had perhaps been chosen by her grandmother, on boxes padded with sacks.

People are coming from the first *minyon*. On the way, several drop into Zublun's or to Pinykhe (Pinye Josef Szepke's wife) in order to take a drink, to drink a small glass of whisky and to have a snack, to take sustenance before beginning the day-to-day work. Here the baked goods from Malka are brought, bagged bread and fresh, crusty rolls and other rolls. Josef-Mendel, Malka's husband, sets up his stall. The Jedrzejower baker has already completed his stall of greens on the other side of the market women. Pesha-Jute's daughter has put out her three troughs of fresh, crisp bagels. Mothers hurry to buy several bagels and several rolls for their children to take with them to *kheder*.

Peasant wagons arrive from the nearest villages, loaded with birchwood, potatoes and wheat. Eggs, cheese and butter. Men are still going to the *Beis-haMedresh* to pray or to the Hasidic *shtiblekh*. On the way they haggle with the peasants; one haggles over a little wagon of wood and he goes home with the wood, or with other bargains. Then they go to pray in a good mood, satisfied with the bargain.

[Column 493]

And once Shmulye Feyde said to a peasant while haggling;

– You want two *gildn* for such a handful of wood (30 Russian *kopeks*). I can carry it home on my shoulder!

– If you carry it home all at once, take it without cost! – The peasant said to him.

– Shmulye said, I hold you to your word.

Meanwhile a group of men gathered, a rope was brought and the wagon of beams were firmly bound together. Help was given to Shmulye to put them on his shoulder and a dead silence arose. No one believed his own eyes… Shmulye would actually carry the entire wagon of wood home? It was thought, here he would collapse. However, he walked. Jews and Christians, old and young, whoever was then at the market, accompanied Shmulye. He had a distance of approximately 300 meters to his house. He hurriedly threw down the wood under his Window. The wood fell with a crash. However, it was not heard because of the bravo-applause and the shouts of hurrah from the surrounding mob. Then as he straightened himself, the peasant first offered his hand, crossed himself and said – *Khodzshmi do Yankelia*! (We are going to Moshe Yankel's.) This was the most distinguished tavern in Czyzewo. And there, several glasses of 95 proof spirits were drunk, roasted goose was eaten and they went as good friends.

[Column 494]

The church bells for morning prayers are heard. The opening locks of the shops in the market, which are found in two rows of low, little wooden houses in the middle of the market, also ring. They form the "business center" of Czyzewo. The food shops and textiles, haberdashery, ironware and so on, are found there, as well as two *khederim* [religious elementary schools], Boruch Krajndl's and Shimon Nusan's, right opposite the church.

The butchers come out and each carries a standing stool and lays a plate of nailed together thick boards on it and his table is finished. Then he looks for the butcher block which urchins rolled somewhere at night. It also happened that on the night before they were to leave for military service, the recruits heated the bath with such a butcher block, if they were not satisfied with the gift the butcher had given to the recruits, which was the custom in Czyzewo at that time.

The butchers each had their spots just as the baker and the female stall keepers. The two Ziske brothers and Yankel Bolender near Malka's bread stalls. And on the other side of the vegetables, opposite Pesakh SurowItchker's wall, stood the "Pejsakes." These were the two brothers, Pesakh's sons Mendel and Moshe. And opposite Ezra's, Eleizer the butcher and Zelikl had their official residence.

Meat was not sold in any butcher shop, but on the street. The butcher himself *hot getreybert* the meat [removed the forbidden vein and fat to make meat kosher]. There were no specialists who removed the forbidden vein and fat.

[Column 495]

Several small merchants hang around the market and wait. Perhaps a peasant will come from a village and some sort of a small bargain could be bought from him, a little wheat, chickens, or eggs, butter, and later the merchant will leave for the village and perhaps buy a hide or a calf or a little pig hair. People come together at random; groups are created and discuss world politics. They worry about world politics. They care about every country, people, cities and *shtetlekh* and the merchants from the shops opposite take part and then return to the shops when a customer appears.

Every Tuesday was a market day, if there was no Jewish holiday. The market would become filled with peasant wagons on both sides of the shops. The peasants from the surrounding villages would arrive very early, bringing their goods to sell in the town. Then, with the money, they would buy products, meat, naphtha, sugar, salt and various other goods, haberdashery, textiles or redeem pelts from the furrier, a fur coat from the tailor, and so on.

Friday seemed to be an unofficial market day in the town. Peasants would come with various products to sell and the main fish sellers, Yehoshua and Ezra, occupied a respected place in the market with their barrels, baskets of various fish, in honor of *Shabbos*.

The market began emptying after noon. Men hastily went to the *mikvah* [bathhouse]; during the summer they would also go to wash in the river. These were the only options for washing oneself during all of the years of Czyzewo's existence.

[Column 496]

A Fair

When a fair was scheduled in the neighboring towns around Czyzewo, and even in those not nearby, such as, for example, Lomza, Wyszkow, Ostro-Mazowiecki and so on, the *shtetl* would be awake almost the entire night. There were already peasant wagons that had arrived earlier in Czyzewo the previous night in order to unload the goods which needed to be taken away to tomorrow's fair. Textile shops and haberdasheries, furniture makers, shoemakers, tailors and blacksmiths brought their goods to the fairs. An effort was made to go earlier in order to find a better place for their stand. And even at the fairs in Czyzewo, the local merchants erected their tables and butcher blocks at night, before those from outside would arrive. A fair was not missed, even if there was a downpour or snow and a hard frost. The market became full of mud from the rain or snow. This, too, did not interrupt the commerce. It did lower the amount made from sales, but the trade continued, particularly in the horse market that was located on Ciechanowiecer Road and the cattle market between the Czyzewo synagogue and the *mikvah* [ritual bath]. The mud would be up to the knees near the old cemetery where there was no paving.

The fairs gave the *shtetl* its livelihood, which was more than during the time between fairs. Whoever had been helped by God that he have a good fair and had earned a great deal was happy. He could return the borrowed interest-free loan money. He could come with an open face and ask for a loan again.

[Column 497]

There was no shortage of those who provided interest free loans in Czyzewo. And there was also no shortage of those who took the loans. Almost every merchant borrowed an interest free loan after every market and before every fair and in the last years before the Second World War, which brought the downfall of the *shtetl*, an interest free loan office was created.

A Wedding in the *Shtetl*

The invitations were printed on a standard form. It was only necessary to write in the names: of the groom and bride, the in-laws, dates. However, notice of the wedding hall where the wedding would take place was given orally when the wedding invitation was delivered at an address. The wedding invitation was always sent by way of the *shamasim* [plural of *shamas* – rabbi's assistants], Ahron and Yisroelke, and they would earn several *gildn* for delivering them. But on the wedding day, Ahron was sent with a special list to guests who were unconditionally invited to take part in the ceremony.

The wedding hall was no problem. The most comfortable salons were in the Christian tea house in Berish Frydman's house, or at the homes of Pesakh Ourowicz, Zawel Edelsztajn, or at the soap boiler Rabinowicz. There were salons in these places, larger than average rooms. These places were not paid for; everyone was ready to give his apartment to celebrate a wedding ceremony there, which lasted at least half the night. At the beginning of the evening, the bride, already in her veil and wedding clothing, would be led away.

[Column 498]

The "bride's throne" was already prepared in the corner of the salon. It was an overturned baker's trough (half a barrel in which the dough for rye bread was kneaded). This was a talisman that the marriage would prove successful. A half or entire armchair stood on the trough covered with a white sheet. And on each side, there were candlesticks on stands in which burned colored, braided *havdalah* candles.[1] After Yudl *Badkhn* [a *badkhn* is a wedding entertainer who specializes in sentimental rhymes], with his hoarse voice, celebrated the bride in song, congratulated the in-laws and the bride in rhyme, he invited the *klezmorim* [musicians who play secular Jewish music] to play the music and the bride was led, going on foot, into the wedding hall where she sat on her "throne."

The girls and young wives, friends of the bride, or young daughters of guests, familiar and unfamiliar, were assembled in the salon and they prepared themselves for dancing. No men dared to dance with them, although there were some who would have done so. The religious ban was voided first in the 1920's and men and women danced, undisturbed.

Yudl *Badkhn* was the only *badkhn* in the town. But in the time of the Germans[2], Josef, Shmerl's son wanted to compete with Yudl as a *badkhn*, but without success… It was inconceivable that it was possible to celebrate a wedding without a *badkhn*. Or that one would bring a strange *badkhn*. Yudl had his separate price for each class. Rich, middleclass and poor. He alone decided to which class the in-laws belonged. In addition to the wages, he would receive a percentage of the wedding gift money. He was also used in the neighboring villages and surrounding *shtetlekh*. Along with his earnings from repairing rubber galoshes, he had an income and led a middleclass life. Particularly after his children grew up and helped.

[Column 499]

The *klezmorim* consisted of fiddle players, a clarinetist and a drummer. The fiddle players were Itsl the *klezmer*. His livelihood came from watchmaking. And Yitzchak the *klezmer*. The clarinetists were Avraham Josef, Itzl's son. And Yitzchak's brother, Meilekh. Both brothers were *tsitses*[3] makers by trade. Drummers would be found among the young. The *klezmorim* would receive wages, just as Yudl *Badkhn*. And in addition to the wages, they were paid by the dancing young girls. A certain sum for each dance; each dance had its price and the money was collected from the girls who took part in the dance. At that time, the dances were the *Patispan*, *Vengerke polka*, waltz and *Sherele Krakowiak*." These were the popular folk dances.

The Order of the Wedding Ceremony with the Groom

The invited male guests sat at the white covered tables supplied with beverages, sweets and fruit. And at the head of the table sat the groom and the fathers-in-law who bargained over various trivialities. About the promised part of the dowry in cash, about the *kest* [support by his in-laws for a fixed period of time] and the obligations of the groom's side. And in the time of Reb Josef-Shlomo, the Szniadower *shoykhet* [ritual slaughterer] (He came from SznjaDov. He came to Czyzewo at the time of the "quarrel" about the Wizner *khazan* [cantor] and he took over the Wizner's position.) wrote the *ketubah* [Jewish wedding agreement] in his beautiful, rounded handwriting. There was no printed *ketubah*.

[Column 500]

The tables covered with wine, fruit and candies were in the second room, or at a neighbor's. Here sat the women guests. And while the Szniadower read over the signed *ketubah*, Yudl *Badkhn* sang about the groom and *klezmorim* played a *freilekh* [happy song] and a *mazel-tov* [good luck] was wished. They had a taste of all of the good things from the covered tables. When the crowd was well satisfied, they dressed the groom in a white *kitl* [white linen robe worn on Yom Kippur and by the groom at his wedding] and a coat on top and he was accompanied by all of the guests to the *badekhn di kalah* [veiling of the bride prior to the wedding ceremony]. Yudl called out loudly – "*Mitn rekhtn fus in a mazeldike sho*! [With the right foot in a lucky hour.]" *Klezmorim* went in the front and played the *Skarbown nigun* for leading a groom to the veiling of the bride.

Entering the bride's room, the groom was strewn with a rain of confetti by the young girls gathered in the room who stood in two rows.

After *bedekhn* the bride with a specially prepared white silk kerchief, the in-laws took the groom, arm-in-arm, and Yudl *Badkhn* again called out – "*Mitn rekhtn fus in a mazeldike sho, tzu der khupa* [to the wedding]!"

Klezmorim played their traditional march to the wedding and, accompanied by wedding guests and the curious, proceeded to the wedding canopy waiting at the synagogue. First went several men, who had changed into various masks and figures, carrying burning torches in order to light the way to the wedding. There was no electric lighting then and the streets were dark if there was no moon that night. And just as it was a traditional custom to throw stones on the roof of Golde's daughter Gitl on *Tisha b'Av* [the 9th of Av, which usually falls in July or August is a fast day commemorating the destruction of the Temples in Jerusalem], so it was a custom to throw rotten apples, or even pickles, at the groom on his way to the wedding. And snow balls in the winter. The groom's short walk from the wedding hall to the *khupah* [wedding canopy] was perhaps the most difficult in his entire life. A large, curious crowd was already assembled at the synagogue so that tomorrow they could describe how the groom looked standing under the *khupah*. Every *yidene* [a somewhat derogatory term for a Jewish woman] described him differently. One said he had the face of an angel. A second like a fool. Or like a Cossack or that the Divine Presence had rested on his face. He had then shone like the sun on a clear summer day. And so on and so on.

[Column 501]

When the groom had been brought under the wedding canopy with *mazel* [luck], the *klezmorim* and Yudl *Badkhn* went back to the bride.

Almost all of the women and young girls in the *shtetl* were assembled in the hall or outside. A large number of them carried lit braided *havdalah* candles or colored Chanukah candles. And after Yudl *Badkhn* celebrated the bride in song, with a serious rhymed poem, which brought tears to the eyes of the women, the mothers-in-law took the bride arm-in-arm and the assembled young girls shouted: "Make way, the bride is coming!" Two rows were formed of girls linked hand-in-hand like an avenue of living people. The bride was called to the wedding canopy with a wedding march.

After the wedding ceremony, the groom and bride were led home to one of the in-laws where a meal of fish and meat and specially braided wedding rolls was celebrated. Soup with several almonds was served in tea glasses. And here the male guests sat separately. Only the groom sat with the bride at the women's table.

[Column 502]

Before reciting the blessings[4], the groom was invited to the men's table and Yudl *Badkhn*, frequently disguised in another pose, made the crowd happy with his humorous songs and stories and comic announcements of the wedding gifts that the guests had given, objects or cash. And Yudl licked off a fat bone from the cash.[5]

The tables were taken out after the blessing and the young people again began to dance until daybreak. But in the middle of the dance Yudl *Badkhn* called out: "Now we will dance the *mitzvah tantzl*"[6] Or as it was also called, the *kosher tantz* [kosher or pure dance]. He offered his large red pocket kerchief. The bride held one corner and the groom the other and whoever had God in his heart and a long arm held the kerchief with at least two fingers. The *klezmorim* played a "lively one" and everyone, men and women, turned in circles. And unnoticed, the groom and bride left the dance. The *kosher tantz* was the only one in which everyone was permitted to dance together, men and women.

In the morning, there was again a celebratory meal, more music, dancing and Yudl *Badkhn* made the guests happy while they ate. After *maariv* [evening prayers], a *sheva-brokha* [seven wedding benedictions] was celebrated and with this the "holiday in the middle of the week" ended.

Translator's notes:

1. Havdalah is the ceremony that concludes *Shabbos* and marks the start of the week. A special braided candle having more than one wick is lit; wine and spices in a special container are also part of the ceremony.
2. The reference to "in the time of the Germans" may refer to the period of the First World War.
3. *Tsitses* are the four-cornered undergarment worn by pious Jewish men, which have a set of fringes at each corner.
4. Blessings are recited over the wine and bread before a meal and after a meal is eaten.
5. He received a good percentage of the cash gifts.
6. The *mitzvah tantz* or *tantzl* [diminutive] is a traditional wedding dance using a handkerchief or napkin permitting men to dance with the bride without touching her, which is prohibited by religious law.

[Column 503]

My *Melamdim*

By Dov Brukarz

Translated by Gloria Berkenstat Freund

My *Melamdim* [teachers in religious schools] had the greatest influence on me and my behavior. From my early youth, my father was almost never home and thus had no opportunity to take part in my education. Therefore, the responsibility fell only on my mother. An average Czyzewo woman, for whom education had consisted of knowing how to write a little Yiddish, knew how to pray very well, almost from memory, she was a pious Jewish woman as they were at that time.

She lived with the name *Americanke* [American woman] for almost all of her years.

Therefore, she could not give me any other kind of education than that in which she herself was raised. I acquired the *alef-beis* [alphabet] from her and nothing more.

She did not receive any money with which to send me to the best teachers in accordance with my father's approval, although he toiled very hard to support his family in Czyzewo.

He really did not achieve wealth although he acquired the efficient running of his household in Czyzewo. Therefore, my teacher led me in their [my parents'] path, against which I never revolted and I am happy that I received the opportunity to perpetuate their memory in the Czyzewo Yizkor Book that will serve as a headstone for all of those for whom no trace remains of where their bones rest after the cemeteries in Czyzewo were destroyed along with the community.

[Column 504]

My mother, Chaya Hinda, who in full measure drank from the cup of the trials of bringing up children. She died on the second Nissen 5700 (1949) in Brooklyn.[1]

My first teacher was the *Shmidl* [little blacksmith].

My father, Reb Shimon, who lived for almost his entire life in America, separated from his wife and children, none of whom he had the honor of leading to the *khupa* [wedding canopy]. He died on the 22nd of Menakhem Av [consoling month of Av] 5715 (1955).

[Column 505]

I barely reached the age of four when my father, of blessed memory, wrapped me in his *talis* [prayer shawl] (a hope that a child will grow to be a good Jew) and carried me in his arms to *Shmidl* and his *kheder* [religious primary school].

The teacher sat me at the long table and began to show me the *alef–beis* on a large blackboard. However, I looked at my father and mother more than at the blackboard, so an angel suddenly threw a kopek right on the *alef–beis*.

This was the first little bit of work of the inclination to good to take me under its influence, making use of the temptation for money and it helped. I constantly looked up to the angel over the blackboard.

No one was interested in where this teacher received the name *Shmidl* and he carried the name with complete naturalness, just as his beard and *peyes* [side curls] and the need that was a frequent visitor in his house. He later left for America.

[Column 506]

When I was in America in 1953, he was still alive. He was then over 100 years old.

Reb Binyamin–Sender Rubinowicz

He was my second teacher.

When I left *Shmidl* and came to his [Reb Binyamin–Sender's] *kheder*, I already knew how to *daven* [pray]. Here I began to study the *Khumish* [the Torah] with Rashi [with Rashi's commentaries].

Reb Binyamin–Sender's *kheder* was one of the "legal" ones. It had a permit because it was located in a special, large room. Therefore, he had to send the students to study at the gentile *folks–shule* [public school] three times a week. However, in time this edict was annulled.

Teaching was not his only source of income. He owned two wooden houses, which brought him a little bit of rent income, and his wife, Yuta–Mindl, sold dairy products from their two cows.

She made the cheese and butter herself and carried it to her usual customers.

Reb Yankel *Melamed*

He taught writing in Yiddish for one hour a day. He was very fastidious about beautiful handwriting. He once caught me writing in a notebook that I held on my lap while he was teaching a *Gemara* [Talmud] lesson and, although he was very strict, he only warned me with a sharp word: "Let this be the last time."

[Column 507]

He loved students with a beautiful calligraphic handwriting.

Although he had a large *kheder*, teaching did not give him enough on which to live. His wife helped by selling a little bit in the market.

Gitl–Golda's son, Moshele Perlmuter

He would also teach writing between subject, but not only Yiddish, but also Russian.

And because he also taught us *Tanakh* [Torah, Prophets and Writings – the Hebrew Bible], which at that time was [considered] more improper than [teaching] Russian by the Hasidim, they [the Hasidim] took a dim view of him. In addition he continued to teach the *Haftorah* [Sabbath reading from the Prophets] with the musical accents and was an Amshinower [Hasidim from Mszczonow, Poland] Hasid.

He did not retaliate against anyone and taught *Tanakh* with great love.

[Column 508]

His *kheder* was small so that in order to have enough income he had to supplement his income by repairing galoshes in the winter and, during the summer, he sold fruit from his own trees.

Reb Moshe Perlmuter, called Reb Moshele Gitl–Golda's

Bine–Boruch's son, Reb Dovid–Leib Garde

A modest Jew and a very learned man.

He lost his vision in his older years; he taught his students by heart.

He was versed in the entire Talmud and commentaries.

The main wage earner was the *Rebbitzen* [rabbi's or teacher's wife] from her work as a seamstress of clothing for village peasant women.

She had two sewing machines and employed girls. In 1905, at the time of the wave of general strikes in Poland, Russia at that time, the Czyzewo strikers also demanded a 12–hour workday from her.

No serious incidents occurred, but she had to work behind closed doors and windows during the nighttime hours.

Reb Hersh Velvel

A great scholar and a modest person; he never had any grievances or complained.

His *kheder* consisted completely of six to eight young students. Although, he received high tuition payments, his wife had to work as a *tsitsis* [fringes on the talis and four–corned undergarment worn by pious men] worker to earn money.

However, she worked only with her son–in–law, Reb Yehosha Nisen, may his memory be blessed.

His *kheder* was at a high level. They also studied *Toyfus Maharsho* [commentaries by Reb Shmuel Yudeles] and he himself had to prepare a "reading."

He himself examined his students every *Shabbos* [Sabbath], repeating the lessons for the entire week.

[Column 509]

We would come to him on wintery Friday nights at around four o'clock at dawn [most likely early on Saturday] to study *Mishnius* [written compilation of the Oral Torah], but not all of the students took part in this learning.

There was a time when my brother, Mordechai, of blessed memory, and I were the only ones at these Saturday mornings.

Kiva's son, Reb Itshe Stolowicz

In addition to *Gemara*, he also taught writing Yiddish, Hebrew and calculations.

In the later years he also was occupied with making honey, not from bees, but artificial, fabricated.

In time, he also began to fabricate candies until he completely gave up the *kheder*.

Reb Itzik Stolowicz [Itshe is a diminutive of Itzik]

[Column 510]

I Become a *yeshiva* Student

Reb Hersh Velvel, may his memory be blessed, was my last teacher.

I became a *Bar–mitzvah* with him and right after I became a *yeshiva* [religious secondary school] student.

I traveled out into the wide world for the first time.

Under the influence of my comrade, Mendel Goldberg – today in America – I went to the *yeshiva* in Ostrowa.

Despite the fact that my mother could give me enough money to eat in a restaurant, be on my own *kest* [meals and other expenses given to a yeshiva student, usually by a father–in–law, but meals were also provided by a town's Jews], at that time, however, it was disrespectful for a respectable *yeshiva* student not to eat any "days" [the townspeople would pay for the meals for a student for a day or more]…

There were people who considered it a *mitzvah* [commandment, commonly translated as good deed] or an honor to give food to a *yeshiva* student one day a week for an entire semEsther.

Not every *yeshiva* student successfully obtained [meals] for all seven days. Therefore the well–known philanthropist, Chana–Meyzl, took care of it in Ostrowa.

She organized a "kitchen" just for this purpose, where the *yeshiva* students, who did not have meals for all of the days of the week would eat.

The food was free.

However, one did not feel that the food was just a supplement there. The food was very good and there was enough. The kitchen carried the name, All Who Are Hungry Will Eat.

The name was very appropriate for it.

[Column 511]

From Ostrowa I went to study in the Praga *yeshiva*, under the leadership of the well–known giant of his generation, Reb Menakhem Ziemba, may his memory be blessed.

Here there also was a special restaurant for *yeshiva* students, but my "father's child" did not want to go there to eat, and on the days [when meals provided by townspeople] were lacking, he provided for himself.

There was an institution in Praga whose purpose was to encourage yeshiva students to want to learn. The institution paid a student who could learn 10 pages a week by heart a half ruble.

If one could learn 50 pages, he would receive a five coin piece along with a special present.

I received as a gift in addition to the five rubles, a watch with a dial on which were the *alef–beis* instead of Roman numerals.

[Column 512]

As can be seen, fate decided that I would begin to learn the *alef–beis* [alphabet] with a gift of money and end [my studies] with a gift.

The sweet dream of my mother, may she rest in peace, that her son would grow up to be a scholar, a rabbi, also ended with this.

My father, may he rest in peace, returned from America and began to search for some purpose… But before he had time to think of something, I became ill. I was taken in serious condition to the Jewish hospital in Warsaw on Czista [Street] from which I returned at the outbreak of the World War in 1914.

Translator's note:

1. There is an error in conversion of the date of death: 5700 in the Hebrew calendar converts to 1940.

[Column 511]

Types in the *Shtetl*

By Dov Brukarz

Translated by Gloria Berkenstat Freund

Gitl-Golda

Who in Czyzewo did not know Gitl-Golda of the Blacksmith Street? Old and young, even children knew who Gitl-Golda was. First, because of the matzo bakery, secondly, because of the only tin roof that existed in the *shtetl* [town], which she had in partnership with Moshe-Yossel the shopkeeper.

As a widow, she and her daughter and grandchildren lived in an apartment that consisted of a large room with an alcove. Until deep into her old age, she supported herself with her own work. On the market days she purchased a piece of butter from the peasants, a few eggs, a little wheat, sheep's wool for the *tsitsis*[1] maker, feathers, a piece of homemade linen and she supported herself with this for the entire year. But during the weeks before Passover, her apartment was turned into a matzo bakery, preparing it in advance according to all laws. Even kosher *Mehadrin Min Hamedrin* [the highest level of performance of a *mitzvah* or commandment].

[Column 512]

Several weeks before Purim, Gitl-Golda was already busy preparing the bakery, buying wood, gathering people, young men, young girls and married women for rolling. She would actually choose the best and the most capable and the most responsible. Only the kneader and the one who slid the matzos into the oven were unchanging, the same ones every year.

Long, newly planed boards were placed on casks and boxes to make tables that ran around three sides of the large room. The oven, which was not used for the rest of the year, was on the fourth wall and it was still heated intensely lest there be, God forbid, any suspicion of *hametz* [non-Passover foods].

[Column 513]

A box was placed in the alcove that served as a table on which stood the large brass basin in which the dough for the matzos was kneaded. On the side stood a wooden barrel of water which was brought from the Brak River because the water from the well used in the *shtetl* was not kosher enough for the matzos. It had to be drawn with *hametzdik* [not kosher for Passover] pails.

Gitl-Golda watched over everything. Her sharp eyes penetrated every corner. Gitl-Golda's voice, which gave instructions, made observations on each movement that could, God forbid, give rise to *hametz*, was heard non-stop everywhere. Although the rabbi employed a special *mashgiakh* [supervisor of dietary laws], Gitl-Golda did not only rely on him, but controlled the rolling pins, the board and the hands of the male and female rollers herself, if God forbid, dough from an earlier piece of dough for matzo remained.

She gave the completed matzos to the customers herself; she kept the accounts in her head without a pencil and never made any errors. Only when the Hasidim came on *erev Pesakh* [the eve of Passover] to bake *matzos mitzvah* [matzos baked right before the start of Passover for use in the Seder], did Gitl-Golda not have access to the bakery. Everything was done only by the men.

Just as the baking of matzo would be repeated each year, so did the throwing of stones on Gitl-Golda's roof on *Tish b'Av* after [the reading of] *Lamentations*. Immediately on leaving the synagogue, the crashing of stones hailing over the thin roof of Gitl-Golda's house was heard across the *shtetl*. Along with the noise of Gitl-Golda shouting, not knowing even who the throwers were. Up to the First World War it was almost like a tradition. After throwing bristles in the beard of the synagogue *Lamentations* reader, the throwing of stones on Gitl-Golda's roof began and only on the half of her house and never on Moshe-Yossel's part. It would always begin just at the time when the women sat in Gitl-Golda's large room on low chairs or boxes holding tallow candles, which gave light to those listening to Gitl-Golda's reading of *Lamentations* in a crying voice, lamenting the destruction of the Temple [in Jerusalem]. The reading would be disturbed because of the stone throwing; therefore, she could never finish the entire reading of *Lamentations*. She read loudly from the large *Tsena uRena Teytsh-Khumish*,[2] which was already yellow with age. She inherited the *Teytsh-Khumish* from her mother, who inherited it from her parents and grandmothers, over many generations.

[Column 514]

The train of inheritance ended with Gitl-Golda. Her daughter did not inherit the *Teytsh-Khumish*. Gitl-Golda died just before the Second World War, as it is told – over 100 years of age. Her daughter and her family perished in the Czyzewo destruction.

Meir Ganer

Meir Ganer [gander] was his name during his life and it remained his name after his death. No one was interested in knowing his true family name.

He had his income from a little shoemaking; sometimes as a bathhouse attendant and the main income came from the fact that his wife, Rywtshe-Rojze, was a regular kneader for Gitl-Golda's matzo. She bound *tsitsis* [ritual fringes] for Itshe Meir, the *tsitsis* maker, plucked feathers and knitted socks and gloves (at that time no machine-made socks were used in Czyzewo). He had a beautiful tenor voice and he would pray at the lectern in the large house of prayer on *Shabbos* and the holidays.

[Column 515]

He was one of the people, who founded the *linas hatzedek* [society to provide medical assistance and medications] during the time of the cholera. On Purim he would be among the disguised who went to gather gifts for the *bikor kholem* [help for the sick], etc. However, he mainly dedicated himself to the children *tinokot shel beth rabban* [the children who study at the Rabbi's house]. Chanukah, when Ahron the city *shamas* [sexton] would bless the Chanukah candles in the large brass Chanukah lamp that stood on the long table on the south side of the large house of prayer, Meir would gather all of the children and after each blessing the children's choir would sing out the amen with their thin, little voice, accompanied by Meir's tenor. At the *hakofes* [procession with the Torah scrolls around the synagogue] on *Simkhas-Torah* [holiday celebrating the completion of the annual reading of the Torah and the start of its yearly reading], which lasted late into the night and in the morning for the entire day, he was surrounded by children and *kheder* boys and he would loudly shout out each verse of the *hakofes* and also "the Holy Flock!" later in the street. The children immediately rang out, "*Me-e-e*," with their childish voices… Thus he went around the *shtetl* with them throughout the day of *Simkhas-Torah* and imbued everyone with the child-like joy, with the song and with the dance, which he danced with the children.

After his death, Yossel the *tsistis* maker, or Yossel, Zawel Leib's son, as he was known, did the same thing. However, he was unsuited for it and the children did not go along with him as with Meir.

[Column 516]

Years later, Avraham, the son-in-law of Yossel Ahron the *melamed* [teacher], again carried out the custom of shouting out, "the Holy Flock." However, there was no longer the enthusiasm, the joy in the *shtetl* as with Meir Ganer, of blessed memory.

Shmuelye Czender (Goldberg)

He was a tinsmith by trade and a locksmith. He devoted himself to being a *feldsher* [barber-surgeon]. He was trusted as much as the Christian *feldsher*. He would give medicines, *shteln bankes* [cupping], but mainly he was occupied with squirting [sprays] into throats. Shmuelye was called immediately for the more severe throat illnesses. He would immediately start spraying with the sprays he created himself, in which there was so much belief as in the best medicines. Spraying was a constant fear among children when they were bad-tempered.

In old age he fell off a roof of a two-story building. He was ill for his remaining years, but even then he did not stop his work as a *feldsher*; he was occupied with spraying for as long as he could walk.

Brocha the *Doktorke*

She was the cake baker, but she was occupied by accompanying the doctor on his visit to the Jewish sick, therefore, she was called the *doktorke* [female doctor]. She carried out all of the doctor's instructions, including *shteln bankes*, giving injections and… if it was needed – charmed away an *ein-hore* [evil eye] or poured wax (this was also a means of help against an *ein-hore*).

She was called to the sick before the doctor was called; she decided who needed to be called, Shmuelye or the Christian *feldsher* or actually the doctor. There were cases in which she believed that no one needed to be called, that it was enough to charm away an *ein-hore* or to pour wax. She would also serve as a midwife, but in difficult cases she would ask that Sheine-Khamke of Brik be called. The women giving birth felt more secure with her [Brocha], but she herself often did not want to leave it even to Sheine-Khamke and would ask that the Christian, qualified midwife or the doctor be called.

[Column 518]

Chaim Dovid Tsimes

Chaim Dovid took over the role of *feldsher* by inheritance from Shmulke and Brocha when they no longer were alive. He was a *tsitsis* maker, but he always found the time to go to help someone ill. When he came to someone without economic means, he did not want to take any money for his trouble. He would spray the chest, *shteln bankes* and if he saw that it was necessary, he would himself go to call the Christian doctor (the only doctor in the *shtetl*). And then carry out the instructions.

Translator's notes:

1. The ritual knotted fringes worn by pious Jewish men on the corners of their prayer shawls and special shirt worn under their clothing.

2. A *Teytsh-Khumish* is a translation from Hebrew to Yiddish of the book from which a congregant reads the Torah portion on *Shabbos*. The *Tsene uRena – Come Out and Behold* – is a 17th century Yiddish book containing stories and commentaries tied to the weekly Torah portion read by pious women who could not read Hebrew.

[Column 517]

Czyzewer Tsitsis and Tsitsis-Makers

Translated by Judie Ostroff Goldstein

As for Czyzewo, exactly as for the other villages around it, there is absolutely nothing to make their existence known to the world at large. Czyzewo did not give the world any famous people, no great intellectuals who made the world better for humanity. But Czyzewo, more than her neighboring villages, was known throughout the world due to "pogroms and *tsitsis*" [four tassels that hang from four cornered garments].

However it is difficult to cite a lot of dates for the pogroms that were perpetrated in Czyzewo (except for the last one in 1937 and the one four years later during the destruction of the Czyzewer Jewish population by the murderous Hitlerites and their Polish assistants). But *zaydes* [grandfathers] knew and told us that in the last years of the 1700's, during Kosciuszko's reign, there were fights around Czyzewo and the Jewish population paid with innocent blood. Later, in 1836-1838, during the uprising in Poland, again innocent Jewish blood was spilled. Generally the fear of a pogrom, that would erupt like a gray storm from time to time, always hung over the Czyzewo Jews.

[Column 519]

I do not exaggerate when I say that the *tistsis* production in Czyzewo was one of the oldest and only occupation that had through the decades developed and served a world market.

As a matter of fact, in 1913 *Reb* Yehoshua Kanet *z"l* [of blessed memory] a grandson of a Czyzewer *tsitsis* maker, died in Jerusalem at the age of one hundred. At the beginning of the 1930's, *Reb* Josef Kanet died in America, a younger brother of *reb* Yehoshua Kanet, a grandson of a *tsitsis* maker. This is sufficient proof of generation after generation producing *tsitsis* in Czyzewo.

Reb Yehoshua Kanet,
the first pioneer from Czyzewo,
who went to Israel – died in 5673 (1913)

The largest market for Czyzewo *tsitsis* was, until the First World War in 1914 – Russia. Afterwards it was America, Canada, England and Poland. Daily hundred *poods* (a Russian weight measure equaling about 16 kilos) of *tsitsis*, packed in small bales were shipped from Czyzewo. Naturally one *tsitsis* maker must not know the address of the second's merchant. This secret was well guarded by the expediters, because this is how they made their living.

It is understood from the name "*tsitsis* maker" that this article was not made in a mechanized factory.

[Column 520]

According to Jewish law it is forbidden to use any means other than man's strength to make *tsitsis* (not even any women). At every stage in the complexity of making *tsitsis* the worker must always keep in mind that his work is "*l'shem tsitsis*". [for the sake of the commandment of tzitzis] Also before beginning work he had to say the following verse: "Harini ose mlakha zo, l'shem mitzvah tsitsis". [I am doing this work for the sake of the commandment of tsitsis] Later on the rabbis declared it legal to use women for specific production jobs, for example, to wash the threads and to gather the *tsitsis* in small bundles of 16 threads per bundle (12 threads and four threads "*shamas*" [rabbi's personal assistant]).

The only *tsitsis* maker in Czyzewo who did not deviate from the principle "man's strength" was *Reb* Shmulke Fiszel's (for many decades was the leader of morning prayers in the synagogue during the Days of Awe [from New Year through Day of Atonement]). People said that *Reb* Shmulke used only wool that he himself sheared from the peasants' sheep in making his *tsitsis*. He made the *tsitsis* by himself, without any help. His *tsitsis* were sold only to selected Jews such as *rebbes* [Hasidic rabbi, teacher] and rabbis and for a much higher price than those for export.

Many years ago, the only ones to produce *tsitsis* in Czyzewo were the Kanet family and *Reb* Shmulke *z"l*. The Kanet family employed workers who years later began producing these articles themselves. Most of them remained small enterprises except Itchke Meyer Parizer who progressed with the help of his mother Chana Liba the wadding maker and his father-in-law *Reb* Yudel

Stoliar. He became the strongest competition for the Kanet family. Then came *Reb* Yehoshua Nisen Kupiec *z"l* who took over from his uncle *Reb* Shmulke *z"l*. There were also small *tsitsis* makers such as *Reb* Szepsl *z"l*, an uncle of Josef Kanet, *Reb* Meyer Wengerka a brother-in-law, Simcha the *tsitsis macher* and Yosel Zanwel Lejb's [son] – Kotliarek.

[Column 521]

But the time also brought permission to use machines that were run by manpower, beginning with spinning the wool to finishing the threads (naturally the machine produced *tsitsis* came out much nicer than those made by hand). The first spinning machine was used in Ciechanowiec, about 20 *versts* [Russian measure of distance – about .66 of a mile] from Czyzewo. There was no train going there - only *Reb* Leizer with his horse and wagon. This was the only means of transporting the wool to Ciechanowiec and bringing back the spun threads for the *tsitsis* makers.

During the First World War, when the machines together with the entire city of Ciechanowiec burned down, Yossel-Zanwel-Lejb's fixed up a spinning machine in Czyzewo along with the other machines that were necessary, a carder and a *"Tsezvooker"*. The force that moved the *tsevooker* was *Reb* Shmuelje whose origin nobody knew and nobody was interested in knowing. Every *tsitsis* maker used his own strength to turn the carding machine. But for the spinning machine there was only one specialist in Czyzewo, *Reb* Leizer (Mont) one of Itchke Meyer Parizer's brothers-in-law

In between, the *tsitsis* makers used a hand machine that was made up of a large wheel. The wool was carded and then spun on the wheel. The large spinner machine could produce 60 threads at a time, the hand machine only one at a time.

[Column 522]

In the 1930's, Pinya Zysman, a son-in-law of Josef *tistsis macher* fixed up a spinning machine and the other necessary machines to occupy his brother Moshel.

After the First World War when Russia was behind the iron curtain, the largest market for *tsitsis* became America. But they were not shipped directly there from the producers. Religious article merchants came to Czyzewo and bought the *tsistsis* and they in turn had them transported them everywhere where Jews were found.

Reb Josef Kanet,
lived to a very old age, died in New York

In 1922 Mendel Kanet's family went to Israel and produced *tsitsis* for Israel and a small amount was also sent to America. In 1935 Yehoshua Nisen Kupiec's family arrived in Israel and also made *tsitsis*. Josef Kanet left Czyzewo for America and also kept busy with *tsitsis*.

[Column 524]

Murdered *tsitsis* makers during the destruction of Czyzewo were:

1. Ostrorzanski, Simcha
2. Ostrorzanski, Szmerl (one of Simcha's brothers)
3. Bronsztajn, Fiszel
4. Wengerka, Meyer
5. Wengerka, Yehoshua
6. Wengerka, Moshe
7. Zysman, Pinchas (the last of the Kanet family *tsitsis* makers)
8. Tombek, Yechiel (a son-in-law of Szepsl *tsitsis-macher*)
9. Zysman, Moshel (one of Pinchas Zysman's brothers)
10. Slucki, Avraham-Yossel (one of Yitzchak Ahron 's sons)
11. Slucki, Benjamin, one of Yitzchak Ahron 's sons
12. Cegel, Mendel (was called Mendel Teltses, a brother-in-law of Simcha's)
13. Kotliarek, Yossel (or Yossel Zawel Lejb's)

The above mentioned were murdered with their families *h"d* [may G-d avenge their blood].

With the death of the murdered *tistis-machers*, the world renowned production of *Czyzewer tsitsis* also died. Their deathbed ended the inheritance of many generations, from parent to child and relative. Their merit will not depart from us forever.

[Column 523]

Reb Mendel *Tsitsi* Maker (Kanet)

When I knew him he was already middle-aged man. He was a tall man who always had a smile on his face that was encircled by a long, black beard that ended in two points. When people saw him in the street, they noticed an intense man full of energy.

[Column 524]

I don't remember when it was, or what he said that first time, *Rosheshone* [*Rosh Hashana*, Jewish New Year], or *Yonkipper* [*Yom Kippur*, Day of Atonement], as he sang with his sweet, sincere tenor "Anaim Zimros" at the start of prayers and soon after "*adon olum*" and "*ygadol elokhim chai*" before ending with blessings that were accompanied by "*baruch hu v'baruch shmo*" and "amen" and it echoed all around the walls of the synagogue.

Standing at the cantor's desk and wearing a white *kitl* [[white linen robe worn on solemn occasions], wrapped in a large wool *talis* [prayer shawl] thrown over his head, he face shone like the sun. He stood there firm and tall like a pine tree and for a long time and slowly moved. You could hear every word he said.

In the jam-packed synagogue it was quiet. The congregation was waiting to hear more of *Reb* Mendel's voice.

Reb Mendel Kanet,
called Reb Mendel *tistsis macher*,
died 21 *Adar* 5700 (1940) in Tel-Aviv

[Column 526]

The congregation soon began praying. The voices, full of sincerity, carried throughout the synagogue like a storm driven wave and the people seemed to move like a forest that sways in a light wind.

It soon became quiet again when Reb Mendel continued the service. And so it continued, with each chapter until he began the last verse with a weeping plea and a shiver ran through everyone like a lightning storm through the body. It made hearts heavy and tears flowed.

[Column 525]

Rojza-Leah, Mendel Kanet's wife,
who was a real helpmate and carried the yoke with him
– to make a living. She died 14 KisLew 5705 [1945] in Tel-Aviv.
By her side is her daughter Chawa, today in Israel Chawa Vitriol

[Column 527]

Each year when the Days of Awe approach, I feel that holy tremor and hear the words exactly as if I was hearing them from *Reb* Mendel.

The Story of a Father's Legacy to His Sons

Reb Mendel Kanet was not considered a rich man from the shtetl, but he led a nice life. Any hungry guest coming into his house left sated and with a contribution in his pocket.

But he was not satisfied with giving help accidentally to guests and poor people. He always knew who was in need and too ashamed to make known his poverty. They would rather go hungry than stretch out their hands for help. But *Reb* Mendel's watchful eye discovered these poor families and gathered money, clothing and other necessities, such as wood and potatoes that he would anonymously provide to those in need of them. Mostly those who received these goods had no idea who had helped them or from where the help came.

To help a needy sufferer – this is the highest basis of the Torah, which *Reb* Mendel inculcated in his children as well other good habits and Jewish customs. People would often see one of his daughters, together with a friend, carrying full aprons with various food products (it was not the fashion then to carry hand baskets), such as honey, sugar, beans, kasha, bread and even meat or potatoes in sacs, thrown over their shoulders. They gathered the food stuffs from the rich and middle class houses and then carried it to poor families.

[Column 528]

So that is how his daughters lived during their youth. And that is what they still do today.

In 1914 *Reb* Mendel left for America. His family stayed in Czyzewo. The First World War and the German occupation severed their contact. His family endured difficult times.

But even though they were having a hard time, they did not forget to provide poor families with the necessities of life.

In 1921 *Reb* Mendel returned to Czyzewo and due to the distinct signs of anti-Semitism that he saw at that time, he decided to leave Poland. The only question was where to go. He chose Yisrael.

What was the reason – why Yisrael? *Reb* Mendel's parents had died in Jerusalem and therefore he decided to live in the country where his parents were laid to rest.

[Column 529]

On a summer's day Czyzewo accompanies the Mendel Kanet's family, a total of 9 people, (daughters and sons-in-law) to the train to see them off to Israel. Along with the Kanet family – the Rubinowicz family had liquidated their farm in the village of Chelenowo (near Czyzewo) as well as their possessions in the shtetl. Both families did this to the surprise of the Czyzewo Jews and Christian acquaintances – the pioneers, the first scouts, who went to Israel.

In Yisrael *Reb* Mendel renewed his way of living as in past years in Czyzewo. He became a prayer leader during the Days of Awe and he organized a small *tsitsis* factory in his own house that he had built in Tel-Aviv. His children continued to bring help to the needy, just as they had done in Czyzewo.

Two documents that are proof of the attention and responsibility involved in *tsitsis* production in Czyzewo.

Documents that prove the great responsibility that was involved in *tsitsis* production

Regarding the Subject of Tsitsis

Here I will point out the many problems with regard to the making of tsitsis, and provide great detail about the stumbling block with regard to silk, which is completely unfit, for they are not spun and twisted together for the sake of the commandment of tsitsis, but rather folded into a silk lattice that looks like tsitsis. Therefore, it is appropriate to remove this stumbling block from the midst of our brethren, and to point out that silk tsitsis are completely invalid. Heaven forbid that one should purchase them. There is a great prohibition upon merchants to sell them, so as not to mislead the public. It should also be pointed out that one should not purchase woolen tsitsis without certification that they were made in the prescribed fashion – that the pre-spinning, and also the spinning and twisting should be done by a person, as is the tradition, for the sake of the commandment of tsitsis. For there are those who do the pre-spinning by a power machine, which is forbidden by the leaders of the generation, such as the Gaon of Tarnow and the Gaon of Bielsk of holy blessed memory the author of "Shaarei Tzion"; and by those are alive including the mighty Gaon of Dvinsk may he live long. Therefore it is fitting to make haste to remove the stumbling block for the sake of the precious commandment of tsitsis, which is considered to be equivalent with all the commandments.

Darchenu, Tuesday of the Torah portion of Haazinu, the eve of Yom Kippur 5695

Rabbi Shmuel David Zabludower, the head of the rabbinical court of the community of Czyzewo

Regarding the Subject of Tsitsis

With respect to the words of the rabbi, may he live long, the head of the rabbinical court of our city, in the first issue of Darcheinu of this year, we come as Orthodox people in Czyzewo, who have been familiar and expert with the tsitsis making industry in our city for several decades already – to publicize the details regarding the aforementioned serious matter, in all of its minutiae and ramifications. As is known from the Shulchan Aruch (code of Jewish Law) and the legal decisors, the work of making tsitsis must be performed manually, by Jews, for its own sake, from beginning to end. In any other manner, it is not only that one cannot fulfill the commandment of tsitsis, but, on the contrary, one would violate the transgression of wearing a four cornered garment without tsitsis. An incident took place in our city even before the world war that one of the tsitsis makers began to make use of a machine that was harnessed to horses to make the cloth and the pre-spinning. The rabbi may he live long protested, through an exchange of letters, regarding the questions and responsa of several of the great leaders who stated that even the pre-spin that is performed by a machine powered by steam or horses is forbidden because it is the beginning of the spinning. The cloth mat is forbidden because it is combed better. The Maharal of Prague was also stringent regarding the combing On account of the protest, that person stopped his work by horse-powered machine, and resumed his work manually, in accordance with law and tradition.

[Column 530]

Thus did the tsitsis making work continue until five years ago, when some irresponsible people arose and began to find pretexts to compete with those who do the work in accordance with the law. (It is known that it is more expensive to do it manually.) From then, the breach grew, and questions arose regarding the presumption of kashrus (i.e., presumption of halachic validity) that the tsitsis makers of our city always had. The breach continued to grow without bounds. For at first, some people in our city attempted to do only the combing by machine, and now people in other towns use steam powered machines even for the spinning. If in our city there are only few who transgress the law and do their work deceitfully to mislead the masses – there are already people in other cities who do not know their right from their left, and perform the work of tsitsis making like any other job, without concerning themselves with the great responsibility that rests therein.

All the aforementioned refers only to woolen tsitsis that are made under some sort of supervision. However, the silk tsitsis that are sold in all factories are invalid and completely forbidden, since the merchants purchase silk thread in Lodz and make bundles of tsitsis from them. The breach is very great. According to the Torah leaders, it is urgent to deal with this matter in all of its ramifications.

[Column 531]

Reb Binyamin the Tailor

by Gorzalczany/Petah Tikva

Translated by Gloria Berkenstat Freund

Monday at dawn, right after the first *minyon* [prayer group], he threw his sack in which among other things were his tailoring tools, needle and thread and the large tailor's scissors that was dozen of years older than he was, on his shoulder. The scissors were an inheritance. For the first time, he left his small house that was located on Bod Street for Ciechanowiecer Road to try to find some work with the peasants in the nearby villages.

With the arrival in Czyzewo of tailors with sewing machines, no one any longer ordered any clothing from him, even for children. Until the arrival of the sewing machines, Reb Binyamin was overloaded with work. He was a specialist in sewing by hand, making new, small kaftans for *kheder* [religious primary school] boys out of old goods and special winter padded kaftans and even padded pants. It had been a long time that he had sat at his large table, blackened by his work and no customer opened the door. Therefore, he would try his to find his good fortune with the peasants in the villages to be able to support his family.

[Column 532]

Going a short way from his house, he heard the voice of his wife calling him: "Binyamin! Binyamin! Come here, I want to tell you something!" He turned around; he knew what she would say to him.

– He asked her with repressed irritation – What do you want?

– What will happen to them? – she said, holding in the tears and pointed to the two boys, shriveled, with small, pale faces who stood near her holding on to her dress and the nursing child in her arms – There is not a *groshn* of money in the house, not even a piece of bread.

[Column 533]

– In a choked voice, he said, - Try to go to Arke the baker; tell him that, God willing, I will go to him [after] *Shabbos* and pay him.

– But Arke said that he cannot [give bread] as long as our debt is not paid.

– What do you want from me? Do you want me to stay here, not go? Good. Let it be as you wish. I will stay here, but what will come from it? You know that there is no work here. Perhaps in the village God will send a little work. So. Be healthy!

With these words, Binyamin turned around and went on his way. Tears fell on his face…

– He consoled himself - Unfortunate one! He was ashamed of himself – I am crying?

He was then 40 years old. Suffering from poverty and a bit of hunger was not new for him. And yet his heart was not that of a woman. It was petrified under the yoke of his bitter fate that had not left him from his birth to this day. No, he was not a man of tears.

Such tears cannot make the pain easier; they cannot console the unfortunate. These are the tears of misery and desperation.

With his sleeve he wiped the falling tears, which ran across his shriveled cheeks, falling on his wide beard. These were tears of bitterness and terrible poverty. A man can only cry like this under oppressive need when the heart melts looking at his hungry and naked, shriveled small children.

[Column 534]

But he still did not lose his hope. He strove with all of his strength to find the opportunity to nourish his family. Perhaps God would have mercy, take pity.

Bent under the weight of the sack on his back, his tired feet carried him further on the road. In addition to his tailoring tools in his sack were his *talis* and *tefilin* [prayer shawl and phylacteries], a prayer book and a book of Psalms. While at work in the house of a gentile he did not forget for a minute his duty to He who lives eternally, as well as his duty to his family. He protected like the eyes in his head the little bit of money that he succeeded in gathering with the bitter sweat on his face, sitting an entire day at work. Not one penny did he use for his own pleasure, not even for a glass of whiskey to refresh his faint heart.

– No! He would not do this! He knew very well that his wife and children desperately longed for, waited for his return for *Shabbos* [Sabbath]. He did not forget them for a minute because this was the only consolation in his poverty.

Years pass, time flies, one becomes older and elderly. Children grow to be adults; one already had lived through bitter need, through the hardships and pain that were brought by the years of war. His son, Mordechai, the youngest of two brothers was called for Polish military service and the sad news arrived, Mordechai and three other Jewish children from Czyzewo were shot by the Poles.

Yitzchak-Ahron – the Modest Man

by Dov Brukarz

Translated by Gloria Berkenstat Freund

"He found only poverty capable of preventing them from sin."

(*Chagigah* 9b [Talmud Tractate])

He was an example of modesty, an unassuming man.

He never complained about his poverty to anyone. Day and night, for example, he was engaged without complaint with what was decreed from heaven.

His brief biography was given to me, which I provide here for the Czyzewer who never knew about him.

He married his second wife in Zambrów [Zambrów], where she had a nice haberdashery business. He, the great scholar, Hasid and very observant Jew, a believer and man of faith, took on the path of "Torah and respect." He devoted himself to commerce with the same enthusiasm as setting aside time for learning Torah, earned money and was happy with his lot.

However, the idyllic life was disturbed when, God help us, a fire broke out one day and Yitzchak-Ahron's shop disappeared with the smoke, became a mountain of ash; not even one thread was saved.

As is the custom for a Jew, a God-fearing person, a Hasid goes to his rebbe before he opens a new business.

He presented the rebbe with *kwitl* [note requesting the rabbi's intervention with God for a marriage for a child, a child for a barren woman, success in business, etc.] and the rebbe gave his assent and a blessing for the future, but something extraordinary happened here. The rebbe, after reading the presented *kwitl*, took out a ruble and placed it in his [Yitzchak-Ahron's] hand.

Yitzchak-Ahron understood what the rebbe's donation, the ruble, signified. This meant that he [Yitzchak-Ahron] no longer needed to run any business, but was to live with help from people.

Coming home, he told his wife about the *tzedakah* [charity] and she added:

"Just as we bless the good, we bless the bad." Both accepted the *din* [religious decree].

They moved to Czyzewo.

The *shtibl* [one-room synagogue] made sure that the Jews who studied day and night lacked nothing.

He quickly became part of a study group.

His wife was busy with selling soap on the market days and at fairs, with very little success.

The soap maker would not take any of her unsold goods; her brother, Yoske Zysman, who had a food shop near the Czyzewo station, took them from her.

The Agudas Yisrael Organization of Poland, Czyzewo branch

[Column 537]

The *Purim-Shpiler*[1]

by Dov Brukarz

Translated by Gloria Berkenstat Freund

Purim is known as a very cheerful holiday. In Czyzewo, Purim was notable for the cheer of the *Purim-shpiler*. Arrangements for the Purim banquet were made as for a wedding. Various cakes were baked, [foods] were roasted, cooked and a table was readied with candles lit, around which we sat from early evening.

The banquet would usually last until the middle of the night. Various couples would come who would collect donations for various charitable institutions that existed in the *shtetl*.

Groups disguised in various masks and costumes would also come. These were the distinguished members of the middle class, community workers for the *Bikor-Khoylim* [assistance for the sick], *Talmud-Torah* [primary school for needy boys], *Hakhanas Kahlah* [help for poor brides] and the like. There also were those needy people who, in masks, made use of the opportunity and collected donations for themselves, for their hungry families.

Each man of means had ready piles of small change and it was distributed generously to those coming in for donations; drinking a small glass of whiskey, wishing each other a joyful *L'Chaim* [To life] from deep in their hearts. All in addition to the donation.

The *Purim-shpiler* had an entirely different character. This was a group of young men who collected money for a special purpose. First of all, for those who needed to enter military service and did not have the means to take the necessary equipment with them. Then, there were also those who needed to be ransomed so that they would be freed from military service.

[Column 538]

These young men organized according to the model of a wandering theater troupe. They would not be satisfied with small donations. They only went to the wealthy houses; there they performed short scenes from the "Selling of Joseph," of how Jakob's sons sell their brother Joseph to the Ishmaelites. This was performed in the most heart-breaking manner. Both the players and those listening would take this tragedy to heart and, the main thing, the rich men did give rich donations.

Der Ashmedai [The *Ashmedai*], the legend in which the Ashmedai drives King Solomon from the his seat of power, spits him out far away from home, where no one knows him and no one imagines his extraordinary wisdom, is among the best in the repertoire of the *Purim-shpiler*. But King Solomon again attains the seat of power and begins a struggle with Ashmedai, the King of the Demons.

This *shtik* [piece] was filled with songs, each performer sang a solo as well as in the chorus. Later, the songs went through the *shtetl*. Here is one that remains in my memory:

[Column 539]

"You should go there on the mountain.
It is high and very strong.
There you will find Ashmedai
In a very deep well…
Go into it,
Make him drunk with strong wine,
He will become confused
And you will take him in chains."

[Column 540]

The preparations for the performance lasted for weeks; special costumes were prepared that cost nothing. Everything was donated.

The *Purim-shpilers* ceased their activities around the years 1907-1908. But those in disguise who collected donations for important purposes were still present many years later.

Translator's note

1. A *Purim-shpiler* was a person who went through the *shtetl* [town] on Purim performing short plays in return for which he would receive money, food or drink

[Column 539]

A Visit to the *Shtetl* After 13 Years

by Dov Brukarz

Translated by Gloria Berkenstat Freund

It was in August 1935, exactly 13 years had passed since we had left Czyzewo for *Eretz Yisrael* [Land of Israel], August 1922.

We had lived in *Eretz Yisrael* for 13 years and had not stopped longing for the simple, primitive *shtetl*, Czyzewo, until … we made the excursion.

We arrived from Warsaw close to midnight. Velvel Jabka was already waiting for us at the train station with his *britshke* [half-covered wagon] and he brought us to the sleeping *shtetl* [town].

The road to the train, the length of two *viorst*,[1] had not changed at all; the white stones that stood at the edges on both sides of the highway were a sign in the dark night that here is the edge of the highway and that a canal began.

[Column 540]

The alder trees stand on the other side from which a faint noise is heard. Opposite us are the houses of the Czyzewo village right at the bend; on the left we recognize Hersh-Natikhe's low, small house that was burned with its four windmills and all of the other surrounding houses in 1914, during the First World War.

We rode the length of Kolye Street to Zbulun's inn, lighted by a large paraffin lamp, or as they were called "kerosene lamp."

"We only have electrical lighting until 11 o'clock at night" - Velvel, who had been quiet the entire time, with his face to the horses, told us. We entered the large market; we recognized the shops there that run along the entire length of the market up to the Catholic church. We stopped at Shmuelye the tailor's house where Velvel's brother lives: we will stay there during out stay in Czyzewo.

[Column 541]

I think this is the same *shtetl* Czyzewo, the same wooden, low, small houses with the sloped shingle roofs, from which people with blackened faces looked out, houses built of brick standing in a row like soldiers, but little changed. The outer walls to the front of the street are painted with lime, mostly with white lime.

The well, built with a surrounding thick wooden wall a meter in height, was in a part of the market between Yossel-Boruch Lapek's brick house in the row of stores and Sura-Ete's wooden house from which two windows look out from the upper room.

[Column 542]

Opposite stands the water pump just as neglected as 13 years ago so that the water is not used as drinking water, only for putting out the frequent fires that occur in Czyzewo. The canals, in which the dirty water that is poured out of the houses, the so called *kanalizatisia*, is carried away to the river which cuts through the width of the *shtetl*. Beginning at the slaughterhouse, it cuts through the Blacksmith Street and Andjowe's "orchard" until it falls into the Brak River.

[Column 543]

Here the images consist of places partly covered with wooden boards that do not stop the odor that comes from there in summer. The Brak River is used to wash clothing, to swim in during the summer - for taking drinking water, ignoring the fact that the water later returns to it. Never mind - it is flowing water and they manage…

The people have changed greatly during the 13 years.

Children have grown up. Young people have become old and the older ones have become old men. But many of the former old men could not wait for our visit and they have returned from whence they came [i.e. they have died].

From right to left: **Yehoshua Lepak, of blessed memory, Pinye Zysman and his daughter, Hodes, of blessed memory** and *lahavdil* [to distingish] between the living and dead - **Berl Brukarz and Berl Gorzalczany**
Sitting, from the left: **Dvora Gromadzyn and Nekhkama Zysman, of blessed memory** and *lahavdil* between the living and dead - **Dvora Brukarz, Sheva Gorzalczany**
Third row: **Shepsl Zysman and Yehoshua Lepak's son, Shmuelik, of blessed memory**

As we were the first family that took all of its belongings and 13 years ago departed for *Eretz-Yisrael*, we were also the first, and perhaps only one that brought greetings to Czyzewo from *Eretz-Yisrael*.

Every day, when we first appeared in the street, we were surrounded by curious people and we were sprinkled with a flood of questions and then asked to compare the life "there" (*Eretz-Yisrael*) and here (in exile). Everything interested them; they wanted to know about everything; many would wonder about "there" and regret that "here" the life was so difficult, taxes, lack of income and the like.

We did not feel safe with our lives when we went out at night. In the best case we received painful blows from the anti-Semitic neighbors.

[Column 544]

Often after we would leave the group, someone would remember and run after us to ask us something. I remember how Avraham Yossel, Yitzchak Ahron's son, remembered that he had not asked me, is it true that there I work on the second day of a holiday and I put on *tefillin*?[2]

– Yes, it is true - I answered.

Once, Yossel, Zawel-Leib's son (Yossel Kotliarek), approached me and asked me to agree to go to his rabbi and ask how I should behave on the second day of a holiday and particularly regarding praying on *Simkhas-Torah* [fall holiday commemorating the end and start of the yearly Torah readings]?

The acting rabbi was then Rabbi Levinson, the son-in-law of Rabbi, Reb Shmuel Dovid Zabludower, may the memory of a righteous man be blessed, who had then become ill. The rabbi advised me that in the morning I should put on *tefillin* privately and later come to the synagogue and put on the *talis* [prayer shawl] without a blessing and I could take part in *kiddush* [blessing on the wine] with the congregation, as is the custom, but I should not ask to be called up to read the Torah.

I prayed in the Zionist Club, which also served as the synagogue for praying on *Shabbos* and the holidays.

The visitors at the praying were young men and young boys, who at my departure from Czyzewo were even younger, or grown children of those who I remember and who perished at the hands of the Germans: Pinye Zysman, Yakov Jablonka, Yehoshua Lepak, Shmulke Wengorz, Shalom Grynberg (Czelonogora), the Grynberg brothers and others.

After praying, friendly conversation or reports about various local, communal and political problems would take place.

[Column 545]

The reporter and leader of the discussions for the most part was Berl Gorzalczany. The building in which we came together, a wooden one, was already finished. It only lacked an oven for heating in winter. A banquet was arranged for the close of *Shabbos* for the departure to *Eretz-Yisrael* of comrade Yitzchak Szlaski and his wife, Chana. I was given the honor of toast master; I used the opportunity then to give the *misheberakhs* [blessing for a person or group] to everyone present at the banquet and because of "promises of a contribution" asked how much was promised for a "cockle stove" [stove made of Dutch tiles]. A large sum was actually collected.

In the morning, Sunday, the group came to say goodbye to us. The last ones to remain were Yehoshua Lepak and his son, Dvora Gromadzyn and Pinye, his wife, Khome (Nekhema) Zysman, of blessed memory, Berl Gorzalczany, long may he live and his wife, Sheyve.

"It is a pity for those who are gone and no longer to be found."

Translator's notes

1. A *viorst* is a little longer than a kilometer
2. In *Eretz-Yisrael* some religious holidays are observed for one day rather than the two days in *golus* - exile.

In the Days of the Polish–Bolshevik War

by Dvora Brukarz (Dwasza), Tel Aviv

Translated by Gloria Berkenstat Freund

Every change in the ruling power in Poland began and ended with Jewish blood and Jewish tears. Thus it was in the years 1914–1915, the years of the Russian–Polish War, when the Russians left Poland and the Germans occupied it. It was the same in 1918 when the Poles took over the government [and] drove out the Germans. And it also was in 1920 at the time of the Polish–Bolshevik War when the Bolsheviks occupied Poland and, later, were again driven out by the Poles.

On the last day, when the Polish soldiers had to leave Czyzewo, escaping from the Bolsheviks, heartrending screams were heard at night from the shopkeepers and other Jews in private houses who were robbed and beaten.

[Column 546]

Living in our house were my mother, may she rest in peace, and my sisters. We decided to tear out the floor, dig a pit and hide all of the more useful household objects, linen, furniture and other things of value until the storms of war passed. Meanwhile, these things would not be stolen, although we knew this work was dangerous.

On a day when people were grabbed to drive cattle, the news reached me that a soldier was waiting in Berl's house to take him to drive cattle. Perl, Avrahamtshe the tailor's [wife], had brought me the news. (Although she already had a second husband, she was referred to with the name of her first husband).

My brother began doing the work with the help of his comrade, Berl Brukarz (now my husband). By the light of a small kerosene lamp and [behind] a well–closed door and Window, after several hours of heavy work, a large enough pit was dug out. Suddenly, we heard knocking in the door and in Polish we were ordered to open the door. We all stood frozen in fear. We understood how great the danger was in opening the door. They would see the pit. They would accuse us of hiding gold for the enemy. There were many such similar accusations at that time. Not opening? It was no less dangerous. They would break in the door. Meanwhile the knock became stronger and more arrogant. We opened it.

[Column 547]

Two Polish soldiers came in and with leisurely calmness asked for bread or for whatever there was to eat. They did not appear cruel. We took whatever bread we had and gave it to them. However, they said that it would be much better for us if we heard knocking on the door a second time and opened the door right away. We thanked them and breathed freely because he [Berl] was in the other room and because of the darkness.

In the middle of the night shouting was heard from the neighboring house. We recognized that the shouting was [in the house of] Yudel the carpenter. Soldiers were demanding money from him and he said that he did not have any, so the soldiers severely beat him. One soldier firmly held his hand and the second one poured gunpowder on his palm (surface of his hand), lit it, did not let go until the gunpowder had burned. His [Yudel's] shouts were heard throughout the street, but there was no one to take the risk and come to his aid and they would not have been able to help him. Meanwhile, other soldiers robbed and beat [him], broke everything that came into their hands.

There still was heavy shooting in the early morning; we again heard banging on our door. The pit in which we had hid the bed linen, underwear, furniture and other things had been covered, the dirt that had been dug out had been taken to the garden under the house; the boards that had been torn out had been replaced as if nothing had happened. My brother opened the door at the second knock. The same two soldiers entered. But they looked different than before, agitated red faces, wild burning eyes and as soon as they came in, one shouted to my brother: "*Żydzu, otday twoi pieniądze!*" [Jews, give your money] and he immediately put both his hands in [my brother's] pocket. He found a silver cigarette case and took it without saying a word. He took Berl's watch with its good chain and immediately ran out of the house. A miracle occurred now, too, that they did not look in the other room. Who knows if they would have noticed that there was a hiding place.

[Column 548]

In the morning, no Polish soldiers were seen in the streets and also no civilians. This shtetl looked as if it was Yom Kippur, closed doors and windows everywhere. A contingent of soldiers was first noticed in the afternoon coming from the other side of the train line, and in scattered rows they neared the direction of Szmidiszer Street. Shouting was heard – Bolsheviks are coming!! People came out of their houses and went to meet them. They immediately recognized that these were Polish soldiers. The people ran away quickly. The soldiers shot after them. Luckily, they did not shoot anyone.

It again became quiet after this and a few hours later the Bolshevik reinforcements appeared. The Poles did not enter the city.

[Column 549]

The "Attic" – A Place of Refuge

One room was taken from us at the time when the Bolsheviks were in Czyzewo. The commissar of the *Chrezvychaynaya* [*Cheka* – Soviet secret police] was quartered there and various people were brought there; mostly from the Polish intelligentsia, the priest, the apothecary and others. However, their rule did not last long.

When the Bolsheviks left Czyzewo and the Poles again became the boss, they threw fear on the Jewish population. Soldiers went through the streets and into the houses and grabbed men for all kinds of forced labor and to drive cattle from one city to another. This "cattle driving" was a good opportunity to have a little fun at the expense of the Jews. This was the greatest danger for those who fell into this work. Whoever was permitted to return home did not return whole, but was exhausted and beaten. Jews with beards returned home with half their beards torn out. The Jews without beards were beaten because they did not have beards, with screams of mockery – "*Zyd* [derogatory Polish word for Jew] – where is your beard?" Or they would be asked to shout:

– *Niech rabin żyje, a ksiądz niech gnije* (Let the rabbi live and the priest should rot). And immediately after this a flood of blows poured forth on the Jews for cursing the priest. It was not better for those who did not want to shout or for those who did not shout loudly enough.

[Column 550]

There was a large attic over our house that served as a workplace for making *tsitsis* [fringed undergarment worn by pious men] and because the house was a meter lower than the one next to it, a second roof was built there where neighbors hid from police raids to capture men to drive cattle.

On a day when they were grabbing men for driving cattle, the news reached me that a soldier was waiting at Berl's house to take him to drive cattle. The news had been brought to me by Perl, the wife of Avrahamtshe the tailor. (Although she had a second husband, she was always referred to with the name of her first husband). Hearing the news I left my housework and in desperate fear, I went to Berl. At that moment I did not even think if I would be able to do something to help him. No pleading or tears was of help with them [the Poles]. When I reached the house I saw the soldier walking around with his rifle on his shoulder at the entrance. I walked by with the pretense of nonchalant calm and entered the house. The picture I saw there remains before my eyes today.

Berl's parents stood as if they were frozen. From their stiff, dark faces screamed out the grief of the torturing that took away their son. His brother, Mordechai, may he rest in peace, also was hiding somewhere and they knew nothing about him. Berl, pale as chalk, had wanted to leave the house… But suddenly…

– The only possibility to save him!

[Column 551]

– If only he could come here he would be saved!

I pointed with my hand in the direction of the window that looked out onto the courtyard, I said quietly, but loud enough for Berl to hear:

– Run out of the window! In the middle of the backway – quickly to the attic!… He remained standing, not moving, for a moment, thinking. It looked as if he had not understood what I was saying to him. However, he immediately came to himself and reached the attic safely.

I then began to think about what would happen if the soldier saw that his victim had escaped from him… Suddenly the soldier outside shoved open the door and shouted: "What is taking so long?" For a while we were terrified of the shouting. Berl's mother, may she rest in peace, went over to the soldier:

– My son has already left to go to you…

And she quickly took a piece of brown bread weighing several pounds and a sack of apples. Offering them to the soldier, she pleadingly said to him: "I beg you to take this package with you and give it to my son. He did not take anything with him…" The soldier, starving, greedily grabbed the package and left the house. Everyone breathed easier… We did not feel the earlier tears of joy that had poured over our heated faces that we had succeeded in saving Berl.

[Column 552]

A few hours later I heard running outside and a soldier shouting: *Stoj! Stoj! Bo ja strzelę!*" (Halt! Halt! I will shoot!). This was Avraham–Boruch Lepak. The soldier wanted to take him to the cattle drive. Passing our courtyard, Avraham–Boruch quickly escaped and went up to the attic. The soldier had lost sight of him when he grabbed his gun to shoot him [Avraham–Boruch]. He [the soldier] walked around the entrance to the attic and shouted like a confused animal:

– *Psia krew! jJak ja tego zyda złapię jak ja tego zyda złapię, to go zastszeljas jak psa*! (Blood of a dog! When I catch the Jew, I will shoot him like a dog). Roaring in this way, he thought for a long time and then went up to the attic.

The attic was empty and light. The soldier remained standing at the entrance. He looked around and saw that it was impossible for someone to hide here unnoticed. At the entrance one could not notice that at the other end lay more than 30 people holding their breath with their hearts beating in fear.

The soldier grumbled, as if to himself:

– *Psia krew! Nie ma nikogo*! (Blood of a dog! No one is here!) And he came down from the attic exasperated. Today, I still shudder when I think about what could have happened if the soldier had uncovered the hiding place and had found so many Jews there.

A large number were still alive until the annihilation of Czyzewo and perished with all of the Jews. May their memory be blessed!

[Column 553]

How Cossacks Arrested Me as a German Spy

by Simcha Glina, Tel Aviv

Translated by Gloria Berkenstat Freund

This was on a Monday morning. The Germans had withdrawn and the first divisions of the Russian Army had entered the *shtetl* [town].

First, they began with our mill and started to break the blades. When I asked them why they were doing this, they answered that they needed wood to cook their food.

It occurred to me to wind the blades of the mill so that they could not reach them. I thought that they would give up and I went home.

It did not take long and three Cossack officers came into the house. There was a soldier with them who immediately pointed to me.

Leading me outside, they immediately began cursing me:

– You *Zydowski Shpion* [Jewish spy]; you think that we do not understand that you have tricked us? You have let the Germans know where we are…

The soldier tied me to his horse and pulled me through the road to the station where the Russian chief commander was located.

[Column 554]

The streets and roads were empty; only the sky was red with the reflection of fires. The *shtetlekh* [towns] and villages around Czyzewo were burning.

I was injured [and] the Cossacks took me to the headquarters, reporting that they had caught a Jew, a German spy.

The commandant, also a Cossack, attacked me with clenched fists, cursed and reviled me with obscene words, adding that he would not play with me for long, that I would be hanged immediately.

Meanwhile he locked me in a separate room and placed a Cossack as a guard.

I saw myself as doomed and quietly made a spiritual examination of my conscience and made a confession of my sins.

I do not remember how long I sat. Suddenly the door opened and a commanding voice shouted:

– Come!

I was sure that they were taking me to the gallows. My wife and my six–month old son appeared before my eyes; I strongly wished to say goodbye to them, to look at them in the last minutes of my life.

[Column 555]

When I was taken past the train station I saw a train standing full of Jews. Among them were the Lubelcziks, Yisrael–Nakhman and his family, and Mordechai. I saw the certainty on their faces that they were being taken to be hanged.

The soldiers who walked behind me did not say one word. Their steps with their hob–nailed boots echoed in my ears as if they were counting my last minutes. In a moment they would stop somewhere at a prepared gallows and be finished with me.

We already had walked for a while onto the Ciechanowiec highway and stopped near some sort of low buildings. I searched with my eyes for a gallows, but the soldiers brutally shoved me into an open room where an officer was located and reported to him that they had brought a spy.

The officer eyed me from my head to my feet and began to scold the soldiers as to why they were driving him crazy with a Jewish spy. He ordered then to take me back to Czyzewo to the commandant in charge of prisoners. He would know what to do with me.

The soldiers saluted and led me outside.

The sky looked as if the entire world was on fire. The shooting grew heavier with every minute and echoed in the emptiness of the road with frightful horror. The soldiers did not know where to look for the prisoner commandant. It turned out that he had already left the *shtetl* and they remained standing with a dilemma: what should they do with the Jewish spy?

[Column 556]

They spoke quietly to each other and then informed me that they had decided to hand me over to the Czyzewo village magistrate who should be responsible for me and guard me until an order arrived about what to do with me. They only wanted to know if the village magistrate was a Jew.

Hearing from me that the village magistrate was a Jew, they again had a dilemma. They were firmly determined not to leave me in Jewish hands and began to rack their brains for where there were authorities with whom they could entrust a Jewish spy.

Finally they wanted to find the local authorities where they could leave me and receive confirmation [that they had left me]. However, the building was bolted and nailed shut. There were no living souls around. A strange, almost frightening stillness reigned except for the echoes of the distant thunder.

The soldiers already were tired from looking for an authority to take the Jewish spy and began to grumble among themselves: was it possible that they would not find a Christian village magistrate here?

I got the idea that they should take me to Bartek, the village magistrate, who lived at Modlin [Street] and was an acquaintance of mine.

They gladly accepted my proposal, but arriving at his house we met his wife. Bartek was not at home.

[Column 557]

My hope again ended. The fear of the gallows again began to stick in my heart. The solders became angry and decided to take me back to the train station to the Cossack commandant. He should finish with me.

Bartek came at the same moment as they were leaving with me for the station. He stopped with surprise that they were taking me. The Cossacks said that I was a spy and demanded that he give his signature that he had received the spy and was responsible for me when they left me.

Bartek went to sign but his wife appeared at the same moment with a lament. He should not take upon himself such a responsibility for a Jew.

Bartek stood for a minute with hanging hands and did not know what he should do. He immediately came to and blew up with impatience at his wife:

– Quiet!

[Column 558]

He signed.

The soldiers left and I breathed a sigh of relief. I finally was free, but where would I go now at four o'clock in the morning. I could again have an encounter with some Cossack patrol and be held as a spy.

I chased after the soldiers and promised to pay well if they would take me home. They watched me closely; did I mean to entice them into something? But it turned out that they recognized in me that I did not have any bad intentions and one quickly whispered as if he wanted to be persuaded if this inviting idea would result in confusion.

– Well, come quickly.

I ran as if with wings and the soldiers followed me.

Several minutes later I was in the house. No one was asleep. Everyone had waited for a miracle.

This cost me a copper 10–piece coin.

[Column 559]

My Good Father

By Simcha Prawda

Translated by Chana Pollack and Myra Mniewski

I am venturing into the sensitive memories of my childhood kingdom in the small *shtetl* of Czyzewo, where I was born, bred, and grew up. There was so much beauty there, orchards with red cherries and juicy apples, green meadows, a forest with thick leaved trees and squirrels on the branches.

The rustle of the forest and the song of the river sound so sad to me now. None of those lovely and hearty figures, who are engraved in my memory forever, exist today, and no power in the world is strong enough to tear them from my heart. They are revealed to me in my nightly dreams and in lifelike visions at twilight and when I lie with eyes open waiting for the arrival of dawn. So much beauty shines from them, so much life, Jewish faith, Jewish stubbornness in waiting for the messiah. My father's *ani ma'amin* resounds in my ears, his strong voice, which in difficult times comforted and encouraged, "Jews, don't give up, salvation will surely come."

My father was a quiet Jew, an ordinary fellow with a little blond beard. He was a humble Torah scholar. He wore a black caftan woven in accordance with ritual law. His kind honest heart trembled when he heard a child cry or someone in pain, even if it was a stranger.

The modesty of my father's heart was always with me. More than once, in my rushing about, I would suddenly long for the comfort of my father's *talis* and *tefilin*, just like I longed for the homey taste of the coarse black bread following the recitation of the weekday *hamoytse*. And above all, I longed for his virtue, which he exhibited in all his worldly endeavors.

It was my father's habit, on his way home from the prayer house in his cowhide boots, to quietly whisper the daily psalms. And as he walked he thought of me, his Simcha, who was *keyneynhore* [1], growing up already and plans for his future had to be made. But at the bottom of his heart he believed that his son, with God's help, would grow up to be a mature, respectable, honest Jew.

[Column 561]

It happened on an ordinary market day. The market and the little streets were full of peasants. Women, overworked with haggard faces, their bonnets tilted on their heads, were bargaining back and forth with each other. Sounds of the marketplace filled the air. My father was busy in his shop. But he remembered to send me off to school.

As I passed Motl's shop, I felt something under my feet. When I bent down, I couldn't believe my eyes— it was a wallet with money. This happened so suddenly that in that minute I forgot everything I had been taught at home and in school about the great sin of taking what was not mine. I put the wallet in my pocket and hastened my footsteps turning to look back often to make sure no one was following me.

In a quiet alley I counted the treasure. There were ten rubles and ninety kopecks in the wallet. In those days that was a large sum of money.

I did not go into the study-hall but held the wallet tightly in my hands as I proceeded to find my friends: Simkhl Gromadzyn, Shmulke Lazers, and Leybish Berishes, and we all went to play cards in the women's section of the *shul*.

We played for a few hours, until I lost all the money. On my way home, sad, with a bitter taste in my mouth, I heard crying screams on our street, coming from Motl Feyge-Peyes store, "Give me back my money."

My heart felt like it was breaking. With hesitant steps, I drew closer. A Jew with an old fashioned caftan—his cries, hoarse and pained, quietly complained that he was ousted from Mishenitz and that that money was his whole fortune. He was about to buy some green soap, but now he was lost.

Motl Feyge-Peyes cursed and swore on her life that she didn't know anything about it and hadn't seen any money.

The Jew was in despair, releasing a sigh that cut through my heart, "*Oy*, kind, merciful Father, what am I going to do now?"

I wanted to scream out, "Sir, I found your money!"

[Column 563]

But I was immediately frightened by my own idea. Where was I going to get the money to pay him back? I had lost it all.

For a few minutes, an internal struggle raked me. I felt I had committed a horrible crime and, if I didn't correct it now, I would never be forgiven and I'd go around with a guilty conscience for the rest of my life.

I tore away from where I stood, ran to the despairing Jew and, trying to control the uproar in my heart, asked him quietly, "Tell me, how much money did you have in the wallet?"

"Ten rubles and ninety kopecks," The Jew turned his gaze on me, his eyes full of pain, grief, and pleading. For identification purposes, he added, "There were also two buttons in the wallet, and one button was broken."

"Come with me, I found your wallet."

I didn't want to think about what would happen next, how I would get the money to pay him back. I knew that he had to get his money back and I was prepared to endure the greatest sufferings.

Bobe Sore tells 6 grandchildren a story

On top: her daughters Rivke and Perl as well as herdaughter-in-law are listening to her sweet tale

[Column 565]

In a few minutes I was in my father's shop with the Jew. I didn't wait for my father to ask, but hastily spoke out instead, "Father, you may do whatever you wish to me, I will accept everything with love, but return the money to the Jew. I found it and lost it playing cards."

I wanted to continue to talk, plea, cry, but the words remained stuck in my throat. My father's face grew strict, as if he were getting ready to execute a sentence. Then within a moment his gaze shifted like an extinguished flame which had suddenly been blown out by a cold wind. With all the strength of my boyish heart I wanted to shout, "Hit me, and kill me! I deserve it! But the Jew should not suffer!" But before I even managed to open my mouth, my father turned to my mother and called out, "Sura, cut three yards of linen for a frock for the Jew."

Upon turning back to us, his face was again transformed. A warm, bright smile shone in his eyes as well as on his whole face, "Not a *groshn* will be missing." He walked over to the drawer, counted ten rubles and ninety kopecks and gave them to the man, while my mother measured the linen.

Later, my father sat with the Jew, invited him for *shabes* and schmoozed with him as if he were a welcomed guest, a close friend.

He didn't scream at me. It was clear to me that in those moments, when my father looked deep into my turbulent heart, he was comforted knowing that his Simchale was fulfilling the commandment of returning a lost object.

Shabes arrived. It was the nicest and grandest *shabes* of my life.

Soon it will be fifty years since that happened and my heart still quivers, as if it were yesterday.

You are always with me, dear father, everyday of my life. Your hard lived life, or unlived life, will accompany me like the sun, even more radiant than the sun. Your deeds will forever illuminate my disposition.

Translator's note:
1. May you be protected from the evil eye.

[Column 567]

My Homily

Simcha Prawda

Translated by Chana Pollack and Myra Mniewski

In my *shtetl*, I was considered an *"apikores"* [heretic]. But God only knows what the nature of my heresy was. I rocked with the same enthusiasm as all the other young hasidic boys when I prayed; I recited the *ani m'a amin* with great devotion every day; I kept my *peyes* [side curls] very long. When I got a haircut I was very careful to make sure Ruven, the religious barber, should, God forbid, not inadvertently let the scissor touch a single hair of my *peyes*. What then was my sin to be deemed an *apikores*?

The answer to this may be as follows:

I once showed up in the hasidic *shtibl* with a short jacket and no hat! This so-called " sin" sealed my fate and brought to pass that I should never again lay eyes on my beloved Aleksander *shtibl*. From that accursed day I was forbidden to set foot in the *shtibl* and the hasidim began to regard me as a dissident.

Having no other choice I went to pray with the *minyen* [quorum] of the *Tiferes Bokherim*[1] which had just been established. There, after prayers we gathered together, gave Zionist sermons and full of longing for Zion, sang the song, *"Al eim haderech shama misgoleles, shoshana haklilas einayim."* It was there that we decided to perform the play, " Village Youth," as a benefit for the library. Everyone was given a role. It was my lot to play the part of Reb Khatsye, which entailed giving a *drashe* [sermon].

[Column 568]

This role was sent to me straight from heaven. It was there, through this sermon, that I was given the opportunity to get even with the hasidic *minyen* who had wronged me by banning me from the *shtibl*. In my sermon I gave my all to making fun of the hasidic fanaticism in Czyzewo. I rehearsed my lines day and night and when I enunciated the words, "When a Jew sins with "something" in this world, what happens to him in the next world?" I gesticulated with various hasidic grimaces to the nth degree.

Despite the fact that we rehearsed in secret in the firehall, news that we were preparing a play somehow became public. Women in the market secretly passed the word to each other, from mouth to ear, wringing their hands.

The *shtetl* was in a fuss, but we, prepared for the performance with all our fervor.

One *shabes*, after the morning prayer, as soon as they took out the Torah, Avrom Yoysef the hasid, agitated, his arms flailing, ran into the Gerer *shtibl* screaming, "*Gevald*, Jews, we're on fire!" There is no need for prayer and there is no need for learning, *'It's time to do the Lord's work; your Torah has been undone'*. The *forces of evil*, may God protect us from them, are surfacing in our *shtetl*." He screamed inflamed, his adam's apple bobbing up and down, his pointy little black beard jutting in rhythm, "*Vey, vey*, Jews, why are you just standing there? There's a fire burning up our homes, our whole *shtetl*, the fire is coming from the firehall and it's consuming our children! *Gevald* Jews, rescue! *'Whoever is for the Lord, come with me!'*"

[Column 569]

The crowd left the Torah on the table, as if in disgrace, and still wrapped in their *taleysim* [prayer shawls], went directly to the firehall to extinguish the blaze. At that moment, the Aleksander hasid, Reb Velvel Shmuel Zeligs, stood in the doorway of our house with his head down, looking like a mourner just returned from a funeral, God help us.

My mother, frightened at seeing Velvel in this condition, screamed, "Ahron, what happened?"

"They say, that your Simchale," his voice cracked not completing the sentence, and all the while standing with his head bent.

[Column 570]

"What about my Simchale?" My mother asked, her eyes bulging, terrified.

"Your Simchale," Velvel began again his voice sounding as if it was coming out of an empty barrel, "*Oy vey, gevald*, God in Heaven—boys and girls, may God protect us, get together and play *treyater* and your Simchale is the big *makher* among them and you are silent?"

"My Simchale?" My mother, already calmed a bit, asked. She raised her modest eyes to heaven, as if to thank God that at least I was alive, and again asked, "What are you talking about Reb Velvel, my Simchale? Aren't you mistaken?"

"Yes, your Simchale. I am not mistaken," Reb Velvel drew out his words, "Who is closer to a child than his mother? You must see to it that your dear brat allows his father, the *tzadik* Reb Shlomo, to rest in peace in his grave. You must see to it that he not play in any *treyater*. That is how you can save the entire *shtetl*. The curse on the *shtetl* will be lifted, children won't be taken from us before their time, and all ills will be cured."

The whole time he was speaking my mother wiped her tears with her *shabes* apron and as soon as she saw me entering the house she looked into my eyes with weeping eyes and asked, "Simchale, you play *treyater*?"

[Column 571]

"How do you know mother?" I answered with a question.

"The whole town is fuming over you," my mother, wringing her hands and sobbing asked me again, "Is it true?"

Silently, I let down my head and didn't answer.

"*Vey* to the mother who has lived to see this! Woe, woe is to me that I have to witness this, and *vey* to your father in his grave, *nebekh!*"[12]

"Simchale!" she began to plead, "Don't disgrace your father in his afterlife, obey your mother. Is it suitable for Shlomka Prawda's son and Moshe Prawda's grandson to congregate with cheeky girls to play the *treyater*?"

My mother's tears and pleading voice literally broke my heart. I decided not to go anymore and promised my mother, "My foot will not cross their threshold!"

Simcha Gromadzyn-Gordon, New York and Simcha Prawda, Mexico

But soon after, I thought to myself, "How will I be able to do this? How could I keep my promise after I had already invested so much work, rehearsing my part with the sermon so many times and especially since the profits were designated to maintain the library. And what will Libshe, the fishmonger's daughter, say? She is expecting me with her infatuated eyes?"

[Column 572]

Indeed, I soon regretted my holy promise to my mother not to act again. As soon as my mother fell asleep after supper, I crept out gingerly, and as if chased by a gale, went straight to the hangar where they were already waiting for me and immediately immersed myself in my role.

As soon as I saw Libshe there, I totally forgot about the promise I had made to my mother and began again to rehearse my role. When I got to the *drashe* I gave it my all, screaming with all of my might. It felt as if I wanted to pommel those *frume yidn* for my mother's tears, for disturbing our *shabes*, and for forcing me to deceive my mother.

When I finished Yelling out my sermon, applause broke out in response to my acting. No one knew however what was going on in my heart at that moment.

Dear mother, forgive me!

[Column 571]

The Holy Billy Goat

Simcha Prawda

Translated by Chana Pollack and Myra Mniewski

Among other things, Czyzewo was blessed with goats and billy-goats. Day and night the goats used to roam the shtetl's streets and alleys, chewing their cuds and leaving tokens of their visits.

[Column 572]

Each goat procured its food in its own way. One grabbed a little grass off an unhitched wagon, another noshed from a sack of potatoes on a peasant's cart. Another took the opportunity to stick its head into a mare's feedbag when the mare was taking a break from eating to shake off some flies. The goat continued to munch away until the mare flared its nostrils in a loud snort frightening the goat who ran away offended.

[Column 573]

There were goats that staved off hunger with a handful of cabbage or even an apple. In a pinch, a roll from Malka the baker would also do.

That is how every goat procured its little bit of food, with no dearth of fear and often actually accompanied by the crack of a whip or hard stick over its brittle bones. That is why, when it came to milking, every goat knew who its owner was and only the owner had the right to some of its rich milk. It was never arbitrary.

Amidst the herd of Czyzewo goats, a "*bokher*" that freely roamed. He had a lengthy, dignified little beard and pious eyes that were overshadowed by his broad overhanging ears.

He would turn his bushy head this way and that as he strolled the streets, bleating in his hoarse little voice, "Meh, meh, meh!" This was an indication for all to make way; the city's he-goat was coming through! Respect for the city's holy billy-goat! And people actually honored him and made way; no one wanted to get caught in his pointy horns.

The only one in town, who not only didn't honor as befit the *shtetl's* one and only billy-goat, but instead scornfully doled out heaping portions of blows, was Reb Itzl Kayles (his wife's name was Kayle). He was the goat's rightful owner, who according to Jewish law, was supposed to be allowed to roam freely because he was a first-born male.

[Column 574]

As soon as the little goat arrived into the world, Reb Itzl Kayles had already calculated how many pots of milk this little goat would produce when it grew up to become a goat. With great joy he tied a red ribbon around the beautiful little goat's forehead which was marked with two adorable little patches. This served as an amulet against the evil eye. Reb Itzl was never stingy about giving the little goat milk to drink. No worries, it would, God willing, return a lot more than that.

And that's how things went along calmly and undisturbed, until. . .

One fine day, Reb Itzl noticed that the young goat was beginning to sprout a little beard, that was growing longer with each passing day and…that it was actually a he-goat and that he had been fattening up a freeloader who was sponging off him. From that day on, Reb Itzl began to decrease the goat's food ration, until one fine morning, he stopped feeding him altogether and in a huff banished him from the shed where he slept.

So the billy-goat, *nebekh*,[2] had to wander through the *shtetl* alone in search of its daily sustenance. But the day came when the billy-goat grew lonesome for his former owner, Reb Itzl. As it happened that day turned out to be the day that Reb Itzl forgot to lock his granary where sacks of wheat and flour were stored. The billy-goat leisurely strolled in and with great pleasure began sating his hunger. He buried his head and beard in a sack of barley, ate a while, tried a bit of wheat from another sack and washed it down with some buckwheat from a third sack. But when he was working on dessert, slurping from a bag of wheat-flour, an unwelcome Reb Itzl showed up at the door and without even saying hello, threw a weight he just happened to be holding in his hand at the goat.

Luckily, he missed him. Confused and embarrassed because he was caught stealing red-handed, the billy-goat let out a heart-wrenching "mehhhhhh!"

[Column 575]

In his language this meant, "Why are you beating and berating me? Is it my fault God created me without an udder and I cannot give milk? Am I supposed to go hungry?" But Itzl Kayles had no intention of suppressing his anger and didn't stop beating and cursing his poor *bokher* for breaking into the granary without his knowledge and stuffing himself on all the goodies.

At a certain moment, the billy-goat froze in its tracks, as if he might have found a way to flee his undeserving master, but he didn't. Instead he sneezed loudly. Reb Itzel spat right in his face and chased the thief into the street, giving him one for the road with a stick across his emaciated back.

A few days later, after the aforementioned incident, Itzel suddenly noticed an eruption of warts on his face. It was the talk of the town that this was Itzel Kayles' punishment for torturing and spitting in the face of his holy *bokher*. From then on he received a new name, no longer Itzel Kayles, he was now called Reb Itzel the Wart.

After this incident with Itzel, every one was very careful not to lay a hand on the holy *bokher*. He, the holy *bokher*, roamed the *shtetl* freely paying visits to grocery stores, produce stands, even visiting bakeries to snack on some baked goods.

[Column 576]

The billy-goat's first visit, after his unfriendly reception at Itzl's, was at the grocery store of Reb Itzl's neighbor, Reb Dovid Sura Etes (his wife's name was Sura Ete.) With his little beard, he rummaged in a sack of oats, "and he saw that it was good." Realizing its true taste he dug his chin deeper into the oats and had a go at it. From Sura Ete's store, he went for a walk around the marketplace, grabbed a lick of farina at Mendel Liev's and saw that this too was not bad. He then honored the widow Sura Rachel with a visit, to satisfy his taste for some ground chickpeas followed by some sour pickles from the barrel at the entrance.

The townsfolk, *nebekh*[2], watched the antics of the holy first-born and, suppressed their anger, pursed their lips and remained silent. One may not disturb the *bokher*. No one dared throw anything at the billy-goat or hit him, because, God forbid, he might become afflicted as punishment for one of the worst sins, not a trivial matter. The *bokher*, according to Jewish law, is free to do his want, and our holy *bokher* indeed behaved as though unbridled.

When Yutke, Yoske Nisl's wife, saw the he-goat approaching her grocery store knowing how he freely roamed through the shops, mercilessly gorging and swilling, she was enraged. Knowing that she begrudged her own children a little farina to cook up for themselves how could she let this glutton feast free of charge? Even if he is a holy *bokher* was she obligated to let him gorge? Isn't it enough that he depletes everyone else's stores and no one does anything about it? Where is the judge and where is justice? No! She would not be silent!

[Column 577]

She grabbed a rolling pin and determined, ran out into the marketplace, straight over to the billy-goat. The goat reared up on its hind legs, pointed his goatee in her face and let out a drawn out "mehehehhhh," baring his pointy horns. All of which meant the following in goat language:

"Yutke, Yutke, who do you think you are going up against with that rolling pin? Against the "holy billy-goat"? Against Itzl's *bokher*, his only-son? I'll impale you on my horns and show you who's boss! Show some respect for the holy *bokher*!!!"

Only then did Yutke realize her mistake. She was not dealing with just any he-goat, but with the *shtetl's* esteemed he-goat, who, according to the law, should not be harmed. God may punish her, heaven forbid, as he did Itzl Kayles, may the merciful one protect us.

She spat three times saying, "May only my enemies suffer so."

The holy goat again strode daintily around from shop to shop, from trough to trough on an eating spree from the nicest and best and no one disturbed him.

[Column 578]

We *kheyder*[3] boys who enjoyed catching billy-goats in order to ride them would make a game of chasing them until they collapsed with the rider on their backs, having no more strength to stand back up. But Reb Itzl's holy first-born was treated with great respect and love. We were afraid of him, caring for him as if he were our own eyes. We fed and protected him for we were scared we would wind up like Itzl Kayles, God forbid, with a face full of warts. Along with the fear we also pitied him and felt badly that Itzl had abandoned him. Indeed every boy tried to oblige the holy-billy-goat, one with a piece of bread, another with a potato or beet that was taken out of the house behind their mother's back. But, as we later learned our kindness turned out to be too good.

It happened on an ordinary Wednesday. We wanted to prepare a festive meal for the holy-billy goat and brought all sorts of treats. Everyone strived to bring the most that they could and we gave it all to the billy-goat. He inhaled everything with gusto, apparently very hungry. Suddenly, he let out a resounding lament, the sound of which carried through the *shtetl*. People ran from all over to see what was happening. A horrific scene—the holy billy-goat is lying in a pool of filth thrashing in anguish from side to side. He raises himself up on his forelegs digging them into the earth, kicking, and ramming his horns into Mendel Liev's stone floor. In great agony he falls down, tries to get up again but cannot, groans loudly and remains on the floor stiff.

[Column 579]

His holy soul ascended!

***

A quorum of Jews raised the holy goat, carried him into the *hekdesh*[4], washed him and wrapped him in a white sheet.

[Column 580]

The whole *shtetl* took part in the funeral. He was carried to the cemetery and every one of the assembled asked forgiveness of the goat, in case someone, God forbid, had caused him pain when he was alive. Everyone felt s/he had a part in the death of the holy-billy goat. But we boys felt clean of sin.

Translator's notes:

1. First born male
2. pitiful
3. school
4. The poorhouse

[Column 579]

Czyzewo *Klezmorim*

by Avraham Yosef Ritholc, New York

Translated by Gloria Berkenstat Freund

I am the great grandson of the Ritholc *klezmer* [musician] family. In Czyzewo, however, my memories barely reach back to my grandfather, Reb Gedalye the *klezmer*, may he rest in peace, whom I as a child would lead for prayer to the house of prayer every day during his old age.

At this opportunity it is worth mentioning that I was the first and perhaps the only one in our family who merited being called by my family name in Czyzewo – Ritholc. However, this first happened during the First World War 1914-1918. Until that time I also was no exception. It was the custom in the *shtetl* [town] to be called by a father's, grandfather's or father-in-law's and mother-in-law's name and even by a wife's name and often according to one's trade or employment.

My grandfather, may he rest in peace, actually was called Gedalye the *klezmer* and I was known by the name: Avraham-Yosef-Itsl the [son of the] *klezmer*.

To Christians I was known as Gedalczuk, after my grandfather's name[1].

[Column 580]

Although my father and almost the entire family, just like my grandfather, drew its pitiful income from watchmaking, that is, from repairing watches, they were called *klezmer*.

In contrast I, who helped my father from childhood on earn an income from [playing] *klezmer*, and later made use of my own strengths and my acquired serious knowledge in the art of music for communal purposes such as the organization of and leadership of an orchestra for the Jewish theater and entertainments, did not however acquire the "*klezmer* title."

Perhaps, it is because it was not my source of income.

My grandfather left four sons and one daughter. All of them were involved with the playing of *klezmer* music.

However, the playing did not provide enough income for even a dry piece of bread; particularly because every family was burdened with several children, everyone had an additional source of income.

[Column 581]

My grandmother, may she rest in peace, would sell small cakes that she would bake at fairs and on market days.

My father and uncles were employed at watchmaking.

However, the *shtetl* and its surroundings were too small to be able to support a large watchmaking family, so we would be a little hungry.

Not having any other alternative, the *klezmer* family began to disperse.

Velvel, the oldest of the brothers, moved to Ciechanowiec and there he and his children created a band.

Ahron, the youngest, moved to Zambrów and also created an orchestra of his own [family] and hired people.

My father and his brother, Yudel, both remained in Czyzewo and were busy with both ways of earning a living (playing *klezmer* music and watchmaking), which was only enough for their families to be hungry for most of the days of the week until my Uncle Yudel finally left for America.

My father remained in Czyzewo. He put a band together and was the only watchmaker for many years.

The following people belonged to the ensemble: my father Itsl – first violin, Yitzchakl the *klezmer* – second violin, Yitzchakl's brother Melekh and my older brother Ahron Dovid – trumpets, the writer of these lines – clarinet or flute, Ahron Leibel and Itshe (both porters) were "basses," Yosl Daniel's [son] – drums.

[Column 582]

Years later the orchestra grew significantly smaller. There only remained: both violin players, and I would help with the clarinet. There were voluntary drummers from among the adult young idlers.

In its blossoming years, the above-mentioned orchestra played at local weddings and sometimes at other happy occasions in the surrounding *shtetlekh* Janczewo, Zambrów or Sokola, even at balls in the surrounding noble courts and Christian village weddings.

It happened often that the groups in a nearby *shtetl* or village would for various reasons forget to send a wagon for the *klezmorim*. The whole orchestra would go on foot (the wages for playing were not enough for hiring a wagon).

For balls, when more music was required, players were hired from other cities and even from Bialystok.

I will only describe two of the episodes, both comical and serious, that would take place, especially at the village weddings and balls.

The first episode shows that with his complete simplicity my father possessed the strength of one who "has great self-control."

It happened in the village of Sudki.

On a beautiful summer day, a Sunday afternoon, we were brought into the courtyard to play at a ball under the open sky. Richly covered tables on which were served various fruits, candies, expensive chocolates and bonbons and various drinks were set out along blossom-lined paths. [There were separate tables on which various smoked and roasted meats were served, which strongly teased our hungry appetites. It really caught our breath.

[Column 583]

The servants knew that Jews do not eat with Christians at the same table. They asked us if they should prepare a separate table for us. We agreed to the proposal not waiting for my father who had gone somewhere to pray the afternoon prayers.

However, the door opened suddenly and my father appeared when we already were sitting around the table laid with chickens fried in butter and other fragrant meats and were ready to start the feast.

It is difficult to say how long the silence lasted in which we all sat as if frozen with fear. Suddenly my father began to scream with superhuman curses:

– Leave! Gentiles, *treyfniakes* [those who eat non-kosher food]! Out, Out!

The band quickly ran, jumped out of the windows and… we had to be satisfied with bread and butter, hard-boiled eggs and tea that my father had prepared while we had been sitting around the non-kosher table.

None of us even thought of rebelling against the actions of my father.

My father was a musician in Czyzewo for 40 years, but because of anti-Semitism that developed in Poland and the anti-Semitic agitation that was carried out, particularly in the Czyzewo area, they stopped using Jewish *klezmer* for Christian balls.

[Column 584]

* * *

I heard the episode that I will now relate from my father when I was a child. Although I am not a follower of spiritualism I will, however, pass it on because the seriousness with which my father would describe this information is deeply engraved in my memory:

On a *Shabbos* night when my grandfather was still a very young man, right after his marriage, two well-dressed noblemen came to him and said that they wanted him and his band to go with them to a ball that they were having that evening.

They mentioned the name of a village with which my grandfather was not familiar. Yet he agreed and called together the group.

They were seated in a beautiful carriage harnessed to three horses and after half an hour of traveling they arrived at a magnificent courtyard where the guests already were gathered.

The musicians were led into a giant dance hall and couples began to dance.

Suddenly [my grandfather said] we noticed that the people dancing had chicken feet.

A terror fell on the group of players; but we didn't know how to get out of there.

We played further, but we agreed among ourselves that we would not eat anything.

[Column 585]

We had to play for several hours because the dancing couples did not want to stop.

It already was close to midnight when the two nobles who had brought us there, approached us and said:

"We are very happy with your playing. What do you want us to pay you with, with gold or with chicken manure?"

"With gold," my grandfather answered in fear.

All at once there was a terrible storm; it became dark and they suddenly found themselves in mud, in a forest. Their violins were hanging on the trees and the violin cases were filled with garbage. They took the violins from the trees with great effort and barely reached home, tired and muddied.

They all went to the house of prayer on Saturday and *gebentsht goyml* [recited the prayer said after escaping from great danger].

* * *

[Column 586]

Before the First World War in my barbershop that I maintained in Reb Yeshayhu Gorzalczany's house and then in the house of Pesakh Turowicz or as he was called, Pesakh the *soltis* [village magistrate], I arranged a voluntary music class.

The most capable ones taking part in the class were:

Shmulke Wengorz, perished at the hands of the Hitler bandits, Moshel Litman's son, shot by the Poles, and Itshe Lubelczyk, died in Syria, and Yudel Lechaim Simkha Gromadzyn, today in America. After my departure from Czyzewo, he became the leader of the orchestra that played for the Jewish theater.

I have to thank my father and my grandfather for the spiritual inheritance, for the strength and love of music that I still have today.

My father, his three brothers and sister all died in their deep old age, in the golden land of America.

May Their Souls Rest in Peace

Translator's note:

1. The "czuk" suffix means "son of."

[Column 587]

Gentle Souls and Kind Hearts
of My Little Town Czyzewo

By Chaikeh Cikrovich (Prawda)

Translated by Chana Pollack and Myra Mniewski

How precious your name sounds to me like the best symphonic music, a symphony of memories of happy childhood and youth.

Who could have imagined that I would lose my dear ones and not even know what became of their remains? But the horrific storm perpetrated by the German murderers, with help from the pious Poles who attacked and murdered you, resulted in the most ghastly reality.

Everything I experienced there is etched in my mind's eye and I'll never forget it:

Our textile shop, which my Grandfather Reb Moshe Prawda, *z"l* inherited from his father and afterwards left to my father Reb Shlomka Prawda. Later, we inherited the textile shop which was located between the two strips of stores that divided the big marketplace in Czyzewo into two parts.

Today, no remnant remains of these shops or their owners.

When spring came and the surrounding orchards began to bloom their fragrance wafted through the *shtetl*. We children, enchanted by the strong fragrance of lilacs in the priest's garden couldn't stop ourselves from plucking them. But alas we weren't always successful because of the angry dog and even angrier caretaker who dwelt there.

[Column 588]

So instead we went to the field in search of flowers. But they were very scarce so we lumbered over to the river to bathe. Little imps that we were, we bathed and caught fish, which were actually not fish at all, but little frogs.

It was so good for our young little souls to run around while our brothers sat and studied, the younger ones in the *kheyder* and the older ones in the small hasidic *shtiblekh*.

We even had a Jewish doctor, indeed a real Jew, who spoke Yiddish, but with a Warsaw accent.

Soon after his arrival in Czyzewo we all fell ill. First my sister Rivka got sick, then my second sister Sheyne-Perl, and soon enough I was also struck – all with typhus. The Jewish doctor healed us.

We were his first patients.

A short time later his wife arrived, a very beautiful woman of average height.

She was a daughter of the Rabbi of Radom, *z"l*.

She opened a school and we were among her students.

There was also a Christian school which one had to attend on *shabes* and the young hoodlums threw stones at us preventing us from playing with the Christian girls. That is why Jewish children didn't go there.

[Column 589]

Our joy was beyond description because our thirst for learning was so strong but not every Czyzewo father could afford the luxury of sending his children to school. The school was nonetheless very crowded to the point of having to take on another teacher.

That was Alte Blajwajs, the *kheyder* teacher, Shaul Hersh's daughter.

Our studies were however quickly interrupted due to the outbreak of the Polish-Bolshevik war.

As soon as the Russians entered Czyzewo Mrs. Gelbojm began teaching us Russian, but before we even managed to learn the Russian alphabet, the Poles were again in charge and arrested our teacher accusing her of being a spy and Russian collaborator.

The horrible news that our teacher was going to be executed spread quickly.

Her husband Dr. Gelbojm was abroad completing his studies. He knew nothing of the tragedy awaiting his wife.

We children cried day and night. Our parents fasted and the boys prayed and at the last minute right before the shooting a decree came down to, "Cease! Release."

The tragedy actually occurred a few years later when Dr. Gelbojm had a successful practice in another city. The doctor's wife died of cancer, leaving behind two daughters. May her memory be a blessing.

[Column 590]

It was then said that the cancer was from the stress she endured during her arrest.

My father, Reb Shloyme Yishay Prawda, z"l, was also a victim of the Poles.

When the Polish army returned after ousting the Bolsheviks, the first thing they did was set out to get even with the Jews in the *shtetl*. They proceeded to incessantly torture Jews by conscripting them into forced labor such as herding animals from one city to another.

One day they seized my father as he was going to pray with his *talis* and *tfilin* under his arm.

He was assigned to a group who herded animals to the front but he couldn't keep up with the march, so the soldier in charge, the only one who was armed, beat my father to the point of his not being able to herd the animals.

He was put on a wagon and taken to Zambrów. There, at his request, his brothers, Chilke and Velvel Prawda, paid a large sum of money to free him from the hands of the murderers.

My father then returned the money to his brothers. He later developed a tumor in his head from the beating and died in his late thirties.

We honor your memory!

Center, Chaikeh and her husband Simcha

I will now return to the time when our teacher was freed from imprisonment.

The years passed quickly.

We grew up; the teacher came and left; those of us between the ages of 12-15 got together to create a youth library.

We raised money, bought various books, recruited members and before we knew it had several hundred books.

[Column 591]

A group of school children

The founders were:

Fayge-Feye Gorzalczany, Sheyne-Perl Prawda, Rochel-Lea Litmans, Lea-Gitl Lubelczyk, all of whom were murdured, may God avenge their deaths. The following survived: Pesha Lepak; Khantshe Gorzalczany Frydman; Yosfe Kandel, in Israel; Chaikeh Prawda, in Mexico; Sluvke Kimovits, in Israel.

When classes resumed, we brought the books to school where they remained with the teacher. Our goal was to found an independent youth library by creating a drama group that would present performances of which the income would go to purchase books. The youth library later became a general library with over 2000 books by the best authors, Yiddish, Polish and Hebrew.

[Column 592]

I remember:

A stormy winter night, my head on my mother's lap, my father engrossed in a holy book. I hear my mother telling my father that someone is stealing wood and coals from the shed. The wood and coal is being depleted. She can't understand who the thief could be?

Only after my father's death was the secret revealed:

My pious father was discreetly distributing money, wood and coal to poor women and families.

When my mother learned of this she upheld my father's deeds. Every Friday she prepared a package and sent me to deliver it to a poor family saying to me, "Chaikeleh, bring this there, but make sure that no one sees you delivering anything. Give it to the woman and leave immediately. Don't say who you are or who sent you and don't tell anyone, not even your best friend. One must help the poor but take heed they not be shamed."

My poor unfortunate parents, your good deeds will accompany me forever.

Blessed be your memory!

[Column 593]

Khevra Mishnius

by Simcha Gromadzyn

Translated by Gloria Berkenstat Freund

My father was the *gabbai* [sexton] of the *Khevra Mishnius* [*Mishnah Society* – group that studies Talmudic commentaries] for many, many years. He also was the bookkeeper as well as the heater of the oven at the *Khevra Mishnius* prayer house.

It was a small house of prayer; a room rented from Shmulke the tailor, right across from the large house of prayer. At that time, they came here to pray only on the *Shabbosim* [the Sabbaths] and the holidays.

Later, in 1909, the *Khevra Mishnius* built its own house of prayer where they prayed three times a day and studied *Mishnius* every dawn and in the evening, between *Minkhah–Maariv* [afternoon and evening prayers]. On winter Shabbosim the studying began at three o'clock before daybreak and in the evening from nine to 11. Then, they celebrated the *Melave Malka* ["ushering out the queen" – the meal evening meal at the end of the Sabbath].

Rabbi Yisrael Tyktin, an iron shopkeeper, a great scholar, was, in addition, a genteel Jew, with aristocratic bearing and, at the same time, he warmly welcomed every Jew. He studied *Mishnius* with a group on *Shabbosim* and during the Days of Awe. Reb Shlomo, Yisrael–Gdalye's [son], the baker, taught. He was a quiet and honest Jew.

[Column 594]

Both of them evoked respect with their erudition, but the men bore no arrogance.

After my departure, I heard that Boruch Szapira, Yoske Grynberg's son–in–law, taught the group. In 1921–3, seven young men studied at the *Khevra Mishnius* house of prayer with Reb Ahron Wajntraub, who today is in Jerusalem. Four of the seven today live in Israel, one is in Mexico and two perished.

On a winter day, the young men woke at four in the morning. They would be awakened by Avraham Chaim the [waker]. He awoke much earlier. He would recite Psalms, heat the oven and go through the streets in the great frosts and tap his path through the dark and knocked on the shutters of the seven young men to wake them for studying.

[Column 595]

The house of prayer built by the *Khevra Mishnius* in 1909 burned during the First World War. Over time, until the new house of prayer was rebuilt, they prayed and studied in our house on *Shabbosim* and holidays.

The meeting at which it was decided to build the new house of prayer on the same spot on which the old one stood also took place in our house.

The new house of prayer, in which we prayed and studied all during the year, existed until the beginning of the great catastrophe in 1939.

Jews from all strata of the Czyzewo Jewish population, merchants, artisans and shopkeepers, belonged to the *Khevra Mishnius*.

Moshe–Mendel Gromadzyn

Standing: **Leibel Eides, New York, Simcha Lew, Yankel Ostrozanski, both perished**

Sitting: **Dov Gorzalczany, Yechiel Eliasz (both in Israel), Yudel Richter, perished**

[Column 596]

A *siem* [celebration of the completion of the collective study of a Talmudic tractate] took place every year, which was celebrated with great solemnity, once [at the home of] Yisrael Tyktin and once [at our house]. My mother and the other wives, who came to help, were occupied all day with preparing, baking and cooking all kinds of good things.

On the walls of the house of prayer hung a large, beautifully drawn *Mi Shebyrekh* [He who has blessed] and "And when the ark would journey…" [Numbers,10:35] that Berl, Szimela's son (Brukarz), had drawn.

We would spend winter evening here and talk about familiar matters, about politics. Kalman Kirczner returned from America and everyone listened to his descriptions of bridges that hung from poles, about trains that ran over the roofs.

My Uncle Nuska, who was the only newspaper reader at that time, brought the latest news of the world.

The *Pinkes*

The *Khevra Mishnius* possessed its own *pinkes* [book of records or register] in which each member of the *Khevra Mishnius* had his own page artistically decorated by Moshe Dovid the *soyfer* [scribe]. This *pinkes* was protected by my father as the most valuable treasure. It lay on the top shelf of our cabinet among the clean holiday tablecloths.

All of the boys would take eagerly to it and eagerly thumb through the pages. Written names, Yitzchak–Hersh the *malamed* [religious teacher], Nuska and Mendel Gromadzyn, Shlomo, Yisrael–Gdalye's [son], Moshe and Mendel, the butchers who were brothers, and Yankel Wibitker.

[Column 597]

The Bridge

by Elihu Gora, Tel Aviv

Translated by Gloria Berkenstat Freund

Our house was located right next to the bridge that also was a boundary of the *shtetl* [town], which was surrounded by innumerable large and small Polish villages. A small and clear river flowed under the bridge for a few dozen kilometers until it emptied into the great Bug River.

The bridge evokes many beautiful and pleasant memories as well as melancholy and difficult ones…

I remember the rabbi going before Passover with the respected people of the *shtetl* to draw water that had stood overnight for *shmura-matzo* [watched matzo – matzo that is made according to rigorous religious standards]. The sun went down, lower and lower and its gold shone in the rabbi's eyes, in the eyes of all the Jews who drew the water from the river.

On Rosh Hashanah, the entire *shtetl* passed by our house [going to the bridge]. Men, women and children walked with holiday prayer books in their hands to *tashlikh* ["cast off" – the ritual of casting away one's sins in a running body of water], shaking out the sins from their pockets into the river.

They came from the entire street and from the surrounding alleys to do wash in the river.

[Column 598]

Every woman had her own stone on which she beat the wash with a wooden handle (a *kjanke*).

Elihu Gora and Ahron Melcer

Here, my friends from *kheder* [religious primary school] and I as children, went in the evening to bathe, swimming and splashing in the water. When we already were young men we walked in pairs to the woods. The road was called the kissing alley… The stroll, the intimate conversations in the moonlit night were unforgettable.

[Column 599]

The two Jablonka brothers

[Column 600]

Here, over the bridge, we went with books by Spinoza and Spenser, by Shalom Alecheim and Peretz, with all of the books that we had to hide from our parents. Here we carried out fervent discussions about the new world opinions that sneaked into the *shtetl* in the same way. Here we sang Polish, Yiddish and Hebrew songs. Here we experienced our first loves and our first opinions. Many secrets were absorbed by the alleys beyond the bridge; many longings and strivings for a better and more beautiful life, with the deep conviction that the world goes forward toward beauty and justice.

Czyzewo, the *shtetl* of my childhood and youth, is now a deserted ruin and [its people have been] bloodily exterminated.

[Column 599]

Bright and Dark Days

By Mordechai (Motl) Szczupakiewicz

Translated from Yiddish by Judie Ostroff Goldstein

This happened in 1938, a year after the famous unrest in the shtetl.

Czyzewo was once again peaceful. The Jews were trying to keep body and soul together, trying to make a living in commerce or as laborers. The youth dreamed of going to Israel and their parents had worried faces and bowed shoulders. In the hunt for any odd job nobody had time for serious thought. Nobody paid attention to the sea of enemies that abounded around us.

[Column 600]

I have to admit I was one of those who did want to think about the anti-Semitism that became more threatening every day. I did business with Christians in the area, became rich and behaved the same towards Jews and Christians. Business was not bad and therefore clouded my memory…

[Column 601]

An evening's entertainment had been planned for officers returning from maneuvers. I was invited and could not refuse to attend. The evening's entertainment took place in the "Rolnik Hall".

The mood was joyous, like a holiday. Everyone forgot about the crisis, danced and was happy. The tall officers in their stiff jackets bowed and were very polite to the Czyzewers and appeared cordial. One of the officers, who was slightly tipsy, embraced me and talked to me very sincerely about the difficult problems facing Poland. The most difficult problem is how to free the country from Jews…

The officer did not realize that he was a little drunk. He was steady on his feet and spoke fluently, elegantly. However, my legs were wobbly. I suddenly felt all alone, like a stable in the field open to all the winds…

The officer noticed the change in me and tried to end the conversation. He actually ended our talk by saying that the Jews are very bright and there was even a period, a long time ago, when they brought much needed knowledge to the country…but today times are hard. The people are needy and hungry and the Jews are living well on the backs of the Polish people.

[Column 602]

Now he spoke more soberly and cruelly. "Three million Jews live in Poland, busy with parasitic businesses. Three million hungry Poles could take their places and restore the country."

I became angry which paralyzed my tongue. The words stuck in my throat. At that moment I decided that it was time to leave Poland. The words of this "polite" officer persecuted and whipped me. They spit in my face.

Was this then the only time that it was made clear to me that there was no place for Jews in Poland?

There were worse situations and more painful, but the deliberate manner in which the officer spoke that happy evening surpassed in vicious truth every slap until now.

I left the officer standing there with his fancy boots and went home through the sleeping Czyzewo streets thinking back on my entire life in the shtetl. I think of how the Christian population benefited from us and instead of gratitude I saw the bared teeth of an animal that waits for the moment when the country will be "freed" from the Jews and allow them to go on a spree with Jewish property, with Jewish blood.

I remember a dawn in 1926. A red flag was hanging at Lubelczyk's house. This brought the police and terrible troubles. The police took out their anger on the Jews in the shtetl.

[Column 603]

At first light somebody knocked on my door. Two policemen came in and carried out a search. They knew they would not find anything in my home. Still they searched with such intensity as if they would find an arsenal of weapons in my house.

When they stopped the search, everything was upside down as if there had been an earthquake. One of the policemen said that they were searching for Communist literature in my home.

He said this with a straight face, but his thoughts were viciously mocking me: we know that you are rich and have nothing to do with those who want to overturn the government and think you are their enemy. But you are a Jew and therefore we will stick you with everything possible.

The policeman said: "We have an order to bring you to the precinct in Ostrowa."

It was clear he was trying to provoke me and I did not say a word. The policeman felt uncomfortable and asked: "Do you want to go by train or by bus?"

The entire day in Ostrowa I was questioned about my connection with hanging the red flag and the Communist party.

After bothering me for a day and a night they finally let me go home. It was already Friday afternoon when I arrived back in the shtetl. The Jews stopped me and peppered me with questions. My arrest seemed a bizarre event to them. They saw this as an omen of difficult times ahead.

[Column 604]

Kowalski, the shtetl Chief of Police was in the street. He knew me very well. But now he had a serious face and yelled: "Why are you people gathering in the street? What kind of illegal meeting is being organized in the shtetl?"

The Jews stood there for a minute staring, then frightened turned and went on their way.

I stood there alone, not saying a word to the Chief of Police who had more than once received fat bribes from me and now it seemed that he absolutely did not want to remember.

The sky was getting dark and the flames of the *Shabes* candles could be seen in Jewish windows. The entire shtetl fell into a holy quiet. I immediately forgot the disturbing and insulting experience.

Jews dressed for *Shabes* in silk and satin *kapotes* [long, black coat worn by Orthodox Jews] were going into the synagogue with the young boys lead by the hand or following behind, dressed for *Shabes*. It warmed by heart.

No, in those days I did not think about leaving the shtetl.

[Column 605]

The Mob a Wild Animal

As the years passed more and more young people thought about leaving. *Halutzim* [pioneers to work collective farms in Israel] left for Israel and others went to America. Houses that had stood here for generations were now deserted. Deserted by fathers, a man or a grown son. The youth organizations carried on heated discussions, disputes, hearing ones fill about parties, ideology and programs. But all of them already carried deep in their hearts this yearning to be a part of the world at large, to re-build their lives on new foundations.

At that time suddenly a pogrom broke out. It started with those picketing during a Tuesday fair. The young mischief-makers were from the estates and villages. The majority, led by students, stood at the Jewish stores and watched so that no peasant would enter.

When the signal was given, a entire gang, organized and well prepared, with sticks and poles, set off for the Jewish stores. The air was full of screams. The fighters were Jeling and those beaten were wailing. The police intervened and captured the hooligans. But the same day a disturbance broke out in the horse and cattle market. There were a lot of badly wounded and a dark cloud of need and want hovered over the shtetl. The final hope of making a living ran out. The idea of leaving became stronger.

At that time a committee was sent to Cyzewo from Warsaw in order to determine the cause of the unrest. They were disguised as peasants and went into the villages, among the workers, spoke for a long time with them and wanted to find out why they wanted to throw out the Jews.

[Column 606]

Some of them stayed overnight in our house, secretly. I wanted to know the results of their inquiry. One of them told me:

"The people! The common man is not capable of thinking on his own. He is really incapable of understanding and is worse than an animal. At least an animal, when sated, does not attack. The common man always turns out to be the most disgraceful criminal."

This person who had so philosophically spoke about the common people was perhaps ashamed to mention those who incited the people. The great majority of the newspapers published in Poland sympathized with these hooligans. Also the Polish intellectuals in our shtetl did not show any understanding or sympathize with the Jews, but just the opposite, they were vile, false and hypocrites.

My Departure from Poland

A month before the war, in August 1939, the possibility of travelling to America came about. The famous exhibition was taking place in New York. I never thought that the war would break out in approximately a month. Even though the political situation was strained, nobody thought that the Germans would actually attack Poland. I had already decided to have a look at America to see whether it would be possible to stay there and leave Poland forever.

[Column 607]

However, I did not take any money with me. I travelled light. This would prove to be a mistake.

After arriving in America I decided to stay there. I felt like a shipwrecked man who swam to a strange shore. I had no one to turn to.

The entire first year in America I worked at night in a bakery. The conditions were terrible and the work – very hard. But not for one minute did I lose hope and I waited for the opportunity to use the initiative that was in me.

After a year I went into business for myself. Carefully I set up the business for which I had all the qualifications from the old country where our mill was known throughout the region.

In the mill business I was a specialist and I went into the flour business.

I had to overcome a lot of difficulties that stood in my way. The most difficult of all was the question of working papers that I did not have.

I put all doubts behind me and the flour business was not bad. I mainly bought flour for export to South American countries. Later I also went into leather. But that is a whole other story.

I stopped feeling so lonely and began meeting Czyzewer landsmen. Azriel Belfer, who had left Czyzewo many years before already had a fine business, a well-organized meat business belonged to Berkowicz.

[Column 608]

Mostly I met them in the Andrzejewer Synagogue where the Czyzewers prayed every *Shabes*.

After prayers we talked about Czyzewo and shared the news about Poland that everyone received through various means.

Then the idea of bringing the Czyzewer rabbi to America was brought up. Really we were already looking for ways to get papers for him. Later we realized what a naïve idea it was. We had not given any thought to the great pain the rabbi had gone through with the other Czyzewer Jews in the ghetto that existed then and was already doomed to extinction.

At that time, we received the first news of those Jews who had wandered through various countries and were searching for a safe haven. We received news about the Jews who were waiting in Vilna at the consulates of various countries. In America there was intense activity. From everywhere men were prepared to help the Jews who were trying to save themselves from Hitler's Poland.

Then we thought about the rabbi's son-in-law, Rabbi Lewinsohn. This brought a lot of joy. We got right down to work and began to organized papers that would allow the rabbi to come to America.

[Column 609]

When our work was crowned with success there was quite a celebration.

Rabbi Lewinsohn arrived in America from Shanghai at the height of the war. He arrived together with his wife and son.

The rabbi's daughter, Freidel Lewinsohn is today one of the most active among the Czyzewer women in America.

Eternal Mourning

People cannot mourn forever. For a long time we simply did not want to believe that this could happen. An entire Jewish community wiped out, murdered in such violent deaths. But it soon became clear that it was true. We were crushed and shaken up. But soon we received news about the individuals who were still alive, who had been saved from the gray hell. And what if people had thrown up their hands and given in to sorrow?

To start with I sent packages. Then I had the idea that I must do everything possible to bring these people to America.

[Column 611]

Among those I brought to America at that time were Zelig Gromadzyn, Yankel Mankuta, Zysze Slucki, Yisroelke Fenster and my sister Perl Spolienec who brought us the news of the dreadful pogrom that occurred in Czyzewo. Their faces spoke louder than words, the terror and fear in their eyes.

Today these people are installed, working, earning and have re-built their family nests. But the sorrow that they experienced is buried deep in their hearts and will never leave them, will always be there as a reminder and a warning.

And so the deep ties to our shtetl, that was a ring in the generations long chain of Jewish life in Poland, cannot be erased.

It was and is no more.

When the axe of Hitler's executioners was let loose on the Jewish people in Europe, our branches also were cut down.

Jewish Czyzewo is no more. A city with Jews was destroyed in great pain, in inhuman agony.

We will never forget, write and tell about it …in memory of the people.

[Columns 611-612]

My *Shtetele*

by Arya Gorzalczany

Translated by Gloria Berkenstat Freund

Whenever I meet a survivor of the great destruction of my *Shtetele* [small town] at a memorial evening or at a celebration, the synagogue, the houses of prayer, the entire past *shtetl* and its streets appear before my eyes.

With them pass [before me eyes] the fathers, the grandfathers who embellished the shtetl and were so tragically annihilated.

Here they are! *Shalom aleichem* [hello] Berl, *Shalom aleichem* Reb Shaya. The same businesslike wisdom and wit comes from the calm words of his son, Berl, as from his father, Shaya. And a Pinya says with a smile what great joy he has had from a book that he had read and also the smile of disdain for the [secular] world of his father, Reb Yakov, Leizer's [son].

What kind of significance do they, the gentiles, have, he would argue, when we possess the Torah?

And here is Yitzchak, my friend from the *shtetl*. Again he mentions the *shtetl's* pure souls at the memorial evening. With a repressed cry, with his naïve eyes, he never stops asking, like his grandfather Reb Alter, why? Why such a punishment inflicted by God?

My glances fall on the survivors of the gas ovens, the beautiful Sheva, who reminds a young man of what has disappeared forever. My eyes become moist; I see them annihilated somewhere in a mass grave, young and old, fathers and grandfathers in the reflection of the likenesses, in the individual surviving sons and daughters, here in our own land.

I do not know if I am fortunate that I, who felt the coming deluge of the *shtetl*, saved myself in time, and so I think, if I, who lived to be here in Israel, remain all alone in the world, am I really the more fortunate one who saved myself and remain alone in the world or am I only… one who is accursed…

[Columns 613-614]

Chaim–Judel Tracz[1]
(from the provincial past)

by Arja Gorzalczany

Translated by Gloria Berkenstat Freund

The courtyard at the Synagogue Alley, across from the house of prayer, was fenced in with a high wooden fence. Inside were found boards, beams and various lumber, sorted according to size and width, under a long wooden roof. All of this belonged to Saneh, the wood trader. The courtyard was called Saneh's storehouse in the *shtetl* [town]. A quiet reigned over the courtyard in the winter, as if there were no wood storehouse there and when thick layers of snow began to cover the courtyard, the wood storehouse looked like a giant mountain of snow had been brought here from outside the city and placed opposite the house of prayer.

All of this was in winter, but as soon as the summer began to arrive, the appearance of the wood storehouse changed. Suddenly the courtyard became full of long wooden blocks. Gentile men, sawyers, arrived with sharp axes and long saws that had two-sided handles on each end. They worked all over the block with the sharp axes and then with a long string that was smeared well with black charcoal, marked the block for cutting the boards and both raised it on their shoulders the way one lifts a coffin and they laid it on two, high sawhorses and the courtyard became filled with song and sawing that mixed with the *Gemare* [Talmud] melodies carried from the open house of prayer.

[Column 614]

Chaim–Judel the Hasid began to appear at the house of prayer during the midday hours. He sat with a Book of Psalms, took the ends of his dark beard between his teeth, bit, let go of it, took them [in his mouth] again, stood up from his spot, went to the window, moved the width of his body into the window, pushed his hat up on to tip of his head. His large, sad eyes looked with amazement at the saws that were speeding up and down in the hands of the sawyers and again sat down in his previous place. This was repeated for several days and he would stare more "intently' with his eyes at the work of the sawyers. There was wonder in the house of prayer that he was distracted from the Psalms and kept looking at the sawyers. Was it the first time he had seen this? Until once, Chaim–Judel jumped up from his spot in the middle of reciting Psalms as if someone had driven him from the house of prayer. He ran and entered Saneh the wood merchant's storehouse, whispered with Mikolaj the sawyer. Mikolaj smiled into his long, yellow whiskers, slapped him [Chaim–Judel] in a brotherly way on the back, as if he had said to him: So Judka [diminutive of Judel], show what you can do. Here we saw Chaim–Judel throw off his *kapote* [caftan] and stand in his wide *talis–katan* [undergarment with fringes at each of four corners worn by pious men]; he took the handles of the large saw, held them firmly, as he did when he went to hakofes with a Torah scroll [circular procession on *Simchas Torah* marking the completion of the yearly Torah reading], *lahavdal* [word said to separate the sacred from the worldly]. Mikolaj nimbly grabbed the block and both sawed. We saw Chaim–Judel's rapture, until he was covered with sawdust. When he finished the work, he entered the house of prayer, went to the ritual washstand, washed his hands and said to us: "You understand that there are Jewish artisans, tailors, shoemakers, quilters, hatmakers, all such sitting trades. There is one blacksmith in the area. Well, such people as Saneh need to know that there are also sawyers present among us…"

[Column 615]

[Column 616]

Chaim–Judel constantly grew in esteem in our eyes from then on. And if I would sometimes remain in the house of prayer at night, I was not afraid to go home. I also was not afraid of the dogs that the gentile boys often set on us because Chaim–Judel was with me and in my childish mind I imagined such fantasies: when the first welcome of *Moshiakh* [the redeemer] occurs, I would not choose Ben Tzion, the teacher in the *shtetl*, but him, Chaim–Judel, Chaim–Judel the sawyer.

When I became older, with Chaim–Judel's strength, I became the first *halutz* [pioneer] in the *shtetl*.

Translator's note:

1. Sawyer, a woodcutter

[Column 615]

Yudel Wapniak

by Arya Gorzalczany/Petah Tikva

Translated by Gloria Berkenstat Freund

I remember my annihilated *shtetl* [town] Czyzewo; the House of Prayer Street appears as in a dream. The half-fallen small house appears before my half-closed eyes with pits of slaked *wapne* [lime][1] From behind the small house a figure shuffles out and I recognize by his slow and fine steps that this is "Yudel Wapniak."

He looked taller than average height, dressed in a pair of large, hard boots smeared with lime. His face was enveloped by a long, faded, bushy, grey beard. He crossed his hands in front and put them in his sleeves. His creased hat was pushed up on the tip of his head as if he was absorbed in an important matter.

[Column 616]

– Do you hear? – he says, taking his hands out of his sleeves and taking his bushy beard in one hand – Do you hear? I say to you, the best food is when one crumbles a piece of old *challah* [egg bread] in a bowl of boiling water. First, it is very economical; it swells from a small bit of *challah* into a full bowl. And secondly: it truly melts in your mouth like a mushroom. What a pleasure. No enemy should know its taste. Ha, ha, ha – he laughed out loud –Alas, what do those rich men know of life? Do they know what is good?

[Column 617]

Yudel Wapniak argued like this with Shlomo's son Mendel-Yisrael, meeting him in the alley of the house of prayer with his *talis* [prayer shawl] under his arm, going to pray in the Gerer *shtibl* [one room house of prayer] that was located [in a room] above the house of prayer. Mendel listened to him calmly and smiling he went on his way.

Yudel Wapniak turned to the market to bring documents to the village magistrate and incidentally to take a look at the peasants in the *shtetl*. And he thought at the same time he would look around and maybe he would detect a customer for a *pood* [Russian weight measurement equaling about 16 kilograms or about 36 pounds] of lime.

Walking in the market between the wagons filled with various grains, potatoes, chickens and various other village products, Yudel remembered that he had no potatoes at home. He stopped for a while, covered his eyes with his hand, searched, looked around on all sides. Perhaps he would see a familiar gentile and would receive a quarter weight of potatoes on credit.

Yudel walked like this all day, from the market to his house, from his house back again to the market, looking for a *groshn* of redemption [to earn some money], until the sun began to set and the time for *Minkhah* [afternoon prayers] neared. Then, walking this way, Yudel first realized that he had spent the entire day and earned nothing. He left the market and ran in haste to the *shtibl* [one-room prayer house] to recite the afternoon prayers. Having finished his prayers, he sat with the usual small group behind the oven talking until *Maariv* [evening prayers] and as always he listened to the story-teller [tell] of the new edict that would torment the Jews, Heaven forbid. He bent closer to the story-tellers when they spoke about the news of what had happened in the *shtetl* that day – about which of the shopkeepers in the *shtetl* had the police chief issued an official report, who had had a *shwarts-Shabbos* [a Sabbath or week marked by calamity] when a confiscator went to the drawer and swept out all of the cash earnings for the entire day – for the taxes that he demanded. And when in the middle of the conversation, someone was heard moaning – *Gevald Yidn* [Help, Jews], how will we be able to bear this? – How will we be able to continue living?! – Yudel Wapniak joined the talk, interrupting the moan with a shout:

[Column 618]

– Quiet Jews. You will live! You will survive! There were worse times than today. Ask Yudel Wapniak. He will tell you. Meanwhile, he took a tasty pinch of snuff from Reb Berish, squinted his eyes and swayed in the length and width, as if he had just learned a page of *Gemara* [commentaries] and began singing a *Gemara* melody. – Of course, you remember just as I do what I will tell you now. But nevertheless, listen closely:

– As the Bolshevik-Polish war grew closer to the *shtetl*, the politicians began to grab Jews for work. Do you remember that being caught for work meant coming home from the work battered, sick, with smashed ribs and, no need to mention, with a torn-out beard and blackened eyes? As you know, we hid in the attics, in the cellars. I said to myself: Yudel, why are you hiding? I asked myself, Yudel, have you stolen something? Or perhaps, God forbid, you killed a man or just did something bad to someone? What kind of hiding place in the cellar is this? May the enemies of Zion hide like this; may they be buried in the ground! I took a handkerchief and wrapped it around my face so that only my eyes were seen, took off my clothing, put on a long shirt and went to bed and I said to my wife: Bayltshe *kroyn* [crown – a term of endearment – my precious], put a chair next to the bed with a glass of tea and a spoon. Have ready a handkerchief so that when you see the angel from hell you can wave at me with the handkerchief and beg me to take a spoon of tea.

[Column 619]

A wild chase for Jews had begun in the *shtetl*. A non-Jew with a rifle appeared on the threshold of my house and when he saw me lying in bed and that my wife was waving a handkerchief over me and was begging me to have mercy on myself and take a spoon [of tea] and that I kept moaning so that it could move a stone, he whistled, gave me several military blessings, left immediately and thus I was saved. Thank God, I escaped from non-Jewish hands. The real war began when the Bolsheviks escaped and the Poles again entered. There still was a deadly fear among the Jews to appear in the street. The fear was still great even after the entire military had passed through the *shtetl* because *khapers* [men who seized Jews] suddenly would appear as if out of the earth. However, a Jew would want to go to the synagogue, to prayer and to study, too. I sneaked through a side alley and entered the house of prayer. However, before I had completely closed the door, what, eh, a gentile was standing next to me with ignited, red face, holding a rifle stretched out toward me, looking right into my face. He was silent, but suddenly he began an echoing wild laughter, "Ha, ha, ha, *Zydek*" [pejorative Polish word for Jew] and again *Zydek* and [he] laughed and shouted *Zydek*, until it appeared that he was very pleased with my bushy beard, because very unexpectedly he braided his fat peasant fingers in my beard and pulled it once to the right and once to the left and did not stop and again stronger and faster. I shouted to him: "*Panie lebn*, [Dear Mister]. Let go; it hurts!" [He answered] "I want it to hurt." And he tore [my beard] in earnest and I bent with it just *lehavdl* [word used to separate the sacred from the profane] like at *nanium* with the *lulav* [motions made shaking the palm fronds [*lulav*] on *Sukkos* – the feast of the tabernacles], but it appears it became tiresome to pull me back and forth. He left my beard alone a little and said to me: "Shout '*Niech cię nasza Polska*' [Leave our Poland] three times and dance!" I thought doing this would not hurt, what does one do if only to be able to emerge alive from Esau's [gentile's] hands? I began to hop, hop, hop, danced, and shouted with all of my strength: '*Niech cię nasza Polska*' and danced. But it appeared that as I danced he took a liking to my boots, because suddenly he roared in a wild voice: '*Żyde otdav mnie twóje buty*!' [Jew, give me your boots]. I said to him:

[Column 620]

– *Panie kroyn* [Dear sir], how can I give you my only pair of boots and then go home barefoot?

He roared more strongly and wilder: '*Te buty zdiancz*!' [Take off these boots!] I fell and said to him: "*Proszę panie* [Please, sir], is it nice that a Polish soldier would take the boots from a poor Jew?" His impure blood boiled even more and he gave me a blow and a scrape with his rifle butt. "*Cichy*!" [Quiet]. When I heard *cichy*, I realized that he was afraid that I would scream. So with my entire strength I screamed such a "*cichy*" that it seemed that the walls of the house of prayer were screaming with me because it was beyond my strength to scream in this way. So the Red Esau was stunned when he heard my terrible screaming and jumped out through the window and, at the same time, baptized himself in the very impure pit of dirt that was under the window. I tell you, Jews, that I believe I still smell the stench from that time when he bathed there.

[Column 621]

– I turned to Shlomo Dovid, the confused one who was sitting in his usual quiet way, but from time to time he was heard talking quietly to himself - Perhaps you would open a Window?

A quiet laughter fell in Shlomo Dovid's yellow-grey beard. He pushed up his hat and again was quiet.

– And what do we Jews heed? I tell you that we must not lower our heads and shout that things are not good! Let our enemies shout not good and they will be our scapegoat! We need to be ready with the three things our Patriarch Jacob taught us: "With a gift, prayer and war." Listen to a story – I was a bit of a village magistrate. I once went to a market day with Bartusz, the village mayor, going from stall to stall so that he could collect duties, payments. One Jew, who stood at his boot stall, promised to make a payment, which Bartusz heard. He was drunk. He grabbed his chain (you know what that signified, putting on a chain), this likely meant jail!

[Column 622]

Leave the *Żydłak* [derogatory word for Jew]. So, do you think I did not prevail? He smiled, took off the chain and nothing happened. We only need to know how to talk to them.

When the Germans, may their names be erased, pushed the Czyzewo Jews into the ghetto, Wapniak lost his bushy beard and *peyes* [side curls], along with his Jewish face. However, the smile never left him. He always walked among the people and awoke courage in them: "Jews, do not be disillusioned," he said, and if he heard a moan from someone, he pinched his nose and shouted: "Jews, run from him. He stinks of despair!"

I do not know if Yudel Wapniak outwitted the Germans and died a natural death in the ghetto or if he suffered the same fate as all of the unfortunate Czyzewo Jews and breathed out his holy soul in Szulborze or somewhere in a gas chamber with his customary smile on his face frozen for eternity.

May his soul be bound up in the bond of life!

Translator's note:
1. The surname Wapniak most likely is derived from lime – *wapne* – the product the family sold.

Yitzchak, Son of Bunim

by Arya Gorzalczany/Petah Tikva

Translated by Gloria Berkenstat Freund

[Column 623]

Tall, overgrown, with a long, wide, grey-haired beard that had not yet tasted the charm of a comb; it covered the greater part of his elongated face in which were deeply set a pair of grey, smart eyes.

I see him, Yitzchak, son of Bunim (Blajwajs), pensively standing behind the oven in the Gerer *shtibl* [one-room prayer house], warming his back and having both hands in the sleeves of his worn-out kaftan, listening to a Hasidic teaching or a story being told by Avraham-Yosl, the Hasid. From time to time he lifted his downcast, half-asleep eyes, shook from great bliss, snuggling in his old, worn-out kaftan.

Was Reb Yitzchak, son of Bunim, really such a poor man who did not have any decent clothes to put on?

No, this was not the reason.

Yitzchak, son of Bunim, simply did not believe in the foolishness of putting on a new kaftan or polishing boots and going out in the street like a "dandy."

– Oh, that is only for a haughty person. It is a waste to me, he would say. Does God need Yitzchak, son of Bunim, to dress up for Him? "Rakhmana Liba Boyeh" ["It is our hearts that God desires of us."] The main thing is that we need to go in the path of God, pray, study and be a Jew!

[Column 624]

And Reb Yitzchak, son of Bunim, observed this although he ran many businesses, sold lime, bricks, mortar and brooms. Yet he was seen in the Gerer *shtibl* more than in the street and when the holy *Shabbos* [Sabbath] arrived, his house was the Gerer *shtibl*.

Reb Yitzchak once stood at his usual place near the well-heated oven on a Friday night, after the *Shabbos* feast. The entire *shtibl* was filled with light from the two large mantle lights that illuminated the walls, the tables with the light of *Shabbos*. Even the simple windows shone today more that on a weekday. There was the impression that the "*Shabbos* queen" was hovering here with her outspread wings that filled the entire *shtibl* with a loving *Shabbos* warmth and melted Yitzchak in all his limbs.

He thought – So, the *tish-zitser* [those who sit around the table]: Reb Berish, Avraham Yosl, Reb Ben-Tzion and others would soon enter. They will tell of the miracles of the *Chiddushei Ha'Rim*,[1] may the memory of a righteous man be blessed, of the Kotzker Rebbe, may the memory of a righteous man be blessed. The *shtibl* will be filled with wonder and *Torah*.

[Column 625]

Suddenly the door opened and a Jew, a poor man, entered and stood behind the oven.

– Eh. What a bitter cold it is outside – the Jew said as if to himself and pressed closer to the oven and groaned from time to time – it is a delightful warmth. Eh-h-h, it is a pleasure to stand at such a warm oven – he said to Reb Yitzchak.

– Funvanen is a Yid [Where are your from] – Reb Yitzchak asked him.

– What difference does it make where I am from? – answered the Jew – I am a vagabond.

– Where have you been eating on Shabbos? – Reb Yitzchak asked again.

– The poor man answered – With Yosef the tsitsis-maker [maker of fringed undergarments worn by pious men].

– So, was it a good feast? – Reb Yitzchak again asked the Jew.

– All Jews should have such a good one – was the Jew's answer – a good piece of fish, a tasty bit of whiskey after the fish, a fat soup with noodles and rice. Then various meats, sheep meat, goose, tzimmes [a sweet carrot-based stew]; tzimmes and compote. What should I say? The tsar himself could have eaten there…

But here the poor man stopped in the middle of talking, raised his reddish eyes and his bushy, black beard and measured Reb Yitzchak with a glance from top to bottom, observing his clothing.

– I see you are one of us. I do not have to tell you. You know as do we vagabonds, who suffer in snow, rain and cold. When do we see a respectable meal? Our feasts are always a thin piece of bread with the head of a herring and we drink a dipper of water and here, with Yosef the tsistis maker, I saw a feast, a great delicacy. When they served the first portion, I ate it up with my eyes. I swallowed the second portion like a wolf and they kept asking me, "Reb Yid [Sir], perhaps another piece of challah? Perhaps a little bit more soup? Perhaps and perhaps, so be a thief and refuse, say no, why should I talk to you too much, when it came to the meat, I thought that I already was full… Forgive me; I could barely hold myself in until after the blessings…

[Column 626]

– And you? The poor man asked his dear friend behind the oven – Where did you eat? How was it with you?

– I? I ate with Yitzchak, son of Bunim – Reb Yitzchak answered.

[Column 627]

– So, was it a good feast?

– Yes, there is no better – Reb Yitzchak answered with disdain.

– What? He did not give you something to eat? – The Jew was curious.

– I know, there [he] gave you a piece of old bread and salted herring.

Reb Yitzchak Blajwajs, son of Bunim

– What do you say! He gave you old bread with salted herring? Wind in his eyes and gangrene in his intestines, your Yitzchak, son of Bunim!

– Reb Yid, one must not swear! – Reb Yitzchak reproached the Jew – Did you give him any kind a donation? – Reb Yitzchak said as if scolded – Did you put anything into the pledge to him?

– I did not make a pledge to him – the poor man said, and while speaking, his face looked as if a fire had been ignited – but if you take a guest for Shabbos, give him a Shabbos meal, do not shame a poor man!!!

[Column 628]

– Perhaps this Yitzchak, son of Bunim, is himself a poor man. It was as if Reb Yitzchak wanted to defend his ostensible boss. But does he not also want to have the merit of taking a visitor for Shabbos?

– Ha, ha, ha – the poor man began a subtle laughter, as if he were choking – are you a Jew, a "beggar"? You may not desire any guests[2] for Shabbos. I, the prosperous one, will take a guest for Shabbos? When he is again a rich man, may God take pity on him and take him from the world, so he will be spared from taking the poor for Shabbos and making fun of them.

Quietly, with suppressed laughter, Reb Yitzchak, son of Bunim, listened to all of the curses that came from the poor man's mouth and they felt like heavy stones on his head.

Translator's notes:

1. Yitzchak Meir Rotenberg-Alter, the first Gerer Rebbe, was known as the *Chiddushei Ha'Rim* from the title of his book *New Concepts of Rabbi Itche Meir* - his responsa on the Torah, using an acronym of his name "the Rabbi Itche Meir."

2. Jewish families provided *Shabbos* meals for poor men, inviting them into their homes.

[Column 629]

The Testament of Leyzer, the Son of Yosl

by A. Gorzalczany/Petah Tikva

Translated by Gloria Berkenstat Freund

He belongs to those figures who remain in my mind and fill my thoughts with substance that has not faded… I see him particularly sharply before me when the Days of Awe arrive. Then his figure comes from deep within me. I think that unseen footsteps follow me and his voice: "Be a Jew," wraps me like a *gartl* [a belt signifying the separation of the sacred from the profane] and does not leave me alone. This brown face entirely overgrown with a black beard, the nostrils spread wide open, which appear to know what lies buried in your depths with their sense of smell. His hat always lifted to the tip of his head: "*Shalom Aleikhim* [Peace be upon you], Reb Leyzer, the son of Yosl! *Aleikhim Shalom* [Unto you peace]! First, my child, a Jew must have faith. Then everything goes well." Thus answered Leyzer, the son of Yosl, to the young house of study man's question about how he was and he hummed a Days of Awe melody. And as Leyzer, the son of Yosl, hummed the Days of Awe melody it was a sign that the God-fearing days were already here. What was chasing him from here? He remained a little longer than usual after praying at the house of prayer. What opportunity would he miss? Another *pood* [Tsarist Russian measure of weight equaling about 16 kilos] of flour or two that he would sell. What was this worth compared to the holy days that were coming! In any case he would not arrive in the after-life dressed up in gold. He entered for the Psalm of the day, for a chapter of *Mishnius* [oral Torah]. When he finished, strolling through the length of the house of prayer, he approached Shlomole, who was sitting with his head bent over his reading desk with an open *Germara* [Talmud]. He pinched his cheek, "Eh, you are hiding from Leyzer?" He spoke to him insolently… "You have forgotten, Shlomole… that the Holy Days are coming? We need to prepare ourselves for religious prayer. For God's sake, yield to me. We will need to repeat the prayers." Shlomole shook his head: "Of course, Reb Leyzer, of course, we need to prepare." The dark eyes, the beard, the entire face of Leyzer, the son of Yosl, smiled with satisfaction.

[Column 630]

He took the *talis* and *tefilin* [prayer shawl and phylacteries] under his arm and left the house of prayer with slow steps. Leyzer, the son of Yosl, was busy with trade the entire year. He ran from one baker to another to sell a *pood* of flour, another sack of flour to earn money for his household. His steps became restrained, slower when the days of Elul [September or October] arrived. He completely forgot that he was named Leyzer, the son of Yosl, the flour trader. He stood with a customer, showing him various samples of flour. A religious melody came to him that showed him that *Zokhreinu L'Chaim* [*Remember Us for Life*] was appropriate. Then he completely forgot the flour samples and when the customer reminded him: "So, Reb Leyzer, how much will it cost?" he woke up as if from a dream. He stopped trading completely on the last two days before the Days of Awe. It was rare when he was seen in the street. He shut himself in a separate room with Shlomole and began *Mekhaelkl Chaim* [He who supports the living – start of Days of Awe prayer] and Shlomole answered, "*Beseder*," [By grace] with his small soprano voice.

[Column 631]

Leyzer, the son of Yosl, sang prayer after prayer and Shlomole floated after him, supported him. The singing tore through the windows, getting lost in the distance. Reb Leyzer, the son of Yosl, did not know that near the window stood women as if glued [to the spot]; Jews listened in amazement to his sweet prayers until late at night. On the Day of Judgment [Rosh Hashanah], Leyzer, the son of Yosl, did not remove his *kitl* [white kaftan] for a second. He stood at his reader's desk like a lion, his head raised. His nostrils spread apart as usual and he sang aloud, "*Hineni*" [Here I am]. But suddenly his voice broke as if a tiny child was crying into his mother's apron, he cried into his open *Mokhzor* [holiday prayer book]. Suddenly, he girded his loins and with his entire strength he shouted: "And restrain Satan that he may not hinder me." It seemed as if the walls of the house of prayer were trembling. The foundation of the ground shook. The worshippers moved their *talisim* [prayer shawls] deeper over their heads as if they were afraid to look outside.

Leyzer, son of Yosel, stretched [it] further, "*Yisgadal*" […will increase…] and Shlomole jumped to a higher pitch, *oy, oy, oy* and everyone answered, "*Sh'may rabo*" […May his name become great]. The house of study filled with song as if flutes were playing and cymbals were being stuck. After the quiet *Shemoneh Esrei* [central prayer of Jewish communal prayer], Leyzer, son of Yosel, argued things out with the Ruler of the World in his manner, with a plea, with anger and with deep love, "I remember you the kindness of your youth…when you went after me in the wilderness…" As Leyzer, the son of Yosl, ended the praying, he started dancing before his reader's desk and Shlomole danced after him. The congregation of worshippers grew brighter as if they had put down an invisible burden from their shoulders, certain that God had forgiven their sins in merit of Reb Leyzer. It would be a good year, what else? And they wished each other: "*Gut yom tov, gut yom tov*" [Have a good holiday].

[Column 632]

* * *

An edict was issued in the ghetto. Every Jew must wear the *Mogen-Dovid* [Shield of David – a Jewish star] mark on his clothing. Alas, Leyzer, the son of Yosl, was the first one who sewed the *Mogen Dovid* on his kaftan. He asserted to the Jews in the ghetto, "Look at what a holy people we are! We have been marked with 'Torah decorations in the form of an ornamental crown.'" He believed that a kaftan with a *Mogen Dovid* was as holy as a *talis* [prayer shawl] and he wore the kaftan to pray. Leyzer, the son of Yosl, had the merit of dying a natural death in his bed. Before his death, he called for his youngest daughter, Toybele: "My child," he stammered with half rasping words, "I have a request of you." Toybele cried. "What father?" "I want to be buried in my clothing. Bury me in my kaftan with the *Mogen Dovid* symbol." These were his last words; this was his testament…

[Column 633]

The Nightmare Persecutes Me

by Malka Lubelczyk-Malinowicz – Ramet Gan

Translated by Gloria Berkenstat Freund

Only sorrowful thoughts remain for me of our *shtetl* [town] Czyzewo. Dark clouds have even covered the times of my happy childhood years and of my beautiful young days. Those last years with all of the difficult events that led me to leave my birthplace forever are etched in my memory.

I also do not feel any joy from the knowledge that I was saved from the murderous Nazi hands thanks to my forced escape from Czyzewo. Knowing that I will not see my most beloved and dearest, will not hear from them again, that I do not even know the location of their sacred rest has extinguished every spark of joy in me. This often gives me an apathetic indifference to everything and everyone.

My parents would pull me out of my warm bed and carry me out or drive me out into the cold night air because of the frequent fires that would break out in Czyzewo. This would happen during the summer and winter, in rain, snow and mud. Helping to pack up the goods from the shop at each fire and, later, the weeks' long work of rearranging the goods on the on the shelves would leave a crushing feeling in me and made my life miserable.

[Column 634]

In addition, my school years arrived and the gentile boys with their cynical laughter when they *shouted Żydówka do Palestyny* (Jewish girl, to Palestine) and the teachers with their masked anti-Semitic faces that would overflow with sweetness in affably reciting the verse: *Żydówka tylko nie rozmawiać po żyDovsku* [Jewish girl. Just do not speak Yiddish]. We Jewish children would feel insulted and ashamed as if we had been caught at a serious crime.

[Column 635]

The worst came at the time of the of the *Endeke* bandit [members of the anti-Semitic Polish National Party] rampages by Arganinski's scoundrels. Our business that was in the center of two rows of shops in the middle of the market and was the one that suffered the most from *Endeke* pickets. In the beginning they only came on the market day. However, later they were there every day. They placed themselves at the doors and would not let any customers in and if a customer succeeded in entering, the *Endekes* went inside and scooped up the customer and pulled him outside with force and even beat him, not only the Christian customer, but also the Jewish merchant.

In one such case, an *Endeke* threw a bottle at my mother's head. She was bloodied and we were afraid to open her mouth. The fear was very great.

I often asked my mother and my sisters:

"Let us sell everything and leave Czyzewo. Here we will not have a good life."

The Malinowicz family
In the center: **Chanatshe Malinowicz**
The first from the left: **two Malinowicz sisters**

My sisters answered me:

"You make a start. We will follow later."

Alas, they did not live to do so.

It often happens that I find myself in a state as if I am dreaming although I am awake and I hear that I am being called: Malka, help! Help us!

I am sure that this was their last cry in Szulborze, standing near an open grave.

After such a dream I feel terribly broken. I blame myself. Why had I not forcefully pulled them out of the hell? My only answer for myself is this – that I came to Israel illegally and not more than two months before the outbreak of the war with Poland. I had no chance to even think of bringing one of my closest ones here.

[Column 636]

For years I could not make peace with my thoughts, that I had no one there. My heart began to pound every time the door of my residence would open: perhaps it was one of my sisters.

Finally, I clearly told myself that this would never happen. Not one of my closest and unforgettable has avoided the brutal fate of the Czyzewo Jews. May the Lord avenge their blood!

What My Grandfather Said
- The Apothecary's Friendship

by Malka Lubelczyk-Malinowicz – Ramat Gan

Translated by Gloria Berkenstat Freund

My grandfather was Leizer, Solte's [son] (Wengorz). Every year at *Tu B'Shevat* [1] my grandfather would bring home a large bag of various kinds of candy and fruits from *Eretz-Yisrael*, *bokser* [karob], figs and dates. He would divide all of this among his grandchildren.

– I asked, Grandfather, from where are you bringing all of these good things?

– His answer was, from the apothecary.

– I was with him today to wish him a good year. Today is again a new year; he gave me all of the things. And every year when it is Rosh Hashanah, he first sends me a Shanah Tovah [good year – a new year's] card and later he comes to me to wish me a "good year." It has happened like this for many years.

[Column 637]

– However, he is still a big anti-Semite and an enemy of the Jews, I insisted.

– My grandfather answered, so I want to tell you from where such a good friendship comes.

And he related:

This was during the time when the Bolsheviks entered the city, during the Polish-Bolshevik War. They then arrested all of the Polish patriots and [members of the] intelligentsia. The apothecary was among the arrestees. When after an investigation, the arrestees were driven on foot through the city (it was whispered that they were being taken to be shot). I saw the apothecary walking with his head down and went closer to him and said: "gey gezunt un kum gezunt [go in health and come in health]."

[Column 638]

This was a risky act on my part, but I had thought about what to do.

When the apothecary returned home later, he came right to me and said that they had all been lined up to be shot, but as a miracle from God, an order was received at the same time: "Run away quickly, the Poles are here!" And the soldiers ran away and everyone was saved.

The apothecary added:

"I am completely certain that your blessing saved me from a certain death. I will never forget it…"

I remember later when my grandfather lay sick. Parisz, the apothecary, came every day and sat for hours at his bed and told him various things. He did everything to console and encourage my grandfather. He gazed at him with eyes full of sincere love.

Translator's note:

1. The 15th day of Shevat – usually in January, is often called the New Year of the Trees, when the first blooming trees begin to blossom in Israel.

[Column 637]

Nuska Szejman

by Yitzchak Szlaski

Translated by Gloria Berkenstat Freund

He stands before my eyes in all of his spiritual beauty, a tall, thin young man with a blond pompadour. He had a sharp and deep mind and a sympathetic heart.

His spiritual and fraternal devotion to his closest comrades was such that it left the deepest memory in the heart of everyone who came in contact with him.

[Column 638]

As an orphan, without a father, in *kheder* [religious primary school] I had the opportunity to feel his warm heart. He sensed my helplessness and eased my desolation with extraordinary tenderness. Now when I think of and remember those days I wonder from where did such genteel understanding and such deep human feeling for one suffering come in someone almost still a child? I did not know then, I felt in him a large and genteel heart and I connected with him with my complete childish soul.

[Column 639]

Nuska Szejman

Later, I saw the same internal suffering that did not cease to haunt him when he met the same fate and he was orphaned by his father's death. Yet his sincere friendship was not lessened at all.

Later in the early *Yeshiva* [religious secondary school] years we would have the opportunity to lie around together on a house of prayer bench. During the cold nights I felt as if someone was covering me with his own coat. The thought that one of his comrades was hungry would take his rest from him and he would literally divide the food from his mouth. When a food package would come from home he immediately divided it among his comrades, which was a great pleasure for him. He beamed with joy. In addition he was an exceptional student. Gifted with a sharp mind he would passionately penetrate into the most difficult Talmudic question under study, walk around for hours in thought about some sort of puzzle in the commentaries. Later he devoted himself to worldly education with the same passion with which we both began to strive to be admitted to the Rabbinical Seminary in Berlin. We were helped by the Warsaw rabbi of that time, Prof. Moshe Sher, who made possible our entry into the Jewish Academic Home where, without cost Jewish students were given lectures on Polish literature, history and grammar.

[Column 640]

Nuska read a great deal. His inner world was enriched by new problems, expanded and deepened. However, he did not let himself be ruled by any doubts or ambiguities, but stubbornly held to his religious world view, joining the ranks of *Poalei Agudas Yisrael* [Workers of the Association of Israel – religious labor movement] and worked as an instructor and organizer, appeared with inspiring speeches, wrote articles in party publications. His ideas possessed a synthesis of *Yidishkeit* [a Jewish way of life] and worldliness. At the beginning of the 1930s, when the Zionist idea captured an even larger number of the Jewish masses, Nuska Szejman also was carried away and devoted himself to [Zionism] with the entire zeal of his soul. He became a member of the right *Poalei-Zion*. He dreamed of a Jewish land where the redemption of freedom, equality and brotherhood would be realized.

Returning to Czyzewo, he threw himself with all of his strength into party work and he showed himself not only to be a good speaker, but also as a capable organizer. Later, when the original founders and organizers of *Poalei-Zion* left the *shtetl* [town] and emigrated to Israel, Nuska remained the actual leader of the *Poalei-Zion* organization in Czyzewo.

That was a time of great quarrels. I would have discussions with him. He defended his socialist beliefs with which I did not agree. However this did not bother his natural friendship. After such heated quarrels he would always come to my house and as if nothing [had happened] strike up a conversation, invite me for a walk. With the ability to feel another's sorrow he immediately felt the smallest heartache and in a moving way tried to remedy it.

[Column 641]

Together, we devoted ourselves to the dream of emigrating to Israel. Alas, he did not succeed. In 1935,

we parted. I traveled to *Eretz Yisrael* and he stayed at his post. He later left for Bialystok where he continued to do Zionist work with the same idealistic enthusiasm and he did not cease to dream about going to *Eretz Yisrael*. He did not accomplish his dream. He perished during the annihilation of the Bialystok ghetto, may the Lord avenge his blood.

My Mother – the Teacher

by Yitzchak Szlaski

Translated by Gloria Berkenstat Freund

Born in Czyzewo, she was forced to withdraw with her husband immediately after her marriage to a distant area because he was hiding out so as not to have to serve in the Russian military. Living a number of years in a larger city in Congress Poland, she absorbed, in sufficient degree, information about the Polish and Russian languages. By nature, she was gifted with a natural drive for knowledge. While still young, she was accustomed to reading a great deal and in general loved to page through various books of religious and general content thanks to which she acquired a great deal of information about Jews and *Yidishkeit* [Jewish way of life], Jewish life and Jewish customs as well as information of general worth about the world and people.

The outbreak of the First World War hurt her severely. She became a young widow in 1915 during the first months of the German occupation of Poland. A short time later she returned to her family in her birthplace of Czyzewo with her two young orphans. ⊔ They were physically and spiritually broken because of the events of the war and lived with the poor Jews in the occupied *shtetl* [town] burned by the Germans.

[Column 642]

My mother, Nemi Szlaski, my sister Sura and my brother Chaim Leib

[Column 643]

Like many other *shtetlekh* in Poland at that time, our Czyzewo was backward in its attentiveness to education and secular education. It should be understood that modern schools for children, or, as they were called *shkoles* [secular schools], were rejected by the Orthodox. It was then the tradition that pure Hasidus and non–worldly learning ruled in these *shtetlekh*. As is known, the educational system in the area – at that time – consisted of *khederim* [religious primary schools] for boys. In their homes, in the small, crowded rooms, our old, well–known teachers spread Torah and wisdom. In contrast, there was no place or time for the girls to study, to help them acquire the least of the basic elementary instruction in reading and writing. Sometimes the parents did this themselves, but not all parents did it, because they were able to hire a teacher]. But others did not have the ability to hire a teacher capable of teaching their young daughters to write. This was a particularly grievous problem among the class that was not rich. However, with the arrival of the young widow, Nemi, the daughter–in–law of Alter the *sofer* [scribe] (Alter Shmulkes, as he was known in the *shtetl*) in Czyzewo, the problem was almost completely solved. In her, everyone found a most suitable teacher for their neglected daughters and their children who were lagging behind in their education, small and grown up. And Nemi the teacher, as she was later called, undertook the filling of her holy task intensively and energetically.

[Column 644]

She organized lectures for various groups, for the young and adults in her small room in her residence, where she taught writing and reading in the Yiddish, Polish and German languages and arithmetic. The children mainly would come in groups – organized themselves and matched up by the parents; they would stand outside and wait respectfully for one group [to finish] to be able to enter the hall of culture.

A class at Nemi's headed by the teacher, Yitzchak Szlaski

[Column 645]

They would sit on the wooden bed (*sofke* [settee]) and seats around the small table in the small room and diligently listen with a thirst and pleasure to the teacher's every word.

It is known that in times of deep suffering and pain, in poverty and deep need in one's life, there is a drive to climb higher and stronger, a drive for knowledge, a thirst for the intellect and culture, particularly among us Jews. In a short time, the teacher's small room was transformed into a small, primitive "public school" that laid the first foundation for the further development of secular public education for the young Jews among us in Czyzewo.

The small room teemed with students of various ages engrossed for the entire day, almost to late into the evening, going in and out, with notebooks and books in their hands. They would leave the lectures satisfied and radiant. Every lecture was a separate achievement in itself [and] all the more lectures, all the more knowledge. And the parent, every simple father and mother, took pride. A trifle – their young daughters already could or soon would themselves write a letter and even with the address in Polish or in German. They would praise the teacher for her honest and dedicated work with gratitude and admiration. For that was the reality. Nemi the teacher was not only a teacher of writing and reading. Nemi more than anything else was a devoted spreader of culture and knowledge. She filled every day with intellectual content. When teaching linguistic subjects. she would cite examples of various old and new writers and works, various stories from Jewish history or facts from current life. The students would intently devour every word with open mouths, feeling that their accumulation of knowledge was becoming richer from day to day.

[Column 646]

This era lasted for a number of years. With the end of the [First] World War, a short time after Poland's liberation, the war between the Poland and the Soviet Union began. Czyzewo, which was located at a strategic point (because of the railroad line), again found itself at the difficult war front. It was in the hands of the Red Army for a short time and then back again to the Poles, in the hands of the wild "*Hallerczikes*" [anti–Semitic followers of Polish General Josef Haller]." There was again suffering and pain and after a few years the communal life in the *shtetl* little by little began to normalize. The first Polish public school opened and then the first shoots of a modern Jewish school, organized and led by the devoted *doctorowa* [doctor's wife], wife of Dr. Gelbojm. Most of the female students were already schooled and prepared with the most necessary elementary education that they acquired during the war years with Nemi the teacher, the only one in the *shtetl* at that time. However, with the opening of the first public school, she still did not end her historic task; her students now came from the older young people who had been at the public school and whose education was neglected because of the difficult war years. Most of the young people were saved by her from the danger of remaining illiterate forever. The young men and misses would come to the teacher in her small room at night in the darkness, quiet and ashamed, and diligently listen to her lectures which were given with full understanding and tact, adapted to the capabilities of [absorbing] and intelligence of the students.

[Column 647]

Her educational activities for the students who called themselves *Amerikankes* [female Americans] make up an entirely separate chapter. These were the wives whose husbands were in America.

As is known, during the first 20 years [of the 20th century] there was a great emigration to America. The largest number of the emigrants consisted of women with children who were traveling to their husbands and parents from whom they had been torn and separated for many years both before and after the outbreak of the [First] World War. Our *shtetele* also was blessed with many such as these. The women, the *Amerikankes*, wanted to and even had to prepare themselves with the basic knowledge of reading and writing. The American consul precisely demanded this. Otherwise, he did not want to issue an American visa. So almost all [of the *Amerikankes*] came to the teacher to study and also for her to carry on the correspondence with their husbands because this was not easy and simple for them.

I remember the moments of sudden luck of those poor, broken–by–suffering widows of the living, when they received the first letter from their husbands in America in which were money and pictures from them. Tears of joy mixed with shame and despair. They came to the teacher to have the letter read [to them].

[Column 648]

Pointing to a photograph of her husband, such a person would whisper quietly to the teacher and say: "Woe is me – this is my husband? He looks like a professor! How can I go to him? So faded from suffering, exhausted – what can I do now? What can I write to him?" And she, Nemi the teacher, would console them and say: "Do not worry, everything will be fine." And then she began carrying on a correspondence with a letter from the women to their husbands in American.

She put her warm heart and genteel soul into these letters. Thanks to her wisdom, tenderness and sentimental feelings which she put into the letters, she succeeded in connecting with love, devotion and information man and wife, father and children on two continents, with different ways of life.

She lived and acted quietly and calmly. She did her holy work for an era, spread basic knowledge among the poor, backward population in the *shtetl*. Without commotion, without clamor, without any protest at her difficult fate, she always turned to God and to people, full of gratitude at being able to feed herself and her children during such difficult years. Time did not stand still. The years passed quickly. The small children grew up. In 1935 I, her son, the writer of these lines, emigrated to *Eretz-Yisrael*, carrying in my heart the hope that at some time I would be able to bring her, my mother Nemi the teacher, to *Eretz-Yisrael*. Her letters to me always were soaked in longing for *Eretz-Yisrael*, no less than for me, her only son. However, cruel fate chose something else.

[Column 649]

After the outbreak of the last war [Second World War], when Czyzewo was occupied by the Soviets, I was precisely informed about Jewish life in the *shtetl* through her postcards, which were covered with 50–60 lines of petite writing. She avoided the severe censorship of the Communist regime by using intelligent citations, examples and aphorisms. Along with my mother, I hoped that we would see each other in the freed Israel, but no!

[Column 650]

Here [Czyzewo], my mother shared the brutal fate of all Czyzewo Jews.

May these few words about your modest cultural activities for the Jewish community in Czyzewo serve in place of flowers that are refreshed by the warm tears of my red, tearful eyes.

A garland on the large mass grave of the majority of the Czyzewo Jews in which you, too, found your eternal rest…

Translator's note:

1. In Yiddish a child is considered an orphan if one of its parents has died. Also, the author writes about his mother and "TWO young orphans." In the caption below, the author lists his sister Sura and his brother Chaim Leib, so there apparently would have been THREE "young orphans."]

The Light from Our Home

Berl and Chantsha

Translated by Gloria Berkenstat Freund

To the memory of our parents

I carried the idea of immortalizing the memory of our parents for many years and, therefore, rejoice with the opportunity given to me by the yizkor [memorial] book for our city, the city of my parents and grandfathers.

I strove to fulfill the *mitzvah* [commandment] of "honoring my father and mother" for all of my years. When the new Soviet regime arrested me in 1940 and the investigator actually wanted to know about my family matters, among other [questions] he asked me:

– Do you support your parents?

I could not imagine what he had in mind with his question and answered the complete truth:

– They were independent until the war, well situated. Today they are completely ruined. In addition, they are not young people; if I were free I would have the opportunity to treat them with honor and support them.

[Column 651]

I tried to make the *sliedovatel* [interrogator] understand the great *mitzvah* of honoring one's father and mother, but he was not interested in my strong desire to fulfill the fourth commandment of the "10 Commandments." My answer was useful for his bad intentions and he wrote that we were one family.

Alas, we did not have the opportunity to help and support our dear parents. May this remembrance be a contribution to their honor and memory.

* * *

In my young boyish years I once listened to a conversation between my father and his close friend. It concerned my exchanging my Hasidic garb for European [clothing]. His friend asked:

– You look at him and say nothing?

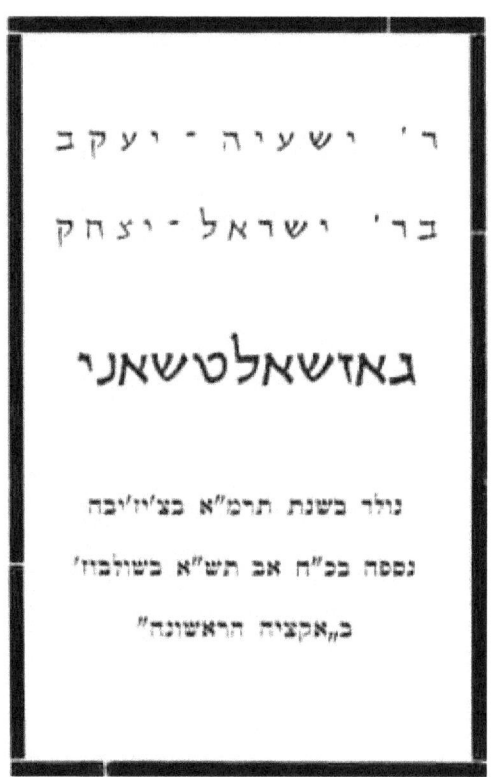

**Reb Yeshaya-Yakov
son of Reb Yisrael-Yitzchak
Gorzalczany**

**Born in the year 5641 [1881] in Czyzewo
Perished on the 28th of Av 5701 [21st August 1941] in Szulborze
During the First *Aktsia* [deportation]**

My father answered with a question:

– Why are you sure that it would help?

[Column 652]

– The close friend advised, you can still try.

– And if he does not obey? – My father asked further.

– Well then, there is no solution; it is hopeless.

– No! – my father called out, "Better he transgress unknowingly than knowing." I have the impression that I will not prevail with him. At least let him not violate his "honor." We children were not the cause of correct relations between our parents and us. But our parents never caused any situation in which we children would rebel against their will.

* * *

We do not know very much about our father's early years. There was no grandfather and no grandmother to tell their grandchildren about their father.

My father was orphaned[1] when his mother died when he was two years old and although the second mother was an aunt, a loving sister of his mother, it was more than natural that the stepchildren would feel wronged in comparison to her own children.

[Column 653]

The other grandmother, Matl Fayga, daughter of Faya Epsztajn, truly made a great sacrifice when she was very young, beautiful and an intelligent girl, taking over the motherhood of four orphans after the death of her young, deceased sister, Yenta-Rivka. She married my grandfather, because that was what the family ordered her to do. She was left a widow at age 45. She did not get married again despite the fact that she was materially well situated. The care of her own five children surpassed for her the question of her own happiness and she was a widow for 35 years until she was murdered by the Hitler bands.

Our father spent part of his very early youth in *yeshivus* [religious secondary schools] and part with his grandfather, Reb Yona in Wysokie Mazowieckie. His grandfather, Reb Yona was a preeminent scholar, a follower of the Enlightenment, a renowned person in Wysokie.

In the year 1946, by chance, I met a Jew, Mr. Tumkewicz who came from Wyskoie, at the *kehile* [organized Jewish community] council in Lodz. Hearing my family name, he asked me if I had had relatives in Wysokie?

– I answered him, "I am a Wysokie grandchild; my grandfather was Reb Yona." Mr. Tumkewicz stood up and asked with reverence:

– A son of Reb Yisroelke?

I told him that he could speak to me while sitting I am just a great grandchild of Reb Yona, a grandson of Reb Yisrael Yitzchak.

My father took my mother from Sterdyn, a small village 28 kilometers from Czyzewo. She was named Yehudis, a daughter of Reb Shmuel Moshe Rozenberg, an aristocratic and noble man from Sterdyn. To the day, the name Reb Shmuel Moshe and the entire Rozenberg family are remembered by all of those from Sterdyn as a model, as a symbol of all good deeds. I remember the year 1932 when my grandfather, Reb Shmuel Moshe, died at a very old age. This was two days after *Shavous* [spring holiday celebrating the "giving of the Torah"]. The Sterdyn Rabbi, Reb Eibeszyc, was with the Aleksander Rebbe for *Shavous*. When he returned a few days after the burial [of my grandfather], he called the entire *shtetl* to the house of prayer and publicly *gerisn krie* [tore his clothes as a sign of mourning]. He banged his head on the wall and cried out: "*Vey, vey is tsu mir* [woe is me], that I did not have the merit to eulogize the great Reb Shmuel Moshe at the open grave." In addition, he gave a eulogy for my grandfather.

[Column 654]

So my father lived in this house for three to four years, *gegesn kest* [had his room and board provided by his in-laws while he studied] and had two children. He later had a shoe business and it was not successful. In addition my father absorbed the original altruistic traits with which my grandfather's house was enDoved. He also absorbed a page of the Talmud studying with my grandfather every day, as was the custom among the Sterdyn Jews.

For several years my father had suitable companionship in the house of prayer. There were then two other *kest* sons-in-law: the future Cienchanowiec Rabbi Brunrut and the Kamanow Rabbi SzuLevic who all were good friends until the end.

He moved from Sterdyn to Warsaw for a short time; also without much success. He finally came to Czyzewo, ran a small grocery store. He at last grew into an esteemed, capable merchant, and built and maintained a beautiful house.

My father was one of the authentic merchants, always searching for new articles, new kinds of goods that had never been brought to the *shtetl*.

[Column 655]

He later was (until the arrival of the state monopoly) the only tobacco wholesaler.

A very large part of the success of the businesses surely belongs to my mother who bore all of the responsibilities for the business with my father and sometimes even more. My mother was greatly beloved by the customers. They would come to her to entrust all of their secrets. They looked to her for advice, expert judgment about a marriage match and the like. Everyone, without exception, had great respect for Yehudis. Male and female neighbors had the greatest respect. The neighbors turned to no one but my mother, Yehudis-*lebn* [dear] and Yehudis-*kroyn* [crown – a word of endearment]. Never in her life did my mother speak a loud word even in serious matters and, as matter of fact, she did not give any [female] neighbor, even the most quarrelsome, any opportunity to speak to her with anything but reverence.

Yehudis Gorzalczany, neé Rozenberg

[Column 656]

Various people came not only to my father for advice. They also came to my mother and not just women. The old Reb Moshe-Mendel Gromadzyn told my mother all of his troubles. Gershon *Yid* [Jew] entrusted his correspondence to his American brothers to no one but my mother.

My mother wrote about everything to his brothers: about his health, about his income, how many horses had been born in a season and the like. Gershon *Yid* was once our neighbor; until the end, he came from very far, from the other side of the city, telling my mother his troubles so that they could be sent in a letter to his brothers in America.

* * *

The Way of Raising Their Children

There were three of us. A sister came much later. We do not remember that there were any conflicts between our parents and we children and also none among us children.

Life in the house of our parents flowed so peacefully, so comfortably. I only remember one slap that I received from my father. It was *Tisha B'Av* [ninth of Av, commemorating the destruction of the 1st and 2nd Temples in Jerusalem]. A group of boys including me prepared a reserve of "small brushes" and threw them in the *shtibl* [one-room synagogue] as was our usual behavior. There was an old Jew there, a poor man. As it usually happened, he was the victim. The majority of the small brushes got entangled in his beard. The Jews begged us to leave in peace. But we did not stop throwing [the small brushes]. Then my father arrived and honored me with a slap. He said angrily:

– Why did you choose the very weakest? Certainly, you should try to throw [the small brushes at somewhere else]…

[Column 657]

Ha, are you afraid that they will break your bones?

Today I am convinced that my father was correct.

In the years 1915-18, during the German occupation, when food was very scarce, my parents worried that, God forbid, there would be a lack of bread in the house. At Kayla the baker's [bakery], they baked dark bread and 80-90 pounds of bread would come out. However, one longed for a white *challah* [Sabbath braided bread] in honor of *Shabbos*, so my mother baked several small, braided *challahs*. And if there was no wine, my father made *kiddush* [prayer over wine] on the *challahs* and gave everyone a piece of bread. My mother saw the longing eyes with which the children looked at the *challahs*. She would convince us that dark bread was certainly good and, perhaps, better with the fish. The children would agree and thus would end the Friday night banquet and a small piece of the *challah* remained.

Dear mother, you worried so much about the holiday and how great was your strength to bear all of the burdens of the entire year. A hidden giant slept in your every limb.

My father lived until the end communally in the Aleksander *shtibl* [one room house of prayer]. He would pray there and he would study and have conversations there all his free hours.

It appears that my father was among the respected men from an early age. As long as I remember, he was one of the leaders of the *Shakhris* [morning] prayers on the Days of Awe, and this was when the old leaders of the *Shakhris* prayers, such as Reb Leizer Solitis and Reb Zelik Yankel Przezakewicz, were still alive. Praying on Rosh Hashanah and Yom Kippur at the synagogue lectern, at that time, was a level that not everyone could attain. My father also had his place at the table among the singers of *Shabbos* hymns during the third *Shabbos* meal in the *shtibl*. He had a sweet voice both while singing and while studying. His *Gemara* [Talmud] melodies in the early morning hours, particularly on *Shabbosim* and Yom Kippur, would put we children to sleep so sweetly…

[Column 658]

My father was the *bal kore* [reader of the Torah during services] on *Simchas Torah* [holiday commemorating the completion of the yearly reading of the Torah and the start of the reading for the new year] and always was the one designated to close the annual reading of the Torah on *Simchas Torah*. The honor obligated a *Kiddusha Rabba* [great *kiddush* – blessing of the wine] and as a right of possession, the entire congregation of the *shtibl* accompanied by all of the children would come to our house to our father for the *kiddush*. How carefully our mother would prepare everything. She welcomed the uproar and noise of the Hasidic *kiddush* with so much satisfaction and a sincere smile. Although the Aleksander Hasidim were a little calmer and behaved quietly and sedately, after the *kiddush* the house looked as if after a wedding and this was repeated twice more on *Simkhas Torah*, at night and the next morning.

Our house was always open at all opportunities for Hasidic get-togethers. Reb Betsalel Yair a representative of the Aleksander court, and others would come from time to time. Such visits by an emissary from the rebbe meant not only a *kiddush* for all of the Hasidim, but also banquets that lasted several days. Male and female Hasidim would come with *kvitlekh* [notes to a rabbi requesting a blessing: for example, barren women asking for a blessing to conceive a child] and various requests. A long chain of people receiving a welcome and, later, those saying goodbye, all of this was a right of possession of *Beis-Yeshaya* [Yeshaya –the author's father's house]. My father accepted this with love.

His excellence in singing nearly brought my father to a conflict with my grandfather. It was at the *sheva-brakhos* [seven wedding blessings that are recited for a bride and groom] in Sterdyn. Before the blessing, my grandfather, Reb Yisrael Yitzchak said to [my father,] the groom: "Sing *Shir-haMaalot* [Psalm 120-134]." My father did not want to sing.

[Column 659]

– Why?

– With that, my father declared, I am even more doubtful about the desire of my father [to have me sing] because the entire intention of asking me to sing Shir-haMaalot is for the group in Sterdyn to hear how beautifully I sing. If I do not sing, they will think that I can sing better than I actually can.

My grandfather accepted the answer and abandoned [the idea].

My father did not belong to the fanatic [believers] of Hasidus, but tradition was one of the highest matters to him. I remember how my father would help the leader of the *Musaf* [supplementary] prayers, Reb Yisrael Yitzchak Janowski, on the Days of Awe with great ecstasy, with the highest notes he could bring out in singing the *Avoyda* [worship service] on Yom Kippur.

For a long time I did not understand the *Avoyda* precisely. He did not belong to a family of *Kohanim* [members of the priestly class]. Recently I have found it said in the book, *Kotzk*, that this prayer was the most prominent in the Aleksander court. The first Aleksander Rebbe was a *kohan* and the rapture comes from this.

My father had an original doctrine in his spiritual life. He really was a Hasid, but with complete understanding. He was a strong follower of Reb Yakov Emden. Our house was conducted according to the prayer book of the "*Yid*" [Jew]: the *erev tafshiln* [food prepared before *Shabbos* or a holiday that falls on *Shabbos*], the Passover Seder plate, the customs for the *sukkah* [temporary structure in which one has meals and may sleep during the holiday of *Sukkos*], *Shemini Atzeret* [the eight day of *Sukkos* – the Feast of the Tabernacles]. The thick prayer book by Reb Yakov Emden was like the *Shulkhan Aruch* [Code of Jewish Law]. He would search in the prayer book for every doubt he had. He would bless the children on Yom Kippur according to the wording of Reb Yakov Emden.

[Column 660]

My father did not belong among the greatly extravagant people, he calculated everything, did not like to overpay in buying goods, but it was completely different with ritual objects, the best *tefilin* [phylacteries], the prettiest *talis* [prayer shawl] with gold or silver embroidery on the upper edges. Months before my *Bar-Mitzvah*, he ordered a pair of *tefilin* from Shmuelka's son, Dov Alter (Szloski).

My father had the character trait of not being proud of his lineage. He simply detested "ancestry" and "pedigrees." My father remained the oldest man in the family after the death of my grandfather, Reb Yisrael Yitzchak, and the death of his older brother, Reb Hersh, and, as a result, he was the representative for various family matters and particularly in arranging marriages for his young sisters.

A match was proposed for his sister, Dvoraka, with a young man from Sokolowa, Avraham Landa. The father-in-law was a prominent Jew, a rich man, a descendant of the Gerer Hasidim. My father was still a young man then. In one of the conversations at completing the marriage negotiations between the in-laws, he said to the father-in-law:

– I will tell you that you are making a mistake if you think you are buying a pedigree from me, but if you think you are selling me your pedigree, it is a waste to talk. I do not buy a pedigree and I do not have a pedigree to sell. My family brings autarkeia [personal self-adequacy] in the area of pedigree. It is enough for me and there is nothing left to sell.

My father also was never stingy with tuition money. My father is not at fault that I did not grow up to be a scholar. He gave me the best teachers, special teachers for six chosen boys. He took the greater burden of paying for the rabbi because others were poorer and could not pay a sixth of the tuition money.

[Column 661]

Our sister, Fayga Faya, was sent to Ostrowa to study because there was not yet a school in Czyzewo. My father would not have so easily sent a girl to a strange place if not for the fact the house of the Kamarower Rebbe would give appropriate supervision.

The Also Were Bad Times

I remember 1915. The Russians left Czyzewo and took my father with them, under the pretext that he had not wanted to make change of one *kopeka* from a ruble at a sale. In those tsarist times this was a sign that Jews were hiding the small coins for the Germans. My mother remained alone with three small children. Yechielka, my father's youngest brother, came to help us pack, so that we could escape quickly, because they were saying that the Russians were setting fires before retreating.

Suddenly, someone knocked on the shutters. We could not tell from the knocks that there was no danger. We had to be ready for anything. However, Yechielka could not remain with us. He had to run home. My mother, her three sisters, young girls, had to be on watch. Night was falling. My mother closed the shutters, locked herself in and sat on the packages surrounded by her small children. Shouting by everyone in distant streets was heard; the bands of soldiers were going around raping, looting.

– Who is there?

– Me, Hersh Mordechai. Yehudis, open up.

– What do you want?

– The officers from the headquarters who are staying with my father-in-law, Reb Zawel Edelsztajn, have sent me to bring them tobacco.

My mother answered him:

[Column 662]

– I will not give you tobacco. Let them come themselves.

A few minutes later, two officers approached. My mother said that she would sell them tobacco on the condition that they would both remain in the house until daytime.

After a short discussion among them, they agreed and sent Hersh Mordechai home to tell the others that they were coming in the morning. My mother made supper for them, unpacked a package of bed linens and made a bed for them.

Late, after half the night [had passed], the officers were asleep; my mother and the children dozed while sitting. Suddenly a heavy knock was heard. They pulled at the door and shouted: "Open!" accompanied by terrible Russian curses. "There are cigarettes here," they said among themselves with echoing curses. My mother woke up the officers, who immediately put on their uniforms and asked that the door be opened. Intoxicated peasants, with curses and dirty expressions in their mouths, poured in like a wave. But the two officers, with revolvers in their hands, stood opposite them:

– Scoundrels! Sons of bitches! What do you want here?

– An order was given: Let no one dare go into the alley.

A guard stood in the street until the day [began] and every new approaching band whispered a secret: "Careful, there is a colonel present here."

Day began. My mother prepared breakfast for them. We heard the front drawing closer. There was shooting on all sides and no one noticed that the two officers had disappeared, leaving their breakfast unfinished. Their hats also remained on the table.

[Column 663]

* * *

My father also maintained the custom of going to the rabbi, to my grandmother Matl and another aunt, Rochel, for as long as they lived, to wish them a happy new year immediately after the prayers on the first night of Rosh Hashanah. For all the years, I was his companion on all these visits.

Hospitality for guests was self-evident. I do not remember any *Shabbos* [Sabbath], even during difficult times, without a guest at the table. There were wandering guests and usual ones. Moshe-Dovid *der Meshugener* [the crazy one] belonged to the usual ones. He actually was normal, nothing more. He had convinced himself that he was the *Moshiakh* [redeemer]. There were guests who lived with us for weeks. The community emissaries from the Aleksander [Hasidic] court were among those who always stayed until all of the court matters in the *shtetl* had been dealt with. Emissaries from *Eretz Yisrael* communities belonged to my father if they prayed at the Aleksander *shtibl* [one room house of prayer].

I do not know why my father never was a *dozor* [member of the synagogue council]. He always was almost forced to be a candidate of the Aleksander *shtibl* [one room synagogue], but he always refused. He would take part in the deliberations, in the preparations, but he did not want the task or the honor for himself.

I once planned to ask my father the appeal of the thing [not accepting the position], but did not have the time. I suppose that he did not want to put on the "clothing" of a *parnes* [elected member of the community council] because his father, Reb Yisrael Yitzchak, was a *parnes* all his life and one of the most respected community workers for public interests. This was to be an expression of "honoring my father," according to his doctrine.

[Column 664]

In contrast, our father was the founder of the Jewish People's Bank. The founding meeting took place in our house and our father was one of the three managers of the bank. Later, our father resigned from public business. His youngest brother, Yechielke, a good head, a man of iron logic, took his place.

In his middle years, our father became a member of the *Khevre Kadishe* [burial society]. He was called to carry out the burial rites for the prominent deceased people. He would fulfill the task with great seriousness and preparation for the ritual purification [of the body].

The Second World War, the general destruction, did not permit my father to leave his children with any material inheritance. Therefore, he left us a spiritual inheritance that we wanted to be worthy of keeping.

We remember his principles and he would recite them to us at various opportunities: that we should not fight someone even when we are correct; that if we were upset, it is self-evident that a person always needs to think that he cannot be an objective judge of his own deeds.

At an opportunity, my father told of a case when my grandfather, Reb Yisrael Yitzchak, convinced him in his youth that he should study *Khoyshn Mishpet* [fourth part of the *Shulkan Arukh* – Code of Jewish Law] [and] *Yoyre-Deye* [second part of the *Shulkan Arukh*] – he meant that he should prepare to become a rabbi. When my father did not obey, my grandfather asked him why? You will not live and behave according to my guidance? My father answered, "Father, I am following your ways exactly. You did not obey your father, the *misnagid* [opponent of Hasidus] and [you] became a Hasid, and a *tish-zitser* [one who follows a particular Hasidic rebbe] in Aleksander. I do not obey my father and do not want to become a rabbi." Alas we children did not have enough sense to record all of the words, rules of life and logical thoughts that our father would say to us, that I know that my material achievements up until the war in 1939 were the result of his help and even more thanks to his encouraging, smart advice and showing me what to do and how to proceed. I did not consider any matter or did any business without receiving approval from my father. My mother was a living witness against the customary opinions about wives and mothers-in-law. Speaking very little, answering one for every ten, she always listened thoughtfully to what was being said to her and never interrupted the speaker. There also were cases when my mother did not want to listen until the end. This was when a neighbor or an acquaintance spoke *loshn-hora* [speech critical of or derogatory about another person]. Then, my mother would interrupt the story with a scornful expression: "Never mind! Everything can be said and what wives can tell!"

[Column 665]

The only daughter-in-law my mother had would not tell her secrets and business to her own mother, but to her mother-in-law. She always found an open ear with her mother-in-law. She would tell her [her mother-in-law] all of the eventual complaints about her mother-in-law's son and my mother always decided that in principal she [the daughter-in-law] was right.

[Column 666]

Our father was one of the first who went to his death in Szulborze; accompanying him was our sister, Fayga-Faya, and her husband Chaim.

Our mother and our young sister, Surala, went over the Bug [River] to Sterdyń. Our mother perished on the 12th of Tishrei 5702 [3 October 1941]. Our sister Surala was hidden in terrible conditions until January 1944 when she was killed by a band of Polish murderers, Hitler's devoted assistants.

Translator's note:

1. A child was considered an orphan [*yosem*] when one parent had died. When both parents were deceased, a child was a *keylekhdiker yosem* [a circular or complete orphan].

Our sister Fayga-Faya and brother-in-law Chaim Zylbersztajn and their small daughter Chanala. Perished in Szulborze

Our youngest sister, Surala, perished six months before the liberation, in the Sterdyń area

[Column 667]

The Pogrom in Czyzewo Described in the Yiddish Press of That Time
Der Moment [The Moment] number 101, Friday the 30th of April 1937

Translated by Gloria Berkenstat Freund

The Great Trial About the Czyzewo Unrest

Detailed report from our special representative.

The trial for the anti–Jewish events that took place on Tuesday, the 5th of January 1937, in Czyzewo and made a ruin of this densely populated *shtetl* [town], where Jews and Christians lived peacefully together for many years, began last night before the Lomza District Court.

According to a series of accounts that arrived from Czyzewo, the matter unfolded thus:

[Column 668]

There was a fair in the *shtetl* on Tuesday, the 5th of January. It was apparently anticipated that the market day would be "lively." Many policemen, with the commissar and the *starosta* [village chief] at the head, were assembled in the *shtetl*, as was usual on a market day during the previous months in the *shtetlekh* [towns] in Bialystok province. At that time, pickets stood in front of Jewish shops with white and red ribbons on their arms and stood watch… When several hours had passed and the peasants had earned a considerable amount from the products they had sold, one of the *Endeke* ["*Endecja*" – "*Narodowa Demokracja*" – anti–Semitic, Polish Nationalist Democratic Party] comrades, a certain Cimer, gave the signal and an entire gang immediately went to the Jewish shops with sticks and crowbars. Chaotically, Jews began to lock the shops and close the shutters. Police at once began to react in the strongest manner and chased the hooligans from the market, driving them to where the horse and cattle market was located.

[Column 669]

The sad results in Czyzewo were:

Zelig Jelin, a wagon driver, 38 years old, was severely wounded, alas, by the hooligans when he wrestled with them, wanting to save a calf – his entire worth. Jelin was taken to Warsaw in his dying condition, where he exhaled his soul in the hospital on Friday, the 8th of January.

Yisrael Baran, a 58–year old butcher, was severely wounded and was also taken to Warsaw.

Ditto, the 22–year old Mindl Kowadle and the 19–year old Henya Fajngold, who had a few bones broken by blows from an iron bar.

Efroim Grzibak received a hole in his head. Yosef Kasower, a blacksmith, escaped with a split head.

The horse–trader, Chaim Jablkowski, had a foot and a hand broken. His son was severely beaten.

Also severely wounded were the cattle trader Shimon Goldberg, Szifman, Wajnbrum, Nisen Feldman and Berl Lapka, a resident of the nearby *shtetl*, Jedrzejów.

[Column 670]

The 36–year old Esther–Shayna Bronsztajn received wounds to her feet. Rivka Slocka, a pregnant woman in her later months, was "treated" with a rusty nail in her stomach. The latter two were taken to the Jewish hospital at Czista.

In addition, 25 Jews received light wounds in various parts of their body and face.

Since then, disregarding the fact that four months have already passed, Czyzewo has not been able to return to normal. Extraordinary need and want reign in the *shtetl*; the recovery is as if cut off; all of the sources have run out; dozens of families have left the *shtetl*. The majority settled in nearby Bialystok. Many families, previously very distinguished and well–to–do had to receive charity. Donated money arrived from many places (over four months, the Bialystok aid committee itself sent 3,000 *zlotes* to Czyzewo).

Now the entire *shtetl*, Jews and non–Jews, lives under the effects of the trials. The two dozen Jewish witnesses, starving and tortured Jews, have mortgaged their last rags and appeared at the trial.

M. Goldman

The Trials

Lomza ([reported] by telephone). As was anticipated, the *Endekes* decided to make use in their political propaganda of the trials [resulting from] the bloody events in Czyzewo.

[Column 671]

They transferred the defense of the accused to the authority of four prominent *Endeke* men, the lawyers Barowski, Jeczarski, Niebudek and Mieszkowski.

The *Endekes* were well represented among the representatives of the press.

Endekes aged from 20 to 28 occupied the 34 seats for the accused. The 35–year old Antony Cimer, who previously was accused as the main organizer of the unrest, did not find himself on the seats of the accused. The trial against him was vacated, because during the examination it was established that he was mentally unsound.

It must be remembered that Cimer confessed during the first examination of taking part in the unrest and the accusing witness, *Przodownik* [the leader] Czechowski, had designated him as a notorious rascal and adventurist.

One of those who also played the first fiddle during the unrest was the accused Kraszewski, who was exiled to Bereza [Kartuska Prison] with the *Endeke* lawyer Marian Arsz and Arganinski.

The Jewish lawyers Grozbard from Lomza and Karniol from Warsaw presented themselves at the trial; the widow of the martyr Jelin was the plaintiff. They demanded 500 *zlotes* for moral losses because of the unrest.

The *Endeke* lawyer Barowski made a vehement argument against the Jewish plaintiff, but the court decided to permit the *Endeke* demand to call additional witnesses on the part of the defense, the lawyer Jursz from Wysockie Mazowieckie, one of the leaders of the anti–Semitic boycott in that area, also was accepted.

[Column 672]

After taking care of the family questions, the chairman read the act of accusation, which said very little about the anti–Jewish unrest. On the contrary, much was said about the anti–police demonstrations by the accused.

We Approach the Witness Interrogation

The first group was 17 witnesses from the local regime against the accused. The witnesses categorically stood firm about the guilt of the accused as direct participants in the unrest and attackers of the police.

During the interrogation of the witnesses, Paprocki began a debate about the ideas of the boycott and *bojka* (fight).

The witness attended a conference with the *starosta* [village elder] from Wysockie Mazowieckie and the *Endeke* representatives whom the *starosta* warned against organizing unrest. Therefore, the witness said, the *starosta* had declared that he was not against a *szlachetny bojkot* [noble boycott]. But when the plaintiff's lawyer, Karniol, asked what he understood by the concept of *szlachetny bojkot*, the witness drew back and said that he had made a mistake. The *starosta* had said that they could carry out a *szlachetny konkurent* [noble competition], not a boycott…

The *starosta* also warned the *Endekes* that he would ask that the *Endeke* pickets be cleared if the smallest attempts at terror and violent acts were noticed.

[Column 673]

Lawyer Karniol asked one of the witnesses if he knew that the *Endeke* leader from Czyzewo, Adgoninski, would lend Jews money with interest.

The chairman withdrew the question because Adgoninski was not on the accused bench…

Call for Help from the Czyzewo Jews

Warsaw (JTA [Jewish Telegraphic Agency]). JTA has received the following appeal from the Aid Committee for those who have suffered in Czyzewo.

Because of the violent agitation that is continuing, the Jewish population in Czyzewo finds itself in a sad state. The shopkeepers have already consumed their goods, artisans are hungry, the [conditions for the] *dorfs–geyer* [those who go to the villages to buy and sell things] are impossible.

Now the question is: Passover is coming. Where will those suffering get their matzos and potatoes?

It is hoped that the Jewish communities as well as the well–to–do individuals will not forget their duty to ease the need of the Czyzewo Jews.

Donations [should be] sent to this address:

Rabbi Sh. D. Zabludower, Czyzewo

(From a trip through the "Valley of Death." Written by Wolf Szliapak)

Czyzewo has around 400 families. Recently over 50 of these have left the *shtetl*, spread all over Poland. The city is known for [having] pickets. This plague continues there all the time without interruption. There are well–known signs in the villages that it is forbidden for Jews to enter.

[Column 674]

The shops in the *shtetl* were transferred to non–Jewish owners. They sold the last little bit of goods or many of the household goods and they only had a piece of bread to eat.

Thirteen cripples remain in the *shtetl* from last Tuesday, the 5th of January 1937, when the martyr, Jelin, was murdered.

We visit the houses [and find] pictures of poverty and illness. Almost 300 families are in immediate need of medical help, bread and coal.

The majority of the sick are spitting blood; these are victims of the time. We are followed by many Jewish artisans; several toiling Jews stick out their hands, half ashamed, and ask for bread for their children. The epidemic of children's diseases has led to the fact that six Jewish children have died in one week, among them the martyr Jelin's youngest child.

We visit the former butcher of the *shtetl*, Hatskl Igla, 50 years old. Last Tuesday, hooligans threw him onto a fence and broke him in two. He lies all day riveted to his bed in great suffering. He spits out his cut–up lung and his children sit in the house without any bread to eat. Today is already Monday and they live with a little warmed up potatoes, which remain from the *Shabbos cholent* [Shabbat stew].

[Column 675]

Who is Guilty in the Events in Czyzewo

It appears that the sad pattern of the boycott campaign in Wysokie Mazowieckie County did not yet satisfy the blood–thirsty *Yidn–fresers* [Jew–eaters – persecutors of Jews] because the *Dziennik Narodowy* [*National Journal*] in last night's edition – a day after the funeral of Jelin, the Czyzewo martyr, and the death of Mrs. Gwardiak by an accidental bullet – provides a description whose intent is clear and distinct:

– The special representative of *Dziennik*, Bidgadski, describes the terrain on which the unrest in Czyzewo occurred.

"The businesses there are all Jewish. There was a certain Szimonowski, whose son, a priest, is a well–known activist in Lodz. He could not support himself. His business is run by a brave Polish woman.

"I want to travel by bus – [but the only one is] Jewish. The bus to Nur, to Dambrow, to Czechowice (all well–known names now) belong to Jewish enterprises."

These are such innocent observations and now comes the true "description."

– [According to Bidgadski] During the past weeks, four Polish businesses have been founded in Czyzewo. This past week a Polish iron shop was opened. All of this irritated the Jews. They actually became wild. When a wheat firm arose, there were denunciations.

– The position of the Jews has continually become aggressive. (?) This has been a blow to their wallets. They wanted there to be outbursts; that windows be broken. The constant acts of denunciation to the *starosta* and to the provincial governor, in Warsaw and to their journalists terribly provoked the Poles…

[Column 676]

And what was with the *Endeke* fighters, who terrorized the passersby and did not allow any customers into Jewish shops. This was all "forgotten" by the *Endeke* and not mentioned and according to his description was understandable because the Jews intentionally created the excesses against themselves…

The *Nara* [anti–Semitic political party] newspaper, *Jutro* [*Tomorrow*] sent a representative who described the place of the events in a similar objective way as the cited *Endeke*. The representative provides an interesting detail that right at the moment when a conference took place of all of the village magistrates from the entire county and the *starosta* from Wysokie Mazowieckie, Dr. Szwiantkiewicz, about maintaining calm and order, an official ran into the room with a shout: "It has begun." The unrest actually had broken out.

The *Endeke* representative writes further:

– The population of the poor villages, Godlewo, Lipskie, Skórki Milewek, Uścianek and Biedrusk took part in the unrest.

Today Czyzewo possesses an unusual picture:

Police patrols march in the streets and through the market. It is quiet in the city.

The local Jews complain about the boycott. Actually, no Poles enter any Jewish business. The peasants come into the city only to buy in the new Polish shops; the Jews chase after the customers without success.

[Column 677]

The Jews in the surrounding villages cannot buy anything. The Jewish women tried for several days to buy milk in the village, but the Polish peasant women did not want to sell and the majority of Jewish women returned home with nothing. Only a few of them received milk from the peasant women, but the milk did not reach Czyzewo because other peasants took the cans and poured out the raw milk into the ditch. As the Jewish merchants said, almost no one could buy a trade license for the new year.

Der Moment [*The Moment*] number 10.

Tuesday, the 21st of January 1937

(Y.B.) Last night when the *khesed shel emes* [mitzvah – commandment – to accompany the dead to their burial] hearse car arrived in front of *prosektorium* [Polish word meaning "dissecting room," but more likely meaning "morgue" in this sentence] to remove the dead body of Reb Zelig Jelin, may his memory be blessed, the commissar from the 11th commissariat already was there with a platoon of policemen. The hearse car immediately stopped with the corpse at the nearby cemetery, which also was guarded by police.

[Column 678]

A large group of Jews was assembled at the cemetery.

The tragically deceased was eulogized by Rabbi Zylbersztajn, Rabbi Fetman, Reb Shlomo Aldfang and a representative of the Czyzewo *kehile* [organized Jewish community]. Heart-rending scenes occurred at the funeral on the part of the widow and orphans of the deceased. A brother of the deceased recited *Kaddish* [memorial prayer].

Heint [*Today*] number 7

7th January 1939

Again anti-Jewish events in Czyzewo.

Twenty-nine Jews wounded – six seriously wounded victims brought to the Warsaw Jewish hospital. One victim died – a second is near death.

Anti-Jewish events in Czyzewo are not news. As our readers remember, several weeks ago the *Endekes* there showed what they could do. They beat several Jews and looted Jewish possessions.

They designated the day of revenge for Tuesday, that is, the day when a petition was being brought to the *Sejm* [Polish parliament] about the exiled *Endekes*. In time, they admitted this to the police and on Tuesday in the morning approximately 200 policemen and police officers came to Czyzewo.

[Column 679]

Because of the threats by the *Endekes*, the Jews did not open their businesses and did not go to the market with their goods. Mrs. Chava Yehudis Melcer, who was on the street, received heavy blows from the *Endekes*.

The unrest started in the morning because a crowd of young *Endekes* had shouted immediately against the Jews and against the police when the police took away their sticks. They went outside the city and provoked a riot there.

On the way, they encountered the 56-year old butcher, Yisrael Baran of Czyzewo, leading a calf. They attacked him with crowbars and beat him on the head, face and body until he was unconscious and he fell down into the deep mud.

The police had not considered that the hooligans would go to the cattle market. Therefore, there were only a few policemen there.

The eulogy in the name of the Czyzewo *kehile* was given by Mr. Berl Gorzalczany – second from the left

When the rampaging mob arrived at the cattle market, they began beating the assembled Jewish cattle merchants until they fell down unconscious. All of the Jewish cattle merchants and wagon drivers, numbering more than 20, were wounded.

The severely wounded were brought to the Jewish hospital on Czista [Street].

[Column 680]

Yisrael Baran

Yisrael Baran from Czyzewo, 56–years old, a butcher. He was wounded in the head, face and hands;

Zelig Jelin, 36–years old, a wagon driver from Czyzewo. He did not regain consciousness. His skull was split.

Mindl Kowadla

Mindl Kowadla from Czyzewo, 29–years old. The *Endekes* entered her residence, threw stones and wounded her in the head and wounded a few more Czyzewer.

Zelig Jelin died on Wednesday morning without regaining consciousness. In total, 41 people were arrested and accused of belonging to the band [of *Endekes*].

What Do the Wounded Say

Last night our co–worker visited the wounded in the hospital and found Baran's daughter, who did not leave his bedside.

[Column 681]

He [Baran] answered our question [by explaining] while he was walking into the city from the market with the calf he had bought, a crowd of several hundred hooligans appeared opposite him near the cemetery and shouted: "Here is a Jew, let us attack him." They immediately threw him into the mud and began to beat him with tools. He lost consciousness.

His daughter cried at these words. After she calmed herself, she spoke again, saying that around one–thirty during the day, several Christians came and said that they had seen Baran lying bloodied and unconscious on the road. They said the same thing about Jelin.

Truth be told, except for the daughter, people in the city were afraid to go to the place of the incident. However, we forced ourselves and ran there. We saw the horrible picture. The father lay in blood and in a deep mud and did not understand what was being said to him. He was barely revived and carried home.

About Jelin, she said that he had a good reputation in the city as an extraordinarily strong man. Witnesses said that he received heavy blows from perhaps 100 hooligans. He had his money with him, his identification card for his horse; everything was stolen from him. He left a wife and three children, the oldest of which was five years old and the youngest three months old.

She could not gain control of herself and went into a corner, again to cry her heart out.

[Column 682]

Chaim Jablkowski spoke with great difficulty. He said that in the middle of a transaction he heard anti–Jewish shouts from a giant group. He did not have time to look, but he felt blows on his body from sticks and iron bars. One hundred and eighty *zlotes*, his horses and wagon as well as a hooded cape worth 70 *zlotes*, which covered one horse, were taken from him.

At night, after he regained consciousness, he [Jablkowski] found Yankel the butcher in his residence. He was severely beaten and breathless so that he could not speak any further.

Litman Wajnbrum still has not regained consciousness. His condition is hopeless. Miss Kowadla says that there was a fearful mood in Czyzewo last night; they constantly heard anti–Jewish shouts. The city's Jewish population did not go out into the street. The doors and shutters were bolted.

She was taken to a municipal hospital in Warsaw, but they did not want to admit her there, so she was taken to the Jewish hospital at Czista [Street].

Last night, many Warsaw and Czyzewo residents visited the sick.

Heint number 176, 31 July 1938.

Czyzewo already had a rich past in the area of "events" and boycott pickets, of anti–Semitic incidents carried out under well–known signs. Czyzewo lies in Wysockie Mazowieckie County, which has become well–known on the highway of anti–Jewish "strict picket fight."

[Column 683]

The Jewish population of Czyzewo has already suffered a great deal because of the idol that is named "boycott and picket." It is enough to remember Zelig Jelin, who died during the well–known Czyzewo events.

* * *

Trials about the anti–Jewish events occur often in Lomza County Court. However, the trials about the events in Czyzewo on the 5th of April, this year [1937], which were dealt with by the Lomza Country Court on the 21st of this month, earned our attention because it was a clear illustration of the well–known word play of Premier Skladkowski that "it begins with Jews and ends with anarchy."

As always, the events began from the innocent boycott. A certain hero under the well–known sign, Kazimierz Dmochowski, would throw fear into the peaceful Jewish population of Czyzewo with his frequent anti–Jewish outbursts.

The measure of patience by the local safety organs overflowed, particularly when the outbursts of Mr. K. Dmochowski became stronger from day to day.

The Czyzewo police posts informed the vice prosecutor for Polish matters at the Lomza County Court about this, who ordered the arrest of Dmochowski in the event of a further outburst.

And it happened."

On Friday, the 15th of April this year, when the market day fell as usual in Czyzewo, a female peasant dared to buy a kilo of onions from a Jewish street stall owner.

[Column 684]

In the blink of an eye, our "boycott hero" tore the onions from the Christian, which he immediately trampled with his feet.

The Czyzewo police immediately approached the adventurer to arrest him.

Prosecutor Polanski in his speech of accusation strongly demanded that the accused be punished under articles 163 and 129 of the penalty codex because such deeds upset the foundation of communal peace.

Lawyer Kurcyusz, in his defense speech, tried to weaken the conclusion of the act of accusation, declaring that according to law, the collective activity of the accused at a public meeting does not qualify because this took place during the market day, which was by nature a public meeting.

However the court did not take into consideration the interpretation of the defender and sentenced all four of the accused to six months in jail and upheld the appeal of the judgment only with regard to the Tanowski father and son.

The court also decided to free under police supervision the remaining two convicted men, Josef Supczinski and Josef Stakowski.

* * *

Heint, Thursday the 29th of April 1937.

The Trials About Anti–Jewish Events in Czyzewo

Today, the 29th of April, the trial about the sad anti–Jewish events in Czyzewo begins in the Lomza County Court, during which the Czyzewo resident Zelig Jelin died and many other Jews from the *shtetl* were severely suffered.

[Column 685]

What Happened in Czyzewo?

On the 5th of January 1937, several thousand men came to the fair in Czyzewo; of these, approximately 400 were members of the *Endekes* Party.

In connection with the information received about the preparation of the day of anti–Jewish excesses, the police regiment consisting of three platoons was even more prepared.

Before noon, the district leader of the *Endekes* Party, Stefan Kraszewski, appeared in the premises of the town officials, where the Wysokie Mazowieckie county chief had arrived with a demand that the village chief permit – hear and marvel! How far the *Endekes* nerve had reached – a people's militia with bands on their arms at the market in order to keep order during the market day. Therefore, Kraszewski had not forgotten to emphasize that he took exclusive responsibility for the members of the *Endekes* Party.

The village chief did not permit a people's militia and issued a court decree around one o'clock in the afternoon for the appropriate police to be at the market where 18 policemen were patrolling. Excesses, such as pushing and beating Jews by smaller groups, began breaking out in other areas. The policemen ended the events. The mob then began to attack the policemen, who were serving at the market. Some of the mob left for Targowice [Street] and began to beat Jews.

[Column 686]

Small excesses also arose at the train station and in various parts of the city. However, they were ended entirely by police at around four o'clock.

The organizers of the events were: Stefan Kraszewski, who was exiled to an isolation camp at Bereza Kartus, as well as the leader of the boycotters of the *Endekes* Party, Antoni Cimer.

The Sum Total of the Events in Czyzewo

In the course of the events, two police officers were lightly wounded and 17 policemen [were wounded]; of these, two were severely wounded. Fourteen Jews were beaten, five of them severely. In addition, one of them, Zelig Jelin, may his memory be a blessing, died on the 6th of January 1937 in the hospital in Warsaw.

The following wounded Jews were given medical verifications [certifications of their wounds]: Shimon Goldberg, Yosef Fribut, Berl Kapka, Avraham Pelman, Eliezer Kapka, Yisrael Baran, Chaim Jablkowski, Mindl Kowadla, Litman Wajnbrum, Esther Bronsztajn, and Yosef Kasower. As well as the tragic death of Zelig Jelin.

In connection with the cruel unrest in Czyzewo, 35 people were accused of responsibility according to article 163 of the penalty codex.

The Court and the Sides

The chairman of the tribunal will be Judge Sarkowski, the vice chairman of the penalty division at the Lomza County Court.

[Column 687]

Secondary chairmen, the judges: Banikowski and Krater.

The charge will be given by the prosecutor Waclaw Tuszowski, who put together the act of accusation.

Defending the hooligans, I have learned, will be the *Yidn–freserishe* [Jew–glutton – persecuting Jews] lawyers, Stipulkowski, Barowski, Niebudek from Warsaw and Mieszkowski from Lemberg [Lviv]. The well–known Jewish lawyer, Binyamin Blazbard, and other Jewish lawyers from Warsaw will appear in the name of the civil claim of the suffering Jews.

The Witnesses:

Forty–two witnesses will appear on behalf of the accusation, among them, 21 higher and lower police functionaries, with the commissar of the reserve group of the Warsaw police, Kazimierz Drazszrczszuski, commandant of the Wysokier police command, Alieksander Paprocki and police officer, Henryk Nejman from Grodno. Among the police witnesses are several from Warsaw, Bialystok, Ostrów Mazowiecka, Wysokie Mazowieckie and Czyzewo itself.

The following 17 Jewish witnesses have been called on behalf of the accusation: Chaim Markus, Sura Gonczar, Shmuel Wengorz, Chaya Kowadla, Avraham Shmuel Wajnbrum, Zalman Goldberg, Chaim Pesakh Niewad, Yitzchak Zysman, Jakov Kowadla, Ahron Gradus, Yisrael–Ahron Kaza, Chaim Bialystocki, Mindl Kowadla, all from Czyzewo. Chaim Jablkowski from Sterdyn, Litman Wajnbrum from Nur, a Lomza commandant.

[Column 688]

Heint, Thursday, the 7th of January 1937

In Unfortunate Czyzewo

Detailed report from our special representative N. Grobia

"The Czyzewo Intervention"

Tuesday, the labor deputy, Szczepanski, put forward an intervention in the *Sejm* regarding the exile of the Czyzewo *Nara* leaders, the lawyer Marian Jursz and Albin Arganinski, to Kartuz–Bereza. At the same time, he connected his intervention to an address by a minister in the *Sejm*, questioning the minister as to why they were doing such an injustice to the *Endeke* patriots. He had, at the mention of "injustice," the support of his ideological comrades – support without any parliamentary elaboration. – Support which reached the heads [caused beatings] of the Czyzewo Jews, those "guilty" in Jursz–Arganinski's *krzywde* [injury].

Czyzewo Tuesdays

I arrived in Czyzewo on Wednesday evening, the day after the events. The *shtetl* was quiet and empty. It was the quiet after a storm. Reinforced police patrols were walking slowly in the dark at the small market and in the surrounding alleys. They watched every hurrying passerby with penetrating eyes.

Just as two weeks ago, I visited the sad, now well–known *shtetl* [Czyzewo] on the way to Czechowice and it also was on "the next day" Wednesday, after the Tuesday fair before the gentile holiday. All of the "next day" Wednesdays after the Tuesdays in Czyzewo of recent times were similar to each other.

[Column 689]

The events of last Tuesday are actually a sequel of the other Tuesday on the eve of the gentile holiday. Something also happened then. During the fair, *Nara* agitators spread the news among the peasants that the arrested leaders, Jursz and Arganinski had been exiled to Kartuz–Bereza and thus the dark people called for revenge on the Jews who were guilty of this.

Calming Speech by the Vice starosta and Priest at the Market

With good fortune, the sad events in Czyzewo were avoided then. The large police division had energetically intervened and the presence of the vice–*starosta* from Wysokie Mazowieckie, Mr. Rath, had given a calming speech to the agitated crowd at the market and strongly warned against provocation and disturbance of public order.

The young Czyzewo priest, although a *Nara* sympathizer, also went to the *Nara* members and asked them to disperse. The two speeches had an effect and the hooligans dispersed, satisfied with only breaking the windowpanes in a few Jewish houses.

However the problems in Czyzewo did not end then. The members of *Nara*, their murderous ambition unsatisfied, "promised" bloody revenge against the Czyzewo Jews and they kept their word.

A Little History of Jewish Czyzewo

A meeting of local business owners takes place in the residence of the Czyzewo Rabbi Shmuel Dovid Zabludower with the participation of a delegation from the Bialystok *kehile* [organized Jewish community].

[Column 690]

There is an oppressive mood. Images of yesterday's fair day are still in the eyes of those present. They speak to unburden their hearts. Old Jews cry: – What will happen next?

The entire *Megilah Czyzewo* [*Scroll of Czyzewo*] is unrolled here.

The tragedy of 150 families; the ruin of an old Jewish *kehile*, of a *shtetl* where 95 percent of the population is Jewish.

Czyzewo Jews once had good income; the wheat trade was developed here. The entire area was rich; Jews and Christians lived [trading] with each other.

It is superfluous to say that the best relationship reigned between them. But, like all other Jewish *shtetlekh* in Poland, different winds began blowing in Czyzewo during the most recent years. The difficulties of the local Jewish population increased from the day when Czyzewo absorbed a young son–in–law *oyf kest*: Albin Arganinski.[1] [He was] a steward in a noble courtyard in the Pozen region, a stubborn anti–Semite. He and another one, lawyer Marian Jursz, created a *Nara* organization in Czyzewo and the Czyzewo Jews have had hardships since the Days of Awe because of the boycott agitation. They have not earned a *groshn* for many weeks. New Christian shops open every day. And it is truly a miracle from heaven that the Czyzewo Jews are not dying of hunger.

The Events of Tuesday

As usual, a large fair was supposed to take place in Czyzewo last Tuesday after the Christian holiday. Peasants arrived from all directions, from all of the neighboring *shtetlekh* and hordes of *Nara* members arrived, armed with sticks. The police reinforcements, who were sent to Czyzewo to protect it from the events, which incidentally were expected, had just been stationed on the roads that led into the city. The sticks and other weapons were taken from the *Nara* members.

[Column 691]

And as a result, one of the members of *Nara* from whom the police had tried to take his stick staged a revolt and with blood–curdling curses called on his comrades not let their sticks be taken.

This was around 12 noon. Immediately, a mob of *Nara* members left for the market with wild shouts of "Hooray, [get] the Jews!" They began to throw stones. Jewish shops immediately were closed. The hooligans grabbed rungs from the wagons, from street stalls and began to mercilessly beat the Jews who had not escaped in time.

All of the Jews in Czyzewo emphasize the truly energetic, devoted attitude of the police, who did not permit any spilling of blood in the city itself. A larger police cordon blocked the road for the unruly mob that wanted to attack Jewish shops and residences and in an energetic manner chased them from the city. The giant mob of peasants then in confusion began to escape to the villages with the horses and wagons.

[Column 692]

Meanwhile, the escaping young *Nara* members wounded several passing Jews and threw stones into Jewish houses. With shouts of hooray, they left for the cattle market, which was located a kilometer [six–tenths of a mile] outside the city, not far from the Jewish cemetery. Since the police were then concentrated in the city itself and they had not considered the possibility of serious events outside the city, only a small number of police were at the cattle market. The arriving murderous *Nara* members made use of this situation and they carried out their bloody work quickly before police help came from the city. Not many Jews were at the cattle market. They were horse and cattle traders, butchers from Czyzewo and from outside who had come to the Czyzewo fair to buy or sell something. These Jews did not know what was happening in the city itself. The arriving mob of hooligans was a sudden surprise to them and only a few of them had time to escape from the cattle market and to save their lives.

The wild young *Nara* members ruthlessly beat people with wagon rungs and iron bars. Mainly, their entire anger was poured out on the 36–year old wagon driver, Zelig Jelin, a Jew, a strong man. Several dozen hooligans battered him so that he fell on the ground unconscious. He was then taken to the hospital in Warsaw where, as is known, he died on Wednesday morning without gaining consciousness. He left a wife and three children.

A large police division arrived immediately right at the spot of the horrible murder, but the hooligans had disappeared. The police then drove away all of the peasants and then the results of the hooligans' work at the cattle market and on the way to the fair was seen.

In addition to the mortally wounded Zelig Jelin, 15 more were severely wounded and around 30 lightly wounded and beaten. Not all of the wounded were found right away. They searched for Yisrael Baran for a long time and he was found later lying wounded at the nearby cemetery among the headstones.

[Column 693]

Several escaping Jews found a hiding place at the cemetery. A large group of Jewish traders escaped from the horse market into a nearby forest. Others hid at the neighboring farm of a *gospodarz* [farmer]. One Jew, Kszeckower, hid in a Christian street stall that was located at the cattle market. The Christian stall owner had pulled the Jew who was in danger into the stall, covering him with tarpaulins and boxes and thus saved him from misfortune.

The unrest in Czyzewo, in general, lasted until one–thirty. Immediately after the police successfully took complete control and forced the agitated mob of peasants out of the city. The investigating judge and prosecutor immediately came from Lomza. Police arrested 42 *Nara* hooligans, including the leader, Stefan Kraszewski from the village Petrases, the replacement for Arganinski and Neter, a son of the village magistrate from the village Godlewa (Kraszewski, as well as Pat, as recorded, was exiled to Kartuz–Bereza).

The hooligans, who ran so wild, came from the surrounding villages of Godlewa, Gedases, Lipskie, Skórki, Uścianek and Biedrusk, mostly sons of farmers.

At the head of the security action in Czyzewo during the events stood the *starosta* of Wysockie Mazowieckie District, Dr. Szwiantkiewicz, who was accidentally physically assaulted by a hooligan. On Tuesday morning, *starosta* Szwiantkiewicz held a meeting of 30 village magistrates from the surrounding villages at the Czyzewo community offices, among whom, incidentally, was the Jewish magistrate in Czyzewo, Mordechai Rotszkowski.

[Column 694]

The *starosta* called this meeting for the purpose of warning the village magistrates of the plague of the continuous events in Czyzewo in which hooligans from their villages took part. *starosta* Szwiantkiewicz said in his speech to the village magistrates:

"I asked you once nicely to calm the peasants in your villages and to stop them from their outbursts. I see, however, that it does not help. Now I will talk to you with anger. You should know that the responsibility for future events in Czyzewo will fall on you. You will suffer, no one else but you. Village magistrates will pay all of the costs that are caused by the events, such as the losses, the bringing of police and other expenses that are connected with returning order and calm to the city.

Thus, the *starosta* mentioned the name of the above-mentioned village magistrate Neter and demanded to know why his sons were members of *Nara* and taking part in the anti–Jewish events. The village magistrate categorically denied this: It isn't true. His enemies had invented a false accusation against him.

In the middle of the speech, a messenger entered the room and the *starosta* reported that it had started… The *starosta* interrupted his speech and went out into the street to lead the security action. Then, the son of village magistrate Neter was caught during the agitation.

[Column 695]

What Will Happen Next?

So ask Czyzewo Jews with concern. As long as the police reinforcements are present in the city, it is quiet, but there will not always be so many police reinforcements in Czyzewo. What will happen if the usual small number of policemen remains in the *shtetl*? The hate is still great.

The morning after the events, when the Czyzewo milk–women went as usual to the nearby villages for milk, the [female] peasants did not want to sell any milk. And those who did receive milk had the milk poured out immediately afterward and the poor Jewish peasants were badly beaten.

The boycott was strong; the pickets caused misfortune for the Czyzewo Jews. The newly opened Christian shops took the last Christian customers who until then had dared to enter a Jewish shop through a back door. At the new year, the majority of Jewish shop owners had not bought [trade] licenses, simply because there was no reason to do so. Tuesday morning, an official and an overseer from the *urząd skarbowy* [tax office] came to supervise the [trade] licenses and collect taxes. However, they immediately left because of the events…

[Column 696]

Perhaps now that they achieved what they wanted and destroyed an innocent Jewish life, they will leave us alone – grieves a proto–proletarian Jewish woman.

Innocent Jewish life… Zelig Jelin saved other Jewish lives with his own life; when the wild hooligans – it is said now – went to the horse market, the hero Jelin remained and did not move from the spot. He was not afraid; what would they do to him, the strong man, the giant who would stand against 10 attackers at once? However, many more than 10 and more than 20 went after him. Zelig wanted to sell his horse at the market, exchange it for a better one to have for the rides to Bialystok. He was the last to remain at the market, asking all of the Jewish traders to escape and Zelig Jelin fell as a victim at the hands of murderers.

Perhaps now… perhaps Zelig Jelin's innocent spilled blood will also atone for the sin of the Czyzewo Jews. The "sin" of wanting to live on the land and not wanting to die from hunger! May God avenge his blood!

Translator's note:

1. a previous reference to Arganinski has his given name as Albin. The reference to *oyf kest* ,– support given by a father to his daughter's husband so that he could study Torah – is ironic. Arganinski was a leader of the anti–Jewish agitation.

The Scroll of Blood
"Davar" number 3584, 12 Adar 5692 (February 23, 1937)

by Gerszon Gur

Translated by Jerrold Landau

[Column 695]

It is a town with a history spanning centuries, with communal ledgers and lists of its great people, rabbis, and pious ones. It was always quiet and modest, and good, friendly relations always existed with all the Polish neighbors – the farmers of the villages of the nearby region.

[Column 696]

During the time of Czar Nikolai, the city was graced with something more than all the other towns of the area had – a railway station. When they built the first Petersburg-Warsaw line, this was the only city that was on the border of this line. Therefore, already from the time of the Czar, it was the custom to hold a market day twice a week as well as a monthly fair at which the merchants and farmers from all the towns and villages with no railway line gathered in Czyzewo to sell their wares, such a milk, eggs, various grains, etc. – to the Jewish merchants, who brought the merchandise to Warsaw. This continued until the town was afflicted, about a half a year ago, with a new Hitler who came from afar and settled there. From then, the chain of tribulations began. This Hitler began to organize a circle of Nara [a nationalist Polish political party] and would teach them each evening a lesson on boycotts and oppression of the Jews. A group of youths with fists and muscles began to gather around him. They were affiliated with the "Center for Matters of Afflicting the Jews" in Warsaw. From there, they received assistance with a working plan for freeing themselves of Jews in Czyzewo. In addition to the moral help they received from Warsaw, the center provided them on market days with several hundred strong youths with fists and clubs, who received a salary for their "clean" work of providing protection on market days. It has been more than a half a year since these Nara people organized in pairs, with clubs in their hands, in front of the doors of all the Jewish shops and next to the peddlers in the market, preventing any Polish customer from coming into contact with a Jewish seller. They would threaten with clubs and beatings until the simple farmer was forced, against his will, to leave the shop. If there were some who succeeded in evading the eyes of the picketers, they would receive a slap on the face as they left the shop, and in most cases, the merchandise that they purchased was confiscated.

[Column 697]

These deeds urged on the police. Once bright day, searched were conducted on two of the leaders of this gang. The searches revealed contacts with Nazi Germany and anti-government activities. The two were arrested. However, the imprisonment increased the severity of the situation. Members of the Nara conducted demonstrations against the imprisonment of their leaders. Beatings of Jews began with these demonstrations.

In the morning of the day of the fair, the farmers of the region streamed in by the thousands in an unusual fashion, but the attention of the Jews was directed to a new type of "arrival" – of thousands of youth in large camps, armed with sticks. The look on their faces indicated that they had not come for business.

In the afternoon, gangs of youths approached a Jewish peddler and overturned his stall with his merchandise. When a policeman arrived to investigate the deed, the members of the gang immediately surrounded him and began to beat him. A tumult arose. Many policemen came from all sides. The farmers immediately appeared with sticks and axes in their hands, and began to beat the policeman. Even the district ruler suffered no small amount from blows.

[Column 697]

A commotion arose among the Jewish peddlers. They all abandoned their stalls with the merchandise and fled in any direction their feet would take them. The shops were immediately closed. Shutters were pulled down in the residential homes. From between the cracks, people peered at the atrocities perpetrated out the open.

Within a moment, the town turned into a killing field between the members of the Nara and the police. However, as was later clarified, the disturbances were perpetrated in the city in order to draw the government forces from the cattle market behind the city, where most of the Jews were located without defense and protection.

Their plan succeeded.

While the Nara people were fighting with the police, their gangs perpetrated a slaughter of the Jews in the cattle market. They beat all Jews, without differentiating, with iron sticks and knives. Zelig Jelin, the town strongman, died of his wounds in the hospital in Warsaw. His body was full of wounds and knife stabbings. Yisrael Baran, a butcher by trade, was placed on the ground and beaten until they thought he was dead. Currently, he is struggling against death in the hospital in Warsaw. They drove a nail into the belly of a pregnant woman. Many others were injured with serious injuries.

Many Jews escaped from the market and hid in the grove near the town, as well as in the nearby cemeteries. They remained in hiding all that day and the following night, from fear of returning to their homes. The screams and cries of the women waiting for their husbands to return frightened the town.

However, this bloody scroll of Czyzewo had not yet concluded.

Several weeks passed. The town had not yet calmed down, and the fear of that dark day had not yet dissipated. The government banned any gatherings and fairs in the town. The Jews wandered around the town literally like mourners, perishing from hunger.

A quiet, discreet boycott began, which transitioned to disturbances and terrible slaughter, finally leading to general slaughter and death from hunger.

[Column 699]

There Once Was a *Shtetl* With Beloved Jews

by Yitzchak Bursztajn, Uruguay

Translated by Gloria Berkenstat Freund

I left Czyzewo for Uruguay in the middle of the summer of 1930.

I had a premonition that I would not see the *shtetl* [town] again. Alas, this premonition was certified with brutal thoroughness. I had the opportunity to be in Europe twice after the Second World War and it did not come to mind to go to my "city of birth."

What do I have to see there, for what do I have to search there, besides the grave of my father, of blessed memory, if the murderers have not disturbed it?

The graves of all of our beloved and dear were surely not in Czyzewo. The enemy had chased them earlier, tortured them until they were annihilated with the other saintly martyrs of the unfortunate European Jewry.

Of course, it would have been worthwhile to be there, to visit my parents' graves, to leave a tear at a grave of a relative, or just for the Czyzewo Jews who had been dead before [the Germans came] and had to watch the gruesome picture of how the Czyzewo Jews, so unpretentious and sincere, were annihilated. Because of this I had to be there, to look at the destruction, to cry my heart out and to say with a holy, God-fearing tremble:

[Column 700]

Yitgadal v'yitkadash…

I remember Czyzewo. The *shtetl* with its people is so fresh and clear before my eyes, not as it was 30 years ago, but as if I had just seen it last night. I see the large house of prayer, walled in bricks, full of Jews. I hear the quiet steps of the tall, stately rabbi, Rabbi Shmuel Dovid Zabludower, as he would enter on *Shabbos* [Sabbath] accompanied by the small Ahron the *shamas* [sexton] and all of the Jews spontaneously stood at their arrival…

[Column 701]

This was the *Misnagdim* [Orthodox opponents of Hadism] house of prayer and behind it in a wooden building were located several Hasidic *shtiblekh* [small, one-room synagogues]. The Gerer [Hasidim] were in one and the Aleksander Hasidim were in another and above on the second story the Sokolower [Hasidim] prayed with several Amshinower [Hasidim]…

The Hasidic *shtiblekh* did not have women's sections. The wives of the Hasidim had to pray at the women's synagogue of the large house of prayer or of the *Khevra Mishnius* [group which studies Talmudic commentaries].

The tall, slightly bent-over Avraham Chaim was the boss in the small house of prayer of the *Khevra Mishnius*.

[Column 702]

This was a rare Jew, with unusual behaviors. He would wake up from sleep right after midnight and at one o'clock he already was at the house of prayer. In the winter he himself lit the oven and said Psalms.

When the clock struck three, he would start going through the streets to wake Jews for prayer

I remember well how Avraham Chaim would knock on our shutters to wake up my father, Reb Shlomo, and it happened many times that my father had already woken up and was sitting at the window studying *Mishnius* by heart.

My father dedicated a part of his life to learning the "Six Orders of the *Mishnah*" [Talmudic commentaries] by heart. He achieved his ambition and therefore was acquainted with the learned circles not only in Czyzewo but also in several rabbinical "courts."

Avraham Chaim was a little deaf in his last years. Therefore, he would knock loudly on the shutters so that his "clients" would hear him. He would not move from the spot until he was convinced that his knocking had been successful. One had to give him a sign, shout, "Yes, Avraham Chaim, I hear. I am getting up."

It was then that he continued on his route with heavy steps.

Avraham Chaim's fights with packs of dogs that attacked him were often heard in the stillness of the night. He had with him for this purpose a good stick just in case and the stick was a good remedy for not being deterred by dogs in his holy service.

Avraham Chaim was the ruler of a small house of prayer of the *Khevra Mishnius*. He did not dislike being at the lectern. As much as I remember, he read the prayers only for the first prayers of the morning service and perhaps sometimes *Shakhris* [morning prayers] as well.

My mother, sisters and brother

[Column 703]

Reb Boruch Szapira, or as we called him Boruch Yoske's [probably indicating that Boruch was Yoske's son], who had a shop at the market, studied a page of *Mishnius* with the group. He was a Jew, a scholar. In addition, he was a good interpreter [of *Mishnius*]. Although his voice was a little hoarse, he had a strong eloquence and everyone around the table, from one end to the other, heard him well. Reb Shlomo had studied with the group before my father. But when he moved to the Sokolower *shtibl* to pray, he stopped studying with the group. However, he continued to study alone every day at the *Khevra Mishnius*.

Fayge-Malka, wife of Reb Shlomo Pakczarski

I remember a solemn celebration of a *siyim* [the completion of the daily study of the Talmudic texts] that would take place at the *Khevra Mishnius*. Such an event of finishing a sequence of *Mishnius* was celebrated with a lavish banquet. The honored guest always was the Rabbi, Reb Shmuel Dovid Zabludower, who sat at the very head [of the table], with Reb Boruch Szapira on one side and my father, Reb Shlomo, on the other.

Avraham Chaim was extremely happy at such holidays. He made sure that the oven would be heated better than usual, that the lamps would actually shine with light. All participants at the *siyim* felt as if they were at a family celebration, cheerful and elevated.

So in my imagination I see at the table Noske the oil presser, a fine Jew, a learned man, as well as enDoved with a good nature and a great deal of humor. In the early years I still remember him when he was the *baal-koreh* [member of congregation who reads from the Torah] at the *Khevra Mishnius*. Later he became ill. He suffered from a kind of paralysis. His hands constantly shook and because of his illness, he no longer was the same Noske.

[Column 704]

Yudel the carpenter, a Jew, a golden artisan, particularly in building wooden houses, took his place as *baal-koreh*. During my time, he already was an old man. He would work very slowly and did not want to take on any larger work [projects], but the house that he did build was as if turned on a lathe.

His grandson would help him with the work. I think his name was Yosl, the son of Khona Yudl's son-in-law. This Khona – his family name was Treblinski – was a very interesting type who drew special attention to himself even in Czyzewo, with his appearance and with his specific behavior.

He was a harness-maker by trade, but he also was an Uman Hasid, one of the "dead Hasidim" – as they were called. [2]

His piety was limitless; he would put all of his feelings into praying. His beloved place, which he had chosen himself, was behind the oven. However, his voice reached into all corners of the house of prayer.

He would pray with enthusiasm, with fervor, clap his hands and make strange faces. It was rare that one would see Khona's face while he was praying because he would always pull his *talis* [prayer shawl] over his head. When he read the Torah, he also stood at his place behind the oven. However, he lowered the *talis* to his shoulders so he could hear the *baal-koreh*, who was his father-in-law, Yudel the carpenter, an honest, toiling man of the people. Although he was not a scholar, he knew portions of the *Khumesh* [Torah] with their Rashi commentaries and also was not unfamiliar with chapters of *Mishnius* [Talmudic commentaries].

[Column 705]

In the Large House of Prayer

Hundreds of worshippers prayed in the large house of prayer. All of them were *misnagdim* [opponents of Hasidism]. They began their prayers there with Psalm [30] [invoking] a song of dedication to the House.

I still remember as a young boy when they finished building the house of prayer. The first *Minkhah-Maariv* [afternoon and evening] prayers remain engraved in my mind. There was not yet a roof on the building. The celebration in the *shtetl* for the new, beautiful house of prayer was enormous. I also remember they took this opportunity to collect donations to finish the last stage of construction. The contributions were made according to the number of bricks; one donated 100, another 200 and so on.

The Czyzewo *Beis-Medrash haGodl* [Large House of Prayer] erected after the First World War

The same night they also were busy with a list of Jews who were interested in buying *shtet* [reserved seat locations in the synagogue]. It should be understood that each row had its price. The first row near the eastern wall cost more and the back one less. The ark was not excessively luxurious. [It was] simple but finished very beautifully. When the carpenters finished with the communal reading desks that were divided into individual seats and finished all of the other facilities, the reading desk from which the Torah was read, the large, long tables and chairs at each side and two ceramic tile ovens, the house of prayer had a very fine appearance.

[Column 706]

Years later, when Eli the blacksmith became *gabbai* [sexton], painters were brought from Bialystok, true artists, and they decorated the new house of prayer with beautiful paintings. The most beautiful pictures, which represented various musical instruments with a fiddle at the head, were on the ceiling and between the ark and the Torah reader's desk. There were other pictures, several of animals, a deer, a leopard, a lion and others. The pictures did not have any signatures. However, it was easy to see that the artists had in mind with every picture something symbolic, suited to a house of prayer. The music was supposed to bring to mind the Temple [in Jerusalem]; the animals, the [verse] "Be bold as a leopard, and light as an eagle, fast as a deer and strong as a lion."

After the new renovation, the house of prayer achieved a truly majestic appearance.

From early dawn to midnight, the house of prayer was open for worshippers, learners, those reciting Psalms and the remaining Jews who just wanted to take pleasure from the hot oven during a cold, frosty day and to tell stories. On a weekday they prayed there collectively several times. A late *minyon* [10 men required for prayer] could even be found at around 10 o'clock in the morning.

Yitzchak Ahron, who was a collector [3] of "*Boruch hu avuorekh shemo*" [Blessed is He and blessed is His name] and "amens," would run from the Gerer *shtibl* [small one-room synagogue] to the house of prayer to grab an amen…

The house of prayer was full of Jew during *Minkhah-Maariv* [afternoon and evening prayers]. A preacher who gave a sermon came often. It was packed there from corner to corner on *Shabbos* [Sabbath] and holidays; even the women's section was full, as well as the *kehile-shtibl* [the one-room synagogue of the organized Jewish community], which was in the same building, where Zerach Starkowski taught *Ein-Yakov* [ethical and inspirational section of the Talmud] to a group of worshipers also was always full during the week and on holidays.

[Column 707]

Ahron the *shamas* [rabbi's assistant], a short Jew, but an energetic one, had a small room on the bottom of this same building, where he lived with his wife who was very similar to him in height. The functions of the *shamas* were many and responsible. First of all he had to help clean the house of prayer and we must confess in praise of him that he was very tidy. The house of prayer always was cleanly swept and the floors were washed. The lime ovens radiated heat in the winter so one could not touch them, so there was a dear warmness throughout the large house of prayer even during great frosts. Ahron the *shamas* was not stingy with [heating the ovens and] during the great frosts he constantly placed large pieces of coal so that it would be warm enough.

Friday night, Ahron the *shamas* would go through the streets calling out, "*In shul areyn* [go to the synagogue]." This was the official signal that it was time for *Shabbos* to start. The women immediately began to light and bless the *Shabbos* candles.

Ahron the *shamas* was the gravedigger if there was a death; first he would appear at the house of the deceased with a long twig torn from a tree at the cemetery to take a measurement for a grave. He would dig the grave himself (during the last years he had a helper for this purpose and to clean the synagogue) and when the deceased was brought to the cemetery, Ahron the *shamas* first jumped into the grave, took the deceased and laid the body down appropriately. He began calling out the names of those present who had asked for "forgiveness" and laid shards on the eyes of the deceased as was the custom in the old home.

[Column 708]

Ahron the *shamas* also had a part in Czyzewo celebrations. He would bring the *khupah* [wedding canopy; can also refer to the wedding ceremony], which was in his possession to weddings. He would place it in the designated spot, mainly outside, near the house of prayer.

In Czyzewo, weddings would always take place under the open sky. There was never a lack of an eager crowd at a wedding ceremony; [they] immediately surrounded Ahron and grasped at the polls of the *khupah* to have a better view of the groom and bride and the in-laws on both sides.

For many years Reb Yosef Shlomo the *shoykhet* [ritual slaughterer] (he was called the Szniadower *shoykhet*) was the experienced master at officiating at a religious marriage ceremony and also was the only *mohel* [circumcizer] in the city. He was the first one to go under and behind the *khupah* to arrange the *ketubah* [written prenuptial agreement], which he later would have to read. Ahron ran in between to bring the rabbi (the rabbi was at important weddings). Ahron held a carafe of wine and a glass in his oofor the groom to break with his foot. After the *khupah*, when Itsl the *klezmer* [musician] on his fiddle accompanied by a young man, who was called Markl (he was a bricklayer by trade) with a tamborine, played a *freylekhs* [a song accompanied by a circle dance], the fathers-in-law kissed, the mothers-in-law gave each other good wishes and cried. Ahron the *shamas* put together the four "poles," pushing through and hurrying home, looked into the house of prayer to see what was happening, a trifle, so many lamps, *yahrzeit* [memorial] candles, lights at the lectern, heated the oven which needed to be closed or to open the oven slide bolt.

Ahron's functions also included always accompanying the rabbi. The rabbi never went alone. If he had to go somewhere or travel, the *shamas* came to take him.

[Column 709]

The Czyzewo Rabbi, Reb Shmuel Dovid Zabludower, was tall with an impressive figure. His face was round, like the moon when it is full, and his gentleness poured over his face. He also possessed a very pleasant, gentle voice, soft and velvety. His speech had a lyrical, gentle tone.

And who sold the *aliyahs* [honor of being called up for a Torah reading] on *Shabbos* if not Ahron the *Shamas*? At the same time, he also called those for a *sefer* [possibly a reference to the honor of *hagbah*, the lifting of the *Sefer Torah* after the reading]. Was there anyone else who could do this better, more capably, more charmingly than him? When *Simchas-Torah* [holiday in the fall celebrating the conclusion of the yearly Torah reading and the start of the new year's readings] and the *hakafos* [honor of carrying the Torah scrolls in a circular procession in a synagogue] arrived, one could see Ahron's capability more clearly. He showed what a true psychologist he was with much intuition for his complicated task. He would stand like an orchestra conductor at the Torah reading table near the ark and distribute *hakafos*. He included everyone; he did not forget anyone. He weighed and measured who should be chosen earlier and who later with an experienced eye, like a tradesman of many years. He called upon the rich Jews who sat at the eastern wall immediately at the start along with the rabbi. Then he went further and further down until the door, not forgetting one of the artisans who sat off on a side, at the very end near the door where the "ritual washstand" was encased in bricks. There were complaints against him; why he remembered [someone] so late. However, Ahron knew what he was doing and was not lost. He made use of the *oyzer dalim* [assistance to the poor] several times to placate such people. One such Jew, who had a *shtet* on a back seat, was very impatient on one *Simkhas Torah* because he had not yet heard his name called out; he stood up agitated and waited for Ahron to see him, but when this did not help he gave an angry shout: "Ahron, do you not see me? [Can you not see?]"

[Column 710]

His [Ahron's] pay resulted from the "concession" he was given by the *kehile* [organized Jewish community] to go to every house on Friday. So he went around collecting his support for his life. Some gave 10; some gave 20 *groshn* and some nothing. But it must be said that his going through the city by no means had the character of asking for a donation. On the contrary, the coins that he would be offered were given to him with honor and respect, thinking of it as a form of receiving his legitimately earned wages. Where would we find such an honest, idealistic member of the clergy as Ahron the *Shamas* of the Czyzewo large house of prayer today?

Questions and Rabbinical Courts

Without doubt, the Rabbi, Reb Shmuel Dovid Zabludower, was the main figure in the city. Although there was no lack of great scholars and learned men in the city, the rabbi was the central spiritual figure. He was respected in all circles of *misnagdim* [opponents of Hasidism] and Hasidim. Scholars in the city would come to the rabbi's house (he lived on the upper floor of Zelig Leibel the shoemaker's building) to speak and to study. It was a true *beis vaad lakhokhmim* [house in which learned men gather]. The rabbi would ask both sides to sit with an arbitrator for difficult matters. My father, may he rest in peace, was present for many *Din-Torahs* [rabbinical courts]. One such rabbinical court remains in my memory. There was a conflict between Kalman the cap maker and his neighbor Motl. The decision of the court, whose arbitrator was my father, went to Motl.

[Column 711]

Motl was satisfied. However, Kalman was angry with my father for many years. My father was exasperated because they knew each other from when they had both prayed at the *Khevre Mishnius*.

In addition to *Din-Torahs*, there was also a series of questions.

There were women who picked over and searched a chicken for a long time [to make sure it was kosher and suitable to cook] or looked at an egg until they had some sort of question. A woman, Sura Leah, and her daughter, Chana Giska, lived next to us. Her husband was in America. Whatever she touched immediately brought a question. Once, she came to our house on the eve of a holiday and asked my uncle, Reb Shlomo, to give her a holy promise. She said, "You know that it is difficult to cook *tsimmes* [stew usually made with dried fruits, carrots and additional root vegetables]; it burns easily. So I took an oath not to make *tsimmes* anymore. Now, however, on the eve of the holiday, I want a spoon of *tsimmes*." My uncle smiled and said, "According to Jewish law, it is permitted. You can cook *tsimmes* and go in health." Sura Leah left a happy person.

[Column 712]

There were three *shoykhetim* [ritual slaugtherers] in Czyzewo. They were all older men when I knew them, Reb Chaim Shmuel, Reb Yosef Shlomo and Reb Moshe Hersh. In his last years, Reb Yosef Shlomo taught *shita* [the laws and methods of religious slaughter] to his son, Shalom Feivel, who lived with his wife and children and had a small shop in Matisyahu the tailor's building. His livelihood was very meager. His situation improved when he earned a little from slaughtering animals.

The *bale-tfiles* [leaders of prayers] during the Days of Awe were the Hasidim. This Reb Leizer Bitner, an Aleksander Hasid, a good *baal-tfile* and musically talented, was often the *baal-Musaf* [reciter of additional prayers on the Sabbath and holidays] in the large house of prayer. Reb Yosef Shlomo, the Śzniadower *shoykhet*, also recited the *Musaf* prayers there. Sura Misha's son-in-law was *baal-Tekeye* [one who blows the *shofar* or ram's horn] and also a Hasidic Jew, who owned the iron shop. He possessed the [honor] of blowing the *shofar* in the large house of prayer every year.

Translator's notes:

1. *Kaddish* – the mourner's prayer. "Exalted and sanctified be God's great name…"

2. The Breslover Hasidim, which were founded by Rebbe Nachman of Breslov. Rebbe Breslov died without naming a successor and the Breslover Hasidim do not have a rebbe. Therefore, they are referred to as the "dead Hasidim."

3. He went from prayer house to prayer house participating in services.

Painting By Marc Chagall

[Column 713]

A Walk Through Czyzewo's Streets
By Gerszon Góra, Bnei Brak

Translated by Judie Ostroff Goldstein

It is hard to be mute, impossible to remain silent. It takes shape, this Yizkor Book about our shtetl Czyzewo. Several Jews thrown together, one from a city and two from a family, eager to take part in the last "monument" to our shtetl. Among these Jews are also several who jumped from the last death train and others who scratched their way out of the mass grave of our dear and holy ones.

And the book grows page by page telling about the gray days and it constructs a building, that clings to us in our blood-soaked shtetl.

This book, the "closing of the grave," the last word, that is so strongly embedded in our fiber.

And it is difficult to be mute, hard to remain silent.

These are my years – more than two decades ago, from childhood through maturity that I spent in the shtetl thinking, longing for a nicer world. Can one keep Silent? Forget?…

Therefore I will share my memories with you in a last walk through the shtetl. This will be the last time I gaze at and see how it used to look once, once, when we were all still young. When we were together there with our parents, living peacefully, going to *kheder* [Jewish school for young boys], being naughty, playing and freely breathing the clear air soaked with so many dreams and aspirations.

And now I take my last walk through your streets and lanes, roads and highways – my hometown Czyzewo.

[Column 714]

I stand on the bridge at "Sutkier Highway". I gaze at the Brok River which extends the length of the city as far as"Bombelie's", to the water mill, where only good swimmers are able to bathe and fight the strong waterfall of the "Dembe". From the second side of the bridge is the "Bug" River. I think, with what faithfulness had the river served the shtetl inhabitants?

[Column 715]

It cuddled both sides of the bridge, shrank and as if not knowing, would with its calm water purposely wink at the shtetl residents. "Come, draw my pure water. Delight in my cleanliness."

As if still alive, I see the barefoot women standing in the cool water, each with a bundle of laundry, I see the stones on which they will beat the dirty laundry and lay them together in a bundles.

There weren't any washing machines. So, in the primitive manner of the village peasants our mothers stood in the river and washed the laundry for the entire household.

Now it is evening and I see groups of schoolboys (those still alive are now grandfathers) take off their shoes at the river, roll up their pants over their knees and go into the river to catch fish. Everything is so primitive. With only their hands they try to catch fish and whoever has luck on their side brings home a sack of small fish, alive and squirming. What a lovely pastime after sitting an entire hot summer day in the suffocating *kheder*.

I walk across watching the second side of the bridge.

The river continues the length of the "rosher" fields where Friday afternoons the youngsters gathered a variety of colorful flowers. I arrive at the "okof", a place where the river water is deep enough for the men to bathe here. During the summer, Friday afternoons, it swarming with people, young and old. All the men from the shtetl came here to bathe and immerse themselves in honor of *shabes* [the Sabbath]. On this day the village hooligans didn't dare come here, as they would do on other weekdays and throw stones at the bathing Jews.

[Column 716]

Winter

I see the river, frozen, covered in snow, only here and there were holes cut in the ice from which the people living near the river, and the two water carriers "Szie" and Meyer, drew water.

Not only summer, but also in winter the frozen river served as a pastime after a night studying in *kheder*. With lanterns in hand, groups of *kheder* boys went onto the ice to "skate". Some of them had special "liurzwes" [skis] and some only shoes. They would arrive home afterwards red faced and sweaty.

Before Passover

The ice is split and large pieces of ice chase one another. The schoolboys drag these ice pieces with the help of long sticks and chase the pieces of ice the length of the river to where the river rises and carries them under the bridge and a large amount of water spilled from the fields. Pieces of ice would split while moving down river and with miracles and great effort it would climb from icy cold water. The boys would be soaked through and shivering by the time they arrive home.

[Column 717]

During Passover the entire shtetl boycotted the well in order to avoid *khomets* [leavened dough or bread] and drew water only from the river.

Even today the calm river still meanders there and people still bathe in it during the summer and skate on the ice in winter. I search among them for a face I know, a familiar boy, a woman I know at the stones where she beat her wash. None. I see only strangers' faces. There's nobody. In "Szulborze" the bones from all of them were hidden, those I search for and can't find anymore, parents, brothers, sisters, relatives, *hy"d* [may G-d avenge their blood].

I run from the bridge and enter the road to the shtetl.

Right by the bridge, at the first boundary point of Zambrówer Highway, I see a lone house, my parents' house in which I spent my childhood in sweet bliss and lived through my first disappointments. This is the house of my grandfather and grandmother, of my great-great grandparents. It is the house of three families joined together: Blajwajs, Rotenberg and Góra. And there is the "szlaban" [tollgate] that marks the entry to the shtetl, or the exit. People don't pay a toll if they travel over the "Rogatkowe" bridge.

This triggers the memories of my grandfather Hershel. My great-grandfather Hershel Blajwajs was the first to whom the Russian government rented the "Rogatke". The "concession" was taken over as his inheritance by my grandfather *Reb* Aba Rotenberg who left it to my father Lejbl, known by the name "Lejbl Aba's" [son].

[Column 718]

Therefore it is worth it to tell about an episode about the arrival of my grandfather *Reb* Aba in Czyzewo.

My grandfather *Reb* Aba *z"l* [of blessed memory] was a Litvak from Lithuania, an ardent *misnaged* [opponent of Hasidism]. But as fate would have it the Litvak *misnaged* came to Czyzewo, a Hasidic shtetl and became united through marriage with *Reb* Hershel Blajwajs, one of the ardent Pszyscher" Hasidim.

My grandfather *Reb* Aba, one of the sons of Eli Rotenberg from Suwalk, was a good and assiduous student. As was the custom in those times, his father sent him to the famous Wolozyn yeshiva. This was a city full of clean *misnagdim*, who considered Hasidim to be a sect, may the merciful G-d save us.

This was during the time of *Rebbe* [Hasidic rabbi] *Reb* Bunim from Pszyche and *Rebbe Reb* Mendel of Kock *z"l*. When the Hasidim began to look for places to spread Hasidism, one of the Kocker Hasidim when to Wolozyn and he made the acquaintance of yeshiva students in order to steer them towards Hasidism.

Little by little he was able to persuade several young men and they agreed to travel to Kock so they could see with their own eyes the greatness of Hasidism.

Secretly, they hired a wagon and set out on their travels, a trip that would last several weeks. On the way, they would stay in cities and villages, on their route to Kock, to eat and sleep. One of the villages was the Hasidic shtetl Czyzewo.

In Czyzewo, the first shtetl where there was a Kocker *shtibl*, the guests were welcome with open arms and warmth and the Kocker Hasidim took special care of the young men from the Wolozyner yeshiva.

[Column 719]

One outcome of the Wolozyner yeshiva young men meeting with the Kocker Hasidim, among them Aba the Suwalker; it laid the foundation for the continuation of the "toll gate concession".

Aba, on arriving in the Kocker *shtibl* was not interested in anything. He immediately sat down and began studying. He caught the eye of my great-grandfather *Reb* Hershel Bajwajs and several days later this young man from the Wolozyner yeshiva was already betrothed to *Reb* Hershel's daughter – Szejna-Chomke.

So Aba did not go to Kock with the wagon. But this decision haunted him all his life. Why did he give up the opportunity to travel to Kock because that same year the Kocker *rebbe*, *Reb* Menedele died and he gave up the chance to visit him while he was alive.

My grandfather married and as it was told he made a deal with my grandmother Szejna Chomke. He would always sit and study and she would run the Rogatke.

[Column 720]

Then my father inherited the Rogatke. My mother was my grandfather Aba's daughter and when she married a Hasid who was a scholar, she inherited everything.

My father and mother *a"h*[may they rest in peace] took over from my grandfather *a"h*. My mother was in charge of the business and my father sat studying Torah and Hebrew. With the outbreak of the First World War in 1914, the income from the tollgate came to an end.

The last three survivors from the old toll gate were my mother, her sister Faja Szwarc, her brother Itchke Meyer Rotenberg and they made *aliyah* [immigrated to Israel]. They died in old age and all three graves are in one row in the Zichron Meyer cemetery, Bnei Brak, may their souls be bound up in the bond of life.

I take a step further and look around the narrow room, small than four by four. There lives Shlomo *der shuster* [the shoemaker] known by the name Shlomo "mlocz". The room serves as a workshop, a kitchen, a dining room and bedroom. There is great poverty here. But it would become even greater when Shlomo was drafter in 1914 to serve in the Russian Army and his wife Gisia, became a grass widow. She became quiet and suppressed hiding her circumstances, living off support for the poor that the shtetl doled out to her, like other in her position.

[Column 721]

One step further and I am at a wooden two-story house where Yankel *der melamed* [the teacher] lives. It reminds me of my *kheder* [religious grade school for boys], days and nights spent in that poor-man's narrow, one room *kheder* that contained everything. There was a *kheder*, a kitchen, etc. But is sorrow to be found here? No, the murders' hand did not reach here. The entire family immigrated to America before the Holocaust.

A little further is another two-story house that belonged to *Reb* Berl-Dawid, the gaiter maker. He was a short man with a long, gray patriarchal beard who looked like a *rebbe* and stood in the workshop the entire day shaping gaiters or "boot legs". He would say that the art of gaiter making lies in understanding how to cut the hide. There mustn't be any off-cuts. That is the entire Bible on gaiter making. He was always seen holding the leather in his hand and turning it around and around in order to properly cut the gaiter. This family also escaped the murderers. His sons Nyska, Isi-Henich, Szymen and Yudel (twins) and the daughter Hai'czke live in America. Only his wife Szejna-Malka was killed by a piece of shrapnel during the First World War.

Gitl Roiza and two sons
The youngest is saying Psalms from *Mana Loshen*
["Answer of the Tongue", title of a book
containing prayers recite at graves] at
the grave of my father *Reb* Lejbl Aba's [son].

At *Reb* Berl-Dawid's

Friday afternoon, coming home from the bathhouse he already possessed the *neshome yeseyre* [the additional soul which is said to possess a Jew on the Sabbath; hence, Sabbath festiveness]. He had already removed himself from weekday materialism and was prepared for *shabes* [the Sabbath]. He had arranged a *minyen* [quorum of ten males required for certain religious services] where men prayed on *shabes*. Before prayers started, he studied *midrash* [a body of post-Talmudic literature of Biblical exegesis].

[Column 722]

Sura-Malka and her four sons lived on the ground floor of this house. The oldest son, Abraml, a Gerer Hasid, was his mother's "crown". Shalom and Yankel ran the family grain business until the Hitler-catastrophe. The youngest son, Itchke, died young during an operation in Warsaw. This is the Kitaj family, known as "the Kitajces". They were the largest grain merchants in Czyzewo. They owned their own horse and wagon. The majority of the peasants would sell their grain only to the Kitajces. Shalom and Yankel, when they were boys, were leaders in Zionist youth organizations. Only Shalom's three children were save from the great destruction. The oldest, Avraham-Shimon went to Israel with an illegal immigrant ship. Yentl and Motke, still only young children, were by a miracle saved (there survival is told about in the Yizkor Book). All the others were murdered *hy"d*.

My parents moved into a long, small room in the same house, after the Polish authorities had thrown them out of the house at the Rogatke soon after the installation of the Polish government. Our family had lived more than two hundred years in that house, at the Rogatke.

Our family also managed to slip through the murderers' hands. The two eldest, Yitzchak-Hersh and the author arrived in Israel in 1933-1934. After a wave of pogroms and before the devil had spread his destructive wings over the three million Jews in Poland, we brought our mother with two more brothers to Israel. Our father was already not among the living.

[Column 723]

On the second story of the same house lived *Reb* Itsl Jablonka, known by the name "Itsl Jididjes". He was of medium height and always wore glasses and was a wise man. He was a fruit merchant and bought from the peasants' orchards. They stood watch so that their fruit couldn't be stolen. He was one of the most respected Gerer Hasidim. He would tell stories in the *shtibl* [Hassidic prayer house] and was an advIsser for community concerns. When he went to do business at the orchards, he and his father Jididje would consider every tree, appraising how much fruit the tree could produce and there quietly (so that the gentile would not hear) whispered to his father:

"Give him 30 Rubles". Generally his appraisals were right on. Itsl had eight sons. Three of them were saved. Two live in America and one in Israel. He used to say to me that he had sons of every kind: Agudaniks, a Zionist writer, American and yeshiva *bokhers* [young men studying in a yeshiva].

He left his mark on his children, as he was a committed Hasid. He would look at all the books his children read. But it also happened that he would find a book that was "not kosher" according to him and he would burn it without delay.

Next to Berl-Dawid's house is Berl Kukalka's. He was tall, with a long, neat beard and he paid attention to his clothing. He was a simple Jew who understood little about the finer points of Judaism. He was an observant Jew and went to the synagogue twice a day. On *shabes* he used his free time to say Psalms.

[Column 724]

Once he asked a Hasidic Jew: "Tell me, I beg you, why this year was my father's *yahrzeit* [anniversary of person's death] date changed? I remember that my father died during the time of the non-Jewish holiday "Czy-Krulia". Today it is long past that non-Jewish holiday and my *yahrzeit* has not yet arrived" (the sexton would remind him of *yahrzeit* date).

Another time he said: "The apothecary, Czyzewer landowner and the priest, the went to secular schools, therefore they aren't fools. So how is that they believe in Jesus?"

He was a tailor, but only for peasant clothing. His wife Henia Rivka had her own money and with his knowing she would give to charity.

In the same house, Berl Kukalka's, there was a small room, where Mendel Yisrael-Shlomo's [son] lived. He returned from Russia in 1919 after the First World War. He had grown tall, like a cedar tree, had a curly gray beard, walked with a firm, sure step, was imbued with Russian experiences, with Russian customs. He was one of the idlers in the *shtibl*, not a scholar, but a smart man. He always sat near the oven and told stories about Russian life, about the life of the Jews in Russia, about the overthrown Tsar Nikolai, etc. We, the young men in the *shtibl*, after studying, liked to listen to his tales. His stories (in this department he was a "genius") opened new horizons for us.

[Column 725]

He was also called *Reb* Mendel *gute-yorn* [good years]. He was also the opposite of *Reb* Yudel Wapniak. He, Yudel, believed that in the old days people live much better and that life was easier than today. People did not know about or need all the luxuries. The cost of living was lower, clothing was plainer and everybody was happy. This new way of living brought worries. Bread with herring or with sour pickles is already not a meal for them. Old challah soaked in hot water with onion is today beggar's food.

Mendel would refute this and prove many times over that today the times are better than the past. Take for example electricity. Once people sat with kerosene lamps that always smoked. Today, turn the button and we have light. There's no wick, no glass chimney that need cleaning every Monday and Thursday. Or take the hard boots that we used to wear. Today we wear light shoes. In the past people used wood and peat that always smoked. Today people sit near an oven like a prince. People aren't fools. People live much, much easier today than in the past. Now, these are the good years. Those who listened could never decide which one of them was right. Both had good arguments for their beliefs.

Where are you today. You bold, lovely fellow Mendel *gute yorn*? Your body and that of your wife are not in "Szulborze". Bitter fate exiled you to Russia where you both, from hunger and cold, gave up your holy souls. Far, far away, there in the Siberian whiteness, where nobody can go, there you found your rest. There in the cold steppe is your grave and nobody knows exactly where it is. May your soul be bound up in the bond of life.

[Column 726]

The second house, another tailor, but already a cut above. Here lives Shmuelje Gutman-Lejb's [son]. He was tall and had a beautiful long beard that ended in two points. He was the "Hasidic" tailor in the shtetl. When a father gave Shmuelje a *kapote* [long, black coat worn by Orthodox Jews, in Poland] to remodel for his son, the son would be in seventh heaven. Shmuelje would put his soul into every stitch. The sleeve, shoulder, breast, everything has to be perfect. When the coat was perfect he did not disguise his pride in his wonderful creation.

He did not know any joy on earth. His only daughter died after she married. His only son, Chaim-Boruch, a highly respected young man in the Gerer *shtibl* immigrated to America immediately after he married.

In a small room on the side at Shmuelje's, lived a young man by the name of Shlomo Calke's [son], a son-in-law of Yitzchak-Hersh *der melamed*. He was short, always had a smile on his face and had a coal black long, wide beard. He was the heart and soul of the *Agadas Yisroyel* [Orthodox youth group] movement in the shtetl.

[Column 727]

He was the leader of *Tzerei Agudas Yisroyel* and later he became a rabbi in a far away shtetl.

I walk to the Modlin area, at the corner of New Street that runs to Kalje Street. I come to Eliezer *dem "strikher's"* (even today I still do not know the meaning of the word *strikher*. His family name was Krystal and that is how he was, "kishmo ben hoo") [like his name so he was (a Hebrew expression that means the same as the preceding Yiddish explanation)]. He was of medium height and broad shouldered. He was the best brick mason in the shtetl. He was a great scholar, a Gerer Hasid. After a hard day at work he would not forgo coming to the *shtibl* to study a page of *gmore* [the part of the Talmud that comments on the *Mishnah*]. His only son Izak, the best of the young men in the Gerer *shtibl* was the first to present the idea of *Agudas Yisroyel* in the *shtibl*.

During the time of the Russian invasion [after W.W.I when Poland had been given independence] Izak had to leave Poland. He went to Kowno, Lithuania, leaving behind his father and sick mother Mirjam who worried about his situation. A short time later Izak left Lithuania and came to Israel. He also brought his parents here [to Israel]. They settled in Jerusalem. *Reb* Eliezer also worked here in construction. And this must be said, to his credit for many years, so many that it was possible to come to the Western Wall, he never missed a day getting up in the pre-dawn hours to go there to pray. There were times when the entrance to the Wall was blocked with enemies, but he found a way to get there to pray.

Before leaving Czyzewo Eleizer always said: "Every artisan must travel to Israel and would enjoy the fruits of his labor."

[Column 728]

He and his wife were fortunate and died when they were very old. They were buried on the Mount of Olives.

Izak Krystal lived in Jerusalem and took a respected position with *Histadrut*.

Here is Mendel *der shtrik-macher's* [rope-maker's] house. He is a special example. As far as his trade was concerned, he had no equal in the area. From the early morning hours until late at night he would draw flax from the bundles and make a variety of ropes (different thickness). Under the open sky was a stand on which was fastened a large wooden wheel that was turned by cheap labor or by amateur labor – child volunteers. Nearby stood his partner Avraham'cze's wheel. Both were also *Einglezer*.

Avraham'cze lived further into the Modlin house area. Years later they dissolved their partnership and each worked making rope and *einglezerei*. Later Avraham'cze stopped making rope and became a horse merchant. Then Mendel was the only rope maker. He was a good natured man full of loving kindness and a member of *Hovevei Zion* [means Lover of Zion. It was the first Zionist organization] and he would also claim that for Jews there was only one place as sweet as Yisrael that was among the leads of the *Khevra Mishnayes*.

From there I see Leizer-Yossel's house, or Leizer Moncarz. He was also called by his family name Leizer Bitner. From a grain merchant he became a baker. Actually he did not become a baker but the owner of a bakery. He was a tall man and not too fat. He was also covered in flour from head to toe. Only a lock of black hair, which was partially white, peeked out from his floured face.

[Column 729]

When speaking with him about business or world affairs one heard a quiet, sincere tenor. Everyone felt that grain was not his life, that there was something nobler, nicer, deeper fermenting in him. But when *Shabes* or Jewish Holidays arrived, especially the Days of Awe, then his soul soared to greatness. Then he became *Leizer der bal tfile* [the prayer leader]. Then he became through and through the "kneader" of melodies. Whether walking, standing, sitting or thinking it was always accompanied by his sincere tenor.

In the large synagogue, it was quiet when people heard that Leizer *der bal musef* [cantor of the additional morning prayer recited on the Sabbath and holidays] is going to the cantor's desk pouring out his heart, with his sweet tenor, before the creator of the world. And perhaps also there in Szulborze, Leizer *bal tfile* sang prayers soulfully:

Asarah Harugei Malchut and Eileh Ezkerahin in his last minutes before jumping into the already prepared mass grave with his fellow Czyzewers?!!!

I soon arrive in the street where the second *bal tfile*, Szoel-Hersh *der melamed* lived. He was a thin man with two skimpy points in his beard. He had a Kocker soul. His pace, his work, his speech, everything he did in a rush, so daring. He had a spirited mind. To speak to him was always enough to give an innuendo to a wise person (an Aramaic phrase). His wife Bluma ran a bakery and he was a *gemore and toisefes* [additions, critical glosses on the Talmud] *melamed*. He taught his students with a special flair. He led their souls into the depths of debate. In the Gerer *shtibl* he was among the town notables. He prayed sincerely and with eagerness. He was not a cantor only a genuine Hasidisher *bal tfile*. When he prayed he took everyone to another world. When he would sincerely proclaimed and all human beings pass before him as young sheep (a quote from the Unetane Tokef prayer on Rosh Hashanah and Yom Kippur Mussaf), everyone saw how every living thing passed before the Master of the World like a small sheep.

[Column 730]

He was active in the *Bes Jakob* School and *Agudas Yisroyel*. His daughter was one of the first teachers to graduate as a teacher in Krakow. His son *Reb* Naftali Herc Blajwajs was a rabbi in Jakblonka.

I zig and zag and end up in the clean furnished room of *Reb* Yehoshua Kotliarek and his wife Rasza. He was a rare individual. The older he became, the younger his dreams and longings became. He garret room was the "Bohemia" for the young, orthodox literary forces. While he was a young bachelor he was adventurous. His parents were Yossel and Szejna-Gitl Kotliarek, one of the richest *tsitsis* makers in the shtetl and he was their only son. He suddenly left home and traveled to Grodno, Wilno and for a short time was also in Amdur. While there he studied and became fluent in Hebrew. Then as if he had forgotten why he had left, he returned and with great fervor he threw himself into working in orthodox circles. A short time later his first poem *"Tshuva"* [Repentance] was published in the monthly orthodox magazine *Dglnu*. The poem reflected the world through his inner struggles. His wife ran the manufacturing business which made it possible for him to have enough free time to set day and night poring over secular and religious books.

[Column 731]

From time to time his essays, poems and articles would be published in orthodox periodicals. He felt a great need to further his education and he struggled to do so. A lot of evening he would go to the Christian Doctor Szenicki's where he could obtain books that were necessary for his self-education. We called him the "veteran". He took an interest in young people who had a literary aptitude. He was a tall, broad man young man with a blond beard. As he was nearsighted, he wore glasses that always shone.

Coming down the stairs I stand for a while. It is difficult to visit everyone. I cannot even though I would like to. Now I am at Gromadzyn's, or Nuska the oil makers. He was paralyzed during his last several years. He was a smart man. Since he founded the synagogue from the *khevra mishnayes* that is where he and his son Shlomo'ke read "holy books" [Hebrew books].

In the same street lives Izakl *der shuster* [the shoemaker]. I would rather call him Izakl *der tilim yid* [the Psalms Jew]. The synagogue was always open for him to say Psalms.

Now I am at Rubin Szmercak's, a grain merchant, a Hasid who only prayed in the large synagogue, a great scholar.

[Column 732]

Going back the length of the street I come to the market place entrance. I quickly pass by the corner house belonging to the Christian baker Grochowski. I'm not interested. Who knows how much Jewish blood flowed through them? I come to the two brick and stucco houses. The first is Jeszaja Calinowicz's. He is short, and bent over. He wears a small gray beard on his shrunken face. He was a manufacturer and very rich, never enjoyed his wealth. His only daughter died young leaving him to raise her small child. His only son Dovidl grew up to be a true rebel who saddened his father's life, even after he had left Czyzwo for who knows where. He still brought grief to his father, even from there. *Reb* Jeszaja would sit and study a page of *gmore* in the *shtibl* with such fervor that people saw that this was perhaps the best hours in his life. That was when he rid himself of all his sorrow. He was one of the notables in the shtetl.

Here, wall to wall is the brick and stucco house of *Reb* Zawel Edelsztajn. He is another sort of man. A rich manufacturer, short and sturdy, with a long patriarchal gray beard, who paid attention to his clothes. He always had the air of an aristocrat. He was so princely that he could not go to the town *mikveh* [ritual bath] – he could not bear the odor. However he never avoided every Friday and once a week going to immerse himself in the early morning hours in the Brok River, summer and winter, even when the river was frozen.

[Column 733]

In the Gerer shtibl he had a permanent place where he would sit for several hours every evening studying a large *gmore* from the Wilno *shas* [a set of books of the Talmud]. The melody he used while studying was full of grace and warmth.

He was a charitable and hospitable man. Visitors were sent all the time to his house and it was not necessary to advise him beforehand. Every guest, no matter how many, always had a place and he planted the idea of *hakhnoses orkhim* [Sabbath shelter and hospitality for poor wanderers] in his wife and children. He was counted among the notable old men of the community.

Now I arrive at *Reb* Fiszel Lubelczyk's, a respectable man of the multi-branched Liubelczyk family. He ran a large wholesale business and was not a Hasid and had no ambitions to become a scholar. But in his bookcase there was a large, beautiful Wilno *shas*. Being a *dozor* [member of the Jewish community council] he associated with the Hasidim. He was lucky as two of his children and grandchildren are living in Israel.

I look behind Fiszel's house and there is a small house that is the resident of Moshel *Yapanisher* [Japanese]. This is not his family name. It is a nickname that was used to describe people. During the Russo-Japanese War he was an ardent supporter of Japan. He would become incensed if anybody had a good word to say about Russia. That was when he was given the nickname *Yapanisher*. He was of medium height, with a scraggly blond beard and always held his head high. The visor of his faded, colorless hat was always turned to the side and never took his pipe from his mouth. During market days he wandered among the gentile wagons and bought a little grain that would have to bring in enough money to last the entire week. The rest of the week he sat in the Gerer *shtibl* talking politics with Yitzchak Bunem's Blajwajs. Yitzchak was his political opponent all those years. Moshel's wife (nobody knows her name) was exactly like her husband, always dressed in clothes where the undergarment was always longer than the outside one. The outside garment was always shiny from fat and their hands were always behind their backs. The only difference between husband and wife was that he was skinny and of medium height, he was tall and broad.

[Column 734]

Slowing down, thinking about the dear, simple Czyzewo Jews, I go step by step and stand in front of the shoe store belonging to Henich *Czewiki*. *Czewiki* is the Polish word for shoes, but in the Gerer *shtibl* he was called Henech Shlomole's [son]. He was a quiet, calm man whose forehead was deeply furrowed with wrinkles from worrying about his childlessness. Most of the clients in his shoe store were Christians. He was a religious Jew, said Psalms and quietly devoted time to *gmiles khsodim* [loans without interest] and *biker khoylim* [visiting the sick].

Reb Zindel Lew, one of the notables of the Aleksander *shtibl*, was his neighbor. He was a scholar with a nice blond beard. His steps were counted and deliberate. He always gave a lot of thought to everything before doing it. He was the only one who broke the custom of not teaching a trade to a child. When his son Simcha had already completed *kheder* [religious grade school for boys] there was a decision to me made – what yeshiva should he attend and "Tov Tora Im Derekh-Eretz" was chosen. But prior to that he apprenticed his son to Berl-Dawid *dem shteper* [the quilter]. A short time later he opened a quiltery in Zindel's house under the direction of his son Simcha who was also a religious man.

[Column 735]

Between Zindel Lew's house and Henech-Shlomole's [son] house is Lejbl *watnik's* (he worked with wadding) house. He also had a soda factory with an ice cellar and would also make ice cream. He always prayed in the Gerer *shtibl*. His wife Frejdke and the children ran the "soda and ice cream factory". He worked the wadding himself as well as *grempliarnie*.

Further along in my walk I arrive a Pinya Szewkes. He had a tavern that his wife ran. She was known as "Piniche". Besides a good lunch, one could get the best liquor there even during the time when liquor was banned and later under the Polish government when it was forbidden for Jews to be in the liquor business. Piniche's tavern was always full. He, Pinya was busy with his grain business. But when there was a drunken gentile who felt a desire to create a tumult or start a fight, Pinya would arrive. He would take him by the collar and with his knee gave him a push and the gentile was already rolling down the stairs and remained lying flat on the pavement. All the gentiles knew that at Pinya's one must behave. He was a tall, fat man with a pair of broad hands, a deep voice and one look from him made every gentile shake. His wife was cut from the same cloth. Both were calm, quiet and dear people. He was a generous man and always prayed in the Gerer *shtibl*.

[Column 736]

I go a step and I'm already at Pejsach Murawicz's two-story brick and stucco house that has a bakery and meat market in the cellar. The brothers-in-law Ben-Cjon Kitajewicz and Judel Chaim Mondry, two kind-hearted Hasidic young men, lived upstairs. Ben-Cjon spoke like a Lithuanian (studied in a Lithuanian yeshiva) and therefore he was called *der Litvak*. But he came from SniaDovo (near Lomza) and from a Gerer family. He always traveled to the Gerer *rebbe's* court. He was full of temperament, whereas his brother-in-law Judel Chaim was a quiet, modest young man who ran the bakery. They both sat and studied in the evening.

Judel Chaim, despite being a Radzyner Hasid, always studied in the Gerer *shtibl*. They were always seen with smiles on their faces.

With Zindel's house that is close to Pejsach Murawicz's, we come to the end of the houses on the market place and Kalja Street begins.

Zebulun Grosbard was a quiet, modest man and looked like a man who had nothing to say. But in truth he was very knowledgeable, a clever writer who had mastered Hebrew and Polish.

[Column 737]

He was well versed in the law of the land. He also knew about business transactions and income taxes and was busy in many of the town's institutions.

Modest Zebulun had a tavern and the wagon drivers and porters gathered there and only there. He had to listen to curses and abusive, obscene language that his clients hurled at each other. His business opened in the pre-dawn hours and closed very late at night. He politely served his guests, swallowing all the mean language that his clients spewed forth. None of this had any affect on him. He always spoke quietly and respectfully.

He was the *kehila* [Jewish Community Council] president. With the arrival of the Germans *ym"sh* [may their names be erased] he was forced by the authorities to be chairman of the "*judenrat*" [council set up by the Nazis through which their orders were passed on to the general population]. Within a short time he resigned in disgust and contempt.

Reb Zebulun was one of the noblest men in the shtetl. He was one of the few elected heads of the community and volunteered at many of the shtetl's institutions.

Now I want to walk through the two rows of stores that are located in the middle of the market place. There is Elijahu Dimentman's store. He was the shtetl''s expediter. His shop is jam packed with goods. He spent the entire week in Warsaw buying the small orders from merchants. To send these orders out one at a time wasn't worth the trouble. In the course of the week, his wife emptied out their store and at the end of the week he would arrive with the small orders and fill it up again.

[Column 738]

Eli was a tall man with a blond beard. He always had a smile on his face. He was considered a smart man in the Gerer *shtibl* as everything he spoke out about in regard to town concerns came to pass. He was active in *Bes Jakob* very generous with his time to anything concerning *Agudas Yisroyel*. He never represented either of these institutions in an official capacity because he did not want to, but he had little to do with the elected leaders.

I pass Zawel Edelsztajn's and Yeshaya Kalinowicz's dry-goods stores that are always full of Christian clients. I look in Chaim Yehoshua Tencza's shop. He had the same goods as in the other dry-goods stores. But he, Chaim Yehoshua was an exception. He was short with a neat blond beard and wore glasses. He looked like a modest and bashful man. But he was a deep man.

[Column 739]

He was an Aleksander Hasid and the shtetl teacher for a lot of years. The most fanatic Hasidim did not approve of his teaching methods but nobody dared to say a word. He was a religious Jew who kept all 613 commandments. Besides Yiddish, Polish and arithmetic, he also taught *loshen kodesh* [Holy language; Biblical Hebrew] and also Modern Hebrew. He had Krinski's "*HaDvur HaEvri*" and "*Hasgnun HaEvri*" and other chrestomathy. He was the only teacher who taught Hebrew to his pupils in Hebrew. Many times he would walk with his students (all Hasidic young men) and the *Khevra Ashkenazy* [Society of Ashkenazy Jews who spoke Hebrew using Ashkenazy pronunciation. The Hasidim used Sephardic pronunciation that is used in Israel] speaking *loshen kodesh*.

And while I am already there let me have a look at what is doing in the stores of the two widows, Chaya Sura *di Monczerka* and Fejga Bracha Szerszyn. The stores are in front of the large market place. Two widows who were forced under the yoke of earning a living and in their widowhood ran their businesses. Chaya Sura *di Monczerka* (the widow of Yossel Moncarz) was a grain merchant. The store was full of various kinds of grain, white, korn, sifted, etc. Fejga-Bracha's store was half-empty. She only dealt with the peasant on market days, buying grain and then selling to grain merchants. Fejga-Bracha was fortunate to make *aliyah* [immigrate to Israel] in 1925 where years later she died at a very old age.

Fejga-Bracha Szerszyn
Died in Tel-Aviv, Israel

[Column 740]

Ahron Tofal owned a button store. He was a tall, thing young man with a black beard who looked like a *yeshiva bokher* [a young man studying in a yeshiva] and was far from being a merchant. He wife and daughter-in-law ran the store. He was entire superfluous to the running of the business. But in the synagogue he was well respected. He was very religious and prayed earnestly. When he came to pray, he would always early in order to gather a *minyen* [ten males needed to perform public worship]. A *minyen*, to be able to pray, was all he wanted from life.

Now I am in the large dry-goods store belonging to Yitzchak, Chaim, Judel's Wasercug together with his son-in-law Yehoshua Kotliarek, Yitzchak's father. He was one of the former distinguished leaders in the shtetl. He was Kocker Hasid and then became a Gerer. He traveled as a messenger, doing a good deed, to Israel and died in Constantinople, not having completed his mission. Yitzchak had a stately appearance and was a quiet and modest man who had suffered a lot since he could never make a living. He had daughters who had to be married off. He was calm by nature. For a short time he was the bath attendant in the shtetl. A simple carcass in the marketplace, but do not come to rely on other people (A Talmudic reference indicating that one should earn a simple livelihood even in a difficult fashion rather than come to need support from others.] was well engraved in his memory and according to the community he always behaved. In the Gerer *shtibl* he always had his seat of honor and respect.

I go on further and stop at Avrahamel Landa's small store. He was an Aleksander Hasid, a committed *Hovevei Zion* [lit. Love of Zion, the first Zionist group established, adults only] and was active in *Mizrakhi* [religious, Zionist movement]. Avrahamel Landas, Matel-Fejga-Faja's son-in-law was a quiet, calm man who ran his small business but did not escape the misfortune that descended on all the Czyzewo Jews *hy"d*.

[Column 741]

I will now push through the narrow streets that end up at the front of the large market place. Here I am at Dawid Preter's house. Engraved deep, deep in my memory is an image of old Dawid Preter. I see the image, but it is a little hazy, as well as the image of his brother Yankel. He already had grey hair and was very old but he walked well, was shortly thereafter he gave up the bakery and immigrated to America with his family.

Dawid Preter, an old, wrinkled man with a white beard never took his long pipe stem from his mouth. Years later, when I heard stories of *rebbes* who smoked tobacco from long silver pipe stems, old Dawid would appear before my eyes, with his pipe that reached almost to the ground. It seemed as if he were calmly standing there among us curious to hear the stories that he used to tell with such humor that people split their sides from laughing. This was his "Talk on Ordinary Matters of Scholars".

He had a cigarette factory and was always afraid of the Russian police (it was called a "*treyf fabrik!*" [illegal factory] because he did not have a permit from the government to produce cigarettes. He was strong competition for the official cigarette manufacturers of Grodno, Bialystok and Warsaw. His cigarettes were the same quality but cost about 50 percent less. 12-14 year old girls made the cigarettes in a primitive factory.

[Column 742]

When the Germans invaded in 1915, he lost his living making cigarettes. Dawid Preter's daughter Malka Preter inherited the building. Her husband's name was Perec Moncarz but she was always called Malka Preter. The large cigarette factory became a small dry-goods store from which they could not earn a living.

Now I visit *Reb* Shlomo Joel Szejman's *z"l* [of blessed memory] haberdashery. He was a tall, thin man with a blond beard, a distinguished scholar and a Gerer Hasid. In the *shtibl* he was always engrossed in the "Debates of the Talmudic doctors Abaye and Raba". He studied *gmore* with all the commentaries and was always debating with the great scholars. He never became involved in community affairs. He was weak and pale. The sudden premature death of his son Ajsze left him dejected. He died in middle age leaving a widow with three orphans. His wife who was called "*kleyn vaybele*" [little wife] ran her business and managed to make a living. Her three children, Malka, Leah and Nuska-Natan, became community activists when they grew up. The last two died young during the great misfortune that befell the shtetl *hy"d*. Malka Szejman lives in Israel.

The neighboring haberdashery belongs to *Reb* Shmuel Jakubowicz. His wife ran the business. He was a writer at the lumber warehouse belonging to Saneh Stuczynski. In those days there wasn't any need for bookkeepers in Czyzewo. A "writer" was sufficient. He would record the client's accounts and add up the bills. *Reb* Shmuel was really a good writer. He had a nice handwriting, he quickly calculated the lumber meterage and was loyal. He was a Gerer Hasid, a scholar. After finishing his work at the lumber warehouse he did the accounts for the haberdashery and he never failed to study his daily page of *gmore*. People always saw him either in the early morning hours or late at night siting over the *gmore* humming his special melody. He never noticed what was going on around him, he simply sat and studied.

[Column 743]

First I enter Matel-Fejga-Faja's [daughter's] large haberdashery. Here we get the impression of a now grown poor, rich person. There remains very little of those past good times. Four stores were made from this large one. But after her husband *Reb* Yisrael-Yitzchak Gorzalczany passed away, she kept the business going herself with the help of the children but it was not what it was before. The majority of their income, like everywhere else, came from Christians. The peasants knew that what they could not find in other stores they would find at "Mateljave's".

Matel was an intelligent, noble woman. She stood in her store wearing a nice wig and married her daughters to noble young men, good-fearing scholars.

[Column 744]

With reverence I step into the room that not more than 4' x 4', if that large. This is the *kheder* and dwelling of my *rebbe* [teacher] *Reb* Boruch Krejndel's [son] *zz"l* [blessed be the memory of the righteous man] (*Reb* Boruch Hershman). This little room stands out, despite being squeezed into this labyrinth of stores, with the same purpose as a mother's lullaby: "Torah is the best merchandise".

I spent several summers and winters in this room. Long benches stood around long tables where about twenty children, aged 8-10, sat. *Rebbe, Reb* Boruch had the seat of honor. On his gray head he wore a satin *yarmulke* [skullcap] and his bright face was crowned with a two-pointed white beard. He was a strict and fastidious man.

Reb Boruch *melamed* [teacher] was not always stern with his pupils. There were times when he would be jusjt like us, a big child among young boys. He would throw himself into our child's world and was good to us, like an angel. Mostly during winter nights he would gather us together and tell us wonderful stories of great and good Jews.

He was the *gabe* [trustee] of the *khevra kadisha* [burial society]. On his bookshelf was the society's *pinkus*, a thick, leather bound book in which hundreds of historical shtetl events were written along with the names of all the former members of the *khevra kadisha* for several hundred years. Every year, *erev rosh khodesh shevat* [eve of the new month *shevat*, generally January] the *khevra kadisha* members observed a fast day and the evening after the fast they held a great feast when they memorialized all the members of the society who had passed away.

[Column 745]

One moonlit winter night, with freezing cold temperatures, everything was covered with snow. The bright moonlight made the snow shine like crystal and underfoot the snow creaked from the cold. That night four of us decided to go out and amuse ourselves in a crazy game.

At that time there was a goat, a male, who wandered around the shtetl because his owner had forgotten to sell him before he was born. So he more or less belonged to everyone and he wandered everywhere. For *kheder* boys he was the object of pranks. The young boys shared their food with the goat, food that their mothers prepared for them to take to school. Sometimes the boys would give the goat all their food. The goat became fat and what a joy it was to get up on his back and go for a rid. In vain, his owner tried to find blemishes on him. The schoolboy society took good care of the goat and watched over him so that nothing would happen to him. He knew all the places where a *kheder* was located and he would wait close by for his portion.

On the evening, above mentioned, we decided we wanted to go out and ride the goat. Each in his turn asked to be excused from from class to see to our needs (this was called going to the field out of the shtetl, as there was no other place in Czyzewo at the time). We soon caught the goat and one of us sat on his soft back, one led him and the two others drove him from behind. There was nothing to compare to this fun. We forgot entirely about *kheder*. We forgot that the *rebbe* is *Reb* Boruch, we did not even think what awaited us when we returned. After about two hours of pushing the goat around we realized what we had done.

[Column 746]

Let me see what's doing at *Reb* Shlomo-Isy's, or as people called him, Shlomka Prawda. He was a religious, naïve man, a respected Aleksander Hasid. He had a dry-goods store but he only helped his wife and children on market days. They ran the business. All the other days of the week *Reb* Szlumke could be found in the *shtibl*. His son was one of those who left the *shtibl* and entered the "organizations" [Zionist organizations] as he, *Reb* Shlomka, called them. But even though he was already not that religious, he still prayed in the morning and still put on *tfillin* [phylacteries]. But *minkha-maariv* [afternoon-evening prayers] he had was able to forget. His naïve father could not imagine that it was possible to forget *minkha-maariv*. This happned on a *rosh khodesh* [beginning of a month] in the afternoon. *Reb* Shlomka sees his son walking in the street and says to him "Symchla, don't forget to say "*yayla veyove*" ["may it rise and come", name of a prayer said on the new moon] during *minkha*. He immediately answered his father "Dad, shouldn't you first ask if I usually go to the *minkha* service?"

Reb Shlomka thought this was a witticism because otherwise it would not have made any sense to him. A Jew does not skip *minkha-maariv*.

[Column 747]

I will soon end my walk among the stores. I have come to the two stores selling hardware and building materials. The first belongs to *Reb* Yosel Boruch Lepak, a *dozor* [warden] of the Jewish community and Zionist spokesman.

The second hardware store belongs to *Reb* Yisrael Tyktin, a tall man with a nice, black beard. In fact his wife ran the business. *Reb* Yisrael Tyktin was active in a variety of societies in which he read lectures, such as *khevra mishnayes* which he in fact hadd founded. And in the synagogue, he studied *midrash* and *gmore* with a group. He also had his circle in the Aleksander *shtibl* where he read a lecture.

His wife, Sura Misza, a short, thin woman was in every corner of the business. She went to Warsaw to purchase product. She was the saleswoman. She oversaw the delivery of the merchandise. People called here "quick silver". It is rare to find only one person running this kind of business that takes so much energy. After *Reb* Yisrael's died he ran the business with her daughter's help and later when she had give the business to her daughter, she continued working with the same fervor. Her son-in-law, *Reb* Itchke Zylberman who was one of the Prager [a suburb of Warsaw] rabbi's sons became one of *Reb* Yisrael Tyktin's sons-in-law on the condition that he would always pray and study in the Aleksander *shtibl*. He always respected this condition but when it came to politics he always sided with the Gerer Hasidim.

[Column 748]

I am now taking my steps in the corridor between the stores and enter the two food stores that once were the brightest and richest in the shtetl.

Reb Moshe Yosel, a Gerer Hasid, never became involved in community affairs. Every morning *Reb Moshe Yosel* could be seen with his *tallis zak* [prayer shawl bag] under his arm returning from prayers. Then he and his wife went to open the store that had three entrances and was full of food products.

Reb Yoske Grynberg, *z"l* [may his memory be blessed] a former rich man, a Gerer Hasid, also had a store with three entrances and an upper floor that served as a warehouse. After *Reb* Yoske's death, the store was divided between the two brothers-in-law, *Reb* Boruch Szapira and *Reb* Berish Zak. But the brothers-in-law did not have any luck and they both became poor men. Therefore they both became great scholars. *Reb* Boruch was a great-great grandson of the famous *gaon* [eminnet rabbinical scholar] *Reb* Boruch the Czyzewer *rebbe*. His son Yoske lives in Israel and a second son in Paris.

Reb Berish Zak, one of the famous Biala rabbi's sons had permission to be a rabbi [had a diploma] and could have been a rabbi in a large city, but he bore his poverty with affection and never mentioned his sad circumstances and never arranged marriages for his daughters. His children often had nothing to eat. In the *shtibl* he was a treasure trove of Hasidic stories and legends of great pious men.

I am taking my last steps in my shtetl where I will never come again. I skipped over a lot of house and not mentioned a lot of people. There are still a lot of streets and houses where dear Jews lived. Every house in the shtetl was like a "temple". Every table was like an "altar". Every Jew lived his life following the commandments and at the tables Torah was read.

[Column 749]

I want to take a last look at all the neat, bright faces that day after day, in my youth, were a part of my life. I want so much to see once more a winter morning in the large synagogue, at the first *minyen* when all the artisans, wagon drivers and porters prayed. And behind the oven stood the two water carriers Meyer and Dovidl wrapped in a *tallis* and *tfilin*, looking in the prayer books and praying to the Master of the Universe, with a wink in their shiny eyes, because, they should forgive me, they did not know any Hebrew.

[Column 750]

I would like to list all the other people, the scholars, artisans, former merchants, Hasidim and porters and wagon driver, but I cannot remember all their names. There were lanes and corners where Jews of all kinds lived, Hasidim, scholars, Litvaks, pious women, young wives, children who lived quiet, honest lives day and night, weekdays and Sabbaths and holidays.

I ask forgiveness of all the souls in heaven if I have forgotten them. It was not my intention, but my memory fails.

This is my last walk through Czyzewo. The last walk in the shtetl where my parents, grandparents, and great-great grandparents live and led a Jewish life, generation after generation.

Painting By Marc Chagall

[Column 751]

Water Carriers
by Dov Brukarz, Tel Aviv

Translated by Gloria Berkenstat Freund

My memory reaches only to the three: Shaya, Surale and Meir.

There were always three; the number was never surpassed. It remained three throughout the years.

There are no indications as to when the business of carrying water began, who was the first water carrier or to whom the first pail of water was brought.

Each of the three had his own characteristic methods and customs. There was never any competition among them and never any cooperation. Each had his households to whom he brought water, even when the household moved to another street. I will attempt to describe each one with his characteristics and appearance.

Shaya Water Carrier

There were two brothers. One was a shoemaker, a Czyzewo businessman, a person who got along with everyone. He was in America during his last years and died there.

It appears that the second [brother] – Shaya – must have been a failure and therefore took to carrying water.

He was a completely normal man according to his appearance, quiet, calm; he had a wife, two children – a son and a daughter. He was seen going to the house of prayer to pray in the very early morning. He also never missed *Minkhah* and *Maariv* [afternoon and evening prayers]. We cannot know if he really could read the prayers.

[Column 752]

His spot in the house of prayer was behind the large, tiled oven.

He was a *kohen* [member of priestly caste] and this led to him avoiding being present for the *Toykhekhe* [biblical passage listing punishments for disobeying the Divine Will]. At that time respected artisans were not called up [to read the Torah] for the *Toykhekhe*.

He also would not go for the priestly blessing; he actually never received an *aliyah* [called up to read the Torah], except on *Simkhas Torah* [holiday commemorating the completion of the yearly Torah reading cycle]. Then the *gabbai* [synagogue official] could not turn away from him.

His wife and his daughter, when she grew up, washed laundry, flicked feathers, and so on. His son helped a bricklayer during the summer, kneading the lime. In the winter, he was a porter and often helped his father carry water.

[Column 753]

Surale the Water Carrier

According to the name it would appear that this was a dainty girl, a young woman. She was actually wide and thick, of average size. It is difficult to say if she actually was so thick or if she only appeared so because of the thick quilted jacket and pants over which she pulled on a thick muddy flannel dress that was as hard as a sheet of metal and therefore she appeared extraordinarily thick and wide.

She wore a pair of heavy boots made of coarse leather on her feet. Their color could not be recognized because of the thick layer of mud that always lay on them. Her head was wrapped in a dark kerchief of crude fabric that hid both her neck and face. Only her small eyes were visible, which looked out alarmed from under her swollen eyebrow less eyelids. Yet, it could be seen that she had a red nose and fat lips that always were closed, locked. She never spoke to anyone and no one heard her voice.

She was dressed this way and quietly did her work both summer and winter. During frosts, her frozen clothing reverberated like steel with each step and touch of her pails.

She drew the water from the small well that was right next to her house, but only when no person stood there. However, if she saw someone from a distance, even a child, standing near the well, she remained standing as if welded to the spot until the person left. When she saw no living soul, she went to the well quickly like the wind and hurriedly drew the water and left with her pails.

[Column 754]

Her clients consisted of several mistresses of neighboring houses on Nurer (Ciechanowiecer) Street. After carrying in the water, she closed herself in her one–room apartment until the morning.

No one knew when she provided herself with food and what she ate. There never was any smoke coming out of the *dimnik* [chimney].

Kheder–yinglekh [religious school boys] said that "devils" lived with her and she spoke unintelligible, cut off words to them [that sounded] as if it came out of an empty barrel.

Meir the Water Carrier

His family name was Brisel, but who in Czyzewo was interested in family names!

There were three brothers:

Hershel, Leizer–Henekh and the youngest, Meir. Hershel and Leizer–Henekh were shoemakers by trade. In their circle they were considered respected businessmen. They owned a wooden house in *Shmidisher* [Blacksmith] Street. Every day between *Minkhah* and *Maariv* [the afternoon and evening prayers] they were reliable listeners to *Haye–Adam* [*The Life of Man* by Rabbi Avraham Danzig], which was read by Reb Yakov, son of Pesha–Yite, to a large group in the large house of prayer.

Meir was a little shorter than average height, his face framed with a small, round, black beard. His family consisted of a wife who was much taller and a son.

He was not capable of any work. He simply was backwards in intelligence. When Motl "Bilke" (Kohan) died, his [Meir's] brother Hershel put a [yoke] with two large wooden pails on him and Meir became a water carrier.

[Column 755]

Water carrying was suited to Meir. He specialized in this, that not one drop would be spilled when he carried the two full pails of water. He said, "I have to give 'a good measure.' I cannot cheat if I am paid for full pails."

His clients were the heads of households from the area near the bridge. Therefore, he drew water from the River Brok and very rarely from the "small well." He only drew water from the well that was on *Shmidisher* Street for his brother Hershel.

The approach to the River Brok was sloping. Meir used the "approach" only when he went to draw water. But he would go along the shore up to Modlin with the full pails and there he would turn and go uphill, which led into the city. And if Meir was asked: "Why do you not come back the same way that you went? That way is closer."

– Because that way I do not have a place to rest – was his answer.

He was serious about it.

One of his clients was Esther Mindl, the wife of Zawel Izaks Abes(Edelsztajn). There, in addition to carrying water, he also did other work. He carried out the kitchen garbage, brought in wood and coal from the small shed in the courtyard. Therefore, he always would receive the leftovers from breakfast, lunch and the evening meal. On Friday he would carry a chicken to the *shoykhet* [ritual slaughterer], then flick the feathers and for his efforts he received all of the giblets, the feet, the wings, the head and the neck and the gizzards… However, *erev Yom Kippur* [the eve of the Day of Atonement], he received the giblets, a half of the chicken from the *kapore* [chicken used in ceremony to make amends for one's sins] and a challah braided to look like a bird.

[Column 756]

He prayed in the city's large house of prayer. He always carried a large *talis* [prayer shawl] bag in which was a very large, yellowed–with–age, woolen *talis* with authentic *tsitsis* [fringes]. His seat in the house of prayer was near Shaya, behind the tile oven. The *gabbai* [beadle] always honored him by calling him up to the lectern for the *Toykhekhe* [list of calamities that await one who does not follow God's law] and the next morning gave him [Meir] an entire 10 copper *tsener* [10 piece coin] (a Russian coin worth five *kopekes*).

This was the only coin Meir knew. He did not want to take any of the others in his hands. Alas, this gift created a hidden "jealousy" in Shaya.

[Column 755]

The Dear and Naïve Water Carriers

by Ahron Jablonka/ Tel Aviv

Translated by Gloria Berkenstat Freund

They voluntarily took upon themselves the yoke of providing and serving water to the Jews in the *shtetl*.

The women of the house knew how to appreciate their provider, knew that he did not work for a five–piece coin, but was responsible for the water corner of the kitchen, eliminating the worry of empty pails.

[Column 756]

On the day of remembrance for the general destruction and ruin, let us also remember and mention their qualities.

[Column 757]

Meirke

For the longest time he was the most experienced in the *shtetl* in his line of business and therefore probably the most noble of them. He himself determined the rank of his women of the house:

This is the first one. This is the second and so on. Until the end of the workday. Influence or money incentives did not exist for Meir.

He was a silent one. He was sparing in his words, not because he considered himself higher than his women of the house and bread givers, God forbid, but because he did not have anything to say or, God forbid, did not want to be insulted by them.

Meirke simply did not have time for foolish talk.

His coattails were rolled up, placed and hidden in his *gartl*–string* that was always tied around him. Sensibly they would not dangle between his feet nor get wet or hinder his walking.

*[Translator's note: a *gartl* is a cloth belt worn by pious men. It symbolically separates the sacred from the profane.]

He valued and thought out every minute. It happened that a Jewish woman approached opposite him and tried to bribe him with a sweet smile: "Oh, Reb Meirke, the pails [of water] are dried up. I cannot provide the noontime meal, wash the potatoes…" He listened calmly. He did not, God forbid, stop. He gave an angry shake of his head, half angry and said: "I know myself that one must have patience."

Meirke did not have any time to be confused in the middle of his work to the detriment of someone who was waiting for the two pails of water.

Meirke did not take any new customers during his last years. His list was too full. Meirke would refuse apart from exceptional cases, such as when a child of one of his most beloved [customers] got married, who already had left *kest* [room and board provided to a son–in–law for a period after a marriage] and began to have responsibility for leading his life by himself. He sneaked off to the house of prayer for hours. At *Minkhah* [afternoon prayers] he uttered the "Blessed is He and blessed is His name" endlessly.

[Column 758]

Meirke no longer carried water from the river. The river water was the source for Binyamtsh and Dudek, not for him. It once occurred in the morning that Meirke carried his first two pails of water for his Esther Mindl and, as if out of spite, a fire broke out somewhere. Large and small, people ran with pails both full and empty, shouting: It is burning, water, water… But Meirke did not turn his head. He was carrying water for Esther Mindl now.

If there is a fire, must Esther Mindl suffer?

He could not read or write. However, he knew precisely, exactly, how many five– coin pieces he was owed from each woman of the house. How many "pairs" [of pails] he had brought and in which week there were two days of holidays and so on.

Meirke was a widower for many years. He had no time to be involved in finding a match, but Esther Mindl influenced him and he agreed to a marriage contract with an orphan from a nearby village.

However, nothing became of the marriage contract. Meirke persuaded Esther Mindl that he was not enough of a skillful person and he could not leave his regular customers and thus must abandon the match.

Binyamtsh

The second one, in order of inheritance in the dynasty of water carriers was Binyamtsh.

He was short with a short beard, a calm and eager face and was the complete opposite of Meirke. He had time for everything and for everyone, knew all of the news and events, who had a child or, may God protect us, in contrast, where someone had suddenly died and had left the world, who had gone abroad last night or the opposite, who had come from America for a visit as a guest to parents, to relatives. He carefully told and spread all of the news in a few words, quickly cut off.

[Column 759]

Binyamtsh the water carrier

Dudke

He was tall, strong and broad–boned, with a round watermelon–head and a pair of fleshy, droopy lips and two large, naïve eyes that were interested in nothing. He always walked with his head down[looking] at the ground and his two large, strong hands were held close to his body and he would slowly place his bear–like steps in this way. He always wrestled greatly near the river until he succeeded in filling his pails and was careful that they not be too full or that there was too little [water] so that they not spill on the way. Large drops of sweat hung and slid from his forehead and trickled down, down to his chest during the hot, long summer days. But Dudke walked nonchalantly like a horse harnessed to a wagon; he did not stop to wipe the sweat, as if he was on a mission to the river and back.

[Column 760]

The young people did not forget Dudke during the holidays or just for a celebration; they looked for him and gave him a drink and were joyful. They liked to watch how Dudke raised heavy, bearish feet and danced a *Krakowiak* [fast, Polish folk dance from the Krakow area].

The young people laid down a small stick or simply straw and bet a glass of vodka if Dudke would dance by and not touch the straw. They stood around Dudke and the laughter echoed through the entire street as Dudke stood intensely and made minute, long preparations to be sure that he would show that he could dance across the straw and not fall.

I only remember him walking without pails on a few weekdays. This was when his mother died. He was very sad and at every greeting he made it understood how difficult it was for him. His mother had been so healthy, young; Dudke did not know how old she was, perhaps 70 or 10 years older, but she was so healthy, such a good mother…

[Column 763]

People and Personalities

Translated by Jerrold Landau

As we pieced together the building materials from our memories for the chapter "People and Personalities" of the Book of Czyzewo, we concerned ourselves and worried lest, Heaven forbid, the memory of even one soul is omitted, be they from this city or another, whether they are one of the communal notables or the poor of the nation, whether a communal leader or a teacher of children. We are certain that as soon as word had it that the Book of Czyzewo was under preparation, all of the survivors of the city, whether in the Land or the Diaspora, would immediately awaken and send in their contributions of sections of memories about the generation of the fathers. We spared no effort to turn to the survivors of our city in various countries and to ask them to give over another image and another vision. To our sorrow, the collection of images is small. There is a long list of those who live on in the hearts of their children and relatives who are not memorialized on the pages of this book. We satisfied ourselves with a little in order not to delay the publication of the book. However we have endeavored to make it such that the light of all of these shall pour out from inside, that these images shall portray a picture of the life of all sides and the reality of all those who lived in our city during those days.

Reb Meir Richter

By Yisrael Wajntraub of Tel Aviv

Translated by Jerrold Landau

With the publication of the book in memory of the martyrs of Czyzewo, may G-d avenge their blood, I will also present some lines about one of the most prominent men of our town, Reb Meir Richter of blessed memory. Who does not remember this man in whom Torah and greatness were merged in one place. He was a Hassid of the Rebbe of Aleksandrow, the author of "Yismach Yisrael", of holy blessed memory. There he also found as a groom for his granddaughter Chaya Bracha the daughter of his son Avraham, the genius Reb Ahron Wajntraub, the son of the rabbi and Tzadik of Radomsk Reb Yaakov David of holy blessed memory. He spent a great deal of money over this, and received him as a grandson-in-law. The Holocaust survivors of Czyzewo relate – and there are still some that remember Meir Richter – that this was his greatest hope in live, to find grooms for his daughters and granddaughters who were great in Torah and fear of Heaven. Reb Leizer Czyzewer was also an in-law.

His son Avraham merited to make aliya to the Land six weeks prior to the outbreak of the Second World War, and died in Jerusalem on Shmini Atzeret of the year 5602 (1941).

If someone were to ask if the personalities of our city were known outside our community, it is worthwhile to point out what Yehoshua Mordechai Rozenblum wrote in his book "My City Czechowice" that was published in Tel Aviv in the year 5701 (1941, page 24. In it you will find these lines:

"In the community of Czyzewo, there were three merchants, three personalities, three outstanding personalities, and these are:

The family of Richter (Judge) that was founded by Reb Meir Richter, the family of Prawda (Truth) that was founded by Reb Moshe Prawda, and the family of Frydman (Man of Peace) that was founded by Reb Pineh Frydman [1].

People said that in this community, the adage of our fathers is fulfilled: "On judgement, on truth, and on peace. [2]

Reb Meir Richter

[Column 765]

**Reb Avraham Pinyas Frydman
with his grandchildren**

Reb Yechiel Asher Prawda of blessed memory

By D. Gorzalczany

Translated by Jerrold Landau

With holy trembling and admiration of his personality and character in his personal life, and his faithful dedication to the Zionist movement, I recall the name: Reb Yechiel Asher of blessed memory, may G-d avenge his blood.

He was born in Czyzewo at the end of the 19th century into a home saturated with Jewish Hassidic tradition. In addition to the watchful eyes of his G-dfearing father Reb Shlomo Yishai – he stood under the strict supervision of his grandfather Reb Moshe Prawda of blessed memory, in whose company he used to visit regularly during his youth the court of the Rebbe of Aleksandrow. From there, he absorbed the Hassidic atmosphere that pervaded there, and he remained faithful to this Hassidic tradition until the end of his life.

He obtained his Torah education from the Yeshivas of the cities that were near to our town. There, he was numbered among the best of the Yeshiva students. He also was considered one of the finest young men in the Aleksandrow Hassidic circles of Czyzewo, among whom he regularly studied Talmud and Halacha.

[Column 766]

He was serious in his thought, studies and prayers. Every day, he repeated with great concentration the prayers: "And a redeemer shall come unto Zion", "And let our eyes witness the return to Zion". With the founding of the Mizrachi movement in Czyzewo, he was one of the first to join its ranks. He dedicated his best efforts, activity and years to it. He restricted his private, family and economic life in no small manner on account of it.

Reb Yechiel Asher was one of the leaders and advisors of every Zionist institution. There was no activity in any Zionist institution that was not directed by Reb Yechiel Asher, with regard to its planning and actualization. In the demonstrations against the "White Paper" and against the evil activities of the British Mandator in the Land of Israel – we see Reb Yechiel Asher at the head of the marchers. Reb Yechiel Asher was one of the chief organizers of the festivities celebrating the opening of the Hebrew University on Mount Scopus. Reb Yechiel Asher appeared as the prime speaker at the public gatherings in the synagogue or under the open sky. His pain and anger infected the community as he demonstrated his protest against the disturbances in the Land of Israel in the years 1929 and 1936.

[Column 767]

He established the first committee for the Keren Kayemet LeYisrael (Jewish National Fund) in which he served as the first director. He participated in all activities on behalf of the fund. Reb Yechiel Asher regarded the placing of the blue and white boxes as now less of a Mitzvah than the fixing of a Mezuza upon a Jewish doorpost. He carried our every activity for the benefit of the Keren Kayemet with a heart full of love and dedication. He performed every activity, small as well as large, with a spirit of holiness and awe. There was no activity whose performance he felt beneath his dignity. Reb Yechiel Asher was among the first organizers and first donors at the founding of the Keren HaYesod.

**Reb Yechiel Asher Prawda,
his wife, and five children**

The question of education was the chief of all of his desires. Even though he himself received his early education in the old, traditional cheder, he felt an internal need to change the course of education for the younger generation, and especially the need to instill the Hebrew language to them.

To that end, the Modern Cheder was founded, where they studied all of the Jewish subjects in Hebrew, which eventually pushed aside the Yiddish language completely. In addition to Hebrew, the Polish language and arithmetic were studied, so that Jewish children would not have to attend the non-Jewish public school.

His faithfulness to the Zionist idea and his dedication to Zionist activity placed him in a very serious situation. On the one hand, Reb Yechiel Asher of blessed memory, a keeper of Jewish tradition, was careful about all of the commandments, easy and hard. He sported a trimmed beard, wore a traditional kapote, and had a Hassidic hat on his head. He was numbered among the Hassidim of Aleksandrow, with whom he worshipped and studied. Every moment of his free time was spent in the Hassidic shtibels, which were the "rock from which he was hewn". When relations deteriorated between the Hassidim and Zionists in our city, Reb Yechiel Asher of blessed memory was asked to forego his Zionist idea and to desist from all Zionist activity, or to forego and leave the shtibel. It was evident that he was suffering from deep internal agony. His education and habits drew him near to the atmosphere in which he was raised, however the Zionist idea did not take leave of him. With great heartache and agony, he left the shtibel. The commandment of Zionism grew and was victorious over his habits.

[Column 768]

The emotional and dear man went around during the last months of his life in solitude, lost in his thoughts. How did his bright thoughts end? When his eldest son grew up and concluded his course of studies in the town, he did not send him to continue his studies in Yeshiva in one of the towns of the Diaspora, but rather to the Yeshiva of Harav Kook in Jerusalem [3]. His plan was that he would also send the rest of his children to Jerusalem when they grew up, and that he would make aliya later on. However, the bitter fate had different plans, and he himself did not merit to make aliya. He was too late.

He, who was beloved and close to people for his entire life, and always worked faithfully in communal affairs, was not able at all, and did not agree to take on any task that was offered to him in the Judenrat. Until… the bitter day came, the 8th of Av 5701 (1941), when the threads of his life were torn apart by the German murderers and their Polish accomplices. He was deported with the first transport to the village of Szulborze and he perished along with the entire community of Czyzewo.

There, in a communal grave, his sublime dreams and plans were buried along with him.

His body is buried "there", but his pure soul hovers in Israel along with the rest of the martyrs of our nation. May G-d avenge his blood.

Woe about those who are lost and who will not be forgotten.

Translator's notes:

1. The words in parentheses that appear in the text are translations of the meaning of the names – the first and third from German / Yiddish, and the second from Polish / Slavic.
2. A statement from the first chapter of the Mishnaic tractate of Pirke Avot: "On three things does the world exist, on judgement, on truth, and on peace."
3. Jane Prawda, Jechiehl's granddaughter, states that her father never went to this school, but rather to Kfar Hanoar Hadati, and was of the first graduating class.

[Column 769]

Reb Alter the Sofer Stam[1] of blessed memory

by Yitzchak Szlaski

Translated by Jerrold Landau

Indeed, my brothers and friends, natives of my town of Czyzewo! When you read these lines about my grandfather Reb Alter the *Sofer Stam* of blessed memory, you will also remember important personalities and wonderful people who lived in our town during those years. The images of the faces of these fathers and grandfathers, with their noble spirits and spiritual traits, who dedicated their lives to the sanctification of the Divine Name, will once again appear before the eyes of your spirit. All of them were like these, weak in body and strong in spirit. Even the ugliness and degradation of Diaspora life did not overcome them, for they were holy and pure, dedicated and faithful to G-d and His nation.

Let us guard their eternal memory, for from them we will constantly draw strength for our souls and spiritual inspiration for us and our children, forever.

He would isolate himself for most of the hours of the day in the triangular space of the gable atop his living space, for he lived honorably in the attic of his son–in–law Mordechai Raczkowski (the baker). There, up above, he set a quiet corner for himself for his work, the holy work of a scribe combined with Divine service.

From my early youth, when I became orphaned, he, my grandfather of blessed memory, spread his fatherly and educational protection over me. I regarded him as a pure, pious, G–d fearing man in private and public; a great scholar who comported himself modestly with G–d and man. His great righteousness and modesty was matched by his great poverty. Nevertheless, he never complained about the deeds and caprices of humans, and of course, never about the ways of G–d.

Reb Alter the scribe, or Reb Alter Smuelke's as he was called, was known and recognized by the people of the town – for his name more than for his actual image and presence. Aside from his family, only the Hassidim and sublime people of our town knew him from up close, for he would discuss with them Torah thoughts, Hassidism and at times also the holy work that he was doing, such as a Torah scroll, the writing of the sections of *tefillin* and *mezuzot*, and other such things.

[Column 771]

He would perform her work with holiness and purity. He would immerse himself in a kosher *mikva* [ritual bath] prior to writing the name of G–d, and he would also recite *Leshem Yichud*[2] out loud with awe and trepidation. When he finished a certain portion of the work, he would review, correct, and read every word he wrote with enthusiasm. It was recognizable from his face that he enjoyed the beauty of the writing and the sanctity of the letters.

The following story testifies to his trait of innocence:

Once Reb Yeshaya Gorzalczany, one of the important people of the city, a wealthy man and a scholar, a Hassid of Aleksander, desired a *mezuza* written by Reb Alter the Scribe. He came to his house to purchase the *mezuza*. Reb Alter showed him a *mezuza* that he had just completed. For a long time, he stood and explained to him with special joy and enthusiasm about the holiness of the letters and the tittles that were written in accordance with all of the principles of the *halachic* books and the innuendoes in the books of kabala, etc. At the end of the explanation, Reb Alter folded the *mezuza* with awe and trepidation and put it in Reb Yeshaya's hands. He took the *mezuza*, and asked incidentally, "Reb Alter, what must I pay?" "So," smiled Reb Alter, "Pay me one zloty." Reb Yeshaya was surprised and said, "How is that Reb Alter? One pays more for a regular *mezuza* sold by those with outstretched hands at the entrance to the synagogue, and now for a *mezuza* written by our own hands, you do not request more than one zloty?" "Yes," replied the old man and apologized, I did not know. Reb Yeshaya placed a significant sum of monetary bills in his hand and left.

[Column 772]

In order to fulfill the adage of the sages, "A man's disposition should always be pleasant with his fellowman," he would frequently take interest and ask about the affairs of the family members of neighbors and relatives who would come to him to consult about various business matters. He would willingly listen to their problems with great interest, dissect all the details, and only then express his opinion, with for or against.

On the market days that took place on Tuesdays and Fridays, or a day of a fair, he would go down from his attic to the bakery of his son–in–law Mordechai the Baker to help him a bit with his hard work. He would watch the children and check the accounts to see that no error had been entered. When things were crowded and cramped due to the great number of purchases, he would also guard the cash till from the evil eye of the gentiles.

Reb Alter Szlaski

Reb Alter Szlaski with his family

He would worship privately on most days of the week, uniting himself with his Creator up there in the attic. He would worship out loud, and pronounce every word clearly, without adding any unnecessary sound. In the evening, he would go to the Hassidic prayer house for the evening services. He would remain in the *shtibel* for a long time while perusing a book or discussing matters of Torah and Hassidism with the elders of the Hassidim. Many of them would take that opportunity to ask his advice or discuss their worries and tribulations with him in order to relieve somewhat the stress of their hearts. This is in keeping with the adage, "A worry in the heart should be discussed." He would often return from there sighing, pained and grieved over the tribulations of others.

[Column 773]

The story that I heard from Grandfather about Reb Zanwil Edelsztajn, his close friend, is typical.

Reb Zanwil was a stocky man with a quick gait. He was aging, and his long beard flowed down over his garments. He was a scholar who feared Heaven, a wealthy merchant who owned a store for manufactured goods. He was an honorable personality in town.

One evening, I was with Grandfather as he returned from the house of worship sighing and smiling alternately. After a little while, he started talking and said:

"Today I learned a new issue called: Everything in accordance with its measure." He continued on and related:

"Reb Zanwil Edelsztajn told me about his difficulties – that his children do not satisfy themselves with small amounts. They waste a great deal of money on clothing, trips, and all types of other enjoyments. He does not have the strength to stop them and disrupt their deeds. Having no choice, he decided to do as they do. If everyone is grabbing, he said, I too will grab! Therefore, he started to distribute charity with greater energy and in a generous fashion. He did not satisfy himself with one guest for the Sabbath, but rather invited two. He would bring a guest home every morning after services. If he did not find him in the *shtibel*, he would search in the *Beis Midrash* or even on the street – so long as he would not return home without a guest for breakfast. He would do other such deeds of charity, *mitzvot*, and good deeds. Reb Zanwil would do a great deal, so as to not be disadvantaged in his competition with his children."

Grandfather praised these deeds of Reb Zanwil, and incidentally explained the verse in Proverbs to me.

"A person with a wise heart will grab *mitzvot*." The *midrash* explains in the Torah portion of *Beshalach* that this refers to Moses. At the time that those who were leaving Egypt were occupied with the spoils of the sea, the verse says of Moses, "And Moses took the bones of Joseph with him, for he had made an oath…" He repeated this and said with great devotion and emphasis, "Indeed, all should grab…"

[Column 774]

Despite his great diligence in the study of Torah, in keeping with the adage, "a mouth that does not desist from learning," he found time to take interest in every important issue in the town or the Jewish world in general. He did not read newspaper, but he would listen with great interest to the reading of the news from the newspapers. He would ask and take interest in the details, and express his opinion on the various problems of the world. Despite this, controversy or disputes of any kind were foreign to his spirit, even a dispute apparently for the sake of Heaven, such as regarding Hassidism or religious extremism, against the younger generation and Zionists of various types. I recall incidents of delay of the reading of the Torah on Sabbaths in the Hassidic House, for most of the worshippers would utilize this means as a way of forcing an individual to straighten out matters that were in dispute. During such a forced interruption, Grandfather would sit looking into a book, wrinkling and rubbing his forehead from pain and anguish over these incidents that caused a delay in the reading of the Torah.

He loved the Land of Israel with his whole heart and soul. An expression of internal joy and soulful gladness would come over his face as he heard things about the Land of Israel. Every story of the building of the Land or a new, interesting movement in Jewish life in the Land caused him great satisfaction and spiritual happiness. It is no surprise, therefore, that his astonishment was great whenever he heard factual information about the land of Israel and its pioneers and builders from the mouths of G–d fearing Hassidim. He would say, "They are involved in the building up of our Holy Land. Heaven forbid that we speak bad of them." I remember once that a young Hassid from the zealots of Agudas Yisrael came to him complaining about his grandson (me) – that I had entered into a bad crowd, Heaven save us, and I had joined the faction of pioneering Hassidim, etc. He asked innocently, "What is wrong with this? He wants to make *aliya* to the Land of Israel? On the contrary, I wish that we could all make *aliya* there speedily in our days!…"

Once he was present at a debate on Zionism that was conducted between me – the Zionist – with one of his other grandsons who was a member of Agudas Yisrael. He listened and smiled with great satisfaction on the expertise that we displayed with our proofs and details regarding the building of the Land. However, at the same time, he would hold his anger and turn his head to the side when he heard words and expressions denigrating the Land of Israel and its builders as my interlocutor said such in the heat of the debate. He would often tell me with his customary innocence, "I understand the trepidation of the Hassidim who fear the word of G–d toward our Holy Torah and the fulfillment of commandments, but why are they so opposed to the Land of Israel? This is a contradiction, and as such, I do not understand it at all."

[Column 775]

As has been stated, he took interest in everything that took place in the Jewish world. The atrocities of the Nazis and the attacks upon the Jews that began even before the enemy, may his name be blotted out, ascended to government caused him a great deal of anguish. He would literally cry like a baby with copious tears over each peace of news that arrived and that he heard.

In 1933, when he found out about the ascension of the Nazi foe to government, he groaned deeply and said, "Master of the Universe, give power and ability to your nation to leave and escape from the inferno and hell that is Germany." As if it were a prophecy emanating from his throat, he would repeat each time, "Jews must also get out of here and escape to any place overseas that they can, so long as they do not remain here." He took great comfort in that his only son was in the United States, despite his great concern as an Orthodox Jew for the religious situation in that country.

In the late summer of 1935, I told him double news – that I was going to get married, and to make *aliya* with her to the Land of Israel. Our decision to build our household in the Land of Israel gave him great joy. From that time, he would attempt to talk with me every day in order to find out every detail about my preparations for aliya. Even more than I was, he would be sad at every difficulty or obstacle that arose in this matter for some reason or another.

Early on Sunday morning, *Rosh Chodesh Cheshvan* 5696 (1935), I went to bid him farewell. He got out of bed, got dressed, washed his hands, recited the *Shema* prayer aloud in accordance of his custom, and then turned to me with a voice choked with tears of joy and gladness. He explained me how great was my merit that I merited to make *aliya* to the Holy Land, to live there, and to continue the chain of the eternal existence of the People of Israel. The tone of his voice increased. He spoke about the commandments that are dependent upon the Land, the holiness of family life, the holiness of the Land of Israel, etc. Then, he hugged me strongly, smothered me with kisses, and said:

[Column 776]

"Indeed my son, you have merited something that many people greater than you have not. May G–d grant you success in your journey." He accompanied me outside and parted from me… forever…

A few weeks after I arrived in the Land, I went to Jerusalem and visited the Western Wall. Immediately thereafter, I wrote him a letter with my impressions of my visit to Jerusalem and the wall. After some time, I received a letter from my grandfather, written with the strong script and ink of a scribe. He expressed his satisfaction, joy and gladness about everything that I had written to him about ourselves and the Land. Then he wrote several pages of words of Torah and *halacha* regarding the blessings one recites before partaking of food. This was because the Land of Israel is a country blessed with much fruit. Every month, different species of fruit ripen, and therefore there is a need to know the laws and sources of the blessings.

When the Nazis invaded Czyzewo, his house was destroyed and burnt completely. He moved to the home of his daughter who lived in the village of Szumowo next to Zambrów. There he was murdered by the impure murderers. May G–d avenge his blood.

Translator's notes:

1. A *sofer* is a ritual scribe. *Stam* is the acronym for *Sefer Torah, Tefillin, Mezuzot* – i.e., a ritual scribe who scribes Torahs, *Tefillin* and *Mezuzot*.
2. The introductory two words of a statement of intention before performing a *mitzva*.

The *Shofar* Blower

by G. Gora

Translated by Jerrold Landau

He spent his last days there in the small attic atop the bakery of his son–in–law. I did not know him during his prime, for when I was still a child; the hairs of his beard were already silver. He lived in poverty and meagerness throughout his life. During his old age, he used a wooden cane to assist his unsteady gate.

He went to the *shtibel* only in the morning and evening. He sat all day at his table to work at his trade of scribing.

He did not have to earn his livelihood from the toil of his hands, without accepting help from his son–in–law, the owner of the bakery. He was satisfied with a bit of bread and a measure of water. How can one sustain oneself from writing *tefillin* scrolls, *mezuzas* and Torah scrolls. All of this was no small matter. This is not the writing of Torah thoughts, or, on the other hand, the writing of secular matters and accounts. The entire Torah and its letters are holy. Therefore, how can one write the names of G–d without any preparation and intention?

[Column 777]

Therefore, the piece or scroll of parchment that he was working on was always resting on the table, with the duck–feather quill dipped in scribes' ink at the side. He, Reb Alter Szmelkes, would pace around the room a bit, whispering his ideas and purifying his thoughts before each word and at times before each letter or tittle. He fortified his mind, body and soul all at once, dedicating them to the task of writing and the meaning of the words and letters. There were also times before the writing of the names of G–d that he would find it necessary to immerse his entire body in order to purify it.

On occasion he would complain quietly to his friends about those scribes whose work was performed "as a spade to dig with" [1], and would write tens of *mezuzas* or *tefillin* scrolls during a single day. For them this was a trade, a job like any job.

Despite the fact that there was not always a coin in Reb Alter Szmelkes pocket, and he lived his entire life in want and poverty, and were he to have devoted himself to the labor of writing with greater strength and speed he would have been able to live properly and not be in such meager straits; he nevertheless did not want to forego even the bottom part of a yod [2] from his Divine service. He would carry out his custom of writing and immersion throughout his days.

Therefore, his renown spread afar. Orders for scrolls and *tefillin* would reach him from far away. Fathers would rejoice and sons would be full of happiness when they succeeded in purchasing from him for the Bar Mitzvah of their sons or grandsons. It was know that every letter and tittle of *tefillin* parchments written by Reb Alter Szmelkes was written in holiness and purity.

Sometimes, literally in the middle of writing, in the middle of a line, he would put down his duck quill and open a book of *Zohar* or other book of *kabala* that was always on his desk, and begin to peruse them. He would say, "Scribing and *kabala* are intertwined. How can one write a parchment of a *mezuza* or *tefillin* or entire section of a Torah scroll without understanding the value of the holy names written there in accordance with the explanations from the books of *kabala*?"

[Column 778]

During the morning or evening hours, he would sit at the table in his corner in the shtibel and continue with the hidden and concealed Torah [3]. He was taciturn, keeping himself discreet, barely talking to anyone. He constantly guarded his set corner and perused books, with his mouth uttering silent words, in keeping with the verse, "Only her lips were moving and her voice was not heard" [4]. He was uttering words and lines of the *Zohar* and other such books.

Nevertheless, he was considered to be among the men of deeds and Hassidic elders of the *shtibel*, and whenever the *gabbaim* [administrators] of the *shtibel* had to carry out some responsible matter, they would ask for his opinion. However, none of this was known about him, for he never got involved with internal matters of the *shtibel*. When he expressed his opinion about some matter of the *shtibel* about which he had been asked, he would give a brief answer of one word: "yes," or "no." He would not say more, and this response was decisive and sufficient, for everyone knew that the "yes" or "no" of Reb Alter Szmelkes was not simply an answer from the lips to the outside, but rather a response that was well thought out and deliberated in his sharp and clear mind.

He would minimize his speaking. Speech is one of the adornments of man, and therefore one must guard it and protect it that it not be defiled with meaningless things – he would always respond when someone approached him and wanted to disturb him with idle chatter devoid of spiritual content. On the other hand, he was like an open wellspring to the young men or Hassidim who occupied themselves with *Zohar*, and were searching for explanations in known places. Then, Reb Alter would explain every matter. Nevertheless, it was difficult to express his living and intellectual thoughts with clear explanations.

Thus was his wonderful daily schedule during his nearly 70 years in our town: *kabala*, *Zohar*, writing *mezuzas* and scrolls for *tefillin*, immersions of ultimate value in a mikva, deep intentions before each and every name of G–d, and morning and evenings spent with the Hasidim and elders, bent over books as he was fully immersed in the eternal gift, pondering the sublime books with his intellectual eye and entering the 49 gates of wisdom that every man must attain, standing on the ladder at the summit near the 50th gate to which no man ever attained. This is how the chain of his life unfolded. It was an independent and fundamental life, without entering into any issues with his fellowman, and keeping away completely from any communal position.

[Column 779]

There was one exceptional and decisive thing. Despite his constant principle of distancing himself from communal positions, he did accept – through the urging of all the honorable men of the *shtibel* decades earlier, most of whom who have already passed away – the position of being the regular *shofar* blower in the *shtibel* on the High Holydays. He accepted this position without any attempts at refusal.

The blowing of the *shofar* is an art and not a labor. This, however, is only with reference to the *shofar* blasts themselves, i.e. the production of normal sounds through the *shofar*. However, the *shofar* blasts are more than an art or a labor according to the holy books. The blowing of the *shofar* is a service of the heart, with a great deal of intentions in the brain. Who would be more fitting for that important service on Rosh Hashanah, the holy and awesome day when all people pass before G–d like sheep, if not Reb Alter Szmelkes, the pious and modest Jew, who in his daily work is a continuum of service of the heart and sublime thoughts of the mind?

Therefore that day when Reb Alter Szmelkes took it upon himself to accept the appointment as *shofar* blower, was a day of great joy for the important men of the *shtibel*. "Finally," they said to themselves, "we have found an appropriate man whose *shofar* blasts will certainly tear up the Satan and the forces of impurity.

Reb Alter preserved this task from year to year with simple faith and soulful love.

"Can a *shofar* be sounded in a city and the people not tremble?" [5]. A *shofar* has two facets: the first is to arouse the hearts and bring them to repentance in accordance with the words of the verse. The second is to confound the Satan, the accuser who stands prepared on the Day of Judgment to impede, Heaven forbid, the prayers of Israel and prevent them from reaching the King of the World.

Ever year, this new *shofar* blower dedicated himself fully to issues of the *shofar* already from the first day of Elul, when the first blast is sounded after the *shacharit* service.

[Column 780]

Next to the table in the attic of his house, along with pieces of parchment and scrolls, with the duck quills and sinews, there was a small *shofar* next to a stack of various books that he prepared for Rosh Hashanah. He would look into them to research various intentions and thoughts of the unity of G–d, in accordance with the kabalistic ideas related to the blowing of the *shofar*. He prepared every day to blow the hundred blasts. He also focused his studies on all matters relevant to those mystic blasts, which make such a great noise throughout the heavens when blown on the Day of Judgment that they completely confound the Satan throughout all the hours of his work [6]. When Reb Alter came to the *shtibel* on those days, everyone began to look at him in a completely different light. He was no longer the scribe as per his day–to–day routine – a quiet and modest Jew sitting in his remote corner. Everyone began to feel that in a few days he will be the "supporting pillar," the "wonderful image" in the cast of characters of Rosh Hashanah. Everyone would look deeply into his pale face and the pieces of parchment that filled his home, and upon his silvery beard that contained fragments of the sinews he used to sew together the parchment folios of a Torah scroll. Above all, everyone knew on those days to refrain from bothering him about other matters, and not to ask any question even if it pertained to Torah. They all together realized and saw in his eyes that every moment was holy and precious to him, and that when he looked into the books, only one thought was with him, catching his very essence. His whole life was for the blowing of the *shofar*.

On the morning of Rosh Hashanah, Reb Alter would be dressed in his white *kittel* and covered entirely in his *tallis*. He stood at his place for the entire *shacharit* service. He would not sit down during the service even during his final years when age caught up with him greatly. He would shake back and forth with very great enthusiasm. It was impossible to look at his visage and his motions, for, as has been said, he was completely enwrapped in his *tallis*. Nevertheless, anyone who looked at him for one minute and saw his body motions would see that he was completely overtaken by a flame and burning as a torch. At times, one would hear him utter a heartfelt, strong sigh that broke forth from his very midst. Everyone rested during the break between *shacharit* and *musaf*, some reading the *mishnas* of tractate Rosh Hashanah, and others with the heartfelt prayers and psalms of the Son of Jesse. However, for Reb Alter, these moments were the most difficult and serious of the entire year. He felt with his entire soul that he was to be the emissary of the congregation, and that he had to open up the upper heavens with his *shofar* blasts for the prayers and supplications of his congregation.

[Column 781]

First, he removed his *kittel*, and walked quickly to the mikva in order to immerse himself properly 49 times, as was his custom every time he went to the mikva. From the *mikva*, he went to the attic of his house when he spent a full hour reciting statements of the *Zohar*. Before the *shofar* blowing, he went again to look into the books that he had been learning for the entire time, which indicate the proper intentions that a G–d fearing *shofar* blower must have during the time of the blowing. After he checked the *shofar* for the last time, he literally ran like a child to the *shtibel* with large steps, despite his advanced age. Almost every year, he arrived very late for the time set for the *shofar* blowing, but nobody complained about him. Everyone knew and appreciated that with Reb Alter Szmelkes, the blasts were not just ordinary blasts that emanate from a *shofar*, but rather something more, for which one must make great preparations.

Then, having donned his *kittel*, wrapped himself in his *tallis*, being fully covered in a sea of sweat, he approached the table and began to recite *Lamenatzeach* [7] aloud.

[Column 782]

After *Lamenatzeach*, he recited the verses that begin with the letters "*Kera Satan*" [8] with his own unique melody, and everyone felt as if they saw with their own eyes the Satan being torn up to pieces with each verse recited by Reb Alter with great feeling and intention, even before the *shofar* was sounded.

The caller called out the blasts, and Reb Alter raised his head, took out the *shofar* from under its cover on the table, placed it in his right hand, and moved it to his mouth as he was trembling and swaying. Even at his mouth, the *shofar* was swaying like a drunkard. A few seconds passed before the first blast, apparently through additional preparation for the many intentions that had to be thought and contracted into the *tekia, shevarim, terua,* and *tekia* [9]. These were mystical emanations in the silence of the *shtibel*. These were not the blasts of a *shofar*, but rather of a soul overtaken with enthusiasm and depression for the upper worlds…

This is how the sets of *shofar* blasts went every year in the *shtibel* with Reb Alter Szmelkes. Thus did Reb Alter serve the Hassidim, the splendid ones of the town, in a faithful and dedicated manner with his whole heart and soul, beginning from his one–of–a–kind work as a scribe and ending with his role as *shofar* blower, through which he gained renown throughout the region.

Translator's notes:

1. In order to earn a livelihood.
2. The smallest of letters.
3. A reference to *kabala*.
4. Referring to Hannah's silent prayer in I Samuel 1:13.
5. Amos 3:8.
6. This is in accordance with the *kabalistic* thought that the Satan stands ready to accuse the Jews on Rosh Hashanah, and the *shofar* sounds confuse him.
7. Psalm 47, recited seven times prior to the blowing of the *shofar* on Rosh Hashanah.
8. After the recital of Psalm 47, and prior to the blessings of the *shofar*, six verses are recited that start with letters that form the acrostic *Kera Satan* – which means, let the Satan be torn up.
9. These are the names of the *shofar* sounds.

[Column 781]

Reb Alter Wolmer

by Dov Gorzalczany of Tel Aviv

Translated from Hebrew by Jerrold Landau

He was born in 1896 in Sokolow Podlaski, and educated in his parents' house in the traditional, religious style. Slowly but surely during the time of his studies in the Yeshiva of Sokolow, he dedicated some of his time to secular studies, and diligently completed studies as a bookkeeper.

He moved from Sokolow to Jandziw[1] or to a nearby village, where his father-in-law owned a mill. Nevertheless, he did not remain in the village for a long time, for during the 1920s, the attacks anti-Semitic ruffians of the N. D. reached their peak of infamy – especially in our area.

[Column 782]

They caused many villagers to uproot themselves from their place to go to the nearby towns.

Reb Alter Wolmer moved to Czyzewo.

He set up his house in a lot next to the post office. He earned his livelihood as an official with the Szopkowicz Brothers Forestry merchants. He later became their partner. Still later, he became the partner in the flourmill of Messrs. Lepek and Szopkowicz.

[Column 783]

Since he was of pleasant manner and liked by people, he quickly stood out and took his place among the honorable families of the town. He also had a recognizable place among the Hassidim of Aleksandrow. His deep knowledge of Torah and holy books, in addition with his broad, variegated general knowledge, earned him a most honorable and prominent place among the community of Hassidim. Everyone revered him. He added to this reverence by slowly earning a place in the wold of Hassidic cantors, since he worshiped wit a sweep voice – at first with Lecha Dodi on Friday nights and at the end as the leader of Shacharit on the High Holy Days.

His excited dynamism in all areas brought him to a strong economic position. His name went before him, and his fame went out as a successful businessman. His abilities stood out everyone, and the "Aleksandrowers" did not hesitate to choose him as their representative in the only "Cooperative Bank" in our town. His place was not missing even on the communal council. Later on, when the influence of the Hassidim of Gur declined, he was elected as the head of the Czyzewo community. He served in that lofty position for many years, and he fulfilled his duty faithfully and responsibly, as befits his uprightness.

The manner of Reb Alter in communal and social affairs was crowned with success. First of all, this was with regard to conducting services, with regard to which this wonderful man brought great satisfaction to hearts and souls.

His home turned into a place that served the community. His faithful wife, Bashka, also gave over a great deal to visitors and those who turned to her for help as the chairwoman of Linat Tzedek. Her efforts were directed to the assistance of the ill and needy, as she concerned herself with arranging hospital stays, lending out of sanitary equipment, and cleaning the equipment after it was returned.

[Column 784]

**Alter Wolmer, his wife,
daughter and mother-in-law**

The years of the terrible Holocaust brought Reb Alter Wolmer, together with Reb Zebulun Grosbard (the head of the community and head of the Merchant's Union), and Yehoshua Lepek (one of the chief Zionists and activists of the "Zentus") to the Judenrat. After Reb Zebulun was fired, Reb Alter filled his place.

He did not take the opportunity to flee and save himself. However, he did attempt to hide his family. He almost chased away his eldest daughter and forced her to flee – however he did not listen to the pleading of his daughter Mirl who urged him to flee. His responsibilities to the community to which he was so faithful removed this thought from him. He preferred to remain with the community and to share in their common fate.

He went on his final journey with the remnants of the Community of Czyzewo. He was taken to Zambrów and from there to Auschwitz – the vale of murder.

The death of this finest of people breaks the heart.

May his memory be blessed!

Translator's note:

1. I cannot accurately identify this town. Perhaps it is Janiszewo.

[Column 785]

Reb Szmuel Zeev and Lea Kandel

By Yosfe Kandel (Okon), Yafa Kandel (Grinwald), Yaakov Kandel and Avraham Kandel

Translated from Hebrew by Jerrold Landau

He was born in Czyzewo in 1887 to his parents Jakob and Sura Rachel. He married Lea (nee Baron) from the nearby town of Zaromb in 1908. She was an intelligent and refined woman, a woman of valor and a dedicated mother who always supported her husband. Thus was our dear mother.

Our father of blessed memory observed tradition and was careful about the commandments. He also worked all of his life to earn his bread by the sweat of his brow. He always found time for communal service, in particular with the Mizrachi movement in the town, in which he found content and a purpose for life.

Among other things, his activities to found the Modern Cheder, which would operate in the spirit of the times, must be pointed out. On account of this, he was forced to abandon his regular and beloved place of prayer in the shtibel of the Mszcznow Hassidim. He moved over to worship with the masses in the Great Synagogue, and later to the Szlamburger Shtibel that he established along with Reb Yosel Baruch Lepek.

The flame of Zionism in the prayer "And may our eyes behold your return to Zion" comforted him throughout all of tribulations of life. Four of his six children are found in Israel.

Father, Mother and our two brothers Yitzchak Noach and Chaim Zebulun were brutally murdered by the murderers of our nation in the year 1941. May G-d avenge their blood.

[Column 786]

Szmuel Zeev Kandel, his wife Lea, and four of their children (two of whom are in Israel)

The Lithuanian

by Gerszon Gora

Translated from Hebrew by Jerrold Landau

[Column 785]

Reb Pesach was one of the honorable people of the town. His house was the only one in the entire town that was built with two stories of red brick, in contrast to the other houses that were build of wood. He was very rich, and was liked by all circles in town. He frequented the Hassidic houses. He himself was not a prominent scholar, but he knew very well how to cleave to Hassidim. In the middle of one of the bright nights of Elul, prior to the holidays, when the horses were hitched to the wagon and the Hassidim were preparing to travel one by one to travel to the Rebbe, Reb Pesach went along with his splendid suitcase that contained provisions for all of the travelers.

[Column 786-787]

Our Reb Pesach also had a daughter who reached the age of marriage, and was perhaps even a bit beyond that age. The matchmakers were not quiet and did not rest. They occupied themselves with this matter greatly, but help from Heaven was not forthcoming.

Year after year went by, and a match was not found for the daughter of Reb Pesach. The Hassidim encouraged Reb Pesach and said to him, "Don't worry, forty days prior to the creation of a child, his match is decreed from above. It must be that the proper match is yet to come. One day, the salvation will come with the blink of an eye."

Indeed, thus it was.

The match from Heaven appeared with all his glory and splendor.

Reb Pesach made a match with an excellent boy from a Lithuanian family, one of the choice ones from the large Lithuanian Yeshivas, whose was known to be an expert scholar.

However, at first it was difficult for Reb Pesach to decide on the matter. How can he bring a Lithuanian into the Shtibel? How could this young man find his place among the Hassidic young men, who speak to each other in the second person and do not treat each other with respect? How would he be able to tolerate seeing a young twenty year old man talking to a ninety year old in familiar language?

However, he had no other way. He had found no other match, and, after all, he always desired to marry off his daughter to a scholar. Therefore, when they advised him about Ben-Zion the Lithuanian, he did not hesitate until he had concluded this fine match.

It was no wonder that everyone talked and was astonished about this match.

The young Hassidic men talked among themselves, "What was Reb Pesach thinking, that he would bring to us a veteran Lithuanian, whose entire essence is formality?"

However the elder Hassidim, who were more level-headed and broadminded, received with joy the news that, with the help of G-d, Reb Pesach had finally succeeded in finding an expert scholar as a match for his daughter, who would be supported at his table for many years so that he could continue to study Torah.

There was one old man there who had himself traveled several times to the Rebbe of Kock. He looked upon this matter positively, and turned to the grumbling young men and said to them:

[Column 788]

"Why all the noise? 'Litvaks' should indeed come to us. It is up to you to draw them near, to expose them to the treasures of Hassidism, and to bring them into the Hassidic mysteries."

The elder continued on, saying, "Remember that when that young man comes to you, whom you call the 'Litvak', you must draw him near and introduce him slowly to our way of life."

The words of the elder influenced the young man, and they all decided to draw the Lithuanian near, and to make him one of the group.

On the first days after the seven days of celebration[1], when Ben-Zion the Lithuanian entered the Shtibel, he sat in front of a large volume of the Vilna edition of the Talmud that he had received from his father-in-law as a gift, and began to study in the Gemara-melody that is known from the Lithuanian Yeshivas on account of its stress on each syllable – the young men looked upon with wonder and were silent. His methodology of study surprised them. They gave him leeway of a few days to continue with his method. For the first days, they also overlooked his manner of speaking, in which he used the formal style even to a young child. This is nothing – they thought – this is dough that can be kneaded.

Ben-Zion the Lithuanian had all of the character traits of a Hassidic young man. His gait was quick and elastic. His new ideas on Torah that he presented to the young men of the Shtibel testified to his sharpness of mind, brilliance, and exceptional grasp. He disliked verbosity of words, and matters that were off topic. He stated his words in brief and with reason.

He was of middle height. His build was thin and lean. His beard was short and groomed in accordance with custom. He had penetrating, dark eyes. They always exuded a thirst for knowledge; a desire to obtain knew facts that would augment his store of knowledge.

During the first days, he recognized the division between himself and the rest of the young men. Even though he studied his Talmud all day, he silently felt within himself a sort of desire for both worlds. Everything was new to him. He saw Jews who wrapped themselves in tallises and put on tefillin in a manner that was different than what he was used to in his youth. All of their customs and manners were different than those he was used to. They all made various strange movements during the time of prayer and study. This one made motions of devotion; the other one paced back and forth, and then went to the corner, with his tallis covering his entire face, and his entire body trembling.

[Column 789]

A desire was awakened in his heart to probe into the character of these young men and to understand them. He wished to understand them and their manners. In particular, their camaraderie amazed him, as they sat around the table after the services and drank a cup of "96" liquor, wishing each other blessings from the depths of their hearts. How strange is it, he thought in his heart – for what does liquor have to do with a Beis Midrash, a place where one studies Torah?

From examining them, he realized that all of these young men were cut from one mold. There is no "I" and "you", just "we". The "I" is subordinate to the "you", and the "you" is subordinate to the "I", and thus they merge into the "we".

Slowly, a meeting of hearts took place between the young men and the Lithuanian, who began to look on this entire matter with different eyes. The young men began to invite him to the Rosh Chodesh feasts, and on occasion urged him to look into some Hassidic book before going to sleep. Thus, from both directions, the closeness was forged and grew from day to day. There was now only one final barrier between them – the Lithuanian "Misnagdish" education that cannot be uprooted from the heart in one day.

However, the day finally came where this barrier was removed. Ben-Zion the Litvak became completely involved in the life of the Shtibel and became an inseparable part of Hassidic life.

This took place on the heels of his first visit to the Rebbe, along with the other young men, before the holidays. The splendor and glory that pervaded in the court of the Rebbe, and the "still, silent voice" that rose above the thousands of Hassidim, who were crowded together and absorbing each expression with awe – these removed the final obstacle from his heart.

He then understood the concept of "faith in Tzadikim" and finding shelter in the shadow of a Tzadik.

Being in the presence of the Rebbe was equivalent with all of the discussions and statements of the young men before this trip.

[Column 790]

He said to himself, "On occasion, there is a certain unique experience that awakens sublime feelings, which can have more influence than an entire book".

When he returned from the court of the Rebbe along wit the rest of the group, he felt himself as one of them in every manner, and he told them:

"Please don't continue to call me a Litvak. I am one of you."

With the passage of time, Ben-Zion ascended the rungs of the ladder of Hassidism and became a pillar of the Shtibel. He was the living spirit of the camaraderie. He was active in charitable matters and in helping those in need. "Lithuanianism" was no longer recognizable in him.

Nevertheless, he continued to be knows as, "Ben-Zion the Lithuanian" among the townspeople.

Translator's note:

1. Traditionally, seven days of celebration follow a wedding.

The Waker

by Gerszon Gora

Translated from Hebrew by Jerrold Landau

Most of the townsfolk did not know him very well. To them, he was a simple Jew, who did not stand out from among the other residents.

The called him Avraham-Chaim the "Kayatz"[1]. This nickname stuck with him for tens of years, and I never thought about looking into the source of this name, for it was used by everybody as if this was his surname.

Twice a week, on Tuesdays and Fridays, the market days on which farmers from the entire area filled up the streets and alleys of the town with their wagons and horses, as they brought all sorts of merchandise for sale – Avraham-Chaim would wander around between the wagons of the farmers with the other merchants of the marketplace, touch the sacks and packages, and turn to each farmer with the same question, "What is for sale, mister?"

Avraham-Chaim was not like the other merchants who had special storehouses and would purchase large quantities of grain to fill up their storehouses. He was a small-scale merchant. It was sufficient for him to purchase two or three sacks of wheat, rye or other types of grain on a market day. They sold it to him as if it was especially designated for him. There were those farmers to whom the "Leviathan" merchants did not pay attention to, because their quantity of merchandise was small.

[Column 791]

On those market days, one could see Avraham-Chaim walking through the streets with an empty sack under his arms, or carrying a quarter of a sack full of wheat on his back, bringing it to his own room that served as a dining room, bedroom, kitchen and grain storehouse all together.

The townsfolk would run into him on those days and ask about his wellbeing. He would answer everyone: "Thank G-d, everything is good. May it only be that G-d gives me years to live, and I will certainly not be lacking anything."

This simple Jew was without any makeup or rouge. His beard had not yet become completely white, which took years off of his withered body. His face was furrowed, and his hands were very callused.

He did not worship in the Shtibel and did not travel to the Rebbe. He also did not attend the Great Synagogue. He was the pillar in the "Chevra Mishnayos" Synagogue – the founder, Gabbai and Shamash all together.

During the time of the lessons, when the householders of the town crowded together around the tables, Avraham-Chaim took a place at the edge of the table near the door. At such times, he gave the impression of a guest who had come for a moment to hear the lesson.

Nevertheless, it was obvious that something was agitating in his heart when he sat at the table with the people attending the Mishna class. This was an internal happiness that enveloped him in the presence of the dozens of householders who were sitting at the tables studying Torah.

During those moments, he would completely forget about his narrow room full of wheat, his barren life and his gray, boring work in the kitchen. He turned his attention away from all of the gentile farmers among whom he circulated and conducted business twice a week. He forgot everything about the life of vanity and physicality. These minutes were to him like his entire life – minutes of boundless spiritual joy, or sublimity and splendor.

The householders of Chevra Mishnayos treated him with appreciation. They valued his extra dedication as a Gabbai and Shamash combined, and attempted to assist him in any way that was possible. However, he refused to accept any help at all. He would say the following to anyone who volunteered to help him sweep the synagogue, or perform any other task:

[Column 792]

"There is no need. This job is upon me, and please do not disturb me, for this work is very pleasant for me."

He had one special trait. This trait was known to several dozen scholars in the town for many years. We, the nine and ten year old children, found out about it incidentally.

It took place on a winter day. We, eight boys, studied in the large cheder of the town. At that time, we were studying the discussion regarding Rabbi Chanina the deputy Priest in tractate Pesachim – this was a discussion that was totally new to us. Each day, we would enter into the depths of the laws of ritual purity and impurity, and we would be astonished at the various levels of impurity: first degree, second degree, third degree, etc. We were very proud that the Rebbe involved us in such a deep section. We studied all day with diligence. We hid among the recesses of the new halachot. New vistas opened up before us. It was as if we received a short vacation from the Talmudic sections of "Nezikin" (Torts) and "Moed" (Festivals) in order to breathe for a few weeks in clear, pleasant air, among the thick oaks that were planted by Rabbi Chanina the deputy Priest. The new learning refreshed us to such a degree that even the Rebbe recognized a change for the better among us, in our studies and our diligence.

One day, the Rebbe turned to us and said:

"Children! I advise you to wake up for one week at 5:00 a.m. At that time, it is still dark outside, the cold is very strong, and it difficult for children such as yourselves to wake up then, but you must remember the first paragraph in the Shulchan Aruch (Code of Jewish Law): 'Be as strong as a leopard.' You must overcome all of the difficulties and obstacles, for then you will feel the true essence of the study of Gemara. During those early hours, the brain is clear and the mind of man is fresh, as if it was just created. It is possible to understand and grasp everything. I am certain that throughout the week, we will be able to review the entire section about Rabbi Chanina the deputy Priest, and you will know it all thoroughly."

The words of the Rebbe were a pleasant surprise to us. On the one hand, we desired this type of "exercise" of waking up while it was still night, and trudging through the snow to study. However, on the other hand, the "evil inclination" portrayed to us the strong cold that was outside, the deep darkness, and the warm bed that we were to have left prematurely.

[Column 793]

"However, who will wake us before dawn?", we asked the Rebbe.

"Leave that concern to me", answered the Rebbe with a bright face. "If you decide to get up, I will concern myself that there should be somebody to wake you."

We all agreed to the suggestion of the Rebbe.

We were still children and did not appreciate the value of this decision, for to us, every matter of getting up early on winter nights was seen as a "trick" and nothing real.

We doubted whether the matter would actually come to pass. We thought that it would be impossible to wake us all up at one time. The following question particularly bothered us: who would be the one to accept upon himself such a difficult task, to go around in the darkness and cold of night throughout the city and to wake up the children to study Torah?

However, all of our doubts were resolved. That very night, when I was in a deep sleep, I was suddenly awakened to the sound of a strong knock on the windowpanes next to my bed. I immediately turned my ear, and heard a voice calling:

"Gerszon! It is already ten minutes to five. Get up to study!"

I was completely surprised when I recognized the voice of Avraham-Chaim the "Kayatz". However, I recovered from my astonishment within a moment. His hoarse voice of the waker hurried me to get out of bed. I got up quickly despite the cold and darkness, as I imagined before eyes the first paragraph of the Shulchan Aruch. I felt myself as a small lair of leopards.

Within the span of a few minutes I washed my hands, got dressed, took my Gemara and flashlight, and hurried to the Beis Midrash of Chevra Mishnayos, the place where our cheder was located.

I thought that I would undoubtedly be the first, for I had hastened to get up without any delay. However, when I arrived at the Beis Midrash, I was surprised to see the Rebbe and the rest of the students waiting for me. At that very moment, the clock on the wall struck five.

We were all emotional, and given over to the experience of waking up before dawn. We were particularly moved by the fact that the waker was Avraham-Chaim the "Kayatz". Even though we were studying the first early-morning lesson with great diligence and with a clear and pleasant frame of mind, we would still glance on occasion to the corner near the lit stove where our "waker" sat, hunched over a book of Psalms, as he was reciting the Psalms of the Son of Jesse with great concentration.

[Column 794]

Avraham-Chaim continued on with this tradition for fifteen years. As has been said, only a few special people knew about this, only those who fulfilled the adage, "night was only created for study". He was the living alarm clock of the town. He would awaken every night at 2:00 a.m. light his kerosene lamp with a small piece of paper, and go out to his holy work.

He would traverse the dark streets and alleys of the town in the midst of the night, and on occasion cut through the night silence with his hoarse, yet strong voice. His route was planned out ahead of time. He woke everyone up at the time that they wanted, having being asked to do so. Thus did the four Beis Midrashes of the town fill up at each night with early risers.

The "Kayatz" was diligent in his holy task for fifteen years, and there never was an interruption. In nights of dense fog, during snowstorms, just as in bright, moonlit nights – he would always go out in the same heavy clothes and large boots in order to awaken the Jews to the Divine service.

He never complained about a Jew who did not wake up to his call. He judged him favorably: surely there was a reason. Even on the foggy winter nights when strong winds blew through the town, when almost nobody would be found in the Beis Midrash, he not angry and did not complain. "It is nothing", he would say. "Even if only one out of ten came, it was worthwhile for me to wake up all ten".

He did not only expend his efforts for great scholars, but also for schoolchildren. When some Rebbe asked him to awaken several students and a specific time for a specific lesson, he would immediately add the children to his list.

[Column 795]

Thus was there in his heart a strong love for the study of Torah. Thus did he bear the difficult task that he took upon himself, to awaken Torah students to the Divine service. I am certain that he continued on with his task until his final moments, until the terrible destruction of the town.

Translator's note:

1. The waker.

The Cantor of the Town

by Gerszon Gora

Translated from Hebrew by Jerrold Landau

Cantorial issues never affected the town. There was never any need to advertise prior to the High Holy Days that they were searching for a qualified cantor for the Musaf services, as was the case in many other town where the issues surrounding cantors took a very important place.

Reb Eliezer the cantor of the town was a "Cantor" in the full sense of the word. He served as the prayer leader in the Great Beis Midrash and was the cantor of the masses of people in the town, of all of the artisans, merchants, and workshop owners who were not of Hassidic extraction and who had worshipped for generations in the Great Beis Midrash in accordance with the Ashkenazic prayer rite. He was especially the cantor of hundreds of pious women who on the High Holy Days all looked similar to each other, like cherubs with their white, shiny, clear clothing. These were pure and sincere women, who never turned their attention to differences of opinions and the opposing views of Hassidim and Misnagdim, or between the Ashkenazic, Sephardic, Chabad, and Arizal prayer rites. It was the woven prayer of a Jewish woman coming from her heart.

In the women's balcony, which was like a large gallery of pillars that occupied half of the space of the Beis Midrash, all of the women of the town gathered together in one unit, or more accurately – with one heart. There worshipped the wives of the Hassidim and Misnagdim, of the Zionists and Agudists, of the Aleksandrow and Gur Hassidim. When on occasion the modern elements recommended bringing a modern cantor for the High Holy Days, a cantor who knew how to sing with a choir, who worse a tall, velvet hat and held a tuning fork in his hands – the Gabbaim (trustees) of the synagogue would push aside this suggestion immediately, without bringing it to deliberation. For it was sufficient for these Gabbaim to hear the enthusiastic opinion of these women about the prayers of Reb Eliezer, which they found to grow more meaningful and sweeter every year, in order to push aside any recommendation of this nature.

[Column 796]

The songs and melodies of Reb Eliezer the Cantor were the topic of the day among all that came to the Great Synagogue on the days of Rosh Hashanah and Yom Kippur.

Reb Eliezer was not a "Prayer leader" like Reb Shaul Tzvi in the synagogue of the Gur Hassidim, Reb Jeszaja of the synagogue of the Aleksandrow Hassidim, Reb Baruch the teacher in the synagogue of the Sokolow Hassidim, Reb Yankel Wibitker in "Chevra Mishnayos" or the other prayer leaders of the Hassidic prayer halls of the town. He was called "Reb Eliezer the Cantor" and that was fitting for him. His manner of standing at the prayer podium, his motions and enthusiastic melodies, as well as his clear, fine voice – all of these gave him the character of an experienced, professional cantor. I can still remember the unique image of his face, as if he stands alive before my eyes: He was of average height. He had a dark beard that was divided into two sections. The edges of the sections had turned silver, as if they were singed by the flame of advancing age. His cheeks were thin and sunken, which made his high, wide forehead stand out even further. His eyes were always raised upward, so that your gaze would never meet his. He could chat with you for hours without gazing directly at you with his eyes. He always made the impression on everyone that he had a special relationship with Heaven, a certain soulful attraction.

He occupied himself with his profession all the days of the year – or to be more specific, his wife and daughters worked at their profession – the baking of black rye. This bakery was called by his name: the Bakery of Reb Eliezer, even though he himself did not know how to place dough into a bucket.

His only occupation was to assist from time to time some sort of good deed in order to ease the burden upon some person. He spent the rest of his time in the Hassidic synagogue or in the Beis Midrash in front of an open book, as he silently hummed heartwarming melodies. He was always engrossed in thought. When he walked along the way, when he was standing, when he was sitting with a book, his thoughts always enveloped him completely. He always seemed like one who was caught in a place that was not his own, as if he was a wanderer in a strange place. For what was the purpose of all of the days and nights of the year, when it was impossible to pour himself out before the podium with prayers and supplications to the Holy One Blessed Be He, and to express the feelings of the heart and soul with such heartwarming and awe-inspiring hymns?

[Column 797]

Indeed, this was the nature of Reb Eliezer the Cantor. It was as if his soul was created on the six days of creation for the sole purpose of the prayers on the High Holy Days, and the purpose of his life was only for those pleasant Musaf services that he performed with his voice in the town. Therefore, his life throughout the year was like a life lacking in content. Only as the High Holy Days neared, when Ahron the Shamash announced on Friday night his traditional announcement that on Saturday night at midnight, the Selichot service would take place, did the fire of life burn n the eyes of Reb Eliezer. His eyes appeared as burning coals.

To what is this similar? It is like a fish that is taken out of water, that flutters about and struggles bitterly as it does not have a drop of water to breathe. At the moment that it is returned to the water, it turns immediately into a new creature, influenced with pleasant, effervescent life.

Those days, the days of Selichot and the Ten Days of Penitence, were to him like the source of living waters, clear, fresh water, which restored his soul to its full life. Then, all of the melodies and tunes that were hidden away all year in the recesses of his heart were reawakened, and began to break out.

During those days, when he sat in his home, when he ate his meals, when he walked around the streets looking for a good deed to perform, one could hear from his mouth the pleasant melody of a hymn or a prayer. This was a sort of practice, a preparation for the High Holy Days, when the tune would break out with its full strength and sweetness.

Reb Eliezer did not conduct himself like other cantors, who would practice for many weeks with a choir prior to the High Holy Days, in order that the prayers should sound "just so". He did not follow this pattern. He would say, "A cantor does not perform tricks. He has to prepare his heart, and the tunes and melodies would come out properly."

The impression of those High Holy Days is still etched deep inside of me. The synagogue was filled to the brim, especially on Yom Kippur when even the "barber", the only Sabbath desecrator in the city, was not missing. All of the worshippers were dressed in festive clothing. Meir and Binyumche, the two well-known water drawers whose characteristic pictures were publicized by the American "gazettes", were seated next to the western table. Behind them were the porters and wagon drivers, who used to worship at the early Minyan, before sunrise, throughout the year. The women of the town peered through the windows of the women's gallery at the large congregation and the cantor standing next to the podium like a conductor. The cantor was standing there, his face like an angel, covered in his white Kitel and his Tallis that was decorated with many silver decorations. He was assisted by his two sons. He supplicated, sang pleasant melodies and poured out his prayers as an emissary of the congregation standing before the Holy One Blessed Be He.

[Column 798]

Reb Eliezer composed new, original tunes for "Kevakarat", and "Heyey Im Pipiyot"[1], etc. The congregation of worshippers reached the peak of emotion as he recited the hymn "Eleh Ezkera Venafshi Elay Esphecha", whose theme is the Ten Martyrs of the Roman Government. His voice was soft or was weeping as he poured out his heart to all of the themes described in the moving words. The men and women of the congregation wept together with him.

Reb Eliezer was weak by nature. His shriveled and lean body always suffered from various ailments. Nevertheless, despite the fact that he poured out his entire essence and blood in his prayers, the High Holy Days were to him the source of health and strength. It was as if he did not live throughout the year except for the merit of these days.

Reb Eliezer's tenure lasted for tens of years without interruption. Throughout those years, he bestowed the best of his melodies, enchanting tunes and heartwarming singing upon our townsfolk, until that bitter and violent day when they were all brought to slaughter and buried in a large communal grave. Then Reb Eliezer the Cantor perished as well, may G-d avenge his death, and his voice was silenced forever.

Translator's note:

1. These are two segments of the Musaf of Rosh Hashanah and Yom Kippur.

[Column 798]

In the *Sukkah* of Reb Itzel

By Gerszon Gora

Translated from Hebrew by Jerrold Landau

Reb Itzel's father, Yedidya, was one of the simple householders of the town, whose knowledge of the "small letters"[1] was very weak. He was one of the worshippers of the first minyan [prayer group] in the large synagogue, along with the rest of the tradesmen, peddlers, and craftsmen. He would participate in the recitation of Psalms on a daily basis. In the evening, after the Maariv service, he would sit at the edge of the table of those who studied *Ein Yaakov*[2], and pay attention. The legends that he heard at that time would remain etched in his memory, and would later bring him a benefit in his livelihood. There were indeed many legends that were too complicated for his understanding, but he believed them in a straightforward fashion, for they were secrets of Torah that are only clear to scholars and people of good deeds.

[Column 799]

He would earn his livelihood from the market days of the town, particularly from his business with the gentile[3] farmers. There was nothing that a farmer brought to town for which Yedidya did not know the price and did not purchase. He would buy all types of grain, legumes, butter, eggs, and fruit. He would also buy the textiles of the farmers, used clothing, empty sacks, and all types of furniture. Even wagons laden with wood for the winter or potatoes, honey, and wax – were valid items of merchandise for him.

Yedidya was expert in the language of the farmers. He understood their spirit, and knew how to draw them near. Often the statements of the sages, which he would tell over in the language of the gentiles, would serve as a tried–and–true means of obtaining their merchandise at a fair price, and often for a much cheaper price than the farmers were accustomed to receiving from other Jews. For the gentiles loved to chat with him, and he knew how to capture their hearts with his intelligent, sweet talk.

He was called by them "Yedidya the Wise." Indeed, Yedidya was a wise, intelligent Jew, who grasped everything clearly and delved into the depths of matters of his fellow.

He was of average height. His body was gaunt, and he wore spectacles over his eyes. For the most part, his spectacles were tied to one of his ears with a string. His gait was slow and deliberate, and his words were weighed and measured. He did not like chatter and plays of words. Anything he said was stated briefly and to the point. His wisdom was in that he knew how to be brief and hit his mark. He could influence any person, Jew or gentile, with one word.

His eyes would also participate in his art of speaking. At times, when someone was trying to blame him for something or simply being lighthearted with him, it would be sufficient for him to place his spectacles on his forehead and give him a stare or a wink for the other person to lower his eyes in embarrassment.

Nevertheless, with all these traits, he did not succeed in become wealthy. His livelihood was earned with difficulty and in a meager fashion.

He sensed a lack in study of Torah even more than a lack of money. In his inner heart, he longed to become a scholar through the influence of the worshippers of the *shtibels* who would travel to the rebbe. Therefore, he attempted with all his energy to rectify this lack through his only son, Reb Itzel. Even though he was far from being wealthy, he gave his son over to the best teachers in the town, with whom only the children of the wealthy studied. He was indeed helped from heaven, and Reb Itzel grew up and became a serious scholar.

[Column 800]

As is known, "a son takes after the father," and "the deeds of the fathers are a portent for the children." Aside from being a fine scholar, Reb Itzel inherited his father's traits and excelled with his intelligence. He was involved in the life of the town. Aside from that, the events of the world at large came his way. Even though he was a G–d fearing Jew who was exacting with the light and difficult commandments, he absorbed the knowledge of the world at large, and would at times peruse the news in the Hebrew newspapers, such as *Hatzefira* and others. Incidentally, he would also glance at the words of literature written there. These things would shake him up deeply, and he would mutter to himself, "Complete heresy… of the students of Moshe the Dasoi"[4]

He became very extreme because his knowledge of the secular world, and if they would refer to secular books as wicked a sinful in the Hassidic House, he would add many more sharp words to the description.

"These are not just wicked or sinful. They incite people to apostasy, Heaven forbid, and one must keep far away from them."

In the Hassidic House, Reb Itzel was the only one who brought news of the outside world. He would add his own commentary in accordance with his world outlook. Everyone liked to be near him. During the break between services and study, or late in the evening, many would gather around him and drink up his words with thirst.

It was a spiritual pleasure to listen to his discussions on various matters, such as Hassidic issues, stories of *Tzadikim*, political events of those days, or on the deeds of the *maskilim* who were destroyed the vineyard of Israel[5]. He would always spice his words with a statement of the sages or with the incidental words of scholars.

[Column 801]

It fell to the lot of Reb Itzel, who specifically knew the source of evil, who understood the world of *Haskalah* and was alert more than anyone else in town to the danger lurking for anyone who has contact with that world, and who zealously opposed the reading of outside books and books of *Haskalah* – to be stricken by this plague in his own home. Baruch, the oldest of his eight children, looked into the outside books and was damaged…

One could not notice anything in the home. Baruch – or as he was called: Butsha – was apparently a lad like all other lads of the shtibel. He wore Hassidic garb and observed all the commandments of the Torah. He would also read a great deal of Hassidic books and stories of *Tzadikim* – books which his father provided him in abundance. Even so, his father noticed with his sharp eye that some sort of change took place in his manner of thinking, and some sort of strong internal ferment was taking place. He began to follow him with open eyes and to pay attention to any word that came from his mouth, until one day the cat came out of the bag, and the mask was removed from the face of his son. That took place on the holiday of Sukkot.

Reb Itzel's *Sukkah* was known throughout the town, not because it was graced with special beauty and eye–catching decorations. In these matters, Reb Itzel's *Sukkah* did not stand out from the other sukkot in town. It too was built from several old boards and covered with branches from the two trees that grew in his yard and was designated for this purpose. The uniqueness of Reb Itzel's *Sukkah* was that it was large enough to hold several *minyanim* [tens], and was designated to serve the needs of all the neighbors around him. On the eve of the festival, when the framework of the *Sukkah* was set up, all the neighbors would gather, fathers and children. Each would bring their contribution to the *Sukkah* of Reb Itzel. Some brought branches, others brought paper decorations, others brought carpets and white tablecloths, while still others brought poles and planks to finish off the *Sukkah*. At that time, Reb Itzel would stroll in his *Sukkah* as an expert builder, giving orders to his workers. He supervised the work with all its detail, and ensured that all the laws pertaining to the *Sukkah* would be followed. On the one hand, he wished that his *Sukkah* would exemplify all his "erudition," and would demonstrate the laws of *Levud, dofen akuma, tzurat hapetach*,[6] etc. On the other hand, he wanted his *Sukkah* to be kosher according to the most stringent viewpoints. At the end, he blended everything together. Within a few hours, his *Sukkah* was ready and prepared for the neighbors.

[Column 802]

This was the procedures for the *Sukkah* of Reb Itzel every year.

On the night of the festival, immediately after *Maariv*, all the neighbors would gather in his *Sukkah*, which had enough space for 30 people. Reb Itzel sat at the head of the table, wearing a black, velvet hat on his head, surrounded by his eight children. Behind him sat the neighbors with their children – approximately 20 additional people. All partook of the festival meal together. There were long breaks between each course, since the housewives had to bring the food from their distant homes. Reb Itzel would utilize those times to deliver pleasant words of Torah as well as stories related to issues of the day.

After the Grace After Meals, the children and simple householders exited the *Sukkah*, leaving behind only about ten scholarly Jews to fulfil the commandment of sitting in the *Sukkah*, as is written "you should dwell there as you normally live." Then Reb Itzel renewed his rich treasury. This time, he discussed more lofty and sublime matters, for he knew that his audience consisted of scholarly Jews at his level. He would bring his listeners into the world of kabbalah, the mysteries of the *Zohar*, and the ten spheres; or he would bring them into the forests of the Baal Shem tov or the tables of *Tzadikim*. At times, he would discuss didactics related to issues of the festival, or open the window of the world at large to them as he would discuss the *maskilim* and the perverters of religion. These discussions would extend for many hours. At times, people would go directly from the *Sukkah* to the *mikva*, since dawn was breaking and it was not worthwhile to go to sleep.

On that festival night, the meal was taking place as always. Reb Itzel delivered his Torah discussions as usual, and nothing special was noticed. At the end of the meal, most of those present left the *Sukkah*, and only Reb Itzel's cronies remained. Reb Itzel did not say anything for a long time, for he was immersed in his thoughts. Those at the meal waited in anticipation. However, it was as if he had become mute. It was obvious that something was bothering him.

[Column 803]

He suddenly became aroused, turned to the others, and said:

"This time, I will tell you a story that happened to me, in my house. The event itself is nothing to be happy or proud of, but it is appropriate that everyone know about it, so that one can keep away from evil and guard one's house carefully."

"The topic is a about my eldest son Butcha," continued Reb Itzel after a deep sigh. "I have known for a long time that something was not proper with this son. I was suspicious that he was reading outside books, but I could not catch him in the act. Once, a few days before Sukkot, late at night, I went to his bookshelf to get a specific book. To my great surprise, I found a book written in Hebrew, which I opened and recognized as an outside book. It was written by a well–known *maskil*. I realized immediately that he had forgotten about it and left the book among the rest of his books. I said to myself: "I will look into it and see what is this poison that these books imbue to their readers." I read a story that could apparently have been written in holy books. It was a story about a Jew who was sanctifying the moon with holy intentions. The book describes the Jews in a nice fashion, as a Hassid and a holy person, and the moon as a creation of G–d, who lights up the face of the Jew as he sanctifies it, and listens to every prayer and every verse that emanates from him. As I was reading, I almost turned into a follower of that book. However, I knew that "A Torah scroll written by a heretic should be burned," and how much more so such a book. I decided to look through it and to search for the heresy and impurity that they bring into the holy – until I found it. After all his fine and heartfelt descriptions, the writer ends his story with a brief sentence, that when the Jew returned home, he was killed… It is easy to understand his improper intention. The sages have said that the sanctification of the moon saves a Jew from a strange death. This heretic came and invented a story to contradict the words of our sages. The worst thing is that he began with nice words in order to capture the hearts of the pure youth."

[Column 804]

After a bit of time, Reb Itzel continued to relate:

"That night, I turned on the winter oven, I ignited a bit of paper which contained ashes from the oven, I poured kerosene on the ashes, I place the book upon it, and set it on fire. This was in order to fulfil the command, "A Torah scroll written by a heretic should be burned.""

Reb Itzel continued to discuss a great deal about this topic, instructing his listeners how to guard and protect themselves from the net of the *Haskalah*.

When the conversation ended and all those at the feast returned to their homes, Reb Itzel felt an easing in his heart. He felt a bit calmer, for this matter weighed upon him like a heavy load. Since he discussed what was on his heart and warned his listeners of the danger of secular literature, he felt as if the load has been removed. He sighed a calm sigh.

Translator's notes:

1. The "small letters" refers to the rabbinical commentaries and glosses on the Talmud and codes of laws, generally written in smaller font than the main text.
2. An anthology of the aggadaic lore as opposed to legalistic] material of the Talmud.
3. The word used here for gentiles is *arelim*, literally "uncircumcised," implying a slightly derogatory tone.
4. Referring to Moses Mendelsohn who was born in Dessau. See https://en.wikipedia.org/wiki/Moses_Mendelsohn
5. i.e destroying the purity of Judaism.
6. *Levud* – that if there are spaces in the walls below a certain width, the wall remains valid; *dofen akuma* – that if the *schach* (foliage cover of a sukka) does not extend all the way to the wall, and the space without *schach* is covered by some covering, the wall is considered to be valid, but one may not sit under the covered area; *tzurat hapetach* (literally: form of a door), that if a wall has an opening in the form of a doorway, with two doorposts and a lintel, it does not invalidate the wall.

The Prayer Leader

By Gerszon Gora

Translated from Hebrew by Jerrold Landau

That morning, we felt a change in everybody. Apparently, no change was noticeable. The studies took place as every day – the same *Gemara*, the same Talmudic discussion, and the same names of the Talmudic sages. However, the tune of the studies changed. The melody was different.

Even the atmosphere in the *cheder* was different from the usual. The echoes of the new studies touched the hearts of each of us. We felt that a new period of time had begun. We entered a period of seriousness and self–reflection.

We were still young and tender. It was before we got to know the world, and its various sins and iniquities. That trembling of the soul that awakens in the hearts of adults, as they go into seclusion with their souls, in moments of self-reflection – that was still strange to our hearts. For what business do we have with reckoning of sins and feelings of repentance?

We were already three years old, and we were hitched to the yoke of Torah, as all children of the towns in those days. We studied prayer, *Chumash*, and *Gemara*. We did not know any other studies. We were connected to the rebbe, the *cheder*, *Chumash*, and *Gemara* from morning until evening. Was there any place for self-reflection and thoughts of repentance in the hearts of children such as us, students of the *cheder* of Reb Shaul–Tzvi?

Despite this, we felt as if some change had taken place inside us that morning.

[Column 805]

Our rebbe, Rabbi Shaul–Tzvi, would start every day before the *Gemara* class with a joke, a pleasant statement, or a regular short story. However, this time, the rebbe had a serious look on his face, and he said with emotion:

"Children! Today, the month of Elul begins. Starting from today until after Yom Kippur, even the fish in the water tremble from fear of the Day of Judgment. Every one of you must, therefore, increase your diligence in the study of Torah, pray with more intention, recite many Psalms, and get up early every morning for Selichot. Remember do not forget, today is Rosh Chodesh Elul!"

From that morning onward, Reb Shaul–Tzvi taught us with a melody that shook up the heart, unlike every day. The statement, "the rabbis teach"[1] had a unique ring to it, arousing latent feelings in the heart.

Everything changed. It was like a new creation.

The Talmudic discussion of "one who exchanges a cow for a donkey"[2] was blended with the tunes of "The soul is Yours and the body is Your handiwork[3]. The Talmudic discussion of "Abandonment without awareness" blended with the tunes of "Kingship, Remembrances, and Shofar"[4].

Even our day–to–day conversations were more enthusiastic and soulful.

For Reb Shaul–Tzvi, the entire month of Elul was a sort of lengthy Rosh Hashanah. Since he was the prayer leader in the shtibel, the representative of the congregation of those Hassidim and people of good deeds, and in his modesty, he did not feel that he could even reach the ankles of any of them – he already began his holy work from the beginning of Elul.

He was not a cantor. He did not sing lengthy tunes or repeat each word two or three times. He was also not one of those prayer leaders who fit melodies into the prayers.

"G–d wants the heart," he would say. "The main thing is the heart, the feeling." One must pronounce and enunciate the proper words with which we plead and supplicate before the Holy One Blessed Be He."

This was his primary power as a prayer leader.

When he would teach us *Gemara* and *Tosafot*, he would include the echoes of the Selichot and the prayers in the lesson, to arouse our tender hearts and instill the seriousness of the month of Elul and the High Holidays into them. During recess or at times when we would review the lessons, he would open the large *machzor* [holiday prayer book] adorned with various commentators, and study carefully all the hymns and prayers, to understand their meaning and delve into the depths of their intentions.

[Column 806]

Indeed, song and melodies are good before the Holy One Blessed Be He, but only when it comes hand–in–hand with the supplications of the heart and prayer that bursts forth from the recesses of the soul.

Therefore, Reb Shaul–Tzvi did not place the emphasis on the melody itself, but rather on understanding the prayers and hymns. He did not enchant his listeners on account of the tunes – even though they were very pleasant and sweet to the ear – but primarily with his heartfelt singing, full of emotion, as if he was "explaining" the content of the words coming from his mouth.

I remember the day after that day, when I was completely under the influence of our rebbe Reb Shaul–Tzvi, when I had felt the special atmosphere of Elul for the first time. I got up early, went myself to the river at the edge of the town, a small tributary of the Bug, and stood at the bank for about half an hour. I contemplated its clear waters that flowed peacefully, with the current speeding up in the morning and the early evening, as they passed the "Kessel Grob" (Kettle Pit) (a deep place in the river outside the town), flowing toward the village of Rus.

With special attention, I followed after the school of fish swimming in the middle of the river. I saw and felt the trembling passing through the water as they swam to and fro in the water.

This vision illustrated before my childlike eyes the words of the rebbe:

"During the month of Elul, even the fish in the water tremble from the fear of the Day of Judgment."

Every day, the rebbe dedicated a special period of time to explain the Selichot and hymns of the High Holy Days.

[Column 807]

On such a day, Elul left its mark on the entire town as well, as the people greeted it with an investigation of their deeds and thoughts of repentance.

The synagogues were filled more than usual. Many attendees were tradesmen and merchants who were often absent from the synagogue due to their occupations. However, they came to the three daily prayers every day during Elul. Idle conversation between people was minimized. Relations between people became more heartfelt and more imbued with mutual trust.

The ambience of Elul was felt the most within the walls of the Hassidic Shtibel. The sounds of Torah burst forth from it day and night. The number of those delving into Hassidic books continually increased. The young men began to look into their deeds and make an accounting of their souls. As they prepared their souls for the advent of the Days of Awe, their hearts were filled with longing and anticipation for the prayers of the prayer leader Reb Shaul–Tzvi. Everyone waited impatiently for the first *Selichot* – for that hour in the middle of the night when Reb Shaul–Tzvi would sound his voice that penetrates the innards and the heart.

This hour arrived.

On Saturday night in the middle of the night, the Hassidic House was overflowing with worshippers, elderly and young adults, youths, and children, all still wearing their Sabbath clothing. *Gartels* and *peyos* were waving in all directions due to the longing for devotion and emotion. Then a middle–aged Jew came forth from the congregation and ascended the prayer podium. He had a thin body, pale, wrinkled face, eyes burning like fire, and thin, trembling beard. When he reached the podium, he stood bent over, exemplifying his modesty and broken heart. This was the prayer leader Reb Shaul–Tzvi.

[Column 808]

"*Yisgadal Veyidkadash...*"[5] His voice carried through the space of the prayer hall, and the words were enunciated with the special melody, without decorations and screeches, as if they rose up themselves from the depths of the heart and immediately penetrated the hearts of everybody.

"Unto You, Oh L–rd, is righteousness..."

The enthusiasm increased. The voice of the prayer leader rose from time to time, and a holy awe filled all the worshippers. Every person imagined that the cantor directed his enthusiastic, penetrating voice directly to the individual alone.

"Unto You is the day, and even the night, You prepare the lights and the sun."

"Unto You is the heavens, and even the earth is Yours, You laid the foundation for the earth and all therein."

Here, his voice rose over all the other voices, and his wonderful intonation captured the sublime moments expressed by those verses. "Unto You is the heavens, and even the earth is Yours" – so clear and understandable are the words.

It was if a magic wand brought all the wonders of nature – the burning heat of the summer and the depth of the cold of the winter, the mighty Leviathan, the sea and its waves, the mighty rivers, the large serpents, and all the mysteries of nature — before the shtibel, to the eyes of the congregation of which he was its emissary. It was as if he showed them how the waves break up, how the rivers and seas dry up, and the heads of the Leviathans shudder under His wondrous providence; by the sublime, elevated "You"[6] before Whom everybody is pouring out their hearts, and from whom they are asking forgiveness before the Day of Judgment that is approaching.

Thus was the prayer of Reb Shaul–Tzvi. He did not follow the normative path of all cantors, but rather knew how to emphasize and to enunciate properly specifically the sections that no cantor pays attention to. This was the grandeur of his influence.

[Column 809]

This was a recitation of "Hebrew" more than a cantorial rendition. Just as with Selichot, he would enunciate each words of the High Holiday prayers with sweetness, as he breathed a soul and living spirit into each verse.

Many roles were placed upon him: he was a teacher of children, a prayer leader, an advisor and leader in all aspects of the Aguda, an activist in matters of Beis Yaakov[7], a director of Gemilut *Chasadim* [charitable fund] into which he invested the best of his energy and efforts. However, his primary praiseworthiness came through the merit of his prayers. He gained renown throughout the entire area by virtue of being an exemplary prayer leader.

Translator's notes:

1. A common introduction to a Talmudic discussion.

2. Mishnah Bava Metzia 7:4.

3. A section of the *Selichot* [penitential] service of the High Holy Day season.

4. Three sections of the Rosh Hashanah *Musaf* service.

5. The opening words of the *Kaddish*, sung with a special, powerful melody on the High Holy Days.

6. The "You" in this verse refers to G–d. These opening verses of the *Selichot* service, describing G–d's control over nature, are taken from Psalms 74.

7. An Orthodox girls' school.

Shmuele the Walker

By Gerszon Gora

Translated from Hebrew by Jerrold Landau

Nobody knew how or when he arrived in the town. He snuck into town several decades previously without anyone knowing, as one of the groups of beggars who made the rounds to the doors. Like them, he too made the rounds to the doors of the town that winter to collect donations. He also extended his hand in the various *Beis Midrashes* of the town. He would sleep in the poorhouse at night along with the other indigents. Nobody paid any attention to him, and nobody cared whether he remained in town or left along with a group of wandering paupers.

Just has his arrival was unknown, without arousing any attention, so was his sojourn in town, which was without any impression or notice. Nobody cared about him or followed him.

Like a shadow of a passing image, he would appear every day in the synagogue during the early hours of the morning. With silent steps, he would slink over to the table next to the western wall, the place of the simple Jews, the hewers of wood and drawers of water. He would recite the Shacharit service in his regular corner, and then recited several chapters of Psalms. Immediately thereafter, he disappeared, and nobody saw him until the next morning, at the same time and in the same corner.

Nobody took interest in him, not when he arrived and not when he left. Nobody was curious to known why this itinerant pauper set up residence in this town, after spending tens of years living the life of a wanderer.

[Column 810]

He was always immersed within himself, and fully enveloped with secrecy and mystery. He never spoke to anybody, or raised his eyes to look at anybody. He also stopped making the rounds to the doors and sticking out his hand for donations, as if he had suddenly become wealthy, and had some wonderful treasury of gold and pearls in his wanderer's sack that was always on his back.

Indeed, he actually became wealthy in town. He displayed a treasury of energy, power, and work, and he used this treasury to its fullest extent. That treasury was precious and important to him more than all the treasuries of gold and silver.

A desire to work, to earn his livelihood through the sweat of his brow and to earn his bread in truth and uprightness arose in him while he was living in town. He started to work in the tzitzit [ritual fringes] factory. He did not concern himself with wages, nor did he take interest in work hours. He made no conditions. He worked in accordance with the verse, "In the morning, man goes out to work and labor until evening."[1].

He would sit all day next to the spinning wheel, and spin the wheel incessantly, producing large quantities of wool strings with the machine that would serve for the production of the *tzitzit*.

He was closed into himself at the workshop as well, as if he locked his heart with seven locks. He did not exchange a word with any person during all the work hours. The only sound that could be heard from his mouth was the sound of sighing and groaning that burst forth from the depths of his soul from time to time.

His heart told him that his personal secret cannot be told. Nobody must know that a small piece of paper with a small notebook waved fluttered atop his stormy heart, below his cloak, as he turned the spinning wheel.

Given that this was a secret, it was necessary to be quiet and lock his lips forever. Thus, he spent his final years next to the spinning wheel in a remote place, far from his place of birth, in constant muteness.

All this had to happen.

If he made a decision on that decisive day, and if those numbered words were already etched on that small note – that nobody will read until after he left the town for good – he was dutybound to guard the second item related to this, that I the complete science, the decisive muteness.

[Column 811]

Days, months, and years passed, and that stranger who arrived in town from afar guarded his secret, maintaining his daily routine. He never left his regular place next to the western wall in the synagogue, and next to the spinning wheel in the *tzitzit* factory. Similarly, the "small note" never left the region of his heart – the small ledger with the note that caused a change in his life and turned him into a different person, a person who bears the obligation of mystery, and upon whom quiet had been decreed for all the days of his life.

The tragic day finally arrived when the deep secret became known to everybody. He was childless and isolated in his death. He gave up his soul in the workshop, among thousands of bundles of wool, next to the spinning wheel. Incidentally, the wheel was spinning.

For the town, however, his death lifted the veil from his secret. It quickly became a wonderful legend, that became a point of conversation for men, women, and children for many years.

Now, the riddle that perplexed many people was solved: For whom did he work? Why did he dedicate all his energy to his work, when one work day per week would have been sufficient to provide for his meager livelihood?

This is what was written on that note attached the small ledger:

"Here I am, alone and abandoned, without a wife and children. I have wandered in cities and towns, made the rounds from door to door, collected donations, and gathered coin after coin. I deposited everything in the post office, as is listed in the loan ledger. Finally, I started working in the tzitzit factory and increased my income. After my death, I bequeath this entire treasure to this town, to build a Talmud Torah to educate young students, so that this will be my final legacy after my *kaddish*…"

[Column 812]

He came to town anonymously, along with a group of wandering paupers. He lived in the town for decades as an anonymous person shrouded in mystery, surrounding himself by utter silence. However, after his death, he became famous throughout the town and the region, thanks to the Talmud Torah building that was built from his money, which flourished into an institution of pride.

Translator's note:

1. Psalms 104:23

Flocks of Holy Ones

By Gerszon Gora

Translated from Hebrew by Jerrold Landau

The townsfolk waited impatiently for the festival of Simchat Torah. The elderly, middle aged people, and especially the "white crowd" – the six or seven–year–old children, and even younger ones – all waited.

That day, it was as if the entire town, with its houses, streets, stones, and clods of earth, turned into one splendid celebration.

Everyone, without exception, from all strata, classes, and groups of the town, celebrated that splendid holiday.

The worshippers of the *Beis Midrash*, the simple Jews of the entire year, the tradesmen, tailors, shoemakers, porters, hewers of wood and drawers of water, did not understand the intentions and internal depth of the festival. For them, it was simple! Jews were rejoicing with the Torah, and therefore they danced in the Torah processions, kissed the Torah scrolls with awe and love, and paid dearly for the *chatanim*[1]. Everyone made sure to get an *aliya* to the Torah. Then, the celebrated a *Kiddush* together, with the gabbai [synagogue trustee], the head of their community, as they rejoiced.

To them, Torah was simple. They would put on their *tefillin*, recite the three daily prayers, recite a chapter of Psalms, and that was the entire Torah – the written Torah, the oral Torah, with all the commentaries around them.

The worshippers of the study groups already felt more sublime feelings on Simchat Torah. The *Ein Yaakov* and Mishnah study groups already felt the sweetness of Torah the entire year. Therefore, to them the Torah scrolls were not white parchment with holy black letters, but rather all their studies from the entire year – the legends told by the teacher of the class, the feeling of the study of Torah, times and seasons – all of this came before them on the day of Simchat Torah. In honor of this, they organized a large *Kiddush* in their *Beis Midrash*, and sang and danced almost all day.

[Column 813]

After the simple, pure Jews moved the celebration to the Hassidic House, where the festival encountered its full fulfilment. There, they unified the "body" and "soul" of the festival. The festival spread forth from there. It burst forth from the narrow confines of the synagogue and *Beis Midrash*, and moved to the street, outside, to the town under the skies, and even amongst the uncircumcised gentiles.

Avraham Yosel the teacher was almost the only one who brought the festival of the Torah to the outside. The uncircumcised gentiles came from the villages to see him at his work.

He was a short Jew with a beard divided into three parts – a bit of hair under his chin, and two bundles of hair coming out of his two jaws, as a segol symbol.

He earned his livelihood as a teacher of young children from those days. That is to say, he lived a life of poverty and want, living in a one room with his large family. The children of his *cheder* also studied with him in that room.

However, none of this is interesting to our topic. The main essence of Avraham Yosel was in the shtibel in the Hassidic house. There, he was no longer a teacher, and a poor, suffering Jew. There he was the head, the leader, the educator, and the guide.

He sat in one place in the *shtibel*, and could not restrict himself to sitting next to a book for a half or quarter of an hour. Rather, he was always in motion and wandering around.

He opened a book, placed it on the table, looked into it for a moment or two, and began to pace to and fro without stopping. He then looked into the book again, and again wandered about… From time to time, he would utter some sort of silent moan, or raise his hands above.

This was his way of study.

All the books of Hassidism and Kabbalah were clear to him. He knew many chapters of Zohar by heart. At times it seemed that he lay down on the bench in the shtibel, and rested with closed eyes late at night. In truth, he was reviewing then what he had studied as he was wandering about a brief time before.

[Column 814]

His work in the *shtibel* was primarily with the young men, the "blossoming Hassidim." He had to direct them in the path of Hassidism, and bring them into its main room.

Therefore, we could meet him suddenly when he was strolling with some new young man who had recently arrived in town to be supported at the table of his father–in–law. He would stroll with him and explain the way of life to him.

Throughout the year, one could not notice any special feelings of joy on his face or through his way of life. His strange mannerisms in the Hassidic House, his way off study, his many quiet discussions with the young Hassidim, his constant delving into books of Hassidism and Kabbalah imparted a serious appearance to his face. This was despite the fact that he was always among the initiators and activists for communal meals, such as the *Rosh Chodesh* feast, the *Melave Malka* meal, or a regular meal among friends in which one could delve into Hassidism and the service of G–d.

The day of Simchat Torah was different. On that day, Avraham Yosel the Teacher went outside his usual bounds. He was no longer as he was, he was not a teacher, a Hassid, a Kabbalist, or a guide to the older lads that day. On that day, he took on a special cloak, the cloak of Simchat Torah.

The following was the order or his day, or more accurately, the order of his service, similar to the service of the High Priest.

Simchat Torah [Rejoicing of the Torah]– that was the name of the festival. Therefore, one had to toss out all bad events from the face, and one had to begin to rejoice, to dance, and to celebrate with the Torah.

Already on the eve of Simchat Torah, Avraham Yosel the teacher would turn the Hassidic House into a sort of wedding hall in which people would rejoice under the canopy of the Torah.

[Column 815]

Already before the processions and before the services, they would bring out wine and liquor. Avraham Yosel would direct the activity, distributing a portion to everyone, and forcibly bringing them into the dance circle in the Hassidic House. He danced, sang, jumped, shouted, and responded to every shout, every commotion, with the following words echoing after every verse:

"Simchat Torah – Simchat Torah."

He barely slept that night, and did not let many of his lads sleep, for how could one sleep. The day was short, the work was great, and one must rejoice. It is a commandment to rejoice, and what joy, and what festival – other than Simchat Torah.

One the day of Simchat Torah, his primary role, for which he had a tradition for a long time – on that day when he became the shepherd of the holy flock and the patron of the young children who were standing under the *tallis* for *Kol HaNearim*[2] – was to concern himself with them so that they would not miss out on anything on that day.

As was his way in holy matters, on that day he went from *Kiddush* to *Kiddush*. His mouth did not stop that day. He did not go alone, but rather with his entire entourage. About 30 or 40 children accompanied him all day. Their parents knew about this, and granted special permission for them to go with him. He brought them into every place where a Simchat Torah *Kiddush* was taking place. He looked after them as a faithful shepherd. He took charge in every place. He became the distributor. He distributed the first portions to his "holy flock." The young ones followed after him like sheep following the shepherd.

When the *Kiddush* participants formed a circle and the dancing reached it pinnacle, he raised his voice in ecstasy, and directed his words to his entourage, who joined him in the dance:

"Who are you?"

"The holy flock."

"And does the flock say?"

"Meeh, meeh, meeh."

[Column 816]

The dance then continued on.

That is how he brought them from place to place throughout the entire day, until after they had already concluded the *Mincha* service with his group in some final place toward evening. Then they finished the final *Kiddush*. He then went out with them all to the main street of the town. Then almost all the townsfolk, including the gentile men and women who were standing at the side, knew that Avraham Yosel the teacher was about to conclude the Simchat Torah festivities.

He conducted and led his flock, the flock that he tended.

Again, the same thing, the continuation of what happened previously.

"Who are you?"

"The holy flock."

"And what does the flock say?"

"Meeh, meeh, meeh."

All the bystanders on the street joined his entourage in the responses of "the holy flock," and the shouts of "meeh, meeh, meeh." Even the gentiles assisted in the shouts of "meeh, meeh, meeh."

The voice of Avraham Yosel the teacher continued for over an hour, and for more than the hour, the responses of the children of the "holy flock" resonated through the atmosphere of the town.

Each year, it was the tradition of Avraham Yosel the teacher to celebrate Simchat Torah with the children, and to imbue their hearts with waves of joy. In order to influence them, he descended from his staircase, attired himself before them as a shepherd, and continued to present his questions to them, in order to receive their faithful response – the response of the children of Israel, the response of the pure, clear souls and hearts, responding the clear answer to the entire area on the festival of the Torah:

"Who are you?"

"The holy flock."

It is no wonder, therefore, that the name of Avraham Yosel the teacher, Avraham Yosel the master of the "holy flock" was guarded in the mouths of these children, the "white group" of the town.

Translator's notes:

1. The special Simchat Torah honors of being called to conclude the annual cycle of Torah reading, and begin the new cycle.
2. The portion of the service when all the children are called up in unison to the reading of the Torah.

My Parents

by Isachar Okon/Tel Aviv

Translated by Gloria Berkenstat Freund

[Column 817]

My father, Alter–Mendel, was born in Czyzewo in 1870 and I do not know if he acquired his love of work during his childhood years or later when he married my mother, dear and kind Liba, the daughter of Shlomo–Ber Kaczanek. Her parents lived in Kosk, two kilometers outside Czyzewo. They had a windmill there, the only one in the area.

[Column 818]

Right after the wedding, they lived in Bialystok for a while. First, in 1895, after the death of my grandfather, Shlomo–Ber, my father took over the windmill and with it began to carry on field work for his own use. He had five acres of land, cows and chickens.

[Column 819]

We were eight children, four brothers and four sisters. The boys would go to kheder [religious primary school] in Czyzewo every day and one of them would take along a small container of milk for the Czyzewo rabbi's family. My father was proud that he did not let any other milk be used in his house.

On Shabbos [Sabbath], my father and we went to the Czyzewo house of prayer to pray. My mother also went to the city to pray on the holidays. I often heard how women praised her as a genteel, bright soul. On Yom Kippur, she did not let the Makhzor [holiday prayer book] out of her hardened hands.

When we grew up, we helped with the work, worked at the mill and so on.

Our economic worth stood particularly in the field, located a half kilometer from the village.

She toiled for her entire life, my dear mother, quiet, patiently carrying the burden for the entire house and she helped my father in all his work. In 1920, when the Hallercziks [followers of the anti–Semitic Polish General Josef Haller] entered Czyzewo, they severely beat my father. He was covered in blood from the wounds on his head and over his entire body. My mother bit her lips so that my father would not hear the cry of her grieving heart. She suffered silently and did not leave his bed, changed the bandages on his wounds day and night and when he finally got up from bed, everyone saw it as a miracle from heaven, as if he had really been resurrected.

There also was constant danger in continuing life in the village. When their sons grew up, they all received permission to carry weapons. My brothers were known for their courage and strength and they evoked fear in the young rascals in the area.

My mother Liba [Liba in first paragraph], brother Shmuelka, sister Gitel, brother Noachel, sisters Etel and Chayatsha, last at left, my small daughter who perished

[Column 820]

Bands of robbers who attacked the peaceful residents came to that area from time to time. But they did not dare come near us. It was not worthwhile for them to challenge our heroic family. In 1937, during the pogrom in Czyzewo, my brother Shmuelka stood guard with a weapon in his hands and helped the Czyzewo Jews day and night.

Reb Yankel Wapniak lived in the neighboring village of Brulin, a slight distance from us. We would meet him sometimes and speak about the situation and with worry remember that we lived in a God forsaken place, cast aside, with gentiles. At the beginning of the 1920s, Yankel Wapniak and his family moved into the city [Czyzewo] and our family remained alone.

In the late 1920s we, the adult brothers, decided that it was time to bring in a motor that would help the wind drive the windmill. It was lively; there was no lack of income. But the times were turbulent. The boycott actions began in Czyzewo, which poisoned the peasants' minds and agitated their mood. The situation grew more bitter with each day and in 1938 the situation was unbearable. Two brothers and one sister emigrated to Uruguay, Israel and Argentina. My parents sold their possessions and left for Bialystok to begin a new life that did not promise anything good.

[Column 821]

Our Parents

by Ch. Kirszenbojm

Translated by Gloria Berkenstat Freund

Yakov–Leib Kirszenbojm was born in Lomza in 1878. His father, Reb Shalom, was a teacher and later he became the *mohel* [ritual circumciser] at a *misnaged* [opponent of Hasidism] *yeshiva* [religious secondary school] in Warsaw. He raised his only son, Yakov–Leib, as a good student, sent him to a *yeshiva* and married him off when [Yakov–Leib] was still young to the youngest daughter of the well–known merchant, Reb Mendel Siedlisker (Zysman), among the first settlers at the Czyzewo station.

Reb Mendel Siedlisker was a rich man and probably had promised the *yeshiva* student a good dowry and for the first three years provided him with *kest* [support given by a father to his daughter's husband so that he could study Torah].

Yakov–Leib Kirszenbojm

[Column 822]

The first conflicts in the house began after the *sheve–brokhes* [seven blessings recited for a newly married couple during the end of a meal within the first week of their marriage]. The grandmother, as was her habit, prepared the table for breakfast and laid down a rustic brown bread. The new young man [the groom] did not know how to deal with it. Finally, he decided to ask if it was possible to have two rolls. He was not accustomed to eating anything else for breakfast…

Hearing such talk, the grandmother decided in her heart that the son–in–law was, alas, sick, and her daughter was in a bad marriage.

[Column 823]

However, she kept silent.

This is how our father's first days in Czyzewo appeared, according to what we heard in various interrupted conversations in the house. However, we do not know if our grandmother gave him, her son–in–law, our father, rolls for breakfast or if our father, having no other choice, became accustomed to and adapted to eating the rustic brown bread. On the contrary we know that at the time of the first Days of Awe a sharp incident occurred between the son–in–law and the father–in–law, which led to the first serious calamities.

Although my grandfather was not a very fervid Hasid, he would go to his rebbe every Rosh Hashanah and proposed then that his young son–in–law go with him.

My father, the son of a *misnagid* [opponent of Hasidism], categorically refused. There was a sharp exchange of words and my grandmother became involved, saying that it was not worthwhile to maintain such a sick *misnagid* in their house… She proposed a *get* [religious divorce].

Rayzl Kirszenbojm

Her daughter, our good–hearted mother, already had love for her husband and in no way did she want to hear about a get.

However, the atmosphere in the house again became heated and father–in–law and mother–in–law decided to provide money for the son–in–law to become his own boss.

Thus it happened that our parents were able to open the first tearoom and guesthouse at the Czyzewo train station.

Thousands of people, merchants and wagon drivers, well–bred Jews and artisans, [Hasidic] rebbes and rabbis came into our guesthouse. Our teahouse was designated as a meeting place for arriving brides and grooms. Banquets were held there for weddings and in honor of a *siem* celebration of the completion of new Torah scroll. They would come to us from neighboring shtetlekh, particularly from Wysokie and Zaromb. Our guesthouse had a good reputation in the entire area.

[Column 824]

Our mother was the one mainly occupied with the tearoom. Our father ran large businesses, was a wholesale grain merchant and was involved with loading and unloading wagons. In addition, he never refused to accept a task on behalf of the community–at–large. He was the *gabai* [assistant to the rabbi] at the house of prayer. And he always found time to read a religious book. He was beloved for his honesty and affability. He was esteemed and loved for his erudition and his good, humane traits and his constant smile.

In our memory remains his quiet and mild persona, which glowed with love for the family and with good will and devotion. He believed in the victory

Brocha Kirszenbojm

of good over evil and that God would not allow Hitler to annihilate His people.

[Column 825]

They remained in Czyzewo their entire lives until the liquidation and [they] perished at the hands of the Nazi murderers in Szulborze and Auschwitz.

[Column 826]

May our few words serve as an eternal headstone for our unforgettable parents, brothers and sisters.

Reported by:

Itsl Kirszenbojm, New York
Gitl Kirszenbojm–Cukert, Kfar Saba
Sura Kirszenbojm, Tel Aviv
Shalom Kirszenbojm, Tel Aviv

[Column 825]

Reb Mendel, the Son of Israel–Shlomo

by Dov Gorzalczany

Translated by Gloria Berkenstat Freund

Only a few people knew that his family name was Glina.

At the end of the 19th century, he inherited the windmill from his father, which he ran with his sons until 1915. However, when the Russian military withdrew from Czyzewo during the First World War, his mill and the three other windmills [in Czyzewo] disappeared in smoke.

Reb Mendel already was in Russia when the mill burned. He had succeeded in escaping with the last troop formation. In general, Reb Mendel was strongly sympathetic to Russia. He showed this during the years of the Russo–Japanese War. He was a constant opponent of the well–known "Moshel Japonczyk," who was against the Russians.[1]

Reb Mendel did not lick any honey [did not have an easy life] and he was homeless in the vast, raging Russia. Over the three years that he was in Russia, he was the *shamas* [assistant] to a local "rebbe" and he could live on his income, although he was very impoverished. Returning to Czyzewo in 1918, he did not bring any possessions from Russia. However, he brought with him a *shlal* [large number] of stories and tales.

[Column 826]

I remember only one of his stories, which Reb Mendel loved to repeat at every opportunity and I provide it here:

It happened in the same year when the tsar was overthrown. One of his most esteemed and richest Hasidim came to the rebbe. It should be understood that Reb Mendel immediately led him into the innermost and most important place, right to the rebbe, as with everyone like him. But in a short time, the Hasid came out of the rebbe's reception room agitated and very irritated and left without saying goodbye, also forgetting to give the *shamas* a "going away present. When he, Reb Mendel, later was alone with the rebbe, he asked the rebbe what had happened and what did it mean, why had the Hasid been so upset?

The rebbe explained:

– The Hasid had proposed his son as a groom for the rebbe's daughter and [the rebbe] rejected the proposal without delay.

– How is it possible? – Reb Mendel wondered. The richest man among the Hasidim, a well–known merchant, a big manufacturer. It is said that he possessed perhaps 250 factories, such wealth, such a good match. How is it possible that the rebbe dismissed it? The rebbe answered in this way: "My 250… there are many, many more dear for me than 250 factories.

[Column 827]

And Reb Mendel added:

Although the rebbe had perhaps no more than 250 Hasidim [followers], he had great inspiration. And a short time after the story the Bolshevik Revolution made a ruin of the Hasid's possessions and of his mill.

After returning to Czyzewo from Russia, Reb Mendel no longer showed any initiative. He maintained himself with a small teaching position. However, he was a presence at all communal occurrences. For example, I remember:

Reb Mendel stood in a circle of various people in the middle of the large market, very angry at the incorrect and dishonest tax evaluation. To my question about how much the estimate had been, he answered, nothing

–So, I asked again, why are you shouting, Reb Mendel?

–This is still too much, he replied with a tit for a tat.

The Jew had an eloquence, a really amazing thing. If he had only wanted to, he could purify a crawling animal with 150 impurities and if it really pleased him he could make the red heifer[2] impure with mere words.

Reb Mendel did not lack time. Therefore, he carried on conflicts with young and old, openly, in the Hasidic *shtibl* [one–room house of prayer] and wherever he found someone. His constant "partner in conflict," Reb Yudel Wapniak (he traded in lime), built a house. Reb Mendel asked him:

[Column 828]

"From where and from what?"

– One walks around, Reb Yudel answered him.

– So, let me try, said Reb Mendel. He stood up and began walking back and forth.

From this you can build? – he asked.

Or during the constant debates with the socialists:

– Why did the tsarist time not please you? Is today better? You could cook a pot of noodles for five kopekes and today there is scarcity. May God protect and save us.

Reb Mendel had a completely different theory about life and death. He argued, "It is not true that death is unavoidable; dying is just by chance. Whoever it happens to, it catches up with him. The old die; the young die, middle aged and, God preserve us, even children. Everything is nothing more than chance and not a must.

And Reb Mendel actually was correct. In 1940, he and his wife were sent out and this time in a sealed troop transport to the Soviet Union, somewhere very deep in distant Kazakhstan and as long as packages of food could be sent from Czyzewo, Reb Mendel and his wife, Nekha, could labor on the cold Soviet steppes. But after the occupation of Czyzewo by the Nazi hordes for the second time in June 1941, help ended from his home city and both old people, Reb Mendel and Nekha, breathed out their souls and left their bones somewhere on the distant cold steppes.

Actually, true, an "accident." May his soul rest in peace!

Translator's Notes:

1. Japonczyk is Polish for a Japanese male
2. The ashes of a red heifer without impurities were used for ritual purification during the time of the Temple in Jerusalem.

[Column 829]

Reb Fishl Lubelczyk

by Bat–Sheva and Shlomo

Translated from Hebrew by Gloria Berkenstat Freund

Reb Fishl Lubelczyk was the third generation of the main branch of the Lubelczyk family that settled near the Czyzewo train station just when the train line was built.

There were three brothers: Shlomo, Chaim and Yudel. Shlomo and his wife, Sheva–Ita, had four sons and two daughters. The oldest son, Yisrael–Nakhman left Czyzewo during the First World War, evacuated to Russia and returned to Warsaw from there, began trading and ran a large business. Of his family branches, only one son, Dovid, remained near the station where he continued to handle the shipping until the end at the outbreak of the Second World War.

Sheva–Ita Lubelczyk
See the picture of Shlomo Lubelczyk on page 86

[Column 830]

The second son, Mordechai, also moved to Warsaw after the First World War and became known in the commercial world. He and almost his entire family later emigrated to *Eretz–Yisrael* and he died here in deep old age.

The third son, Avraham–Berl, and his wife, Yakha, left in 1915 in the flow of refugees to Russia from which they never returned.

Fishl, Avraham–Berl's only son, was born in 1890 and had a good upbringing with his father. As an experienced merchant, he raised his only son for Torah and commerce. As a young man of 18, he [Fishl] was betrothed to the daughter of a well–known rich and well–established man from Serock [Poland], Yisrael Yankel Zabuski, a distinguished family, large forest merchant and contractor for the Russian government.[1]

This Reb Yisrael–Yankel was the main provider of building materials for the construction of the Kierbedzia Bridge between Warsaw and Praga over the Vistula River.

Fishl Lubelczik lived in the city; he continued to carry on his father's business and before the First World War he had great contact with the large cities and giant Russia from which he brought various food items.

[Column 831]

After the rise of new Poland, his mother Yakha, a smart and good–natured woman, of good ancestry, a granddaughter of Reb Yerukhem Altshuler, famous *gaon* [sage], Bodker rabbi and one of the four sages who were called the "*Arba Khayot*," returned from Russia. Hundreds of Jews from the area would make a pilgrimage for the *yahrzeits* [anniversary of a death] of the four.[2]

[Column 832]

His [Fishl's] wife, Elka and the children also returned with his mother. At the time of the German occupation, Fishl remained alone in Czyzewo because he could not manage to leave. He eventually built one of the most beautiful houses in the *shtetl* on the main street.

His house was known as an open house for visitors, for all local charitable purposes. He always was one of the first donors.

At the start, he prayed in the large, city house of prayer, which was built during his term as a *dozor* [member of the synagogue council] and with his active participation. Later, he went to pray in the Aleksander *shtibl* [small, one–room house of prayer].

[Column 833]

His father was not a fervid Hasid, but he would travel to the Otwocker [Rebbe] from time to time. Given that there was no Otwocker *shtibl* in Czyzewo, he went to the Aleksander [*shtibl*], where he occupied a distinguished place. He was again elected to the *kehile* [Jewish community] council.

As a sympathizer of the Zionist movement and a member of *Mizrakhi* [religious Zionist], he later took part in founding the *Kheder Metukan* [modern religious school]. He was generous with his donations to Zionist funds.

Yerukhem and Elka Lubelczyk

Yokheved Lubelczyk

He tried to raise his children as religiously observant and intelligent people. He was one of the few who sent his children to study in the *gymnazie* [secondary school] in Lomza and Lublin.

There were four children in the home. Two of them are in Israel. His daughter, Leah–Gitl and her husband Yehuda perished at the hands of the Nazis. The youngest son, Avraham–Berl, fell at the front, fighting in the ranks of the Soviet army, immediately on the first day after the attack on White Russia by the Hitlerists. The father and mother perished at Auschwitz, may the Lord avenge their blood.

[Column 834]

Leah–Gitl and Avraham–Berl Lubelczyk

Translator's notes:

1. The Avraham–Berl mentioned in this paragraph is Fishl Lubelczyk's father. Fishl's third son, who carried the same name, was named after Fishl's father.

2. *Arba Khayot* – the four creatures, often referred to as the "angels of fire, who hold up God's throne."

[Column 833]

Memories

The Jewish Town that Was Destroyed

by Yerucham HaLevi–Kopiec of Tel Aviv

Translated from Hebrew by Jerrold Landau

There are fruits that ripen in the middle of the summer, and there are fruits that ripen only in the late autumn. There are flowers that blossom in their full beauty during the spring, and there are flowers that display their beauty when the breath of winter can already be felt.

So too the garden of childhood, from which we have already been expelled, opens its gates for us with childhood memories that are always precious to us. Now, they elicit great love from us in our era, the era of the worst atrocities within the history of martyrology of the People of Israel.

[Column 834]

We are the children and siblings of those who suffered the tortures of hell and who were murdered with hellish deaths; those forced into ghettos and death camps and who were cast into pits and bushes poisoned with the venom of the snakes of Europe; those into whom the human beasts of the land of Germany – the land in which the cradle of culture and spirit stood – stuck their monstrous talons.

From the time that news of the annihilation of the Jewish population of Europe began to arrive, the thought arose to set up a memorial monument to both the great ones of the nation and the simple folk; to a Jewish town in which we saw pure warm-hearted people of pure faith – people with pious souls, souls that we all know, and with whom we were raised.

[Column 835]

In those day, the childhood years – we lived in the era of the Garden of Eden. Our childhood cradle stood in the Jewish town before we ate of the Tree of Knowledge and discovered that we were naked, before we knew the stormy sea of life. At that time, did we know to pay attention and understand the life in the small town? During difficult days, childhood memories rooted in a Jewish town float before us. At that time, how great are the rays of light and warmth that penetrate our hearts!

Then, when we were children, our small world was full of content and change. Now, we see those days with their full splendor and glory, with the power to awaken within us deep experiences and strong longing.

The cheder in which we studied, in which we were raised and spent the days of our childhood – how many pleasant feelings enter our hearts as we remember it.

The new generation that did not know the *cheder*, the romanticism in it, and only looks at the external form, the "shell" rather than the "content" is astonished with us as we speak of these "strange" things and express these "unusual" feelings of our hearts.

If we look at the Jewish family life of the town, we uncover love, dedication, wholesomeness, and the ideal life. Unconsciously, the call bursts forth from your heart: How much light, joy, and festivity exalts the soul.

It is difficult for us to portray on paper the full image of the Jewish town. It is impossible to describe in a plastic manner the town; whose soul was greater than its body and whose content exceeded its externals. The joy of commandments in the town, how much sublime beauty can one find there. When we look into it, we see a broad portrait of local Jewish life. The simple, natural life of the Jewish street had not yet been disrupted by inter–generational battles.

After we survey it and see the special importance and greatness f the Jewish town in various realms of life, we understand that we have exited from one world into another, from the world of the past to the word that is springing forth from the ruins of the previous world, the world of yesterday. This exit was not due to a rebellion against the former, the old, but rather due to the paths of life that opened before us.

[Column 836]

This is like a person who leaves his parental home to go afar. On the porch, he turns around and gives a final glance, a long, focused glance, a glance of longing, a glance suffused with pain and grief over the house inside, in which the memories of early childhood remain, for imprints of life that once was, and is no longer.

Czyzewo – One Among Many

By Pinchas Frydman of Ramat Gan

Translated from Hebrew by Jerrold Landau

It was a pure Jewish town, one of many in the Diaspora of Poland.

Before me pass the days of my youth, the time that I spent among all those noble personalities who placed their stamp upon the character of the town.

I wish to recall two unique individuals who influenced me and others like me. The first is Reb Yechiel Asher Prawda, may G–d avenge his blood.

He was my teacher and guide in the doctrine of Zionism. He was one of the few progressive people in our town and our generation, "the final generation of slavery, and the first for redemption." He was a scholarly Jew, a scion of a Hassidic family. He observed the commandments of G–d faithfully, and with a pure heart. He was the first founder and chief spokesman of Mizrachi in our town. He gathered around him *Beis Midrash* youth who were seeking new horizons, and brought them into the concept of Zionism. He had a strong belief in the justice of his path. He was the living example of an activist with many activities. He was of clean hands and upright heart. He gathered crowds in public and preached to them on the topic of the redemption of the Land. He comported himself in the manner of the early Hassidim who never concerned themselves with their private affairs. He neglected all his private affairs and dedicated himself to communal needs with no thought of receiving remuneration. He was always ready to help and guide, even when he was overly busy. His opponents caused him pain on more than one occasion, and he accepted everything with love. He was revered by his friends who expressed love and appreciation to him. He dreamed all his days of *aliya* to the Land of Israel, and did not merit… He remained in the vale of murder. May G–d avenge his blood.

Reb Moshe Hershman, may G–d avenge his blood.

[Column 837]

The Tzadik, the young son of my revered teacher Reb Baruch Melamed, should be remembered eternally. He was a noble young man graced with a progressive spirit. A mysterious spirit covered his face. He went into seclusion, dreamed, and prophesied discretely. He was a Hassid of Kock. His entire essence spoke, "G–d is the L–rd, and there is no other than Him."

We worshipped together in the Hassidic House. His preparation for prayers took longer than the entire public prayer service. He would mention the elder Admor of Kock with awe during his conversations. It was as if he stripped off his materialism and fluttered in the heights. His face was pale even without this. He would become even more pale as he overflowed with Hassidic words. In his opinion, this is what brought the fire to ignite the hidden point in the heart of every Jew, so that he will sense the truth of "There is none other than He."

[Column 838]

I wanted to know other paths…

I did not add understanding… but I always revered that noble soul from previous generations that dwelled in the pure body of that youth.

[Column 837]

My Town on Weekdays and Festivals

By Ahron Jablonka of Tel Aviv

Translated from Hebrew by Jerrold Landau

The town of Czyzewo is situated on the railway line from Warsaw to Vilna, 70 kilometers from Białystok, and not far from the vale of murder in Treblinka, the furnace of destruction and annihilation.

As a neighbor of tens of similar towns scattered along the bustling railway line, Czyzewo was also connected to all those who found their paths to the central cities of the country such as far–off Warsaw, Łódź, and Danzig, as well as to the Jewish centers such as Białystok, Baranovich, and Vilna on the other side of the line.

Only two kilometers separated between the houses of the town and the railway station – between the quiet, idyllic town and the railway tracks upon which trains led by engines plied the lines day and night, with their echoing, elongated whistles. They frightened the town and left black billows of smoke in the air that could have affected the lungs of the townsfolk, had it not been for the fresh winds that blew them in all directions.

a)

Czyzewo was a small town. Most of its houses were wooden, built in the village style of that day. Most were one story high. Their ample gardens were covered with wooden shingles handmade by the expert in that craft in the town and the district, Reb Yankel Pesha–Yutes, or as he was called by others, "Yankel the Dreier" or "Yankel the Rebbe's."

[Column 838]

The houses were crowded and paired up next to each other. Their common walls embraced each other. When we would look up to the rows of houses and buildings, it would seem to us that even the few that were built on the streets surrounded by fences with spaces between them were leaning over in order to connect to each other, as if they wanted to move themselves by force, to crowd together more, and to close up the breaches, thereby leaving no empty space between them, to live together in accordance with the adage "two are better than one"[1]. It was as if they wanted to join forces in the wake of the storms and thunder, to put up a strong stand, so that they will never be uprooted from the world of the living. It was as if the walls felt sensed some sort of mysterious sense of the future – of the destruction that would take place.

Several new, modern, two or three story, stone houses stood up straight among the low houses in the center of the city. They stood out as children of giants, as Nephilim[2]. They prided themselves in a haughty manner above all the houses of the town.

The house of Reb Zevulun Grosbard stood at the corner of the railway station (Kalia Gasse) at the end of the row of houses. He ran his coffee house and inn from that house.

[Column 839]

The wagon drivers and porters of the town set up their place in it and around it. Reb Zevulun was a quiet, modest man, and a scholar. He was the town administrator, and in the final years before the Holocaust, also the head of the community. He was held in honor and appreciation by all strata of the town population. Fate fell specifically to him to be the one who ran an inn that catered primarily to the wagon drivers and porters. It was specifically him who was forced to listen to the words of their mouths throughout the day until a late hour at night, and to pretend that he was "not listening."

Two covered towers in the middle of the marketplace in the center of town formed the business center. The bustle due to an abundance of business was not particularly great. The shopkeepers were free to stand outside alone or in small groups to wait for a customer, or to engage in a brief conversation on some topic between customers – on daughters who reached marriageable age and for whom a match must be found, on sons studying in *Yeshivos* in far–off towns and who have already reached marriageable age. From family matters, they would move on to general world matters, current events of the town, commentary on the days news of the country or of the world – to didactic discussions on Torah, Hassidic stories, one of the jokes of Reb Yudel Wapniak with the sense of humor, or, a witticism of Reb Mendel Yisrael–Shlomo's, the wise man of the town. The latter was a professional arbitrator who would straighten out and resolve all the disputes of the townsfolk. However, when a customer appeared from afar, the conversation would end, and the group would immediately disband.

b)

Our town appeared as a small, grey community during the six weekdays. However, in truth, a special feeling could be felt, of tradition and piety along with alertness to what was taking pace in the study halls. In later years, the worshippers of the Hassidic prayer halls also opened a large window in the heavy, rusty iron gates that closed them off. They carefully followed the national struggle that was taking place and had conquered thousands of Jewish communities throughout Poland in its storm. Many of their sons later became the builders and actualizers within the young, national camp that arose within this bustling Jewry. Despite the constant dispute between the Hassidim and Misgagdim [opponents of Hassidism], as well as internal struggles within Hassidism, the residents lived under one roof, with one city rabbi, Rabbi Shmuel David Zabludower, whose influential personality intervened and solved every dispute and struggle.

[Column 840]

The Jews of the community of Czyzewo forged a well–rooted Jewish way of life for themselves. Aside from the study of Torah, they occupied themselves in benevolent deeds, giving of charity in a discrete fashion, and especially in tending to guests.

Tens of poor guests from the scattered towns always appeared at the *Beis Midrash* and Hassidic houses of worship on Sabbath eves. They would stand silently around the porcelain ovens or lean against the western wall, with thoughts about their family members whom they were forced to leave behind, for they did not have enough money to buy them even a dry morsel of bread. They were wondering if they would be invited to a Sabbath meal. In the end, however, these suspicions were for naught, for the gabbaim [trustees] concerned themselves with this matter while it was still day. While there was still time, they recorded the number of guests in the *Beis Midrashes* and *shtibels*. This endeavor was a full partnership, natural and devoid of any anger. It broke down the barriers between Hassidim and *misnagdim*, and between Hassidim of Gur, Aleksander, and others. A single, unified spirit pulsated in the hearts of everybody.

The service of welcoming of the Sabbath concluded, and the worshippers would return to their houses. The Jews of Czyzewo strolled peacefully though the quiet streets of the town, with their children and guests accompanying them at their side. Almost every householder was accompanied by a guest. They appeared as children of angels, as literal angels – for "this day is honored about all days, for the Rock of the Worlds rested on it."[3]

The two dear, sublime images of Reb Zanwil Edelsztajn and Reb Berish Frydman, may their memories be a blessing, stood out above them all. They were always the last to exit from the house of worship after the Sabbath eve service. This was due to the concern lest a guest be forgotten and left behind without being invited to a Sabbath meal. Then, they would be prepared to host them in addition to their other guests. The number of guests was no issue at all. It was as if the walls of the houses expanded themselves at the beginning of the Sabbath to enable the hosting of any number of guests. It was as if the walls were making efforts to take part in the commandment of hosting guests, thereby exalting the Sabbath Queen.

[Column 841]

c)

Apparently, Czyzewo was a town like hundreds of other such towns in the country, devoid of horizons and depth. It did not have a *Yeshiva* or a *gymnasja* [high school]. Therefore, many of the youth left and wandered to distant places of Torah, whereas those who remained were forced to acquire knowledge through their own initiative through various groups and correspondence. Despite the lack of conditions and means for organized education, the town was blessed with youth of natural, rooted intelligence.

This youth, educated in the *Beis Midrashes* and *Yeshivos* for the most part, without recognized degrees or external crowns, had been forged through the internal, glowing flame, and were graced with a constant desire for spiritual elevation.

They left the *Beis Midrash* and the *shtibel* due to the storms of the years, however, they did not abandon the Hassidic spark. It was carried inside of them and accompanied them on all their paths.

Wherever they wandered, the always carried the memory of their youth and connection to their hometown on the tablet of their hearts. Even with a distance of thousands of kilometers and after several decades, and especially after the terrible destruction, the town still stands before their eyes as in previous times.

These are not just blurred memories, but living memories of the childhood landscape. They arise anew from beneath the threshold of our daily lives, and shine before our eyes with their colors. Decades have already passed, and the hidden source of memories, experiences, and childhood and youthful impressions that have been hidden as if forever open to us. Excavations, excavations, each of which raises pages of love and disappointment, wounds that healed and were forgotten, and once again… we feel their pain.

d)

The town of Czyzewo stands out among tens of medium size villages surrounding it on all sides. Since it was close to the railway line, it served in a natural fashion as a center of marking the produce of the villages, and provided them with all their needs. The business connections and friendly relations between the Jews of the town and their gentile neighbors were conducted for many generations in simplicity, as if the matter was established from the six days of creation. It never entered the mind of any of them that this ancient order would ever change.

[Column 842]

A picture is drawn before my eyes – containing my father and brother Yaakov of blessed memory, and at times even my elder brothers, may they live, Bucze and Yisrael. They would be meeting a landowner or farmer with a farm on Friday afternoon, whom would be treated with delicacies for the Sabbath, and especially with a respectable glass of liquor after the gefilte fish prepared by our late mother of blessed memory, the diligent and dedicated wife. They warmed up so much that their stuffed faces reddened from great pleasure, as their mouths did not cease to utter words of praise for the taste and aroma of the Jewish Sabbath delicacies.

From this perspective, our house was not alone, but rather one of the many who acted in such a fashion.

The rainbow of livelihood of the Jews of Czyzewo was variegated. There were merchants, shopkeepers, tradesmen, small–scale industrialists, wagon drivers, porters, and laborers – simple people of dark toil who served each other to the extent of their ability and talents, in accordance with their trades and employers. Most of them inherited their trades from grandfather to father, and from father to son.

They would often go out to the villages of the area and even farther afield for commerce or labor. They would often remain in the villages for the entire week. On Fridays, one could meet tradesmen returning home, resting at the side of the road or in a field after a week of backbreaking work and a journey by foot of tens of kilometers with their thick knapsack (a gift from the farmer, his employer) on his bent back.

The two regular market days, Tuesday and Friday, served for the merchants who went outside the town for livelihood as a sort of early meeting place with the farmers. The farmers would come to the town market with their produce. Immediately after exchanging good morning greetings with the farmer, the Jew would be invited up to the wagon, and the business would be conducted as they traveled. If they did not succeed in concluding the business before they arrived at the edge of the town, the Jew would not leave the farmer, but would accompany him to the market as they discussed business.

The merchants of the town, especially the small–scale ones, were never wealthy. They struggled hard for their day–to–day existence. Most of them only managed thanks to the charity and the loans that they received from friends, acquaintances, or the town bank. They always struggled to obtain the sums to pay back loans or to pay for necessary purchases.

[Column 843]

Those who were more firmly based tended to their livelihoods by anticipating what was to come. They conducted themselves as merchants with a developed sense, who understood the need to invest a long time with a perspective requiring patience.

As in all aspects of life, the adage "cast your bread upon the waters"[1] applied in commerce.

e)

Different eras passed over the Jews of Czyzewo in their difficult struggle for existence for their staff of bread. However, the final period before the Second World War, from 1936–1939, was more severe than the previous eras. The anti–Semitism that spread throughout Poland at that time, and was supported overtly or covertly by the authorities throughout the entire country and in all aspects of life; the persecutions; the general boycott; and the deliberate displacement of Jews from their sources of livelihood – none of this, of course, passed over Czyzewo. The evil winds of hatred and disparagement toward the Jews of the town began to blow among the gentiles – both among those in town and the farmers of the region. The boycott and terror increased constantly. Guards were placed outside Jewish businesses and shops to prevent the gentiles from having any business contact with Jews.

In response to the appeal of the Jewish Sejm representatives to the interior minister of Poland, the minster declared loudly to all the elected officials:

"To physically strike, no; to boycott, of course."

Thus, the boycott in Poland received public affirmation from the elected officials of the state.

This declaration, "to boycott, of course," spread as quickly as lightening and ripened the seeds of poison that had found fertile ground on the soil of Poland. The Jews of Czyzewo felt its stringent meaning on their skin and flesh.

The transition from this declaration to actual violence did not take long. An attack against the Jews broke out on the market day of January 5, 1937. The results were one casualty and many injuries. Hillel Zelig Jelin, may G–d avenge his blood, fell on that day.

He was one of the powerful men of the town. He was the first victim in the town during the era before the outbreak of the Second World War – before the approach of the terrible, bloody storm.

[Column 844]

In effect, this was a hint to the nearby western neighbor. A clear hint with an obvious echo:

"The soil of Poland is a sure ground for your Satanic plans!"

Indeed, the enemy, may their names be blotted out, understood the call correctly. After the conquest of 1939, it chose the soil of Poland as the comfortable stage to carry out its plans – as the central place for the death camps, the crematoria, and the burning of the bodies of its victims.

For many decades, through many generations, the Jews of the town forged a modest way of life with a populist bent. They were always whole in their body and calm in spirit, until the troops of Hitler arrived and destroyed everything with the wipe of a murderous hand.

Czyzewo my town, they washed the stones of your roads with rivers of pure blood.

The traditional friendship and business relations that existed with their gentile neighbors for many generations did not stand up for the Jews of Czyzewo on the day of trial and test, just as they did not stand for all the Jews in the hundreds and thousands of other communities of Poland and in the other lands of Nazi occupied Europe. Our town was wiped off the face of the earth without any remnant and memorial of what was. It was destroyed and uprooted completely. It was destroyed to its foundation, along with all its multi–colored, lovely, and bustling life. It once was…

It was the 8th of Av, 5701 (1941).

That night, shortly after midnight, the Jews of the town were summoned together with their elderly, women, and children. They were hauled and beaten, as they were accompanied by tens of armed S.S. men to the central market square. Rabbi David Zabludower, may G–d avenge his blood, the rabbi of the community, was among them, paralyzed and bedridden. Approximately 1,800 Jews stood in the square, subdued and in despair. They stood and waited, forlorn, for their final moments, until they were hauled by the murderers to the communal pit of death that had been prepared from them along the road from Czyzewo to Zromow in the village of Szulborze.

The communal death pit in the village of Szulborze on the main Czyzewo–Zromow road swallowed up everything. It is not possible for us to come to supplicate over this mass grave and to pour out our bitter words.

[Column 845]

Indeed, there is no stone or marble monument over you, the martyrs of Czyzewo. It is not stone or marble that will perpetuate the holy memory of our parents, siblings, relatives and friends that are dear to us. The pages of this memorial book are dedicated to all of you as a community and to each of you as individuals, as limbs of a family – of a single family that unified its life together and gave up its soul in holiness and purity.

[Column 846]

Let the pages of this Yizkor Book serve as a monument and memorial candle burning in the "Holocaust chamber"[5] in our hearts. It will be a monument and eternal flame for many generations to lament over the small, wonderful community that was and is no more.

Translator's notes:

1. Kohelet [Ecclesiastes] 4:9.
2. See https://en.wikipedia.org/wiki/Nephilim
3. From one of the Sabbath hymns.
4. Kohelet [Ecclesiastes] 11:1. retn
5. This is a play on words, as Martef Hashoah (Holocaust Chamber or Cellar) is a Holocaust memorial institution in Jerusalem that preceded Yad Vashem. See https://www.martefhashoah.org/

[Column 845]

The Bridge

By Eliahu Gora of Tel Aviv

Translated from Hebrew by Jerrold Landau

Twenty years ago, we both stood on the bridge and took photographs for the eternal memory of us and those that will come after. This was the last time that we walked upon it.

I recall our house, the last and the first in the town, that stood next to the bridge over the small, clear river that wound over several kilometers and poured into the large Bug River.

For the small handful of Jews who lived in Czyzewo, our town was a small fortress in the midst of a large forest of many villages populated by Polish–Christian farmers. The bridge was the boundary.

The bridge reminds me of many fine, pleasant memories, as well as difficult, gloomy memories.

I recall before Passover, when the rabbi of blessed memory went out with the communal notables in the evening to draw water[1] for the matzo *shmura* for Passover. How lovely and pleasant was this ceremony, which was an honor to all of us. I will never forget the splendid procession on Rosh Hashanah for *Tashlich*. The entire town, from young to old, women and children, walked with *machzorim* [festival prayer books] in their hands to pour out their prayers to G–d, that He forgive their sins and grant them a good, fortunate year.

I recall how the entire neighborhood went every day with their kitchen utensils and pots in their hands to wash and clean the dishes. They also went to the river with their laundry. Everyone would choose a stone for themselves to beat the laundry with a wooden handle.

I recall how groups of children and adults went in the summer to bathe in the river via the bridge and the fields far from the town so that they would be safe from the gentiles who would attack us from time to time.

[Column 846]

I will never forget the groups of children and women who would gather the sorrels (szczaw) in the fields. Who can describe the beautiful evenings and nights when the older youth would stroll in groups or couples over the bridge between the two rows of trees, to the road to the grove leading to the house of the landowner of our area. They called it: the valley of kisses… The intimate conversations on lovely moonlight nights while sitting on the roots of tree stumps. The murmur of conversation was swallowed in the sound of the trees surrounding us.

We will not forget the classes that we studied over a long period: Spinoza's Ethics. The clear, fresh air around us helped. We absorbed many secrets amongst the avenues and trees behind the bridge along the route that led to the house of the landowner. It was life, grace, joy, happiness, love, and disappointment. All this was uprooted by the cruel hand of the Nazi enemy with the assistance of Polish anti–Semites. All this was erased forever.

How can I not recall the songs that we sang in groups and pairs – songs of love, songs of the homeland, Polish songs, in Hebrew and Yiddish. Their echoes could be hard afar, and blended with the nature and the songs of the birds around.

Similarly, I recall the time when I saw together with my friends, as we read books and debated about entire worlds and sublime ideas, about how to step out to greet the life of the future.

Translator's note:

1. Literally "Mayim Shelanu" which means "Water that has remained" i.e. water that has remained overnight. According to Jewish law, the preferred way to bake matzos is with water drawn in the evening, and left overnight to cool.

[Column 847]

The Footsteps of the Early Ones

By Yerachmiel Eliasz of Moshav Chibat Zion

Translated from Hebrew by Jerrold Landau

A monument to my late sister Esther of blessed memory As I recall my small town of Czyzewo, with it streets and alleyways, the Zionist youth, and especially the fathers of the youths with warm Jewish hearts, happy to hear any greeting from the Land. And who did not have at least one family member in the Land?

My heart pines inside of me, in which today only a memory of all that was good and precious remains. I further recall when Esther of blessed memory became connected with the Zionist youth chapter of Czyzewo despite the opposition of Uncle Yaakov–Pinchas, despite his promise that he would send her soon to the Beis Yaakov teachers' seminary in Krakow. Despite the charm of this promise, it was not attractive to her, and she chose something "actual." The connection with this Hashomer Haleumi youth movement stemmed from the Zionist idea. This concept existed with all the youth, including Esther.

The principal activists among the General Zionist youth movement at that time were: Dov Gorzalczany, Yitzchak Szlaski, and Aryeh Gorzalczany (all in Israel). The best of the youth of the town were gathered in this movement. The counselors gave the best of their time during the days and nights. They also did not spare their money, especially to maintain the headquarters where the people would gather every evening to learn and teach.

During the evenings, when I went out to the street and heard the rejoicing and song bursting forth from the headquarters, I would find myself inadvertently standing next to the windows, peering in and being jealous of those who merited to be inside that building. I followed in Esther's footsteps not long after she joined the movement. I joined the Zionist youth movement.

[Column 848]

Thus, I too merited to be guided, and, within a brief period, to be a counsellor.

As a member of the Zionist youth, I was faithful to the movement. The opposition was very so strong that it did not make sense. However, honoring our parents remained our chief concern. Every younger or older youth with self–respect would be very careful to avoid angering and vexing their parents. This was especially expressed by going to the *Beis Midrash* on the Sabbath and festivals. All the youth from all factions would fill the synagogues and shtibels only out of concern for the honor of their mothers and fathers. After the festive Sabbath meal, the youth would go out to the streets bedecked in their shiny uniforms – each movement with its own colors.

Esther Eliasz

It is too much to describe today.

My great dedication to the youth movement can be seen from the following story:

One day, the Hashomer Hadati chapter of Czyzewo set itself up. Out of fear that the new chapter would attract members from our ranks, we decided to perform a brazen act: to steal the flags of Hashomer Hadati. This is what happened:

[Column 849]

All the members of Beitar were invited to a large celebration organized by the chapter of Hashomer Hadati, but the members of Hanoar Hatzioni were not invited. We knew that the main point of this celebration was the inauguration of the flags of the groups. We decided to steal the flags and destroy them, so that there will not be much value to the celebrations (or so I thought in my naivete). One night, Hershel Belfer of blessed memory, Alter Landau, and I broke into the chapter and carried out the activity fully. At that time, I felt that I had performed a daring and "patriotic" act.

[Column 850]

My sister Esther of blessed memory made *aliya* to the Land shortly after I did. We remained faithful to our Zionist and pioneering education that we received in the chapter of Hanoar Hatzioni in Czyzewo. We spent our first years on a Kibbutz. This was a time of disturbances in the Land. A difficult life of toil and defense activities were the lot of every lad in the Yishuv. We too went through all this with strength and pride, thanks to the nationalist ideals that we absorbed into out blood there in our small town of Czyzewo… Honor to its memory.

[Column 849]

My Small Town

By Dalia Schneiderman of Tel Aviv

Translated from Hebrew by Jerrold Landau

It was the warm hours of the afternoon. The sun was in the center of the sky, beating down with heat. Nobody was seen on the streets, aside from the postman. He brought me a large, brown envelope that was sent to me, as it was to all the natives of Czyzewo, and seemed somewhat strange. It contained the request to write a composition on a specific topic about the town in which I lived many years ago, until I made *aliya* to the Land.

Suddenly, I forgot where I was. I forgot that was I was in my residence. Everything seemed dim, grey, stormy, and unclear. I was no longer in a room of my house, but rather in a small town somewhere in the expanse of Poland: I was a young girl, smiling and joyous, and strolling leisurely on the streets of our town Czyzewo. Oh, how I loved it. Everything was bustling and quaking, enthusiastic and vibrant. I know; indeed I know that my ancestors who lived there experienced disturbances and pogroms. However, this did not stop them from continuing with their lives, the life of the Jewish people in the Diaspora with its experiences and common way of living.

I then left my house. The sun peeked out of the clouds with a mischievous smile and melted the white snow that covered the roofs. The flowers and trees began to blossom, and their green color beautified the streets. I continued to stroll leisurely and arrived at the synagogue. The elders of the city could be seen through the window sitting in ne of the corners, bent over thick volumes of Gemara, as their white, splendid beards swayed with the swaying of their head. In another corner one could see the young lads, bent over books as the rebbe warns them to study and not occupy themselves with meaningless pursuits.

[Column 850]

A winter day. The home of Reb Avraham Szwarc

[Column 851]

I continued along my way and arrived the town market. Here we see the female hawkers shouting to the heavens, debating, bargaining, and announcing their merchandise with great noise. In the houses, the housewives were sitting, cleaning, washing, fixing, and polishing the old silver vessels that they had inherited from their grandmothers.

In the evening, when everyone was washed, clean, and calm after a day of work, the youth began to meet here, in the center of town, for discussion about the problems of the world. Since our youth was progressive, gaining world culture along with their own culture, with all its storms, battles, and spiritual and economic upheavals; they would arrange social gatherings and performances in the evenings. They would organize their lives on the fine side, lives of experiences, interesting culture, and contentment.

Then the Sabbath arrived. Oh! This was the wonderful day for everybody, the day when everything was clean, shiny, and sparkling. The marketplace was clean, and the sounds of the hawkers were no longer heard. The booming voice of the rebbe with his young students was no longer heard in the cheder. Everyone was joyous, happy, and content on the day of rest. This was a day that was full of splendor and holy grace. Even the trees laughed, and it was as if the color of the flowers became more beautiful, festive, and joyous.

The entire town participated in weddings. Everyone rejoiced with the joy of the bride who was wearing the traditional white gown given to her by her mother, for she too got married in the same dress. Everyone was happy when the bride became betrothed under the *chupa*. The entire town came to rejoice in her grace, for everyone was brethren, brethren in heart and soul to one nation, one religion, one town, and a common aspiration for the homeland.

This was what life was like in our town, the life of traditional Jews rooted in the land for generation after generation, a life of happiness and joy at times interrupted with sorrow and weeping.

Despite all this, everyone aspired to leave, to leave the place where generation after generation had lived, for the Jewish spark was never quenched, and the hope to return from the Diaspora to the Holy Land continued to burn. Indeed, many left the town. Then, the terrible enemy came, murdering women, children, and men without mercy, and without leaving a survivor. These people fell upon the altar of their nation without any fault on their part. These were people whose full desire was to make *aliya* to the Land of their fathers, and they did not merit to do so – good, upright people whose place of burial we do not even know – people who had warm, pure, Jewish hearts.

[Column 852]

Again, the same silly, grey, stormy, non–understandable vision returned to me. I again found myself in my room sitting next to the table, writing the musings of my heart, memories, thoughts and wonderful pictures that seemed to me as literally from a dream – about the wonderful days that we had during our childhood in the small town somewhere in the expanse of Poland, a place that will never rise up again. These wonderful childhood days will never return.

Father!

By Rachel Wengorz (Gorzalczany) of Tel Aviv

Translated from Hebrew by Jerrold Landau

This took place on a day in October 1944. Snow, shiny in its whiteness, already covered the fields of Siberia. Our family consisted of three people. We lived in an old, creaky, train wagon that stood on a side railway track. My father was a political prisoner somewhere. It had already been two years since we last heard from him, and our hope of seeing him again was dwindling.

A strong wind blew outside. I was busy with housework. Suddenly, we heard the whistle of an approaching train. The children outside raised a great tumult. As would any curious 12–year–old girl, I too went outside and joined the groups of noisy children. The train stopped, and we spread out over the platform as we peppered the travelers with hundreds of questions, hoping to receive something from them.

Suddenly a bearded man wearing worn out clothing exited from one of the cars. He stopped the children one after the other and asked them if they knew where the Gorzalczany family lived. I pointed to the wagon in which we lived and returned to the group of children on the platform. Something pushed me to return and look at this man. When I turned backward, I saw the beard, and noticed that he had wrinkles under his forehead. Suddenly he stretched out his arms to me and asked in a choked voice: "My daughter, do you not recognize your father?

[Column 855]

Destruction and Holocaust

The Death of the Jewish Population in Czyzewo

by Shimon Kanc

Translated by Gloria Berkenstat Freund

Czyzewo, a *shtetl* [town; the plural is *shtetlekh*] in the Bialystok *wojewodshaft* [region or province], experienced the same fate as the other *shtetlekh* in this region. The Hitlerist occupiers also created a separate ghetto here. The life of this ghetto was not different in principle from life in all of the other ghettos of this region which were under Soviet rule until the German attack on the Soviet Union.

The Jews of this *shtetl* actually lived as if in a ghetto before the war. But despite the fact that, in the first months of the German occupation, Jews came running here from other *shtetlekh*, the Germans drove the Jews out of their houses, restricting their right to live only in several streets.

The bell that the commissar asked to have made in order to make it easier to call the people together in the middle of the night earns particular attention here. This shows that the regime in the *shtetl* knew that the ghetto would exist for many days and gave it the character of an interim camp that they could liquidate at any moment at once.

[Column 856]

The reason here was not the need of residences for the non-Jewish population because the apartments, half in ruin, burned, long stood empty. Rather it was a result of the system to torture the Jews, humiliate them with inhumane living conditions. After the first *aktsia* [action – usually a deportation], the ghetto was reduced to five houses. With the return of the escaping Jews, it [the ghetto] was given the opportunity to be used again.

At the beginning, the ghetto was not closed. The residents could move freely, go to the villages to obtain food. The Germans shut their eyes to this. This took the burden of feeding the ghetto from them. The Jews worked for absolutely no pay. After the first *aktsia* that took place on the 1st of November 1942, the ghetto was fenced in with wire. It appeared that the ghetto lasted longer than the Hitlerists had calculated for unanticipated reasons. It happened because of the necessary work carried out by the Jews.

[Column 857]

In the various ghettos in Poland there were often transfers of Jews from one ghetto to another. The Hitlerists used these policies as one of the instruments to annihilate the Jewish population, leading them to a condition of apathy and passivity.

The Germans also looked the other way and pretended not to see the arriving Jews. There was even a case when the commissar sent a special representative to the surrounding *shtetlekh* recruiting Jews for Czyzewo. The commissar did this because of a shortage of working hands. The representative came back without anything because Czyzewo was well known in the area as the place that was designated to be liquidated more quickly.

Few of the escaping Jews who wandered about on the roads and in the forests and villages decided to return to Czyzewo. Many Czyzewo Jews perished in other *shtetlekh*, murdered by the Polish gangs and local peasants.

When the war broke out there 3,000 Jewish souls in Czyzewo.

According to the witness testimonies of the survivors, over 1,500 Jews were driven out during the first *aktsia*. Later, over 2,500 souls were taken to Zambrów[Zambrów]. This shows that there were people from other *shtetlekh* in Czyzewo who came here during the first days of the war.

Despite the great poverty, the population in Czyzewo ghetto did not experience the typhus and dysentery epidemics. However, they were not spared later when they were in the Zambrówer barracks with the thousands of Jews from other *shtetlekh*.

[Column 858]

The plan of the Gestapo to liquidate the Czyzewo Jews was not distinguished by any particular preciseness. As in many other areas they economized on transport for taking them to Auschwitz and other death camps and annihilated them just several kilometers from our city.

The Hitlerists prepared the first and largest mass-*aktsia* two months before they took over the *shtetl*. It should be understood that the members of the *Judenrat* [Jewish council] did not clearly know about the plans for annihilation. They went through the houses and convinced the Jews that they should not escape because, as they were told, it was usual to be recruited for work.

This shows that just as everywhere else, the Germans also placed a great deal of thought here into the assistance of this Jewish administrative body that they installed. The methods of the *aktsia* itself also were the same. The ghetto was surrounded with a strong cordon of gendarmes, S.S. members and Ukrainian and Polish *granatowja policja* [Blue Police, popular name of the police organized by the General Government]. Driving those remaining and hidden Jews onto the collection point was first carried out by the Polish police. After them, the German S.S. members entered the residences to verify and finish the work.

The most capable were left for work in the German enterprises. The old and crippled were murdered on the spot. The faces of the Hitlerist criminals were twisted in devilish grimaces, having lost every human expression. The *aktsia* was carried out in conditions of increased terror, inhuman screams and terrible bellowing from the members of the Gestapo who operated with whips and shot blindly at innocent people, surprised and frightened. There could be no talk of the least resistance. Every thought of overt action was shut off by fear.

[Column 859]

In these conditions every initiative to escape was truly heroic. There were many cases in Czyzewo. There still lived in people a strong will to save themselves.

No civilians took part in covering the holes in Szulborze. Evidence of this is that the peasants from the surrounding villages did not clearly know about the mass murder. Rumors went around, accompanied by mysterious superstitions, about devils and specters. It appears the work was done by Polish policemen.

The peasants in the Czyzewo area, who had not lived badly with the Jewish population until the war, were under terrible fear after the second *aktsia* and, therefore, did not show the appropriate readiness to help the Jews who had escaped from the ghetto. Of the hundreds of Jews who strayed to the villages and forests, not more than several score survived; of them a number perished after the liberation in the pogrom that the Poles carried out during the first weeks of the liberation.

[Column 860]

No organized resistance took place in Czyzewo. Only several young people succeeded in reaching the partisans who fought in the Baranowiczke Woods, near Bialystok. There were cases of passive resistance that expressed itself in sabotaging the work, not registering, scorn at the Jewish policeman and the escape to the forest that did not always come as a result of fear of death. Facts show that during the *aktsia*, Jews were not aware that they were being taken to their death. During the selection no one wanted to be one of the few whom the commissar let remain. The commissar had to carry out the selection with force.

The Czyzewo ghetto did not have any contact with the ghetto in Bialystok. The young did not have any knowledge of the heroic resistance that was put up by the young Jews in Bialystok. But among those fighting in Bialystok itself were also found several Czyzewo young people. Members of the Zionist organization.

During the "Quiet" Days

The Beginning of the Second World War in Czyzewo

Yitzchak Worona

Translated by Gloria Berkenstat Freund

[Column 859]

Friday, the 1st of September 1939, around four o'clock in the morning.

[Column 860]

The larger part of the Jewish population was still absorbed in deep sleep. Only a few women, who were hurrying to prepare for *Shabbos*, were already awake. And suddenly there was a strong thunder that came closer and became stronger, noisier, but no, it was not thunder, it was airplanes; they were coming closer to Czyzewo. Then they were over the city and disappeared with frightening noise. People ran out of the houses in fear, lifted their eyes to the sky; whose airplanes were they? Polish on maneuvers? A second squadron flew in and disappeared in the direction of the first. Everyone already knew: it was war! Their mouths had not yet said this. Mothers thought of their children in the firing positions! Who knows? No one knew that the airplanes had already destroyed all of the Polish trains, all of the Polish military collection points, deep into the east.

[Column 861]

At nine o'clock the radio reported that Germany had attacked Poland without a declaration of war. The Jewish population received the news with a heavy feeling and with fear, but externally calm. So passed several days.

The mobilization was expanded, new groups, new age groups were called and, at the same time, many of the mobilized returned. There was not enough clothing for the large army, not enough weapons. Contingents came and contingents went. The scenes of departure were dreadful; mothers accompanied their children, wives led their husbands, and children held on to their fathers. All cried and mourned the fate of those mobilized who were leaving Czyzewo and, at the same time, there were reports of the first Czyzewo fallen, Feivel Wajngold, Yosl's grandson, Moshe, and still others. The same reports said that the Hilterists were marching, destroying all positions of resistance. The number of fallen Czyzewers at the front reached scores.

[Column 862]

Day after day, enemy airplanes flew over the *shtetl* and dropped incendiary bombs. This enveloped the entire *shtetl* in flames of fire. And the first victims of the bombings were: Mordechai the baker and his son, Leibush the *Szlachtchenike*'s [the generous person's] son-in-law and others, up to ten men. The mood was mournful; people went around dejected. It is impossible to describe what Czyzewo Jews lived through during the sad days. People ran like poisoned mice; they wanted to save what they could. One carried a pillow, one a piece of furniture, one a child who had fainted. The wives of the first fallen ran around demented with wild voices. The special militia drove the residents to their homes. The firemen's siren warned with an alarm that they should quickly seek protection against the incoming airplanes, until they finally became indifferent to the alarms.

A squadron of German airplanes appeared on the third of December; the street emptied quickly. Strong explosions were heard; all of the Jewish houses were immediately in flames. They could not think of slipping out of the city. Everything burned; all of the streets from one end to the other. People ran out of the burning houses. The smoke choked. They ran to the open fields and when the German tanks entered Czyzewo, the *shtetl* was already one large ruin.

An order was issued; the entire population, young and old, had to register for work. Up to the 300 people must appear each day; the work was very difficult and they were often rewarded for their heavy labor – with blows.

According to the agreement by the Germans and the Soviets, Czyzewo belonged to the Russians. The last act of the German retreat was to brutally beat everyone they encountered. When the Russians entered the *shtetl*, we wished ourselves *mazel-tov* [literally, good luck, but also used to mean congratulations].

[Column 863]

* * *

Let us be permitted to remember the names of my closest and dearest who perished at the hands of the fascistic murderers:

[Column 864]

My mother, Tsibia, my sister, Czarna, and my brother, Yudel.

May my words be a contribution to the *Sefer Matzeyvah* [*Book of Headstones*] in memory of the Czyzewer Jews who perished.

[Column 863]

Desolate Days and Nights

Yentl Kitaj

Translated by Gloria Berkenstat Freund

I am one of the very few survivors of Czyzewo from that ruthless time of annihilation.

I was then still a young girl, barely 13 years old. Where can I find the strength to report the pain of a child who sees how all of her closest were being murdered and herself looks death in the eyes every day?

How much and what I write is not significant and pales in comparison with what I lived through.

However I know that this is my duty, the sacred duty of a Czyzewer Jewish child and it is like erecting a monument, a book of headstones for our destroyed, former Jewish *shtetl* [town], Czyzewo.

Therefore, I will attempt to communicate here at least a small part of my experiences during that ruthless time.

[Column 863]

Upcoming Storm

The fate of the Czyzewer Jews was – with certain nuances – similar to the fate of the Jews in other *shtetlekh* [towns] in Poland. It was quiet in the beginning. The bullying of the Germans did not take on a mass character. When they cut off the beard from someone, gave a slap, even shot a Jew somewhere outside the city, they found some kind of reason for it. The public began to be calm and to think that "the devil was not so terrible as he was portrayed."

There began to be heard those who decried the pessimists, those who did not want to be calmed and believed that it was a

[Column 864]

bad situation. The talk of those who did not allow themselves to be thrown into melancholy began to be listened to, those who boldly and often appeared at the market and said that no community of Jews would be slaughtered.

There was no great activity in the *shtetl*. In 1939, many Jews, after their houses were burned, moved to live in the surrounding villages. Many Jews did not want to stand out and seldom left their homes.

The Death Gang

Permanent torture of the Jews of the *shtetl* began with the arrival of the commissar. Jews were driven daily to work where they had to endure various afflictions. In addition, through the *Judenrat* [council of Jews created by the Germans] the commissar imposed on the shtetl a mandatory contribution of money.

[Column 865]

It began to be said that the Death Gang, which was known for its savagery and sadism, would be coming into the *shtetl*. My cousin, Dovid Kitaj, warned me:

[Column 866]

– Go to the forest. Save yourself; I am telling you that we need to get through the war.

There was confusion when a decree was issued that all Jews, small and large, needed to appear ostensibly to travel to work. Some left the *shtetl* entirely; others consulted one another on what to do.

[Column 867]

Arguments also took place in our house, whether to appear or not.

Kraszewski, a peasant from Holdoki, an acquaintance of our father, came to our house. He saw what was going on in our house and shock appeared on his good-natured face:

– The luck that the Swabin [Germans] will give you, you will never be late for. Meanwhile come to me, Shmulke. To the village for as long as it is not a risk to our lives.

Everyone in the house agreed that we needed to go to Kraszewski.

It was quiet on the road; Jews went back and forth. Some sighed; some were hopeful that Jews would somewhere survive the calamity.

Ruchtshe Lew, whose child was murdered by a bomb, came from the village with a small leather sack. Sweat dripped from her face. She stopped and wanted to know what was happening in the *shtetl*. I told her that many Jews were escaping, hiding. Not me – she said with resolve – What happens to all of the Jews will happen to me.

We were well received in Kraszewski's home, were given food to eat, but the food stuck in our throats. Who knew what was happening with our mother? My brother, Motke, and my father consoled me that they had made arrangements with Nowicki that he would take care of her. She was sick, had to stay in bed; when the police raids stopped we would return to the *shtetl*.

The Echo of the Shooting

Thus we lived with Kraszewski in the attic and looked through the holes at the lonesome trees in the courtyard with its storage sheds and stalls. I thought about my mother, who lay alone in the house and my heart grieved but I could not cry. I knew that we must sit still, without a rustle.

[Column 868]

Suddenly, a distant bang was heard that terrified us as if the bullet could reach us. It became quiet for a while after the first bang. We soon heard another shot and several more that quickly followed one after the other and soon a faint noise of automobiles reached us and a little later heavy shooting was heard. My father murmured quietly with a lowered head:

– They are shooting with machine guns, the murderers.

When it became dark, Kraszewski came up to us. He left bread and milk for us and sighed:

– Shmulke, it is bad. I did not imagine this… We do not spread calves out [for slaughter] like this in the middle of a clear day, like here…

He stood dejected with lowered hands and explained how the Jews in Czyzewo were loaded into automobiles and driven on foot to Szulborze, to the anti-tank trenches.

From there – he ended – no one came back.

Kraszewski went down bent and we remained sitting on straw, dazed, huddled together.

Later we learned that when the *aktsia* [action, usually a deportation] had just begun, Nowicki took my mother in a wagon, told her that he was taking her to us and took her to the Shul Street where all of the Jews stood to be sent out. Immediately after, she was loaded into the automobiles with the other women.

"Where is the Jewish God?"

When everyone was standing in the street, the gendarmes and the Polish policemen began to run through the houses and pulled out whomever they found, beat and shot them. Those who watched immediately felt that something very bad was being prepared and many took advantage of the police being occupied and ran in various directions, to the villages and forests. Zisha Slucki, who is now in America, also escaped then.

[Column 869]

The Germans wanted to enjoy themselves and they began to ask about the rabbi. When they heard that he lay paralyzed, they went into his house where he lay with an open religious book near him.

– Tell us, old devil, where is the Jewish God? – They shouted with wild voices and laughter, pulled him across the ground and threw him like a pack of old rags into an automobile that was fully packed with women and children.

A *gestapowiec* [member of the Gestapo] sprang to him lying in the automobile and whispered in his ear. The rabbi began to shake as if poisoned, trying to murmur something with his open mouth and could not bring out anything. He looked at the people surrounding him through his yellow, dried out eyelids as if he was asking that they help him cry out at least one tear from the large cracks that were his eyes. The women around him broke out in a loud cry.

The *gestapowiec* and the Polish policemen laughed.

On this day, the 25 Av [18 August], 1941, 1,750 Czyzewo Jews perished in Szulborze.

The earth still heaved in the following days. The peasants were afraid to go out to work in the fields.

[Column 870]

The Ghetto of the Survivors

A small number, more than 100 people, succeeded in saving themselves. The commissar, himself, had chosen young, healthy people. In the morning, after the slaughter, he created a ghetto of them, led them into the small houses near the train line and sent them to various work.

Still more Jews came later, among them, some who escaped during the deportation and went not too far away. They had to go out to work every day, to build the highway to Wisoki, to the noble courtyards and to the railroad to load scrap from the bomb blasts.

My father considered everything to escape farther from Czyzewo, from the great misfortune. But this was not an easy thing. The roads were being watched by the Polish bandits who attacked the passing Jews. Murdered Jews were often found lying on the roads. Yet, we got through as far as Malkin where we stayed until things would get calmer.

I went to Sterdyn to an acquaintance. But I was not there for long. My father, who remained in Lachow, where Jews lived, later removed me. But before that, I succeeded in surviving the *lapanke* (round-up) for Treblinka.

Lachow lay on the road to Treblinka. Here I saw the transports to Treblinka pass through. The train wagons were fully packed with people. Fainting faces looked out through the window holes.

The Priest and the One who Jumped from the Train

Once, when I walked from the village, laden with a basket of food, a long train with dark red freight cars suddenly sped by; in the small windows appeared pale, fainting faces. I remained standing with my heart throbbing heavily. The deafening bang of the wagon wheels was in my ears. My feet became clay-like and I could not move from the spot.

[Column 871]

Suddenly I noticed a bent figure getting up from the ground not far from me; it straightened up, looked around on all sides and slowly, cautiously, with shaking steps was going in the direction of the village.

I stood frozen to the earth for several minutes and tried to recognize who this could be. I had met people several times in Lachow who had escaped from Treblinka, but they were barefoot, half naked. The figure appeared to be well dressed. This was a woman.

Suddenly I heard booted steps. Several peasants who seemed to lie in wait for victims sprang out from behind the bushes. They tore her clothes from her. The woman began to try to argue, but probably thought that it was better than again falling into the hands of the Gestapo.

The nervous strain reached the highest level in me. I barely kept myself from screaming. I wanted to attack them, scratch, beat, fall to their feet, asking them to leave her alone.

At that moment, the priest came from the village with fast steps. He immediately approached the group of peasants.

[Column 872]

— Why? – his low voice reached me – why are you doing this to her? It is still a crime.

— She is Jewish – several voices spoke up at the same time – she sprang from a train car, from a transport to Treblinka.

The priest was not surprised. He stood erect, with outstretched hands.

— Leave her alone. She has been punished enough and God will forgive your sins.

I saw the woman quickly turn around and enter the village. The priest also went in the same direction, a great distance from her.

My heart became lighter. I wondered if he was not one of the *lamed vovnik tzadekim* [1] thanks to whom the world still exists.

The Czyzewo Ghetto is Liquidated

Word would come from Czyzewo that it was calm there. The several hundred Jews were working and no one bothered them. In contrast, it constantly got worse in Lachow. Jews were grabbed for work, where they were beaten, tortured. The smell of those burned in the crematoria of Treblinka reached here. And the word was passed about a deportation that would occur in the nearest days. My father told this to a member of the *Judenrat* who advised him that he should quickly leave Lachow.

We returned to Czyzewo, but at the last minute, my father stopped and did not want to enter the *shtetl*. He left Motke in a village, in Rush, where he became a shepherd. He parted with me with tears in his eyes:

[Column 873]

You will be with Uncle Yankel in Czyzewo. Meanwhile, I will search in the villages; perhaps someone will take pity and I will find a place for me.

His heartbroken words came out of a choking throat and I cried. I understood that my father did not believe they we could save ourselves in Czyzewo.

I worked for several weeks on the highway. The mood in Czyzewo was tense. The rumors of what the Germans were doing in Wysokie, Zambrów and Ciechanowiec reached here. A deportation was also expected in Czyzewo.

— Today smells of some kind of abomination – Kraszewski once said to me, and then he told me that the Germans had ordered wagons from the peasants to carry people, probably Jews, who else?

When I came back to the *shtetl* and told this to my friends, they laughed at me. They clearly knew that the commissar was looking for workers and we did not have to be afraid of any deportations.

At night, my father came to take me away to a village. He also knew about the wagons, but I repeated what the girls has said and maintained that there was no good in showing such fearfulness.

My uncle, Yankel, urged me:

— Go, child, with your father. My heart is also telling me that something is not good.

Something stirred outside. The watchmaker, Motl Stalowitch, said that the office commissar had called him to repair his clock and simultaneously to hire him to ring [the bell] at four o'clock in the morning. People were certain the office commissariat wanted him to thus give him a sign and to show the Jews that something was being prepared for them.

[Column 874]

In the morning, the *S.S.* members and gendarmes actually did come and in their way, with shooting, blows and wild cursing drove out the Jews, took them in-the peasant wagons to the Zambrówer barracks, from where in two months they sent them to Auschwitz.

The ghetto in Czyzewo was entirely liquidated.

In the Peasant Attics, in Hunger and Thirst

My father had taken me away to Pienki, to Janczewski, a rich peasant with a good character. He had compassion for us and could not watch how we ran around as if chased by dogs. He did not think to take money from us. In general, he spoke very little. When my father took Motke from Rush and brought him here, he did not say one word. Then I thought that he had great compassion for us.

Rumors about raids of hidden Jews spread in the village with the arrival of the freezing temperatures. The *S.S.* members warned the peasants that they should turn in all of the Jews to the Gestapo. Janczewski began to be afraid and blurted out harsh words for us.

We understood the hints, but we did not have anywhere to go. The peasant began to starve us, not giving us any bread for entire days.

At night when the village had begun to fall asleep, my father trudged out of the courtyard and each time asked another peasant for a piece of bread, listening to the stories of newly caught Jews in the villages.

[Column 875]

Janczewski became more sour and more bitter from day to day. He stopped bringing us water. It was dangerous to go to the well and we had to be satisfied with snow, which substituted as water for us.

There would be very snowy nights and we did not have any fear that someone would hear the splashing from the pail in the well so Motl [2] would go to take a pot of water that we kept for several days.

My Father's Death

On the night of the 22nd of February we lay in the attic and waited for the last noises of the village to be stilled. We had not had a swallow of water in several days and Motke needed to scrape along to the pond to take a little water. A door still creaked somewhere; a shutter closed. A murmur of a couple and a suffocated laugh was carried from behind a fence. When it became quiet, thirst dried the gums and excited the brain.

Finally it became quiet. The village slept; the littlest rustle could be heard for a mile.

Meanwhile, Motl also slept. My father did not want to wake him and took the dipper himself and began to creep out of the attic.

Something in me began to shiver.

– Father, I will go with you…

– It is not necessary – my father barely moved his lips – two make more noise.

[Column 876]

I could not lie still in the attic for long. I went down, pressed myself to the wall and waited, listening to the rustle of the night.

Suddenly I heard a scream:

Halt!

Soon a shot echoed and it again became quiet.

I felt a cold shiver go through me and I went back up to the attic, told Motke about the shot. He was confused and I felt how he shivered and his teeth began to chatter. We again heard footsteps in the silence and the thump of spades in the ground.

We did not close our eyes for the entire night. When it began to dawn, I went down to the well and saw the dipper lying empty. A bit of dug dirt caught my eye. However, I did not think that this was the grave of my father.

Later, Janczewski came up to the attic and said that our uncle, Yankel Kitaj, had been shot that night in the village.

I told him about our father's departure and that he was sure to be frightened by the shot and was hiding somewhere and was afraid to come out.

We waited impatiently the entire day for our father to come. Late at night I fell asleep and I suffered terrible dreams. I saw myself lying with my father in a river of blood. Wild horses sprang over us, stepped on us…

Janczewski came to us again in the morning and soon declared that the person shot was not our uncle, but actually our father himself.

[Column 877]

I buried my face in the straw and sobbed bitterly. Janczewski's words that we had to go away from here because the entire house smelled of death reached me as if through a fog.

I said nothing. Motl lay with wideopen eyes as if mixed up. Only when the peasant went down did he turn to me:

– What will become of us now?

I felt his hot tears on me.

The Awakened Conscience of the Dejected Peasant

The peasant did not give us any food and we did not go anywhere to seek bread. Through a crack we watched when the dog was given food and each time one of us went down and divided [the food] with him. The dog watched with great understanding eyes, let himself be petted and wagged his tail as if he were satisfied by his friendly action…

We lost count of the days and weeks. Some sort of non-Jewish holiday arrived and relatives and neighbors came together in Janczewski's house; they danced and frolicked. Someone played a harmonica.

Suddenly a fight broke out there and the curses became louder and wilder.

We lay with a death wince in our hearts and pictures of the house being set on fire swam under the lids of our closed eyes; we saw ourselves running and everyone was starting after us.

[Column 878]

Suddenly it became quiet. The crowd dispersed. Someone harnessed the horses to go to call a doctor for the badly beaten Janczewski.

Janczewski came up to us in the morning. He was completely bandaged and was barely able to hold a jug of milk and white *challah* [bread eaten on the Sabbath] in his hand… His conscience had begun to torture him that the misfortune had come to him because he had let us starve.

Better, more satisfying days began for us. They came just in time because we were so exhausted from the hunger and thirst that we felt as if we were losing our last strength.

But soon he came with the frightening news that they had learned about us in the village. Someone must have noticed us in the courtyard and we had to leave. The police could come at any minute.

He was pale and had an insane look full of fear. He breathed with heavy gasps:

– For this comes death…

He accompanied us out and showed us his field stable from afar, where we meanwhile could stay. He would not be responsible if we were caught.

We, I and Motke, held each other. I felt a painful vertigo and my feet felt as if they had been cut off. Motke frequently fell. Wanting to pick him up, I felt at once that I was sinking into the snow, that something heavy had slammed me over the head and Janczewski stood from afar and looked at us.

[Column 879]

Alone in the Field

We were exhausted and weakened from walking. Here, in the field, we breathed easier, although the dangers were much greater.

We had to learn new methods of caution and to rely on our memories. We were stuck for the entire day in a hole that we had hollowed out in the sheaves of straw and artfully disguised. We crept out at night like animals being chased, trembling as if a hyena would spring out from where it lurked at any time.

There were still beets in the fields and they had to be ripped out in such a way that no one would notice that someone had been here. We fed ourselves from them for a long time.

One night we stood in the middle of the field and looked towards the village where the lit small windows winked at us like scores of eyes and told of a sated, calm life, of warmth.

At that, it occurred to Motke:

– I have not eaten a piece of bread for so long, have not warmed myself … perhaps we should go to a peasant?

At first, I shook off this idea. There were peasants who gave every Jew they encountered to the police either because of meanness or because of cowardice. The better ones who did have mercy were also afraid to help. Rarely did a peasant want to take a risk.

We had an idea and stole into a stall where there were pig pens and we took a few potatoes from the pigs. The dog already knew us and did not bark.

[Column 880]

Crawling once to such a stall, I noticed a peasant acquaintance who led horses to be watered. I went to him and simply asked him if he would be able to give me a piece of bread. He told me to wait and immediately brought out an entire bread. Later, we went to other peasants who I believed would not do anything bad to us.

Tired from an entire night of creeping around, we went back before the first rooster cry to our hiding place, where we had to lie immovable the whole day.

With the Two Girls from Zaromb in the Icy River

Once lying down at night, I felt someone pulling at the sheaves. Our hearts withered. But before we had time to do anything, we saw two girls standing in the opening.

These were Jewish girls from Zaromb. The same fear blew from them as from us.

Our family grew larger. The anxieties of getting food also became greater and we had to think about new ways of supporting ourselves.

The girls were furriers. We went into a village where no one knew us and presented ourselves as Polish girls who could sew pelts and were looking for work.

We spoke a peasant language and the peasants believed us, although once when we went to a shoemaker, he received us well at the start, smiled, but his smile changed immediately into a mocking grimace and he began to speak to us with a Yiddish accent.

[Column 881]

We were unmasked.

Drawing back by a side road, we saw the same shoemaker was already waiting at the exit of the village. He had a bicycle and there were two others with him.

– We are lost! – one of us said, expressing what we were all thinking.

In great desperation, we instinctively began running. From where did we get such strength? The non-Jew on the bicycle had trouble following us. But we felt that the distance between us and he was becoming smaller. The road was bad, with pits, but he did not stop. He saw fat prey before him. Three girls – three portions of kerosene, sugar and, perhaps, alcohol.

We ran where it was advantageous for us, where we knew it would be difficult to ride on a bicycle. We had already run past the last hut and felt as if our last strength was leaving us. The non-Jew had to feel it. We thought that he was laughing, he was sure he would win. But, suddenly, a dog ran out from somewhere with a resounding bark. We did not turn our heads. Yet we heard a wrangling. The dog had grabbed the non-Jew by the foot and threw him off the bicycle. The non-Jew's curses reached us, but running, running, we did not look at him.

We ran in the direction of the river. We reached it. The trees on the shore were naked; the river was covered with white frost but only with a thin, icy membrane. It broke with the first step, but we did not stop. We went up to our necks in the water.

[Column 882]

Later, when we lay in the bushes soaked, gasping, without breath on the other side of the river, we saw the shoemaker running with other young peasants who he had called for help. They stood at the shore and looked in all directions. Nervous, windblown, choked with rage, they searched along the entire shore. It never occurred to them that we had crossed the river.

With effort, we moved ahead on all fours. I felt a strong pain in the joints with each step. The pain went through my entire body. My friends remained behind for a minute, but soon they were ahead of me. I saw the trembling of their shoulders as if they were wrestling with someone who wanted to stop them.

None of us said a word. We did not feel the frost, the pain from the prickly bushes that irritated us on the road. Yet moans came out. The other's moan seemed as if it had come from one's own breast.

We finally left the forest. It was night. A village with fires lit lay to our right. Oh, if we could only warm our soaked bodies somewhere!…

But gendarmes were stationed in that village. We had to avoid it. We went across the bare fields. The cold hurled us to the ground like frozen birds from a tree.

A shudder went through our bones. We again stood up, ran a little way. My knees bent and my body shook on them. I sank down frozen

[Column 883]

on the ground. Other frozen hands helped me get up. The wet clothes pasted to the ground, ripped with pieces of skin.

We, three Jewish girls, frozen, desolate, went through empty fields, where no sign of a person, of a settlement was seen from afar.

– *Oy!* – Another one gave a shout, like a child, who wants to go and cannot.

– Let us rest for a minute.

My head began to bang, my ears grew deaf. I began to dream… It was dark in front of my eyes and the night was so vast, a deep and velvet one…

The dream lulled me to sleep.

A girl's hand pulled my shoulders, my face. She spoke with a steamy, tender, desperate, suffering voice:

– Do not sleep… You will die.

With the last strength of someone dying, my hands shook; my entire frozen body.

– Oh, a little warmth to release our frozen blood.

But there was only hard, wintry darkness around. No rustle, no movement from a human step and no breath from a living being.

We dragged ourselves farther, tired, fainting, without strength.

Late at night we arrived at our hiding place.

We Are Surrounded

During the night, we again crept over the field and dug for beets like moles. This was now our only food because, after our failure, we did not dare go into a village for a long time.

It was already the middle of the night. Motke and the two girls carried the beets. They went bent, separated from each other and I ahead, the spotter, if the enemy appeared – a shadow of a person.

[Column 884]

We were not far from the barn; I suddenly heard a suspicious, faint noise. Dark shadows moved in the darkness, surrounding the field and the barn.

It was as if my blood gelled. From surprise? Were we not then prepared for this? We made an agreement with ourselves every night before going out into the field that if something happened, we would meet in another place.

And so this happened.

We were surrounded, lost.

Willingly I would have opened my mouth and would have screamed into the night as a cow bellows when she senses the arrival of death.

But I did not scream. Like a good spy I only murmured quietly and so that each word would reach everyone without any mistake.

– We were surrounded.

We all threw away the beets and scattered, each in another direction. I remained lying in a furrow, stretched out, as one with the ground.

The idea of time did not exist then. The darkness was vast and good, and possessed a heart that beat. We wanted it to be thicker and to stretch even longer.

An alarm rang in a nearby village. I understood that the raid, the search for us had moved to the village.

[Column 885]

We met at the arranged spot in the morning, in another stable. Each told how they had saved themselves. The girls had lain the entire night buried in a potato pit, covered with potatoes.

The sheaves in which we lay hidden little by little became fewer. The covering, a thin one, let in the cold. However, still worse was that it no longer disguised us. Every move was seen from the outside.

It happened. A peasant, traveling past, heard our whispering and tore apart the sheaves. A brightness hit us in the eyes. But, for us, it was black and dark… We cried, a cry of desolation, helpless ones who no longer had anything with which to defend themselves.

The peasant stood surprised, as if turned to stone. His eyes, which were glued to us, sparkled and froze. In a moment, he ran to his sled and eagerly went to the village.

Singing in the Darkness

We recovered quickly and began to think about what to do. There was a fear about remaining here because it was possible that the peasant would alert the police in the village.

We entered Sutker Woods. It was the middle of the day. Cuckoos and crows pulsated over the trees. Their unease promised fresh snow. The wind turned in the air like a mill plastered with withered leaves that still remained in the trees from summer. But each rustle rang in our ears likes steps that chased after us.

[Column 886]

The short winter days finally ended and in no way could we find a place to hide.

Snow fell in the forest, a wet one that stuck to the branches and melted, fell on the ground and melted, with such desolation, just like us.

We hid under a tree, seeking protection, but the wind threw wet handfuls [of snow] in our faces. Dampness penetrated our bodies, ate into our limbs.

A frightening unease enveloped us. Where would we hide our tired, damp and broken down limbs? Our eyes searched, groped…

– I am hungry – one called to the other.

– We will die of hunger and from cold – another quietly murmured – Let us at least not stand in one place, let us go.

– They can still see us.

– Let them see – a drawn girlish hand was raised in the air – Let death come… Dying little by little is still worse than suddenly.

We held hands and left the dark forest. But a thick darkness also hung over the fields that did not allow us to look in. A heavy sky hung from above that merged with everything all-around, with the darkness and our hearts.

We walked. We barely placed our feet. We did not hold up our heads, the wind cut our innards like a knife. It seemed to us that we were dragging ourselves without end and a sweet dream wanted to comfort us. Colorful flames swarmed in our eyes.

– We could yet fall asleep walking – I called – let us sing. Think of some sort of song.

[Column 887]

– The Germans will hear – Motke pleaded. He was then 13 years old and so fervently did not want to die.

– Let them hear – said the furrier from Zaromb, and immediately began to hum some sort of Polish song. She sang quietly; we helped her with clenched teeth. When she finished one song, she began another, a third. Later someone remembered a Yiddish song about a lonely tree on the road to *Eretz-Yisrael*. We all were more caught up in our own singing that became louder, at ease, flowed like a river in the dark night.

The hunger, the tiredness, weakness and fear left. We expressed all of this loudly in our singing. Every minute someone could have heard us. Maybe it would be better this way. The readiness to perish eliminated the fear of death, which had no reality.

Who said that we are weak, cowardly? Let the Germans come with their raised guns and bloodhounds. We had been escaping from them in panicky fear for two years. Now, this all looked like a wicked joke. Futile, there was no way out.

It became day, light; no one appeared from anywhere. We dragged ourselves back to the Sutker Woods like wounded animals that drag their wounded bodies somewhere to a hole, ready to die. It again began to snow. It did not fall, but attacked. Because of its thickness and brightness, we could not see what was a step in front of us. The snow also Landad on us, grew, raised itself. We stood doubled up, hunchbacked, like white hills in the woods. Only inside were the thoughts veiled in a heavy fog like an eternal, endless night had settled in us.

[Column 888]

The End Comes and I Remain Alone

Hiding in the wheat became easier with the arrival of summer. Eating also became better. The peasant more readily gave us bread.

The front neared. In addition to the mindless rumors that reached us, we sensed something from the bread that the peasant would throw to us. The closer the front was – the larger the portions were.

The days began to pass more quickly. The front was very close and there was turmoil in the area and energy. They burned entire villages near the Ostrower highway. They dragged people from hiding places to dig trenches and here, suddenly, Motke, who had already indulged in a peek in the village in the middle of the day, was seized for digging trenches.

I ran around as if poisoned. I looked for a way to save him. In Janczewski's house I learned that he [Motke] had escaped from the trenches. No one knew where he was. I did not find him in any of our hiding places. After several days, I found him lying in the middle of a field covered with straw.

But after a few days, the same thing happened to him. I again started to look for him and I suddenly saw that they were leading him, injured, on the road. I looked at him. My look asked:

[Column 889]

– How did this happen?

I tried to go to him, but I thought he was winking at me that I should not come near, not reveal myself and him.

They took him to a hospital that was quickly taken by the Russians and they took him to a camp near Moscow. They thought of him as a German prisoner of war.

In order to learn all of this, I had to run around all day and look at the military locations. During one of the searches I met a Ukrainian who recognized me as a Jew and I just succeeded in saving myself.

Later I learned that Motke, and other such "prisoners of war" as he escaped from the camp and went to Moscow on foot. The road was difficult. They could not endure it and in the middle of the road, turned back to the camp. Motke was the only one who reached Moscow, entered a synagogue where the Jews helped him to explain his situation and prove that he was a Jew.

During the last days, Janczewski permitted me to stay longer in his house and talked with me, remembering the names of Czyzewo Jews with whom he had been acquainted and friendly for many years, went to their homes, knew their children, their entire lives during the week and on *Shabbos* and holidays.

– They were such good people – Janczewski sighed.

[Column 890]

– There are none of them, none – I looked at Janczewski with a stiff look. In that minute I relived the days and nights in his attic, with no bread or water, the death of my father.

He probably understood what I was now reliving; he lowered his eyes and spoke quietly:

– Who could anticipate such a hell? Only accursed devils could invent it… Such slaughter, so many people killed.

– Now I was alone. From where would I get the strength to survive so much bitterness?

– You must strengthen yourself – Janczewski spoke weakly – forget everything that was and start anew.

– Forget? How could one forget all of this? "But we will have to start anew" – Then I thought for the first time that everything anew can only be begun in *Eretz Yisrael*.

The reverberation of the battles reached here in the village that day. A powerful blow suddenly shook the walls and rang in the panes of the windows and we immediately heard the echo of shooting by a machine-gun and guns. There was an echo, another blow and another one…

I went out in front of the gate, inflamed by eager waiting, listening to the roar from the front that grew in waves.

I stood entirely without fear and watched the retreating Germans who were not interested at all in what was around them. If they looked to the side, their look was not that other well-known look of one who believes he is the subjugator, but the look of a surrounded hare. It appeared to me as so similar to the look of their Jewish victims. It could seem that their own shadows threw a fear of death on them.

[Column 891]

A considerable time passed and Soviet soldiers in hordes entered the village. They were smudged. They had tired, browned faces; they ran in a disorderly way and lugged the various sorts of burdens of war, machine-guns, artillery guns.

Suddenly right near me stood a young, smiling officer.

– So, young girl, see how they run, the nobles, ha?

[Column 892]

I stood distraught for a minute. The spoken foreign language words were understandable to me. A strange person stood in front of me, armed from head to foot and I had no fear of looking right in his face. He saw my confusion and pointing at the courtyard, he asked with the same smile:

– Your cottage? You live here?

It was as if I had awakened from a deep sleep.

– No, no. I am not from here… I am from Czyzewo, from Czyzewo.

After three years I smiled for the first time. This was the first elemental outbreak of the newborn freedom.

Translator's notes:

1. The 36 righteous men upon whom rests the existence of the world. The Hebrew letters *lamed* – 30 – and *vov* – 6 add up to 36.
2. Motl and Motke are both diminutives of the name Mordechai.

[Column 891]

The Walk Through Every Hell

Motke Kitaj/Ellis Island

Translated by Gloria Berkenstat Freund

I was not in the ghetto on the day when the Jews were driven out of Czyzewo to Szulborze. I was hidden at that time with a peasant, for whom I did various work. On that day I had gone out to the pasture with his cows. I rode a horse and thought about the peasant's words that something was likely to happen in the ghetto. Each event in the ghetto created a certain stir among the peasants. No one expected anything good. There were those who were happy about it. However, there were also peasants who had regrets and were sympathetic, although they could not show it.

[Column 892]

I rode slowly and strained all of my senses. I wanted to see something in the empty distance. But it was quiet around me. In my heart arose a hope: perhaps the Germans would not do anything to the Jews. It is understandable that I was happy that I would come to my father and tell him that it is calm in the ghetto.

Suddenly I heard shooting from the side of the *shtetl* [town] and something like a lament began to grow and to reach to heaven. It did not take long and I saw the Jews were being led out.

Small, gentile boys came running from the distant fields and shouted to me:

[Column 893]

– Escape, Motke, escape!

I sat on the horse as if nailed to it and could not move from my spot. A penetrating cold overcame me. The large horde of people came closer near the bridge across the Riszer courtyard; Chaim Dovid Tsimes and Eli Ruwin Salman were dragging themselves. They could not move. A German gendarme ran toward them, pulled out his revolver and shot. They fell backward with arms spread.

My throat became dry and my heart grieved with a painful cramp. I tore away to Kruszewski in Aldaki where my father was hidden. The neighboring peasants did not know about him. Several hours later, they asked me outside if my father had appeared. If yes, he was no longer alive. All of the Czyzewo Jews had been shot.

I was still just a child and could not tell any lies. I just kept quiet and could not understand how they could speak so indifferently about death.

The fear of death persecuted me. I felt it around me. The last day before the death of my father, I begged him and my sister:

– Save yourselves. Remember, I feel death approaching…

After my father's death I suddenly felt like a grown man. My sister was completely broken. She walked around disheveled with flattened hair and became indifferent toward death.

I encouraged her, strengthened her, told her that we must live through the difficult time, that the war would end, that the sun would shine for us, too.

[Column 894]

Her state of mind alarmed me and caused a great deal of worry. I left her in a stable and went along to gather food. I crawled through the stables and milked the cows myself.

There were peasants who knew of this and pretended not to see. When they wanted to give me food to eat, they were afraid and gave hints that I should take food. If I were caught it would appear that they did not know about it.

Rarely would it occur that a peasant would openly show me compassion. One such peasant, Grucki, a good, humane heart, had 16 children. When I would come to him at night, he sat me down with all of his children and made sure that I would have enough to eat to satisfy me.

I felt calmed under his warm look. However, I immediately remembered that my sister was alone in that village, hungry and frozen and the soup remained in my throat.

It became more difficult each day for me to ask for a piece of bread from the peasants. I proposed that I do work, but fear paralyzed their desire to employ me.

Sitting in the forest, we decided to make baskets and brooms and bring them to the peasants. In this way it was easier to take a little food from them.

Later my sister helped carry baskets. I knew all of the roads and made a pretense of hope for my sister, although it was difficult for me, myself, to control the unease, knowing the danger that hung over us.

[Column 895]

The responsibility for my sister made me uneasy. I felt freer and surer alone.

While walking alone one night, a group of peasants, who were coming from Pienki, surrounded me. I grabbed a stick and took them on. This happened unexpectedly and they wavered. One of them shouted to me:

– Leave our village and we will not do anything to you… You bring misfortune here.

Later when the two girls from Zaromb [Zaremby-Koscielne] sareturned to us and they went with my sister to the village to earn something I remained alone for the entire day. I had food, but the anxiety over their fate terrified me. I did not stop trembling from the moment that they left at dawn that they would return peacefully.

Until the day arrived when a shoemaker in the village recognized them as Jewish girls and dragging themselves they barely escaped with their lives, wet, semi-conscious and frozen.

All three lay for many hours and were silent. They simply could not move their lips.

The girls did not have any underwear into which to change. I left for the village and I was successful in taking several pieces of women's underwear from the attics so that they could change their clothing.

That night I said to them that they would no longer go to the village; I myself would provide food.

The distant echoes from the front began to come closer to us.

[Column 896]

Creeping through the stables and doghouses, where the dogs were accustomed to me, they quietly watched as I took a half of their portions. They quietly caressed me and their canine eyes looked at me with human sympathy. I petted them and listened to the distant cannons that resounded like music in my ears.

Once wandering this way I feel asleep somewhere under a tin roof of a fallen house. In the midst of sleep I suddenly heard a shout:

– Stand up! Hands in the air.

Three German soldiers stood near me, aiming automatic weapons at me. I was stricken, not knowing what was happening to me and not having the strength to move a limb.

– Out! – It thundered in my ears. But I did not move from the spot. My hands and feet were as if paralyzed. One sprang towards me, grabbed my by the hand and stood me outside.

They led me to the woods where their headquarters was located. Several German officers sat there. One of the soldiers reported that they had caught a young Jew.

I stood lost and told myself that this could be my last moments if I did not succeed in convincing them that I am not a Jew.

I made a half-witted face and said in Polish:

– What kind of Jew? There have been no Jews here for a long time. All of them have been taken away…

[Column 897]

The officer became angry:

– We have other things to do before we occupy ourselves with the disgusting Jews. Take him, shoot him, liquidate him quickly so that he does not take root here.

The soldier straightened himself, saluted and dragged me to the nearest tree, took sever steps back and aimed the rifle at me.

I took my last look at the officer and succeeded in seeing his stretched out figure. Someone with a high bulbous nose looked at me with a gloomy look. I closed my eyes and waited for the shot. I thought that my sister would not know what had happened to me. At the same time I heard a shout:

– Halt!

I opened my eyes. The gloomy officer shouted to the soldier. It would be better to give me a spade and I would help to dig the trenches on the line.

I was confused and did not understand what he was shouting and when the soldier pushed the spade into my hand, I was sure that this meant that we were digging a pit for ourselves.

Later, I saw that they did not intend to shoot me. The soldier brought an interpreter who translated his questions into Polish: where did I live and what was I doing in the ruin? I answered that the ruin had been our house and my parents had left to work. Only I myself remained to take the cows to pasture. Soldiers had taken them from me. When I saw they were shooting, I hid.

It appeared that the soldier had reflected that my words have been believable to him.

[Column 898]

The translator told me to recite the morning prayer. This I knew very well. My sisters would teach it to me every day so that in case of danger I could say that I was born a gentile boy. Now it became useful. My listeners were convinced that I was not a Jew.

The German even took my suffering to heart. For the fact that I had lost my parents. I was given enough to eat and placed in an auto; they wanted to take me to my parents.

We traveled through the surrounding villages. I met many peasants whom I knew. They were sure that the Germans were taking me to be shot and they looked at me, some with regret, some with malignant joy.

The German frequently turned to me and asked me if I recognized anyone here who could inform me about my parents. In the end the matter became tiresome to him when I shook my head no to everything and he asked me to get out and to look on foot. He explained to me that he did not have the time. The enemy was close and I would certainly find my father and mother somewhere here by myself.

Here, at this place, the Germans were preparing to strengthen their positions. Hundreds and thousands of peasants, whom the Germans had dragged from their huts to dig trenches, swarmed around. I was the only Jew here; every minute one of the peasants recognized me and pointed me out the Germans.

I felt lonely and helpless. However, I recognized that every minute I stood unhidden could cost me my life.

[Column 899]

Looking around I noticed in the distance that the German military kitchen was distributing food to the peasants. I did not think for long, took a kettle and stood in the line for food.

I was not accustomed to such a large portion and right after finishing I felt cramps in my stomach. They drew me to the ground. I lay down, howling from pain. However, this would bring me the attention of the peasants and I bit my lips until they bled and created a mask on my face of nonchalance, of being carefree. Seeing that a German officer was approaching, I was the first to go to him and to talk to him, stuttering:

– I…am looking for…work…

He measured me with a penetrating look and I winked brotherly, licking my dry lips from the cutting pain in my stomach with my tongue. However, I did not want to let him look at me for too long and I made various gestures with my hands of what I wanted to say, that my work would be 10 times faster.

– What do you want to do? – the German asked in a tone of interest while showing an absentminded demeanor.

– Guard…I answered very earnestly.

The German's eyes brightened with a lively gleam. My suggestion evidently pleased him and he made me the overseer of a work sector. When he left, I breathed with relief. I did not become an overseer; I wanted to work more, just as everyone, in order not to be conspicuous.

[Column 900]

For the fourth month, the front stood on the Narew, between Rozan and Ostrolenka. It was a frosty January and the Polish peasants and I dug the trenches. The Germans rushed, faster, faster. They barely had turned away and we already were standing. Suddenly a young gentile boy pointed to me and said: "He is a Jew… We have to finish him."

An older peasant wiped the icicles from his whiskers and as if not hearing the other's talk, said very quietly:

– There is something fishy today…

– But we have to make an end of the Jews – the other one did not let go.

– If you have no sense, what is there to talk about…

– What is it?

– Because it is being said that the Germans will take their boots from here at any minute… And you are thinking about such nonsense…

The other one roared something with puffed out lips at my side, like a infuriated cat and ended it.

The work with the spades started again. No one looked at me as if they had tried to forget that a Jew was working with them.

Suddenly a mighty thunder shook the air. Frightening shooting became thicker with each second. The bullets and shrapnel exploded near us. Each time we heard new moans from the wounded and dying. There was nowhere to hide from the bullets. Suddenly I felt a sharp pain in my arm. I tried to stop the blood with my hand, but at the same time, the people began to run out of the trenches.

[Column 901]

Civilians and soldiers stepped over the wounded and dead. I ran with them not knowing to where.

Running a bit I encountered a military patrol, which stopped me, but seeing the blood that ran from my arm, the soldier took me into the vehicle and took me to the nearest hospital.

There actually were swarms of the wounded who lay on stretchers and on the ground. The air was filled with moans and laments. I was one of those who stood with my own strength. But everyone, the doctors, the nurses and soldiers were drawn to me like one of their own, a war wounded.

The situation became more difficult with each hour. This could be seen on the faces of all of the hospital personnel. Everyone thought of his own skin more than saving the wounded.

The evacuation began immediately. I was taken with the other wounded soldiers to Allenstein, which is a Polish city today and carries the name Olsztyn.

I did not have much rest there for long. The powerful Russian offensive surged like a sea through an eroded dam. The Germans ran away from Allenstein and left the wounded to God's care.

When the Russians appeared I tried not to distinguish myself from the other German wounded. I was afraid to reveal that I was a Jew. The fear of revealing my origin already had been pressed into my soul.

[Column 902]

It was difficult to free this from all of my nerves.

Several days later came an order that everyone who could walk should report to a certain point in order to register to travel, each to their home city.

Arriving at the meeting spot, first, everyone's watch and other valuable things were taken. I immediately felt that the Russians had no honest intentions in gathering us. I want to an officer and told him that I am a Jew and how I had fallen in the hands of the Germans after being wounded in the trenches.

The officer listened to me attentively and assured me that I would be freed, but I did not see him again.

We were placed in rows and created a train of thousands of people. There were Germans and Poles, French and Italians among us. Ragged, hungry, tired, we dragged ourselves over hundreds of kilometers to the nearest train station.

The Russians stubbornly insisted the entire time that we were being taken to Warsaw, but no one believed them any longer. Everyone felt the arrival of dark clouds.

A bird, a page, a button on a shirt can bring a greeting from the home in a distant land. Also, after a night's sleep in the moving train, I suddenly felt that we were stopping at the Czyzewo train station. It was as if I smelled the earth of home, the old home.

It was in the morning. It was quiet and dead. My thoughts excited me and my feet began to rush to spring from the train wagon. But a young officer immediately stood near me:

[Column 903]

– Where are you going, *bratak* [brother in Russian]?

I knew that I had to tell him that I was going to look for a little water and when he turned around I would run. I still knew all of the hidden paths. But against my will I said to him:

– This is my city.

I am sure that he could see in my eyes all my longing and my burning impatience to feel the familiar earth under my feet.

However the officer placed his fist at my nose and shouted as an order:

– Get into the wagon quickly… Forget from where you come. You will never again see your city before your eyes…

There was a disturbance. Soldiers sealed the doors, retreated and stood on guard with their automatic weapons in front.

No one dared to stick out his head. I looked at the Czyzewo fields through the small Window and on the blue horizon the forest was covered entirely by clouds. I thought I saw the souls of the thousands of slaughtered Jews…

We arrived in Shatura, a settlement near Moscow with a giant electrical station and large peat plants, after several weeks of traveling.

The wagons were opened and there were many dead Germans who could not endure the hardship, the hunger.

We were given food to eat for the first time in the camp. Our stomachs did a dance and we ran back and forth… Many could not endure and fell dead…

[Column 904]

In the morning, the individual investigation immediately began:

– Tell the truth! Who are you, from where?

The methods, the threats and torturing were reminiscent of the *S.S.*, the Gestapo.

It was the same at work. They stood in mud over their knees and shaped the peat. The soldiers chased them without stop. People fell like flies.

I wanted to have revenge on the Germans. Had they not tortured the Jews in Czyzewo, in Zambrów, everywhere, exactly in this way? However, I did not feel any joy in this. We were molded from entirely different clay. The human pain moved me. I helped anyone I could.

I began to think about getting out of there. The area was full of bogs and all of the roads were guarded. Yet, I noticed that people decided to escape. I noticed how they communicated with each other, often in sign language, only with the eyes and they disappeared together into the dark night. How far they went – I did not know.

I also did the same thing; I started on the road at night with a young Polish peasant from the Czyzewo area.

It was the middle of the night. Everything around appeared to be sunk in a deep sleep, a stillness, dark, cold. The sky was covered with heavy clouds.

Suddenly I saw how people were moving along, looking at everyone and hurrying farther. Like shadows or like spirits, everyone in the same direction.

We followed them, although we knew they did not know the way better than us.

[Column 905]

Walking began to be more difficult. The shadows suddenly disappeared from our sight. From time to time a shout was heard from somewhere. However, we did know from which side it came. Suddenly we felt that we were sinking.

We were in slimy mud.

A frightening fear ruled us even more. The mud reached to our chests.

I began to tap with my hand to find something to hold onto. My eyes bored through the darkness and I saw a young tree not far from me. I began to reach for the tree with all of my strength. Finally, I succeeded in grabbing the branches and felt the hard ground under my feet.

I looked around and saw that my comrade was standing in the same place, mud up to his chest. I shouted to him, but he could not take a step.

I succeeded in finding a long pole and went back into the mud as far as for him to be able to grab on the pole and I pulled him to the shore with all of my strength.

After going several kilometers, I saw that he was falling off his feet. He sat down and said that he would not be able to go far. His strength was gone. He was drawn back to the plank bed.

I began to go alone.

Finally, I returned to the Sztol train line. I waited for the small train to arrive that carried peat and I jumped on a wagon full of peat as it rode by.

I traveled covered with wet peat across hundreds of kilometers.

[Column 906]

However, the wagon was an open one and when day began to dawn I had to jump down at the first station.

It was a small *shtetl* where I seldom met a passerby, only individual peasants with milk and small cakes, who had just returned to the marketplace near the station. I was hungry, but did not have any money to buy anything.

A peasant noticed how I looked at the small cakes with hungry eyes and gave me one, pouring me a glass of milk.

When I greedily drank it up, he simply told me that his village had been alerted at night to be aware if any escapees from the camp were hiding in the area.

He looked at me with searching eyes and I understood that he realized who I was.

It was clear to me that I had nothing to lose. In addition, the peasant evoked trust in me and I openly told him that I had escaped from the camp, where I had been sent through an error.

The peasant endeavored to make a pretense that he did not hear what I had said to him and so again as normal talked about which was the best road to take to Moscow.

I lay stuck somewhere in a corner the entire day. When it got very dark, I again jumped onto a small passing train and buried myself under the peat.

Through the cracks I saw going by high chimneys from giant factories that in the night looked like black giants who were chasing me, threatening: your escape is useless!

[Column 907]

Suddenly I felt as if the train had crossed an iron bridge across a lake. According to the peasant's instruction, the train to Moscow had to pass here.

I waited until the train decreased its speed a little and jumped off.

Judging from the fires, I understood that I was not far from the station. I approached cautiously. In the dark I ran into a shadow. At first my heart stopped in fear, but I immediately realized that this was as lonely a dog as I. I was the first one to begin a conversation and it appeared that he was going to Moscow without a ticket, without money.

The freight train to Moscow arrived. It did not stop, only went a little slower. We took advantage of this and jumped onto a step of the wagon.

There was a strong wind. Our bodies became stiff from the cold and fear. We could fall from the step at any moment. The train went at terrific speed and we desperately held onto the iron handles of the wagon.

It was already dawn when the train approached Moscow. We said goodbye, sprang down from the train and headed to Moscow in various ways.

[Column 908]

Arriving at the electric station I immediately recognized a Jewish woman among the waiting passengers. This was my first encounter with a Jew since I had left for the woods.

I went over to her, began to speak Yiddish and told her in short words who I was and how I came here. She did not want to speak with me. She looked away to all sides with fear in her eyes and advised me that I should quickly return to the camp because they would not help me in any way here.

I left her dejected, but I did not think of returning to the camp. I saw before me the troubles I would have to go through, but I did not want to give in.

I immediately noticed a second Jew. I went to him, but I decided not to be so open and did not tell him that I had escaped from the camp. I told him that I had come from Tashkent.

Perhaps the other one immediately recognized that I was not telling the truth. He walked with me quietly through the noisy streets. In his house, he asked me to sit and immediately said:

– It would be better if you told me the entire truth. Perhaps I will be able to help you in some way… At the same time, he said to his wife:

– He must be hungry. Cook something.

His wife immediately cooked potatoes and borscht for me. How many years had it been since I ate such a human lunch in a Jewish house at a table with people!

It turned out that the way in which I ate said everything to the Jew because he said quietly to his wife:

[Column 909]

– You see then that he has not eaten for a long time. Give him more.

Calmed, I told him everything. He listened to me earnestly and said that my situation was really difficult, but that the worst was behind me; I should not worry but be very careful.

He gave me an address for a Jew at a Moscow synagogue and 20 rubles for my first expenses.

It was already late when I arrived at the Maroseyker Synagogue. No one was there. I stood worried and not knowing what more to do. Suddenly someone stopped near me and asked who I was looking for in Russian.

I immediately recognized that this was a Jew. I thought that in a Jew who was walking near the synagogue I could have trust and I told him everything. He took me home with him, let me spend the night, gave me a fresh shirt, fed me and, in the morning, he gave me the address of the union where they needed to accept me. He told me that they receive a great deal of help from Jews abroad and I should be bold.

At the union I was sent to Ber Mark, the chairman of the Jewish committee of the union. I again lost my confidence and said to him that I had come from Siberia where I had remained all alone.

Despite all of my experience, I had not learned how to tell a lie. They immediately recognized that I was hiding something. Ber Mark, listening to me, strongly warned that he would not be involved with me, would not give me any help, if I did not tell him the entire truth.

[Column 910]

It was only when I told him everything that he checked the lists of the surviving Jews. My sister was not there. He told me about the pogrom that had taken place in Czyzewo after the liberation. I believed that my sister was alive and asked him to help me to return home.

Ber Mark promised me to do everything. Meanwhile, I received a provisional document and a place to sleep in a hotel outside Moscow.

The help that I received was not enough. I had a considerable hunger. Bread was still rationed and I could not dream of this.

All day I would walk through the Moscow streets and at the metro stations where the stream of millions of people flowed without stop. I slowly lost the ability to differentiate who was a Jew. People who to me appeared similar to Czyzewo Jews turned out to be pure… Armenians, Syrians, Persians and Georgians.

The hopes that I placed in Ber Mark ran out little by little. He actually could not help me to leave Moscow in a legal manner.

I, myself, began to look for a way to leave the Soviet Union.

I walked around the train station for several days, looking for the possibility of getting onto a train that was going to the Polish border.

Once while walking in the White Russian train station, I noticed a Lithuanian refugee family that was returning home… They had many packages and several small children. I helped them carry things into the train wagon and when the train moved I did not descend and traveled with them as far as Molodëzhnyy.

[Column 911]

When the train stopped in Molodëzhnyy I suddenly noticed a transport that stood ready to go to Poland. Without thinking a great deal, I immediately entered this train.

Finally we traveled past Plock; I heard how they were shouting Plock. I sprang down with joy. I immediately realized my mistake. This was Polotsk, the Russian *shtetl*.

My nerves were strained by the continuous anxiety and I began to jump from one train into another, and fell into the hands of an NKVD [Commissariat for Internal Affairs, the Soviet secret police] inspection. My provisional documents from the Union of Polish Patriots surprised them. They did not know what to do with me and left me alone.

Finally I arrived in Bialystok.

I did not meet one Jew in Czyzewo. I went on foot in the village to Janczewski, who gave me food and several *zlotys* and told me that my sister was alive, but that he did not know where she had gone.

It was as if I were being chased by a fever. I immediately ran to the train and in three hours I was in Warsaw.

I did not see anyone in Warsaw then. However, the destruction that was revealed to me made a terrible impression on me.

[Column 912]

Solitary, I wandered through the streets, among the ruins and gravel, in the direction of the ghetto. All around there was only destruction, ruins.

I felt as if the ash lay on my heart, on my young shoulders, but I bore all this with an anxious stubbornness.

I left for Praga, There I met several Jews; they walked around like shadows. Some were still searching for someone; some already had lost any hope.

One asked the other:

– Why did you come here? Who are you? How long do you contemplate remaining here?

I was advised to go to Lodz; there were more Jews there. Perhaps, I would find someone.

Arriving in Lodz at dawn, I saw a long line standing near a meat store and I realized that they were arguing in Yiddish.

To my question if anyone knew someone from Czyzewo, someone in the line said that he knew a Jew from Ciechanowiec [Ciechanowiec is about eight miles from Czyzewo], who was named Slawaczik and who lived on Zawadzki Street, no. 15.

Arriving at the house at the address I was given I felt as if I were in a foggy vision, where the brain is over-strained and one begins to dream while awake. The young man who opened the door said something into the second room, from which I heard the voice of a woman:

– Motl!

[Column 913]

This was my sister.

She had just gotten up from sleeping. In her dream she had heard my voice and sprang up from bed and we both cried.

This was a cry of joy and sadness all in one.

However, it is wonderful that after such tears it becomes easier. My sister took me with her warm and sure hand and took me with her.

We were together again, but not for long.

In May 1946 I traveled to Germany with a convoy and my new wandering began through German cities, across Austria and Italy and back.

I was drawn into the life of the former concentration camp inmates, who were involved with commerce in all of the countries.

It was illegal to sell; the police and secret agents always chased us. Once such a police agent caught me and placed me under arrest. I hit him, tore myself away and escaped.

[Column 914]

Police began to chase me along with Austrian civilians and in the end they caught me. At my trial I said that I had thought a Nazi was attacking me with a gun and so I defended myself.

Several years later, in 1949, I came to the same Austrian city, Salzburg, as a soldier in the American intelligence service.

While in a restaurant I met the same agent and paid him for the trouble he had caused me.

I was in the army until 1953. I was demobilized in America. Later I worked as a salesman in an iron business where I learned to be a locksmith.

In 1956 I bought the business from my uncle.

I married a *sabra* (a Jew born in Israel during the establishment of the nation) from Israel. My life was renewed. But I will never forget everything I lived through. Each name of the annihilated Czyzewo Jews is dear and sacred to me!

[Column 913]

The Road of Suffering

by I. Nowinsztern

Translated by Gloria Berkenstat Freund

A.

When the war broke out I was serving in the Polish military in the third *pulk* [regiment] of the cavalry that was then stationed in Sulwak. This was during the 11th month of my service. In the barracks a murmur began. The officers ran around without their heads and waited for an attack. On the third day we finally moved in the direction of the Prussian border.

[Column 914]

The march passed through almost without interference. A spirit of combat reigned among the soldiers. The blood in the veins gurgled and [we were] full of expectation of a clash with the Germans.

During the evening we finally arrived in the German village. A voice, drunk from aroused blood, echoed from the forward rows:

[Column 915]

– Attack, brothers… Hey – Ha!... Charge, Brothers!

We ran, ran into the night and nothing happened. A cannonade of fiery, exploding shrapnel and artillery shells poured in the darkness of the night with flaming rain and concussed the air and the earth. We saw nothing and ran, ran.

I ran just like the others. The fire of revenge flared in me. The insulted and persecuted Jews of Zbaszyn[1] were before my eyes, all of the Jews from Germany and Austria who Hitler had driven from their homes like mangy dogs. I felt the menace that he brought to the Jewish homes in the Polish cities and *shtetlekh* [towns] with the attack on Poland. I did not think then of the possibility of such horrible death for millions of Jews. But I felt in the Hitlerists the greatest enemy of the Jewish people and I felt joy at the opportunity to strike at their wild, twisted faces and feel how they fell at our hands.

I did not remember how long this lasted. Suddenly the order came to withdraw. We again crossed the border and began to go through the dusty roads. No one knew exactly how the situation looked on the other fronts. We only knew that the Germans were far away and that fighting was taking place deep in the country. It was possible that already we were completely surrounded.

During the day we lay in the forest in order not to be noticed by the German airplanes that flew across the sky and scattered their fire, lighting fires in village huts. The entire area was agitated and confused. Thick clouds rose over the fields. Peasants from burned huts packed their things, pulled their horses and cows out of the stalls and went to wait in other villages.

[Column 916]

We found ourselves in the Golasze Forest. I knew the area well. My parents lived in a village not far from there. I took a moment and I went to see them. Their joy was great. Everyone began to ask that I remain in the house. But I could not convince myself to become a deserter. I did not want to admit the idea that everything was lost.

My parents' situation deprived me of my rest; I could not find a place for myself and volunteered for the most difficult tasks, went on intelligence [missions]. Once, I again dropped in to my parents, sat with them for the entire night and talked. We did not talk about me remaining. They saw that they would not convince me. My sister, who lived with our parents, also sat at the table and comforted them that a soldier feels the changes less, is accustomed to wandering and does not think about what tomorrow will bring.

My father sighed that a Jew is a Jew everywhere and it is always worse for a Jewish soldier than for another one. Who knew what the Germans would do with the Jews?

When day began to break I untied the horse and rode to my two comrades, with whom I had gone out on patrol at night and had left to sleep in the forest. They were well rested and were sitting under a tree. Instead of answering my greeting, one of them, the *plutonowy* [sergeant], looked at me like a wild cat:

[Column 917]

– Where were you the whole night?

– I was with my parents – I pretended not to understand his anger and offended tone – they live not far away.

– Do not confuse me – the *plutonowy* hissed between his pressed lips.

– You are a spy, a German spy.

He sprung quickly onto the horse. The second soldier did the same thing. The *plutonowy* pointed his hand imperiously at me: "You take your horse by the bridle and you will go in front."

I did not understand exactly what this signified. Perhaps he meant to punish me in this way. However, going several steps I heard suspicious whispers behind me. I turned my head. The *plutonowy's* eyes shone. His head stretched out belligerently in front, as if he was ready to throw himself on me. His free right hand manipulated the lock of his rifle.

In the blink of any eye I understood with painful clarity that my minutes were numbered and that I must quickly defend myself with all of my strength. I held my gun in front, with the barrel down. As if in a trance, I stopped, standing face to face with him. He was visibly surprised by my sudden stop. His hands stopped manipulating the rifle and in the same blink of an eye, I shot.

His brown, boney face immediately became wax-like; some kind of stale, threatening roar tore out of him. His hands moved in all directions in the air and he fell off his horse, like a crow that had been shot down.

His horse began to run wildly among the trees. The other soldier, who I had almost let out of my sight, suddenly turned his horse and began to go back at a gallop.

[Column 918]

I was frozen stiff from terrible fear for my own deed for several minutes. Simultaneously I was engulfed by a strong joy that we had succeeded in saving ourselves from a sure death. I rode away in the direction of headquarters.

B.

For several days, large German forces drove through on the Czyzewo-Dambrowa highway: tanks, motorized infantry, heavy artillery and mine launchers, horse encampments, sanitary battalions and military engineers. The noise of the wheels and the deafening noise of the motors filled the forest where we were hidden and we looked with eyes red from lack of sleep at the highway over which hung thick clouds of dust that did not conceal from our eyes the order in the ranks of the German military.

Even a civilian who was not skilled in military matters felt and saw the immense strength that was descending on Poland. The hopelessness of our poorly armed resistance was clear. Yet, when the Germans caught us and there was a fight, we hit them relentlessly and did a great deal of damage to the Germans. We withdrew to Bialystok in the evening; outside the city we learned that the central regiment already had been imprisoned by the Germans.

Withdrawing, we regrouped in the village Hryniecwiczwe that lies on the Lapy-Bransk highway.

German motorcyclists patrolled the highway without stop. Large trucks carried supplies and ammunition.

[Column 919]

In the evening our patrol reported that the road was free and we began to withdraw from the village. When we arrived at the last hut, fire that came from the highway began to rain on us. Our ranks began to break. Horses and men fell. Groans were heard in the darkness. It appeared that those remaining would very soon give in. I was mainly afraid of that. However, it happened thus, that we staged a stubborn resistance all as one and suddenly we noticed that the Germans were beginning to withdraw.

"Chase them!" – came the order from our officer and we started off after them in a gallop with a wild shout of hurrah. Suddenly everything stopped. Shooting at us started from all sides. Everything swirled together, moaned and wheezed. My horse fell to his knees. I bent down and felt the hot horse breath from his nostrils. Foam remained on my fingers. His large eyes looked at me with fear and regret. Later, when I would find myself in great danger, face to face with death, this equine look would appear before my eyes, which tore my heart with sorrow and pain.

A small group of us remained from this struggle; with its last strength, it barely forced itself through to the woods and started for Volkovysk on foot.

In quiet Volkovysk there was an uproar from the soldiers running in, who were reorganized and sent to Lithuania. Arriving in Styczyn during the day, a major greeted us and informed us that we were being hit on both sides. The Russian army was also going into Poland.

He now spoke to us not as subordinate soldiers, but as to his own, his friends.

– We have lost the war – he spoke with clear pain – not only the buttons that [Marshal Edward] Rydz-Smigly boasted he would not surrender, but we have even lost the land. Yes, my brave soldiers, you are freed from your oath, save yourselves as you can… I will remain here, whoever wants can remain with me.

The news had a crushing effect on the Jewish soldiers. Several hours later we were surrounded by the German Army, which took the city without resistance.

Now I had only one purpose: to reach Czyzewo even more quickly, where I expected to find my parents.

The roads were full of danger. White Russian bandits attacked and murdered Poles, Jews; the Polish uniform was hated by them. After Skidel [Skidzyel, Belarus], I fell into the hands of such a band, which began to carry out the death sentence over us. We were saved by chance. Out of one danger and into the second one. The Russians, who could not figure out what kind of people we were, held us under arrest. Again a chance occurred and we succeeded in freeing ourselves and after great hardship, came home to our parents who were still in Dąbrowa, a quiet village seven kilometers from Czyzewo.

[Column 921]

C.

We already felt winter in the air. Therefore we stopped moving into the city. We remained living in the village and did a little trading. There was turmoil in Czyzewo. The Reds raised their heads. Denunciations flew. Some Jews were taken away to Siberia. It was quiet in the village.

We did not stop talking in the house about moving into the city for the entire time. Although the peasants in the village had a good relationship with us, a strange unrest was in the air. The peasants told various stories. When the first spring sun began to dry the winter dampness of the earth and of the nearby fields, we in the house decided that we had lived long enough in the village and one morning my father finished eating the dark village bread, drank up the sour milk and left for the city.

– Perhaps we will be helped – my mother said half to herself, half to me. I looked at her dreaming eyes in which lay all of the tempests of the village and it pressed against my heart. I understood how much she wanted to live in Czyzewo and it hurt me that I could not help with this.

My father returned late at night and said that there were no apartments to be had in all of Czyzewo and there was no other solution than to build our own house with someone else. He even had discussed this with Shmulke Wengorz. He should start building immediately.

My mother looked at us and was silent. I saw now she had wiped her damp eyes and smiled to herself.

[Column 922]

– Our own apartment in Czyzewo… Will our luck also brighten?

Poor Mama! She was not destined to live in her own apartment in Czyzewo. They did start to build the apartment but in the midst [of the building] the war broke out between Hitler and Russia.

The war began Sunday morning. The buzz of the airplanes flying began to rustle in the village and a distant echo of rapid, dense cannon-fire and explosions of bombs. This lasted three days. The German military already was in Czyzewo on Tuesday night.

The news was brought to us by the peasant, our neighbor, who looked us in the eyes with an overwhelmed face, wanting to read the answer to his silent question: What will happen to you, Jews? What will you do now?

The first days passed quietly. Everyone sensed that it was not good. However, no one dared to say anything. The fear of the Germans was greater than the terror from the bombs.

My mother was the first to decide to go to the city to look at what was happening there.

This was Friday, the sixth day after the outbreak of the war.

My mother did not remain in the city for long. When she returned, her face was darkened, covered with wrinkles even deeper than before. Fear remained in her eyes of a corpse that she had seen lying near the train tracks. This was Leyzer Bytner. *Shabbos* in the village was a sad one, a melancholy one.

D.

We all left the village on Monday on the road to Czyzewo.

[Column 923]

Many German autos and motorcycles rode along the road. None of them bothered us, did not look in our faces to see if we were Jewish. From time to time an auto stopped, or a motorcycle, asked the way to Szepietowo and traveled further.

We were near the village of Dmochy when three Polish militiamen on bicycles drove by us coming from the opposite direction. I recognized them from afar. Michalczik and Kaczimierczak were familiar gentiles. Pawel Dmochowski was an agent with Yakov Litwak. They stopped. They did not answer our greeting, only asked why we were not wearing bands on our arms and, before we had a chance to answer, they began to beat us over our heads, hands and backs with sticks. They were tall, sturdy and hit with cold-calculated fury; when one of us bent to avoid the stick, they were ignited with fury and began to hit with more fervor.

– Now you have yours – Michalczik finally said and turned to the comrades – Come, they have enough for now.

Calmly, they sat back down on their bicycles and left.

The sufferings of this day did not end with this. We met German soldiers near the city who were singing as they marched. Seeing us, one of them sprang out of the ranks with a scissor in his hand, ran to my father, grabbed his beard and cut it off.

My father stood for while without speaking, with closed eyes. These sufferings were probably more difficult for him than the earlier blows with the sticks.

[Column 924]

The soldiers rolled with laughter.

We barely managed to reach the *shtetl*. The streets in Czyzewo were empty. We did not see a living soul. I looked at my father – he was as pale as the wall. I sensed a strong pain in his heart.

We did not know what to do. All of the doors were bolted. Fear hung in the air.

We knocked at the door of Josef-Mendel the baker. It took a long time until the door opened. He looked around carefully on all sides.

Inside he welcomed us, quietly looked my father's cut beard, at our swollen faces and after a long time sighed:

– Thus, they have mistreated you?!

My father said quietly:

– It probably would have been better if I had stayed in the village. It is quiet there.

– It is a quiet before a storm – Josef-Mendel said – one way or another, here we are among Jews…. It is not good, perhaps a miracle will occur.

– But where do we find an apartment? – My father moaned.

After a long search, we met Shlomo Cziwice, who agreed to let us into his house.

We immediately got a small wagon, loaded it with a few things, said good bye to our neighbors; the older peasants looked up with sad eyes from under their dusty eyebrows. The wives of the peasants crossed themselves.

[Column 925]

We sat closed in our homes for entire days then. Rarely someone furtively approached and told us something he had heard from someone else about the war, about new murder victims shot by the Germans.

At night, we left discreetly for the village through the back roads to gather something to eat.

Thus, the despairing days passed. The *shtetl* looked as if it was without an owner, subjected to the whim of the murderers.

Suddenly, information reached us that the German field commander had settled in Banucke's building and that he was beginning to make order in the *shtetl*.

The Russians had begun building a secondary train line a short time before the war, but were not successful in completing it. The Germans resumed building it and gave an order that all Jews in Czyzewo from 13 years of age and older had to report to work to build the train line.

Everyone went on the first day. The work was difficult and there was no payment for it. Little by little the people began to escape and not go to work. Simultaneously, the Germans became stricter from day to day; they invaded the houses and whoever was caught was taken to work. They invaded our house several times, but we succeeded in hiding in the courtyard in a pile of wood. Every day my father went to work alone.

Several days passed and something new again happened. A commissar arrived in Czyzewo.

[Column 926]

He immediately sent for several people. Sender the miller, who until the last day remained his right hand, became his closest crony.

Before long there was a *Judenrat* in Czyzewo into which entered Shmulke Wengorz, Yeshaya Lepak, Alter Walter and Dovid Lubelczik. Zebulun Grosbard was the chairman.

At first, no great changes took place. The Jews continued to go to work and did not receive any payment. German soldiers again went through the houses to look for those who were hiding. Those caught were subjected to various suffering.

It dragged out like this for the entire summer until the building of the railroad was finished. However, the capturing of [people for work], which was a daily phenomenon, did not end with it. There could be no talk of earning a livelihood. No Jew dared to open his shop. Only the Polish shops were open.

A gendarmerie was created under the leadership of the national commissioner, Sadovski. A commissioner arrived named Heyman. The commissioner for the noble courts was Bibow.

The torture of the Czyzewo Jews now became more organized. Despite the need that reigned in the *shtetl*, demands began for contributions. The commissioner summoned members of the *Judenrat* and demanded large sums of money, furs, silver candlesticks from them, providing short periods of time to gather them.

Seeing what was being done, Zebulun Grosbard immediately resigned. His office was taken by Alter Walter, who became chairman of the *Judenrat*.

[Column 927]

Czyzewo received its first Jewish militiaman at that time – Ruwin Mlodz, who kept watch on the social fabric that was set by the commissioner.

Meanwhile, driving Jews to work continued, to clean the streets, to various labor in the noble courts, to blowup the bunkers that the Russians had built on the Bug [River] and to load the scrap iron in the wagons.

E.

Panic began in the *shtetl*. The members of the *Judenrat* went through the houses endeavoring to calm the mood, saying that no one should escape, not run away, because they knew precisely that this was only about work.

Actually, at the new synagogue building stood *Wehrmacht* [Defense Forces – German armed forces] soldiers and weavers, cabinetmakers; they took them away to work where they even received food. As for those remaining, an order was issued that everyone must appear at three o'clock at night. The *Judenrat* then informed everyone of this. The turmoil in the *shtetl* grew. Even more people believed that they must save themselves; that they must find a way to escape.

That day, Sender was seen busily going through the houses, where he asked everyone not to run because, God forbid, a calamity for the Jewish people could come. The Germans could be made angry and it would be worse. Other members of the *Judenrat* did the same thing. They assured everyone that this just was about work for the Czyzewo Jews.

[Column 928]

My brother worked with the carpenters at the *Wehrmacht* on that day. My mother and my father and my sisters left for the village. At night I saw the panic; I could not wait for my brother and I also went to them in the village.

The *shtetl* became agitated that night. Men said goodbye to their wives and children. Grown children said goodbye to their old parents and to young brothers and sisters. Crying was carried through the streets: "May you return soon." No one slept without their luggage with them. They were uneasy and, yet, believed that this would not affect them. They would not be sent away. The market was covered with security police, members of the Gestapo, Polish militia as well as members of the *Judenrat*.

All of the assembled Jews stood in long rows; they followed every movement of the Gestapo men moving around with stress and in great anxiety. The Polish military men ran around the houses and dragged out whomever they found. They dragged the old Wengerka in a wild manner through the street. Disheveled, he wrestled with the gendarmes, fell, stood up on his knees and implored them. The gendarmes pushed him, dragged him and threw him among the Jews at the market. The same was done to others, who had foreboding of the threats of death and clung to life with all of their strength.

This lasted until seven o'clock in the morning. Then soldiers and an officer of the *Wehrmacht* suddenly appeared at the market and removed the woodworkers from the rows. My brother again was among them.

[Column 929]

The Jews were anxious. They did not know what was better, to go with the *Wehrmacht*, to remain waiting for their individual fate. When other soldiers came several minutes later and demanded locksmiths and other artisans, no one made themselves known. Everyone was afraid to step out from his row. There was dead silence. The angry voice of the *Wehrmacht* officer, who turned to those who stood closest to him, was the only thing heard; "What are you by trade?"

When everyone's answer was evasive, the commissioner himself began to choose: "You, to the right, you right, right, right…" He counted out 108 young people in such a manner and placed them on one a side.

Black covered automobiles immediately arrived, in which the wives and children were loaded. The remaining men, surrounded by the Gestapo, went on foot. Where? This no one knew.

The rain poured down the entire day. The policemen and Gestapo were dressed in rubber coats. All the while, their loud laughter at the soaking wet Jews was heard, which reached the ears of the broken, moaning. The weeping of the children, who had been torn from them with such frightening savagery, still rang.

Yet, there were those who made use of the strong rain, which did not stop whipping the face and forced the policemen to pull the rubber visored caps deeper over their eyes, and they escaped to the empty field, hiding in the pits in mud, waiting until it would get dark.

[Column 930]

The policemen pointed out many of them to be shot. The road was spread with the murdered. Dead also lay at the market in pools of blood. These were the sick who could not walk faster. Shprinca Krzanski, the cripple without feet who scraped along the ground, also was murdered. The policemen chased her from her house. When the Germans noticed her, they immediately shot her.

The murdered lay in the street all day. The 108 people, who the commissioner had chosen, went to work at the *Wehrmacht* and returned at night. The commissioner waited for them and allocated houses for them to spend the night.

One hundred and eight people were led into three houses, into Saneh Stuczynski's, Shlomo Cziwice's and one other. On the same evening more people who had saved themselves appeared among them. Shlomo Feivel Cukrowicz, the son of the *shoykhet* [ritual slaughterer] was also among them. The number saved increased. However, none of them dared to enter the street to see what was happening.

The rain stopped late at night and I ran into the city to learn something about my brother. I moved near the wall of the emptied houses and wanted to hear some kind of rustle. But a dead silence reigned everywhere. A frightening terror hovered everywhere, from every corner. Fear and despair shook from the thrown open doors and windows. A white, half-torn curtain flew out of a Window in the courtyard, waved in the wind. Torn like the lives that were now being torn.

[Column 931]

Suddenly I heard a choked murmur from Shlomo Cziwice's house. I knocked quietly. However, no one answered. Someone opened the door when I began to call my name. It was quiet for a while, like in a grave. Everyone was silent. I stood frozen and could not say a word. With frozen wonder, I tried to bore through the darkness. My lips whispered something of which I myself was not aware.

When I had recovered a little and spoke with the people, it appeared that my brother definitely had not returned from work. He had remained overnight in the workshops.

Trembling completely, I left the house and began to go through the dark, empty alleys. Heavy thoughts bored into my brain; what will happen next? How can my parents be saved? Somewhere near the mill, I remained standing without strength. Everything in me cried from desperation and helplessness.

F.

I arrived in the village late, after midnight. Everyone lay in bed in darkness with open, watchful eyes. I told them how the *shtetl* looked. My mother moaned quietly:

– And will we be able to save ourselves in the village? This misfortune will not pass us by in the village. It is better to be among Jews.

Yet we all remained in the village for eight days. The peasants showed us mercy. On the eighth day, my mother could not bear it and left for the *shtetl*.

[Column 932]

She returned late in the evening and told us that it was a little calmer. She saw her brother there. Everyone was working for the *wehrmacht*. Ruwin still was a policeman.

We were in the *shtetl* again. The national commissar announced that he was creating a labor camp in Czyzewo, in which no child must be found. Everyone would receive a half-kilo of bread a day and was placed under the decrees of the *Judenrat*.

The feeling of deep pain began to wither little by little. More Jews, who had been hiding in the villages and furtively smuggled themselves back in the *shtetl*, arrived everyday.

The commissar knew nothing about this and did not say anything. The opposite, it seemed that he was satisfied with it. He once sent for Sender and confided in him that men were needed for work near the train and Sender immediately traveled to Ciechanowiec to recruit Jews for Czyzewo.

The commissar then permitted five houses to be added and they all were fenced in with a wire fence. A gate was erected and nearby – a post on which a bell was hung that rang as a signal for gathering all of the Jews in cases when the commissar would come to visit the labor camp.

The fencing created a bit of panic among the Jews and many Jews began to escape. However, eight days later they again returned. Death lay in wait on the roads and in the villages.

[Column 933]

Large groups of Jews were driven daily to work, where they had to endure various hardships. They had to do the heaviest work until late at night under blows from rifle butts and whips, in the rain and later in the snow.

There was no information about the Jews who were taken on that Thursday. This day entered the history of Czyzewo as "the bloody Thursday." When someone wanted to describe the time of something that happened, he would say: "this was before 'the bloody Thursday' or this was after 'the bloody Thursday.'"

For a long time, Bloody Thursday was the day of terror for the remaining Jews in Czyzewo.

G.

Little by little the fate of the deported Jews, women and children became clear. Peasants brought the news about the place and the last days of their mass death.

The Jews were held all of Thursday in the school of the village of Szulborze, eight kilometers from Czyzewo. On the second or third day, they were led out in groups to the wide anti-tank pits that had been dug out long before. The pits were a meter deep and three meters wide. The party consisted of 40 people; up to 20 were shot in the pits.

The gates of the school were opened the entire time and new groups, new victims were pushed through them.

The peasants, who drove past later, saw the earth rise. They crossed themselves and quickly drove away. Various versions about frightening specters were spread in the surrounding villages.

[Column 934]

At the beginning no one wanted to believe this. Later it was confirmed by Moshe-Ahron, the lame one's son, from Zaromb. There, an order went out at the same time that the Jews should be sent to Czyzewo, but they were stopped on the road and they were murdered in the same way. Only he managed to jump down off the wagon in time and he crawled to the field on his hands and knees. From there he watched everything with his own eyes. He lay in the field for several days and was afraid to leave.

Autumn passed with grey fogs and rains. Snow and blizzards arrived. The roads, the roofs of the inhabited and abandoned houses became covered in white. Only the spirits remained dark, somber.

Yet, there still were those who did not believe in the story of Szulborze. Sender, who still was an intimate of the commissar, took care of the matter of contributions and lived outside the fenced in camp, received permission from the commissar to travel to Szulborze. He wanted to show everyone that the story of the murder of an entire congregation of Jews was a lie. The commissar himself had told him that they were working somewhere in a camp.

He returned from Szulborze with a lowered his head and sorrowfully distracted eyes. We could barely get a word from him. He said, "It is not good. I found nothing there, only a sleeve from a shirt, a shabby man's jacket, a bone from a hand that stuck out of the ground…."

[Column 935]

Jews went from house to house, again and again repeating the unbelievable thing. We were lightheaded from knowing the bitter truth. If there was still a hope – it disappeared. If someone had pity for oneself – it disappeared. If the thought of saving oneself arose again and one asked: why, because of what, because of whom? – This also was dulled.

The winter was frosty, biting, with angry winds. We went to hard labor every day. Our tired feet hardly lifted – tired heads barely held up. There were days when we actually lost the feeling that we were alive, that we were going to work and returning. We thought that we were standing up to our throats in thick, muddy water, that we would drown, be covered, be flooded.

And then many days and weeks passed, we again had the strength to cling to life. We sneaked into the villages, traded something for bread, bought a little from a Polish baker. The Germans looked away, did not even insist that everyone wear the yellow patch in the street. If they caught someone in a sin, they could be bribed. Hershel Mond was caught slaughtering a calf that he had procured somewhere in a village; Sender went to the commissar and arranged for him to be let out immediately.

The terror of waiting for "news" eased a little. The wives and children of several members of the *Judenrat* began to return. This opened the people's wounds and brought out bitterness.

[Column 936]

In the middle, Moshel Zylbersztajn, another Jewish policeman, arrived in the *shtetl*.

Someone once asked him:

– Moshel, is it appropriate to be a policeman? He had a ready answer.

– Do I have a choice?

There was no lack of work. There was after all a lack of workers. In addition, many people avoided going to work. I was one of them. Pity for my parents, for my sister, was a weight on my heart and I went through the villages every day to find them something to eat.

However, Shmulke Wengorz had an eye on me. Once, at night, the Germans demanded 20 new people to clean a field of stones brought by the Russians. You will not escape now, he said to me.

Do not be stubborn, my sister begged me, we could pay with our heads…

– You will work for several weeks. Perhaps things will calm down… Mainly, let us be healthy and endure.

It was *erev* [the eve of] Passover. The sun again rose over Czyzewo, a spring-like one, but it was not bright in the *shtetl* and it also was not joyful. Only the Germans stood more erect and even more harshly chased the Jews to work. I could not endure carrying the stones and after several days of work I escaped from the village.

This was repeated several times. The entire burden of providing food for the house lay on me. Therefore, I ignored the warnings that I would be arrested. Once, Marcziniak, the Polish policeman, even came to look for me.

[Column 937]

I learned of it earlier and hid at Riba's [house] under a bed and when it got dark I sneaked out of the ghetto and for two months no longer came to my parents to spend the night.

I worked the entire day in the field with the peasants, gathered the sheaves like everyone else and when it got dark I sneaked into the *shtetl*, brought some food for the house and ran back to the cut fields to spend the night in a haystack.

New Jews, individual people from other *shtetlekh*, began to arrive, bringing new information about liquidated ghettos and death camps, about Treblinka. The people, who had survived death in various ways, were emaciated from being hungry for so long.

Once, standing at the point where Alter Wolmer distributed the bread, a woman returned. The nightmare of pain and deadly fear, which she had lived through in that other place from which [people] were being sent to Treblinka, still appeared on her face. She asked for bread that cost 20 pfennigs. However, she did not have anything with which to pay.

The woman remained standing and at a loss began to look around for some kind of salvation. Her eyes became damp and I thought that blood would soon begin to flow from them.

I took out 20 pfennigs and gave them to her.

H.

It was *Sukkos* [Feast of the Tabernacles] time, 1942.

There was a renewal in the *shtetl*. The commissar ordered us to dig mounds of potatoes that we had to prepare for winter. We immediately [created] five piles of potatoes. This gave us the security that we would be allowed to survive the winter. This provided courage and we went to our exhausting work with more enthusiasm.

[Column 938]

The commissar's right hand now became Shmulke Wengorz. Sender died in a mysterious manner. It was said that he was poisoned. The commissar regretted his death and gave a speech at the cemetery, saying that he was a capable and loyal person.

The commissar became even more hostile and stricter.

One night, we suddenly heard the ringing of the bell that stood in front of the gate. A frightening panic broke out in the house. Shouting was heard: "They are going to take us away, to kill us. The end has come."

There were those who dared to jump over the wires, running away from the *shtetl*. The commissar himself shot after them. Enraged, the Polish policeman Marcziniak ran after the people. He immediately shot one who he caught right on the spot. He split Kosower's head and he led him covered in blood, shouting:

– One does not run away from us. We are the ones who send people away… to the other world. But first you have to finish the work.

– It appeared that the commissar only wanted to see if everyone was here in the house and that everything was in order. However, that night left a heavy feeling among the people that something terrible was coming closer with each day.

[Column 939]

The 1st of November 1942.

It already was dark. The people had begun to come together from work. Suddenly a bit of news was distributed that the Germans had arranged for wagons in the surrounding villages. There was great turmoil. Some saw the end in this; that they were going to take us away. Others consoled themselves that the vehicles were needed for the planting of new trees. There were those who knew for sure that new work of chopping wood in the forest was beginning and, therefore, the vehicles were needed.

It was clear to everyone that something new was going to happen. And even those who had consoled themselves felt a painful unease in their hearts that took sleep from their eyes.

The group that worked building the new highway outside the city, feeling the unease, went back to working on the night shift. Others left discretely outside the wire fence.

Shmulke Wengorz arrived. He walked in the middle of the street and his face did not seem as hopeful as earlier. He first went to the commissar who denied the whole story about the wagons.

The denials strengthened the suspicions even more. My mother and father now allowed themselves to be persuaded that I should leave the *shtetl*. My sister ran into the house, tore some clothing from hangers and threw them to my brother and me to carry and she herself began to make a small pack for her and our parents.

When we went outside into the dark night, my mother turned around all of the time and sighed, with her head cast down to the ground:

[Column 940]

– Woe, woe, is me…

– We were not the only ones – my father reassured her.

And there were frightened whispers carried in the air. Bent silhouettes crept through alternate roads. Hearts raced with unease and fear. As if ashamed, the sky donned dark clouds.

At one thirty at night, the policemen and members of the Gestapo suddenly surrounded the few fenced in houses and they started shooting at the houses. This was a warning that no one was permitted to move from this place. Those who attempted to jump out of the windows immediately were shot.

The sound of the shooting reached the places where the Jews were working on the night shift, but before they could determine what was happening, uniformed S.S. members and policemen appeared there and took them to the ghetto. Here there also were those who tried to jump out of a window and they were murdered immediately. Esther Gonczar also was murdered then. There was no way to escape, nowhere to run. Gendarmes and policemen stood watch on all roads and fields. We, too, had to return to the ghetto.

At seven o'clock in the morning, a member of the S.S. informed us that everyone was being taken to a special labor camp and we needed to take food and cooking pots with us.

The hour that we were given to prepare lasted as an eternity, difficult and terrifying. No one tried to pack his bag with anything, not with food, not with clothing. Everyone was convinced that we were going to be taken to Szulborze where the same fate of the earlier transports awaited us.

[Column 941]

The wagons into which we were loaded were waiting outside. Polish policemen searched every corner until they brought out the last Jews.

They left on the Zambrów road guarded on all sides. Choked sobs were heard. Children clung to their sobbing mothers and burst into tears. Adults drilled holes in the ground with their looks. It was a weight on their minds and it blunted every thought.

Hundreds of people knew that they themselves were the corpses and they themselves were going to their death, mourning themselves.

I.

No one noticed how we arrived at the barracks in Zambrów. There was a tumult of thousands of Jews running to meet us. People recognized each other and broke into tears. Others laughed and joked with the humor of one sentenced to death, who in the last moment had not lost their connection to life.

Captured members of the Red Army, who had all died of typhus, had been held earlier in these barracks. Large wooden toilets were located in the courtyard of the barracks that had been remade by the Germans into barracks with three story plank beds. The Jews were pushed into these.

There were Jews from Lomza and Lomzyca in block numbers 1 and 2 and in the third from Zawada, Wizna and Zambrów. The Czyzewo Jews were driven into the fourth block; the Wisoki Jews were located on the lowest plank beds.

There simply was no air to breathe in the barracks.

[Column 942]

Stifling smells, like stale meat, floated from the people… [Lying with one another's] heads on shoulders, feet and hands on [each other's] stomachs; they created an impression that piles of human limbs had been thrown together. Women and children were mixed with grown men. There were those who sat like hens over the packs that they had succeeded in smuggling past the gendarmes who had taken everything at the entrance. They stubbornly clung to the belief that they would survive their fate. Others destroyed everything that they had saved and hidden up to now.

We were not given food on the first two days. No one looked at us, as if someone outside was waiting for us to die off.

On the third day we noticed a commotion. They began to organize field kitchens in the courtyard. A loaf of bread was given for every 10 people. Peasant wagons brought potatoes, beets and wood.

Despite this, dozens of people died day after day. Various illnesses spread. My father also became ill. There was no one to determine the illness and no one to cure it. The Germans only permitted all of the sick to be taken to one barracks.

No one knew how many Jews were in the barracks; it was said that there were approximately 16,000, [the number of whom] became smaller with each day. People fell like flies.

When the cases of death increased, the gendarmes assigned a small wagon to carry out the dead and bury them. The gun barrels of machine guns looked down from the observation towers ready to shoot at every attempt to escape.

[Column 943]

Hunger, illness and death did not cease to rage. Pain and dirt was the daily bread here.

There was nothing with which to sweep the dirt. We persuaded the gendarmes that several people be permitted to go to the nearby words to cut branches to sweep and clean the barracks and the courtyard. In the bundles [of branches], they smuggled in bread and fats that they had bought from the peasants.

Moshel Rajczik, who brought the kettle of food and divided it among the people who stood in line with their cups, quietly with shaking knees, bent, hungry, was chosen as guardian of order.

Zelik–Leibel, the shoemaker, stood in line with his [cup] in his boney, out–struck hands that shook like an old man's. When Moshel Rajczik poured in [his portion of food], [Zelik–Leibel] at first brought the cup closer to his eyes, then gently shook it – only water, not one piece of potato…for the children. He poured it out in Rajczik's face.

Rajczik, pale, did not say one word.

The camp elder arrived at the same moment and called to him.

Zelik–Leibel barely moved. We saw that it was difficult for him to move his own limbs, but he did not release the empty cup from his gripping fingers. His children cried: father, father…

The dogs sprang on him with a wild fury as soon as he appeared in the courtyard; they began to tear his clothes from him, pieces of his body, fingers, arms.

[Column 944]

Zelik–Leibel's frantic screams tore through the entire courtyard. He did not hear someone call to him from a corner that he should lie down on the ground. Then the dogs would withdraw from him. However, the camp elder heard him and the dogs were set on him, too. He did not even try to throw himself on the ground. The dogs did not let them catch their breath, tore pieces from their half naked bodies. Their laments split the heavens.

J.

The 24th of December 1942.

I decided to escape from the barracks. Others had done so before me. The way was simple. One had to make one's way to the group that went into the forest to cut branches. There, one bribed the watch and escaped.

Yet here the danger was greater. One could be noticed by the guard and shot on the spot.

I passed through all of the dangers. It was a cold winter day, dark clouds covered the sky and I ran through the dark forest in great haste. My foot somehow got caught in a branch and I fell. For a second I thought I would catch a bullet. I lay for several minutes with my face to the ground and I did not hear any shots, any steps. I crawled on my stomach, continuing further and further. I did not know the time of day. It suddenly became more overcast. I was afraid that they would notice in the barracks that I was missing. They would run out with bloodhounds to seek me. The dogs would tear me apart…

I finally arrived at the edge of the forest. I remained standing for a minute and a frightening question began gnawing at my heart: Where to?

[Column 945]

I looked into the cloud–covered sky that hung heavy on the naked fields as if it was absorbing the grief and pain of the Zambrów barracks and searching for where to pour it out.

Suddenly I heard the hum of a motor. There was a machine somewhere not far away. Not yet, I was not yet free. Death still hovered on all sides. Where does one go? Where does one hide?

I knew the roads here well and I decided to avoid Czyzewo and to go to Dambrowa, to the village where we had lived. I did not tell the peasant whose house I entered that I had escaped from the barracks or that I had been in Zambrów. I learned from the peasant that there again was a ghetto in Czyzewo. With enthusiasm, the commissar had started to bring together the scattered Jews who had avoided the deportation and after a short time they again were sent to the barracks. Those closest to the commissar were now Moshel Zylbersztajn and three other Jews, among whom was a furrier who had escaped from Ciechanowiec during the deportation.

I remained in the village over the Christian holidays, regained my strength and began to think about how to help my parents and my sister and brother who remained in the barracks.

I packed several loaves of bread in a small sack and left for Zambrów.

Finally, after a difficult journey, I arrived at the gate of the barracks. I was surprised by the calm manner with which I began to think about how I would smuggle in the food.

[Column 946]

Suddenly I heard someone from inside call me by name and I saw my mother and my sister. A painful despair poured from their faces. Other women with wrinkled coats and dirty hair approached. They came closer to the wire fencing. I heard voices: Run away…come inside…run away!

I stood, soaked by the wet snow and sweat from going such a long way through the fields and I did not know what to do. My mother's quiet eyes pulled me. I approached the gate.

The shouts of the gendarme woke me from my immobility, but my mother's eyes still pulled me. I let him take the bread from me. Only the fats remained with me. When I was inside, my mother fell on me crying and I felt as if a vise clung internally to my neck.

The situation in the barracks had changed completely, become stricter; no one was allowed to go out to the forest to gather branches. A boy who had tried to sneak out in a peasant wagon was shot in the presence of all of the Jews who were driven from the barracks to watch the execution. Something new, bitter hung in the air.

K.

It was the 2nd of January 1943. Deportations of Jews from the barracks to Auschwitz, to the death camp, began on a frosty night. The German chief of the barracks had made an announcement about this earlier. He said that we were being taken to work. He ended his short talk: "Whoever does not believe this should step out and say so."

[Column 947]

The deportations took place at night. Each night up to 2,000 people. It took place under heavy guard, furtively, secretly. We felt the breath of death.

For now, they were taking [people] from No. 1 and 2. We lay entire nights with open eyes. The orders of the German gendarmes who were administering the deportation rustled in our ears. I heard how dogs were set against people, desperate screams of weakness and fear that cut into the soul like sharp knives. This was death, death. In my brain were tangled thoughts of how to get out of this hell.

I was not the only one who thought of this, but we did not hear of anyone who succeeded. Those who tried to escape through the wires at the change of the guards, using prepared shears, all were shot. Three young Kosower young people bribed a guard who took their money and, when they left, shot one of them. The two remaining managed to draw back in time.

And yet a hope awoke in me that I would be able to escape.

The Czyzewo block was taken during the course of two nights. The first transport began on Friday night. My father gladly agreed that we should avoid this transport and go the next day at the end of *Shabbos* [Sabbath].

A strange delirium now trembled deep in my subconscious. "We must escape" – I said to my parents who sadly shook their heads in agreement. My sister pointed to her two children, one three years old and the other one eight months old. "Perhaps they will let us live. Where will I go with my babies?

[Column 948]

I felt guilty and came to an agreement with my brother that we will take the children. But she remained categorically against this. "I will not run anywhere." She became stubborn.

During *Shabbos* I tried to convince others from Czyzewo that we need to escape. I told Esther Riba that if we succeed in escaping, we would be in Dambrowa at the Drengowski's.

It began. We were placed in rows. Warmly wrapped S.S. men sat in sleighs and we, a group of 800 people, went on foot to the train station where there already were train wagons prepared for us.

I did not wait long. At the first small bridge we passed on the way, I nimbly shuffled down and lay with my face to the ground.

I heard people walking over my head. I did not know if my brother had noticed in the darkness that I had left. My mother and my father remained slightly behind me with my sister. I felt a strong desire to draw them to me. But, I was afraid to raise my head.

The frost was very strong, burning, searing. The air stuck us like the tips of knives. It was difficult to raise the chest and to breathe. However, the footsteps over me and the voices of the Germans who shouted, "*Laus, schneller!*" [Louse, faster.] rang with a sharp metallic echo and poured into my ears like buckshot. The blood in my veins became as heavy as lead. My eyes began to stick and I do know how long I slept. Suddenly I felt a stabbing in my toes that penetrated through my entire body.

[Column 949]

I quickly stood up and listened in the frosty night. It was quiet around me. No breath of air, no people, still and dark, blue snow and a black night.

I started to walk, dragged myself, stepped on the frozen ground, wobbling, shaky. Later, I began to crawl on my stomach, on all fours, to the forest that was at most 100 meters from me.

It was quiet and dark. I walked for an hour [or] two and felt that my strength was leaving me and then I fell down on the ground. The frost was still burning and searing. A shiver penetrated my bones. I bit my lips from the cold and shivered, shook, and my teeth chattered.

The night lasted for an eternity. I had to sit down to rest after every [few steps]. A fever banged in my temples. My eyes half-closed, stiffened: my body shook. Do not fall asleep!

Things became worse for me when night had withdrawn from the forest, from the sky. A burning pain lay heavily on my head and tired, weakened, without strength, with dried lips and leather gums, I could barely drag my feet.

– Alas, if I could warm my body somewhere!…

A little warmth to thaw my frozen blood…

Nothing more, just to warm myself a little…

I arrived in the village at six o'clock in the evening and went to the Drengowskis.

– Woe, woe! The peasant women commented – See what the bandits have made of a person.

[Column 950]

Her husband said to speak quietly and both of them began to rub my nose, my feet. My stiff, frozen limbs began to defrost. They broke the ice from my limbs with experienced hands and warm hearts. Finally, I began to feel the warm trickle of my blood.

In the morning at sunrise, Esther Riba and Zeylik Gromadzyn sneaked into the cottage. The peasant woman wrung her hands. Their appearance evoked compassion from her. Simultaneously, she was afraid that someone would learn of their arrival. [Things] were very strict then and there were threats that one would pay with their life.

Every once in a while she went outside to see if someone had noticed their arrival. When they revived a little, she said with a worried face that we would not be able to spend the night in the house because the police creep around and search in every hole. We could go into the barn. If we were caught, let it seem that we entered without their knowledge.

We remained sitting helpless. Our limbs, our toes still hurt us from the frozenness. The peasant woman turned around and sighed. She went to the door, listened to the noises that carried from the village street, the normal noise of an ordinary Monday. She was somewhat calmed.

– People have large ears and long tongues – she quietly said – some misfortune could to us and for nothing…

Her talk pressed into our hearts like pliers. Esther Riba let out a sobbing cry. Her entire body began to shake.

[Column 951]

Tuesday, in the morning, my mother suddenly turned up unexpectedly. I barely recognized her. She stood over us shrunken and bent. Her blue lips murmured quietly:

– My children…

We forgot about the cold and sprang out of the straw, crying and hugging each other.

– How, Mama, how did you succeed in escaping?

My mother shook her head.

– At the train, I saw that you were not there, so I also left.

Her forehead was even more deeply wrinkled; her eyes looked sadly worried as if she was considering [our] great misfortune.

– What will happen to father?

Drengowski came in and asked us to talk more quietly. It would be better if we did not talk at all among ourselves.

In hiding, we listened to every rustle. However, we only heard the beating of our own hearts. It was quiet. From time to time, we heard the passing of a fast sled with a jingle of bells that hung on the wagon shaft, on the manes of the horses.

My mother could not restrain herself:

– My heart tells me that we will not survive here. I am afraid…

I took her hand to calm her down. Her hand was as cold as a piece of ice.

On the fifth day of our lying in the barn, in the evening, Drengowski came in. He remained standing with his head down and looked for a while with blind eyes, as if someone had taken his ability to speak.

[Column 952]

– What has happened, Pani [Master] Drengowski? – I asked. His appearance awoke a sleeping fear.

– It is bad… Police are maneuvering around the village… You have to leave from here.

We held our breath and listened more carefully. However, it was quiet outside, so that the stillness rang in our ears.

The peasant became impatient.

– Now is the best time to get out… You must go.

L.

In addition, the frost outside seized my breath. No living soul was seen anywhere. The village was at rest, [people] warming themselves near the ovens. Even the dogs stayed in their doghouses. A black crow cawed somewhere on a low, snow-covered roof. We walked faster. We wanted to reach the forest more quickly.

There was a bunker located in the forest near Dombrowa. This bunker now seemed to be our only salvation. For how long? No one would have thought about that then. One thought, one desire: save oneself. Let it be for a week, a day. Perhaps later the great salvation would come. However, does a hunted animal think about later? We already had stopped thinking of ourselves as people. Is not the dog in the doghouse better than us?

We were in this bunker for several days. In the village that I would [sneak into] to gather something to eat, I immediately heard that the peasants were saying something about the bunker and [this information] could reach the police any day. Therefore, we began to dig another bunker deeper in the forest for ourselves. In the midst [of our digging] several more Czyzewo Jews arrived who were wandering around in the forest. We took them in. A new snow fell when we finally finished. There could be no talk of moving; the footprints in the snow would betray us immediately.

[Column 953]

I became sick, had a high fever and thought the end was coming. My mother sat over me and her lips trembled. She asked God for her child's health. She could do nothing more for me. There were no medicines, nothing to eat.

Despite all of this, the illness passed quicker than at home. I stood up. My shoulders, my left side still throbbed, but I braced myself. We had to take care of the bunker.

It was very crowded in the bunker and we had to speak about dividing the people. Half went to the second bunker that we had dug earlier.

On the same day, I went to the village. My mother insisted that she wanted to go with me. But she was unable return. The Drengowskis permitted her to sit near the oven for the entire night.

In the morning, we took several breads with us and left for the forest. My mother could barely stand on her feet.

We suddenly heard shooting from the direction of the bunker as we reached the edge of the forest. This was the first bunker in which several people remained.

There was no place to run. When the Germans were finished with the first bunker, they could continue searching and also discover the other bunker.

[Column 954]

I took my mother by the hand and left for the other end of the forest where we lay shivering the entire frosty day and listened to the echoes that came from the other end of the forest.

When it grew dark, we sneaked into the village. The Drengowskis told us of the entire progression of the police search.

The Germans learned that Jews were hiding in the forest and brought several peasant women with them who could show them where the bunkers were located. A grenade was thrown out at the moment when they approached the bunker. This was the only grenade located in the bunker. Later, everyone had to leave the bunker and they were shot immediately. Only a boy was allowed to live, so he could show them the location of the second bunker. However, that bunker already was empty. Everyone had run at the echoing of the shooting.

– What would become of us? Where would we go?

The peasant was quiet. His wife said:

– You have to look for hiding place somewhere. It is terrible in the village…

– I will not begrudge you food.

She said that 12 Czyzewo people were hidden in Cetki. There were Shmulke Wengorcz's son [and] Lepak's son. The police discovered them and shot them along with the peasant.

We went outside.

I felt a violent beating in my temples. My feet did not want to obey at all and bent to tumble. Everything began to spin before my eyes.

[Column 955]

My mother noticed this and ran back to the peasant, asking him that he at least let me stay here overnight. She would go to the woods.

I walked like a lunatic with shaking steps. My mother led me. I think that her feet also were breaking and I wanted to hold her. But she whispered quietly:

– My child, you should get well. Lie calmly.

I do not know how many days I lay in the barn. Suddenly I felt someone was shaking me and trying to awaken me. I opened my eyes.

– Water… Water…

The Drengowskis stood over me, dressed in furs as if they were going to go on a trip. The peasant's wife let out a suffocating shout:

– He is alive!...

It became apparent that they were sure that I was dying and wanted to take me away to the forest. Opening my eyes and asking for water was something of a miracle from heaven to them and they did not touch me.

In the morning, when my mother came to see how I was, the Drengowski's told her:

– We have children, too… Take him away from here. A misfortune can occur at any minute… Your son is strong and Yakosz [the article writer's nickname] will recover in the forest.

I barely dragged myself to the forest. Sweat poured from my feverish forehead and cooled. My mother said that if I was sweating it was a sign that I was getting better.

However, several day later abscesses appeared over my entire body, ran and drew my last bit of strength.

[Column 956]

Who thinks that a person is a weak creature? No. There is nothing stronger than a person. The illness that I survived was severe typhoid that takes weeks and months to heal. Here in the forest, I was healthy after several days and felt like I had been on a trip to a distant land. Everything I had lived through seemed so distant and I suddenly received new strength.

I again went to the village, helped Drengowski at work and, therefore, I received bread from him, for me, for my mother.

M.

The dangers increased and became greater with every day. The Germans knew that individual Czyzewo Jews, who had escaped from death, were wandering around the villages and they lay in wait for them with various ruses. For a Jew who was caught, they [the Germans] promised the peasants kerosene, whiskey, sugar. There were Wolomin peasants who wandered through the roads all day and threw themselves on every Jew they found, as if at winnings.

A band of Polish thieves was rampaging the Czyzewo area at the time that was led by a Jew. In addition to stealing pigs, he took as his task the elimination of those peasants who were involved with catching Jews. He was spoken about in the village with reverence and fear. Many peasants did not point out a Jew just because of the fear for this band.

Among the Wolomin policemen, there was one who was considered a big anti-Semite, who only sought to murder Jews. Unexpectedly it was shown that he was a Jew. The Germans shot him. However, the peasants believed that there were still many such who disguised themselves and took revenge for the killing of Jews.

[Column 957]

Once, going in the village at night, I met the teacher, who recognized me immediately and greeted me in a friendly way. I knew that he would not turn me in and I stopped to talk with him.

He told me that one of his uncles received a card from my younger sister who had lived in Bialystok for the entire time. She asked about us since she had learned that we were living somewhere in a village.

The card did not let me rest and after a long effort I finally received it.

I carried it around for several days and did not know what to tell my mother. I knew that this would overwhelm her and it could have an effect on her health.

Again lying in the bunker in the dark, my mother began to speak about what had happened to the entire family. I felt how she rolled and writhed in the pain of suffering. I wanted to console her and the story of the card that was needed to convince her that my sister was alive tore out of me.

I immediately realized that I had done something terrible, but it already was too late.

In the morning, early, she left on foot for Bialystok and immediately fell into [the hands of] the gendarmerie.

After the liberation, when I looked for traces of my vanished mother, I accidentally met a Polish girl who was employed cleaning the gendarmerie. She told me how the Germans took my mother to the courtyard and set specially trained dogs on her, who threw themselves on her and tore her to pieces.

[Column 958]

N.

I was left alone.

Various news items reached me every day. Zelik-Leibel, the shoemaker, was found murdered after the harvesting of the wheat. Chaim the Cheek [a nickname] had taken all of his possessions to Dmochy, to Kraszewski and left his son with him. Kraszewski took all the money and murdered the boy. Yakov Jablonka, who hid somewhere for a long time, met several peasants on a foggy, autumn day, who attacked him with poles and axes and murdered him in a frightening manner.

The bunkers were very unsafe hiding places and, therefore, I spent time in the barns. Every night I spent the night in another barn and during the day, when it had barely turned grey, I left discretely so no one would notice me.

Summer arrived. Everything blossomed, turned green, like years past, [like 12 months ago], just as nothing was happening in God's world.

It would happen that I lay entire nights in the rye and thought about the day I had just lived through. Everything looked hopeless, without relief, chased during the day and at night, without hope that it would end at some time. The entire world looked just like the moon, so far away and cold that I trembled, perhaps it was not necessary to torment myself so much!

I later heard that the peasants were saying that something was threatening in the wheat, sighs with such a frightening echo.

[Column 959]

Sadovski, a peasant from Dabrowa, with a genteel heart, told me this. He knew the truth, what threatened me and would bring me a newspaper, a piece of bread and warned me about and from where danger could come, where it would be better to hide.

It already was the end of July. I hid at the edge of the forest near Sadovski's field and waited for Sadovski to come. Suddenly I saw a dark cloud nearing the field that soon was filled with a loud conversation, shouts and the tumult of German soldiers with rifles outstretched and the barking of dogs.

I ran with all my strength, not looking back. I crossed the 300-meter field that cut across the forest as if in one leap. I finally stopped when I was outside of Dmochy, stretched out on the ground and listened to the distant noises that came from the right. The Germans had departed on the [Krzeczkowo] Bienki [Road].

[Column 960]

I lay down and closed my eyes. My heart beat in fear. It already was the third day that I had not had a piece of bread in my mouth. Running had completely exhausted me. I barely drew breaths. Will it be death after I succeeded in saving myself from the Germans?

Bobe Sore tells 6 grandchildren a story
he Christian woman who hid Avraham Krapik's grandchild, now the
wife of the rabbi in Lodz

No. I would not die. A powerful desire to live struggled in me. It was nine in the morning. I had never dared to enter the village at that time. Now I did not want to think of any danger. I had only one goal: food, food to maintain my soul and to remain alive. Let it be the life of a hunted dog, but life, life!

Women peasants crossed themselves and, reading the hunger on my face, brought out warm milk and pushed pieces of bread into my pockets.

I left quickly.

It was near the end of summer. The fields were golden yellow after the harvest. I would have loved to look at the golden fields, but now I could not enjoy them. I had to lay hidden in the bales because with the approach of the front there were more Germans in the area. The peasants spoke about the frightening cruelty of the retreating Germans. The peasants themselves prepared bunkers outside of Dabrowa to hide when the military entered the village.

[Column 961]

Lying once this way in the sheaves, I felt that the earth suddenly began to tremble from distant explosions. I was enveloped by a strong joy. I barely waited for the arrival of night to run to the village to learn something about the front.

Drengowski told me that the Russians would arrive any day. He invited me to the table and offered me a plate of borscht.

He permitted me to remain in the courtyard. The cannons thundered for the entire night. Machine guns banged without end. Beams of light cut through the darkness with enormous strength as if they strove to drive out the night. The sky was red with the glow of distant fires.

At dawn military vehicles drove into the village with a great uproar. I left for the bunker. There was a confusion in my head. I wanted to imagine myself liberated, among my own, found, alive. I wanted to remember faces, but my head became heavier and heavier. I feel asleep.

I was awaked by a great commotion over my head. I strained my hearing and began to move to the exit. The German soldiers reinforced positions right near the bunker. They were occupied and did not notice me leaving.

The village was starting to bustle. The peasants brought apples to the German positions and looked at me with disbelieving eyes that I was moving around the German positions. Had I lost my senses?

I began to run from one place to another. Near the forest I saw that it was full of the German military.

[Column 962]

I lay for a long time in the shelter, curled up with a heart that banged like a hammer. A German soldier ran by every few minutes. And I thought that they were piercing my hiding place with their looks. When it became quiet I ran back to the village.

The Germans ran around agitated and confused, grabbing peasants for work. I was pulled in among a group of young peasants who were sent to dig trenches.

I did the work willingly and diligently dug the earth with my shovel and listened to the hiss and whistle from the unseen shrapnel. It groaned, seethed and roared from all kinds of machine guns somewhere very nearby.

I was gratified that everyone was occupied and did not pay attention to me. However, suddenly one of them somewhere shouted:

– As God loves me, this is the Jew, Yankel!

There was a tumult. Someone's strident voice was heard that they should tell the Germans while there was still time…

In a minute a silence arrived as if they were thinking about how to do it. It was a strange moment and I did not stop digging with my shovel.

– People! – one of the peasants suddenly called – Are you crazy? At such a time, when the Swabians [Germans] are counting their last moments, such foolishness is still in your heads?

The other's face became fire red; no one said anything more about it.

The Russians forced their way through the secondary train line on the same day and began to shoot at the Germans from behind. Individual Germans fell, shot.

[Column 963]

Noise from the exploding hand grenades and the motors starting rang from the right.

The German were running away.

Suddenly I felt what had made me so terribly tense. It became still, entirely still. The tumult from the front rolled away somewhere far outside the village.

I suddenly trembled and lifted my head. I saw that all of those who had been digging with me had sprung up, carefully stuck out their heads and listened to the suddenly distant noise.

We watched and could not understand anything. Were there really no Germans here? Other feelings bubbled now in me: I was free, free!

Where do we go now?...

A strange fear again fell on me with this thought. I was afraid of learning the truth about what I often thought about during the days and nights of being chased, although I chased away my dark thoughts. I wanted to convince myself that they are alive, that they were wandering somewhere in the fields just as I was.

Now this thought seemed still more remote than before. I wanted to know the truth and, at the same time, I was afraid of it.

I spent the day with the peasant, washed myself, ate, not the same as usual. Drengowski also was different from usual, changed, affable.

He asked me what I was thinking of doing, where I wanted to go now. He himself was happy that the Germans had left, but did not know if we needed to celebrate with the Russians. They could bring in the *kolkoz* [collective farms] and then all would be lost.

[Column 964]

When it became dark, neighbors with mysterious faces sneaked into Drengowski's cottage. Seeing me, they slyly squinted their eyes and smiled:

– From the other world, Yankel, huh?

One said that they met Jews who came out of the forests on the roads now. However, the *esenzetowices* (members of the Polish underground party) were shooting at them. They shot two Jews who were hiding with a peasant in a neighboring village. The peasant barely succeeded in receiving a pardon for his life.

This was beyond belief to Drengowski and he frantically, silently shook his head. I understood the fear that enveloped him. I already knew this fear very well, during the few years I spent with him.

He wiped the anxious sweat from his brow and indistinctly mumbled under his breathe:

– Nerves!... what do you think, such danger…

This also was not the first time I had heard this and just as before I knew that now I must not be weak and must pull myself together.

I quickly left the house.

I thought things over, that I should not take to the road now where I could meet the *N.S.Z.*[2] It was terrible in the forests, too.

I again slept in the barn.

On the third day the Russian military entered the village. The roads became animated with Soviet trucks and jeeps. They entertained civilians, laughed, sang. It became tumultuous in the village.

[Column 965]

I left on the road to Bransk. A peasant told me that there were Jews there. For the first time I felt that I was walking as a free man, that I did not have to look around on all sides.

I did not celebrate my freedom for long. A military patrol arrived at the crossroads. The soldiers asked me for documents and looked at me with suspicion. When I told them that I had lived for three years without documents, they earnestly, with outstretched guns, led me to Szepietowo and placed me in some sort of hut where an officer was also quartered.

The officer was busy and did not have any time for me. However, I had to wait. A soldier stood outside at the door and kept watch.

Peasants, who brought food products from Dabrowa, arrived late at night. When they heard that I was being held because I did not have any documents, they immediately turned to the officer.

– *Tavarish* [friend] commander… This is Yankel from Czyzewo, a Jew… We know him.

The officer flashed his teeth and broke into a wide smile:

– *Vos-zhe zitstu?...Gegesn hostu shoyn?* [Why are you sitting?...Have you eaten already?]

The officer was a Jew.

Back in Czyzewo

I stopped before entering the *shtetl*. I felt a strong anxiety; deep in me something rejoiced and yet I thought that I was falling into a dark abyss…

Would I meet anyone?

So I was in Czyzewo. The same alleys, small houses. But would I meet one recognizable face from them?

[Column 966]

There was something heavy on my chest and it restricted my breathing. Czyzewo! There was very little movement in the alley. They looked at me with strange looks and one asked another:

– A Jew?

I went to the market. Perhaps there would be someone there, an acquaintance, a family member.

I met Hershel Mant, Zelik Gromadzyn. The suffering they lived through still raged from their faces. We began to talk about examples of experiences with interrupted words. Everyone had cheated death in a different way.

Leibush Frydman's daughter, Shmuel Ikir's daughter arrived. Later, Yosl Gonczar came, too. All rejoiced, but there was great weeping in their joy.

I said to Gonczar:

– Yosl, let us leave here. It is difficult to breathe here.

– Where will you go?

– Let it be to Wysoki. I feel bad here.

Yosl was quiet for a minute as if he was reflecting. Later he spoke up.

– So, we will temporarily live here. No one is bothering us. Commerce is beginning here.

I rejected this:

– I do not like this.

On the same day I left for Wysoki.

Before Passover, the news reached me of the great slaughter by the Polish bandits in Czyzewo.

My pain from the terrible loss was very deep. I knew what the Jews in Czyzewo had lived through until they achieved liberation. Their cruel death placed a terrible burden on my soul and it has not abandoned me to this day.

Translator's Footnotes:

1. In 1938, the German government expelled German Jews who originated in Poland, who had had their German citizenship taken away or did not have German citizenship, to the Polish border town of Zbaszyn

2. *NaroDove Siły Zbrojne* – National Armed Forces – a Polish resistance organization. There were reports that the *N.S.Z.* murdered Jews who survived the Holocaust.

[Column 967]

In the Valley of Lament and Fear
- From My Diary –

by Etka Cukerman, Haifa

Translated by Gloria Berkenstat Freund

October 1942

A cold, cloudy day. It is still dark in the soul; death reigns around us.

I am alone with my eight-year old sister. I think aloud, audibly:

"How do we have a chance to survive? How do we save ourselves from death?

From where did she get so much wisdom? She said with the complete seriousness of a mature person:

– Etka, you must learn the Christian prayers; you will be able to pass for a gentile; you will be able to go through the villages asking for work, bread.

Surprised, I looked at my young sister and asked her:

– And you? Will you do the same?

She said:

– I? Do I look like a gentile girl? I am such a weak one… You are strong and already grown… You will do well and will remain alive.

I was then 13 years old.

A few weeks later, the ghetto in Czyzewo was liquidated. The Germans released a rumor that Jewish children up to 12 years of age needed to return to the ghetto and nothing would happen [to them].

[Column 968]

I did not believe this, but my small sister already was tired of wandering around through peasant stables. Every day it became more difficult to find a peasant who would let us spend the night or give us something to eat. She said:

– In any case, we will not survive.

We said goodbye and she returned to the ghetto.

The Poles said that on Christmas day the Gestapo shot several children at the Jewish cemetery. My young sister was among them.

December 1942

I write these words in a field where I have already sat hidden for three days. The "police search" is still going on. They are looking for Jews. My heart dies in me with every rustle. I think that the various animals, who run around here, feel freer than I do.

A person is worse than an animal.

I did not know where to run. I was chased everywhere. Peasants came today not far from my hiding place and began to chop down trees and almost have reached here [where I am hiding]. The rope around my throat is getting tighter.

[Column 969]

Things were good for me for a month. A peasant who knew that I am Jewish suggested that I hide in her cellar. In exchange I would knit and sew for her.

It was dark in the cellar. Mice ran around. I worked all day by the light that came in from a crevice. It was good for me in darkness.

I was asleep when the peasant came in with a shout to me:

– Out. Leave. There is a police search…

I sprang up from my straw bed, confused, lost.

– Why are you standing? I will not die for you!

– Where should I go?

– Go, leave!

It was snowing outside. A frosty wind went through my body. Where to go? Why is the entire world so bad to me, a child who did nothing bad to anyone? I know that I committed a serious crime; I was born a Jewish child… I have to perish… Death hovered from everywhere.

I was so hungry.

I had already eaten all of the bark from the surrounding trees. I was afraid to go further. The snow had stopped and my steps could be noticed in the snow.

I sat on a tree, doubled over, twisted together. How good it would be if I could straighten out my feet.

One could not. One could not move.

Perhaps I would survive in this way.

Night would come and perhaps it would start to snow and I would climb down, straighten out my feet and walk around so that I would not fall asleep, not freeze. I do not want to freeze.

[Column 970]

I was so hungry and I badly wanted to go to sleep.

* * *

It was a horrible night.

It rained the entire night. It only eased up when the train with the Jews began to leave from the market. The Jews walked in rows, four in a row. In front went the young and the old were in the back.

The entire train was guarded by six armed *S.S.* members.

Six *S.S.* members for over 1,000 people.

The six *S.S.* members ordered the Jews to sing and dance and the Jews sang and danced.

The Poles, who were standing on the side, laughed.

I, a child, stood among these Poles. My heart cried and everything in me shouted as the heartless laughter of the Poles at the mockery of the Jews drilled in my ears.

– Why do they submit?

– So many men and only six Germans.

Suddenly shooting was heard. The first victims fell before my eyes. They had tried to escape and fell at their first steps.

The laughter from the Poles did not stop.

Again, someone tried to escape, not far from my spot. The bullets from the *S.S.* members reached him where he stood. This was Lopata. His sister worked in the village of Chelenowa with me. He probably also thought about saving himself there and hiding [in the village] with his sister. He fell dead on the spot.

[Column 971]

The rows moved ahead. The interrupted singing, mixed with the crack of the rifles and the last screams of the dying, was renewed at the order of the members of the *S.S.*

The trucks of Jewish women and children drove after them.

The shooting lasted the entire day.

The Poles said that the Jews were taken in the direction of the Szulborze Woods, where the Russians had dug trenches. There, they were arranged in long rows and shot. They fell into the pits, dead, wounded, alive.

I went there two days later. The earth was split and rose. A peasant said that those buried alive were moving.

May 1943

On a spring night after a day of heavy labor in the field, I left for the village. Succulent greenery was around me but my mood was poisoned. The memories of the death of those closest to me, of all of Czyzewo, did not leave me for a minute.

I immediately saw in the village that all of the roads were blocked by German soldiers. Someone told me that they were searching for a Jewish girl who said she was a Christian from Warsaw and was hiding in the village. He added that she was wearing long braids.

I understood that this meant me. Someone had denounced me to the Gestapo. I wrapped my head even more with the cloth I wore on my head so that my hair would not be seen. I saw a pail somewhere and I wanted to leave the village with it, under the pretense that I had forgotten something in the field. However, the Germans who sprang out of every corner, would no long let anyone leave.

[Column 972]

"This is the end," I thought. All of the torments that I had gone through that entire time, it all was useless.

The members of the *S.S.* went to all of the peasant cottages, searched in every corner. There was no way out. I had to again play my role of a gentile girl to the end. My heart was gripped by fear. However, at the same time I wanted to laugh; look at how many Germans were searching for me, a forlorn Jewish girl. I was 14 years old then.

However, I did not laugh; all of my limbs sagged in fear.

The door suddenly opened. Five gendarmes quickly entered. A Polish policeman accompanied them. He immediately recognized me and pointed at me:

– Here she is, the *Zydowka* [Polish word for a Jewish woman].

I showed my Polish documents, but the gendarmes brutally pushed me out.

I was led away to the chief of prisoners by whom I was employed. He also was a German and he became very angry when he learned that I was Jewish. Blows began to fall on me and shouts that I tell with whom I had hid and from whom I had received the Polish documents.

I knew very well then that I must not confess because that meant death. I stubbornly maintained the song I learned: "I am a Christian girl from Warsaw. My parents were taken to Germany. Since then I have wandered from one village to another and work to survive."

[Column 973]

The time was drawn out and the gendarmes did not get tired. When they saw that hitting me did not accomplish anything, they tried to be nice.

– Tell us who hid you and we will leave you alone.

The *sturmfuhrer* [assault leader] even tried to smile, [said] that I was still a child and it would be shame for them to kill me. However, I no longer was a child. My experiences had made me mature and old. I had no doubt that they only wanted to get the names of more victims from me. I bit my lips and said only the few words I had learned, mechanically.

– We have to finish with her, the chief said, I should be taken out, placed near a tree and a pistol aimed at me.

I looked at the pistol with wide-open eyes; just in a minute, everything would be over. Now, when it appeared to me that the end of the war was approaching.

However, my heart did not want to stop; I really wanted to live and I begged them: "Do not murder me!"

They said something to each other and led me back into the house. Again, they began to pelt me with questions and torture.

– You are a partisan! One of the investigators suddenly had an idea.

[Column 974]

A short time earlier partisans had attacked the village and he wanted to convince me [to admit] that I was their spy. I had the impression that he did not believe this himself, but he wanted to frighten me so that I would confess to being a Jew.

His speech and sharp looks spun and drilled in my brain, which became foggier. My will also was weakened. It appeared to me that I would soon say everything that he wanted me to say, but I clenched my teeth, bit my lips… I fainted.

I do not know how long I lay in a puddle of water. The German, who stood over me, said:

– You are alive. Nothing will happen… Ask her to recite the evening prayer.

I knew the Christian prayers very well. I knew what a good weapon they were in the struggle to live and I sang them like a born *shiksl* [gentile girl]. They made a strong impression. They looked at each other. The German mumbled something, again took my documents, looked at them on all sides. Finally, he said:

– Go home and you will report here tomorrow. Your documents will be here.

His voice echoed in my ears like a voice from the other world. I was heavily beaten and could not move from the spot.

The peasants from the village quickly learned everything. I do not know what they thought. When I began going on the road to Czyzewo in the morning I saw the peasants accompanying me with eyes as if they were accompanying me to my death.

[Column 975]

At the Czyzewo Gestapo it looked as if they were waiting for me. Curses and blows began to fall on me. Although I was a little stronger from my success at yesterday's exams and had decided that I would not collapse from the blows and threats, there came a moment when my nerves could not endure and I again fainted.

When I came to, the Gestapo member sat opposite me without remorse. He told me to go home and come in 10 days for the documents.

I understood that they would again research the correctness of what I had said. I began to feel terror when I thought about this. But I did not see any way out and I therefore patiently waited. On the designated day I again went to the Gestapo. It appeared as if they had found such a family. Therefore, they accepted the documents as correct. But there was another drawback: I had said in my statement that my parents had been sent to Germany. However, it appeared that only the father had been sent…

[It was as if] a bone had gotten stuck in my throat and I could not utter a word. He would again lift his boots over me and let them down slowly, slowly… He knew that the fear itself was worse than the suffering. I wanted to shout from pain, but a thought entered my brain at that moment and I began to cry that they not sent me back to my mother because she beat me terribly…

This worked.

[Column 976]

The Gestapo member began to laugh. His face became distorted in such a foolish grimace.

"Run, run to wherever your eyes take you," he shouted to me.

He gave me back my documents. I again was free.

* * *

It already was several weeks after the liberation.

How strongly I longed for it in the empty days and dark nights. Now it had come. I was free!

And yet – –

What do I gain with my freedom?

True, I no longer was afraid of the Gestapo and did not have to escape to the forest and tremble at the bloodhounds, but death still hovered. Deadly danger threatened on all sides.

The Poles whom I met in the city and in the village looked at me with fear and hatred. They saw in every Jew one who had come to demand of them the possessions that they had stolen.

I took a piece of bread with me and went back to Czyzewo on foot.

My melancholy attacked me more strongly the deeper I went into the *shtetl*. There were no familiar faces. Everyone looked at me with hate. Their glances asked: "You are still alive?"

So I listened:

> "On the preceding night, the Polish bandits barged into the house in which the Jews who had returned from the forests and villages lived and they murdered them all."

[Column 977]

I sensed from the words of the Poles that they knew who had done it. I went for the militia. From my intestines came a scream of bile:

– Why are you not doing anything? Why are you not capturing the murders? Is Jewish blood forgotten?

The militiaman spoke calmly, going through me with his sharp look and he considered his every word:

– Who had asked them to return here? What were the Jews still looking for here?

The officer in the Russian command did not want to intervene.

[Column 978]

I went to Szulborze, to the mass grave of the Czyzewo Jews.

There was no trace of the cruel crime. The entire square was overgrown with grass. Cows with full udders ate, grazed.

Several genteel Pole, recognizing me, were sorry about my situation. They had a way out for me: I should convert. In any case, the Jewish people no longer exist.

I ran away from them, crazy, broken and disappointed.

Czyzewo was liberated! A Czyzewo without Jews, without me.

I have nothing to do here.

[Column 977]

How I Smuggled Food into the Zambrówer Barracks

by Yeshaya Wyprawnik, Los Angeles, California

Translated by Gloria Berkenstat Freund

When the Czyzewo ghetto was liquidated, I left with everyone for Zambrów where we were driven into the barracks. There were already thousands of Jews from Zambrów and Ciechanowiec and other *shtetlekh* [towns]. There was no food. The people sat on their packs with down cast heads. Illnesses began to rampage.

I sneaked out of the barracks on the third day and started to go in the direction of Czyzewo; I did not enter the *shtetl*. I imagined how it looked there.

I went through the villages, sneaked into barns and doorways, gathered a full sack of food and began to think about how to smuggle the food into the barracks.

I hung around the barracks with the sack on my back and searched for a solution for managing to get in. Here I noticed a peasant traveling in the direction of the barracks with a cask. I stopped him; I spoke to him. I told him that I had food for the Jews, but that I did not know how to bring it in. The peasant shrugged his shoulders and said that he was afraid. When I put five *zlotes* in his hand, he took my sack of food and laid it in the cask, from which came a not good smell. I also jumped onto the wagon and rode inside with him.

[Column 978]

I gave the sack to Avrahaml Makowka, who divided it among the Jews and I immediately jumped back on the wagon and I left the barracks with the peasant.

I was daring and hired myself out to work for peasants. The peasants did not suspect that I was a Jew. I told them a story that our village had burned. My work pleased them. I did not lack strength and I worked with doubled effort in order to earn money for food for the Jews in the barracks.

[Column 979]

Every morning I went there with a wagon and Avrahaml Makowka took the food from me.

Days passed and the discipline in the barracks weakened. For a few *zlotes* the German soldiers were bribed and they let [the food] in. Then, I took Velvel, Avraham Makowka's son, and went with him to the village, received sugar, fats and bread for him. He took it into the barracks.

[Column 980]

He did this several times until the situation became more difficult. They stopped permitting people to leave the barracks. He remained there. Several days later he was sent with everyone to Auschwitz.

A strong frost crackled when I went with my sack for the last time. The wind cut the face and there no longer was any talk of going inside. The German soldiers in fur coats stood on guard surrounding [the barracks]. I learned that they [the Jews] would be taken to Auschwitz during the night. My heart cried and I thought that everything was hopeless. The entire area appeared to me as one large grave.

[Column 979]

In the Circle of the Agony of Death

Simcha (Seymour) Moncarz / New York

Translated from Yiddish by Dr. Jerry Sepinwall

Edited by Judie Ostroff Goldstein

From Czyzewo to Gross-Rosen

The first of September, when the Second World War broke out, the Nazi airplanes had suddenly hailed bombs down upon Czyzewo. Several friends and I came to the decision to flee from Czyzewo. We ran to Ciechanowiec.

On the eighth of September we heard that Czyzewo was burning. Together with Eliahu Wisocki, two others and I returned to Czyzewo.

Entering into the town we found everything in flames and one could not see any living persons; everyone had gone away to the Brak River, near the orchard [of a wealthy individual]. By backroads we were successful in getting back to that place, and there we already saw the tragedy of the Jews of Czyzewo. Mothers searched for their children, children sought their parents, old and young mourned for the destroyed town.

[Column 980]

Until today I still hear the voice of the wife of Moshele the teacher, who lost her mind from fear and she ran around and with a wildness cried out "Shma Yisrael." Ш

I, Chaim Visotsky and the Rav, Rabbi Levinson, Jakob Plocker, Chaim Judel, his brother-in-law Ben-Cjon, Surowicz's's son-in-law, and still others entered into the town, while we were hearing that there were many dead who needed to be buried. We began to look for the ones killed by the bombardment. The first victims were: Leibush Kac, Simcha Raczkowski, Avraham Yosel Maslo, his father-in-law and his wife Doba, Arke the baker's wife and Bluma Kitajewicz.

[Column 981]

Simcha Raczkowski,
among the first victims in Czyzewo

Night fell.

Those who knew gentiles ran away to them and the others ran away to the fields. I searched for my family and we divided up; I and my sister went away to the station and we went in to Melech Rotman's. My parents went away to Rusz to a Christian they knew.

Sunday, the 10th of September, the Germans entered Czyzewo. The only building they found that had not burned was the synagogue. There hundreds of families had sought shelter.

A short while later, when the Russians entered Czyzewo, the Jews breathed a bit more freely. This did not last long, however, and the fighting flared up – Russians against Germans. Once again, bombs fell on Czyzewo, again [there were] corpses and we were once more under the rule of the Hitler murderers. Now there began the great calamity.

A Judenrat was established consisting of the following people: Zebulun Grosbard, Alter Wolmer, Shmulke Wengorz, Jakob Kitaj and Yehoshua Lepak.

[Column 982]

A decree was soon issued that all men had to go to work at the train station. The work was extraordinarily difficult and, moreover, the workers were beaten viciously for no reason. However, everyone had to put up with all of this. While everyone feared that when the work at the station would be completed things would take a turn for the worse, and that is indeed the way things went. The work lasted for three weeks. And when it had ended, the Judenrat let it be known that all people, craftsmen and women had to come out at 4:00 a.m. the next day and to assemble in the town square. This was the 28th day of the month Av, 1941. There was a great turmoil; people could not sleep that night. Everyone had the premonition that a black fate was about to befall the Jews of Czyzewo. A small number fled from the town. With broken hearts and fright, everyone came at the appointed hour, and to whomever did not come, the Judenrat came around to awaken them and to beseech them, "Everyone should come in order not to provoke the Germans, which might then, God forbid, bring a greater sorrow upon the town." Children and people who were sick or too weak to work remained in their homes.

We had to stand in rows and the Official-Commissar selected out craftsmen, such as tailors, shoemakers, cabinet makers and blacksmiths.

**The school in Sember where the Jews were kept.
From there they were taken away to be murdered.**

[Column 983]

The "selection" lasted until about seven o'clock. Gestapo forces from Lomza came with trucks and machine guns and ordered: all persons, women, children, old, sick, must come at once to the square.

I still feel today the horror and the pain from the sight when our great Tsadek and Gaon [2], the Rav Zabludower, was thrown unto a truck. I still hear today the wailing which broke out from the women who had seen this then. It is impossible to describe this horror. All the trucks with the packed-in people drove away in the direction leading toward Zambrów, via the blacksmith's street.

At three o'clock in the afternoon, the street was already cleared, save for us, the group of chosen craftsmen [were] still standing.

It was announced that for the craftsmen, among whom could be found several women, a ghetto was being made ready. This consisted of several houses fenced in by barbed wire. Everyone had to remain there until a subsequent order. The next morning, Polacks already began to tell us that all who had been taken away yesterday were shot in Sember.

We were made to put on yellow patches and herded to work. The craftspeople, who worked at their trades, had somewhat better conditions. My brother Izrael and I found strong favor with the Commissar because of the good furniture which we worked to make for him. In recognition for all this, he freed us from having to wear the yellow patch and ordered that we should be given better food.

On a certain evening, a rumor spread that there were covered wagons that would be arriving the following morning. There was a stampede. Anyone who knew of it ran away. My brother and I took the families and we remained in the cellar, there where we had worked. Remaining in the ghetto were people whose despair had made them indifferent to everything. They said: We do not wish to struggle any more for a life which has, in any case, no worth. At night, we heard a shooting in the street. Everyone was loaded onto wagons and driven to Zambrów. Whoever was found to try to run away was immediately shot. We remained in the cellar two days and nights. We resolved to flee to Sutik to a well-known farmer named Andrzejtyk.

[Column 984]

We gave him money and promised more if he would shelter us until after the war. We made a bunker at his residence, under the floor of a small room. There eighteen persons were hidden: I and my friend, Raizel Brukowski (eshet hayil [2]), my brother Izrael and his wife and children, Moshe Keizmacher with his family, Moshel Zylbersztajn, Feivel Niewad, Eliahu Wisocki, Zelig Gromadzyn's wife and children, Rochel Kachan, Rochel Lichtensztejn and Brocha Kirszenbojm.

Our food every day consisted of a bit of watery soup. Only two times a week did he also give us a piece of bread. It is hard to convey how our existence was in the filth. In the barn there were also hidden three youngsters: Judel Wengorz, Shmuelik Lepak and someone from Zambrów. One can also imagine the farmer's situation. The hardship he had in supplying food to us, even the little insignificant food; however this was also to come to an end.

After laying up in the filthy cellar for 21 weeks, it was on an early Shabbos morning March 20, 1943, the house was suddenly surrounded by police and gendarmes. The first to be found were the three youths and they were immediately shot, and right after them the farmer was shot. They then went to his daughter, they said to her: if she would reveal where Jews could still be found, she would continue to live: but if she would say only that she knew nothing of any more Jews, she would be immediately shot exactly like her father. Trembling and tearful she disclosed our bunker. We were all led out of the pit and we were sure that this was the end.

[Column 985]

The chief of the gendarmes was one of those for whom we had made furniture. He recognized us, looked at us with strong pity. After a brief conference he ordered a wagon to be brought and we were all driven to Czyzewo to the Official-Commissar. We were all stuffed into a dark cell. We were all certain that these were our final minutes. Moshe Keizmacher already had made the final confession with us. We bid farewell to one another. The women and children cried bitterly. The only one who did not cry, rather who comforted everyone, was Rochel Kachan. She said: this is our our greatest good fortune, as we will soon be freed from our suffering. [For a long time already, we should not have been able to endure all of this.]

Around 12 o'clock noon the door to our cell was unlocked. The Official-Commissar appeared with his subordinates. After a brief silence and staring at each face, he turned to me and my brother and asked: "Why did you flee!" I replied: "We are sorry, but we are once more ready to work for the Official-Commissar." After an exchange of words with his people, he decided that I and my brother should be placed into a special cell; all the remaining ones were taken away to Szulborze and there they were shot. Only Moshe Zylbersztajn outwitted the gendarmes and they brought him back and placed him in with us in the cell. He explained to us that the outer garments were stripped off of all of them, they were placed at the edge of a pit and they were all shot with machine guns.

[Column 986]

The Official-Commissar from Czyzewo, dressed in a brown uniform with a black-white armband and a swastika on his left arm, had taken over the house of the General in Czyzewo together with a servant staff of ten people. It was continuously swarming with SS officers and gendarmes. There in the same building, in a room on the second floor, he decreed that we should work. I, my brother Yisrael and Moshe Zylbersztajn worked there for a whole year from March 1943 until March 1944.

[Column 987]

Sunday the 21st of March, in the morning, the Commissar was still asleep. Gendarmes came into our room, chained us one to another and took us to prison in Lomza. We were taken out into the yard each day and beaten viciously. The dogs were incited against us and they [literally almost] tore pieces from us.

Second from left, sitting **Moshele Zylbersztajn**
Standing on the right, **Berel Melamed's grandson**

This is how it was for three weeks, and how it ended up was arranged by the Official-Commissar in Czyzewo, that we should be taken to the cabinetmaker's shop; there we worked for some seven months, our living conditions became a lot better and easier. Germans used to come to stare at us and couldn't believe that we were Jews and could not understand why we were allowed to continue living, while in Lomza and in its surrounds there was no longer a single Jew.

Yisrael Moncarz and wife

[Column 988]

Finally this too ended. The Russians having entered into Lomza, the prison was liquidated. About a 1000 Polacks and we three Jews were packed into wagons and transported to Germany to a concentration camp, Gross-Rosen.

The bitter life and the torment that we suffered in the camp is impossible to write down. Hunger, filth, sickness were there and people were literally trampled underfoot, experiencing various "tsoures." [4] After this we were taken down to the Krupp ammunition factory. We worked there until the month of December 1944 and then were returned again to Gross-Rosen. Only Moshe Zylbersztajn remained in "Funf-Teichen" [i.e. Five Rivers]; he was sick and could not walk. We were subsequently taken to Buchenwald; there I was separated from my brother. I worked after this in Bissingen and in Dachau. Later, in the camp "Allakh" we were liberated by the Americans.

My sister Doba with her husband

Translator's notes:

1. The foundational Jewish prayer: "Hear O Israel, The Lord Our God, The Lord is One"
2. Righteous person and great rabbi
3. A women of valor
4. Kinds of suffering

[Column 989]

In the Ghetto and On the Way to Auschwitz

by Shmuel (Wajsbart) Ben Zahavi

Translated by Gloria Berkenstat Freund

Bela from Janczewo came running to Czyzewo and said that all of the Jews, women and children, old and young had been shot there. Sender told her to disappear so that a panic would not break out.

Similar messages came from the area, but they were all suppressed. One morning it was learned in the *shtetl* [town] that Alter Wolmer had received a letter from his brother in Zambrów who wrote: "No one should appear when an order comes to go out into the street." We first learned of this after the great slaughter on the 28th of *Menakhem Av*.

What would have happened if we had known earlier?

The Tragedy Begins

A cruel order was issued by the Angel of Death on a dark night of Wednesday going into Thursday: "All Jews onto the marketplace."

The Angel of Death in the uniforms of the *S.S.* under the leadership of the murderer *Obersturmbannführer* [S.S. paramilitary Nazi rank] Getsler appeared in the streets. All of the Czyzewer Jews were assembled at the market, loaded into vehicles, driven on foot and brought to Szulborze from which no one returned alive.

The mass grave at Szulborze

[Column 990]

Two large mass graves were created on the field.

There was a heavy rain that day with thunder and lightening. It was as if the heavens were also crying at the mass destruction. Only the murderers carried on their trade calmly and they finished it with the well-known German precision.

The remaining Jews who stayed alive in various ways were divided among several houses behind Jatszak's mill and this was called the Czyzewer ghetto.

They went to work not knowing it they would return home. If yes, they wondered if they would find alive those they had left in the house. My son who had succeeded in escaping from the market during the *aktsia* [deportation] was still alive. Leaving every day for work I would prepare something for him to eat for a day and he would wait for me to return.

Ten days later, after the *aktsia*, the Hitlerist murderers again entered the ghetto and took about 30 children [and] Altke Sura, Misha's [daughter] and her grandchildren and took them to Szulborze and murdered them there. After this it was quiet for a long time.

The only Jew in Czyzewo who had contact with the commissar was Sender. After his mysterious death, the three members of the *Judenrat* [Jewish council created by the Germans], Alter Wolmer, Yehoshua Lepak and Shmulke Wengorz, became acquainted with the commissar. There was a certain relief in the ghetto.

[Column 991]

Several carpenters and I worked for the commissar and for the gendarmes. We received a salary of 10 marks a week and had permission to bring food products into the ghetto.

The *Judenrat* also extracted permission from the commissar to open a bakery in the ghetto and bring in meat. A *shoykhet* [ritual slaughterer] would come from Ciechanowiec once a week.

One day an important S.S. officer was supposed to come from Łomża. The commissar warned that people should be at their work and that they should be cleanly dressed. Neat. During the visit he actually told the officer that he needed all of the people for work and it all passed peacefully.

All three of us, Frydman's son and Moshe Rajczik and I worked for the commissar who had moved into the general's house. Once the Polish policeman Marcziniak came bringing a father and two children with him. We were sure that their death sentence had already been signed because they had come across the border from the other side, a crime for which the only sentence was death.

The commissar appeared on the terrace and Marcziniak asked him if he should shoot the three Jews.

– Quiet! – The commissar thundered at him. He remained quiet for a while. It appeared as if he was devising some kind of death with which to punish the "criminals," but a few minutes later Yehoshua Lepak and Shmulke Wengorz fortuitously arrived. The commissar turned to them:

– What should I do with your Jews?

– There is no room for them in the ghetto.

They answered:

[Column 992]

– If it is this way then I will give them a permit so they will be able to go to another ghetto.

He said that they should be given five marks and bread to take with them.

Later there was another case:

A Jew who had slaughtered a cow had been caught. This also was one of the crimes that was punished with nothing less than with death. Here the Jews again received a fine of four hundred marks.

Life in the ghetto already was seen as normal. The older Jews would come together every *Shabbos* [Sabbath] in Yankel Rajczik's [room] to pray; the young ones went to work. In they evening they would come together in a house where Lubelczyk and his two daughters lived [with] Sura Mishe's son Hershel and his sister Yehudis. Her husband and his brother had been killed. Utshe Malcman and her family and Frydman also lived there. They would spend several hours behind draped windows. Shayna Riba and her sisters Mirl and Esther and still others would also come in.

One day they began to say that ghetto would be closed and all of the Jews understood from this information that 40 train wagons had been ordered to take out the Jews.

But it was not believed that this was true. However, people began to escape from the ghetto, among them my sister and her child.

The news came on Thursday, but it was calm until *Shabbos*. On *Shabbos* night the ghetto was besieged by members of the Gestapo and Polish policemen with machine guns.

Those who attempted to escape were mostly shot on the spot. They were many of them.

[Column 993]

In the morning we were all taken to barracks in Zambrów where they had placed the Jews according to their *shtetlekh*. We were together with the Wysok Jews. We shared the kitchen with them.

They began to liquidate the camp in January. Łomżer were taken on Sunday, Monday and Tuesday, Zambrówer on Wednesday and Thursday, Czyzewer and Wysoker on Friday and *Shabbos*.

We arrived at Birkenau on Sunday at 9 o'clock in the morning. We were told to leave everything in the train wagons as we got off.

We were 2,400 people. Two hundred and fifty were chosen for work. This was permission to live for a while.

We were led away to barracks close to the gas chambers. We were led with music and Moshe Rajczik immediately received a blow to his face and he became covered with blood when he said, "What is this? They are taking us with music?"

We were led into barracks where a table covered with a blanket stood. A *kapo* [prisoner in a concentration camp assigned to carry out various tasks], a Jew, said:

"You, Jewish criminals, may your fathers be cursed, take out your gold things!"

Everyone emptied out everything that they had. Then we were led to change our clothes.

They gave an order:

"Take off your clothes!"

The shaving began after the undressing.

The shavers actually were Jewish, but the pains that we suffered during the shaving were unendurable. They did not shave, but simply plucked the hair. At first it was under the arms and in other parts of the body.

[Column 994]

They took our winter clothing and gave us: a shirt, underpants, a man's jacket and a pair of pants, shoes and socks. Then we were taken to a second block.

There they began to break us physically and mentally. They beat us without a reason and we were not permitted to sit down.

This lasted until Wednesday. We were not given any food.

One of us grabbed a little food from a barrel. This was noticed by the block-elder; he told him to lie on a bench and he began to beat him with club on his bottom. The one who was beaten kept quiet, but when he received a blow over his back, he jumped up from his spot with a lamenting shout. Two porters immediately grabbed him and threw him on the ground. One stood with his foot on his chest and the other stopped his heart with his boot.

They suffocated him.

This was the first victim from our transport. The dead were laid out, crammed like cords of wood in the courtyard – four wide and four across.

Such piles were in the hundreds.

In the evening they put numbers on our arms. From then on we no longer had names, only numbers. Here Avraham Igla and his brother were torn away from us. Moshe Rajczik, Yankel the carpenter's son, Chaim the carpenter and his son and I remained together.

We were taken to Auschwitz.

[Column 995]

When we left Birkenau, the *S.S.* man said to us: "You are fortunate that you are leaving here."

However, this "good fortune" did not make us happy because we already knew that the "Garden of Eden" named Auschwitz awaited us.

We were taken into a courtyard and immediately a hail of blows on us began. This is how we were taken to the bath. There our clothing was taken away and exchanged for camp clothing. From the bath we were taken to a block where remained for three days without any work.

During the fourth week we were sent for carpentry labor. During the three weeks many people had died. A selection took place every few days. The weak were sent to the gas chambers and to the ovens.

The selection was always done at night. We had to take off all our clothing even during the greatest frosts. A drunk *S.S.* man would stand leaning against an electric pole with a thick cigar in his mouth and as we passed by him he would indicate with his hand – go right, or – go left. Right meant "gas chamber."

Left – work.

I met Yehoshua Lepak there. He looked very bad. A week later I no longer saw him.

[Column 996]

I also met Gonczar. He was sick with dysentery and he disappeared several days later. The same thing happened to son of Chaim the carpenter.

One day Moshel Rajczik became ill. I did all of his work then and he received his portion of food. None of the *kapos* noticed this. I did everything so that he would quickly become healthy. To our great joy he succeeded.

Here I also met Leibush Frydman and his son, who quickly disappeared. Leibush fought for his life until July 1943.

On the 18th of May 1944, another transport left for Gleiwitz [Auschwitz sub-camp]. On the 16th of January 1945, the so-called "death march" began.

We were marched out in a group of 4,500 people to Gross Rosen. Only 2,800 arrived there. The others were mostly shot.

We were taken to Buchenwald from Gross Rosen. I remained there for five weeks. Later we were taken to another camp.

On the 13th of April 1945 I was liberated by the Americans.

Translator's note:

1. *Menakhem Av* – "consoling and comforting" *Av* – the period after *Tish B'Av*, the day on which the First and Second Temples in Jerusalem were destroyed – a time of consolation

[Column 995]

I Escaped from Auschwitz

by Sura Ben–Ari. Camp number 33740/Haifa

Translated by Gloria Berkenstat Freund

I was still a young girl at the outbreak of the war in 1939. Therefore, I remember little of the hardships and tortures that Czyzewo Jews endured from the Nazi murderers. However, what I myself survived and saw is enough that I am horrified when I remember and imagine the terror that I experienced.

[Column 996]

Avraham and Fruma Maslo, as well as the grandfather, Mordechai Frydman, fell during the first bombardment.

[Column 997]

Right after the bombardment my parents went from Czyzewo to Bialystok where my father rented a spot for a chemical laundry. Life was difficult in general and for a new person in a strange place in particular.

On a Friday in 1941, the Germans drove as many Jews as could be stuffed into the city synagogue and set it on fire.

Avraham Landa and Yosef Mendel, the baker with many children, were there and they were all burned in the synagogue.

When the entire area around the synagogue began to burn, we ran to Pesakh Maslo, who then lived in Bialystok.

The Germans quickly organized the ghetto. We entered the ghetto to visit Golda Bolender.

From Golda we learned that our uncle, Yankel [Yakov] Bolender, had been shot. My aunt immediately wanted to go to Czyzewo. We did not permit her to go. However, I went there as a Christian girl with a cross around my throat. In Czyzewo I did not meet any of my family. The shtetl [town] had been burned.

[Column 998]

I then put on my "Star of David" patch and went to the Czyzewo ghetto. There I learned that my brother, Yitzchak Frydman, his wife, Szayna–Bayla, their two children, Fruma–Rochel and Sura–Laya, already were no longer in Czyzewo with my aunt, Enya Bolender. Her daughter Zisl and her children and her son Sender and his wife all perished in the sadly famous village of Szulborze.

I learned that my brother, Yitzchak, and his family were in the village of Rosochate. I went again with the "cross" around my neck with great effort and arrived in Rosochate with swollen feet.

The joy was very great. However, we did not know what would happen tomorrow.

I left to return to Bialystok and brought the news to my mother that everyone was alive and healthy. I gave her the signs exactly as my brother had given them to me. But I told my sister Chana–Etka and Golda Bolender the sad truth. Golda Bolender had her father, Ziska, and her sick mother, Zelda Bolender, in Bialystok. They all perished in a terrible death.

Yakov Bolender, his wife, children, grandchildren, sons–in–law, Motl Smolowicz and Fiskha Zysman, standing on the left

Our entire family was driven away to the Pruzany ghetto and from there to Auschwitz.

We traveled in closed wagons, burning with thirst. Many people died en route.

The women were immediately separated from the men and children in Auschwitz.

Going in the ranks to death, I was separated from my beloved and dear ones forever.

[Column 999]

I met a friend of my sisters named Dina Farber and I went with her to the Auschwitz camp.

They took our clothing and shaved our heads. My number on my arm is: 33740.

Instead of food or drinks they gave us blows without cause. We were chased barefoot, without shoes, in the snow. There they treated us worse than cattle. Death would have been better than such a life.

[Column 1000]

Alas, I lived in these conditions for a year and a half. I was saved thanks to a Czyzewo Jew. His name is Chaim Berl Wiferownyk, may his memory be blessed.

He worked in the *sonderkommando* [death camp prisoners forced by the Germans into work units whose primary job was to dispose of the bodies of the victims]. He wanted to take revenge against the Germans for the death of his wife and children. He organized a group and they chopped down the barbed wire so the [prisoners] could escape. However, they were caught immediately and shot on the spot. I succeeded in escaping then.

In the Abyss of Terrible Death

by Moshe Rajczik, Kiryat Motzkin (Camp Number 88925)

Translated by Gloria Berkenstat Freund

These memories were written in blood and tears. A people perished before my eyes in horror and misfortune. The entire time that I unburdened myself, I had the feeling that these are not only memories of my personal experiences. With certain changes, they are characteristic for hundreds of thousands of other survivors of that horrible hell. However, all of those Czyzewer who were closest and dearest to me, who perished with such a cruel death, continue to hover before my eyes. I know from the start that I will not succeed in providing everything that I have gone through in those terrible days of unending pain and death. Not only because many events were lost and forgotten over the course of time. There simply are no words in human language that can reflect the horror of those days. However, I consider it my duty to record my experiences, which are certainly similar to many others people's. I will open-heartedly tell everything here that happened from the first day of the outbreak of the war. I will not hide anything bad and not add anything good, only the truth, as I saw it and lived through it.

On the 1st of September 1939 I was in Warsaw. Seeing the great danger, I decided to return home to Czyzewo.

I had no rest [because] I was afraid that I would remain separated from my home and the fate of all of those close to me.

[Column 1001]

Arriving in the *shtetl* I found it had burned. At the Catholic Church, Polish soldiers still stood, but their weakness and disorientation could be felt. There was no doubt for anyone that they would not be able to hold on for long.

The soles of my feet were scratched, callused and swollen from walking so long. My eyes and lips were dry from the heavy weariness. Despite all of this, when the Germans entered Czyzewo I left immediately for the village of Dmochy-Glinki. I had peasant acquaintances there and therefore wanted to see if they could help me.

A tired weariness lay over the village; doves looked for a place to hide from the gunpowder and the people mimicked them, leaving their cottages abandoned, and went out onto the narrow dirt roads between the fields.

On the road, I met the Chrapker miller, who consoled me that I did not have to be afraid because the Soviets would quickly be here. That is what a German soldier told him.

Meanwhile, the Germans calmly carried on their murderous work. They shaved off the beard of Moshel (Czak) and photographed him with the background of the burning houses. They hanged a sign around his neck, "I am the Jew who set fire to the city."

The Czyzewo soldiers marched out and began to build small houses. I was a carpenter, was a member of the brigade at the workers' cooperative where the [female] representative of the high official was my comrade, Royza.

A kind of unrest already was felt in Czyzewo three months before the attack by the Germans. A Soviet officer, a political commissar, had said to me then that the peace with the Germans would not have any longevity. The border was not far way and there was talk that new soldiers were mobilizing here. The attack hung in the air and sadness and fear prevailed in the Jewish houses in Czyzewo.

[Column 1002]

There were those who tried to console themselves and others after everything; they did not want to allow the idea that the cruel enemy of the Jews would again acquire the *shtetl*.

Suddenly shrapnel and bombs began to fall over the *shtetl*. There were those who were killed. And the battalion that incidentally consisted of many Jewish soldiers withdrew. The attack came unexpectedly for them and created disorder and chaos.

I ran with the battalion. Along the entire road I encountered disoriented soldiers and officers who were running, not knowing where. An officer tried to take over the leadership and, shooting in the air, stopped the running soldiers. He gave an order to leave the wounded, take their weapons from them and go into the woods. I lifted a rifle that had been thrown away and joined the ranks.

We sat down to eat deeper in the forest. Shooting was heard immediately. It was clear that these were the German parachutists. But we did not have enough bullets with which to be able to answer them.

We arrived in Minsk, but it was the same there, the same chaos. The Germans already had surrounded the city. I began retreating with a small group.

We arrived in Bialystok through back roads, among fields, forests, but we were caught here by a German patrol and taken away to the headquarters where the German commandant cursed us with the worst words. That we were damned partisans and he ordered that we be taken out and shot. We were a group of six people, among whom only Moshe-Dovid Slikes and I were from Czyzewo.

[Column 1003]

The German soldiers led us out to the forest and began looking for a suitable place to place us for shooting. However, at the last minute a rider on a sweaty horse rode in and told them about an attack by the 10th cavalry regiment and they quickly led us back to the camp for war prisoners. I tried to convince them that I was a Ukrainian, but they later learned that I was a Jew and they led me with seven more Jews to the barracks where the Jews were located. Everyone was undressed, only in underpants.

On the first night we, several Jews, agreed among ourselves that we needed to dig through to the Russians. However, everyone else was apathetic to our plan and did not want to believe in the success of escaping.

We succeeded in getting clothing from somewhere and when everyone was asleep we sneaked out of the barracks and sneaked through the fence in the darkness up to the Polish barracks. The guard was weaker there and, when the patrolling guards sat down for a while, we forced our way out, jumping over a fence and began running in the direction of the forest.

However, we did not manage to run far and bullets began to fly over our heads from all sides. Seven Jews, among them Moshe-Dovid, fell from the bullets. Only three of us succeeded in reaching the forest. The Germans continued to shoot. However, they did not want to come near us.

[Column 1004]

The shooting did not stop the entire night. We remained lying hidden behind the thin trees, trembling from the cold and fear. When it began to get light we crawled to the highest point, where we sat until it became dark. From afar we heard that the tumult and the uproar that had reigned in the camp had begun to end. The Germans had apparently given up on us.

We descended from the trees and began walking in the dark, without a goal, further away from the camp.

In the morning, [after] walking the entire night, we saw in the distance the cabin of the forest guard. His wife was busy at the entrance.

We held a short deliberation and it was decided that one of us, a blond lad, would present himself to her as a Pole who had escaped from the camp.

Seeing him, the woman crossed herself. She believed that he had escaped from the camp and warned him that the camp was very close by. Shooting was still heard and [the Germans] were still searching in the forest.

The Christian woman invited him in, but her words about the police search scared him. He said goodbye and returned to us.

We realized that we had gone the wrong way and began walking in the opposite direction.

The road continued difficult and long. Every rustle caused fear and there was the worry of doubt in our heads. Were we going in the right direction? We were afraid to meet anyone who might betray us.

[Column 1005]

We finally saw a solitary peasant woman walking by with a basket. The blond boy went over to her to ask her where we were.

She became very frightened. When he said that he had escaped from the camp, she became calm, gave him a piece of bread and told him that her son was also in the camp. She was taking food to him.

The peasant woman showed him how to go by a side road and also told him to be careful because there was great trouble in the area.

In the Destroyed Home

I finally arrived in Czyzewo. All of the Jews were at work, for which they were not paid. There were no S.S. men in the *shtetl* yet. It was only the military from the front and the military commandant had given the order that all Jews must work on the train line, which had to be transformed back into narrow tracks.

After two weeks a special department commissar came to Czyzewo, who began to "create order" among the Jews in the *shtetl*.

The condition of the Jews worsened even more. The commissar ordered the creation of a *Judenrat* [Jewish council}. Zebulun Grosbard was designated as the chairman. The commissar himself came to the *gmina* [community] office and gave Zebulun a slap, saying: "You are the elder. Therefore, everyone must be obedient to you, and you to me."

My father had the surviving *Sefer Torah* [Torah scroll] and from time to time a *minyon* [quorum of ten men needed to conduct certain prayer services] came together [with him]. Zebulun also prayed in our house. They called to heaven for help, quietly, with a choked cry, behind hammered-shut doors and windows.

[Column 1006]

On a beautiful day, all of the Jews were called to appear at the market to register for work. The people no longer believed [what was being said], but they had to [go]. Everyone was then taken away to Szulborze where they all were shot.

The department commissar created the ghetto with those who had survived.

Once on a summer day the commissar approached me and said that everyone had to appear in the street in the morning. Only I and a list of carpenters would not be bothered. Turmoil began when I went to the ghetto and spoke about the list. I made a list of 30 people and the commissar signed it, adding:

– From tomorrow morning until night I will not be the boss of the city. It would be better if you hide until over night…

I returned home with a heavy mood and repeated the commissar's words. Other Jews were present and everyone saw a hidden signal in the commissar's words that we should escape.

There was an uproar in the ghetto. Whoever could, hid. A rumor spread that Hitler himself was leading the deportation. No one appeared at the designated hour.

Sender, who was friends with the commissar, appeared in the street. He often had a drink with him. He went through the houses, said it was not a question of deportation, but only to register.

Little by little the people began to leave their houses and appear in the rows. I went to the department commissar, but he did not want to talk. Later, I succeeded in removing from the line Sura Stuczynski. The department commissar later confirmed that he needed her as a cook.

[Column 1007]

I returned to the ghetto in the evening, where a deadly silence reigned. The Gelbards' three-year old son came out of the small garden near our house in which we had planted potatoes and pointed to the potatoes with his small, shaking hands:

– I hid here… I saw how they took out my mother, my aunt to be shot, so I hid…

We kept the child with us until we were taken to Auschwitz.

Once on *Shabbos* [Sabbath] when a *minyon* had gathered in our house, a Jew, breathless, wild, shaven, came running in the middle of the praying. He barely could stutter: "Jews, give me a *talis* [prayer shawl]."

He cried for a long time wrapped in the *talis*. When it was dark enough, he took off the *talis* and in a quiet voice began to tell how he had escaped from Treblinka and all of the horrors he had seen there. He worked at sorting the clothing that had been taken off by the transported Jews. He changed into the clothing and succeeded in escaping.

We were a small group, veteran soldiers who decided to escape from the ghetto with weapons in our hands and go into the forests to the partisans. Shmulke Gelbard [the name "Gelbard" is spelled in various ways throughout this chapter], Sura-Misha's son Hershel (Zylberman), Shimon the son-in-law of the tailor, Yisrael-Shlomoka the shingler, Yakov Jakubowicz and two brothers who came to the Czyzewo ghetto from another *shtetl*, were in our group.

We contacted a Pole who would enter the ghetto to trade, and who traveled back and forth to Warsaw. Shimon, the tailor's son-in-law promised to pay with dollars for weapons. The Pole promised to bring two pistols and two hand grenades and took a deposit of 50 dollars.

[Column 1008]

Several weeks passed in restless tension. Finally, the Pole appeared again and explained that he had encountered a police search on the way and had to throw away the weapons he had bought. He even wanted to return the money.

We again tried to make contact with a second Christian whom we promised to sew a suit without payment with the condition that he would connect us to the partisans. Again, nothing came of these contacts.

Another illusion vanished.

I saw many terrors during the ghetto days. However, there also were moments of moving humanity. Such was the moment when the Germans demanded of Zebulun Grosbard that he provide 30 people for work and he immediately answered that he had no one. They took him to be hanged and he had to carry his own rope to the gallows, which was made of an electric pole in the middle of the market across from the community building. The gendarme told him to throw the rope. Zebulun tried to throw the rope with his last strength and could not. Then the gendarme threw it. He waited a minute for the Jew to beg him to pardon his life and that he would obediently carry out all orders. However, Zebulun Grosbard stood calmly, ready for death, not giving in to the German murderers and handing over the Jews to them.

The gendarme hesitated for a minute, and finally he shouted:

– Run back to the ghetto.

[Column 1009]

In Auschwitz

The day came of the last deportation and we were all taken to Zambrów, where the military barracks were located, the collection point for the Jews from all the surrounding *shtetlekh*, and from where we were taken to Auschwitz.

We were taken to the train on a frosty night, loaded in the train wagons. Each wagon was packed with people to the edges, without food and drink. Thus we traveled enclosed without a bit of air. We did not know where we were going. Some knew [enough] to explain that the Germans had erected ovens to burn people.

When the train stopped, the doors of the train wagons opened wide and the *S.S.* soldiers, with whips in their hands, shouted, cursed, drove us out and did not let us take our packs.

The tumult among the people was frightening. We were placed in rows, men separately, women separately. The square was a giant one and was lit by spotlights. We were in Auschwitz.

They immediately began to choose people who were capable of work. The weak ones were placed separately. The fate of these people was known. My uncle, who was among the rejected, tried to convince the Germans that he was still young and could work. He received a blow with a whip across his face and immediately was covered in blood.

We were then loaded into vehicles and taken away. The *S.S.* soldiers followed us on motorcycles. We arrived in the courtyard of Birkenau and had to march to the beat of wild music and hysterical laughter from the Germans. We marched and were taken into a bath barracks. It was so crowded there that one literally stood on another and could not catch their breath.

[Column 1010]

The Czyzewers, Wengorz, Lepak, Shmuelka Gelbard, Chaim Stoliar and his son and Leibush Frydman were in this barracks.

When we were led into the bath we thought that they were going to gas us. We looked up to the ceiling from which the gas would stream out. Many Jews made their confession out of fear, but suddenly there was a spray of warm water. Can anyone imagine the wave of joy that the water brought with it?

For two weeks, we, the selected carpenters, did nothing. We received tea or coffee in the morning, a portion of bread with margarine or marmalade. When the bell began to ring we instantly had to be on the roll-call square. We were counted there. We were taught the rules of when to take off our hats. The *kapo* [concentration camp inmate assigned administrative tasks] shouted: "Cap off!" – everyone had to take off his hat – and bang his right foot.

The making of one's bed had to be abided by vigorously. Blows were received for the least inexactness.

There was a *kapo*, a German Jew, a former colonel, who had a Christian wife, over the 100 [people] to which I belonged. His son was a high officer in the Hitlerist Air Force.

Once he did not come to the barracks the entire day. In the morning he said that his son had turned to Hitler with a request in which he pointed out that his father could be of great use to the German Army. As a result of this, he had been called to the camp commandant who asked him if he wanted to go free and enter the military. He answered that he wished to be with all of the Jews in the gas chamber. His son became hysterical and had fainted on the spot.

[Column 1011]

To enter work in the carpentry workshop I first had to pass an exam. I was assigned to make a complicated door with a transom.

The first piece of wood that I brought to the workshop from the warehouse was ruined for me by a Pole, cutting a bad length. It led to a scandal. I tried to tell the Pole nicely that he should not prevent me from surviving the war. As an answer, he slapped me.

I had nothing to lose and, determined, I went to the guard in charge of order, told him that I was being disturbed at work and I did not know how I could carry it out.

The German became furious and wildly ran to the Pole, warned him that if he tried to sabotage me, he would simply be shot. He must learn if the Jew could work…

The Pole shook with fear and no longer disturbed us. My work pleased the Germans and later I succeeded in drawing in Gelbard and Chaim Stoliars son. His father failed the exams also because the Poles had disturbed him.

Once they [the Germans] sent me to fix something at the crematoria. Going closer, I saw Ruwin, the chimney sweep, among the people who walked like shadows while burning the dead bodies that had been pulled out of the gas chambers.

[Column 1012]

Seeing me, he stood for a while as if welded to the spot. Suddenly a short shout of joy tore out of him. He murmured and his face again became human, "You are alive?"

At the same time, Berl the wagon driver approached. He also was happy that he saw a familiar person among the survivors. They placed a golden 10-ruble piece in my hand.

I met with them several times. We could not always stop and converse. We only communicated with glances, which quietly expressed the joy of the encounter. Another day of life, a weak point of hope glowed in our hearts: perhaps we would meet again tomorrow.

The Heroic Revolt at the Crematoria

Suddenly they stopped sending me to work at this crematorium. I learned later that a revolt of the *kommandos* [work units], who were employed with burning the gassed bodies, had taken place there

Usually the separate groups did not dare come together, could not talk to each other. The *kommandos* got drunk before taking the transport to be burned and they did their horrible work automatically.

I did not know the channels through which the people organized the contact and how they communicated among themselves. It is a fact that the initiative came from the group in which Chaim-Leib, the wagon driver, worked. They were the first ones to grab an *S.S.* man and throw him in the burning oven.

[Column 1013]

This was the signal and together everyone ran like a hurricane to the remaining *S.S.* men, tearing the guns from them and shooting them on the spot. Individuals still defended themselves, but the machine guns that they had taken from the guards in the watchtowers already were in Jewish hands. This gave the Jews dominance and in half an hour the last *S.S.* defense point had been destroyed in the area around the crematorium.

The Jews began to run to the exit with weapons in their hands. However, the road was far away and the alerted camp commandant succeeded in sending out reinforcements, a large well-armed *S.S.* group, which immediately began shooting at the escapees from their cars.

A struggle developed that did not last long. The Jews staged a desperate resistance and fell to the last one.

Chaim-Berl, the Czyzewo wagon driver also fell then in the heroic struggle of the Jewish crematoria workers against the Hitlerist murderers.

From then on, I was no longer taken to work there; every day I went from Auschwitz to Birkenau, where different carpentry work had to be done. I was accompanied by an *S.S.* man with a machine gun. He walked behind me, ready to shoot if I made the slightest movement to escape or to communicate with someone.

The road was wide and tormenting enough. I searched with my eyes for a known face. I was answered by fearful looks from tortured faces over which hovered imminent death.

[Column 1014]

Once I noticed a particular movement. The *S.S.* man accompanying me was in a tense mood that day. He hurried me so that I should go faster because he still needed to return to the camp, to accompany another transport.

I just tried to make the road last longer and all the while I was stopped by the passing vehicles packed with Jews. I knew the road well and knew that they were being taken to the crematoria. Particularly large transports arrived that day and many vehicles were mobilized. An armed *S.S.* man on a motorcycle followed each vehicle.

Suddenly a vehicle arrived with small children who lay thrown in, one on top of the other. Terrible crying tore from there. Suddenly I saw a child sliding down and she was standing on her feet. I remained riveted to the spot and I could not take my eyes off of the beautiful and genteel small face of a girl who looked all around desperately on all sides, searching for a person who would help her. She clasped a doll in her small hands.

An *S.S.* man on a motorcycle drove in. The child began to run toward him not letting the doll out of her small hands. It looked as if she was more concerned for the doll than for her own fate. Her childish, crying eyes had a motherly tenderness.

She ran to the *S.S.* man with childish trust. However, she did not manage to open her small mouth. The *S.S.* man's hand had lightning-fast pulled his revolver and its fiery voice immediately reached her small head. She fell down near his motorcycle, not letting the doll out of her small, convulsively gripping hands.

[Column 1015]

The *S.S.* man drove further.

I was at Auschwitz for two years and two days. When the Russians were getting closer, we were taken to Mauthausen.

From there they took me to Ebensee, an Austrian town in the mountains where we were employed at blowing up mountains and building tunnels.

I worked there for six weeks in inhuman conditions, swollen with half-paralyzed feet. I felt that these were my last days and I decided not to go to work any more. It would be better if they shot me on the spot.

I remained in the house and waited for death. Suddenly I heard my name being called. I was sure that these were my last minutes. But the *S.S.* man who appeared at the door of the barracks was calm this time, taking me to an office and, later, going down with me in an elevator deep into the ground where the disguised ammunition factory was located.

The noise from the various machines was deafening. But another regimen existed here, different from the one above. The people, mostly Hungarian specialists, walked around, fully satisfied, occupied. Each had his section, his machine. No one looked at me. Only the foreman hurriedly showed me what I had to do and went to the other end of the room.

After an entire day of work, the same master craftsman returned to lead me out above, where there already were other camp inmates and a *kapo* led us to the barracks.

[Column 1016]

I worked in that factory until the liberation.

Salvation Arrived

This was on the night of the 4th of May 1945. The tension in the barracks turned into chaotic unrest. People walked around and said that there was a secret order to gas everyone and that this would happen after the morning roll call.

The apprehension grew. In the morning, no one wanted to go out to the roll call. The people stretched out on the ground and did not want to move from the spot.

Something was astir and we did not know what the Germans were thinking of doing to us. It appeared that the *S.S.* members did not want to leave anything over and, escaping, they left several Germans as representatives, who were to lead us away. But the several Germans were realistic. They saw that everything was lost and the camp leader himself came to us with the news that he was taking over and had opened the storehouses for us, let us take crackers, cigarettes and, whoever had the strength, left for the city.

We were free!

I cried, not knowing from where I had taken so many tears. My heart hurt for all of those fallen and burned, who did not live to be liberated with me.

I lay on a plank bed and sobbed. No one looked at me. I fell asleep. When I woke up, I no longer heard anyone speaking German.

[Column 1017]

Across Rivers of Tears and Seas of Blood

Yisroelke Fenster – a son of Avrahamtshe, Camp Number 89887

Translated by Gloria Berkenstat Freund

My Experiences of 1941

This was a Sunday in the month of June. They began to attack the city in the morning and the Hitlerists marched in on Monday. We were the first people who were taken to work. The "stationmaster" led us to work. They shot the weak ones on the way.

Thus we were sent to work every day. And in the evening we returned home. This lasted for a time, until an order came that in the morning all of the people aged 15 and older should appear at the market from which they would be sent to work.

At dawn, around four o'clock, the terrible truth was apparent. Men and women were separated and we were surrounded by Polish policemen and the Gestapo. There was a heavy rain, but we stood until eight o'clock, when a vehicle arrived from Lomza, from which descended a Gestapo officer. He exchanged greetings with the municipal commissar, and they began to count and select people who were placed on the side. Black trucks arrived and they began to load women and children and the men were told to go in the direction of the Zambrówer Road. The Polish policemen tried with all of their strength to search out the Jewish children and wanted to pull them out of their hiding places.

[Column 1018]

We, the survivors, about 50 people, were led back to the ghetto. In the morning, we learned the bitter truth, that all of those who had ostensibly been taken to work the night before had been shot in Szulborze.

The number of people in the ghetto quickly increased with the arrival of the escaping Czyzewer and [people] from other neighboring *shtetlekh* [towns]. We numbered around 300. Everyone was quartered in the small ghetto houses with a prohibition against moving from one house to another, under the threat of being shot. The same day several victims did fall. The first was Czarna Silka's daughter; the second was Moshel, Pesha-Yuta's son, and so on.

[Column 1019]

Thus we lived in painful fear of certain death for 18 months until November 1942. One day there was a rumor that wagons were coming tomorrow to bring trees from the forest. There was panic in the ghetto. We already knew from experience what this meant. Many ran away and the remaining were taken to Zambrów, which was the assembly place for the transports to Auschwitz.

We remained in the ghetto for six months; my brother and I, glaziers by trade, two cabinetmakers and two saddle makers. But, as after the first deportation, abut 60 people returned and a short time later they were again sent to Zambrów. Only a few people remained.

Transports began from Zambrów to Czyzewo to the train station so that they could be sent to Auschwitz. Those who died on the way were given to us to bury. From that time on, none of the people in the ghetto could approach us or talk to us. They were shot immediately for transgressions. Dina Szwarc and the sister of Motl the watchmaker were shot, whom we buried immediately.

We were told to go with the last Zambrówer transport. This was my brother and I, Simkha Moncarz, his brother and two others. We were packed in the train wagons without food and without a drop of water.

The trip lasted not more than two days, but it was enough for hundreds of dead to accumulate.

[Column 1020]

Shooting was heard often on the way. Those who tried to escape were shot.

There was an immediate selection when the half-dead people descended from the train wagons at Auschwitz. Those capable of work remained on the spot and everyone else was loaded onto trucks – to death.

The entire work went with the greatest speed; everything was emptied in 10 minutes. Those capable of work were led with music to wash and trim their hair. Our clothing was taken from us and we were given camp clothing. And from then on everyone received a number. My number is "89887," which I wear to this day and will remain with me for eternity.

We were led into the barracks.

I lived in Auschwitz for two and half years without hope of living to see freedom.

On a beautiful summer day, the noise of American airplanes was heard that rang in our ears like the most beautiful music and a hail of bombs immediately fell and I was wounded. I was taken to a hospital where I spent six months.

Every week the very sick were chosen and sent to the ovens. Suddenly an order came to liquidate the camp because the Russian Army was approaching. We were driven on foot, without rest, until we reached a "haven." The weak fell on the road. The survivors were driven to various work.

We were freed by the American Army on the 5th of May. My wife and three children perished. May their blood by avenged!

[Column 1021]

In the First Days of Burning Hate
by Avraham Kandel and Chaim Belfer/Tel Aviv; Gorzalczany/Petah Tikva

Translated by Gloria Berkenstat Freund

1st of September 1939

On this day we sent out a shipment of geese from Czyzewo to Warsaw. The stationmaster at the train station received the goods, but without assuming responsibility. It was not known how far the geese had travelled, but they returned to Czyzewo the next day.

The Czyzewo train station was bombed on the 7th of September.

The Germans entered on the 9th of September right on *Erev* [the eve of] Yom Kippur.

The *shtetl* [town] remained without food. The Germans opened the municipal food and bread warehouses. Everything already was moldy.

The holiday already was disturbed for the Jews. They spoke of Jews caught by the Germans outside the city; they were beaten on their legs and shouted at: "Crawl on all fours"… They were spit at in their faces.

"Your Chamberlains… Your [British Secretary of State for War Leslie] Hore-Belishas!"

Younger people clenched their fists. A fire burned in their eyes; how could we endure this? Creator and Master of the Universe, how could You create such a hell?

The first initiative to escape was undertaken by the *HaShomer HaTzair* [Zionist-Socialists] organization.

Yosef Levi, a party messenger, came and connected us with a peasant. Yosef Levi spoke about the destruction being done by the Germans in the Jewish cities, about Warsaw, where entire streets were erased and people were lying in the streets near murdered horses.

One wanted to stop-up their ears and to not hear any more. Just leave, leave from here, but very few moved from the spot. Their feet were as if riveted, their knees as if filled with heavy lead.

[Column 1022]

We were the first group that moved from Czyzewo. The two Ejnszic brothers and Yisrael Lew went with us.

We traveled to Bialystok by train and through backroads we reached Lida [in Belarus].

We were stopped at the border by a patrol. We barely escaped and again began to wander along the border. We lost our courage. We went from *shtetl* [town] to *shtetl*, from settlement to settlement.

Vilna went from hand-to-hand three times in the course of a month. The Red Army took the place of the Poles and then the Lithuanians came. Life became more difficult with each new owner.

To be frank, the Lithuanians were not in any hurry to take Vilna. Moscow Radio reported on the first days that the Soviets were withdrawing from Vilna and its vicinity, but the Lithuanian rulers hesitated in accepting the gift. This Lithuanian restraint was incomprehensible at first.

Jokers jested:

– They are ashamed to come during the day; they are afraid to come at night…

However, it soon became clear that the Lithuanians were receiving Vilna as a present. But the military bases for the Red Army remained in various places in the country.

[Column 1023]

The tall Lithuanian policeman and the short soldier finally entered. A shudder went through the Jews:

– They are beating Jews.

A pogrom!

People ran wildly through the streets, locked the gates of their houses and hammered shut the shutters. Everything grew louder and the screams came closer: "Death to the Jews."

Heavy stones flew through the windows of the Jewish houses. Shops were forced open and Jewish possessions were looted.

Screams from the beaten and trampled Jews were mixed with the debauched laughter of those doing the beating.

Divisions of the Red Army were still in the city. The officers and soldiers watched what was happening and were silent.

In the morning, the new regime finally quieted the pogrom.

We met the Czyzewo Rabbi's son-in-law, Reb Pinchas Levinzon and his wife, Freidel, and their only child in the Vilna house of prayer.

He studied all day and received support from the Joint [Distribution Committee]. They lived well and even offered to lend us money.

We did not need any money because we were living in a *kibbutz* [community] and received food from the Joint.

There was a Council for Refugees (a committee for the homeless) in Vilna. The Vilna Jews welcomed the refugees. We would take a job at various work, even cutting wood. The [Vilna] Jews pitied and consoled us.

In Vilna we quietly dreamed of going to *Eretz Yisrael*. However it was too difficult to obtain a visa. There were those who were not believers and were successful in not driving themselves crazy with hollow ideas.

[Column 1024]

They were clever and realistic, but our hearts rebelled. In addition, after a short time, they began to issue visas.

How many Jewish tears were spilled in the corridors of the American and English consulates! How Many Jewish hearts left [the consulates] like broken pottery!

The number of those who won the lottery and received an American visa was small. But we lived with the idea of going to *Eretz Yisrael* and this was easier to accomplish. The British consulate gave hundreds of visas, but we did not receive one.

Suddenly, people began to say that the Japanese Consulate was issuing transit visas. It did not occur to us to go there; what would Czyzewo Jews do in the country of the geishas? In addition, we knew that the small Japanese were too friendly with Hitler.

Therefore, we became disoriented and astonished when we heard that the Japanese Consul [1] began to throw visas right and left and almost for free.

This was suspicious. Jews knew that there are no bargains; we must pay dearly for everything. Therefore, the Japanese visas were considered with suspicion.

The relationship between Russia and Japan was strained. There already were rumors that Soviet agents were photographing everyone who went near the Japanese Consulate and that traveling through Russia they would be sent to Siberia.

[Column 1025]

Yes, we were sad, but we decided and later went to the Soviet Consulate for permission to travel through [the Soviet Union] to the Japanese border. So many miracles happened to us. Perhaps further wonders would also happen.

We came together with our Czyzewo comrades and wove the dreams of going, going…

At the Russian Consulate they demanded that we pay for the trip to Japan in dollars.

One of us sent a telegram to an uncle in New York and the necessary dollars arrived in a short time.

Sitting on the train, we did not feel any fear. Each one had a train compartment and a numbered seat, but the door opened hastily outside of Moscow and members of the *NKVD* [*Narodnyy Komissariat Vnutrennikh Del* – People's Commissariat for Internal Affairs – secret police] entered, sized us up with sharp, penetrating glances.

The first inspection and check of our documents had begun.

Everyone held their documents, the passport and the visas in their hands. Long months had passed until they had gathered them and here, suddenly, they were taken from us. One of the members of the *NKVD* gathered them altogether in a pile and did not even look at them. He crumpled them in his fists and pushed them into his pouch.

Leaving, they took Kandel with them.

It appeared as if he had been arrested and we remained confused and lost.

A person has such a feeling of being lost when his clothes are torn off in the middle of the street and he is left standing naked and he must not move from the spot under the threat of an aimed pistol.

[Column 1026]

It did not take long and again we heard a knock on the door of the compartment. We all had the thought, "They finally have come for us."

To our surprise, they brought back our documents, but Kandel did not return.

We traveled further on the train, which moved slowly to Vladivostok, with heavy hearts.

Kandel turned up unexpectedly after we had been in Vladivostok for several days. Until today he does not know what kind of imperfection they had found in his documents. He was summoned to the *NKVD* every day in Vladivostok and his papers were checked again.

The director of the hotel in which we lived was a Jew. He immediately began to shout, rant and curse when he learned that we were going to *Eretz Yisrael*. He made the pretense of being very strict and angry, but quietly, very secretly, he took an interest in the situation of each one of us and gave advice and helped with an intervention to speed up our departure.

We met many Jews during our time in Vladivostok, but none of them wanted to talk with us. They avoided us as if we had a contagious disease.

The days and weeks of half euphoria and half fear flew by. We were aware of how long we had been on an *NKVD* list. Various surprises could happen to us.

No one yet was sure of the accomplishment of their dream of arriving in *Eretz Yisrael*.

[Column 1027]

Finally we were on the ship that took us to Japan.

Representatives of the Jewish section of the refugee committee waited for us in the Japanese port city of Kobe. They brought new clothing, apples and other good things for us.

Kobe was a city with a population of one million… Hundreds of Jewish families. Jewish life existed only in their own club where they came together. The refugee committee was located there.

Our transit visa was valid for 14 days, but the government increased its term without any difficulties.

In general, the relationship on the part of the government and on the part of the population was very warm. We felt this in both official offices and in the street where every passerby, despite the fact that we did not understand their language, tried to express their sympathy and understanding for our suffering in various ways.

In Kobe, new people, from every strata, Hasidim, *yeshiva* [religious secondary school] students, from Zionist youth organizations and even Bundists, arrived every day.

Here we also met our rabbi's son-in-law, Reb Pinchas Levinzon and his family. At every step we felt the help from the Joint [Distribution Committee]. Finally we found ourselves on a Japanese ship going to South Africa.

[Column 1028]

On this road we felt the dispersion and simultaneously the great numbers of the Jewish people. Throughout the world, from Czyzewo to Vilna, from the frosty north to the warm south – there was no place where we did not encounter the sad, Jewish eyes that looked at us with so much warmth.

Meeting these Jews, everything took on a new life, a new light.

This was confirmed for us by the hidden Jews in Vladivostok into whose hands we stuck a red flag and warmed the earth beneath their feet! The few Jews in Japan who felt free there and yet exile did not fall from their shoulders.

We succeeded in calling out: "Jews from every land unite. Come with us to the Jewish land!"

We traveled from Cape Town on an Egyptian ship and at Kantara [Egypt] we were taken over by an English convoy, which accompanied us to Atlit [near Haifa].

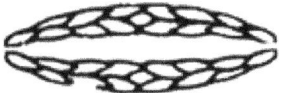

Translator's Footnote:

1. This is a reference to Chiune Sugihara, the Japanese vice consul in Lithuania, who issued approximately 6,000 transit visas to Jews enabling them to travel through Japan.

[Column 1029]

My Experiences during the Years of the Second World War

Mirl Wolmer-Biderman

Translated by Gloria Berkenstat Freund

Eight days after the outbreak of the war in 1939, Czyzewo, our *shtetl* [town], shuddered during a frightening bombardment of incendiary bombs. Very few houses remained undamaged. The Jewish population ran wherever their eyes led them, to the nearby villages and forests. Or even to the fields, under a hail of bullets that the German murderers endlessly shot from machine guns. This continued until night, when we no longer saw the blazing sky and mourned the *shtetl*, our Czyzewo, which had become a ruin.

The German military entered the city. People slowly returned to the *shtetl*, which had been turned into a large mountain of ash. Many families traveled to the nearby *shtetlekh*, which fortuitously were not burned. Several families along with ours moved in with Motl Szczupakiewicz, whose house had remained undamaged. With the little food we had hidden, we lived meanwhile in fear for what the future would bring us.

The German murderers immediately on their arrival began their terror against the Jewish population. Young and old were grabbed for heavy work, with beatings without reason. We were quickly broken physically and emotionally. However, deep in our hearts a weak hope smoldered that the war would end quickly and we would all survive. The situation changed quickly. Poland was divided between Germany and Russia and our *shtetl* became a border city between both parts.

[Column 1030]

We lived under Russian rule over the course of 20 months. It was a strenuous life, but yet we lived. We worked in various cooperatives. People returned to Czyzewo. Building began again a little on plots divided by the government. It appeared that things were beginning to be normal.

One morning, we again unexpectedly heard the thunder of artillery guns and saw how the Russian military was running in haste. The Germans were soon in the street. A panic broke out among the Jewish population. The German murderers immediately gave an order that the Jews must put on yellow patches and bestowed murderous blows just for sadistic pleasure.

A *Judenrat* [Jewish council] was chosen that consisted of four people. They were responsible for carrying out the German orders exactly. The order that a sum of money and gold had to be provided came immediately. People saw a bit of a consolation in this; perhaps our lives would be ransomed for money? However, time revealed that this was only an illusion and disappointment came quickly.

[Column 1031]

On a certain day, an order came: "All people without regard to age and type should come to the market." No one could imagine that this was the call to the death camp. They consoled themselves that they were again being taken to work.

The *S.S.* men took the sick from their beds and small children from their cradles and, with the help of the Polish police, searched for all of the hidden Jews and brought them together to one place; my sick grandmother was among them.

Only those who were considered capable of work were chosen. All of the others were loaded in autos, driven somewhere and we do not know what became of their remains.

Those remaining were taken to several houses outside the city and they declared:

– Only those capable of work remain here. Later, the areas will be fenced in as a "work camp."

I, Rochel Kachan, Horowicz's daughter and several others (I cannot remember their names now) worked in the Czyzewo courtyard near Sokolowski. In order not to have to endure being bothered by the hooligan policemen who would come to visit the work camp every night, we received permission to remain overnight in a house in the courtyard. Rochel Kachan and I lay on a small bench.

The bad news about the annihilation of the Czyzewo Jews spread quickly to the surrounding *shtetlekh*. It also reached Sokolow. Although the Jews there also lived in a ghetto, they had nevertheless convinced themselves that they would avoid the misfortune because they had better conditions. Therefore, my uncle sent a special messenger that we should all come to him in Sokolow.

[Column 1032]

My mother, sister and I traveled with him. However, my father in no way wanted to go because he bore a certain responsibility. He was afraid that because of his departure others would suffer. The Germans would punish them for his disappearance.

After several months in Sokolow, we returned to Czyzewo. We could not remain there calmly, not knowing what was happening to our father. Therefore, we decided to return and whatever happened at least we would all be together.

We imagined that we would live because we still belonged to the labor camp. But on a given day the commissar's Christian cook secretly told us that the alarm clock was set for 12 midnight. This was a bad sign.

Returning to Czyzewo, I was registered for work with the German commissar. Two men also worked there, Feivel Niewad and another one, whose name I do not remember now. My mother and sister worked on the highway.

Returning to the labor camp at night we saw all of the Jews in great despair because they had learned the Poles would carry out their orders very early.

The question was in everyone's mouth:

– What do we do?

But no one could answer. Some ran to the forests, others ran to hide with Christian acquaintances, but what Christian wanted then to hide a Jew? Others ran to their work, thinking that they would not be taken from their work. My mother and my sister also ran to the highway work. Alas, I never again saw them among the living.

[Column 1033]

My father did not want to hide at first. He said that wherever he hid they would find him and shoot him. He was then in the *Judenrat*. What would people say if he also hid?

He went around and recited Psalms.

It was very difficult for me to leave my father and escape. I sat with him until he actually forced me to escape. Perhaps I would succeed in getting Polish documents and as a Christian perhaps I could survive.

These were the last words that I heard from him.

My thought was that I would hide somewhere overnight and in the morning we would be able to see each other. But the two men with whom I worked at the commissar came in and convinced me that I should go with them through the camp fence and we would go to the courtyard of the commissar where his beloved animals were located. From there we would be able to observe everything that was happening in the camp.

It was dawn, still dark, when the wild *S.S.* members surrounded the camp, gathering everyone there, loaded them into wagons and took them to Zambrów. We here, in the commissar's courtyard, waited for a miracle.

[Column 1034]

We sat in the animal garden. When the Christian servant brought food for the animals she also brought a little warm food for us. But none of us could swallow a drop. We had a premonition of what awaited us.

When the *S.S.* finished their work in the camp they came to the commissar, found us hidden in his garden and they reacted like animals. We were sure that they would shoot us at once, but the commissar arranged that meanwhile we would be taken to jail.

This was on a Sunday when the pious Christians went to church. Two policemen took us with loaded rifles the way criminals are taken. The two men were led into a cell and I into another. I counted the minutes the entire day, knowing that these were my last hours and the end would be at night.

Around five o'clock at night the keys in the door of my cell were heard. The policemen reported to me that more hidden Jews were found; they would all be placed in jail.

This was true. All were actually crammed together in the jail that was near the *gmina* [administrative district office]. Now we knew that everyone was being brought together in one place and we would be sent to Zambrów.

But in the morning we received an order to go the work camp. There we were shown three small houses in which we were told to remain. Whoever dared to go out would immediately be shot. Everything that the Jews still possessed was taken out to a clearance sale to the neighboring Poles.

[Column 1035]

There were about 15 people in the camp then, women and men. We were sure that we would soon be taken to Zambrów. Several decided to escape into the forest. Others hid with Christians. I was never brave, but my will to live was so strong that I decided to escape to the Christian world.

Before going away I learned that my mother and my sister Feigel were hiding somewhere. I sent them word that they should go with me, wherever fate would determine for us. But my sister ordered me to go alone because their faces could betray me. They had decided to return to the labor camp.

Before leaving the camp I heard that Rochel Zylbersztajn was hidden in one of the small houses and when she wanted to quickly move to a second house she was murdered by the police.

Due to the provocation of the Poles, it became more difficult to find a hiding place anywhere. We, therefore, made peace with our fate and waited to be taken to Zambrów.

Making use of a moment when there were few policemen, we succeeded in going over to the other side of the camp. Wrapped in a thick peasant-like shawl, I went in a wagon to a village near Zambrów where I had a Christian acquaintance. I could not travel too far. I did not have any documents. Despite this I hoped that perhaps I would be able somehow to help my parents who remained in the Zambrów camp.

[Column 1036]

Alas, I no even had a chance to try to do something because everyone had been sent to Auschwitz from which no one returned.

I succeeded in acquiring Christian documents under the name of Janina Zarczicka. I worked in the village and hoped for a miracle, a redemption.

But fate wanted something else for us and one day Czyzewo Christians, who I knew very well, traveled through the village. They noticed me; they did not say anything and I thought that they would not denounce me. But at night, Marcziniak, the Czyzewo policeman, arrived in the village with an order from the commissar to shoot me on the spot.

The peasants in the village had a little heart and they let me know that they would ask the murderer that he not do it.

The order was that I must come out at four o'clock in the morning into the garden in the courtyard where the murderer would need to carry out the execution.

I strongly doubted whether the good peasants would convince the murderer and, therefore, I spent the night in a nightmare between hope and doubt. I asked myself: is it possible that people would watch a person being shot without asking why and not providing any resistance?

At the chosen time, four o'clock in the morning, I came to the garden where Marcziniak, the murderer, was already waiting. I also saw some Christian acquaintances walking there who assured me that for appearance's sake, Marcziniak would shoot into the air so that it would be known in the village that he had exactly carried out the commissar's order. They told me that a wagon was ready with which I would go away to Lomza immediately after this.

[Column 1037]

In no way could I believe my ears; was it possible? Were they successful in convincing the well known "murderer!"

But it happened as the good peasants promised me. I immediately left for Lomza.

I was also afraid of the bright light of day. Each day it became more difficult to hide. Several Christians from the place where I was staying volunteered for work in Germany. I joined this group.

After going through various inspections, I sat a lucky one on the train that took the workers to East Prussia.

After arriving in Interburg [Insterburg], the labor office sent us to various areas for field work.

I toiled hard for two years with the German peasants. But I lived with the hope that it would end some day.

The day finally came. We heard the Russian artillery fire. The German peasants became very frightened, left everything and ran to the American side. They took us, the workers, with them because they were sure that they would quickly return to their estates and it was a shame to lose the slave workers.

A heavy battle with the Russians took place in the city Keslin. Finally the Russian tanks entered the city where a great number of Soviet prisoners, as well as all of the foreign workers who had wrested themselves from their German overseers, waited for them.

[Column 1038]

Taking their rucksacks on their backs, they immediately began to march back home.

There were no train movements then. So they went on foot.

I traveled for two weeks in this way.

I arrived in Poznan with many other Polish woman and men where we found trucks on which to travel.

On the entire road back I still had hope after everything that perhaps there had been a miracle and I would meet someone from those closest to me.

Arriving in Czyzewo, I went up to an acquaintance in the suburbs of the city in order to learn how the situation appeared in the *shtetl*. As soon as she saw me she ran into the city calling the several Jews who had miraculously survived.

The two Szwarc sisters, Dina Frydman and Grosodzin's sister came. They asked me to come to them to spend the night where we would tell each other of our experiences.

We did not say one word going through the paved streets of Czyzewo. A great pain pressed on our hearts. I felt as if everything was drenched in the blood of those closest to us.

I took out a document with my correct name at the *gmina* and went back to the Christians to spend the night and in the morning to drive through the cities to look for someone from my family, because I already knew that I had nothing to look for in Czyzewo. Everything was lost.

Avraham Igla and the girls accompanied me to the Christians and calmly returned home. At night I heard shooting. I asked the Christian what this can mean. Her answer was:

– The Russian like to shoot at night.

[Column 1039]

But I had a bad premonition and could not fall asleep.

I left very early for the train station. There, a Christian acquaintance told me about the misfortune that had happened to several Jews from Czyzewo who were miraculously saved from the gas chambers or from other dangers and who had barbarically been murdered at home this night by the Polish bandits.

[Column 1040]

I left with the first train for Sokolow, with the hope of finding a trace there of our many branched family.

But here, too, the brown death killed everything that had the name, "Jew."

Also here, I did not find anyone.

As it appears, the fate, the blind fate preferred that I survive in order to be able to tell about those who can no longer speak.

May their memory be consecrated.

[Column 1039]

Through Flames and Smoke

A Czyzewor Partisan's Story

B. Bolender

Translation donated by Andrea Bolender

In loving memory of Benek Bolender

When the war broke out in 1939, I was 13 years old. I didn't yet comprehend what is war. I first came to grips when I had already paid a dear price. I lost all who were beloved and dear to me and their holy remembrance is forever etched in my memory.

I lost my parents and my entire family; I was the only one to make it out alive.

For years, I couldn't fathom that such things could transpire. Unfortunately, I made peace with believing that it was the truth yet I shudder every time I remind myself of it all.

When Czyzewo was bombed by the Germans, we were all lying in a cellar. There were many dead. The city was burning. We were left without a roof over our heads. At that point, my father ob'm, took us to Gromadzyn.

[Column 1040]

There (in Gromadzyn) we got a place to sleep in a stable and we were also able to get by with the food but we weren't able to stay there for long so we returned to Czyzewo. We were taken into a house not far from the slaughterhouse. I don't remember the name of our host, all I remember is that he worked at the motel in the mill.

My father sent me on a train to Lomza, over there my grandfather ob'm had his own house. I returned safely and you can imagine the happiness when the saw me alive.

We said goodbye to all of our acquaintances and friends and left for Lomza (this was already in the time when the Russians were still in Czyzewo). My father would often travel to Czyzewo for business.

In the year 1941 in an early morning, suddenly airplanes appeared in the skies and they were throwing down bombs like a heavy rain. The Russians said that this was military maneuvers but the bitter truth came out later when we saw the destruction from the bombing.

[Column 1041]

The next morning, the Germans were already in Lomza. On the roads we saw Jews who had been shot. A week later, my brother Avrohom Shimon was taken for labor and from that point on I never saw him again.

A short while later they made a ghetto in Lomza where life became unbearable.

One day a order came that all men from a certain age were to gather at a place outside the ghetto. They were all put on black machines and were "officially" taken to work. In reality they were driven to the Tzarvanne wild forest and were all shot. Amongst them was my father ob'm.

Our family now consisted of, my mother, a sister, 2 brothers and myself. A while later they sent me to work in Simova. Over there I worked at the chateau. Later they sent me to work in a stone quarry where I became sick and I later escaped from there to Czyzewo. Over there I met up with my relatives who forced me to go to Dr. Gerlich. He gave me a letter for the German camp commander (stating) that I couldn't work at the stone quarry and they sent me back to the Lomza ghetto.

Life in the ghetto was very difficult. They would suddenly grab people for forced labor. Those who could, would hide on the roofs or in the cellars. At one such instance, I was hiding with other people in an attic. My cousin, Boruch Sendoss was a policeman. The commander ordered him to go up on the roof and see if any Jews were hiding there. When he saw us there, he went down and said that no one was there. The commander didn't believe him and went up himself and found all of the people there.

[Column 1042]

On the spot he shot my cousin, HYD (Hashem Yinkom Domo- G-d avenge his death).

He fell as a sacrifice to sanctify the almighty's name.

The Gestapo demanded from the Jewish council of Lomza "a few bearded Jews". Without warning the Gestapo police began searching on their own. They found my grandfather and another Jew from Kolna. They took both of them away. We learned later of their fate.

This is what Jews from Rutka told over.

When the car which was transporting bound up my grandfather and the other Jew passed a mountain in Rutka the Jew from Kolna managed to free himself and jumped out of the car. My grandfather was a weaker person and therefore couldn't help himself. When the car arrived in Rutka , the German opened the door and saw that my grandfather was alone and he shot him on the spot.

This was told to me by Yidden from Rutka who saw this with their own eyes. One person was named Avrohom Sendattsh Ob'm.

I worked in an artillery factory not far from Ostrova. On a certain day, rumors began were circulating that they'd be sending out the Jews from the ghetto to some work area.

[Column 1043]

I together with some other Lomzer Yidden snuck out of the ghetto by night and started walking towards Lomza where our parents were.

We went the entire way by foot almost entirely through forests. We passed through the area where not long before the Simaver Yidden were shot. Sticking out of the ground were bunches of hands and feet.

We stood there for a while kneeling with our heads bent however we soon schlepped on with our tired feet. We were already used to such happenings.

Entering the ghetto we saw destruction. Nobody knew for certain what was being done with those who were being sent out. With my mother's permission, I together with my older brother Leizer headed straight to the forest.

With a broken heart we said goodbye to our mother, sister and brother and without a word left the house.

We began looking for a way to escape from the ghetto.

After a long search we were successful.

We got going on the path which took us through the forest surrounding Zambrów. Along the way we met up with men, women and children who'd escaped from different ghettos. They told us that "they" were moving out all Lomza Jews to Zambrów.

In a forest not far from Zambrów we met a group of Russian Partisans. They allowed us to join them.

[Column 1044]

The Run from the Russians

They showed us that they considered us all equal in their goal. Each of us swore in his heart to defeat the Hitlerites and to avenge all of the spilled innocent Jewish blood.

Even in the forest our lives were far from certain. Death hovered over from all sides. However, we thought that at least we won't go without a fight. We won't let them lead us to slaughter like sheep.

Every minute of the day we readied ourselves for a German onslaught. Then we had to be careful not to fall into their murderous hands.

"Weapons, give us weapons" the younger people begged from the partisan leader. We'll be victorious!

"In our hands burns the desire to "pay back" the enemies of the Jews for their cruelty".

We did all sorts of hard labor and thought of ourselves as partisans.

Suddenly, when we thought that the Russian Partisans looked at us as their own and loyal to their cause came the tragic turn of events.

"Get away from us!" the Russians screamed, "deal with the Germans yourselves". "We don't want you to follow us".

They took everything from us whatever we had and they left us hungry, broken and totally relying on the Almighty.

We started digging ditches. Tired and hungry we dug with our last strength. The ditches immediately filled with Yidden who wandered in the forest.

[Column 1045]

The worst was the hunger, there wasn't anywhere from where we could get food. Some of the younger fellows went to nearby villages to try to get food.

It was very dark and we were overtaken with fear. We were scared to travel far. When we left our ditches, we suddenly heard shooting in our direction. We quickly hid, each person where he could. Later when it was quiet we went back to our ditches.

While we couldn't see, we could hear the moaning and cries for help from the wounded. Obviously, this was coming from those who were still alive. We had nothing to help with. There were many dead. It seemed like the villagers had reported and shown the forest where the Jews were hiding.

The few survivors decided not to remain in the forest to be shot like animals. We went back to Zambrów in the barrack and happen what may happen but at least together with all the Yidden.

It so happened that I fell into one of the first transports. They packed into wagons thousands of Yidden and took them to the train station in Czyzewo where empty cattle wagons were waiting for us.

We arrived at the station in Auchwitz 1/12/1943 at night.

The station was well lit. We were ordered to leave the wagons where there were many dead and we were ordered to leave everything in the wagon.

We stood outside for a long time and waited. I was together with my mother, sister and brother and suddenly we realized that the Germans were selecting workers.

[Column 1046]

My older brother was amongst those workers.

I was very short and it enabled me to run over to my older brother who was standing on the left side. Right after, vehicles came and took away all those standing on the right. We later found out that a day later they were all burned.

All of the workers had numbers made on their left hand.

Being in Birkenau (now Brzezinska) we saw how every day new transports arrived. Immediately when the train would stop, members of the SS would shout orders for everyone to disembark from the wagons. Whoever tried to take anything with him even a piece of bread was shot on the spot.

Often we would see how on the spot they'd make selections. From large groups of Yidden were chosen smaller groups of young men and the rest of the men with all the women were transported in autos to the crematorium.

It happened that suddenly brought an entire town. Worn out, half dead, skeleton like. The Germans saw that there wasn't anyone to select and they sent them all to the crematorium.

Later in that day, the gas chambers in the death factory Birkenau consumed forever the last remembrance of a Jewish town.

The remaining people from our transport waited for their death. Every day people were hit and beaten to death for no reason.

[Column 1047]

One time they called out that all stylists should gather at a certain place. My brother brought me along although I had no idea about styling.

We came to the place and came under a hail of blows and were then driven into a sauna. They then threw us out naked into 25 degree weather and ordered us to run. While running many people fell. Some of them were from Czyzewo.

My brother Lazer became sick and went to the hospital.

A few days later there was a selection and my brother was amongst the sick who were sent to the ovens.

When we became close to the Russian front the Germans instituted what was called the death march.

[Column 1048]

They led us from one barrack to another. People were falling on the way like flies.

They schlepped us to a territorial city in Czechia.

On May 8th, the Russians came to free us.

I began wandering with a real will to go back to Poland. Maybe I'd find one of my relatives.

When I came to Czyzewo I was notified that the previous night, the Polacks killed the surviving Czyzewer Jews.

I didn't go into the city.

In 1948 after wandering for a long time, I arrived in America.

I have a wife with two children and don't have a bad life however what I witnessed and personally lived through, I'll never forget.

Forever I'll remember you

My father Mottel Bolender and my mother Rochel Leah. My brothers Shimon, Lazer and Chaim Yitzchok. My sister Sora Feiga. My uncles Fishel Bronsztajn his wife Chynka, Yitzchok Starkovisky and his wife Beltshe and their 4 children

[Column 1049]

Czyzewo – Siberia – Canada

Moshel Blajwajs (Edmonton), Canada

Translated by Gloria Berkenstat Freund

My Arrest

It was a Friday night, the 11th of October 1939, two weeks since the Russians, had occupied Czyzewo.

I had just arrived at the house of prayer. A young Jewish man came in right after me. I knew he was the sausage-maker's son. He stood in the door for a minute, as if he was hesitating; should he say something to me. Finally, he hastily said: They are calling you to *Revkom* (revolutionary committee) for a minute.

– Let me make *Kiddush* [prayer over wine] – I tried to speak calmly, seeing the fear in eyes of my wife and children.

The young man was impatient and said that everyone was waiting for me there. They just needed to ask me something and they will let me go right away.

I was led to a room that was full of smoke from cigarettes. Little by little the faces of Jewish communist acquaintances in the *shtetl* [town] were unveiled for me. A uniformed member of the *NKVD* [*Narodnyy Komissariat Vnutrennikh Del* – People's Commissariat for Internal Affairs], who began to question me, sat in the middle at a small table. The others assisted him.

There was cross-fire; they were shooting questions at lightning speed from all sides, one after the other, with no logic, only to confuse me, dull my memory and get an answer that would be worthwhile for them, that would affirm that I was a manufacturer who had used and exploited people and was an officer in the counter-revolutionary Zionist organization, which had as its purpose the overthrow of the Soviet regime.

[Column 1050]

I confessed that I was a Zionist, wanted to go to *Eretz-Yisrael*, the national home of the Jewish people, but never thought about counter-revolution, had never exploited a worker.

The next morning, early on *Shabbos* [the Sabbath], I was taken under guard to the train. On the way I met Jews who were going to pray. Some turned their heads in fear, as if they were afraid that my misfortune would draw them in.

I was taken to Sakala [Sokółka], the district location of the *NKVD* headquarters, which could not find a suitable house for its extensive work in burned out Czyzewo.

It appears that it was known in the *shtetl* where I was being taken. We wife and my oldest son, Simkha, came on foot to Sakala on the same day. She was not permitted to come near me; I could only look at their terrified faces through barred windows.

In the evening I was loaded into a vehicle with other arrestees and taken to Bialystok. There was a terrible frost that stung every limb. I was in a bare jacket.

The basement cell into which I was led in the Bialystok jail was filled with wild, bearded men, blond, dark and grey beards. At the beginning I therefore thought that they were all Jews. It became obvious that this was a mixture of White Russians, Poles, Jews and Ukrainians. The *starosta* [village elder] for the cell, a Vilna Jew, lawyer Prajs, turned to me, speaking in Yiddish. He asked me from where I came, why I had been arrested. Listening to me, he sighed sadly:

[Column 1051]

– It smells of counter-revolution. They will slip you in as a 58 (paragraph, according to which one was judged as an active or passive counter-revolutionary, which could mean from eight-years up to the death penalty).

It already was 1:30 in the morning when the door opened and the soldier on duty came in, let out an inarticulate, angry shout and remained standing: "…to the devil; I have forgotten your name. It begins with the letter 'B'…"

He called out Birenbaum, Binder, Blausztajn. When I mentioned my name, he was happy:

– Oh, I need you.

He ran quickly with me through the corridors and circular staircases, shouting, "*Bystei, bystrei*!" (Fast, fast!). At that time, I barely understood Russian and in my confused mind I mixed up the word *strelyat*, which means shoot. I was sure that he was chasing me to my execution. He had a blanket in his hand. Whenever an approaching step was heard, he threw the blanket over my face. I did not know then that this was done so that the arrestees would not speak to their acquaintances.

I was taken into a room where all of the walls were covered with rifles. This increased my certainty that they were going to shoot me.

An officer entered. He carried a pistol and his belt contained many bags of bullets. He stood near me and silently did not lower his stinging gaze from me, as if he wanted to hypnotize me. Finally, in a hoarse voice, he said:

[Column 1052]

– Do you smoke?

He went to a cabinet, took out two pictures of [Chaim] Weizmann and [Ze'ev] Jabotinsky, showed them to me, asking:

– To which of them do you belong?

It was all the same to me. In any case they would soon shoot me.

I answered:

– To both.

He was very satisfied with my answer.

– So, I understand. Describe what kind of diversions [revolutionary work] they entrusted to you?

– What kind of diversionary work?

– Swine, again you do not want to speak?

Insults, blows began to pour. I was taken back to the cell bloodied and having fainted.

I came to myself a little after a few days. I was called again on the fourth night. This time there were seven officers. Each one had his own particular manner of questioning. The purpose was the same: I should confess and describe my plans for diversions against the Soviet regime.

I was without strength and hysterically shouted:

– Cut me in pieces… I have nothing to tell you. I am innocent.

– Swine, you spoke in the house of prayer?

– Yes.

– Who sent you? What was the purpose of your appearance?

– Collecting money for the Keren Kayemet [Jewish National Fund].

[Column 1053]

– Explain the idea. The accursed fascist ideology and the murders, and the murders that you planned against the workers. Did the workers oppose you, huh? Speak…

The truth was that at the time, when there was the threat of a pogrom, I opposed Lepak, who had called for our appearance in the street with weapons. I believed that we would only agitate the Christian population even more. I tried to make them understand.

They mockingly laughed:

– You yourself agitated the peasants against the Jewish workers. You organized the pogroms… What methods did you use? Describe… My thoughts became confused. I spoke:

– I did not agitate… I did not have any methods… Shoot me.

– You will die in jail, like a dog.

I was not called for any questioning for four months. The cells became still thicker and more suffocating for me. Several dozen people lay on plank beds. Human feet, hands, heads, stomachs, backs, human faces were mingled together. People were covered in lice. No one changed clothes during the entire time, did not wash, [were] sick, swollen. At night when one wanted to empty himself, he walked over the heads, throats, backs, feet. Fights broke out because of a crust of bread, because of nothing. Those who did not have a spot on a plank bed lay on the floor, in all of the crannies, sitting, standing, lying, one's foot lying on the chest of another, and a third feel asleep over them and his foot came out on the throat of the first one… A man whose lungs seemed as if they had been eaten away pushed toward the small-barred window that was always open. But no air came in.

Individual volleys of bullets were heard. Everyone thought: tomorrow could be my turn… From time to time, someone was called. He came back after a few hours, battered, mutilated and crying.

[Column 1054]

After four months I was again led through the corridors and labyrinths with a blanket over my eyes to an investigation.

The officer received me very courteously, so genteelly, that I did not believe my ears that I had heard correctly how he addressed me so politely with *ir* [the formal word in Yiddish for you] and he spoke so civilly that I was hopeful that I would not be treated badly. However, [I was told] it was truly worthwhile not to suffer. I only needed to provide the methods and contacts of our counter-revolutionary leaders and I would be finished with this tiresome investigation.

– I have explained everything. I have nothing to add.

I was again led out, battered and fainting. I was brought to consciousness with a dipper of water, poked from behind, pushed in the front. I was pushed back into the cell.

– Yes, they do this – a Jew sat next to me and helped me bind my wounds with pieces of my torn shirt.

– Why do they not shoot me already? – I asked in pain.

– They do this, too – he answered pensively.

– It is better than being tormented.

– You think so?

A secret wind blew from the question, but I was in too much pain to catch what he meant out of the air. My mouth was full of blood and my ribs still felt the boots of the members of *NKVD*. My loosened teeth struck one another. I barely murmured:

[Column 1055]

– I will finally not endure such a hell…

– They still want us to perish, to be crushed like lice, but we will not die, we endure – the Jew whispered close to my ear.

The days in the frozen cell extended, long and difficult. The nights were full of moans, laments, supplications and curses. We were not permitted to lie down during the day; we learned to sleep sitting up, standing and moving. Sitting with open eyes, I felt that I was sleeping. The brain rested. Near me stood my father with outspread arms, stroking my wounds and talking to me in a soft and warm voice: "You hurt, you hurt badly. But you will endure. Be strong. You will survive."

A shiver went through my body. The dream disappeared, but, I still heard my father's words in my ears: "Be strong. You will survive!"

Several days later I received a package from home. There was a handkerchief, which was cut into pieces by the prison guards so that I would not be able to hang myself; a piece of soap cut into two pieces and a shirt, the first shirt I changed into after five months. This also was the first news for me in the Bialystok prison that my wife and children were alive and were in Czyzewo.

Eight months passed and no one called me. It appeared as if they had forgotten me; that I had been sentenced to die in prison. Is there a more terrible death than the slow dying and suffocation in dirt?

[Column 1056]

I was called again in the ninth month. The officer who questioned me spoke gently and I immediately felt the gentility was not artificial. He often said to me that my wife and children were threatened; they should live Russia. And I? I would probably sit there for as long it would be until I confessed. He did not try to pressure me to confess, not even with questions. He gave me a packet of cigarettes when I left [the interrogation]. He was a Jew.

After 11 months I was moved to a separate cell.

At first I breathed freer, but I immediately felt the horror of sitting alone day and night in the stone grave filled with silence. I wanted to move, to speak, to shout so that someone would hear me. Shouting in a grave. The steps in the corridor – dull blows in my head, blows that dulled, deafened. The longer I listened to the steps, the duller the sound became. Somewhere a door opened and closed. They brought new victims. Orders, echoes of movements. I heard human screams at night of a man who did not want to confess to criminal offenses he did not commit. The screams tore into my head as if thin needles would open wide my brains, smash my skull. The quieter it was, the stronger and more frightening the distant scream rang in my ears.

One night I was taken out into the courtyard. Many other arrestees were already assembled there. All had to kneel down. An officer read the sentence for each one separately, each sentenced in a private conversation among three people who had never spoken to him, had never seen him.

[Column 1057]

My sentence sounded: five years labor camp. We immediately were led in the direction of the train station. Soldiers surrounded us on all sides. The officer warned: "Do not say one word! At every superfluous movement, at every stop of a step on the march – you will be shot immediately."

We traveled; the small windows of the train wagon were barred. We had no food. Over 15 days, they distributed bread and herring twice. We were taken off [the train] at Kotlice at the border with the Komi S.S.R. to a transit camp. There were thousands of arrestees, various kinds of criminals mixed with pale faces of genteel people in giant barracks. Terrible fights broke out. The soldiers, who stood guard, always were on the side of the strong ones.

From there we travelled 10 days on coal and wood barges on the Dvina [River]. The name Dvina reminded me of a Polish river, but this river was much larger, endless and sadder. It [the river] devoured three thousand [people] who had been fed with bread and herring over 10 days, from our transport, which numbered over 6,000 people. They became sick with dysentery after drinking from the river, writhed in pain and had severe convulsions and not being able to bear the suffering, they threw themselves in the river. A typhus epidemic spread quickly. The weakened organisms did not wrestle for long, gave into death. Their neighbors, who were still standing on their feet, silently lowered them into the water. The barges swam further over the sad river.

[Column 1058]

We were taken off somewhere near a forest. Some were sent to hospitals and some to work sawing trees in the forest.

The blinding snow was high. To cut a tree one had to dig into the snow, two meters deep. The standard [quota] was six cubic meters a day. The portion of bread was lowered from 600 to 300 grams for not reaching the quota.

During the work I once cut down a tree badly and it fell in the opposite direction, raising me into the air and hurled me 30 meters. I woke up in the hospital, where I lay for 10 days. I was sent to work as soon as I began to recover. My work consisted of hanging notes on the up-to 500-600 dead who were sent from the hospital.

After several months we were taken several hundred kilometers deeper into the forest to a camp where the conditions were even more difficult. We slept in unheated barracks on the bare ground. The mice crawled over our heads and the hunger frighteningly tortured us.

It appeared to me then that this was the worst hell. Later, I learned that there were many worse in Russia, but this camp also had its bloody history of pain and murder. In 1937 they had begun to build the train line that ran for 2,000 kilometers up to the North Pole. Every meter of the road cost thousands of victims. An old resident of that area once told me: " See, under every wooden railroad tie, lie buried hundreds of people. The railroad here travels over millions of dead."

[Column 1059]

The war broke out. Thousands of criminal [prisoners] were freed, went to the front. However, I belonged to the political [prisoners] and I remained for a long time.

Almost all of the Jews, who constituted five percent of the general number of camp inmates, remained. In free minutes, we told each other about our pasts when we were still people. However, very few such people remained.

Returning from work once, I was told that there was a letter for me at the post office.

Shaking from the cold, hungry, I stood and read the several short lines: "I send you 50 rubles. Write your exact address." It was signed by a Jew who had been with me in the Bialystok jail. It is still incomprehensible to me how he knew in which camp I was located. He also searched the address of my wife and children, who had been sent to Krazna-Kievka, a village near Petropavlovsk and learned where they were. They succeeded in sending me two letters. They did not receive my answers.

Finally, it also was our turn; an order arrived to free all of the Polish citizens, with out any distinctions.

They again spoke to me as to a person. They let me wash, trim my hair. They gave me a clean shirt, as much bread as I wanted.

My first steps were to go to Krasna-Kievka. But I did not find anyone there. They had been taken to another village in Chkalov Oblast.

[Column 1060]

I remained without money, without food. I succeeded in begging for a piece of bread, going by foot from village to village. I went over a hundred kilometers in a week. I completely lost my strength when I finally was near the village. I slowly reached the chairman of the *sovkhoz* [state-owned farm], who told me that it was true, Brajna Blajwajz had been here, but she was sent away by train to other work in Akmolinsker Oblast. Her father and mother were with her. They were not far away, 30 kilometers from here, in the *shtetl* [town], Suchaton.

Again, I went 30 kilometers on foot. I barely dragged my starving body. I had just seen the first houses in the *shtetl* when I fainted.

When I woke up I found myself in a room. The people, who were moving around, spoke Yiddish. In a corner on the floor lay my father-in-law and mother-in-law wrapped in blankets.

There was deep joy mixed with unending sorrow. The two eighty year-olds barely understood what had happened to me. They were completely dulled by the years and the suffering they had lived through.

Here I learned that my wife and children no longer had the strength to suffer hunger and had left for Uzbekistan. But a letter immediately came from there. Yes, the children are very sick in a dying condition in a hospital and their mother did not have the means to keep them alive.

After long hardships, they returned to me in Suchaton where I worked and earned barely enough for dry bread.

[Column 1061]

Our luck lasted for several months. My oldest son was taken in the military. My wife traveled by train, wanting to produce a few pieces of goods that she wanted to sell in Suchaton to earn expenses. But the militia, which caught her traveling on the train without a ticket, took her off the train and searching her found the goods. The court sentenced her to five years in a labor camp and exiled her to Karaganda [in Kazakhstan], where she was for four years at hard labor in the coal fields.

I remained alone with the three children.

Days passed slowly. The war was ending. A wagon suddenly pulled up to me with a member of the *NKVD* and he invited me to go with him. He spoke very politely and tried to pretend that this was something of a usual formality. But a terrible premonition immediately hung in the house. The children cried, hanging onto the wagon and begged the man from the *NKVD*: "Do not take away our father from us." The man from the *NKVD* whipped the horse and we left. The cry of my children accompanied me the entire way.

The officer, who was waiting for me, read from a paper that on this-and-this day I had said to a worker that it had been better for me in Poland than in the Soviet Union. I could in no way remember that I would have said such a thing. A worker appeared immediately, and as if he had memorized a Psalm, said to me to my face: "You had talked to me that way, that the fascist Poles were good for you!"

None of my entreaties helped. I was again ordered to jail. I was sentenced to eight years in a labor camp.

[Column 1062]

I was in the camp, which was somewhere on the road to the North Pole, until 1947. My wife came to me there two years later. The children had left for Poland in 1946 from which, through various ways, they arrived in Canada.

An amnesty for the Polish arrestees came in 1947. On the night of our departure from the camp we were surprised to notice the chief of the *NKVD* at the camp, a captain, put on a rifle and take over our convoy. On the way, he said to me in simple Yiddish: "Go slightly slower, let the gentiles go in front…"

When I remained behind with my wife and another Jew, Fiszman, who is in Israel now, the captain came to us and quietly said: "Do you understand why I went along with you? My intention was to say goodbye to you as a Jew to a Jew."

It was a long time since I had heard such humane, moving talk and this was from an *NKVD* captain, who was the specter of fear for the entire camp. Who could imagine that under the hated uniform beat such a warm, Jewish heart?! He spoke with a broken voice:

– As I have looked at you, my heart cried with pity. However, I saw then that I was not so alone. Now, I remain here alone. My daughter, an adult, will marry a gentile. Ech – the life of a dog.

I actually had a great deal for which to thank him. During my last two years in the camp I received work in the warehouse thanks to him and it was a little easier for me. No one recognized him as a Jew.

[Column 1063]

When we were nearer to the train station, he hugged and kissed each of us. He pressed our hands for a long time and spoke with a determined voice: "Do everything so that you do not stay in Poland for long. Travel out from there quickly." I asked him, "Where?"

[Column 1064]

He added, "This is very difficult for me to say. Make sure you go far from Poland."

Alas, I had to wait in Poland for over a year, working in Wroclaw in a small brush factory. At the beginning of 1950 I succeeded in finding an address for my children and, receiving papers from them, we departed for Canada.

[Column 1063]

Propelled by Fear of the Swastika

by Freidel Lewinson, New York

Translated from Hebrew by Gloria Berkenstat Freund

There was immediate darkness in the city as soon as the war broke out. We immediately saw that the world was sinking for us. The Czyzewo train station was bombed on the first day and the fire was seen from all sides. We began to think of escaping. Where? How? No wagons could be had for any amount of money. I went to Yechielke the horse-cab driver, began to ask him to take us away to Cienchanowiec. I offered him 500 *zlotes*; even if he had wanted 1,000 *zlotes*, if only he would take us to Cienchanowiec, because we saw that all of the fire was in Czyzewo. He answered that 1,000 *zlotes* was really a large amount, but first he had to save his wife and children. "You see that I am packing myself and will leave immediately with my family."

I came home and informed my parents that we could not get a wagon for any amount of money. My remarkable father answered thus: "We will place ourselves in the hands of the Creator and stay. We will go to a brick building and the Creator will help us survive the fire that is drawing near us."

[Column 1064]

My Escape with my Child to Cienchanowiec

I became very nervous from the bangs of the bombs that were heard all around. I had a neighbor, Boruch Hitsl's son, Henryk, who was a horse trader. I cried and said that I was a mother and I needed to save my child. He said that as he had a wagon, I should give him 50 *zlotes* and he would make a place for me and my child in his wagon, and that he was leaving Thursday at night.

This was a great favor because he would have received much more if he had said he would take someone. When I asked him to take our entire family, he said that this was impossible because the whole wagon was occupied.

When my father heard that I had said that I did not want to travel alone with my child, he said to me, "I decree that you should leave with your child. We will trust in God and you are so frightened. So go."

[Column 1065]

This was on Thursday night, four days after the outbreak of the war.

We left for Cienchanowiec in a wagon packed with people, with a few things.

I will never forget the trip. All of the bridges were burned; it appeared as if the entire world was in flames and we met almost the entire city on the road. We ran on foot with the small children who could not walk.

We arrived in Cienchanowiec late at night.

We stayed with people unknown to us.

We got boxes in Cienchanowiec and buried our possessions under the floor. The same confusion as in Czyzewo.

The sad news arrived in the morning from Czyzewo that the entire city was in flames. The Germans had bombed Czyzewo and no could enter the city.

Everyone who had left families in Czyzewo regretted that they had escaped.

Suddenly Meir Orkes arrived.

He reported that there were nine Jewish victims and others had saved themselves in the forests.

Meir Orkis [spelled Orkes above] told me that nothing had happened to anyone in our family.

I decided not to escape further and remained in Cienchanowiec until the Germans entered.

We were in a cellar for two days.

When the enemy, may their name be erased, entered, all of the Jews were afraid to stick their heads outside.

[Column 1066]

We were very dejected and afraid, but little by little we began to go out into the street. However, we immediately heard that they already were looking for ways to cause suffering. They ordered a baker to provide a very large quantity of bread. If not, they would murder all of the Jews. A gentile boy had cut some kind of telephone wire; they said that the Jews had done it. They demanded that the Jew who had done it be given to them. If not, all of the Jews would be murdered.

Many German colonists lived in Cienchanowiec and they got along well with the Jewish population. They convinced the German regime that this was not done by the Jews.

We relaxed a little.

A few days later my husband came to Cienchanowiec and spoke about the destruction.

We decided to bring our parents and sister to Cienchanowiec.

One of the most respected members of the middle class in Czyzewo gave us two rooms and our parents came to Cienchanowiec.

Many Cienchanowiec members of the middle class would come to see my father and the Cienchanowiec Rabbi brought my father a few religious books because of his [my father's] entire large library which he had collected for his entire life, he did not have even one book. Everything had been burned.

After a few weeks rumors began to spread that the Germans were leaving and that the Russians were coming.

No one believed this. It was felt that this was a provocation by the Germans.

It was *erev Sukkos* [the eve of the Feast of the Tabernacles] when I went, at the request of my father, to bake a few flat rolls for *Lekhem Mishneh* [two holiday or *Shabbos* – Sabbath – breads for the holiday].

[Column 1067]

The owner had a *sukkah* [temporary structure in which one has meals and may sleep during the holiday of *Sukkos*] and, going to the bakery, I saw [people] were running all over and Russian tanks were entering the city.

I ran home quickly to relate the happy news that the Russians had entered and we were no longer subject to various provocations.

My father accepted the news very coldly and said: "What is the celebration? Previously the body was in danger and now our souls are in danger."

We knew that the Russians persecuted those who study Torah and how would we be able to raise children without Torah…?

The Decision to Travel to Vilna

Immediately after *Sukkos* 1939, a cold winter arrived of which I remember no equal.

Everything was burned after the bombing of Czyzewo, so that I had no shoes and no galoshes because I had left the house in a pair summer shoes. And a heavy snow had started to fall here. We walked in snow up to our knees and could not find any shoes to buy because all of the shops had been burned. We decided to go to Bialystok to buy shoes and galoshes. Traveling involved mortal danger. The bridges had been bombed out and we had to go by boat from Łapy in order to be able to go to Bialystok.

With great effort, we succeeded in reaching Bialystok. There we were able to buy something to wear on our feet so that we would be protected from the cold.

We met a few *yeshiva* [religious secondary school] men in Bialystok who informed us that Vilna was being granted to Lithuania and that there still were a few days in which we could travel by train and that many rabbis were departing. The entire Mirer *Yeshiva* was leaving. As Lithuania was not yet in a state of war, we would be able to travel further from there.

[Column 1068]

We immediately decided that only my husband would leave because we did not have our child with us. The child was with my parents in Cienchanowiec. So we decided that the child and I would go later.

Arriving in Cienchanowiec, I told my father that my husband had left for Vilna. He was very happy. He said: We older ones will still be able to get by somehow, but the young need to leave because this is no place for a young rabbi.

The Czyzewo Jews who had escaped to the villages began to return. Everyone thought about how it had been organized under the Russians; some of them nailed together a bit of a house, some moved outside the city.

The Jews asked that the rabbi return to Czyzewo. They received a room from the brush maker and my parents moved there.

I left for Tyktin [Tykocin], to my mother-in-law's, as there was no room for me and my child in the one small room.

While I was in Tyktin, my husband sent his brother-in-law from Vilna to bring me and our child to Vilna.

He arranged for gentiles to take us across the border when we reached it. But when my brother-in-law told me the plan, I said that I must go to say goodbye to my parents.

[Column 1069]

Traveling from Tyktin to Czyzewo took three days because traveling then was difficult. I finally arrived in Czyzewo.

On a dark evening I said goodbye to my dear, dear parents and my youngest sister, Gitl, who accompanied me outside, and with the blessings of my great father. I left my dear and precious ones that dark night with a small package in my hand.

Arriving in Bialystok, we started on our way. This was in December 1939.

When we arrived not far from the border where my brother-in-law had hired the gentiles, it already was heavily guarded and the gentiles had been arrested. We saw that we could not cross; we went to the nearby city Oszmiana [Ashmyany] . We were advised to wait until New Year's Eve when the guards would be drunk. Then we would be able to go across. However, this idea was incorrect because a terrible frost began. The temperature reached -42 [Celcius; -43.6 Farenheit]. Such a frost had not be seen for more than 50 years.

My child was three years old. We had to go perhaps 60 kilometers [over 37 miles]. It was impossible to walk with such a child; we had to carry the child. I looked among those who were ready to sneak across the border, someone who would carry the child. I wanted to pay well, but it was impossible to find someone. Additionally, the news arrived that those who went with children had had their children freeze to death.

I decided not to go.

[Column 1070]

My child and I were in Oszmiana for three months and we could not cross the border.

There were extraordinary circumstances where people bribed the guard at the border and went across the border in a wagon at night.

Thus did my child and I arrive in Vilna after three months of wandering.

This was before Purim in 1940.

We were almost the last ones who succeeded in escaping from there.

Thus passed a few months and we believed we had saved ourselves from hell until the first day of *Sukkos*.

Suddenly, the news reached us like thunder that the Russians had marched to Vilna and we again were in the middle of fire.

Our running was useless. Our home [country] was again unified with Vilna. My brother Chaim, who had lived in Maladzyechna, which already was occupied by Russia, came to me after the outbreak of the war and someone also arrived from Czyzewo. Dworya Edelsztajn also came to me and gave me a message from home and we believed that we were destined to live under the Russians.

We began to think of getting citizenship and believed there was no possibility of emigrating.

Vilna-Japan

At the time when we thought that we had to take [Soviet] citizenship, it became known that the Japanese Consulate, which was located in Kovno, was issuing visas to Japan.

It soon took on a mass character and every *yeshiva* [religious secondary school] person and a majority of the rabbis who were in Vilna took out Japanese visas.[1]

[Column 1071]

Having the Japanese visa, we had to have transit visas through Russia. No one believed that it would be easy to obtain so many transit visas from Russia. A miracle occurred. No one understands even today why we were immediately given transit visas.

Someone took a chance and went to obtain a transit visa and he was given one. Everyone who had a Japanese visa began to go and for a payment of 150 dollars received a Soviet transit visa.

When we asked at Intourist how we could obtain dollars, when we were not permitted to buy them, that we could be arrested, they answered that you will find a solution.

After paying the 150 dollars per person, we prepared to travel, but no one believed that we would travel safely and would arrive in Japan. It was thought, who knows if we were actually traveling to Siberia.

We traveled 14 days and nights locked in train wagons.

This was in February 1941 when we left Vilna. We arrived in Moscow two days later. We were treated very well there. As foreigners, we stayed in one of the nicest hotels, *Novoia Moskovskaya*.

We were given the best foods, but it should be understood that we did not eat them, except for fruit and sardines, because of *kashrus* [kosher dietary laws].

Seeing how we were treated in Moscow, we began to hope that perhaps they would really let us go.

We traveled for 12 days and night on the train from Moscow-Vladivostok and arriving in Vladivostok, we were all searched. Whoever had money or jewelry had it taken from them. They promised that they would come back and return what had been taken.

[Column 1072]

They took expensive pearls from me, diamonds from someone else, money from another one, but we were satisfied, seeing that they were letting us go.

We arrived in Japan safely on the 24th of February 1941.

We were amazed by this enchanted land. It was spring in February, with wonderful weather, beautifully sunny.

We left Vilna in heavy frosts and arrived in a country that was wonderful. The sun shone, warm, light, clean and magical. The people were sympathetic, welcomed us with smiles, with warmth. This simply amazed us. We had left a civilized land with so much evil and arrived in a barbaric land, where we imagined we would live in a frightening atmosphere and it was such a surprise there.

I remember riding on the bus; looking through the windows, we saw the esthetic displays in the shops. We could not hide our great amazement and kept admiring the cleanliness and refinement of the manner of treating foreigners by the Japanese.

Although they were preparing for a war and there was not enough food, they shared it with us and when we came and stood in the ranks to receive various food that was distributed with [ration] cards, they would move back from their spot so that we would receive [the food] first. This was a piety that must be shown so that it can be seen how they welcomed a stranger and we had so much thankfulness for them that we will never forget. They would pat our children, give them fruit and acted with extraordinary sincerity.

[Column 1073]

While in Kobe we received a letter from home. The parents were very happy that we had safely completed the journey and hoped we would arrive in America, and as we had all survived the difficulties we would also achieve this. I wrote to them until the sad news arrived that the war between Russia and Germany had broken out and every contact with home was cut off.

News arrived after our departure that more people had applied for transit visas and the issuing of visas had stopped and no one could leave anymore.

We tried to send queries, but without success. It was no longer permitted to leave. There were still many learned men who had missed the opportunity. Many of them were later sent to Siberia.

From Japan to Shanghai

Our visas to Japan were valid for only 12 days. Arriving there we immediately met with representatives of the Joint [Distribution Committee] and they helped us extend the visas, each time for a few months, and provided us with housing. It should be understood that there was one room for each family, not so comfortable, but it was a great help in a strange place. There also was financial support from which to live frugally.

Everyone communicated with their relatives or friends in America that they should send us papers of support so that we could travel to America.

[Column 1074]

Those who were the first to receive affidavits were given visas by the American Consul and they traveled to America.

Later, an edict was issued that whoever had relatives in Poland, which now belonged to Russia, could not get a visa. As we had received an affidavit after the edict, they refused to give us a visa. Nothing was of help. They did not want to admit anyone.

Our transit visas for being in Japan were extended for 11 months. Then they did not want to extend them and we had to leave for Shanghai where various illnesses and epidemics raged.

In Shanghai we met many of those who had left previously for Japan. Some of them were sick with dysentery and malaria.

The terrible climate and filthiness that reigned then in that city, affected us very badly.

In Shanghai we took a residence from one of those who had come earlier and had been able to obtain a visa to Israel.

Life was very difficult. There was great scarcity. But my husband succeeded in getting a job in the slaughterhouse as a rabbi [assuring the observance of the laws for kosher meat], with a very small salary that barely maintained the soul. We ate meat once a week and this was just the smell of meat, three-quarters of a pound for three people. A guest would also sometimes share in this. But fish was cheap.

My child, who was then five years old, had not tasted a cup of milk for a year. Later, we searched for and received a glass of milk for the child. Sometimes during the weeks I would buy two half ounces [14 grams] of butter for the child. Thus passed a year until 1943 when the war broke out between Japan and America.[2] The situation then became worse.

[Column 1075]

The Japanese in their own country who had been so good, now being in power in Shanghai, began to show great cruelty to the refugees. Possibly because they were under pressure from Hilter, may his name be erased. One morning an edict was issued that all Jews must live in a ghetto in the quarter that was being designated.

There was a frightening panic and, as the time was short, all of the refugees went to look for apartments in the ghetto and the prices there rose a great deal, although they were the worst residences in the city.

Many did not have any money to rent an apartment, so a committee was created and ruins were bought and small houses were nailed together and everyone was given a room. We also had no money to rent an apartment and we took such a room and when the period had ended for living in the previous apartment we had to move to the ruin. Everyone became afraid when we saw that the Japanese were getting worse from day to day.

Rumors began to spread that we would be taken to forced labor and we lived in fear. The houses were cold, without heating ovens. We had to put ovens in ourselves and it would cost a lot. The circumstances were such that for the first winter we were without heat. There were no heavy frosts during the winter there, but the kind of cold that was worse than frost.

My child caught the measles in the terrible cold. I stood over him constantly, not allowing him to take his hand out from under the quilt.

[Column 1076]

Then my child got sick with dysentery.

We suffered hardships without end until we all pulled ourselves out of it. Then the war began to come closer.

Shanghai was bombed by the Americans, airplanes flew over our heads and we were in great danger again. And in addition to the hardships of illness and need was added the deadly fear of the bombardments.

In one case a bomb entered a house with refugees. Several people perished from bombs that day.

Thus we had new fears every day. We did not have any contact with our home, but rumors went around about the terrible things that were taking place in Poland.

The news came from Russian sources. No one wanted to believe it. It was considered Russian propaganda.

In 1945 when the war in Europe ended and Japan continued the war, we thought that we were all lost because the Japanese had a principle of not surrendering, but to commit *harikari* and to fight to the last soldier. We were all very despondent and then the atom bomb was dropped on Hiroshima.

The news arrived during our great despair that Japan had been defeated.

The joy among the refugees was very great. We saw that we had been saved, but the joy did not last long.

Newspapers began to arrive from America as soon the war had ended: the *Forvets* [Forward] and the *Tog* [Day] and there we saw that the unbelievable was true and the destruction was very great. We almost lost our minds.

[Column 1077]

Had no one survived?

We began to run to HIAS [Hebrew Immigrant Aid Society], where lists of survivors had arrived.

At this sad time, other Czyzewo *landsleit* [people from the same town] in America learned the Czyzewo rabbi's daughter and son-in-law and child were among the survivors in Shanghai. They immediately got in touch with us and began sending packages of food and clothing and money.

The Czyzewo *landsleit* in America showed so much interest in us, even more than relatives.

This was an expression of the great respect that they had for my great father who occupied the rabbinical seat in Czyzewo for 36 years.

Shanghai-America

The Czyzewo *landleit* in America immediately began to think about ways to bring us to America, but as they did not have their own synagogue, they asked the neighboring *landsleit*, those from Jedrzejow, to invite my husband as their rabbi.

The Jedrzejow [Jews] were required to pay a fee for two years to assure that the rabbi would be able to provide for his family.

The Czyzewo *landsleit* collected 5,000 dollars in a week and deposited this money and simultaneously mailed the necessary papers with an invitation [for my husband to serve] as a rabbi.

We received visas on this basis.

We came to America in the month of September.

We did not have to use the money that we had put away.

There was an extra ordinary warmth that the *landsleit* showed us and I will never forget it.

[Column 1078]

My husband was the rabbi in the synagogue for eight years.

While in America the sad news about Czyzewo began to arrive.

In 1947 Reb Zisha Slucki, who miraculously survived, came from Czyzewo and was a witness of the complete destruction of Czyzewo. I learned the tragic truth from him about the death of my great father, the Czyzewo Rabbi, the rabbi and *gaon* [genius], Reb Shmuel Dovid Zabludower, who was known in the rabbinical world as a great *gaon* and *tzadek* [righteous man], may his merit protect us - and my dear mother, Yocheved, and my sister, Gitl, who perished together with the Jewish community of Czyzewo on the 28th of Av 5701 [21st of August 1941] and were buried in a mass grave in the village of Szulborze near Czyzewo.

After the sad greeting I did not have any hope that a miracle could still happen and that I would find someone, including my brother, Chaim, who had married six months after the war in Maladziecna [Belarus] and my oldest sister, Tzvia, and her husband and two children, who lived in Warsaw. I do not know what happened to them. It is possible one of them survived. I have searched for years with no success.

Such a tragedy spread over our generation.

Although we go on with life, we cannot truly enjoy any happiness because our hearts constantly cry for our precious and beloved [ones] whom we will never forget.

This is written by Freidel, the daughter of the Czyzewo Rabbi, who was saved with her husband and their only son, Hershel, may he be healthy, who walks in the path of his magnificent grandfather. We are now in New York.

Translator's notes:

1. These are the visas that were issued by Chiune Sugihara, the vice consul for Japan in Lithuania. Sugihara was responsible for saving the lives of 5,558 Jews.
2. The war between Japan and America began on the 8th of December 1941.

[Column 1079]

Years of Banishment

by Sheva Lubelczyk, Tel Aviv

Translated by Gloria Berkenstat Freund

On that day at the end of summer 1939 in our *dacha* [seasonal house in the countryside] in the *shtetl* [town] of Brak on the Bug [River] there was trouble as dark clouds began to appear in the Polish sky, which carried sad portends. So, on that Friday morning when my husband suddenly arrived in a wagon, I became deeply upset. He simply said:

– There is unease in the *shtetl*.

We loaded our things and returned home, which was simmering with various prophecies and predictions, pessimistic and optimistic.

This unease lasted an entire week. A mobilization began that was declared in great haste. Heartbreaking cries were heard from the mothers mixed with the screams of the young wives who accompanied their sons and husbands.

My husband was busy for an entire week preparing reserves of merchandise, following to the instructions of the regime organs. He already had filled the kerosene reserves and the warehouses with various articles; only sugar was lacking. His last order could not be fulfilled by the *Bank Cukrownictwa* [Bank of the Sugar Industry] because of a lack of wagons, which had been taken over entirely by the military. He had to go to Warsaw to place an order at the nearest sugar factory, which turned out to be a sugar factory near Amniszow. From there my husband brought the sugar by automobile, which later served as the only reserves for those who had not already been annihilated.

Peasants came to the market Friday morning and said that strange bombs had fallen that had made giant pits in the fields. They did not want to believe that a war really had broken out. But the sad fact that the war had happened already was clear to us.

There were those in the *shtetl* who began to speak of evacuating, going further from the *shtetl*, further from the battlefield, somewhere to a village.

We wanted to be far away from Czyzewo, but there were no means of transportation.

Help came unexpectedly from Leibel Krzanski, who had horses and wagons and took us the village of Biali, 10 kilometers from Czyzewo.

[Column 1080]

We spent several turbulent days and nights there. We heard the bombardment, saw the fire at the train station – Czyzewo was burning, particularly our kerosene reserves, and with fear we thought of all of those closest to us who had remained.

Several hours later the peasants came with the news that the Germans were entering the village. Our [hosts] began to be scared stiff. They were afraid of being punished for hiding Jews.

We had to pack our things and go back to the *shtetl*.

All of the roads in the direction of Brisk were filled with Germans in vehicles and on motorcycles.

We walked with hearts beating in fear that they would stop us. However, they did not bother us, only made do with mockery and insulting shouts.

Exhausted, we arrived in Czyzewo and did not have anywhere to go. We wandered from one spot to another. We met a Christian acquaintance, Bralinski, by chance, who later was a real big shot with the Germans. He gave us a house, abandoned and dirty, where the mice ran around freely and were not afraid of people.

For a month we made do with only fear, until the Soviets entered.

The battles in Poland stopped. Warsaw already was defeated and a form of Soviet life began on the territory of western Ukraine and western White Russia [Belarus]. Little by little, the evacuated Jews began to return to Czyzewo, which was included in the composition of the western "White" Russia. Czyzewo began to revive little by little.

Soviet Power in Czyzewo

Autumn ended very early that year and an early and severe winter appeared and was added to the hardships. There had not been such winter frosts as there were in 1939-40 since 1928.

Life in Czyzewo was very difficult during the first weeks of the Soviet regime. The new administrators and managers of the *shtetl* could not cope with the improvisation and they began to seek tradesmen. Fate then fell on my husband who received assignments from the new communist bosses to provide the necessary goods to the shops. One of the most important articles was kerosene and my husband received instructions to provide kerosene for the population and particularly for the authorities.

[Column 1081]

Berl met Reb Yechiel-Asher Prawda, whose sister was a fervid communist in Bialystok, and in her name he told him [Berl] the secret that he should protect himself because there was a decree to arrest him. Reb Yechiel-Asher told him not to return to Czyzewo, but to wait in Bialystok until the fury ended.

Berl could not grasp why they would arrest him. He did not feel guilty. In addition, he saw that the Soviet regime in Czyzewo bestowed trust on him, trusted the providing [of kerosene] to him. He saw before him the Jewish shopkeepers who were waiting for his help and he decided to return to Czyzewo.

He barely succeeded in crossing the threshold of our house. A Jewish militiaman entered at the same time and politely asked him to go with him to the *Narkom* (people's commissariat).

I began to beg him to eat something. But the militiaman hurried and said they would come right back. I just managed to tell him to take a fur with him.

Several difficult hours passed in bitter suspense. Berl did not return and it soon was clear to me that he had been arrested.

This was on the 17th of October 1939. We did not see him until November 1941.

Lonely, broken, I went out to the street for help. I found locked doors everywhere. There was no one to beg, to ask.

Walking, I met Klar, the teacher from the People's School, for whom my husband always had showed a warm respect. No one knew that behind his hypocritical grace was hidden a fervid communist. He answered my tearful plea that he give me advice about Berl with a sarcastic smile.

– You will never see him again.

Later, I learned that this Klar was one of the denouncers and coworkers of the *NKVD* [*Narodnyy Komissariat Vnutrennikh Del* – People's Commissariat for Internal Affairs], who had pointed out my husband as a terrible element, a [Jewish] nationalist and Zionist leader.

Days dragged by, full of suffering and tears. Agitated, I did not stop looking for where my husband had been taken. Finally, in the middle of 1940, I succeeded in sending the first package to the Bialystok jail where the other Czyzewo Jews were located, but one person did not know of the whereabouts of another.

[Column 1082]

The Jews who had not been exiled organized little by little, traded, worked in nationalized enterprises. Several state haberdashery and knitwear stores, a central cooperative and so on were opened.

It continued this way until April 1940 when the families of the arrestees and "uncertain elements" who had been shown as unsatisfied with the Soviet regime began to be exiled.

My two small children and I were loaded into a freight car with 60 more people. We were first given food after a few days, bread and herring. Thirst tortured us more than hunger. From time to time we succeeded in receiving a little bit of *kipyatok* (boilied water) and we saved it for the small children.

Frightful scenes played out on the road. The weeping reached us from the other train wagons of the large transport that carried the innocent name "resettlement," people being taken to live in another place.

After eight days we arrived on the distance steppe. They said this was Kazakhstan. We descended from the train wagons and stood in the emptiness, afraid, despondent. There was no one to ask about our future fate. It seemed like there was no more distant end of the world than this.

After standing thus for several hours in the cold steppe, trucks finally arrived and we were told to load ourselves onto them. The Russians, our guards, were somberly quiet for the entire time, not wanting to say where they were taking us.

In the Kazakhstan Steppe

We again traveled into the unknown, until in the dark we finally arrived at the *kolkhoz* [collective farm], where a wooden barracks stood. There was not enough space for everyone and many remained outside in the cold for the entire night.

It was not much warmer in the barracks. Despite our tiredness we could not fall asleep. We only waited for the day to begin and we could see where we were being taken.

In the pale dawn we saw poor, small houses made of clay and straw. The first people appeared, shaggy, dressed in torn fur hats, *walenkes* [felt boots] and *papakhes* [Astrakhan hats, wool hats]. These were the Poles and Ukrainians, exiled from the border areas. They looked at us with sympathy and tried to console us, bringing us into their only room where there was a lack of even the most primitive facilities. They provided an iron bed and the strange clay house became more familiar.

[Column 1083]

I understood that the difficult time for me and my children would continue and I did not think too much about the terrors, but thinking of Berl did not stop. I thought how fortunate I would be if we were together now in this clay house in the steppe, which appeared endless, without a border, sandy and endlessly lonely.

Thin hazes spread in the mornings and nights. The cold subsided and damp winds began to blow. I began to go out to work in the garden. However, a snowstorm fell in May. Wild winds began to blow with clouds of snow. The small house in which we lived was deep, a few steps down in the ground, and the snow which had fallen the entire night completely covered the small house in the morning and we could not leave the house.

We were confined for four days as if in a cave. The owner did not appear too overwhelmed. In his large fur hat on his head he walked around the burning iron oven, watched the fire like an ancient figure in an ancient cave, shaped bricks made of cow dung and made water for drinking out of the snow. The days merged with the nights and were endless. On the fifth day the neighbors cleaned off the snow and we could go out into the sunshine.

I again left for work in the orchard. The shovels were large and heavy. My palms became full of blisters that burst, which gnawed with sharp pain when I worked.

With our arrival the authorities decided to build their own bakery. I was assigned to the construction work that consisted of kneading lime mixed with straw and cow dung with my feet and with my hands simultaneously pasting the walls, which grew.

Later they took me to thresh the wheat and load it into the high-wheeled wagons.

At night, when bonfires were lit in front of the thresholds to drive away the mosquitos, I returned to the hut, tired, made something to eat for the children and in the growing darkness began thinking about Berl, about whom there had been no news. Fruitessly, I looked for a hint, a clue, for information in every letter and package that came from Berl's parents and from his sister, Fayga-Faya.

[Column 1084]

I knew how difficult it was for them to send a package. The post office in that area did not accept [packages]. They had to travel to Baranowice and this was very expensive.

The days and the weeks crawled wearily and arduously on the steppe. Every letter from home drew me out a little from the oppressiveness. My sister Gitl and her husband, Yehuda, wrote that they were getting ready to build, had already bought wood and other building materials because the war would end soon and everyone would return. The thought – Would it also end for me? – did not stop torturing me.

The last letter I received from my father was dated the 10th of June 1941. He wrote that storks were flying in who were throwing eggs. I saw in this a hint that something terrible was beginning there and I developed severe anxiety.

We received no further letters.

I did not stop writing. In addition to letters home, I also wrote to Moscow to [Vyacheslav] Molotov, to [Mikhail] Kalinin, to various ministries, describing for them the suffering of a lonely woman whose husband had been taken away and only asking for his address.

I did not receive any answers, but I did not tire and continued to write. Once I was even called to the *NKVD* and an officer asked me what kind of letters I was writing. I explained to him and in a categorical tone he said to me:

– One does not write!

Sparks began to fly in front of my eyes. I stood confused for a while. But I immediately became painfully infuriated. I declared with all of my resolve:

– No power will stop me from writing. I will write until I prove that my husband is innocent.

The officer looked at me with sullen eyes and roared:

– You will be badly removed.

His words now did not frighten me and I seethed:

– Shoot… I will still write. For as long as I do not know where my husband is and why he is under arrest.

[Column 1085]

My children were waiting outside and they cried hearing my shouting. But I drowned this out with my own shouting. I saw how the face of the officer was changing. Had he experienced a stab from his own conscience or was everything previous pretense? He began speaking in a different tone.

– Listen, citizen. Your husband is in Bialystok; he was sentenced to many years. This is all I can tell you.

Suddenly desolation began to press on me and I wanted to shout, to lament, but the pain was too great. All sources of tears were shut by the oppression.

In 1941, after the pact between [Wladyslaw] Sikorski and Stalin, the attitude of the *NKVD* to us became much, much milder. We received permission to go more than three kilometers from the *poselok* (settlement) and we made contact with other settlements. People began coming to us who recruited workers.

We were not paid with money for our work the entire time in the *kolkhoz* [collective farm]. The great wage was the food. Now we were considered free people and they proposed that we work at building the new train line and they promised therefore that, in addition to the *stolovaya* [canteen], bread and cloth, we would receive money. Therefore, I decided to go there. Others went with me, most of them Christians, exiles like me.

At the new place we began to build a new train line a distance of 700 kilometers [about 435 miles] through the Russian Kazakhstan steppe to connect the Karaganda coal basin with the metallurgical basin of Magnitogorsk.

We had to travel 13 kilometers with oxen to the Taiantsha train station. It was the end of October. The steppe was empty and a cold, north wind blew. We were dropped off at the Taiantsha station and they told us to wait, that the high official would be there soon and show us where to enter and what we had to do.

We were delayed for two weeks at the station and waited for the high official… But no one was interested in us. The people murmured gloomily: "They apparently have a lot of time. Alas. It is Miserable with such [people]," and continued to wait with resignation.

When the hunger and the cold grew very annoying, the talk of the people began to become passionate, on edge. Someone proposed me as the representative to the high official, whom no one knew and that I should demand work from him. Everyone supported this.

[Column 1086]

I was gotten rid of very quickly when I went to see the high official. "Wait, we will soon call you." But anger and bitterness was sown in me. This and the long days and nights of being quiet and oppressed by my suffering added to my boldness. I needed a humane attitude from him toward those who were suffering.

This helped. In the morning, a freight-wagon was supplied in which we spent three weeks until we were let out at the Batali train station.

Here we built a new train line and all of those newly brought here were employed at unskilled labor, dug, carried beams, unloaded stones from fully loaded wagons that arrived mostly in the middle of the night and we were immediately awakened because fines had to be paid for every hour that the wagons were held.

The days were bleak. A cold rain poured and we were soaked to the bone.

The frosts pushing me with each day pressed even deeper in the steppe. Poverty was not a novelty to us and we bore it easily – in addition, they gave us 800 grams [about 28 ounces] of bread per person.

In the evening, the working groups marched home with their spades on their backs and we cried with longing and I wrested myself from the marching group of women, running in front. Perhaps there was a letter, some news from Berl. I thought Rukhl was running next to me with joyful news.

Rukhela was everyone's darling there. She would write letters for wives to their husbands and relatives in their distant homes and they believed that her letters were lucky because they received an answer immediately. Rukhela was born with a silver spoon in her mouth, they would say with honest thankfulness.

The child felt my quiet pain at that time and not mentioning it she also poured [the pain] into the letters that she wrote for strangers to their closest people.

The end-of-November cold was even sharper; it wore away the people driven together to the most distant border. The ache of separation that burned the heart added to the pain

The weeks extended in over-exertion and toil like a nagging nightmare. I wanted to escape from it with the dear memories of my old home. The nightmare had pressed, drowning the soul like a swelling and here – *Robota!* Work!" There was not even a day of rest. All of the holidays were thrown in the garbage. A world without holidays! Sometimes an exceptional day came and we were not taken to the steppe. It [the exceptional day] spread in the hut exactly like a long night and the sadness, the longing, grabbed one by throat.

[Column 1087]

We rarely had a day of rest. Removed from the world, we felt as if we were totally condemned. One longed, another grieved and everyone lamented and worried about the fate of their closest ones.

Suddenly we were told that the work had ended and we needed to travel further.

We did not work on that day and prepared to leave. But the news arrived here that the locomotive had left the tracks and they were waiting for another one. The next day someone came running and said a passenger train was going to pass through. This would happen once every three weeks. Everyone ran to see it. An internal gnawing drove one to see if a miracle had sent a close [relative]. My Rukhl grabbed her fur and began running in the direction of the station. Wanting to hold her, to have her remain in the house with small Shmulik, I myself wanted to take a look. Perhaps I would just see the former arrestees who had met Berl somewhere in a jail.

By chance, a [female] Christian neighbor, who walked by, looked at me with good eyes, shook her head and said:

– Let her. Let Rukhela run. She was born with a silver spoon in her mouth…

I went back into the house. I thought I heard someone shouting my name. I did not pay any attention. My mind was occupied with only one thought: when would this nightmare end?

Suddenly, someone was knocking on my door and two Christian neighbors called out together:

– Why are you sitting? Your husband has come…

I heard a frightening shriek and did not know that this was my own screaming. I ran out as if dazed. I saw Rukhl walking in a cluster of illegal people with an old man in a torn jacket with a sack on his back. This was Berl. I fell on him, wanted to speak, to cry: Berl, Berl, but my brain could not comprehend. A strange noise, as if from the far sides, reached my ear, started high, higher and finally sank under the waves. I lost consciousness.

When I woke up they told me that I had lain in a faint for several hours. Berl sat near me. His elongated, bony face was unshaven. He said:

[Column 1088]

– Sheva, my Sheva! I am with you. Do you not see?

I still could not comprehend the great good fortune and murmured:

– It cannot be… Is it you?

Little by little I sensed in myself our great joy.

We were together again.

In the morning we both left for work. The grey morning hours woke us up and the late evening hours brought us back home.

Our house consisted of a fifth of a regular 15-ton freight wagon, which according to regulations could only hold eight horses. We were five families who made up of 15 people.

The End of November

There already was heavy frost in that area of southern Siberia. The residences and wagons became unbearable. My husband began to demand that the "foreman" designate permanent quarters as well as permanent work.

The new residence consisted of a corner in a lime hut where in addition to us lived another Polish family of four people, a Russian woman and her children and Russian girls, altogether 14 souls in one room.

After enrolling Shmulik in school, life went on in need and in want, in longing for our distant home. We established letter connections with *Eretz Yisrael* and with America. The warm letters from those closest to us encouraged us a little. We received a food package from Israel, which consisted of canned goods (which we hid for Passover), several pieces of soap and several packages of tea. After giving a package of tea and a piece of soap to the foreman, our conditions greatly changed for the better.

Suddenly, my husband began to be counted among the *Stakhanovces*[11] and occasionally he also received a free day, which was used to carry out the necessary trade transactions in the neighboring *kolkhoz* [collective farm], such as, for example, exchanging several needles for potatoes, a piece of soap for a pail of milk and for tea we could receive whatever the heart longed for.

They did not want to take my husband in General Anders' Army. A worsening relationship between the regime and the Polish refugees developed after Anders and his army left Russia.

[Column 1089]

One morning they ordered that we get Soviet passports. At first they spoke to us nicely, later angrily. Several Polish citizens were arrested and the bread [ration] cards were taken from the others; we were not told to go to work and everyone was taken out of their residences to the empty, wild steppe. This was in March when the weather in this area was still -20 to -25 [Celcius, -4 to -13 Farenheit]. We wandered around the steppe with our children for several days and nights. Some moved in with local residents in their huts in exchange for an article of clothing or some other things. And finally we were persuaded of their justice and took a passport.

Mama Russia, your goodness crosses borders. In other nations, one must live for three to five years before receiving the right to become a citizen, learn symbols, where citizenship is only given at birth. And you gave us the privilege of having the merit to become a Soviet citizen.

[Column 1090]

Life flowed slowly for us in the large Kazakhstan steppe. However, in the larger world, the political situation changed as if in a kaleidoscope. And on one morning my husband was called as a Polish citizen and asked to enter the army that was being organized by the Polish [female] writer and fervid communist, Wanda Wasilewska.

Again I remained alone with the children, but as the wife of a military man I had certain privileges.

With the withdrawal of the Russian Army, we were also permitted to resettle closer to the west.

In 1944 we were in the Kiev area where we worked at heavy labor waiting for the war to end. And at the beginning of 1946 I saw my husband again in liberated Poland.

Translator's note:

1. Alexsei Stakhanov was famous for having exceeded his daily quota as a coal miner. He was used as an example in efforts to increase worker productivity. A *Stakhanovce* was someone who exceeded the work quota assigned to him or her.

[Column 1089]

Blind Fate
From Czyzewo to the Ural Mountains
A Czyzewor Partisan's Story

Dov Saba as a witness, Tel Aviv

Translated by Gloria Berkenstat Freund

Not only I but also those who sent me here to the distant north, approximately 120 kilometers from the Arctic Ocean, did not know for what offense I received this [punishment]. Although I was pelted with enough crimes: chairman of the Zionist organization of the *Tarbut* [secular Zionist] People's Library, of *Tsentos* [organization for aiding children and orphans], others were added: kerosene and coal merchant and so on. However, no case was carried on against me. I simply was torn away from my home and family and exiled there where the majority of crude oil wells and coal pits were and the frost lasted up to 10 months a year.

I would certainly have grown old there in hardship and pain as the Jewish overseer of the camp baths, a former captain in the Red Army, Comrade Lipszic, prophesized – "Your homes! Little brothers" – he spoke sarcastically – "you will never see, just as you will never see your own ears." In short, a part of his prophecy was fulfilled. My old home had disappeared and is no longer there, but I have left paradise.

[Column 1090]

Again, blind fate played first fiddle, because I myself was busy with trying hard to join the category that received 450 grams of bread and could not mix in any political matters, such as, for example, the group was called together one morning and it was announced with a sweet smile on the lips: "Children, you are free, not, God forbid, pardoned. But simply everything that had happened was nothing; every offense is null and void like the dust of the earth."

Fate, blind fate.

This was the same fate that led to the night of the 13th of April 1940 when those who extol themselves with the ideal of fairness and justice loaded up to 40 people in a wagon in which more than eight cows were not allowed to be taken.

[Column 1091]

After several weeks of going through the spaciousness of Greater Russia, we were unloaded somewhere in a faraway Siberian steppe and told that we were free citizens, with the right to move within a circle of three kilometers. In addition we were given the right to work without pay and to be hungry.

The workdays were exactly documented, but there was no one to make payments. As long as one had something to sell and exchange for bread, the soul still remained in the exhausted, worn out body. When there was nothing left to sell, as for example, with Mendel Glina and his wife, Nekhka, they could not endure and died. In contrast, others wrestled with their last strength to keep their souls [not die]. My wife and children were among them.

At the same time, when we had been so generously freed, we went to them with a magnanimous proposal to have us be recruited for regular work, suitable for women and the young to build a new train line in an area of 800 kilometers that would connect the coal basin in the Karaganda with the iron basin in Magnitogorsk. In addition, a great privilege was given here, that each worker had the right to his money to buy the entire daily 800 grams of bread and 400 for each non–working child. There was a rumor that from time to time we would also be able to buy a meter [a little more than a yard] of linen for a dress.

[Column 1092]

It is understandable that they took upon themselves the expense for taking the people from one steppe to another. Wagons harnessed to oxen were provided for their convenience, on which they were taken on the 40 kilometer road to the Sokhotin [possibly the Shymkent] train station.

Whereas we needed to wait for wagons and this was to last for about 10 days, the people, the women and children meanwhile were permitted to enter the open train station, right near the fence. It was autumn. There was not yet any frost, so why should they not be permitted to move in the station, as is suitable for free citizens?

In those regions, there always was movement, particularly in those days, when train formations followed train formations and in great haste they would be held in various stations for hours and days. These were transports of people, freed from the other regions, from which people rarely returned.

In the great game of fate of those days, a kind of coincidence could happen; on a beautiful morning, a young Pole who had more luck than me got off one of the train formations and by chance learned that his old mother was exiled to this area where we now were. By chance, he went over to my wife and asked her if she knew, had seen or had heard of a woman with the name Lutustarska.

– Yes – my wife answered – she had remained in village no. 3. Go to the square, there you will see the wagons or a vehicle from this village where your Mother Lutustraska is located.

[Column 1093]

Said and done. The young Pole immediately ran there. In the morning he and his old mother sat in the train formation and departed. The Pole's trip ended in the distant south, Tashkent area, about four and a half thousand kilometers [2,796 miles] from the Sokhotin train station. It was warm there, did not rain, did not snow. There one could sit in the area of the train station not only near the fence and sit and rest as much as one's heart desires.

I already was an old resident for eight days of this train station, 12 kilometers from the city of Bukhara, which carried the name Kogon. Our train formation stood, moved to a sidetrack as if it had been forgotten.

Our work consisted of waiting to be taken to lunch. We used the time before and after lunch to move around a little among people in the city, seeing how it looked, if there was an opportunity to acquire work.

From time to time we would go to the train station to look at the newly arriving faces and there were plentiful faces, in the thousands. Every free spot among the train tracks was occupied. Old and young, women and children, men. It should be understood that rare ones sat on the packs. One could recognize their origins according to the size of the packs. The tumult was oppressive. The noise from the people, the crashing of the wagons, the turbulence from the wagons merged in a deafening symphony of uneasy longing. Who knew where my wife and children were now wandering?

[Column 1094]

Among the innumerable mob, my gaze fell on an old woman who sat peacefully on her packs and dreamed. I recognized that she was Polish and I went over to her. I asked her in Polish, "Where are you from?"

She measured me with her quiet eyes and answered: "From a village very far from here, from near Zambrów."

I asked further:

– From where have you come now? Do you know Czyzewo? Perhaps you met someone.

– Yes, I know [Czyzewo], she answered.

– And Czyzewo Jews – I asked – do you know or did you hear anything about someone.

– No – she said – there were no Jews from Czyzewo with us.

– Perhaps in neighboring villages – do not give up.

The woman became impatient and replied:

– I know only one woman from neighboring villages. She is named Sheva G. She is here with a daughter, Rochel and a son, Shmuelik… I was brought here by my son who was liberated from a camp and, passing me, took me along… Nothing torments me any longer…

Today who knows if Elijah the prophet, the Tishbite, from the Gilead [region] calls one – it is also blind chance.

[Columns 1095-1098]

Majdanek

by Gershuni

Translated from Hebrew by Jerrold Landau

Shearim, 7 Elul, 5700, August 16, 1945

For us.

The atrocities, murders, death wagons, gas chambers. All these words, that filled the pages of the newspapers for five years to give expression to the terrible cruelty of that evil man – have stopped and have moved aside.

Now there is a new, exhaustive idiom.

We do not need to look for a translation in the lexicon of terrors. To make efforts to clothe the unusual forms of deaths of millions of us in the garb of appropriate expression – is not necessary.

There is one word – and this is everything.

Majdanek.

It is etched in our memories for generation after generation. We know how to mention it among us with anger and wrath. The eyes of our daughters will well with tears when it comes to their lips, and as our surviving brethren return from the fire of the burning of millions, to that town next to the destroyed, ruined Lublin.

Stand silent.

The feet become stone. The clothes are torn to the heart. That gate that is never locked will open wide and be beaten from its great oppression.

For you, every shoe, the thousands, six meters high – is the skull of a corpse.

Every particle of ash in the heaps – is like a grave – that is not a grave, of millions of brethren.

All those rooms that stand as a memorial – to the pillar of shame so high for all the nations.

For there was a time, in their lives, for these five consecutive years.

Majdanek.

For them.

The daughters of the covenant decided that the "factory of unusual death" will remain built up, as a "museum," "a house of the handicapped."

Every clod of earth around us will be protected. Every scorched bone that has not been burnt by the fire of the furnace will be embalmed in a container. Officials will be placed in the room of thousands of shoes, so that they can be guarded in their emptiness so that they will not become smudged with dust.

The tins of gas, thousands of photographed passports, children's games, disinfection rooms, change rooms, etc., etc. – with all the originals.

And around us, this is acceptable

How many tens of benches for waiting will there be. Surviving trees will be transplanted, and flower groves will be planted so that the visitors can wait in a pleasant fashion.

In short:

The visitor, that hard–headed American doctor, will stand for a few moments and survey all these things. He will take a shoe in his hands and feel it from all its sides. He will take interest in the type of shoe, and as he leaves he will murmur:

[Columns 1097-1098]

"An interesting museum."

The cold–headed English gentleman will enter. He will go from room to room. He will tarry for a moment next to the balls among the children's toys. Are they appropriate for basketball? Then he will go on his way.

That Russian "Tobriszcz" will make the rounds through the rooms as a person doing his own thing, with enjoyment and satisfaction, as if to say:

"All this is from us – it is thanks to us that this museum exists. We discovered this place!"

And on the benches for waiting, next to the trees, near the flower groves, that blood sated, wicked Nazi, may his name be blotted out, will sit. He will breathe in the pleasant air, and grumble with his mouth:

"Accursed Jew."[1]

There, in some city on the fact of the earth, a pot–bellied professor will sit, hunched over the manuscripts of the new lexicon he is preparing, as he writes the following lines.

"A small town next to Lublin in the State of Poland. During the great war with Hitler, a museum was set up there by the governments of Russia, England, and America atop the place where people were killed."

And in in the margins of the page, the following word will be written in large letters.

"Majdanek."

Translator's note:

1. I believe this is meant to be an ironic transliteration of "tourist" in a Russian accent.

[Column 1099]

After the Deluge

A Look at My Destroyed *Shtetl*
by Chana Gromadzyn–Gotlib / Haifa
Translated by Gloria Berkenstat Freund

Czyzewo!

After so many years of separation I return to you, *Shtetl* [town] of my birth. You are mine!

As the train gets even closer, my senses become more awake and open. Here already is the iron bridge. From here one sees all of Czyzewo as if on the palm of one's hand. The poplars have grown taller, murmuring with a choked cry and bending their thickly leafed branches to me sadly as before, years ago, when the singing of our Yiddish songs echoed here and a wind carried away our quiet whispers.

The leaves whisper quietly, so familiar and close. I think they want to pass on to me the cries of those driven away, who here went on their final road.

The train stops.

I walk the 15–minute road into the *Shtetl* quickly. The houses begin, Jewish houses without Jews. Strangers stand at the gate, look at me as if at something strange. Their secret whispers reach my ears:

"Look, one of the Gromadzyns has come."

I pretend I did not hear, walk with my head down like a homeless dog. I recognize every stone here. The beautiful houses that stood across from the *gmina* [community or municipal office] are no longer here. In their place stand small, village–type houses.

[Column 1100]

Yankel Gromadzyn in New York with his class of children at the Yavne [religious Zionist] school

I run quickly past the market. Strange faces move around me, they tell me something about that day when death trod here. I do not listen to their talk. The screams of the Czyzewo Jewish community that was pushed with rifles and bayonets to the slaughter in Szulborze echo in my ears.

The same houses still stand on the right of the market, orphaned like nests from which the little birds have flown away. Only the tears left by their owners at their departure still remain.

There is a green square with trees in the middle of the market. These were planted by the Soviets who entered in 1939. I looked on all sides and I thought that there still hangs in the air the last looks of the Czyzewo Jews when they, the unfortunate ones, said goodbye to their homes for the last time and left for Szulborze, for Zambrów.

[Column 1101]

I see them young and old, women and children, with bullet holes in their bodies, with hands stretched out to torn–away parents.

Jewish tears fell here on the bridge, their last words that echo now in my heart.

Where are you, my closest and dearest friends and comrades? Is it possible that on one day you were all so brutally murdered?

Now I go alone through the Czyzewo streets. Here are the Zarembskis, the Nurskis. I think that every stone is dripping with blood. People live in all of the houses now as if nothing had happened. Only I still hear the screams that come from each building.

My parents, Chaim–Ahron and Shayna–Chaya, brothers and sisters

[Column 1102]

I stand at familiar, well–known doors. I want to knock… The doorknobs are red–hot in my fingers…

What am I doing here? I know you are not here anymore, although the house has remained the same. Somewhere in the corners an innocent, childish smile wanders around which once startled a mother's heart.

Here is the house of prayer in the alley where I was born, raised and grew up. I remember melodies that were sung here, the *Shabbosim* [Sabbaths] that were celebrated here. The holidays and *Tisha–B'Av* [ninth of Av, commemorating the destruction of the 1st and 2nd Temples in Jerusalem]; how we sang the Shabbos songs and recited *The Book of Lamentations* and laments. Now only empty winds remain, ashamed, sad. Who here understands their anguished silence?

The house of prayer, which was transformed into a wheat granary, is dishonored. A peasant stands in the distance and observes me with astonishment; from where have I come here?

I go through the entire alley and my memories of all the past years lay like dust. Here was the *Beis–Yakov* [school] for religious girls, several houses along - six rooms, and more, and more, such good, dear houses from which remain only ruins.

I run to the cemetery; the eternal resting place is defiled, too. The headstones lie throw around, broken. Peasants dig in the sand…

Woe to the bones that have no rest. Woe to my eyes that see all of this!

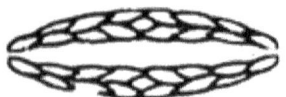

On the Ruins of Czyzewo

by Dov Saba of Shayka, Tel Aviv

Translated by Gloria Berkenstat Freund

This was in August 1944.

The division in which I served stopped on the eastern shore of the Vistula [River] and waited for the order to march further ahead.

There still were several Polish soldiers who were from the Czyzewo area in the division. Just like me, they had been far from their homes for three to five years, but with the difference that they still had their families there. And I?...

Yet we spoke together about "jumping" [leaving without permission] to see what was happening.

It was easy to say "jumping." There was no regular communication in Poland at that time. No trains. No buses. The only connections between city and city were the military vehicles. If they agreed to take someone with them, this was authorized by their captain, who agreed to ignore it when they and the vehicle were missing for two days.

There still remained two "small" matters: a bit of a passport and benzene for the vehicle that could not be obtained. Permission to leave was absolutely necessary because there were Russian control posts every few kilometers.

With a lack of choice they had to connect with me and entrust their secret [intending to "jump"], knowing that I then had the possibility to take care of this matter [getting the necessary benzene].

I already knew then about the great destruction. Yet I could not overcome my desire to see with my own eyes how the *shtetl* looked.

I learned that my cousin, Rivkale, had survived in neighboring Sterdyń. I demanded that we make a detour and travel through Sokolow, Sterdyń and Czyzewo.

This was a very risky step. Making use of military gasoline for private purposes along with issuing an official travel permit and signing it without the knowledge of the *polk* [regiment] commander could lead to a war tribunal.

But in view of the great destruction, could I play such a serious role, particularly when the war was then in full fervor and no one could know what would happen tomorrow, if we would survive the war?

Yet I reflected. My wife, my children, who I had left in distant Siberia, appeared before my eyes. Could I take a risk while their agonizing hearts constantly pleaded that I avoid every danger?

But the idea that perhaps this was the last opportunity to see Czyzewo outweighed [this doubt]. I knew how dear a greeting from our home city Czyzewo would be for me wife.

Despite the fact that we escaped at the maximum speed from the military "sweetness," the trip lasted for 24 hours as we had calculated.

[Column 1105]

We were in Sterdyń.

My memories of the past years in this *shtetl* attacked me in waves. Now it seems very long ago. We would come here from far and wide for *Khol Khamoed* [intervening days of a holiday] days. The horse-drawn coach arrived at the market at my grandfather's house and it became so lively in the entire *shtetl*. Women came out of the shops and spoke loudly among themselves: Look, Ita Minka's grandchildren have come. Eh?

Those who were only close to my mother said:

– Yehudis and her children have come…

Close neighbors came to wish my *Bobeshi* [grandmother]:

– May you enjoy your guests!

– May you live agreeably! – my grandmother answered, not interrupting her toil preparing for welcoming her guests.

Our grandfather's house was welcoming; it always swarmed with people. *Shabbos* night, after *havdalah* [ceremony marking the end of *Shabbos*], Jewish scholars and simple toilers who lived through physical labor came together for a glass of tea and they grabbed a last friendly conversation before the arrival of a week of toil.

From time to time, Jewish merchants and artisans in the dozen would meet together here and return the interest-free loans that were almost the only capital for their diverse livelihoods.

Family gatherings would take place during the Days of Awe. Sons, daughters, grandchildren and great grandchildren came. They came in the tens from Czyzewo, Wysokie, Siedlce, Sarnak, Gorowo, Wladowa, Cienchanowiec, Warsaw and other cities. The pilgrimages to the grandfather were a sacred duty for everyone, accompanied by a great deal of pleasure.

[Column 1106]

No one remained, only the small Rivkala, Uncle Zilke's small daughter.

I met her in the same house where all of the survivors of the great destruction, several familiar faces, emaciated, dejected, having just crawled out of the holes, the fields where they had been hidden the entire time, lived.

The people rejoiced with me and tears ran from their eyes. They cried over the exterminated lives and over their own loneliness and hopelessness.

I learned several facts about the deportations of those closest to me. My mother, Yehudis, lived 14 more months here in Sterdyń after the first deportation in Czyzewo.

On the 28th of Av 5701 (August 1941) over 1,700 Jews were taken out of Czyzewo to Szulborze. My father, Yeshayahu, my beautiful sister, Fayga-Faya, and her husband were among them.

My mother and my youngest sister, Surala, crossed the Bug River then for Sterdyń.

Sterdyń had been under Hitlerist occupation the entire time since 1939. A Jewish *kehile* [organized Jewish community] existed there, which was living in difficult conditions of both a ghetto and not a ghetto, in constant fear of the same fate that had occurred in Czyzewo and the other Jewish *shtetlekh* [towns].

A large deportation took place in Sterdyń two days after Yom Kippur, on the 12th of Tishrei 5703 [23 September 1942]. The Jews were taken to Treblinka, which was located in the area of Sterdyń. A number of members of my family went with them including my dear over 80-year-old grandmother, the small Ita-Minka.

My mother still had a little bit of jewelry. She gave it to a Hitlerlist bandit and asked him to shoot her on the spot.

[Column 1107]

My dear and bold mother! She perished in the same house in which she had enjoyed so much precious joy and in the same house in which 11 years earlier her father, my great and good grandfather, Shmuel Moshe, had died. She had the honor of coming to her eternal rest near the grave of her father.

With a grieving heart, I took leave of the people who looked like their own shadows. My 14-year-old Kwinka traveled with me to Czyzewo.

In the meantime, my Polish friend in the vehicle had detected a place for whiskey in Sterdyń. She was very tipsy when we continued the trip.

The distance from Sterdyń to Czyzewo is 28 kilometers [a little over 17 miles]. Over the entire distance she told me about their experiences. Her glance constantly went in the direction of the highway. I noticed how her face had suddenly changed, had a tense expression.

– Here! – she shouted, pointing to a spot where a village house, with stalls and small rooms, surrounded with a wooden fence had stood.

– Here in this barn – she pointed with her eyes to a place that [as we rode by] became smaller and further – after the deportation, when they took your *Bobeshi* and shot your mother, our family and still others decided to escape. After wandering for a long time, we received, for a high price, a hiding place here in the attic over the barn.

The auto flew at a terrible speed and Rivkala, spoke in one breath, as if she was afraid that she would not have enough time to speak:

[Column 1108]

My father, my mother, my two sisters, Bela and Tushka, a brother, Yankele, and my little sister, Surala, lived there for a long time with the other Jews. The attic was well-hidden, disguised with hay and straw. At night the men would sneak out to obtain something to eat. The front already was nearby. The Russian Army already was at the Bug [River], near Brisk. They counted the weeks; soon they would be liberated… Suddenly, a band of Polish bandits surrounded the entire area, discovered the hiding place and immediately opened fire on them with automatic weapons and rifles, threw grenades into the hay and straw, until everyone perished.

A sharp pain again began to gnaw and oppress. In the month of July 1944 I was among those who crossed the Bug, marched through Lublin, were chased by the Germans up to the Vistula [River]. If this had happened two months earlier, my young sister would still be alive. She aleady was 17 years old when she perished. Would she have recognized me? When I saw her for the last time she was 12 years old.

I shook off the thoughts; Surala is not here, Rivkala's parents are not here, Uncle Zilka and Aunt Chana, her sisters, Bela and Tushka, brother Yankel, their hopes which were just being attained were ended by the Polish murderers.

The murderers were not entirely successful in their work. Rivkala was only wounded and they thought that she was dead. My dear friend, Avraham Sukhe, and his wife, Branka, managed to avoid the bullets and grenades. As well as my close friend, Pinchas Lerman. They were hidden somewhat more deeply in the straw and later healed Rivkala's wounds.

[Column 1109]

Our auto was stopped at Ceranów by a Russian military post, badgering us that we wanted to shoot a Russian officer whom we had picked up on the way.

The questioning began about what were we doing on the road, hundreds of kilometers from our military unit; what were civilian girls doing with us?

We spent the night in jail. In the morning we succeeded in clarifying that as sergeants of the food provisioning division we were traveling to procure products for our unit.

Meanwhile, the commandant of the post noticed a golden watch on one our soldiers (also from Trapei). He exchanged it for his own lead watch and we moved further on the road.

Our auto traveled a little more serenely. The old familiar scenery, the green meadows in the villages awoke in me slumbering memories. Here we passed through the *shtetl* Nur. I remembered the figures of familiar merchants, simple and smart people, with whom I once traded. Now the *shtetl* looked even smaller, more miniscule than before. No Jewish faces appeared, but was it true that no Jews remained here?

The vehicle sped. Here we were passing Godlewo, a village halfway between Nur and Czyzewo. Once it seemed as if they had grown together, like a part of Czyzewo. Here the large, dry pine forest in the hot summer months would be full of Czyzewo Jews who came here to rest, to catch their breathe.

[Column 1110]

Here one could meet the Czyzewo Rabbi, Reb Shmuel Dovid Zabludower, a genteel person, refined in education and good deeds. He would come here with the *rebbitzin* [rabbi's wife]. Both were weak people and the Godlower pine forest was a cure for them.

Chana-Sura Edelsztajn also traveled here for a cure for the health of her son Shimon's lung disease. Tens and hundreds of faces of friends, acquaintances and comrades were revived before my eyes that moment, walking in those woods. Here was Roszke Edelsztajn and her two children, the same age as my older son and daughter, Yenta Lepak and her two sons, the brothers and their wives.

There emerged the Friday nights when the young people, including me, would travel here with their families to spend the *Shabbosim* with them. It was familiar in the forest. Someone would read aloud the larger newspaper in honor of *Shabbos* or a newly published Yiddish book. We celebrated feasts together and, later, strolled, talked, considered problems and worried about the world.

We drew closer to Czyzewo.

Every bit of dirt, every stone was familiar and close to me. Almost nothing had changed in the villages. The houses with the colored shutters, the red spotted cows grazing in the meadows, the jumping horses with the bound feet, which were frightened by the noisy vehicle. Here and there I was made dizzy when passing a skeleton of a burned house, but the calm silence of everything around me brought out an accidental scream, a remainder of the cruel war.

[Column 1111]

There was no time to dwell on these thoughts. The Russian ZIS [Soviet-made limousine] swallowed the kilometers. Here from the distance emerged the village of Kosk with its familiar *wiatrak* (windmill). I remember the Kosk miller, Alter, and his many-branched family. A quiet and honest Jew who would rely on God's mercy to provide the wind just when the peasants would bring their wheat to be ground. He earned his livelihood, raised children and led a respectable house. When he came to the city he would give good contributions for charitable purposes. He gave the rabbi a good donation for the redemption of the *hametz* he sold every *erev* [eve of] Passover.[1]

It continued in this way until the children grew up. They took over the mill and did not want to rely on the wind. They added a motor driven with kerosene. The entire Okin family consisted of nimble and honest merchants.

Across on the right side of the highway was the Kosk court, a rich, noble feudal estate. The administrator, Organinski, may his name be erased, was a bloody enemy of the Jews, an organizer of pickets at Jewish shops. He was the initiator of moving the fairs from Tuesdays to *Shabbos* [Sabbath] and led the pogrom during the fair in the *shtetl*. During this pogrom, the strong man, Zelik Yankel Yelin, died in a murderous way and many others were wounded.

While I was in Wołomin and looked for traces of my sister's daughter, Chanala, I learned that Organinski was shot like a dog by his own worker who served as a spy for many years.

[Column 1112]

Here is the Kosk forest.

We would walk here on *Shabbos* to breathe fresh air (it was located within *tkhum-Shabbos* [the distance one may not exceed when walking out of a city or town]). Once, tens of years ago, the Czyzewo boys and girls came together here and rebelled against the Russian tsar, holding gatherings and singing revolutionary songs.

And we already were at the train embankment, which served as a border of the *shtetl*.

We traveled beyond the train bridge and arrived in an *aleje* [boulevard] of thick and tall trees. This was the street for strolling by the Hasidic Jews from all kinds of small synagogues and *shtiblekh* [one-room houses of prayer]. The Hasidic melodies, which the *shtibl* musicians sang and repeated, echoed here.

Now only the road with its trunks and stumps remained here. The giant poplar trees were cut and taken away by the Germans. My gaze stopped to the right of the highway. On that side of the train route, something strange is noticed, new buildings scattered without any order. Later, I learned that the Jewish ghetto was in this area. The last survivors and escapees from the deportations lived in these houses until the final annihilation. Those driven from the surrounding *shtetlekh*, Nur, Jeżewo and Zambrów, also lived there. There also were other refugees from more distant *shtetlekh* and villages.

The house of my Uncle Mosheka stands orphaned. He, his five sons and his wife put a great deal of effort and hardship into building their apartment. They built it with their own hands, were their own bricklayers, their own carpenters. Now someone strange lives there. Who knows if they had a hand in their death?

[Column 1113]

– Where should we take you? – came the question from my traveling companions as we entered the *shtetl*.

They could not imagine how much pain the question created. I answered:

– Alas, I have no address; let me off in the middle of the market.

They had to drive 10 kilometers [about 6 miles] to Dambrow, on the way to Wysokie. Therefore, we discussed meeting very early the next morning in the same place.

Alone, with my young cousin, I remained standing in the middle of the market.

A strange emptiness enveloped me. The same market and yet so strange, unrecognizable. There was no trace of the two rows of Jewish shops around which it always boiled and hummed. The three brick houses, which once gave the impression of fortresses, were orphaned, separated from the thick labyrinth of small, wooden houses with small shops and moss-covered roofs.

Now there is a square with plants. The evil dream of the Polish anti-Semites, who in previous years had fought to eliminate the Jewish shops from the market and plant a city garden in their place, was accomplished. They demanded it in the name of the urbanistic esthetic and culture. However, even they did not imagine then that with the accomplishment of their dream the Jewish owners would be eliminated from the shops and the houses, all the Jews, who here on a piece of empty field of the Czyzewo noble's estate, would build an effervescent center of trade and craft that served the entire surrounding Polish population with all of the necessary things.

[Column 1114]

Here in Czyzewo at the Jewish blacksmiths and farriers, tailors, furriers and shoemakers, carpenters, harness-makers, the peasant ordered his plow tools, his wagon and sled, had his garments made, a pair of boots and a fur coat for the winter. They worked, the Jewish artisans, literally for bread and water.

The Czyzewo Jewish merchants were the buyers of wheat, rye, clover and various other products, that the peasants would have had to [otherwise] drag for days to the distant cities and sell them for *groshns* [pennies]. The Jewish merchants sent all of the wheat to distant places, even to Danzig. and thereby bettered the prices for the peasants.

How much life did these Jews bring to the entire area! The market always was full of them. They stood in groups and conversed, bickered. None of them are here now. Everything is as if emptied, closed, dead.

I tried to brace myself and turned here and there, listened to the echo of my boots on the stone sidewalk. My thoughts tormented me; would I not meet even one familiar face here?

Perhaps, I would knock on the first, best door. See. Ask. Demand?

Some kind of cold strangeness chased me from the houses, from the new sidewalk that was not here before. The strangeness seized my will, my strength.

Several people approached from two corners of the market, looked at me with strange glances. The Polish sergeant with the automatic weapon carried in front [of his body] began to look familiar to them.

[Column 1115]

– Several voices suddenly cried out, Boże mój, to przecież Pan Berku (My God. It is after all Mister Berka). Someone grabbed my hand, looked at my face and crossing himself said something, with astonishment, wonder, friendship… and fear.

Some, surprised, wanted to kiss me. I did not give them the opportunity, only extended my hand to everyone and impatiently wanted to know if there were any Jews here.

They pointed me to several small, wooden houses that had belonged to Zindel Lew, to Leibel Watnik's Fraydke.

Stanislaw, who as an official from *Rolnik* [organization of farmers], earned *bakshish* (a bribe) from me during my business partnership with Adamski, was very happy with me now and did not leave me alone. He took upon himself to take me to the Jewish houses and tried to speak the mildest words to me.

It was as if my heart had stopped. The moment came that no pen is capable of describing.

Suddenly I was surrounded by Jews, Czyzewo Jews, and so much sincere warmth, familiarity came from them that it took away my breathe and softened my heart for a minute.

Zisha Slucki, Yankel Godliwer and his daughter, Malka Rayzl, Zelik and Rivka Gromadzyn, Avrahaml Szwarc's two daughters and Leibush Gridman's oldest daughter, stood before me

Revived, I asked, "Where are the rest? I want to see them. I soon will need to leave."

Everyone was silent.

[Column 1116]

I did not ask anymore. Their expressions and faces said everything.

I barely absorbed anything from the confusion when they began talking, explaining. The slaughter had begun there. Several steps further, others, a man, a child, were shot. Now, everything was occupied by Poles coming from the surrounding villages. They grabbed everything that they could. All of the Jews lived here together. The door and gate were locked at night.

The tragic foreboding of the great misfortune that came later was in their words, in their voices, of the slaughter that the Poles carried out of these last victims, survivors of the Czyzewo ghetto.

We tried to do something quickly to refresh our hearts and we again went through the empty *shtetl*. The first thing we saw was the house of prayer, which remained completely undamaged. The Hitlerists turned it into a wheat warehouse. So it remained today. Who is there to be interested in it?

We remained at the old cemetery that was next door to the synagogue. The first founders of the *shtetl* had come to their eternal rest here, the first Jews who had come here hundreds of years ago. Only distant, foggy legends about them have reached us, which do not create a clear picture about their life, but only provoke a fantasy. Curious boys would jump over the fence of this old cemetery, strolling between the graves and read the inscriptions on the headstones.

The writing on these simple and crooked stones was rubbed off. Somewhere a name was recognized.

[Column 1117]

It remained etched in the memory for a long time. The name was woven into various legends about the wisdom and piety of the great grandfathers of the Czyzewo Jews.

This legend again lives in my memory now; a naïve charm hovers over them. The secretive voice of a boy sounds in the ears, which relates with such certainty that before the arrival of *Moshiekh ben Dovid* [Redeemer, son of David], the herald, *Moshiekh ben Yosef* [Redeemer, son of Joseph], will come to Czyzewo and stand with one foot in the old cemetery and the other foot in the new house of prayer and will blow the *shofar* [ram's horn] acknowledging the arrival of *Moshiekh ben Dovid*, because the great Jews who rest in Czyzewo have a large part in the redemption.

Now, the boy who repeated it is also now a legend.

The land neighboring the new synagogue, which was burned at the time of the First World War, was considered sacred by the Czyzewo Jews. The land, surrounded by a fence, is now occupied, built on. Strangers live there, perhaps also hostile people.

We moved further from the center, more to the west in the direction of the new cemetery, which was located outside the *shtetl*. Here, too, the fence was taken apart in pieces. The marble headstones that had shown a certain worth had disappeared. The small, older stones lay spread out, broken. It was difficult to differentiate the graves over which the cows grazed in the field.

We stood silently and looked at this destruction and malicious defilement. My hands and feet shook, heavy thoughts filled my brain.

[Column 1118]

The place at which the ghetto was located was across from the cemetery on the east.

The small houses still stand, chaotic, scattered without a plan, without any order. The haste with which they were built can be seen. The surviving remnant of Jews from Czyzewo, Zambrów, Nur and Jeżewo of the first deportation lived here.

The people who accompanied me spoke quietly. Their words often got stuck in their throats. They lay here for months, fenced in by barbed wire, under a constant guard and afraid of death along with the rest of the Czyzewo Jews.

The stories about the *Judenrat*, about the Jewish policemen represent places that are etched in the memory: "See the torn wires? Hersh-Leib was murdered here when he tried to escape during a deportation. Hersh-Leib was murdered two steps from there [the wire]."

Names, names, names of close ones, familiar people whom I would once meet every day, knew every detail, event in their lives, rejoiced together and suffered together. Now I listened silently to the history of their death. Which ones were murdered on the spot; which ones were loaded into a wagon to Zambrów to the military barracks from which they were sent to Auschwitz.

The scenes which people described to me were so painfully clear. In reality I now experienced with them that November day of 1942 when the ghetto was surrounded by gendarmes who began shooting and burst into the houses. The old, the sick and the small children were shot on the spot. And those remaining were loaded into the wagons like sheep for the slaughter.

[Column 1119]

Those who went with me were the lucky ones who succeeded in making use of the pre-dawn darkness and escaped.

– Where did you escape to?

– We did not know then where to escape. We escaped from death not really having a chance to escape from it…

There was no cowardice in the wrestling with death. There was powerful courage, a strength that defeated death.

The day almost was over and I was still walking around like someone sick, and with expressionless eyes I looked at the houses and people who moved around as if under a fog, as spirits going through the streets, as specters from another world.

What was happening here? Czyzewo had ceased to exist. The streets, the houses looked like sick illusions in which lived people whose hands were smeared with the blood of the dead Czyzewo Jews. These were not people. These were shadows of murderers. Night would fall soon. Who knew what dark thoughts still took shape in their heads?

Fear was painted on the faces of those who were accompanying me that I not leave them. The automatic weapon on my arm provided them with security. They would soon return to their disturbing houses, locked with seven bolts, but would it help?

They also looked like shadows, remaining from the innocent dead and tortured Czyzewo Jews.

I walked in the web of shadows – myself a shadow – engrossed in the nightmares I had lived through. I stood near the house of the Szczupakiewiczes. So many memories from my young years were connected to this house. The library was located here, the only center of culture and knowledge in the *shtetl*. Here I experienced my first wrestling with the past, with the Aleksander *shtibl* [one room house of prayer], searching for new horizons that the books revealed for me.

[Column 1120]

This house was the forge in which new types of leaders were tempered, communal, party members, people with a great deal of devotion and ardent aspirations for the accomplishment of great ideals.

Motl Szczupakiewicz, his brother Chaim and brother-in-law Yisroelke and their families also lived in this house. We had a sincere friendship with Motl that had lasted from our youngest years on. In the later years his house was the meeting place for comrades and friends. Deliberations on various community matters would take place here and often simple, friendly conversations that added so much content and color to our lives.

Motl Szczupakiewicz had emigrated to America before the war. His sister and her daughter, Surala, survived in Czyzewo and live now in their own house, in the room that once served as a washroom. The remaining rooms were all occupied by the Russian military.

Mass graves outside the city

[Column 1121]

I remained standing on the threshold. We looked at each other and immediately recognized each other, although both of us looked very little as we once had. I had changed my military uniform. She was pale, emaciated, a shadow of what she had been. The experience of the fear of every rustle that could bring death with it was still visible on the child's face.

Perl led me out the courtyard; stopped at a spot and with an overwhelmed voice said:

– See. My brother, Chaim, lays buried here. He tried to escape during the deportation… He wanted to live.

[Column 1122]

She bowed her head and sobbed.

I returned to my first hosts, absorbed by grief.

I sat with them until late in the night and listened to their frightful experiences, in which they passed on to me what they had seen. Yankel Godlewer and his daughter, Rivka Gromadzyn, both Szwarc sisters, Leibush Frydman's daughters, also were sitting there then. Our eyelids already were heavy, but no one wanted to go to sleep.

Who could imagine that this would be our last conversation!!

A short time later they perished in the bloody pogrom that was carried out by Polish bandits.

Translator's footnote:

1. The foods that one is not permitted to eat on Passover are called *hametz*. A Jew "sells" the prohibited foods, usually through a rabbi, to a non-Jew and "buys" them back after the Passover holiday.

Czyzewo – Today

On the Vestiges of a Disappeared Jewish Life

by Y. Dawidowicz

Translated by Gloria Berkenstat Freund

With a heavy heart I walked around the *shtetl* [town], where a warm Jewish life once pulsed. The soul of the *shtetl* was taken away. It was extinguished as if it had died. It looks as if it had been thrown back to its ancient state of hundreds of years ago before the Jews arrived and it was only a small peasant settlement.

The Jews in Czyzewo were the majority for dozens of years. Their communal life was a separate one, [with a] narrow connection to the Polish population, which lived in separate streets and was under the influence of the *Endeke* [members of the anti-Semitic Polish National Party] agitation against the Jews.

Very few Poles really were friends with their Jewish neighbors. Among the few belonged Makarewicz, a tailor who lived among the Jews, who considered himself as one of them.

When the Soviets occupied Czyzewo, Makarewicz took over some kind of office and was hated by the Polish nationalists in the villages.

[Column 1123]

The partisans in the Polish underground bands caught him in a village where he worked as a tailor and wanted to shoot him. However, the peasants of the village saved him at the last minute when he already had been placed at the wall.

However, the fear of death that he experienced left deep traces in him. He became paralyzed a short time after this event. The illness also took his ability to speak.

This Pole was now the only one in the *shtetl* who "was able" to speak about the former life of the Jews of Czyzewo.

Alas, when I visited him to learn something about the life and death of the Czyzewo Jews, I quickly had to give up. Sweat actually appeared on Makarewicz's face. He tried so hard to create articulate sounds. I felt his sympathy to the Jews and his deeply felt grief over their death. It was impossible to learn anything more.

His 82-year-old mother lived with him.

There was another Pole in the *shtetl* who it is true did not do a lot so that he could be counted among the Righteous Among the Nations, but who it is worth remembering because of his positive attitude toward the Jews and his honesty concerning what the Germans had done, often with the help of the Poles.

This Pole, named Barczik, was a left socialist from a group led by Dubja, before the war. A feeling of justice and brotherhood developed in him that was reflected in his condemnation of the anti-Semitism that reigned among the Polish population. He [Barczik] said to me, "I had Jewish friends whom I will never forget because of their honesty and heartfelt humanity."

[Column 1124]

Barczik was very closely connected to the Szczupakiewicz family. When he spoke of them, the two brothers, an expression of sincere respect and grief over their great misfortune appeared on his face. Let him speak for himself, with his own language and manner of talking:

> "These were capable people, with great initiative and energy. Such people we must esteem when we get to know them well. They were the owners of a mill, a lumber warehouse and a construction enterprise. The *shtetl* [town] would have benefited from such capable people. Now everything lies in ashes, in ruin."

Barczik stopped for a while. On his face hovered a smile. He had remembered that one of the Szczupakiewicz [family members], Motl, had survived because he had left for America before the war. "I still remember him, as if it were now. Over 20 years have passed. He was good-looking, sympathetic and the elegant one in the *shtetl*. He was very successful, even with the Polish girls in the aristocratic sphere. He had luck. His brother and his entire family all perished. Only a sister and her young daughters remain. They hid with peasants in Gedasa.

They had lived in the same village before the war. When the "*aktsies*" [actions, usually deportations] began, they did not appear. The gendarmes came and on the spot shot the husband, son and a daughter, who were buried in their own courtyard. Only she and two young daughters escaped to neighbors and they succeeded in surviving.

[Column 1125]

After the arrival of the Russians, Barczik helped to move their grave, on which he planted flowers. He comes from time to time to water the roses that grow, protected by a gentle hand.

[Barczik said:] "She herself, Szczupakiewicz's sister and her young daughters, settled in Czyzewo in the house that once belonged to them, the only multi-story house on the long Mazowiecki Street. But they could not last there long because death lay in wait on all sides."

The Night of the Long Knives

Kazimierz Barczik rested for a minute. It was a short pause that seemed as if he was looking for the appropriate words for the terrifying [things] that he now was going to describe. His voice was broken as if from a suffocating throat: Our Poles [did] so much cruelty! They saw with their own eyes the worst that not even human fantasy could imagine. They saw how people were transformed into hyenas, into the most horrid animals. Later, they themselves became the same; they surpassed them in their horrible savagery.

This was approximately a half-year after the liberation of Czyzewo from the Hitlerists. Individual Jews began to emerge from the hiding places in the forests, bunkers in barns. In time, their number reached about 20. These were broken people. They all lived together. When night fell they closed themselves in their houses. The fear of death that had accompanied them for years in their hiding places had not disappeared here.

[Column 1126]

However, the leaders of the Polish underground broke into their houses and murdered everyone. Among the Polish population in Czyzewo, that night was recorded as the "Bartholomew's Night" or "the Night of the Long Knives."

Were the criminals apprehended? – I asked when Barczik became quiet for a minute.

– No, they are walking around free.

– Is it known in the *shtetl* who did this?

Barczik hesitated, looked in my eyes questioningly. Finally, he said:

– Yes. There are those who know, but none of them will say anything because… who can know what kind of regime will come to power tomorrow? But even with this regime, anyone who tries to remember and to point at the murderers would not be certain of living.

This is also the reason why no one in Czyzewo knows who waters the roses on the graves of the Spolieneces in the courtyard of the Szczupakiewiczes.

Only a few people survived this night: Zisha Slucki, Zelig Gromadzyn and his mother, Avrahaml Igla, Gonczar and also Mrs. Spolienec and her daughter. The house where they lived was occupied by the Russian military. They [Mrs. Spolienec and her daughter] only had a small room, I think the former washroom. On this night the house became a place of amusement for the military. The bandits were afraid to enter and this saved them.

[Column 1127]

Those who had been saved left the *shtetl* in the morning.

In the *shtetl* they looked at Barczik as a Jewish servant. He helped arrange the formalities under the law at the court for Szczupakiewicz for the land and house that had belonged to them. No Jew could arrange it because he would not have dared to come to Czyzewo, which had become a *shtetl* of pogromists.

Holy Stones

Suddenly I felt very lonely. I walked through the dead streets sunken in sad thoughts. The stones, the houses, everything screamed with the shouts of the most frightening death that man could devise. Individual passersby looked at me secretly, strangely. I read the suspicion in their eyes, on their faces: what was he, the stranger, looking for here? Has he not come to settle a grievance that not one of the current residents had on his conscience?

I also looked questioningly in the people's eyes: perhaps a Jew would appear, a close, familiar face twho would tell me the history of all of the horrors that had occurred on this soil. I felt so lonely; I needed to have someone who could shake off the entire horror of those days, help me demand my due, to scream…

I stood on the spot where the old cemetery had once stood. Today this spot is defiled, contaminated by the absolute nonchalance that reigns here, just as if nothing had been here. There is not one trace of generations of holiness with which the Jews in Czyzewo surrounded this spot. Garbage of all kinds is spread among the newly built workshops and houses.

[Column 1128]

The new cemetery did not have a better fate.

An old Christian woman passing by stopped near me, fixed her gaze on me with her extinguished, dripping eyes. Could she read on my face that I am a Jew? She had felt it from my bent shoulders and downcast head. A voice freed itself from her toothless mouth, as from a sick hen:

– You are alive?

– Then you do not have to cry, *Bobeshi* [diminutive of grandmother]?

– One must, one must; terrible things happened here – she said, as if to herself.

– Speak, *Bobeshi*…

People lost the fear of God and spilled innocent blood. The blood flowed like rivers. Over there, she pointed with her hand, which she quickly drew back as if she suddenly had felt the blood, the earth did not rest for weeks in Szulborze.

She sighed, moved her hand and began to walk with her little steps. I showed her a reddish stone.

– Everyday they pulled out the headstones…

– Why did they do it?

– This is what I still ask? Why do you do this? It is still a sin before God. Sacred stones and you drag them to grind corn, to sharpen axes, scythes… The bread becomes soaked in blood, innocent human blood. They laughed at me, said that I already am too old, that God had nothing against annihilating the Jews… Even the fence, a fence of red bricks, had been taken apart… They came here from the villages and placed their wagons here. Made a market out of the cemetery. First the priest (the name of the priest is Henryk Becza) called out from the pulpit that they should avoid this place that was sacred to a people with different beliefs.

[Column 1129]

For a short time the people stopped defiling the spot. But they immediately forgot the words of the priest and again began coming here with the wagons and cattle. The militia later chased them to the old marketplace.

The old one became quiet and I, too, did not reply at all and we got confused with vague thoughts: actually we all forget our dead; "the deceased are forgotten in our heart after 30 days." The problems of the living cannot bear the constant thought of death, even as terrible as it may be. The choice did not lie in our hands, but here was a case that was different. The holiness of that place was greater and more fearful than a usual cemetery. This was the cemetery of a world that was brutally annihilated.

Everything that was a reminder of that world must be held sacred and dear. There are no designations for those who desecrated it so brutally, so inhumanely with bovine obtuseness.

The old woman stood up moaning and spoke with interrupted words: "All of the misfortunes come to us because… Ragajczyk's two children froze. The wind opened the windows at night. In the morning they were pieces of ice. The hand of God. He [Ragajczyk] had shown the Germans the bunker in which Jews were hiding in the forest.

[Column 1130]

She left murmuring something with her face to the ground, as if she wanted to ask for forgiveness for the crimes about which she knew much more than she spoke.

Is there a punishment for these crimes? Can we speak of forgiveness?

Spirits Want to Take Revenge

Later, I entered one of the houses on Mazowiecki Street and knocked on the first, best door, asked for an invented name and carried on a conversation.

Although I had never been in the house before the war, I was sure that Jews lived here then. I had a need to sit in such a house, to absorb the crying of the walls and see how the Pole, the only resident, would react when I mentioned who the previous residents were, who had built this [house] and had perished so tragically… so dreadfully, wretchedly.

There was a couple in their forties in the house. The man, tall with a somewhat bent back, lay stretched out on the furniture, on one of the two dark-brown wooden beds. His wife, who was busy in the kitchen, at first, animatedly answered my question about the invented name. She asked me to sit. Later, he also sat down. When the conversation was lively enough, I threw in the question:

– Is it true that Jews lived here before the war?

They were undisturbed, did not feel any embarrassment.

– Well, true. Who else could live here? It was a Jewish *shtetl*.

[Column 1131]

– Did no one, not even one survive?

– There were. They were later murdered by ours [the Poles].

I made an effort to speak calmly:

– Our bandits…

– There were bandits, the wife, a stout one, but with a worn-out face, said – many misfortunes had come to the *shtetl* because of them. There is an epidemic every year or another misfortune. Kazimierczak mutilated his hand with an unusual nail and it had to be amputated. Is this not a punishment from God? He had stolen a little in the ghetto. Kazimierczak's bull went insane and trampled his daughter… Who knows how many more misfortunes await us. The horseshoes, which we have placed over our thresholds, do not help. There are angry spirits in the *shtetl* that want to take revenge.

I looked around the house. The poverty screamed out of every corner. Perhaps their consciences still were tormented…

Growing Fear

Here I was in the house of the Czyzewo village mayor, Bronislaw Szienka.

He served me tea and a snack. When he realized where we were going, he did not wait to be asked. Speaking with him was easier. However, for the entire time my head did not stop banging as if with a hammer: "How much had he benefited from the Jews when they were alive and how much by their death?"

I learned that he was the stationmaster for the Czyzewo post office before the war. Yet, he did not remember the Jews by their family names but actually by their first names, as they would be referred to among the Jews in the *shtetl*. Every name brought out a wide smile for him. He smiled to himself, to his own memories.

[Column 1132]

He remembered weddings and circumcisions, arguments and fights. He told a story about a boycott carried out by the Czyzewo Jews of Skarczinski's whiskey refinery because he did not want to sell them the location for a new cemetery. The Jews, God forbid, did not stop drinking and selling whiskey, which they bought in the nearby *shtetl*, Braki, until Skarczinski had to give up and sell the land.

The voice of the village mayor rang dryly and hoarsely; he sighed:

"Alas, there once were times, people… They will never return, not the times and not the people… Never…

I asked myself: "Does he sincerely have regrets? Or does he not himself understand his words?"

He continued speaking:

– How strange it is; is it not true? To live in such a *shtetl* where one still feels and every day one sees everything that the people had built with their own hands, had had to leave everything and… there are none, now there are none of them.

Doubt pierced me; were his words coming from his heart or was he only trying to guess my thoughts?

I said:

– I thought the same thing going through the *shtetl*.

He smoked a cigarette, sat more comfortably in his chair. He was wearing an indoor-vest of the color of tobacco over a white shirt that highlighted his old, wrinkled face that gave me a strange sadness. The small plan of speaking, which I had prepared while walking to him, failed. My host spoke words to me that I had not expected.

[Column 1133]

– I confess my great sin – he said, offering me a cigarette – that also was the sin of many others. We did not help the Jews during their great misfortune. We watched calmly as they were tortured, as they were taken to be annihilated. Yes, yes – his voice became almost hysterical – we knew that they were being taken to their death and we did nothing but watch, as if they were dogs, not people with whom we had lived together for tens of years…

– Hundreds of years, almost a thousand… [the words] escaped from me.

My host smiled:

– Yes, you are correct. We sinned against the Jews, against God. A fear of the punishment that we could receive attacks me often… True, it can still come, it can.

A rising fear appeared on his face.

The Criminals Cannot Be Bribed

The only restaurant in the *shtetl* where I went to eat something was called *Gospoda Ludowa* [People's Inn]. I entered as if with unfamiliar feet, heard half-inebriated talk and laughter around me. In the middle of eating the bad tasting soup, a person with a blond head of hair came over to me and immediately said to me that he knew who I was and that he could help me gather material about the annihilation of the Czyzewo Jews.

I looked at the polite, smiling face of a person over 30-years old and I asked openly:

[Column 1134]

– How do you know who I am and what has happened to me?

"I was a sergeant in the information service of the A.K. (*Armia Krajowa* – Home Army – underground army during the occupation). There are no secrets for me and you do not have to be afraid of me," his voice rang solemnly and with squeaking hoarseness.

I must confess that I was somewhat frightened. Was a trap being prepared for me? I reminded myself how I had been warned before leaving Warsaw: "You are traveling into a bandit's cave. Be careful!"

The person with the fair forelock spoke further:

– I am a person who also can arrange everything. If you are staying the night I can give you a room in my house.

This made me smile a little, but I did not know how to extract myself. If I were to tell him that I already have somewhere to sleep he would ask me with whom. It did not appear that it would be very easy to get rid of him. I thought for a minute that I would take on a mysterious tone that would leave him to think and I would not be obliged with anything. However, I immediately realized that this could cost me too much because too many people were walking around there with the heavy baggage of sin and the demand for an accounting could lead them to further crimes.

Therefore, I tried to divert the conversation in another direction, about life today, about earnings and taxes and the agricultural cooperative.

A fog of smoke floated in the long and dark room, from corner to corner and almost hid the face of those who were sitting with their glasses of whisky and holding cigarettes in their mouths.

[Column 1135]

Suddenly, an accordionist sprouted from among the tables and began to play a joyful jazz melody on the harmonica. Someone rose up from a chair and began to dance alone with a glass in his hand. He created various poses, drunk and lewd. Everyone moved out of the way, clapped their hands and the drunkard spun and hoarsely sang.

Suddenly, the door opened in the middle of the dancing and a wide-shouldered gentile with a blood-sprinkled face entered. The dancing was interrupted and the harmonica stopped playing. Heard was: "Ah, Gandila has come."

Gandila smiled with pleasure and looked at them with irony and disdain. He immediately called to the accordionist:

– Hey, what are you playing there? Play *Rebeka*…

The tumult quieted for a minute. The fingers of the accordionist began to wander around the keys. Trembling notes echoed and then became bolder. Gandila wiped his eyes with a handkerchief…

[Column 1136]

My conversationalist did not take part in the commotion. He bent down to me and quietly said:

– He mourned his own "Rebeka"… A Jewish family had hidden with him in the village; he drove out all of the family, except he left their daughter, a 20-year old young woman. But she did not want to remain and left with [her family]… The Germans shot them all.

I called over a waitress, paid and not saying one word to my conversational partner I went out to the street.

The experiences of an entire day were mixed in a chaos that tortured me terribly. I was tormented by disgust for everything around me and for myself. I had the feeling that I was walking around a terribly contagious filth of crimes and decadence that would not let me buy back [the former Jewish Czyzewo] at any price.

[Column 1135]

"Czyzewo Jews? Where Are They?"
A Visit with the Czyzewo Priest in the Year 1960

by I. Dawidowicz

Translated by Gloria Berkenstat Freund

I heard a great deal from various people, Poles and Jews, about the Czyzewo *proboszcz* [parish priest], the priest, Henrykh Becza. The surviving Jews in Lomza, where he had lived previously and was known as a friend of the Jews, spoke about him especially warmly. His name, as one of the pious and good people among the non-Jews, is connected with individual humane moments in post-war Czyzewo.

[Column 1136]

I decided to meet with this good example of a Catholic priest who tried to maintain the Jewish holy places in Czyzewo.

On a dreary Czyzewo night I again went through the half-dead alleys. With all of my senses alert and open, I listened to each scrape. Perhaps somewhere a trace remained of that ebullent and warm Jewish life. I heard voices, laughter, crying from closed windows. But all of this came from distant, strange and cold people. I had a strange feeling that they, the Poles, still could not accustom themselves to living on the ground, in the houses. After everything, they rummaged like shadows on the edge of life. The feeling of guilt toward the people whom they robbed, whose houses they inherited.

[Column 1137]

The priest received me warmly. I told him that I wanted to express the gratitude of the surviving Czyzewo Jews for his courteous deeds.

He sat on the other side of the desk and looked at me astonished.

– Czyzewo Jews? There are such? Where are they?

I told him about individual Czyzewo families who live in Israel, in America. They cherish the memory of their *shtetl*. Now they were preparing to publish a yizkor book that would be a monument to the innocent, annihilated Jewish life.

I added:

– Your noble character will also be immortalized in this book as an example of humane, courteous goodness.

A deep quiet reigned in the house, although a housekeeper moved around there, a pretty woman of middle age. Yet each corner was permeated with strong smells of hermits and recluses.

Finally the priest began to speak:

– Is there an essential difference between people because of their belief? Is Christianity not a continuation of Judaism?

[Column 1138]

His voice became a little stronger:

– I record each person and his belief. People who perished because of their beliefs and their origin are sacred. Their memory is sacred. It is a sin not to protect their holiness. Our duty is to protect people from sin – the Czyzewo population – I have said - is very sinful in relation to the Jews

His eyes blazed with a very hot glance reflected from the ascetic face of a 70 year-old man. He said:

– It is true that there was a pogrom somewhere. The war made the people wild and brutal. I regret that I did not come here sooner. Perhaps I would have succeeded in protecting them from the great crimes.

We were quiet for a short time. The clock on the glass cabinet chimed the hour with a thin musicality.

– I must also say to you – he responded – underlining the word I – that I saw enough bad not only in Czyzewo. The people in Lomza were not better. There were daily murders. Human life lost its sanctity. Millions perished in the battles, rotted in the trenches in the concentration camps. Jails. Yes, yes, war thirsty people made of the world one giant wild animal. Closed the hearts to every feeling of compassion.

His voice became more like a fiery voice from the pulpit with each second. His words, ignited with humane love, were moving and inspired.

The door opened noiselessly, as if letting a shadow pass through. A woman entered.

[Column 1139]

The same woman who had earlier collected a donation from me. She walked somewhat bent over, had a delicate countenance, young, but her hair was interwoven with silver threads.

He moved his hand toward her indicating that she sit down and shielding me from her said:

– We speak about those difficult and sorrowful days when human life did not have any value.

The faces of both were sadly in thought. I knew that they risked their own lives at that time in order to save Jews. In the village of Jablonna, where the priest lived during the war, he had 11 Jews whom he saved in various ways under his protection in a dark chamber in a masked bed in a tree in the forest to whom he himself brought food. Among them was a child whom he gave to a trusted Christian woman. Later he gave it to a *kibbutz* [collective community] in Lodz. Today [the child] is certainly in Israel.

I knew about all of this, which had been told to me by Jews and Poles before I had come here. I now remembered it in my conversation with him. However, the image of the Czyzewo streets did not cease to press on my heart. The horrible desolation. In my ears still rang the quiet cry of the annihilated Jews, which soaked every stone here. I felt the need to share my pain; full of embitterment, I said:

– If the Poles, Christians who willingly go to church on Sunday had not helped the Hitlerists, many tens of thousands of Jews would have been saved; if they had not shown each hiding place, had not helped to identify the Jew and give him into the hands of the enemy, perhaps it would not also be so mournful in Czyzewo.

[Column 1140]

– Why do you talk this way; were there not believing Christians with good, genteel hearts in Poland? Is this not so … Chanale, a shame she is not now here… in 1941 we found her on a frosty morning sitting on our threshold. "What is your name?" I asked her. She looked with such sorrowful eyes and answered: "Chanale!" I understood everything and did not ask her anything more. A Jewish child already was with me and I gave her to one of my friends. She wanted to convert her, but her husband did not permit this. Perhaps her parents would survive the war and come for her. She remained Jewish and today she writes letters to them from Israel. She married…

I wanted them to understand me better and, therefore, I answered in the same tone:

– Do not think that we have forgotten all of the facts. We recorded them in our books about that horrible time. However we also ask that you not forget that there were not many such facts. Hitler had a great deal of help from the Christian population in Poland, who actively helped to murder hundreds of thousands of Jews. Yet, this was not an accident. It was the result of a generations long attitude in relation to the Jews, with whom they had lived together for 1,000 years and now…

[Column 1141]

I stopped, seeing that the priest had lifted his head in a pose as if he wanted to say something.

As a preface, he began – in my lectures I try to correct the great injustice that was done to the Jews. I was told that even before the war in Lomza, Jewish and Christian children fought. Everyone thought of me as his priest. I also do what I can now. It is not true that Christianity is the cause of hate. Christianity bars every hatred. It often happens that a foreign influence sneaks in from other domains, from chasing after power. You saw the same with the Communists… And where was all of world culture? However, Jews, those who survive, need not lose their belief and pride. You now have your own land, a small one, a poor one, but from it came the prophets, the holy ones who elevated themselves to the Godly light…

[Column 1142]

The clock struck nine when I took leave of the genteel man. The hostess quietly, like a shadow, went into the other room and immediately returned with a small pack of letters. There were Israeli stamps on them. "These letters are from my children," she said.

I went through the dark Czyzewo streets and had not yet returned to reality. I thought: do they belong to the *tzadekim* [righteous ones] thanks to whom the world exists? However, is this enough? Where are the others?

[Columns 1141-1142]

We Will Guard Your Holy Memory in Our Hearts

by Dov Gorzalczany

Translated by Gloria Berkenstat Freund

Speech of Dov Gorzalczany, on the *yohrzeit* [memorial] day of the destruction of Czyzewo, 28 Menakhem Av 5720 – [21 August] 1960, at the unveiling of the memorial headstone for the annihilated Czyzewo Jews on Mount Zion in Jerusalem.

> Of steel and iron, cold and hard and quiet
> Forge a heart, you man – and come!
> Come, go to the city of slaughter; you should see it with your own eyes,
> Touch with your own hands,
> The fences, posts, gateways and walls.
> The dark, dried blood with the brains
> Of your brothers' heads and throats
> On the stones of the streets, on all of the blocks of wood.

Honored gathered survivors of the Czyzewo Jewish *kehile* [organized Jewish community]!

We have come here together today on Mount Zion in Jerusalem to honor the memory of our fathers and mothers, brothers and sisters, relatives and friends, who perished through all kinds of unnatural deaths, were shot, suffocated and buried alive in mass graves in the village of Szulborze. This happened 19 years ago, on that Thursday, the 28th of Av in the year 5701 [26th of July 1941].

We also honor the sacred memory of all of our dearest who were driven from Czyzewo to Zambrów, where a number of them died of hunger. The others were tormented and tortured and taken to Auschwitz in horrible conditions, where they perished in the crematoria.

[Columns 1143-1144]

This happened on the 4th of Sh'vat 5703 [1st of February 1941].

We have gathered here on Mount Zion and join with the souls of everyone who lived through the Seven Gates of Hell and returned to the *shtetl* [town] after the liberation and there were cold-bloodily murdered on the ruins of their homes by the Poles.

This happened 15 years ago on the night of Tuesday, the 10th of Nisan 5705 [24th of March 1945]. May we honor their sacred memory with a minute of silence.

These three dates, which are engraved in this Jerusalem granite, will remain eternally etched in our hearts and minds.

These three dates will always tell us and the future generations about the three waves of enmity and hate, about the three phases of fury and murder, of the bestial savagery on innocent people, on children, women and old people, of the horrid and calculated murder to which there is no equal in the history of humanity.

The first wave came suddenly, in the first weeks of Hitlerist occupation. With the illusion that they were being sent out to work, the Jews assembled at the market from which they were led under a hail of murderous blows and gunfire straight to a giant mass grave that previously had been prepared in the village of Szulborze.

Among those assembled there were many whose parents did not even merit being buried in that grave. Tired, tortured, they could not continue to keep up with the marchers in the pouring rain and were shot on the spot. Their bodies were strewn around the villages of Rusz, Celinów and along the way that led from Czyzewo to Sember.

The first ones who planned the slaughter in Czyzewo were our Polish neighbors who had lived with us for hundreds of years. They turned to the Nazis asking to be freed from their Jewish neighbors and proposed their most far-reaching help, particularly in searching for hidden Jews to make sure they did not escape.

They did it with characteristic brutality and when the devilish work was done, they were paid with permission to loot the Jewish houses.

Very few people succeeded in surviving on that dark night. [Those who escaped] were helped by the pouring rain.

There also were those who succeeded in hiding and did not appear at the market. These miraculous survivors represent the nucleus of the second wave of annihilation.

[Columns 1145-1146]

The second wave of annihilation was well planned, exacting in the smallest details. This was the wave of murder, accompanied by superhuman pain. This was the "Zambrów Exile."

The Jews from the entire region were exiled to Zambrów. Words cannot describe the conditions in which our parents and brothers were squeezed together. Epidemics and illnesses broke out without even the most minimal medical help. There were conditions of hunger and terror. Hundreds fell [dead] every day.

There was heavy frost in Poland during the winter of 1941-42. At that time the Jews were taken in torn clothing to the train from which the transports to their last road left for the Auschwitz crematoria, to the gas chambers where they were bestially murdered. A negligible percent survived that time.

I will remember only an allusion of those frightful events. How pale they appear compared to the phrases from [Hayim Nahman] Bialik's famous *Shita Shtot* [City of Slaughter].[1]

> His eyes beheld these things; and with his web he can
> A tale unfold horrific to the ear of man:
> A tale of cloven belly, feather-filled;
> Of nostrils nailed, of skull-bones bashed and spilled;
> Of murdered men who from the beams were hung,
> And of a babe beside its mother flung,
> Its mother speared, the poor chick finding rest
> Upon its mother's cold and milkless breast;
> Of how a dagger halved an infant's word,
> Its *ma* was heard, its *mama* never heard.

There the small heads of children were banged on stones, on electric and telephone poles.

The Third Wave

The final and savage phase of annihilating the Czyzewo Jewish *kehile* [organized Jewish community] was prepared by the Poles themselves, without the help of the Hitlerist rulers. The liberated Poles could not bear the presence of the surviving Jews and on the night of the 10th of Nisan they came and murdered those whom Hitlerism could not defeat.

They murdered all of those who escaped from the meticulous German annihilation machine. They murdered both sisters in the Szwarc family, the daughters of the Frydmans, of the Gromadzyns, the daughter [and] the grandchild of old Yankel Godliwer and many others.

[Columns 1147-1148]

Human understanding is not capable of grasping the great destruction; there are no words for the misfortune. How can we be in a position to record the facts that have reached us?

Here the dates are etched in granite. We have written about the course of the entire destruction in the Czyzewo Yizkor Book that will be published soon.

Here in the "cellar of death" were gathered the ashes of millions of Jews from all corners of the world who perished in the death camps. Among them are the ashes of the Czyzewo Jews.

In the moment, we feel the spirit of the hovering souls. We take their rage in their last moments of their lives against the murderers, against all of those who nonchalantly watched the bestial murders and were silent.

We, survivors, feel the duty to do everything so that their memory will never be forgotten. We will be a memorial stone and record their memory by telling the history of their lives and tragic death in [this yizkor] book.

Dear souls, we part with you and promise you to dearly preserve your sacred memory in our hearts. We will never cease to demand revenge, as Bialik says:

> What do they ask? Why do they stick out their hands?
> Where is a fist? Where is the great thunder,
> That will take revenge for all generations?

And move heaven and earth, tear the heavens.
Turn over My chair, My divine throne.

Translator's note:

1. This excerpt of Bialik's poem is taken from *Complete Poetic Works of Hayim Nahman Bialik*, edited by Yisrael Efros, vol.1, pages 129-43.

[Column 1147]

Czyzewo Benevolent Association
by Itsl Kirszenbojm/New York

Translated by Gloria Berkenstat Freund

The Czyzewo Aid Union was founded on the 15th September in New York, registered as a legal organization in 1904 under the above mentioned name according to the laws of New York State.

At that time, the majority of the *landsleit* [people from the same town] were in New York. Therefore, they founded their own synagogue, where the Czyzewer came together every *Shabbos* [Sabbath] and holiday. They felt welcome there, in their own atmosphere. Their own *khevre–kadishe* [burial society] also was founded then and meetings were held every year in the Czyzewo manner.

The purpose of the organization was to help out the needy members and newly arrived immigrants. Therefore, a loan fund was founded to make it possible for the newly arrived to bring over their families [from Czyzewo].

In 1920s, right after the First World War, the Czyzewer in New York did not forget their *landsleit* in the old home. They collected money in various ways and sent help to Czyzewo.

[Column 1148]

The *landsmanschaft* [organization of people from the same town] gave $1,500 to the United Joint Appeal (United Fund Raising]. The Czyzewo loan fund in Tel Aviv, named for the Czyzewo martyrs, received 500 dollars. Six thousand dollars also was invested in Israel Bonds.

The synagogue had to be given up when the Czyzewer moved to other areas and three Torah scrolls were given to Israel and one Torah scroll was received by the Czyzewo *landsleit* in Tel Aviv.

There also was a union in the 1920s that was only involved with supporting its own members in New York. When the flow of new immigrants brought young people who knew what the situation in the old home looked like, the Young Friends and Ladies Auxiliary was founded, which collected money at various opportunities and sent aid directly to Czyzewo. This began in 1937. Today, the Ladies Auxiliary is busy only with supporting the needy.

[Column 1149]

List of the leaders of the Ladies Auxiliary:

- Freidel Levinson
- Sonya Kaufman
- Gitl Chedrof
- Itsl Kirszenbojm
- S. N. Selcer

Today [1961] the Society is led by the following:

    Izidor Berkowicz
    Yisrael Lubelczyk Antshel Kawarla
    Itsl Kirszenbojm
    Joe Kandel
    Lou Eides.

[Column 1150]

Charter members: presidents beginning in 1904:

    Max Cohen, may his memory be for a blessing
    Avraham Zylbersztajn, may his memory be for a blessing
    Chaim Zylbersztajn, may his memory be for a blessing
    Avraham Spalanski, may his memory be for a blessing
    Morris Goldman
    Harry Birnberg, may his memory be for a blessing
    Simon Zylbersztajn
    Joe Bernstein, may his memory be for a blessing
    Benny Gordan, may his memory be for a blessing
    David Schwartz, may his memory be for a blessing
    Nathan Berkowicz, may his memory be for a blessing
    Max Kasper, may his memory be for a blessing
    Max Schapiro, may his memory be for a blessing
    Itshe Mankuta
    Avraham Kronenberg
    Azriel Belfer
    Avraham Berkowicz, may his memory be for a blessing
    Izidor Berkowicz.

[Column 1149]

Activities of the Czyzewo Landsmanschaft in Israel
by D. Aba Yitzchaki

Translated by Gloria Berkenstat Freund

The beginning is dated 1944. But the history of the *Irgun Yotzei Czyzewo* [Organization of Former Residents of Czyzewo] also has its pre–history. As is told, a protest meeting was called after the pogrom in Czyzewo in 1937 with the purpose of alerting the Jewish organizations in *Eretz–Yisrael*.

The almost spontaneous meeting took place in the cellar home of *landsman* [man from the same town] and activist, Comrade Elisha Rubinowicz. There were protest speeches from the comrades Izak Kristal–Bedolah of Jerusalem, Avraham Cukrowicz–Cur and Yitzchak Szlosli, then in Rishon LeZion.

The participation in the protest meeting was very large. Almost all of the *landsleit* [people from the same town] who lived in Israel came. The necessity of founding a permanent union of Czyzewer and other things were spoken about at this first, large meeting. In the mean time, the Second World War broke out. The economic conditions in the country worsened. Some activists left for the Jewish Brigade. All of this paralyzed the idea of creating a Czyzewo Union.

Not until the end of 1944, after receiving clear information from the survivors (those saved from death) about the destruction and death of Czyzewo, the comrades, Dov Brukarz, Shimon Zysman, Elisha Rubinowicz and Comrade Isachar Okon held the first meeting, which took place in the residence of Comrade Okon, at which it was decided to call the first "memorial gathering."

[Column 1150]

The first memorial evening took place at the residence of Comrade Rochel Part. A detailed letter about the great destruction and death of the Czyzewo *kehile* [organized Jewish community] was read at the gathering in which all of the Czyzewer took part. The letter was written by Dov Gorzalczany about his visit to Czyzewo after the destruction. A *khazan* [cantor] recited the traditional *El Malei Rakhamim* ["God of Mercy" – prayer for the dead] and at the end the men said Kaddish [mourner's prayer].

It was then decided to honor the memory of the Czyzewo martyrs through the creation of an initiative for charitable purposes and a *gemiles–khesed* fund [interest–free loan fund] that still carries the name:

"Charitable Society in the Name of the Fallen of Czyzewo."

Okun, Brukarz, Zylbersztajn, Zysman and Rubinowicz were elected to the managing committee at the first committee meeting.

The danger for *Eretz–Yisrael* was now far way, but the war had not yet ended. Therefore, the work of the Czyzewo *Irgun* could still not show any great activity.

[Column 1151]

The main work then consisted of social aid, help for sick comrades. The committee prevailed on other *Landsmanschaftn* to take part in distributing help the neighboring families, as for example, Czyzewer [aid] to those from Wysoka or to those from Sokolow. The work of the Czyzewo committee was always crowned with success. Czyzewo communal workers always looked after each other and before the official founding of the Union, when a young Czyzewo woman was left a widow with three small children, without the means for continued existence, the above–mentioned comrades did everything they could to at least partly help the orphaned family. They had already thought about founding an aid union, but they increased their activity at the end of the cruel war.

In addition to the annual memorial evenings, which were devotedly observed and were arranged for the day of the first expulsion on 28th of *Menakhem Av* [the Comforting [month of] Av], other communal gatherings took place, customarily on Chanukah and so on. The committee made attempts to connect with *landsleit* [people from the same town] outside the country. Letters were sent to America, Uruguay, Mexico and so on. The *Irgun* began to occupy a place in the life of every Czyzewo family in Israel. Paging through the minutes book of that time, we find: "Comrade Zysman and his wife spent a certain sum of money in honor of their 'silver anniversary' for the *Irgun* fund instead of an evening of entertainment." The managing committee also charged itself with a "peace– making mission." They made peace between *landsleit* and neighbors for whom conflicts, arguments arose as a result of living in common.

The work of the managing committee was divided into various branches,

- a. dispensing small loans to needy comrades;
- b. dispensing help to the unemployed or sick;
- c. visits to the sick, with participation mainly by the women: Dvora Brukarz, Nemi Brand–Stolowicz and Shoshana (Royzka) Kszinwanogo. They visited the sick Czyzewer in the hospital.

The only source of income was the Levies from the *landsleit*. The collection was made personally by the comrades of the managing committee in the old manner. They went from house to house and asked and the comrades gave as much as they could. The following were engaged in this work:

Zysman and Szliaski, Brukarz and Zylbersztajn, Yafa Raucher–Gromadzyn and Rivka Cohen–Kanet, Rochel Part–Garde and Malka Szejman, Yitzchak Hersh Gora and Elisha Rubinowicz.

[Column 1152]

At a meeting that took place on the 1st of October 1946, we created a project to call for the collection of memoirs about Czyzewo, to revise the memoirs, to publish this in a brochure and to distribute it to the *landsleit*. This decision can be considered as the "forefather" of the later creation of the present yizkor book.

The Czyzewo Union in Israel did not only look for *landsleit* abroad who could help, but mainly tried to make contact with the "survivors" saved from the fire that spread over the entire world. The *Irgun* looked to support the Czyzewo refugees in Shanghai, the Soviet Union and Cyprus and so on with money and food packages and, as always, tried to be a someone "who was meritorious and brought merit to the many," that is, to have a direct influence on the relatives of the refugees in Cyprus that they also fulfill their obligations, to give addresses to the rescue committee of Rabbi Kook, may he memory be blessed, and others through which matzos were sent for Passover and other food packages all the way to the exiled Czyzewo families in distant Siberia.

1947, the managing committee was busy preparing a welcome for the first homeless family that came to Israel. Earlier, the attention of the managing committee had been to distribute help in various forms to individual refugees who had come during the war years through Anders' Army, through Shanghai, Teheran and so on.

1948, a great misfortune occurred to a Czyzewo family in Israel. The committee organized serious aid work of a greater scope. In the meantime, contact was made with the New York Czyzewo *Landsmanschaft*.

The American *landsleit*, with a will to help those in need, turned to the Czyzewo survivors, who were then in Lodz, Poland, with a proposal that they would take on the material support. Those in Lodz diverted the proposed help to Israel where a fund would be created for constructive help for the *landsleit*. Thus arrived the first 100 dollars from the New Yorkers for the *gemiles–khesed–kasa* [interest–free loan fund].

Contact with the Czyzewo organization overseas grew stronger after the rise of the State of Israel. The activity of the Y.F. [Young Friends] and Ladies Auxiliary increased and we received the first direct support of 200 dollars sent with the first Czyzewo tourist. Organizations of Czyzewer, which are in other cities in America such as Detroit, Kansas City and Cleveland, responded. In Cleveland, Mr. Herman, a newly arrived *landsman* [man from the same town], distinguished himself.

[Column 1153]

The comrades Berl Gorzalczany and Ahron Jablonka, new activists, were drawn to the work. The loans given became bigger. New immigrants arrived. Comrades from the managing committee went to the [different areas] to visit needy *landsleit*, to learn their economic conditions. The newly arrived were provided with loans.

The memorial services were organized along with the Zaromber *landsleit* in Israel because of [our] common fate and identical *yohrzeit* [anniversary of a death] day; this continued for several years.

1949, the managing committee tried to help the Frydman family save their child from gentile hands (the current *Rebbitzen* [rabbi's wife] Marina).

Because the Israeli pound was devalued, the activity of the *Irgun* was weakened a bit. A loan of 25 or even 50 pounds lost its worth and was incapable of serving as an alLeviation of need. But the work did not cease completely. Aid collections were organized in the previous way. A booklet was created; comrades taxed themselves with regular monthly payments for the chronically ill members of the union.

The result of the *Irgun* activity was very high morally. But the work of the *gemiles–khesed–kasa* was very modest during the years 1945–1951. Seventeen loans were distributed for a sum of 580 pounds. Stabilization of the Israeli currency began to happen in 1952–3. The monetary support we received from the foreign unions now was worth more. In 1954–1955, 28 loans were made worth the sum of 3,220 Israeli pounds.

At that time, the committee did a great thing. It made possible for a member to move from a tomb–like apartment to a respectable, human one–room apartment with all of the comforts of living. It made super–human efforts then, but it had no other choice. The union was in a dilemma, but the comrade would lose his health in the inhuman apartment. However, the fund atrophied for a short time.

Beginning in 1955, tourists began to visit Yisrael. They became acquainted with the activities of the fund, listening to reports about the needy among the *landsleit* in Israel. Leaving their personal troubles and returning home, they prevailed in having the support for the Israeli loan fund increased. The results were noticed immediately.

[Column 1154]

The number of loans in 1955 reached 17 with a sum of 4,500 Israel pounds.

In 1956 the idea began to mature of memorializing the memory of the Czyzewo martyrs in the form of a yizkor [memorial] book. Simcha Prawda heard about this on his visit to Israel, carrying the idea back to the *landsleit* in America and as a result we received the first 450 dollars collected from eight families as their first support for the project of publishing a yizkor book. This action encouraged the Israeli *Landsmanschaft* and the committee began the work with the hope that the dream of publishing such a book could be accomplished.

All of the preparations for publishing the yizkor book were made and it appears that the fear that, God forbid, as a result, the work of the *gemiles–khesed–kasa* would be weakened was unfounded. The work for the publication of the book went hand in hand with the general *Irgun* work. Contact strengthened among all of the *landsleit* in Israel. A yearly taxation for the *Irgun* from all of the *landsleit* was adopted. Comrades abided by it and answered every call with postal or bank checks. The former system of personal visits was no longer necessary. The activity of the *gemiles–khesed– kasa* also strengthened. The results in numbers were:

In the years 1958–1961, 58 loans worth 12,000 pounds were given out.

In the meantime, a headstone was erected on Mount Zion in Jerusalem, along with those of hundreds of other Jewish *kehilus* [organized Jewish communities].

A very large number of comrades in Israel, and particularly, the *landsleit* [people from the same town] around the world, became active thanks to the work of publishing the yizkor book. In addition to those in New York, there were responses from Mexico, Argentina, Uruguay, Nicaragua, Detroit, Cleveland and others with thanks and recognition of our work.

You, beloved and dear Czyzewo Jews all over the world, have the results of the great undertaking here before your eyes.

[Column 1155]

Dedicated to the Anonymous Donor

[In Hebrew and Yiddish]

by The Editorial Board

Translated by Gloria Berkenstat Freund

This modest page is dedicated to our modest *landsman* [person from the same town] and devoted friend, who doubled the contents of our *gmiles-khesed* fund [interest-free loan fund] with his large financial contribution and also created a fund for founding a house in Israel in the name of the Czyzewer martyrs.

We wanted to portray this wonderful person in this book, in which understanding, feeling and deeds exists together harmoniously.

However, this noble man, who excels with his extraordinary modesty and avoidance of honor, categorically forbid us to publish his name.

The contributions of this anonymous *landsman* is really of a higher quality and is permeated with the feeling of a fraternal relationship to the surviving Czyzewo Jews who take pride in this magnificent personality from our *shtetl* [town].

Memorial Candles

Yiddsh translated by Gloria Berkenstat Freund

Hebrew translated by Jerrold Landau

In fury and deep anger, we recall
For these do we weep

Our mother:

Hudes-Elka

The most honorable wife, God-fearing Jewish daughter, a true Jewish mother. She set herself apart from gossip and always looked to help a neighbor with advice and deeds.

Our father:

Izak-Dovid *haKohan*
[member of priestly class]
Kajzmacher
(Izakl the shoemaker)

One of the good types in the *shtetl* [town]. A Jew, a host [to poor men who needed a place to stay on *Shabbos* [Sabbath], a charitable person. Avoided gossip and speaking ill of people. He spent his free time praying in the house of prayer or reciting Psalms.

Our sister:

Fayga-Rivka and her husband, **Avraham Liampart** and their two small daughters

Our sister: **Dwora Kajzmacher**

Our brother:

Yakov, his wife **Rivka** and two children.

Our sister: **Fruma** and her husband.

The entire **Liampart** family without heir

Those who will never be able to console themselves:
Chaim-Asher *bar* [son of] **Izak-Dovid** *haKohan*
Sura-Miriam *bas* [daughter of] **Izak-Dovid** *haKohen*
New York

[Columns 1161-1162]

Our family members who fell at the hands of the enemy
Woe unto those who are lost and are not forgotten

Our brother **Yaakov**, his wife **Nechama**, and two children

Mother: **Chana Jablonka**

Brothers: **Berl, Moshe and his wife, Shlomo, and David**

Perpetuated by
Bumsha and Yisrael of New York,
Ahron and his family of Tel Aviv

Their memory will never leave us

Father: **Avraham Landau** and my brother Yona who were burnt
In the Great Synagogue of Bialystok

My sisters **Rivka and Rachel**, who perished in Treblinka
My sister: **Feigel**, who fell as a partisan two days before the liberation in Bialystok
Mother: **Devora nee Gorzalczni** who died in 1931
My wife: **Chana-Yetka Landau, nee Karpik**, and my son **David**

In sorrow and agony
Alter-Yitzchak Landau

An eternal monument for my relatives

My father **Moshe-Ahron Kokowka**

My mother: **Doba**

My brothers
Yitzchak-Yudel and his wife and child,
Yosef Leib and his wife and children
Leizer-Velvel, wife and two children
Shmuel-Feivel

My sister: **Yakhad-Miriam** and her husband and four children

Sura and her husband and child

Honored by:
Avraham Kaufman-Kokowka

[Columns 1163-1164]

We will recall our dear ones
In memory of my dearly beloved

| My sister, **Dvora Gromadzyn** | My brother's son, **Moshe, his wife and children** | My unforgettable mother, **Perl Gromadzyn** |

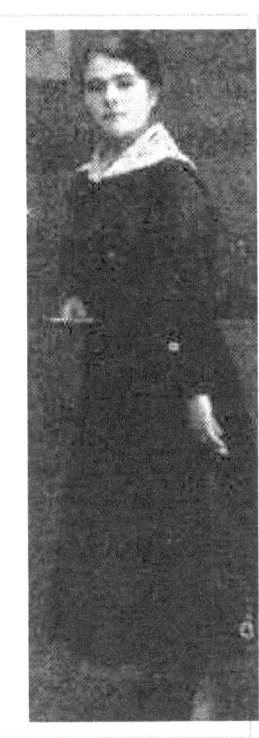  

In eternal sadness:
Chaya-Rivka Gromadzyn, New York

We weep bitterly for our dear ones

Our sister: **Esther-Rochel Orlinsky (nee Szajka)** and her husband **Yakov**

Their daughters: **Sheva, Feigel, Leah, Rivka**

Their son: **Itshe-Meir**

Our sister: **Chaya-Kszonszka (née Szajka)**

Her husband: **Moshe**

Immortalized by:
Bina, Gitl and Shlomo Szajka, New York

We will recall our dear ones
Who perished during the years of the terrible Holocaust

Our sister: **Rivka Plocker**,
her husband, **Binyamin, and two children**

Our mother,
Sura Prawda

Our cousins: **Simcha Lew and wife Rukhtshe and child**

Roshka and her husband and children

Yosl, Yisrael-Yitzchak and **Avraham Berl**

Our sister: **Perl Pinkus** and her husband and child

Our uncle: **Zindel Lew and wife**

Our aunt: **Lew** (the small woman) and **her daughter and grandchildren**

Immortalized by:
Simcha Prawda-Kapczinski, Mexico
Leibel Prawda, Mexico
Khayke Prawda-Cukrowicz, Mexico

We will recall our dear ones

Our brother: **Yosl Litmans**, his wife **Toyba and daughter**, **Esther-Leah and son Avraham**

Our mother: **Peshke Litmans**

Our relatives:

**Esther Markus,
née Baran and her husband and children**
Perished in Bialystok

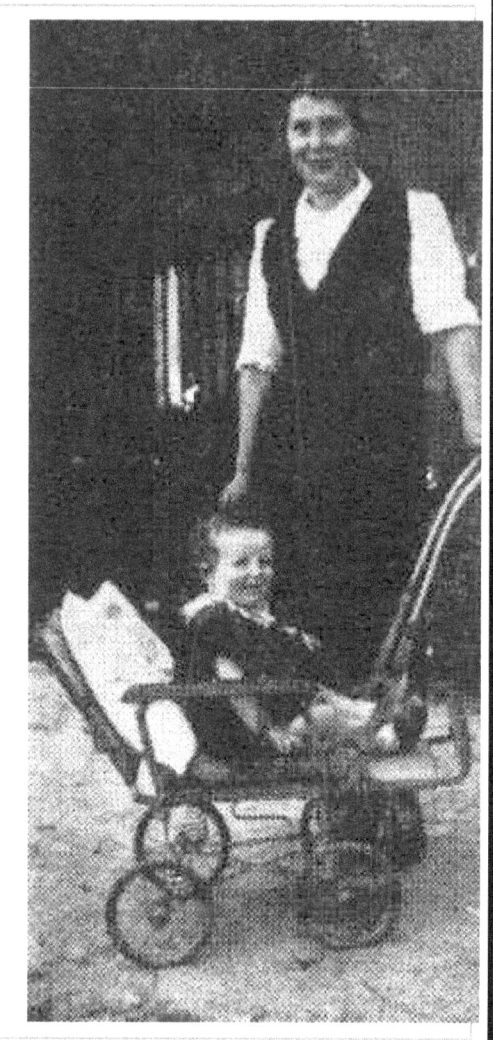

Our sister
Rochel-Leah Litmans
with her daughter

Immortalize their memory
Morris Litman, Isser and Yenta Litman and Ralph Litman, New York

[Columns 1169-1170]

Pure ones who were murdered by the bloodthirsty murderers

My father: **Yehuda Mendel**

My brothers: **Shepsl and his wife**

Yechiel, his wife, Dina, and children

In sadness: **Simcha Cukrowicz**, Mexico

Your refined souls

In eternal memory

Our father: **Reb Shmuel Zangvil Edelsztajn**

His wife: **Chana Sura**

Our brothers **Tzvi-Hirsch and his family Baruch and his family Zisha and his family Noach and his wife Rivka nee Bolender** Their children: **Dvorale, Yisroelik, Shoshana**

Our brother **Moshe**, perished in Vilna

Our sisters:

Rachel Minc and her daughter Rivka Basha Estreich and her family Chava Wajngort, and her daughter **Feiga, Dvora Shprintza** and her husband **Yaakov Pomeranc**

Yankel Farbsztajn, his wife, Pesha and their children

Honored by: sister and aunt
Nakhma Liberman-Farbsztajn

Perpetuated by
The daughters and sisters:
Nechame Malinowicz of Israel
Menucha Edelstein of California
Chaya Reznik of Israel

[Columns 1171-1172]

We will remember the victims of the 28th of Menachem Av, 5701 (1941)

That day shall be dark, may G-d above never consider it

(Job 3)

I have become silent, I will not open my mouth, for You have done

(Psalms 39)

Father: **Reb Yosef-Tzvi HaKohen Czernko**,
who ran like a deer for mitzvah matters
Mother: **Rivka**
Brothers: **Yehuda, Tovia, David, Shmuel**
Sisters: **Leah, Tova**

And the rest of my relatives and family

With tears of mourning

Son and brother: **Yaakov Chernako** of Tel Aviv
Daughter and sister: **Rachel Dagan** of Jerusalem

And my heart is full of tears

Father: **Shmuel-Nathan Jakubowicz**
Mother: **Freda nee Sapir**
Brother: **Mordechai-Litman, his wife Chaya-Sima, and their four children**
Uncle: **Avraham HaKohen Sapir and family**
Aunt: **Sura Sapir-Lewin and family**

As an eternal structure:
Pinchas Jakubowicz of Herzliya

Columns 1173-1174]

I will be full of tears day and night

Land, do not cover their blood

Father: **Shalom Kitaj**

Mother: **Grincha nee Bolender**

Brother: **Leizer-Meir**

Uncle: **Yankel Kitaj and his wife Rishka**

Their children: **Eliezer, David, Avraham, Yitzchak**

Perpetuated by: **Yentel Kitaj-FLibacznik** of Israel
Avraham Shimon and Motke Kitaj of New York

I will be full of tears day and night

Grandfather: **Avraham-Leib Frydman**

My father: **Yaakov Leizer**

My mother: **Chaya Rivka**

Brothers: **Yosef, Gershon, Menachem, Yisrael**

Sisters:
Grandfather: **Avraham-Leib Frydman**

My father: **Yaakov Leizer**

My mother: **Chaya Rivka**

Brothers: **Yosef, Gershon, Menachem, Yisrael**

Sisters: **Miriam, Tauba**

The mourners:
The son and brother: **Pinchas Friedman**
The daughter-in-law and sister-in-law
Chana Friedman nee Gorzalczani

[Columns 1175-1176]

> **My tent is spoiled, and all my cords are broken. My children are gone forth from me, and they are not; there is none to stretch forth my tent any more, and to set up my curtains.**
>
> (Jeremiah 10)

Tortured holy souls

Elimelech Rothman

His wife **Sura-Devora**

> Their children:
>
> **Liba and her husband Chaim Slucki**
>
> **Miriam**
>
> **Hinda**
>
> **Shaul**
>
> **Mendel**
>
> **Shlomo**
>
> The perpetuators: brother, brother-in-law and uncle
> **Yisrael Zysman** of Cleveland
> Daughter and sister: **Malca Rothman–Asher** of Israel

Translator's note:

1. I have taken the translation of the above verse, Jeremiah 10:20, from the Mechon Mamre Biblical translation: https://www.mechon-mamre.org/p/pt/pt1110.htm

[Columns 1177-1178]

These I recall and am confounded

My brother: **Hershel Neimark and his wife Miriam**

Their daughters: **Hadassa, Chaya-Lea**

My sister: **Reichel Handelsman nee Neimark and her husband Berl**

Their children: **Chaim-Leibel, Shlomo**

Grandchildren of Chaim-Leib the bookbinder

Memorialzed by:
The sister, sister-in-law, and aunt: **Rachel Zysman nee Neimark** of Cleveland

[Columns 1179-1180]

Let it not come until you, all ye that pass by – behold and see, if there be any pain like unto my pain, which is done unto me…

(Lamentations 1)[1]

Let Us Remember

Father: **Shimon Zyglbojm**

His wife: **Chana**

The brothers:

Feivel and his wife Lea, and their three children

Moshe-David, his wife Fedia, and their daughter

Yosef

Avraham and his family

The sisters:

Esther

In eternal memory

My mother: **Yuta**

My brother: **Chaim**

His wife: **Feigel**

His daughters: **Dvora, Rivka, Shifra**

My brother-in-law: **Shlomo Spalieniec**

His daughter: **Chana-Rivka**

His son: **Yosef**

I will remember them forever
Motl Stubin-Czupakewicz

Sura-Rivka **Perl and her husband Avraham Szipman, and their two children** Perpetuated by the daughter and sister: **Chaya Zyglbojm-Jakubowicz** of Israel --- **Chaim-Berl Wiprawnik** Honor his memory!	**In memory of our family** **Reb Ahron Hurwicz** His wife **Silka** Their daughter: **Charna** Her husband: **Yechiel Serka** And their children. Daughters: **Sura, Slova, Miriam, Lea** We will never forget you **Rayzl and Yakov Hurwicz**, New York

Translator's note:

1. I have taken the translation of the above verse, Lamentations 1:12, from the Mechon Mamre Biblical translation: https://www.mechon-mamre.org/p/pt/pt3201.htm

[Columns 1181-1182]

We weep bitterly for our dear ones

Father: **Yaakov-Yitzchak Kozlowsky**

Mother: **Naomi-Elisheva nee Smolke**

Our sister: **Chaya-Rachel, her husband Shmuel-Meir Zeliozni, and their children Yospa and Yehudit**

Our brother: **Chaim-Leibel, his wife Alta, and their children Yehoshua-Tzvi and Avraham-Moshe**

Those who mourn bitterly:
Yisrael-David, Gedalia, Fishel Kozlowsky of Israel

Land, do not cover their blood

Parents: **Zavel and Batya Gonczar**

Brother: **Yaakov and sister Naomi**

Sister: **Chaya and her husband Yosef Goldberg, and their son Tzvi**

In eternal memory:
Yaffa Gonczar-Keler, Yosef Gonczar of Israel

In eternal memory

Mother: **Marisha**   Father: **Yechiel Levin**

Sisters: **Chaya, Teibel, Simale**

Weeping for them:
Daughter and sister **Chana Levin - Kizelstein**

> Then fell I down upon my face, and cried with a loud voice, and said:
> Oh L-rd G-d! wilt Thou make a full end to the remnant of Israel?
>
> Ezekiel 11:13[1]

May G-d avenge their blood

My brother: **David Perlmuter**, his wife **Rache-Leah** and their children

My parents: **Moshe Perlmuter** and **Chana Rachel**
Their daughters: **Beila Rachel and Perl**

Weeping in sorrow:
M. Zacharish

In eternal memory

Yechiel-Mordechai Gozlacki
And his wife **Chana nee Malinowicz**
Chana Malinowicz nee Wangocz and
her children: **Freida, Ethel, Shmuel-Meir**

Perpetuated in sorrow:
Moshe-Aba Malinowicz,
Malka Malinowicz-Lyubelczyk of Israel

The sound of their blood rises from the earth

Our father: **Reb Yitzchak Stolowicz**,
our mother: **Rachel**
Our sisters: **Esther-Tauba, Gittel Rivka**
Our brother: **Yehuda (Yidel)**

Weeping for them:
Their sons and brothers: **Zalman and Moshe-Eliezer Stolowicz**
Their daughters and sisters: **Naomi and Miriam**

Translator's note:

1. I have taken the translation of the above verse, Ezekiel 11:13, from the Mechon Mamre Biblical translation: https://www.mechon-mamre.org/p/pt/pt1211.htm

[Columns 1185-1186]

Why shall the nations say, where is your G-d
May the gentiles witness before our eyes the vengeance over our spilled blood

Our dear parents

Reb Chaim-David and Rivka Cymes

Who gave their lives in sanctification of the Divine Name

Our sister: **Matel and her husband Moshe Tulman**

Their daughter: **Dina**

Their sons: **Hershel, Shmuel, and Chaim**

Who escaped from the Warsaw Ghetto and the iniquitous hands of the murderers in Czyzewo

And perished with our holy community, may G-d avenge their blood

Mourning: Their sons in Israel and the Diaspora
Yosef, Moshe, Avraham-Yitzchak & their families

[Columns 1187-1188]

Beloved and pleasant in their lives, and not separated in their deaths

(II Samuel 1:23)

At the headstones at the Czyzewo cemetery in Brooklyn, New York, stands my sister, **Dvora-Elka** accompanied by our cousin, **Toyba (née Szturman)** – on the day of a *yohrzeit* [anniversary of a death]

Memorializing their name:
son: **Dov Brukarz** of Tel Aviv. Daughter: **Dvora Manoach-Brukarz** of Brooklyn, New York

[Columns 1189-1190]

> **I will even gather you from the peoples, and assemble you out of the countries where ye have scattered, and I will give you the Land of Israel**
>
> (Ezekiel 11)[1]

In eternal memory

Our dear father: **Reb Yosef Baruch Lepak**, of blessed memory

Our dear mother: **Gittel**, may peace be upon her

We will always remember the lives cut short of our father, of our brother Yehosha and his wife and children who perished in the years 1939-1943 with the entire Czyzewo Jewish community.

May God avenge their blood!

We will always keep your memory, dear mother. You were worthy of avoiding the unworthy hand of the murderers of six million Jews. However, no trace of your sacred grave remains at the Czyzewo cemetery, which was destroyed.

May their souls be bound up in the bonds of life!

> With our heads bent we express our grief and fury
> Your son: **Mordechai Lepak and family**, New York.
> Your daughters: **Penina Lepak-Markowski and family**, Tel Aviv
> **Tziona Lepak-Rozenblit and family**, New York

Translator's note:

1. I have taken the translation of the above verse, from Ezekiel 11:17, from the Mechon Mamre online Bible translation: https://www.mechon-mamre.org/p/pt/pt1211.htm

Index of Names in the Cyzewo Yizkor Book
Prepared by Jerrold Landau

Notes:

1. This book was translated by several translators, and different name spelling conventions were used by the translators. In many cases, the spelling of names was not consistent even within a single chapter by a single translator. A spelling normalization effort was then undertaken over the entire book, with the aim of introducing as much consistency as possible. My choice of style for the normalization was not consistent in all cases, and may have introduced some awkwardness. Nevertheless, the normalization was necessary given the wide variety of spellings that were found in the initial translated drafts.

2. I did not index the TOC, as any names in the TOC will appear on their relevant pages

3. I did not include names of Biblical figures, or names of generic famous writers such as Sholom Aleichem, Bialik – unless specifically connected to a visit to the town (i.e. the index concentrates on the town itself). I did include article authors who live abroad.

4. This book is paginated by column, with two columns per page. The index entries generally represent the columns. In cases where text spans both columns, as well as in the pages prior to 75, where the original book had no page numbers (page numbers were inserted during translation), index entries refer to the page by the first column number. Furthermore, in pages where there is an article break mid-page, thereby resulting in the top part and bottom part (two separate articles) each covering both columns, the entire page will either be considered as the first (odd column), or the columns will be reset on the second article.

5. In cases where the author is either a famous historical character, a Jewish resident of another town (if obvious from the context), or a gentile, I include an asterisk in the surname. This is to ensure that the regular natives of the town can be differentiated from others.

6. In cases where only a first name is given, I did not include in the index. I do not include even if the first name is identified by the Yiddish possessive (e.g. Shlomo Gedalya's – which means Shlomo, Gedalya's son), or those identified by profession (e.g. Yosel the Melamed). To sum up, only names which include surnames are included. On the other hand, if

only a surname is listed, it is included.

7. In cases where an article appears the same, or almost the same, in Yiddish and Hebrew, and only one version was translated, the index entries will follow the English translation rather than the original text.

8. In cases where only a surname is mentioned, but it is possible to identify the first name from the context, I indexed in the entry that includes the surname.

9. World famous historical characters such as Hitler are not included in the index. More minor historical figures, such as Polish leaders, are included.

10. For the Memorial Candle section, the names were taken from the consolidated list (which includes the scans of individual pages), rather from the actual pages. The page number in this index is the first of the two columns on the page.

11. In cases where a different surname appears with an entry (i.e. not a spelling variation), the second surname is likely either a maiden name or a married name.

Note that the "Columns" are the column numbers in the original Yizkor Book, not to be confused with the page numbers in this translation.

Surname	First Name	Columns (there are two columns per page)
Abarbanel	Shmuel	245, 248
Abramowicz	Dina	107
Abu Szmuel	Dov	157
Adamski *		1115
Adgoninski		673 *
Ajdelsztejn	Zajnvel (Zawel)	84, 189
Akselrod	Chuka	345, 436
Akselrod	Chava	442
Akselrod	Leibel	428, 435, 441
Aldfang	Shlomoh	678
Alter	Avraham Mordechai Rabbi	297
Altshuler	Yerukhem	832
Amsterdam		401
Andrzejtyk *		984
Angres-Bard	Yohanan	434, 435
Arganinski *	Albin	671, 688, 689, 690
Arsz *	Marian	671
Astranzanski	Yaakov	358

Baczan	Yosl	472, 473
Badaczker		422
Banikowski *		687
Banucke		925
Baraczker	Hershel	424, 434
Baran		488
Baran	Alter	103
Baran	Shayna	435
Baran	Yenta	428
Baran	Yisrael	661, 679, 680, 681, 686, 693, 698
Barczik *	Kazimierz	1123, 1124, 1125, 1127
Barowski *		671, 687
Bartusz *		622
Beck *	Josef	444
Becza *	Henryk (Henrykh)	1129, 1135
Belczyk	Levi	103
Belfer		385
Belfer	Avraham Yitzchak	189
Belfer	Azriel	608, 1150
Belfer	Chaim	360, 1021
Belfer	Hershel	849
Belfer	Moshe Ahron	356
Belfer	Zalman	386
Ben-Ari	Sura	995
Berdan	Eli Velvel	416
Berkowicz	Avraham	1150
Berkowicz	Izidor	1149, 1150
Berkowicz	Moshe	237
Berkowicz	Nathan	1150
Bernstein	Joe	1150
Bialik *	Chaim Noachman	43
Bialistocki	Mordechai	321
Bialopolski *		378
Bialystocki		212
Bialystocki	Chaim	687
Bibow *		926
Bidgadski		675
Binder		1051
Birenbaum		1051
Birenbaum *	David Rabbi	325
Birnberg	Harry	1150
Bitner	Leyzer (Leizer)	230, 278, 712
Blajwajs		103, 207, 406, 408, 445, 717
Blajwajs	Bunim	217, 221, 623, 626, 627, 628,

Blajwajs	Hershel	717, 718, 719
Blajwajs	Moshe (Meshal, Moshel, Moshe Leib)	96, 140, 150, 151, 337, 370, 403, 428, 429, 479, 1049
Blajwajs	Naftali Herc	730
Blajwajs	Simkha	1050
Blajwajs	Shaul Hersh (Szaul Hersh)	144, 222, 389, 390, 589, 729
Blajwajs	Yitzchak (Yitzchak Bunem)	623, 625, 626, 627, 628, 734
Blajwajs	Alta	589
Blajwajz	Brajna	1060
Blausztajn		1051
Blazbard *	Binyamin	687
Blumenkranc	Moshe'le	229
Blumsztejn	Yitzchak	345
Bodla	Izak	57
Bolender		385
Bolender	Avrohom Shimon	1041
Bolender	B.	1039
Bolender	Belitshe	424
Bolender	Chaim Yitzchok	1047
Bolender	Enya	998
Bolender	Golda	337, 349, 350, 351, 369, 997, 998
Bolender	Lazer	1047
Bolender	Motl	472, 1047
Bolender	Rochel Leah	1047
Bolender	Sender	998
Bolender	Shimon	1047
Bolender	Sora Feiga	1047
Bolender	Yankel (Yakov)	494, 997
Bolender	Zelda	998
Bolender	Zisl (Ziska)	998
Bolender (Gafni)	Sura Dina	340
Boran	Esther	424
Borensztejn *	Avraham Rabbi	298, 299
Bralinski *		1080
Brand-Stolowicz	Nemi	1151
Brisel	Hershel	754
Brisel	Leizer-Henekh	754
Brisel	Meir	754, 756
Brokhauser *		69
Bromberg *	Rabbi	324
Bronsztajn	Chynka	1047
Bronsztajn	Esther-Shayna	670, 686
Bronsztajn	Fishel (Fiszel)	356, 524, 1047

Brukarz		488
Brukarz	Chaya Hinda	504
Brukarz	Dov (Berl)	13, 57, 103, 153, 181, 183, 420, 422, 424, 425, 434, 471, 473, 477, 483, 489, 503, 511, 535, 537, 539, 542, 546, 548, 550, 551, 596, 751, 1149, 1150, 1151
Brukarz	Dvora (Dwasza)	424, 542, 545, 1151
Brukarz	Mordechai	422, 428, 429, 435, 442, 480, 488, 550
Brukarz	Shimon (Szimela)	505, 596
Brukowski	Raizel	984
Brunrut		654
Bursztajn	Avraham Eli	373
Bursztajn (Dimentman)	Leah	376, 379, 382
Bursztajn	Shlomo	702
Bursztajn	Yitzchak (Yisrael Yitzchak)	241, 243, 372, 699
Calinowicz	Dovidl	732
Calinowicz	Jeszaja	732
Calkes	Shlomo	278
Cegel	Mendel	524
Celniker		223, 385
Celniker	Yisrael Yitzchak	416
Chedrof	Gitl	1149
Chmiel		103
Cikrovich (Prawda)	Chaikeh	587, 590
Cikrovich	Simcha	590
Cimer *	Antony	671, 686
Ciranke	Yakob	428
Cohen	Max	1150
Cohen *	Rabbi Shabtai (Sha'ch)	284
Cohen-Kanet	Rivka	1151
Cukerman	Etka	967
Cukrowicz	Berl	345
Cukrowicz	Dina	1169
Cukrowicz	Feigel	372
Cukrowicz	Jehuda Mendel	1169
Cukrowicz	Shlomo Feivel	930
Cukrowicz	Simcha	1185
Cukrowicz	Szepszl	1169
Cukrowicz	Yechiel	1169
Cukrowicz (Cur)	Avraham	57, 345, 371, 372, 373, 374, 377, 436, 442, 1149
Cymes	Avraham Yitzchak	1185
Cymes	Chaim Dawid	1185

Cymes	Moshe	1185
Cymes	Rivka	1185
Cymes	Yosl (Yosef)	428, 1185
Cynamon	Josef Mendel	238
Cynamon	Malka	238
Cyrelson *	Rabbi R. L.	290
Czak	Moshel	1001
Czarne	Hershel	15
Czechowski *		671
Czeliasniak	Yosef Shmerl	472
Czender (Goldberg)	Shmuelye	516, 518
Czernko	Dawid	1171
Czernko	Jehuda	1171
Czernko	Josef Cwi	1171
Czernko	Lea	1171
Czernko	Rivka	1171
Czernko	Shmuel	1171
Czernko	Towja	1171
Czenko	Yaakov	1171
Czimbam (Goldberg)	Dovid	471, 472, 473, 474
Czinowicz	Moshe Rabbi	294
Cziwice	Shlomo	924, 930, 931
Czczupakiewicz		143
Czelianogora	Shalom	422

Dagan	Rachel	1171
Dancygier	Chaim	189, 215, 220, 221
Dancygier	Tzwi Hersh	225
Dancygier	Yechiel	225
Dawidovicz	I Y (Julian)	29, 73, 1122, 1135
Dimentman	Eli (Elijahu)	175, 231, 737
Dmochowski *	Kazimierz	683
Dmochowski *	Pawel	923
Dombrowski *	Dr.	162, 165
Drazszrczszuski *	Kazimierz	687
Drengowski *		948, 949, 951, 953, 954, 956, 961, 963, 964
Dubja *		1123

Edelsztajn	Boruch	1169
Edelsztajn	Chana Sura	1110, 1169
Edelsztajn	Cwi Hirsz	1169
Edelsztajn	Dwora (Dvora, Dworale)	337, 1070, 1169

Edelsztajn	Menucha	1169
Edelsztajn	Moshe	1169
Edelsztajn	Noach	150, 151, 337, 362, 363, 445, 1169
Edelsztajn-Bolender	Rasza (Roszka)	159, 1169
Edelsztajn	Shimon	1110
Edelsztajn	Shmuel Zangwil	1169
Edelsztajn	Sura	1169
Edelsztajn	Szoszana	1169
Edelsztajn	Zanwil (Zawel)	197, 219, 262, 263, 485, 487, 661, 732, 738755, 756, 773, 840
Edelsztajn	Zisze	1169
Eibszi		654
Eibeszyc		385
Eibeszyc	Ahron	150, 235
Eides	Leibel	373, 595
Eides	Lou	1149
Eiger *	Akiva Rabbi	317, 325
Ejnszic		1022
Eliasz	Botsze (Boruch Yakov) (Botsze)	229, 231, 278
Eliasz	Esther	340, 847, 847, 848, 850
Eliasz	Yechiel	57, 358, 595
Eliasz	Yerachmiel	847
Emden *	Yakov	659
Epstein *	Yechiel Michel Rabbi	300, 301
Epsztajn		226
Epsztajn	Faya	653
Epsztajn	Chaim Leib Rabbi	294
Epsztajn	Jakob	242
Epsztajn	Jakob Yitzchak Rabbi	300
Epsztajn	Matl Fayga	653
Epsztajn	Simcha Rabbi	295
Ewri	Yeshaya	222
Fajngold	Henya	669
Farber	Dina	999
Farbsztejn	Jakob	1169
Farbsztejn	Pesze	1169
Farbsztejn (Liberman)	Nechama	1169
Feigenbaum *	Yitzchak Rabbi	297
Feldman	Nisen	670
Feldsztajn	Fayga	373
Fenster	Avrahamtshe	1017
Fenster	Peshke	345, 436

Fenster	Yisroelke	610, 1017
Fertl	Motl	491
Fetman		678
Fiszer	Yehoshua	167
Fiszman *		1062
Fribut	Yosef	686
Frydman		991, 992, 1145
Frydman	Avraham Lajb	1173
Frydman	Avraham Pinyas	765
Frydman	Berish	133, 187, 189, 207, 219, 220, 276, 279, 389, 472, 478, 840
Frydman	Chaja Rivka	1173
Frydman (Gozlani)	Chana	1173
Frydman	Chana-Etka	998
Frydman	Dina	1038
Frydman	Fruma-Rochel	998
Frydman	Gerszon	1173
Frydman	Jakob Lezjor	1173
Frydman	Josef	1173
Frydman	Lejbusz (Leibush)	138, 143, 144, 145, 161, 222, 389, 966, 996, 1010, 1122
Frydman	Menachem	1173
Frydman	Miriam	349, 350, 351
Frydman	Mirjan	1173
Frydman	Mordechai	382, 996
Frydman	Pinchas	237, 358, 836, 1173
Frydman	Sura-Laya	998
Frydman	Szayna-Bayla	998
Frydman	Tauba	1173
Frydman	Yisrael	1173
Frydman	Yitzchak Dawid (Yitzchak)	215, 220, 998
Fydeto	Jakob Pinchas	152

Gaczer	Shmuelja	101
Gandila		1135, 1136
Garde	Alter	188, 189, 233
Garde	Bine-Boruch	508
Garde	Dovid-Leib	508
Garde (Part-Garde)	Rochel	371, 373, 1150, 1151
Gdiche	Yehoshua	167
Gelbard		1007, 1011
Gelbard	Shmulka	1007, 1010
Gelbojm		93, 101, 103, 207, 427, 489, 589, 646

Gerlich *	Dr.	1041
Gershuni		1095
Glina		81
Glina	Brayna	428
Glina	Chana	435
Glina	Mendel-Yisrael Shlomo	485, 825, 826, 827, 828, 1091
Glina	Simcha	485, 553
Glina-Ginsberg	Hendl	424
Glina-Zysman	Nekhka	424, 828, 1091
Godlewski *	Marzik	79
Godliwer	Malka Rayzl	1115
Godliwer	Yankel	1115, 1122, 1145
Goldberg	Josef	1181
Goldberg	Chaja (Chaja Rachel)	1181
Goldberg	Cwi	1181
Goldberg	Jakob	334
Goldberg	Josef	1181
Goldberg	Mendel	510
Goldberg	Shimon	669, 686
Goldberg	Zalman	687
Goldfaden *	Avraham	437
Goldman	M.	670
Goldman	Morris	1150
Goldsztajn		421, 422
Golombek	Shmuel Zelik	232, 233, 234, 235
Gonczar		996, 1126
Gonczar	Batja	1181
Gonczar	Esther	940
Gonczar	Jakob	1181
Gonczar	Naomi	1181
Gonczar	Sura	587
Gonczar	Yisrael	1181
Gonczar	Yosl (Yosef)	966, 1181
Gonczar	Zawel	1181
Gonczar (Keller)	Yaffa	1181
Gora		223, 717
Gora	Eliahu	57, 355, 358, 385, 597, 598, 845
Gora	Gerszon	215, 223, 285, 293, 303, 713, 776, 789, 795, 798, 804, 809, 812
Gora	Yitzchak (Yitzchak Hersh)	374, 399, 406, 408, 409, 428, 442, 1151
Gora (Gur)	Gerszon (Gershon)	13, 57, 285, 387, 389, 391, 395, 399, 416, 695
Gordan	Benny	1150
Gorde		144

Gordin *	Jacob	427
Gorzalczany		103, 1021
Gorzalczany	Arija (Arje, Arjeh, Arya, Arja)	57, 67, 333, 334, 335, 339, 367, 368, 369, 370, 611, 613, 615, 623, 629, 847
Gorzalczany	Dov (Berl)	13, 57, 75, 109, 129, 150, 151, 337, 362, 370, 385, 405, 411, 433, 445, 531, 542, 544, 545, 595, 678, 765, 825, 847, 1141, 1150, 1153
Gorzalczany	Fayge-Feye	591, 743
Gorzalczany	Matel	743
Gorzalczany	Mendel	825, 826, 827, 828
Gorzalczany	Moshe'ke	151
Gorzalczany	Yechielke (Yechiel, Yechiel Mordechai)	143, 145, 356, 1183
Gorzalczany	Yeshaya (Yeshayahu) (Jeszaja) (Yeshaya Yaakov)	143, 144, 145, 229, 278, 586, 651, 771, 772
Gorzalczany	Yisrael Yitzchakl (Yisrael Yitzchak)	100, 133, 651
Gorzalczany (Malinowicz)	Chana	1183
Gorzalczany Frydman	Chantshe (Khantshe)	159, 591
Grabski *		169
Grade	Berish (Alter Berish)	362, 365
Grade	Chaim	385, 457
Gradus	Ahron	687
Gradus	Gel Grade	165
Graubard *	Isuchar Berish Rabbi	298
Graubard *	Jehuda Lejb Rabbi	298, 299
Graubard	Zebulun	222
Gricer	Feywele	225
Gridman	Leibush	1115
Grobia	N.	688
Grochowski *		732
Grodus	Ahron Hirsz	297
Grodzinski *	Rabbi Chaim Ozer	290
Gromadzyn		84, 1099, 1145
Gromadzyn	Chaim-Ahron	1101
Gromadzyn	Chawtsha	428
Gromadzyn	Dvora (Dwora)	542, 545, 1163
Gromadzyn	Feigel	351
Gromadzyn	Fruma	349
Gromadzyn	Mendel	101, 596
Gromadzyn	Moshe	1163
Gromadzyn	Moshele	364
Gromadzyn	Moshe-Mendel	594, 656
Gromadzyn	Nuska	101, 596, 731
Gromadzyn	Perl	116

Gromadzyn	Rivka	1115, 1122
Gromadzyn	Shayna-Chaya	1101
Gromadzyn	Sheina	345
Gromadzyn	Yankel	333, 334, 338, 339, 367, 368, 369, 370, 1100
Gromadzyn	Zelig (Zeylik, Zelik)	610, 950, 866, 884, 1115, 1126
Gromadzyn (Gordon)	Simkha (Simcha, Simkhl)	425, 428, 435, 441, 561, 570, 586, 593
Gromadzyn (Gromadzyn-Gotlib)	Khantshe (Chana)	428, 1099
Gromadzyn-Kirszenbojm	Chaya-Rivka	424, 435, 1163
Grosbard		385
Grosbard	Baruch	359, 360
Grosbard (Grosbart, Grozbard)	Zebulun (Zvulun)	138, 140, 143, 144, 173, 174, 175, 313, 315, 389, 736, 737, 784, 838, 839, 926, 981, 1008
Grosodzin		1038
Grozbard *		671
Grucki *		894
Grynberg		337, 544
Grynberg	Avraham'l	150, 151
Grynberg	Nisle	484
Grynberg	Yoske (Joske)	189, 215, 483, 594, 748
Grynberg (Grynberg, Czelonogora, Czelonogora)	Shalom	91, 336, 341, 342, 345, 362, 369, 423, 424, 479, 544
Grzibak	Efroim	669
Guterman		211
Gwardiak		675
Hagerman	Jacob Shlomo Rabbi	297
Hagerman	Moshe Joel Rabbi	297, 298, 299, 300
Hagerman	Yitzchak Jehuda	299
Hagerman *	Yitzchak Paltiel Rabbi	299
Handelsman	Berl	1177
Handelsman	Chaim Lajbl	1177
Handelsman	Reichl	1177
Handelsman	Shlomo	1177
Hebel		144
Held	Yocheved	350
Held (Cheld)	Josef	57, 67
Heller *	Rabbi Yom Tov Lipman	282
Herman		1153
Hersh	Yitzchak	101
Hershman	Boruch	133, 745, 746

Hershman	Boruch, Rabbi	75
Hershman	Moshe	836
Heyman *		926
Hirshborn *	Yitzchak Yaakov	297
Hitsl	Boruch	1064
Hitsl	Henryk	1064
Hofman	Rochel	373
Hofman	Shlomo Zelman	97
Horowicz *	Dawid HaLevi Rabbi	297
Horwicz	Ahron	1179
Horwicz	Reizl	1179
Horwicz	Silka	1179
Horwicz	Yaakov	1179
Igla	Avraham (Avrahaml)	994, 1038, 1126
Igla	Hatskl	674
Igla	Moshe-Lejb	161
Ikir	Shmuel	966
Jabka		441
Jabka	Dovid	400, 402, 406, 408, 409
Jabka	Welwel (Velvel)	89, 539
Jablkowski	Chaim	669, 682, 686
Jablonka		223, 488, 599
Jablonka	Berl	223, 416, 1161
Jablonka	Bucze	103, 844, 1161
Jablonka	Chana	1161
Jablonka	Dawid	1171
Jablonka	Itsl	222, 723
Jablonka	Jakob, (Yakov, Yaakov)	150, 151, 428, 544, 842, 958, 1161
Jablonka	Moshe (Moshele)	223, 416, 1161
Jablonka	Nechama	1161
Jablonka	Shlomo	1161
Jablonka	Yisrael	844, 1161
Jablonka (Tapuchi)	Ahron	13, 57, 223, 273, 313, 416, 461, 465, 755, 837, 1153, 1161
Jabotinsky *	Ze'ev	370, 1052
Jakubowicz	Chaja Sima	1171
Jakubowicz	Mordechai Litman	1171
Jakubowicz	Natan	1171
Jakubowicz	Pinchas	1171
Jakubowicz	Shmuel (Shmuel Natan)	742, 743, 1171
Jakubowicz	Yakov	1007

Jakubowicz (Sapir)	Frajda	1171
Janczewski *		874, 875, 876, 877, 878, 889, 890, 911
Jandzewer	Mendel	230
Janowski	Shmulka	428, 441
Janowski	Yisrael Yitzchak	227, 229, 231, 278, 659
Jeczarski *		671
Jeliazny	Jehudit	1181
Jeliazny	Josefa	1181
Jeliazny	Shmuel Majer	1181
Jeliazny (Kozlowsky)	Chaja Rachel	1181
Jelin (Yellin)	Zelig (Hillel Zelig)	669, 671, 674, 675, 677, 679, 680, 681, 683, 685, 686, 692, 693, 696, 698, 843
Jeruzalimski *	Moshe Noachum Rabbi	298
Jursz *	Marian	672, 688, 689, 690
Kac	Leibush	980
Kacenelson	Yitzchak	21
Kachan	Rochela (Rochel)	373, 984, 985, 1031
Kackowicz *	Moshe Ber Rabbi	302
Kackowicz *	Yaakov David	302
Kackowicz	Yocheved	302, 348, 351
Kaczanek	Shlomo-Ber	817
Kaczimierczak *		923, 1131
Kahan		385
Kahn *	Pinkhas	388
Kalan	Ruchele	371
Kalinin *	Mikhail	1084
Kalinowicz	Yeshayahu (Yeshaya)	209, 219, 220, 738
Kaliszyner	Chaim Lejb (Rabbi)	99
Kanc	Shimon	13, 29, 856
Kandel		1025, 1026
Kandel	Avraham	360, 785, 1021
Kandel	Chaim Zvulun	785
Kandel	Heide	167
Kandel	Jacob (Jakob)	57, 785
Kandel	Shayna (Shayndl)	373, 382
Kandel	Shmuel Velvel (Szmuel Zeev)	356, 357, 445, 785, 786
Kandel	Sura Rachel	785
Kandel	Yaakov	358, 785
Kandel	Yitzchak Noach	785
Kandel (Baron)	Lea	785, 786
Kandel (Grinwald)	Yafa	785
Kandel (Okon)	Yosfe, (Joe)	591, 785, 1149

Kanet		520, 529
Kanet	Dwashke	424
Kanet	Josef	189, 418, 521, 522, 523
Kanet	Mendel	153, 189, 522, 523, 525-529
Kanet	Rojza-Leah	526
Kanet	Yehoshua	518, 519
Kapka	Berl	686
Kapla	Eliezer	686
Karan		223
Karesz	Meir	471
Karlbach		388
Karniol *		671, 672, 673
Kasower	Yosef	669, 686
Kasper	Max	1150
Kaszanske	Moshe	1163
Kaszanszke (Szajka)	Chaja Menucha	1163
Katliarek	Yehoshua	389, 391
Katliarek	Yossel	486
Kaufman	Sonya	1149
Kaufman (Kokowka)	Avraham	1161
Kawarla	Antshel	1149
Kazlowski	Chaim-Leib	389
Keizmacher	Brocha	984
Keizmacher	Chaim Asher	1159
Keizmacher	Dvora (Dwora)	165, 1159
Keizmacher	Fruma	1159
Keizmacher	Hadas Elka	1159
Keizmacher	Izak Dawid	1159
Keizmacher	Jakob	1159
Keizmacher	Moshe	985
Keizmacher	Rivka	1159
Keizmacher	Sura Miriam	1159
Kejmowicz		103
Kepak		448
Kerdan	Eli Velvel	389
Kimovitz	Sluvke	591
Kirczner	Kalman	596
Kirszenbojm		442, 446
Kirszenbojm	Brocha	824, 984
Kirszenbojm	Ch.	821
Kirszenbojm	Chaya-Sura	428, 436
Kirszenbojm	Itsl	67, 424, 428, 435, 826, 1147, 1149
Kirszenbojm	Rayzl	822

Kirszenbojm	Shalom	373, 821, 826
Kirszenbojm	Sura	826
Kirszenbojm	Yakov-Leib	821
Kirszenbojm (Cukert)	Gitl	826
Kitaj	Avraham (Abraml)	722, 1173
Kitaj	Avraham Shimon	722, 1173
Kitaj	Dovid (Dawid)	865, 1173
Kitaj	Eliezer	1173
Kitaj	Lezjor Majer	1173
Kitaj	Motke	722, 874, 875, 876, 877, 878, 879, 887, 888, 889, 891, 893, 911, 1173
Kitaj	Rishka	363, 364, 1173
Kitaj	Shalom	356, 722, 1173
Kitaj	Shmulke	867, 868
Kitaj	Sura-Maka	722
Kitaj	Yankel (Jakob)	363, 364, 722, 873, 876, 981, 1173
Kitaj	Yisrael	1173
Kitaj	Yitzchak	1173
Kitaj		385, 449, 722
Kitaj ((Bolender)	Grincze	1173
Kitaj (Slowczyk)	Yentl	722, 863, 1173
Kitajewicz	Bluma	981
Kitajewicz	Belfer (Ben-Zion)	222, 736
Klar		411, 1082
Kliar		103
Knorpel	Dan	143, 144, 145, 150
Kobrin * (Karbin)	Leon	427, 437
Kohan	Motl	754
Kokowka	Doba	1161
Kokowka	Josef Lajb	1161
Kokowka	Leizer Velvel	1161
Kokowka	Moshe Ahron	1161
Kokowka	Shmuel Feivel	1161
Kokowka	Sura	1161
Kokowka	Yachad Miriam	1161
Kokowka	Yitzchak Jydel	1161
Kokowka (Kaufman)	Avraham	1161
Kon		81
Kook *	Rabbi	1152
Kopczyski	Simcha Prawda	15
Kopiek	Fiszel	57, 223
Kopiek	Yehoshua Nisen	154, 155, 520, 521, 523
Kopiek	Yerucham HaLevi	833

Kosciuszko *		107, 518
Kosower		938
Koszleon	Michal	97
Koszleon	Szmuelke	97
Kowadla	Chaya	687
Kotliarek	Sheina-Gitl	730
Kotliarek	Simcha	521
Kotliarek	Yehoshua	223, 730, 740
Kotliarek	Yitzchak	740
Kotliarek	Yosel (Zanwel Lejb's, Yossel)	521, 524, 544, 730
Kotliarek	Zawel-Leib	544
Kowaldo		81
Kowaldo	Hyman (Anshel)	259
Kowadlo	Mindl	669, 680, 682, 686, 687
Kowalski *		604
Kozlowsky	Alta	1181
Kozlowsky	Avraham Moshe	1181
Kozlowsky	Chaim Lejb	223, 1181
Kozlowsky	David	1181
Kozlowsky	Fishl	1181
Kozlowsky	Gedalia	1181
Kozlowsky	Jakob Yitzchak	1181
Kozlowsky	Shmuel Majer	1181
Kozlowsky	Yehoshua Cwi	1181
Kozlowsky (Smolke)	Naomi Elishayva	1181
Krajndl	Boruch	75
Krapik	Avraham	959
Kraszewski *		867, 868, 873, 893, 958
Kraszewski *	Stefan	671, 685, 686, 693
Krater *		687
Krau	Dr.	163, 164
Krawiec		394
Krinski *		739
Kronenberg	Avraham	1150
Krystal	Eliezer	727
Krystal	Mirjam	727
Krystal (Kristal-Bedolah)	Izak	390, 727, 728, 1149
Krzanski	Leibel	1079
Krzanski	Shprinca	930
Kszeckower	Itshe-Meir	400, 693
Kszinwanogo	Shoshana (Royzka)	1151
Kukalka	Berl	724

Kurcyusz *		684
Kuszer	Mendel	206
Lamport	Avraham	356, 1159
Lamport	Fajga Rivka	1159
Landau	Avraham	1161
Landau	Alter (Alter Yitzchak)	849, 1181
Landau	Dawid	1181
Landau	Dwora	1181
Landau	Fajgl	1181
Landau	Rachel	1181
Landau	Rivka	1181
Landau	Yaakov	356
Landau	Yona	1181
Landau (Korpik)	Chana Jetka	1181
Lande (Landa, Landes)	Avrahaml (Avraham)	255, 660, 740, 997
Lapka	Berl	670
Lateiner *		427
Lechaim	Yudel	586
Lepak		103, 143, 444, 449, 782, 954, 1010
Lepak	Avraham-Boruch	552
Lepak	Gitl	1189
Lepak	Josef (Yosel) Boruch (Baruch)	133, 138, 207, 356, 447, 475, 747, 1189
Lepak	Mordechai Max	1189
Lepak	Shmuelik	542, 984
Lepak	Yehoshua (Yeshaya)	149, 150, 151, 159, 165, 167, 176, 336, 343, 362, 369, 428, 445, 542, 544, 545, 784, 926, 981, 990, 991, 995, 1189
Lepak	Yenta	1110
Lepak (Markowski)	Pesha (Pnina)	436, 591, 1189
Lepak (Rozenblit)	Ziona	1189
Lerman	Pinkhus	1108
Levi	Yosef	1021
Levin (Kizelsztajn)	Chana	1181
Levinson	Hershel	285, 1078
Levinson	Rabbi Yosef Menachem HaLevi	211, 285, 544, 608, 610, 980
Levinsztejn *	Josef Rabbi	298, 299
Levinzon	Pinkhus	1023, 1027
Lew	Avraham Berl	1165
Lew	Roszke	1165
Lew	Ruchtshe (Rachcze)	867, 1165
Lew	Simcha	358, 595, 1165

Lew	Yisrael Yitzchak	358, 385, 1022, 1165
Lew	Yossel	1165
Lew	Zindel	138, 231, 447, 448, 734, 735 1115, 1165
Lichtensztejn	Rochel	984
Lipszic *	Comrade	1089
Lipszic *	Aleksander Ziskind Rabbi	298, 299
Litman	Maurice	1167
Litman	Moshel	422
Litman	Ralph	1167
Litman	Simchah	422
Litman	Yenta	1167
Litmanis (Litmans)	Rachel	349, 350, 351
Litmans	Avraham	1167
Litmans	Esther Lea	1167
Litmans	Peshke	1167
Litmans	Rochel-Lea (Rachel Lea)	591, 1167
Litmans	Tauba	1167
Litmans	Yosel (Yossel)	150, 1167
Litmans (Litman)	Isser (Isser)	428, 1167
Litwak	Moshe David	358
Litwak	Yakov	923
Lopata		970
Lubelczyk		86, 350, 992
Lubelczyk	Abram Chaim	84
Lubelczyk	Avraham-Berl (Avrum Berl)	385, 830, 834
Lubelczyk	Chaim	829
Lubelczyk	Dov (Berele, Berl)	363, 366, 1081, 1084, 1086, 1087
Lubelczyk	Dovid	830, 926
Lubelczyk	Elka	831, 832
Lubelczyk	Fayga-Faya	1084
Lubelczyk	Fiszel (Fishel)	143, 175, 231, 356, 733, 829, 830, 832
Lubelczyk	Itshe	423
Lubelczyk	Itshe	586
Lubelczyk	Judel (Yudel)	84, 829
Lubelczyk	Leah Gitl	591, 834
Lubelczyk	Mordechai	555, 830
Lubelczyk	Moshel	422, 423, 424
Lubelczyk	Moshele	434
Lubelczyk	Rukhl (Rukhela)	1086, 1087
Lubelczyk	Shlomo	84, 86, 97, 829
Lubelczyk	Shmulik	1088
Lubelczyk	Szviva	345

Surname	Given name	Pages
Lubelczyk	Yakha	830, 831
Lubelczyk	Yerukhem	831
Lubelczyk	Yisrael Nakhman	555, 829, 1149
Lubelczyk	Yokheved	831
Lubelczyk (Gorzalczany)	Bat Sheva (Sheva, Sheva-Ita)	349, 351, 436, 829, 1079, 1088
Lung	Arke	492
Lutustarska *		1092
Lyn	Chaja	1181
Lyn	Marisza	1181
Lyn	Simale	1181
Lyn	Tajbl	1181
Lyn	Yechiel	1181
Makarewicz *		1122, 1123
Makowka	Avrahaml	978, 979
Makowka	Velvel	979
Malcman		385
Malcman	Elihu (Eli) Ruwen (Rubin)	140, 143, 144, 175, 228, 231
Malcman	Utshe	992
Malinowicz		634
Malinowicz	Etl	1183
Malinowicz	Frajda	1183
Malinowicz	Hershel	133, 231
Malinowicz	Moshe Abba	1183
Malinowicz	Nechama	1169
Malinowicz	Shmuel Majer	1183
Malinowicz (Lubelczyk)	Malka	160 167, 633, 635, 636, 1183
Malinowicz (Wengorz)	Chanatshe (Chana)	634, 1183
Mankuta	Itshe	488, 1150
Mankuta	Yankel	610
Mankuta	Yehuda	436
Mankuta	Sura	428
Mankuta (Berkowicz)	Sura	435
Mant	Hershel	966
Marcziniak *		936, 938, 991, 1036
Mark	Ber	909, 910
Markus	Chaim	687
Markus (Baron)	Esther	1167
Maslo	Doba	981
Maslo	Pesakh	997
Maslo (Masle)	Avraham Yosel	980, 981, 996

Maslo (Masle)	Fruma	996
Melamed	Avraham Yosel	222
Melamed	Baruch	837
Melamed	Berl	986
Melamed	Yitzchak Hersh	278
Melamed	Moshe Josef	266, 270
Melcer		233, 385
Melcer	Ahron	416, 598
Melcer	Chava Yehudis	679
Mendel	Jehuda	97
Meyzl *	Chana	510
Michalczik *		923
Mieszkowski *		671, 687
Milner	Yisroelik	401
Minc	Rivka	1169
Minc	Sura	373
Minc (Edelsztajn)	Rachel	1169
Mlodz	Ruwin	927
Mnakusa		373
Moliere *		437
Molotov *	Vyacheslav	1084
Mondry	Judel Chaim	736
Moncarz		360
Moncarz	Chaya Sura	739
Moncarz	Doba	988
Moncarz	Dovid (David)	365, 371, 382, 437, 446
Moncarz	Hershel	428
Moncarz	Lezjor	155, 728, 729
Moncarz	Malka	340, 343
Moncarz	Meir (Majer, Mejer)	138, 141, 428
Moncarz	Mordechai	373, 376
Moncarz	Perec	742
Moncarz	Simcha (Seymour)	979, 1019
Moncarz	Yisroelke (Yisrael)	230, 984, 986, 987
Moncarz	Yossel (Yosef)	343, 428, 739
Mont	Lezjor	521
Montefiore *	Moses	296
Morgnsztern *		378
Morozow *		472, 473, 473
Murawicz	Pejsach	736
Najmark	Chaja Lea	1177
Najmark	Chaim Lajb	1177
Najmark	Hadasa	1177

Najmark	Hershel	1177
Najmark	Miriam	1177
Najmark	Moshe	356, 357
Najmark	Shimon Nusan	227, 232
Nata	Hersh	81
Nebach	Lezjor	97
Nejman *	Henryk	687
Nidbach (Nitabach)		372
Niebudek *		671, 687
Niewad	Chaim Pesakh	687
Niewad	Feivel	984, 1032
Niewad	Mendel	101
Niewad	Moshe	101
Nikolai *	Czar	696, 724
Nitabach	Moshe	345
Nowicki *		867, 868
Nowinsztern	I. (Yakosz, Yankel)	913, 955, 962, 964, 965
Nurski		1101
Oestreich (Edelsztajn)	Basza	1169
Okon	Alter-Mendel	817
Okon	Chayatsha	818
Okon	Etel	818
Okon	Gitel	818
Okon	Noachel	818
Okon	Shmulka	371, 818
Okon (Kaczanek)	Liba (Luba)	817, 818
Okon (Okun)	Isachar	57, 67, 817, 1149, 1150
Okun (Okin)		88, 1111
Olszewski (commissar) *		107
Organinski *		93, 1111
Orker	Avraham	1177
Orker	Hershel	1177
Orker	Jente	1177
Orker	Lajbl	1177
Orkes (Orkis)	Meir	1065
Orlinsky	Fajgl	1163
Orlinsky	Itche Majer	1163
Orlinsky	Jakob (Yaakow)	1163
Orlinsky	Judel	101
Orlinsky	Lea	1163
Orlinsky	Rivka	1163

Orlinsky	Szajwa	1164
Orlinsky (Szajka)	Esther Rachel	1163
Orner *	Jakob Rabbi	298
Ostrorzanski	Simcha	524
Ostrorzanski	Szmerl	524
Ostrozanski	Yankel	595
Ourowicz	Pesakh	497
Pakczarski	Fayge-Malka	701
Pakczarski	Shlomo	701
Paprocki *	Alieksander	672, 687
Parisz		638
Parizer	Itchke Mejer	520, 521
Paw		81
Pedeto	Jakob-Pinchas	222
Perlman		427
Perlman	Avraham	686
Perlmuter	Bajla Lea	1183
Perlmuter	Chana Rachel	1183
Perlmuter	Dawid	1183
Perlmuter	Gitl-Golda	507
Perlmuter	Moshele (Moshe)	507, 1183
Perlmuter	Perl	428, 1183
Perlmuter	Rachel Lea	1183
Perlsztain	Nechemia	442
Plocker		103, 365, 422, 488
Plocker	Binyamin	412, 1165
Plocker	Feigel	349, 350, 351, 373
Plocker	Jakob Der Rav (Yankel, Jacob)	75, 206, 240, 241, 980
Polanski *	Prosecutor	684
Pomeranc	Jakob	1169
Pomeranc (Edelsztajn)	Szprinca	1169
Porat	Aryeh	361
Portnoy		446
Pozkowski (Pokoj)	Maks	426, 427
Poznanski *		78, 79
Prajs *		1050
Prawda		103
Prawda	Leibel	1165
Prawda	Matisyahu	383
Prawda	Moshe	227, 230, 571, 587, 765
Prawda	Sheyne Perl	587, 591
Prawda	Shlomka (Shloyme	571, 587, 590, 746, 765, 1165

	Yishay, Shlomon-Isy, Shlomka, Shlomo Jiszai, Shlomo)	
Prawda	Sura	1165
Prawda	Velvel	590
Prawda	Yechiel Asher Chilke)	104, 137, 138 ,139, 150, 343, 344, 356, 358, 383, 445, 446, 447, 590, 765, 766, 767, 768, 836, 1081
Prawda (Cukrowicz)	Chaikeh (Chaikeh)	591, 1165
Prawda (Kapczinsky)	Simcha (Simkha, Symchla)	428, 433, 559, 567, 570 , 571, 746, 1154, 1165
Prawda (later Plocker)	Rivka	165, 406, 408, 410, 412, 587, 1165
Preter	Dawid	741
Preter	Yankel	741
Preter (Moncarzz)	Malka	742
Pszakewicz	Zelik Yankel	226, 229, 657
Rabinowicz		96, 385, 497
Rabinowicz	Aliza	57
Raczkowski		385
Raczkowski	Mordechai	694, 769, 772
Raczkowski	Simcha	980, 981
Raczkowski	Yisrael Yona	100, 133, 138, 144, 146, 147, 220, 221, 278, 343, 366, 389, 390, 478
Raczkowski (Ber)	Dwojra'ke (Dvora)	150, 159, 160
Ragajczyk *		1129
Rajczik	Moshel	943, 991, 993, 994, 996, 1000
Rajczik	Yankel	992
Ratman (Rimacz)	Nisl	400
Raucher-Gromadzyn	Yafa	1151
Reznik	Chaja	1169
Riba		937
Riba	Dovid	436
Riba	Esther	948, 950, 992
Riba	Mirl	992
Riba	Shayna	436, 442, 446, 992
Ribak	Meir	428
Ribak	Meir Shimshon	356
Richter	Meir	227, 764
Richter	Yudel	358, 595
Richter *	Mojzesz	424
Ringelblum *	E. Dr.	107
Ritenberg		394, 395
Ritholc		579
Ritholc	Ahron	581

Ritholc	Avraham-Josef (Avraham Yosef Itsl)	422, 423, 425, 428, 433, 434, 481, 579
Ritholc	Shifra	435
Ritholc	Velvel	581
Ritholc	Yudel	581
Rithold	Itsl	581
Rosman		373
Rosman	Luba	373
Rotenberg		717
Rotenberg	Itchke Mejer	720
Rotenberg	Lejbl	720
Rotenberg (Blajwajz)	Szejna-Chai'ke (Szejna Chomka)	83, 719
Rotenberg (Ritenberg)	Aba (Avraham-Aba)	83, 215, 218, 717, 718, 719, 720
Rotenberg *	Pinchas Eliezer Rabbi	299
Rotenberg *	Eli	718
Rotman		371, 446
Rotman	Asher	1175
Rotman	Elimelech (Melech)	981, 1175
Rotman	Hinda	1175
Rotman	Luba	371
Rotman	Malka	1175
Rotman	Mendel	1175
Rotman	Mirjam	1175
Rotman	Sura Dwora	1175
Rotman	Szaul	1175
Rotman	Shlomo	1175
Rotman	Yehudit	360
Rozen *	Rabbi Yosef	284
Rozenbaum		489
Rozenberg	Shmuel	414, 415
Rozenberg (Gorzalczany)	Yehudis	653, 655
Rozenberg *	Shmuel Moshe	653, 654
Rozenblum	Yehoshua Mordechai	764
Rozenblum *	Baruch Zwi Rabbi	298
Rozenblum *	Betsalel (Tsalka)	378
Rubinowicz		529, 1150
Rubinowicz	Binyamin-Sender	506
Rubinowicz	Elisha (Eliasha)	1149, 1151
Rubinowicz	Meitshke Binyamin Sender's	425
Rubinowicz	Yuta-Mindel	506
Rubinowicz (Rabinowicz)	Josef	188, 189

Rubinsztajn	Chaim Shmuel	218
Rubinsztajn	Levi Yitzchak (Lew Yitzchak)	101, 490
Rubinsztajn	Tanchum Rabbi	317
Ruskalonker *	Shmuel Leib	378
Rydz-Smigly	Edward [Marshal]	920
Rziwiec	Zelman Shlomo	22
Saba	Bela	1108
Saba	Dov	1089, 1103
Saba	Fayga-Faya	1106
Saba	Kwinka	1107
Saba	Surala	1106, 1108
Saba	Tushka	1108
Saba	Yankele (Yankel)	1108
Saba	Yehudis	1105
Saba	Yeshayahu	1106
Sadovski *		926, 959
Salman	Eli Ruwin	893
Salte's	Lezjor	92
Sanoker	Simkha	247, 249, 250
Sapir (Levin)	Sura	1171
Sapir Hakohen	Avraham	1171
Schapiro	Max	1150
Schenirer *	Surah	391
Schenirer *	Sura	104
Schneiderman	Dalia	849
Schwartz	David	1150
Selcer	S. N.	1149
Sendattsh	Avraham	1042
Sender		926, 927, 932, 934, 935, 938, 989, 990, 1006
Sendoss	Boruch	1042
Serka	Lea	1179
Serka	Mirjam	1179
Serka	Sura	1179
Serka	Slowa	1179
Serka	Yechiel Ahron	150, 437, 1179
Serka (Horwicz)	Czarna	1179
Shalomberg		151
Shimon	Fejwel	171
Shuskes	Shmuel Rabbi	294
Siedlisker	Mendel	85, 87
Siedlisker (Zysman)	Mendel	821

Sikorski *	Wladyslaw	1085
Skadkowski *	Premier	683
Skarczinski *		1132
Slawaczik *		911
Slikes	Moshe-Dovid	1003
Slocka	Rivka	670
Slucki	Avraham	356, 524
Slucki	Binyamin (Benjamin)	356, 524
Slucki	Chaim	1175
Slucki	Zysze (Zisha)	610, 869, 1078, 1115, 1126
Slucki	Chaim	373
Slucki (Rotman)	Luba	1175
Smolowicz	Motl	998
Sofer	Moshe Dawid	221
Sokolowski *		79
Solitis	Leizer	657
Soloveitchik *	Rabbi Chaim	298, 300
Soloveitchik *	Rabbi Yosef Dov of Brisk	283
Sorowicz	Gedalya	345
Spalanski	Avraham	1150
Spolienec		1126
Spolienec	Perl	610
Spolieniec	Chana Rivka	1179
Spolieniec	Josef	1179
Spolieniec	Shlomo	1179
Srkowicz	Rabbi Zwi	283, 301
Stakowski *	Josef	684
Starkovisky	Beltshe	1047
Starkovisky	Yitzchok	1047
Starkowski		385
Starkowski	Zerach	189, 300, 356, 473, 707
Staroki	Fishl	424
Stipulkowski *		687
Stoliar	Chaim	1010, 1011
Stoliar	Yudel	520
Stolowicz	Esther Tauba	1183
Stolowicz	Gitl	1183
Stolowicz	Itshe (Itzik, Yitzchak)	509, 1183
Stolowicz	Jehuda Yudel	1183
Stolowicz	Kiva	509
Stolowicz	Miriam	1183
Stolowicz	Moshe Elazar	1183
Stolowicz	Motl	873, 875

Stolowicz	Naomi	1183
Stolowicz	Rachel	1183
Stolowicz	Rivka	1183
Stolowicz	Zalman	297, 1183
Stubyn	Chaim	1179
Stubyn	Dwora	1179
Stubyn	Fajgl	1179
Stubyn	Juta	1179
Stubyn	Rivka	1179
Stubyn	Szifra	1179
Stubyn Czopokewicz	Matl	1179
Stuczynski	Akiva	152, 222, 389
Stuczynski	Nesanel (Saneh, Sane, Natanal)	222, 276, 277, 363, 389, 390, 743, 930
Stutszinski	Sura	1006, 1007
Sukhe	Avraham	1108
Sukhe	Branka	1108
Supczinski	Josef	684
Surka	Mordechai-Hersh	232, 233
Surowicz		101, 980
Surowicz	Gedalia	57, 374, 436, 442
Surowicz	Mendel	494
Surowicz	Moshe	494
Surowicz	Pesakh	485, 494
Surowicz	Shayva	160, 165, 472
Szachnerowicz (dentist)	H.	101, 103, 488, 489, 490
Szajes	Berl	225
Szajka	Bina	1163
Szajka	Gittel	1163
Szajka	Shlomo	1163
Szapira	Gitka	318, 324
Szapira	Boruch Rabbi and Admor	99, 225, 317, 318, 320-326, 478, 594, 703, 748
Szapira	Natan (Notke Pilcer)	325
Szapira	Rasha Mirl	323
Szapira	Yaakov Yosef (Yaakov Yosha, Yoske)	317, 318, 320, 478
Szapira	Zusha	321
Szapira	Chaim	144
Szapira	Jakob	215
Szczepanski *		688
Szczigel	Sura	472
Szczupakiewicz		207, 438, 444, 1120, 1124, 1125
Szczupakiewicz	Chaim	140, 336, 337, 363, 1120, 1121

Szczupakiewicz	Motl (Motel, Mottel)	15, 150, 151, 175, 176, 337, 362, 370, 408, 445, 448, 599, 1029, 1120, 1124
Szczupakiewicz	Perl	1121
Szczupakiewicz	Surala	1120
Szejman		223
Szejman	Ajzsze	742
Szejman	Gitka	373
Szejman	Laja	742
Szejman	Malka	372, 381, 742, 1151
Szejman	Shlomo Joel	742
Szejman (Szajnman)	Nuska-Natan	223, 373, 375, 416, 639, 640, 742
Szenicki *	Dr.	731
Szepke	Pinye Josef	492
Szepke	Yosef	472
Szerszyn		422, 488
Szerszyn	Alter	103, 434, 436, 480, 488
Szerszyn	Fejga Bracha	739
Szerszyn	Liba	428
Szienka *	Bronislaw	1131
Szifman		669
Szifman	Avraham	1179
Szifman (Zigelman)	Perl	1179
Szimonowski *		675
Szinman		340
Szinman	Lea	340, 341
Szklarek	Pinkus	1165
Szklarek (Prawda)	Perl	1165
Szlaski	Alter	770, 772
Szlaski	Chaim Leib	642
Szlaski	Chana	545
Szlaski	Nemi	642, 644, 648
Szlaski	Sura	642
Szlaski	Yitzchak	13, 57, 329, 334, 335, 339, 345, 349, 351, 367, 449, 545, 637, 641, 644, 769, 847
Szliapak	Wolf	673
Szliaski		1151
Szlosli	Yitzchak	1149
Szmelkes	Alter	219, 220
Szmercak	Rubin	731
Szniad	Dawid	285
Szopkowicz		782
Szpizman *		378
Szrajer	Artur	107
Szulewic		654

Szwarc		360, 1038, 1122, 1145
Szwarc	Avraham (Avrahamel, Avrahaml)	222, 276, 389, 465, 850, 1115
Szwarc	Dina	1019
Szwarc	Paja (Faja)	720
Szwiantkiewicz *	Dr.	676, 694

Telces	Mendel	169
Tencza	Yankel	449
Tencza	Yehoshua (Chaim Yehoshua)	236, 738
Tofal	Ahron	740
Tojba	Professor	104
Tombek	Yechiel	524
Tombek	Yitzchak	222, 280
Treblinski	Khona	704
Tronk *	Yehoshua Rabbi	298
Troyba		393, 394
Tsalka	Shlomo	390
Tsimes	Chaim Dovid	518f, 893
Tulman	Chaim	1185
Tulman	Dina	1185
Tulman	Hershel	1185
Tulman	Moshe	1185
Tulman	Shmuel	1185
Tulman (Cymes)	Matl	1185
Tumkewicz *		653
Turowicz	Pesakh	586
Tuszowski *	Waclaw	687
Tyktin		472
Tyktin	Yisrael	100, 101, 227, 228, 231, 232, 279, 297, 593, 596, 747
Tyktin	Sura Misza	747

Ungesbard		422

Visotsky	Chaim	980
Vitriol (Kanet)	Chawa	525

Wachs *	Chaim Elazar Rabbi	298
Wajnbrum	Avraham Shmuel	687
Wajnbrum (Wajnbaum) *	Litman	670, 682, 686, 687
Wajngold	Czarna	864
Wajngold	Fawel	861
Wajngold	Tsibia	864

Wajngold	Yudel	864
Wajntraub	Ahron	333, 367, 594
Wajntraub	Avraham	764
Wajsbart (Ben Zahavi)	Shmuel	989
Walter	Alter	927, 937
Wangras		350
Wapniak	Yankel	820
Wapniak	Yitzchak	88
Wapniak	Yudel	617, 618, 619, 622, 725, 740, 827, 828, 839
Wasercug	Chaim Yudel	133, 740
Wasercug	Fejgel	337, 349, 350, 351, 369
Wasercug	Michel	223
Wasercug	Yitzchak	363, 740
Wasermacher	Yitzchak	222
Wasilewska *	Wanda	1090
Watnik	Fraydke	1115
Watnik	Leibel	1115
Weizmann *	Chaim	1052
Welie	Fraydke	472
Welje (Welie)	Mordechai	189, 472
Wengerka		927
Wengerka	Mejer	521, 524
Wengerka	Moshe	524
Wengerka	Yehoshua	524
Wengorz		1010
Wengorz	Berl	189
Wengorz	Judel	984
Wengorz	Lejzer	188, 231, 636
Wengorz (Gorzalczany)	Rachel	852
Wengorz	Shmulke (Shmuel)	423, 424, 544, 586, 687, 921, 926, 936, 938, 939, 954, 981, 990, 991
Wengorz	Yisrael	150, 151, 446
Weter	Ahron	403
Wibitker	Jekel (Yankel)	101, 596, 796
Wiewiurka	A.	265
Wiferownyk	Chaim Berl	1000, 1175
Winder	Meir	426
Wingurt	Fajga	1169
Wingurt (Edelsztajn)	Chawa	1169
Winograd		223
Winograd	Yeshaya (Yeshai, Yeshayhu)	223, 389, 416

Wisenrad		391
Wisocki	Eliahu	979, 984
Wiszniak	Yosef	428
Wizna (Wisznia)		282, 406, 410
Wolfsman	Meszel	89
Wolmer		385
Wolmer	Alter	138, 143, 144, 207, 229, 231, 447, 448, 781, 782, 783, 784, 981, 990
Wolmer	Bashka	783
Wolmer	Feigel	1035
Wolmer	Yehoshua	15, 360
Wolmer-Biderman	Mirl	1029, 1036
Worona		84
Worona	Chaim	57
Worona	Bezalel-Ber	164
Worona	Yitzchak	859
Wyprawnik	Yeshaya	977
Yvablkowski *	Chaim	687
Yafa	Avraham	248
Yelin	Zelik Yankel	1111
Yellin	Dovka	349, 350, 351
Yitzchaki	D. Aba	1149
Yoshi	Shlomo	230
Zabludower	Chaim	196, 197, 285, 358, 389, 1070, 1078
Zabludower	Gitl	197, 1069, 1078
Zabludower	Shmuel Dawid Rabbi (Szmuel) (Shmuel Dovid, Shmuel David)	98, 100, 133, 186, 193, 195, 281, 282, 284, 285, 292, 300, 302, 343, 465, 490, 529, 544, 673, 688, 701, 709, 840, 844, 983, 1078, 1110
Zabludower	Yocheved	283, 285, 1078
Zabludower (Szniad)	Tzvia (Cwia)	196, 285, 1078
Zabludower-Levinson	Freidel	67, 193, 211, 285, 337, 370, 609, 1023, 1063, 1078, 1149
Zabuski *	Yisrael Yankel	830
Zachrisz	M.	1183
Zajfnzider		472
Zajonc	Kelman	101
Zajonc	Rochel	428
Zak	Berish	748
Zaklilowski	Arya-Shakhna	253
Zaklilowski	Dawid	255
Zaklilowski	Gad	253
Zarembski		1101

Zejgermacher	Chaim	222
Zelaznik	Chai'ke	165
Ziemba	Menakhem	511
Zigelman	Chana	1179
Zigelman (Jakubowicz)	Chaya	1179
Zyglbojm		207
Zyglbojm	Avraham	1179
Zyglbojm	Chana	1179
Zyglbojm	Esther	1179
Zyglbojm	Fejwel	141, 414, 1179
Zyglbojm	Fedja	1179
Zyglbojm	Josef	1179
Zyglbojm	Lea	1179
Zyglbojm	Moshe Dawid	1179
Zyglbojm	Sura Rivka	1179
Zyglbojm	Szimon	1179
Zylberman	Eliezer	296
Zylberman	Hershel	222, 223, 389, 1007
Zylberman	Itche	140, 228
Zylberman	Sura-Misha	1007
Zylberman	Itsze (Itche)	207, 222
Zylbersztajn		223, 678, 1150, 1151
Zylbersztajn	Akiva	229
Zylbersztajn	Avraham	1150
Zylbersztajn	Chaim	665, 666, 1150
Zylbersztajn	Chanala	665
Zylbersztajn	Eliahu	358, 360385
Zylbersztajn	Fayga-Faya	665, 666
Zylbersztajn	Leah	89, 432
Zylbersztajn	Moshele (Moshel)	416, 936, 945, 984, 986, 988
Zylbersztajn	Rochel	1035
Zylbersztajn	Simon	1150
Zylbersztajn	Tova	360
Zylbersztajn	Welwele (Velvel)	228, 234
Zysman		1150, 1151
Zysman	Hodes	542
Zysman	Meir Leibel	86, 385, 442
Zysman	Mendel	84, 87
Zysman	Moshel (Meszel)	424, 522, 524
Zysman	Peshke	997
Zysman	Rivka	373
Zysman	Shayna	428, 435
Zysman	Shepsl	542

Zysman	Shimon	1149
Zysman	Yisrael	1175
Zysman	Yitzchak	687
Zysman	Yoske	538
Zysman (Glina)	Nekha (Nekhkama, Khome)	435, 542, 545
Zysman (Sysman)	Pinya (Pinchas, Pinye)	147, 150, 522, 524, 542, 544, 545
Zysman	Rachel (Rochel)	160, 167, 373
Zysman Najmark	Rachel	1177
Zywieca	Shlomo	152

NAME INDEX

Please Note: This is the Name Index for the English Translation

A

Abarbanel, 81

Abramowicz, 33

Abu-Szmuel, 45

Adgoninski, 282

Ajdelsztejn, 23, 58

Akselrad, 178

Akselrod, 134, 173, 176, 180

Aldfang, 284

Aleichem, 4, 120, 124, 177

Aleksander, 29, 30, 36, 38, 39, 41, 52, 53, 54, 56, 57, 58, 69, 72, 73, 74, 75, 76, 77, 83, 87, 88, 93, 94, 95, 96, 105, 107, 108, 120, 122, 124, 133, 154, 182, 198, 233, 234, 271, 273, 274, 276, 277, 295, 301, 311, 312, 313, 315, 316, 328, 364, 370, 503

Al-Fasi, 116

Alter, 31, 38, 40, 57, 58, 65, 70, 72, 74, 75, 76, 106, 144, 175, 177, 182, 194, 197, 254, 260, 267, 274, 327, 328, 329, 332, 333, 334, 335, 336, 357, 375, 410, 414, 437, 441, 442, 499

Anders, 488, 519

Angres-Bard, 175, 176

Arganinski, 262, 281, 289, 290, 291, 292

Arsz, 281

Asher, 31, 38, 39, 43, 133, 140, 141, 149, 154, 181, 182, 325, 326, 367, 483

Astranzanski, 141

Avni, 33

B

Baal Shem Tov, 117, 124

Baczan, 190

Badaczker, 170

Bajwajs, 70, 304

Banikowski, 289

Banucke, 410

Baraczker, 170, 175

Baran, 31, 173, 176, 194, 197, 280, 284, 285, 286, 288, 291, 294

Barczik, 505, 506

Baron, 337

Barowski, 281, 289

Beck, 181

Becza, 507, 511

Beker, 40

Belczyk, 31

Belfer, 57, 140, 141, 155, 156, 252, 375, 455, 517

Ben Zahavi, 441

Ben-Ari, 445

Ber, 46, 49, 109, 357, 403

Berdan, 169

Berishes, 231

Berkenstat, 59, 72, 80, 81, 84, 87, 89, 145, 147, 151, 156, 160, 162, 164, 167, 169, 171, 175, 178, 181, 185, 187, 188, 190, 191, 193, 195, 198, 203, 208, 218, 220, 221, 222, 225, 227, 238, 245, 247, 253, 254, 255, 258, 260, 262, 263, 264, 266, 269, 279, 294, 317, 320, 357, 358, 361, 363, 379, 381, 382, 395, 405, 429, 435, 441, 445, 447, 454, 455, 459, 468, 475, 482, 489, 493, 496, 504, 511, 513, 516, 517, 521

Berkowicz, 78, 176, 252, 517

Bernstein, 517

Bialik, 4, 10, 515, 516

Bialopolski, 150

Bialystocki, 67, 289

Biderman, 459

Bidgadski, 283

Binder, 469

Birenbaum, 123, 469

Birnberg, 517

Bitner, 74, 95, 301, 309

Blajwajs, 28, 31, 39, 41, 43, 65, 68, 69, 71, 146, 156, 157, 164, 166, 173, 193, 242, 258, 259, 304, 309, 310, 468

Blajwajz, 166, 181, 473

Blausztajn, 469

Blazbard, 289

Blejwajz, 165

Blejwas, 129

Blumenkranc, 74

Blumsztejn, 134

Bodla, 14

Bolender, 46, 129, 131, 136, 138, 146, 155, 170, 190, 199, 445, 446, 464, 468

Boran, 170

Borensztejn, 107

Botsze, 74, 75, 95

Breslov, 82, 301

Brokhauser, 19

Bronsztajn, 140, 214, 280, 288, 468

Brukarz, 14, 31, 44, 54, 55, 169, 170, 171, 173, 175, 176, 178, 180, 190, 191, 193, 195, 197, 198, 203, 208, 220, 221, 222, 223, 225, 247, 317, 518, 519

Brunrut, 272

Bunim, 90, 119, 120, 123, 258, 259, 260, 304

Bursztajn, 80, 148, 149, 150, 151, 154, 294

C

Calinowicz, 310

Calkes, 95

Cegel, 214

Celniker, 71, 155, 169

Chagall, 302, 317

Chedrof, 516

Cheld, 18

Chmiel, 31, 46

Cikrovich, 241

Cimer, 279, 281, 288

Ciranke, 173

Cohen, 98, 120, 517, 519

Cukerman, 429

Cukrowicz, 14, 134, 147, 148, 149, 150, 176, 178, 180, 412, 517

Cur, 148, 149, 150, 176, 180, 517

Cymes, 173

Cyrelson, 101

Czarne's, 45

Czczupakiewicz, 40

Czechowski, 281

Czeliangura, 193

Czelianogora, 170

Czeliasniak, 190

Czelonogora, 224

Czimbam, 190

Czinowitz, 105

Cziwice, 409, 412

Czyzewer, 6, 11, 12, 13, 14, 19, 21, 22, 23, 28, 29, 35, 37, 48, 62, 66, 67, 68, 82, 85, 153, 171, 211, 214, 220, 252, 253, 286, 307, 316, 323, 382, 441, 443, 447, 454, 467, 516, 517, 518, 519, 521

D

Dancyg, 58

Dancygier, 58, 68, 70, 72

Danzig, 21, 319, 368, 501

Dawidowicz, 6, 20, 504, 511

Di Monczerka, 312

Dimentman, 53, 75, 151, 312

Dmochowski, 287, 409

Dombrowski, 47, 50

Drazszrczszuski, 289

Drengowski, 419, 421, 423, 426, 427

Drengowskis, 420, 422, 423

E

Edel, 58

Edelstejn, 70

Edelsztajn, 43, 46, 61, 88, 129, 143, 181, 201, 275, 310, 312, 319, 330, 370, 478, 499

Edilsztejn, 43

Eibeszyc, 43, 76, 271

Eides, 148, 246, 517

Eiger, 118, 123

Ejnszic, 456

Eliasz, 14, 74, 95, 131, 141, 246, 374, 375

Emden, 274

Epstein, 60, 108

Epsztajn, 72, 80, 105, 108, 271

Eybishets, 155

Ezkerahin, 309

F

Fajngold, 280

Falk, 123

Farber, 446

Feigenbaum, 106

Feldman, 280

Feldsztajn, 148

Fenster, 134, 176, 253, 454

Fetman, 284

Fishl, 75, 170, 363, 364, 366

Fiszel, 14, 40, 53, 57, 65, 71, 212, 214, 310

Fiszer, 51

Fiszman, 474

Fladeszczike, 193

Freund, 59, 72, 80, 81, 84, 87, 89, 145, 147, 151, 156, 160, 162, 164, 167, 169, 171, 175, 178, 181, 185, 187, 188, 190, 191, 193, 195, 198, 203, 208, 218, 220, 221, 222, 225, 227, 238, 245, 247, 253, 254, 255, 258, 260, 262, 263, 264, 266, 269, 279, 294, 317, 320, 357, 358, 361, 363, 379, 381, 382, 395, 405, 429, 435, 441, 445, 447, 454, 455, 459, 468, 475, 482, 489, 493, 496, 504, 511, 513, 516, 517, 521

Fribut, 288

Frydman, 36, 38, 40, 41, 47, 56, 57, 58, 65, 68, 70, 71, 78, 94, 95, 136, 138, 141, 154, 156, 190, 192, 201, 244, 323, 324, 367, 370, 428, 442, 444, 445, 451, 463, 504, 519

Frydmans, 515

Fydeto, 43

G

Ganer, 209, 210

Garde, 57, 58, 76, 147, 148, 206, 519

Gdalja's, 30

Gelbard, 450, 451, 452

Gelbards', 450

Gelbojm, 27, 31, 65, 172, 197, 242, 243, 268

Gerlich, 464

Gershuni, 491

Getzl, 78

Ginsberg, 149, 170

Glina, 22, 170, 173, 176, 196, 227, 361, 490

Godlewer, 504

Godlewski, 21

Godliwer, 501, 515

Goldberg, 127, 190, 207, 210, 280, 288, 289

Goldfaden, 171, 177

Goldman, 281, 517

Goldstein, 3, 6, 10, 11, 12, 18, 19, 20, 33, 35, 40, 42, 44, 45, 54, 68, 78, 80, 211, 249, 302, 436

Goldsztajn, 170

Golombek, 75, 76

Gonczar, 289, 416, 428, 444, 506

Gora, 14, 92, 99, 104, 109, 124, 139, 141, 149, 155, 156, 157, 158, 160, 162, 165, 166, 169, 173, 178, 180, 247, 248, 332, 338, 340, 343, 345, 348, 352, 353, 373, 519

Góra, 68, 70, 71, 302, 304

Gordan, 517

Gorde, 41

Gordin, 172

Gordon, 235

Gorzalczany, 14, 18, 20, 30, 31, 33, 35, 36, 40, 41, 43, 46, 49, 74, 126, 127, 128, 129, 130, 136, 140, 143, 144, 145, 146, 147, 155, 164, 167, 175, 176, 178, 181, 218, 223, 224, 241, 244, 246, 253, 254, 255, 258, 260, 270, 272, 285, 314, 325, 328, 335, 361, 374, 378, 455, 513, 518, 519

Gorzlaczani, 95
Gotlib, 493
Grabski, 51
Grade, 143, 144, 155, 185
Gradus, 49, 289
Graubard, 71, 106, 107
Gricer, 72
Gridman, 501
Grochowski, 310
Grodus, 106
Grodzinski, 101, 104
Gromadzyn, 23, 30, 126, 127, 130, 134, 136, 138, 144, 145, 146, 170, 171, 173, 175, 176, 178, 180, 223, 224, 231, 235, 241, 245, 246, 247, 253, 273, 310, 420, 428, 438, 464, 493, 494, 501, 504, 506, 519
Gromadzyns, 493, 515
Grosbard, 38, 39, 40, 41, 53, 115, 155, 156, 311, 336, 369, 410, 437, 449, 450
Grosbart, 53
Grosodzin, 463
Grossbard, 141
Grozbard, 281
Grucki, 396
Grynberg, 26, 43, 58, 68, 129, 131, 132, 134, 143, 146, 170, 171, 177, 193, 195, 224, 245, 316
Grzibak, 280
Gur, 108, 121, 122, 123, 124, 142, 293, 336, 343, 370
Gwardiak, 283

H

Hagerman, 106, 107
Halevi, 60, 96, 99, 106, 108, 366
Haller, 77, 171, 268, 357
Hebel, 41
Held, 14, 136
Heller, 97
Herman, 519
Hershman, 20, 37, 314, 368
Herzl, 140, 147, 149

Heyman, 410
Hofman, 28, 148
Horowicz, 106, 460

I

Igla, 47, 282, 444, 463, 506
Ikir, 428
Itsl, 18, 71, 170, 173, 176, 194, 201, 239, 300, 307, 361, 516, 517

J

Jabka, 26, 163, 165, 166, 179, 222
Jablkowski, 280, 286, 288, 289
Jablonka, 14, 31, 43, 71, 92, 115, 169, 173, 187, 188, 197, 224, 249, 307, 320, 368, 424, 519
Jabotinsky, 129, 130, 146, 469
Jakubowicz, 314, 450
Janczewski, 387, 388, 389, 393, 394, 404
Janowski, 72, 74, 75, 95, 173, 180, 274
Japonczyk, 361, 363
Jeczarski, 281
Jelin, 136, 138, 280, 281, 282, 283, 284, 285, 286, 287, 288, 291, 292, 294, 372
Jeruzalimski, 106
Jeszaja, 41, 95, 96, 112, 113, 114, 310, 343
Judel, 23, 30, 71, 254, 255, 311, 313, 436, 438
Jursz, 281, 289, 290
Jute, 58, 199

K

Kac, 436
Kacenelson, 3
Kachan, 148, 438, 460
Kackowicz, 109, 136
Kacowicz, 138
Kahn, 156
Kalan, 147

Kaliarek, 160
Kalinin, 485
Kalinowicz, 66, 70, 312
Kaliszyner, 29
Kanc, 6, 379
Kandel, 14, 51, 140, 141, 148, 154, 182, 244, 337, 455, 458, 517
Kanet, 44, 57, 170, 211, 212, 213, 214, 215, 216, 217, 519
Kapka, 288
Karbin, 177
Kardan, 71
Karesz, 190
Karlbach, 156
Karniol, 281, 282
Karo, 103
Kasower, 280, 288
Kasper, 517
Katliarek, 157, 158, 160, 196
Kaufman, 516
Kayle, 236
Kaza, 289
Kazimierczak, 508
Kazlowski, 157
Keizmacher, 50, 438
Kejmowicz, 31
Kepak, 183
Kerdan, 157
Kimovits, 244
Kirszenbojm, 18, 148, 170, 173, 176, 178, 180, 181, 358, 359, 360, 361, 438, 516, 517
Kitaj, 140, 143, 155, 183, 306, 382, 383, 388, 395, 437
Kitajewicz, 71, 311, 436
Klar, 166, 167, 484
Kliar, 31
Knorpel, 40, 41, 43
Kobrin, 172, 174
Kocmacher, 144
Kon, 22
Kook, 326, 519

Kopiec, 366
Kosower, 74, 415, 419
Koszleon, 28
Kotliarek, 71, 213, 214, 224, 309, 313
Kowadla, 22, 87, 286, 287, 288, 289
Kowadle, 280
Kowalski, 251
Kozlowsksi, 71
Krajndl, 20, 199
Krapik, 425
Kraszewski, 281, 288, 291, 383, 384, 386, 424
Krater, 289
Krau, 48, 49
Krawiec, 160
Krejndel, 314
Krejndl's, 58
Kristal-Bedolah, 517
Kronenberg, 517
Kruszewski, 395
Krystal, 157, 308
Krzanski, 411, 482
Kszeckower, 163, 291
Kszinwanogo, 518
Kukalka, 307
Kupiec, 14, 44, 71, 213
Kurcyusz, 287
Kuszer, 65

L

Lamport, 140
Landa, 85, 275, 313, 445
Landau, 2, 8, 10, 15, 33, 92, 96, 104, 109, 112, 115, 118, 125, 139, 140, 142, 293, 323, 325, 327, 332, 335, 337, 338, 340, 343, 345, 348, 352, 353, 366, 367, 368, 373, 374, 375, 376, 378, 491
Lapka, 280
Lateiner, 172
Lazers, 231

Leibel, 148, 173, 176, 180, 197, 239, 246, 300, 417, 424, 482, 501
Leibeleides, 178
Lepak, 31, 36, 38, 39, 40, 42, 43, 46, 50, 51, 54, 65, 129, 132, 140, 143, 146, 173, 176, 178, 181, 182, 183, 191, 223, 224, 227, 244, 316, 410, 422, 437, 438, 442, 444, 451, 470, 499
Lepek, 335, 336, 337
Lerman, 498
Levinson, 59, 67, 99, 224, 436, 516
Levinsztejn, 107
Levinzon, 18, 457, 458
Lew, 38, 75, 141, 155, 182, 183, 198, 246, 311, 384, 456, 501
Lewinson, 475
Lichtensztejn, 438
Lipszic, 107, 489
Litman, 170, 241, 287, 288, 289
Litmans, 43, 136, 138, 173, 244
Litwak, 141, 409
Lubelczik, 75, 175, 176, 178, 364, 410
Lubelcziks, 228
Lubelczyk, 23, 24, 40, 46, 75, 134, 136, 138, 140, 141, 145, 155, 170, 171, 241, 244, 250, 262, 263, 310, 363, 365, 366, 442, 482, 517
Luria, 103

M

Makarewicz, 505
Makowka, 435
Malchut, 309
Malcman, 39, 40, 41, 53, 73, 75, 155, 442
Malinowicz, 36, 46, 51, 75, 262, 263
Malkarcz, 154
Mankuta, 173, 176, 197, 253, 517
Mant, 428
Marczyniak, 414, 415, 442, 462
Mark, 403
Markowski, 176
Markus, 289
Maslo, 436, 445

Mazowiecka, 21, 32, 40, 289
Mazowieckie, 28, 126, 145, 150, 271, 281, 283, 287, 288, 289, 290, 291
Meizelzon, 105
Melamed, 71, 89, 90, 91, 95, 205, 368, 439
Melcer, 71, 155, 169, 248, 284
Mieszkowski, 281, 289
Milner, 163
Minc, 148
Misza, 316
Mlodz, 410
Mnakusa, 148
Mniewski, 154, 230, 233, 235, 241
Molotov, 485
Moncarsz, 141
Moncarz, 38, 40, 44, 74, 132, 144, 147, 148, 149, 173, 177, 178, 181, 309, 312, 314, 436, 440, 455
Mondry, 311
Morgnsztern, 150
Morozow, 190
Muncarsz, 131
Murawicz, 311

N

Najmark, 72, 140
Nata, 22
Nebach, 28
Nejman, 289
Neter, 291, 292
Nidbach, 148
Niebudek, 281, 289
Niewad, 30, 289, 438, 460
Nisen, 44, 206, 213, 280
Nitabach, 134, 148
Nowicki, 384
Nowinsztern, 405
Nurskis, 494
Nusan, 72, 74, 75, 193, 199

O

Okon, 14, 18, 25, 147, 337, 357, 518
Olszewski, 33
Organinski, 27, 500
Orkes, 475, 476
Orkis, 476
Orner, 106
Ostroff, 3, 6, 10, 11, 12, 18, 19, 20, 33, 35, 40, 42, 44, 45, 54, 68, 78, 80, 211, 249, 302, 436
Ostrorzanski, 214
Ostrozanski, 246
Ourowicz, 201

P

Paja's, 58
Pakczarski, 297
Paltiel, 107
Paprocki, 281, 289
Paris, 27, 49, 316
Parisz, 264
Parizer, 212, 213
Part, 53, 518, 519
Paw, 22
Pedeto, 71
Pelman, 288
Perlman, 172
Perlmuter, 173, 205, 206
Pilcer, 123
Plocker, 20, 31, 50, 79, 136, 138, 144, 148, 167, 170, 178, 197, 436
Plotsker, 65
Pokoj, 172
Polanski, 287
Pollack, 154, 230, 233, 241
Porat, 142
Portnoy, 182
Pozkowski, 172
Poznanski, 21

Prawda, 3, 31, 38, 39, 43, 72, 74, 133, 140, 141, 154, 165, 166, 167, 173, 175, 181, 182, 230, 233, 234, 235, 241, 242, 243, 244, 315, 323, 325, 326, 327, 367, 483, 520
Preter, 314
Przezakewicz, 273
Psbezokowicz, 74
Pszakewicz, 72

R

Rabinowicz, 14, 28, 58, 155, 201
Rackowski, 70
Raczkowski, 30, 36, 38, 41, 46, 70, 95, 132, 145, 155, 156, 157, 192, 327, 436
Ragajczyk, 508
Rajczik, 417, 442, 443, 444, 447
Rath, 290
Ratman, 163
Raucher, 519
Rav, 20, 436, 437
Riba, 176, 178, 180, 181, 414, 419, 420, 442
Ribak, 140, 173
Richter, 72, 141, 170, 246, 323, 324
Rimacz, 163
Ringelblum, 33
Ritholc, 170, 171, 173, 175, 176, 194, 238
Rosman, 148
Rotenberg, 23, 68, 69, 107, 160, 260, 304, 305
Rotman, 141, 147, 181, 436
Rozen, 98
Rozenbaum, 197
Rozenberg, 168, 271, 272
Rozenblum, 107, 150, 323
Rubinowicz, 57, 205, 217, 517, 518, 519
Rubinowitz, 171
Rubinsztajn, 31, 69, 118, 198
Ruskalonker, 150
Rziwiec, 71

S

Saba, 361, 489, 496
Sadovski, 410, 424
Salman, 395
Saneh, 143, 156, 254, 314, 412
Sanoker, 82, 83
Sarkowski, 289
Schapiro, 517
Schenirer, 31, 158
Schneiderman, 376
Schwartz, 517
Selcer, 516
Sendattsh, 465
Sender, 171, 205, 410, 411, 412, 413, 414, 415, 441, 442, 445, 449
Senders, 197
Sendoss, 464
Sepinwall, 436
Serka, 43, 177
Shalomberger, 36
Shames, 45
Sher, 265
Shmulkes, 267
Shuskes, 105
Siedlisker, 22, 24, 359
Sikorski, 486
Skarczinski, 509
Skladkowski, 287
Slawaczik, 404
Slikes, 448
Slocka, 280
Slucki, 140, 148, 214, 253, 384, 481, 501, 506
Smiths, 144
Smolowicz, 446
Sniadowo, 56
Sochaczewer, 107
Sofer, 70, 327
Sokolowski, 21, 460
Solitis, 273
Soloveitchik, 97, 107, 108
Sorowicz, 134
Spalanski, 517
Spolienec, 253, 506
Spolieneces, 506
Srkowicz, 97, 109
Stakhanov, 489
Stakowski, 288
Stalin, 164, 166, 486
Stalowitch, 386
Starkovisky, 468
Starkowski, 58, 108, 140, 155, 170, 191, 299
Stipulkowski, 289
Stoliar, 213, 451
Stolowicz, 106, 207, 518
Stuczinski, 157, 158
Stuczynski, 43, 71, 94, 143, 156, 157, 314, 412, 449
Stuszynski, 71
Sukhe, 498
Supczinski, 288
Surka, 75, 76
Surowicz, 14, 31, 46, 50, 149, 176, 178, 180, 190, 195, 436
Surowitchker, 199
Surowitz, 170
Sysman, 43
Szachnerowicz, 31, 197, 198
Szajes, 72
Szapira, 29, 41, 68, 72, 96, 118, 119, 120, 122, 192, 245, 296, 297, 316
Szczepanski, 289
Szczigel, 190
Szczupakiewicz, 39, 43, 53, 54, 65, 143, 146, 165, 178, 181, 183, 249, 459, 503, 505, 506
Szczupakiewiczes, 503, 506
Szejman, 71, 147, 148, 154, 169, 264, 265, 314, 519
Szenicki, 309
Szepke, 190, 199
Szerszyn, 31, 170, 173, 175, 177, 194, 195, 197, 312, 313

Szimonowski, 283

Szinman, 131

Szlaski, 14, 125, 127, 128, 130, 134, 136, 138, 145, 224, 264, 266, 267, 327, 329, 374

Szliapak, 282

Szliaski, 183, 519

Szlosli, 517

Szmelkes, 70, 332, 333, 334, 335

Szmercak, 310

Szniad, 99

Szniadower, 29, 97, 201, 299

Szopkowicz, 335

Szpizman, 150

Szrajer, 33

Sztatchopakowicz, 129

Szulevic, 272

Szwarc, 71, 94, 141, 156, 188, 305, 377, 455, 463, 501, 504, 515

Szwiantkiewicz, 283, 291, 292

T

Tancze, 140

Tanowski, 287

Telces, 52

Tencza, 77, 183, 312

Tofal, 313

Tojba, 31

Tombek, 71, 96, 214

Tracz, 254

Treblinski, 297

Tronk, 107

Troyba, 158, 160

Tsalka, 150, 157

Tsimes, 211, 395

Tsitses, 44, 203

Tumkewicz, 271

Turowicz, 241

Tuszowski, 289

Tyktin, 30, 72, 73, 75, 106, 190, 245, 247, 316, 477

U

Ungresbard, 170

V

Visotsky, 436

W

Wachs, 107

Wajnbrum, 280, 287, 288, 289

Wajngold, 381

Wajntraub, 126, 145, 245, 323

Wajsbart, 441

Walter, 410

Wapniak, 25, 255, 256, 257, 307, 358, 362, 369

Wasercug, 36, 71, 129, 136, 138, 143, 146, 313

Wasermacher, 71

Wasilewska, 489

Watnik, 501

Weizmann, 469

Welje, 58, 190

Wengerka, 213, 214, 411

Wengorcz, 422

Wengorz, 43, 57, 58, 74, 136, 170, 171, 177, 181, 224, 241, 263, 289, 378, 408, 410, 414, 415, 437, 438, 442, 451

Weter, 164

Wibitker, 30, 247, 343

Wiewiurka, 89

Winder, 172

Winograd, 71, 157, 169

Winszenker, 192

Wisocki, 436, 438

Wisznia, 165, 166

Wiszniak, 173

Wizna, 56, 97, 416

Wizners, 29

Wolfczikhe, 199

Wolfsman, 25

Wolmer, 38, 40, 41, 65, 74, 75, 141, 155, 182, 335, 336, 414, 437, 441, 442, 459

Worona, 14, 23, 49, 381

Wyprawnik, 435

Y

Yair, 274

Yelin, 500

Yitzchaki, 517

Yona, 30, 36, 38, 41, 42, 70, 71, 80, 81, 95, 156, 157, 192, 271

Yudelszten, 195

Z

Zabludower, 29, 30, 37, 56, 59, 60, 97, 99, 102, 109, 129, 132, 141, 146, 188, 197, 217, 224, 282, 290, 295, 297, 300, 369, 372, 437, 481, 499

Zabuski, 364

Zajfnzider, 190

Zajonc, 30, 173

Zak, 316

Zaklilowski, 84

Zarczicka, 462

Zarembskis, 494

Zaremby-Koscielne, 396

Zejgermacher, 71

Zelaznik, 50

Zeligs, 234

Zelik, 72, 74, 75, 76, 273, 417, 424, 428, 500, 501

Ziemba, 208

Zigelbaun, 168

Zilberstzajn, 174

Ziske, 199

Zyglbojm, 39, 65

Zylberman, 39, 65, 71, 73, 105, 157, 316, 450

Zylbersztajn, 26, 71, 73, 74, 76, 141, 155, 169, 278, 284, 414, 418, 438, 439, 440, 462, 517, 518, 519

Zysman, 23, 24, 42, 46, 51, 148, 155, 170, 173, 176, 180, 181, 213, 214, 220, 223, 224, 289, 359, 446, 518, 519

Zywieca, 43

www.ingramcontent.com/pod-product-compliance
Lightning Source LLC
Chambersburg PA
CBHW081420160426
42814CB00039B/263